Cracking Containers with Docker and Kubernetes

The definitive guide to Docker, Kubernetes, and the Container Ecosystem across Cloud and on-premises

Nisarg Vasavada

Dhwani Sametriya

www.bpbonline.com

FIRST EDITION 2022

Copyright © BPB Publications, India

ISBN: 978-93-91030-79-7

LIMITS OF LIABILITY AND DISCLAIMER OF WARRANTY

To View Complete
BPB Publications Catalogue
Scan the QR Code:

Dedicated to

Minu
for shining brighter than the brightest stars,
&
Our Families
for unconditional love and support.

About the Authors

- **Nisarg Vasavada** is an Indian National Hailing from the birthplace of Mahatma Gandhi, **Porbandar**. He is an Electronics and Communication Engineer by Qualification, an e-Learning entrepreneur by profession, and a foodie minimalistic animal lover by heart (oh, and a huge anime fan too, believe it!). He has pursued **BE in Electronics and Communication** and **ME in Embedded System Design**.

  Even during the college years, technical presentations and project demonstrations have been his favorite activities. During his bachelor's at **Noble Engineering College**, he was felicitated with the Dewang Mehta Award for excellence in Communication, which empowered him to consider writing and presentations more than just academic necessities. His master's at the **PG School of GTU** provided him a platform to take his technical writing skills a step further by authoring, presenting, and publishing review and research papers at international IEEE conferences.

  Respecting the essence of education is something that he has inherited from his family. On top of that, he has been privileged enough to work with CDAC ACTS, Chegg Inc., and Loonycorn which helped him get exposure to the front line of virtual delivery of educational content. Presently, he directs video courses for **Cerulean Canvas** on bleeding edge technologies like Cloud Computing, DevOps, 5G, Artificial Intelligence, and the list keeps growing. Just google Cerulean Canvas Courses!

  If you want to share your research (specially on green computing), discuss a course idea or potential partnership, get anime recommendations, or share cute cat or panda videos… he is the one you're looking for!

- **Dhwani Sametriya** is another Indian National Hailing from the food capital and the heart of Gujarat, **Ahmedabad**. She has pursued **B.Tech** in Electronics and Communication Engineering at **CHARUSAT** and **ME** in **VLSI** from **PG School of GTU**. VLSI is not just a topic or major, it is the way of life that teaches you to prioritize even the tiniest details in a way that everything works ever so smoothly and most of the people don't even realize the magic going on inside the chips smaller than their fingertips. She fancies food, photography, culture, well-written dramas, and aquariums!

Be it her casual visits at the Science City as a child, Industrial visits or weekend workshops at College, or research work at CDAC ACTS... "How Stuff Works" has always piqued her interest (nostalgic reference intended)! Her work with Masibus, Knowmore CPH, and Loonycorn has given her the opportunity to write, create, and publish Datasheets, Technical Manuals, Business Presentations, Research Papers, Articles, and Video Courses.

She is a Docker Certified Associate and a Cloud Computing Enthusiast. Currently, she is Cerulean Canvas' Content Producer (just google "Cerulean Canvas Courses"!) and a Member of the Editorial Board at Whioce Publishing.

About the Reviewers

Abhishek Mishra is an architect with a leading multinational software company and has deep expertise in designing and building enterprise-grade intelligent Azure and .NET-based architectures. He is an expert in .NET, full stack, Azure (PaaS, IaaS, serverless), infrastructure as code, Azure machine learning, intelligent Azure (AzureBot Services and Cognitive Services), and robotics process automation. He has a rich 15+ years of experience working in top organizations in the industry. He loves blogging and is an active blogger in the C# Corner developer community. He was awarded the C# Corner MVP in December 2018, December 2019, and December 2020 for his contributions to the developer community.

Saibal Ghosh is currently employed as a Principal Architect in Ericsson India Ltd. He has an overall experience of more than 20 years in different areas of technology including Cloud, Cloud Security, Docker, Kubernetes, databases, and operating systems, and uses his understanding of technology to solve real-world problems.

He is very deeply involved in matching technology with business requirements and these days spends a lot of his time working on the security of the different telecom systems being deployed at the customer locations. He has rich experience in areas like security, solutioning, system integration, and consulting. He obsesses about technology and technical communication and works painstakingly to ensure that technical communication with various stakeholders is precise, correct, and meaningful.

Outside of work, he likes to spend time with his family as well as pursue his deep and abiding interest in yoga and meditation.

Michael Hausenblas is a Solution Engineering Lead in the open-source observability service team at Amazon Web Services. He covers Prometheus, Grafana, and OpenTelemetry upstream and in managed services. Before Amazon, he worked at Red Hat, Mesosphere, MapR, and in two research institutions in Ireland and Austria.

Acknowledgments

Writing a book takes patience and a positive state of mind. These aspects are challenging to maintain, especially during the time of the pandemic. Without direct and indirect support from all directions, this book would have been just a pipe dream.

I (Nisarg) would like to thank my parents **Dr Neeta Vasavada** and **Dr Milan Vasavada**, for raising me as a man who romanticizes the pursuit of knowledge and considers his moral duty to share it with utmost dedication. Mother's selflessness, benevolence, and open-heartedness have always been inspirational, whereas Father's ever so successful efforts of vaccinating hundreds of families and making the world more immune to Covid-19 one jab at a time were nothing short of heroic.

It brings chuckles and giggles on my face while appreciating every single purr, meow, headbutt, crawl, and nibble by my beloved super cute feline family members (cats). Lots of love to you all!

I (Dhwani) would also like to express gratitude towards my family. My mother, **Mrs. Shakuntala Sametriya's** fearless attitude to take on new challenges with all her might and the never-ending wisdom talks with my father, **Mr. Poonamchand Sametriya** have played a huge role in shaping my current self. A big hug to my sister **Shweta Sametriya** for always shielding me and filling my life with laughter. Your expressiveness in the field of design has taught me the importance of individuality in life. It takes a hearty bunch of loving Gujjus to spend lockdowns like a breeze over video calls, home-cooked food, and fruit juices… I am proud to be around them.

Together, we would also like to appreciate BPB Publication. A big thanks to **Nrip Jain**, **Sourabh Dwivedi**, and **Surbhi Saxena** for making this integration possible and carrying it out smoothly. We can't thank **Shali Deeraj** and **Priyanka Deshpande** enough for coordinating with us so well and for tolerating our inconsistent timelines. Special thanks to **Saibal Ghosh**, **Abhishek Mishra**, and **Michael Hausenblas** for reviewing this book with such attention and care. Your involvement has taken this project a notch higher in quality and has helped us grow as authors.

Finally, we would like to express our gratitude to the ever so vibrant DevOps internet community, including but definitely not limited to Docker Captains, authors of various documentations and public projects, and the students of **Cerulean Canvas**. All of you are awesome!

Preface

"Innovation is the ability to see change as an opportunity, not as a threat."
- Steve Jobs (apparently)

Even at this point in 2021, the majority of Computer Science, IT, and Electronics university curricula across the globe haven't advanced enough to train students not to strictly pick between black and white and go for their comfortable shade of gray (no pun intended). To such students, the DevOps philosophy of participating in the best of both worlds (Development and Operations) comfortably, sounds elitist and far-fetched. Conversely, the industry is rapidly migrating towards cost-efficient, cloud-native, AI-driven DevOps workflow, which makes upskilling more of a necessity than an ambition.

To be honest, by the time Containers and their role in DevOps became mainstream, both of the authors of this book had already completed their academics. We were awestruck by the potential of Containers, Docker, and Kubernetes when we came across them. Personal projects, hobby projects, start-ups, enterprises… Everyone can benefit by adopting containerized microservice application model! Their creative and potentially productive ideas can break-free from the shackles of inevitable large-scale IT infrastructure dependence and the financial risks associated with it. We had jumped into the field of e-learning with these topics and have been serving thousands of students virtually ever since. This book is the culmination of our experience and our expressive attempt to make students, professionals, and enthusiasts of all levels appreciate this technology as much as we do.

The writing of this book is aimed to reach a sweet spot between casual comfortable discussions and accurate technical facts. While the chapter and topic sequencing have been carried out to be comfortable to the complete beginners, the information sprinkle is aimed to keep even the seasoned professionals engaged. We have tried to answer as many **Why**s, **How**s, and **What if**s as possible. Almost every topic is explained with practical examples, necessary tutorials and its real-world implications. Codes, commands, figures, and screenshots are double-checked to avoid any misunderstandings. Things that are not supposed to be taken so seriously (jokes, puns, personal opinions, and curiosities) are written in italic to maintain a uniform sense of separation.

To expand the context about the content of the book further, the first page of each chapter is pretty special. The Introduction section gives a brief idea of what you will learn from it, the Structure section provides a list of major topics in the chapter, and the Objective section lets you know how the chapter will serve you in your journey of learning containers (point A to point B stuff).

Here are one liners for what each chapter delivers (after all, we don't want to spoil too much).

- **Chapter 1** explains microservices and establishes the need for virtualization.
- **Chapter 2** explores virtualization and containerization with a little computing history.
- **Chapter 3** introduces Docker with its architecture and a hands-on example.
- **Chapter 4** teaches how to write your own Dockerfiles for Container Images.
- **Chapter 5** demonstrates Container lifecycle and operations with Docker CLI.
- **Chapter 6** covers Docker Networks and Docker Storage objects with their drivers.
- **Chapter 7** construes Docker Compose to easily write multi-container applications.
- **Chapter 8** elucidates Container Orchestration with Docker Swarm.
- **Chapter 9** says "Hello!" to Kubernetes with its architecture, cluster bootstrapping, and an example.
- **Chapter 10** expands upon workload orchestration with pods and its controlling Kubernetes Objects.
- **Chapter 11** digs deep into a diverse range of network and storage options of Kubernetes.
- **Chapter 12** reinforces cluster robustness with Kubernetes access management and security standards.
- **Chapter 13** simplifies Hosted/Managed Kubernetes on Cloud offerings with Google Kubernetes Engine to further leverage Kubernetes' orchestration potential.
- **Chapter 14** dives deep into the Container ecosystem with supportive tools such as Helm, Spinnaker, Stack Driver, Prometheus, and Istio.
- **Chapter 15** glosses over Serverless Kubernetes with Cloud Run.
- **Chapter 16** concludes the journey on an optimistic note (for now).

The book has a prologue but not an epilogue because the containers are still a growing technology, so writing an epilogue would be kind of premature.

We really hope you like this book, and it finds a permanent place in your digital or physical bookshelves, office desks, and university recommendations as the time goes on.

Wish you a very happy and satisfactory reading journey!

Downloading the code
bundle and coloured images:

Please follow the link to download the
Code Bundle and the *Coloured Images* of the book:

https://rebrand.ly/383d55

Errata

We take immense pride in our work at BPB Publications and follow best practices to ensure the accuracy of our content to provide with an indulging reading experience to our subscribers. Our readers are our mirrors, and we use their inputs to reflect and improve upon human errors if any, occurred during the publishing processes involved. To let us maintain the quality and help us reach out to any readers who might be having difficulties due to any unforeseen errors, please write to us at:

errata@bpbonline.com

Your support, suggestions and feedbacks are highly appreciated by the BPB Publications' Family.

BPB is searching for authors like you

If you're interested in becoming an author for BPB, please visit **www.bpbonline.com** and apply today. We have worked with thousands of developers and tech professionals, just like you, to help them share their insight with the global tech community. You can make a general application, apply for a specific hot topic that we are recruiting an author for, or submit your own idea.

The code bundle for the book is also hosted on GitHub at **https://github.com/bpbpublications/Cracking-Containers-with-Docker-and-Kubernetes**. In case there's an update to the code, it will be updated on the existing GitHub repository.

We also have other code bundles from our rich catalog of books and videos available at **https://github.com/bpbpublications**. Check them out!

PIRACY

If you come across any illegal copies of our works in any form on the internet, we would be grateful if you would provide us with the location address or website name. Please contact us at **business@bpbonline.com** with a link to the material.

If you are interested in becoming an author

If there is a topic that you have expertise in, and you are interested in either writing or contributing to a book, please visit **www.bpbonline.com**.

REVIEWS

Please leave a review. Once you have read and used this book, why not leave a review on the site that you purchased it from? Potential readers can then see and use your unbiased opinion to make purchase decisions, we at BPB can understand what you think about our products, and our authors can see your feedback on their book. Thank you!

For more information about BPB, please visit **www.bpbonline.com**.

Table of Contents

## CHAPTER 1

Prologue to the Containers

Introduction

This is an introductory chapter intended to bring a spectrum of readers from different technical backgrounds on the same page. We will explore the current landscape of IT industry and learn how a majority of software ideas are developed and delivered. This will take us to topics like Web applications, DevOps philosophy, and Microservice architecture.

Structure

This chapter covers:

- The web applications
- Agile and DevOps
- Microservices

Objective

Since this is the beginning of the book, the tone of this chapter is casual and lightweight. The context of this chapter focuses on a discussion about the state of internet-powered applications. By the end of this chapter, you will have a clear understanding of when you require microservice architecture and when you do not. Overall, it will play the role of a precursor of the container-focused content in the further chapters.

The web applications

At some point in our childhood, all of us wanted our own version of Dexter's Laboratory in the basement with an intelligent supercomputer like Iron Man's Jarvis. As life took its course, we grew up to realize that most of us are not as wealthy as Tony Stark, and God knows where Dexter's funding came from. Fiction aside, it is not even a distant past when we used to have albums full of Blu-Ray DVDs, portable hard drives full of backup data, and a limited amount of mp3 songs stored in portable USB sticks or memory cards.

Although the lifestyle was not inconvenient, the tech offerings were not designed for scale. Just think about it, with such an evolving volume of growing data and content, it would have been impossible for individual users to have their personal copy of data. For example, how many servers would you need just to store Netflix and Instagram data?

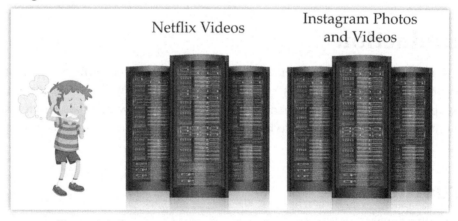

Figure 1.1: Conceptual representation of a world without web apps

As the generations of wired and wireless mobile communication kept evolving, high-speed Wi-Fi, and Mobile Internet became affordable and accessible to people across the globe. This was the trigger for the rise of the client-server application model. Instead of performing computing, data storage, data processing, and data access over your devices, the data would get served to you depending on your request. This gave rise to a lot of possibilities including but definitely not limited to:

- Digital content (music, videos, gaming, and education) at your fingertips
- Access to world Map and live navigation

- Opportunity to socialize with billions of people across the globe
- Data Storage on Cloud
- Cloud Computing
- E-commerce, E-governance, and Internet Banking

All of these services were commonly categorized as **web applications**. The inspiration behind the name is simply their access mode being the internet (mostly HTTP(s) requests). Such a model was not a new discovery. Your television cable operator was "serving" you the content at scheduled times, your telephone operator used switching centers to "serve" you the calls (and eventually messages), Internet itself always operated on data being "served" to you regardless of the type of website (search engines, blogs, content management, and so on). With the rise of internet-enabled businesses, the notion of web applications became more widespread, and the market became more optimistic about the model. Today, almost every aspect of your life is connected to internet in some or another way, and the trend will just go upwards as stronger internet generations, and IoT finds their way in the hands of average consumers.

Agile and DevOps

With the growing web-application market, freemium and ad-based revenue models became mainstream, and the applications started to get competitive. It was no longer possible to wait for 6 months to roll out software updates. Developers started to roll out smaller updates at a higher frequency. Major platforms like Facebook even started to use models like Continuous Integration/Continuous Delivery (CI/CD) that would continuously update some aspects of their services without any need of performing manual application updates. Such fast feature rollout and the development process behind it was called **Agile** *(due to agility of development and deployment)*.

Agile was easier said than done. Transformation in the pace of development and deployment could not be achieved without adopting new work culture and tools. Just the fact that the updates rolled out more frequently did not mean the code could escape the cycles of testing, or deployment would become any less infrastructure dependent or tedious. A buggy, an unstable agile application, was as problematic as a stable but slowly updating traditionally developed (waterfall model) one. The application developers and system administrators had to switch to an intertwined workflow where neither of their work was independent from each other.

The new work approach was called **DevOps** (Developers + Operators) that brought new roles like **DevOps Engineers** into the market. DevOps focused on coordinated application development in smaller but continuously deployable pieces of code.

While programming is still a manual process, many other aspects of the DevOps cycle had to be automated such as code version controlling (using tools like Git), Infrastructure deployment as Code (using tools like Chef or Puppet on premises or using Public Cloud Platforms like Amazon Web Services or Google Cloud Platform), Automated logging and Monitoring (using tools like FluentD, Prometheus, Grafana, and so on), and integration of all of this (using tools like Jenkins). This increased the reliability of the software products, with bug fixes being released quicker and, in the worst case, unstable patches being rolled back. From feedback acquisition to catching up with the competitors, from data processing to pricing manipulation, everything became more efficient. The most significant achievement of DevOps workflow is improving broader contextual understanding and awareness of the application, its performance, and its caveats in the heads of the people working on it (aka DevOps Engineers). This inherently created an informed and coordinated decision-making culture, reducing the risks and increasing the returns. It is no surprise that the bleeding edge IT workspaces offer some of the most satisfying jobs.

Microservices

With developers and the development-deployment models changing so much, the applications themselves had to change as well! Heavily integrated major applications running on a single piece of hardware as a tree of processes and threads were divided into smaller, and decoupled services that would operate independently and communicate data in the form of requests and responses over the internet. Such small services are called **Microservices**. Microservices are easier and quicker to scale (up or down) and distribute over clusters of infrastructures with isolated operation environments (physical or virtual). This makes them dispensable, secure, and avoids single point of failure. It also made planning and execution of updates easier.

At this point, it is quite likely that you came across the existence and title of this book via some microservices on professional or casual social media! Of course, not all applications are microservices. Many of them still run natively on your hardware as traditional apps. If your application does not need to scale or "serve" its clients, you do not have to worry about any of this. For everyone else, this book provides insights and instructions on some of the most important technologies behind DevOps.

Conclusion

In this chapter, we saw how microservice-based web applications created under DevOps workflow are present and future of IT. While microservices are great, they faced a major resource wastage problem in efforts of achieving isolation. In the next chapter, we will look at what are Containers and how they make microservices great again!

CHAPTER 2
Hello Containers!

Introduction

In the introductory chapter, we got a fair idea about web applications, the client-server model, and the microservices. As great as they may be, to use them optimally in ubiquity, we need to address the implementation level issues. One of the issues is efficient resource allocation. Ideally, every instance of a microservices needs a separate system. To overcome this bottleneck, this chapter will explain OS-level virtualization. Eventually, we will move toward Containers and introduce Docker as a utility to make containers handier.

Structure

This chapter covers:

- Virtualization
- Virtual Machines (VMs) and Hypervisors
- Containers
- DIY: Running a Container on Linux
- Basic definition of Containers
- Docker: A Container Runtime Environment
- VMs or Containers

Objective

Let us be honest here. This is not a salient chapter that can add a couple of skills to your résumé. But reading this will reinforce the idea and importance of isolation and virtualization in computing. VMs and Containers are just a couple of variants among a spectrum of OS-level isolation methods. This chapter will also make you realize how tiresome it is to run containers from the scratch without any assisting tool. So, you will appreciate Docker and more genuinely while reading further chapters.

Virtualization

In the previous chapter, we saw how it is important to distribute loads into multiple microservices to avoid single point of failure. But many times, the solution for one problem becomes the root cause for another. Observe the figure below to understand what happens when any application runs on a normal computer system:

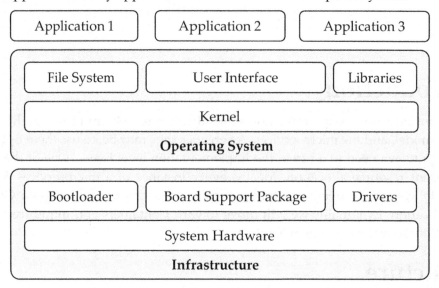

Figure 2.1: Abstraction of a running application instance

To anyone who has gone through a part time training or a full-time course on Computer Science, some if not all of the layers of this figure will ring a bell. This is the well-known, traditional way of running applications on a computer. Generally, we look at such figures from OS or driver's perspective where we try to understand the position of OS components in the abstraction.

Let us change the perspective a little and try to look from Application's point of view. In this case, we have three applications and all of them are running as an individual unit. But the problem is, they are working in the same user space. It means that they can access the same files at the same time. This causes conflicts of operations. To understand this problem better, let us do a practical task. Open a document file, save it and try to delete it while it is open. You will get an error dialog box saying something like the following screenshot:

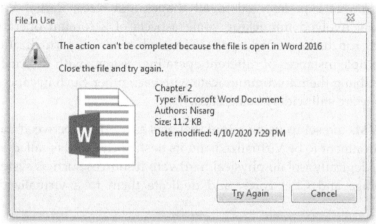

Figure 2.2: *Windows error dialog box*

The windows explorer cannot delete this document file because Microsoft Word is already using it. For manual users like us, this is completely fine as we can just close the file and delete it afterwards; but who will make such a decision in an autonomous system?

Moreover, if we talk about microservices, there can be hundreds of instances of the same application. Just think about running a hundred Nginx webserver instances and all of them are programmed to use port **8080**. One might argue that we can customize them to use different ports but there is no guarantee that the same ports used on testing machines will be free on the deployment system as well. The situation practically becomes a nightmare, and developers have to use those 6 magical words… **"But it worked on my machine!"**

Unfortunately, that is not where the nightmare ends. The most crucial part is the security of the microservices. In the same user space, one corrupted process (or microservice) can act like the rotten mango which ends up degrading the quality of the whole box. All of this leads to a pretty solid conclusion. Hosted applications or services need subtle isolation. This triggered the advent of **Virtualization.**

Not so surprisingly enough, this conclusion is not a new discovery. Computer scientists were working on Virtualization since way back in the 1960s. The idea of logically dividing a computer into two or more smaller computers that could act independently without interfering with one another's processes was both fascinating and advantageous.

Virtual Machines and Hypervisors

Virtualization was experimented in all shapes and sizes. Partial Virtualization or **Emulation** involved mimicking some aspects of a foreign operating system (generally to run unsupported applications) whereas full virtualization allowed running multiple instances of different operating systems with full customizations and even enabling them to communicate with each other. Such instances are called VMs and they are still widely being used.

Generally, **VMs** are setup using **a tool** that acts as a bridge between the operating system environment to be Virtualized and its host. Such a tool is called **Hypervisor**. Hypervisors logically isolate physical hardware resources such as system memory (RAM), storage and CPU cores, and dedicate them to a virtualized guest OS environment.

Types of Hypervisors

There are two types of Hypervisors, Type 1 and Type 2 (*naming creativity at its peak!*). *Figure 2.3* represents the nature of **Type 1 Hypervisor**:

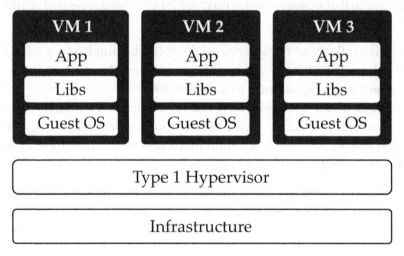

Figure 2.3: Type 1 Hypervisor

Compared to *Figure 2.1*, we have collapsed the Infrastructure and Operating System blocks because now our focus is on Hypervisor and VM. Anyway, you might have noticed that the Hypervisor is sitting right on top of the Infrastructure without any

OS in-between. That is because Type 1 Hypervisors are installed bare-metal. They do not have any Host OS supporting them.

It also means that as software, they are self-sufficient and sophisticated enough to function smoothly without OS file systems, system calls, library functions, and other kernel utilities like scheduling and process management. Just think about it, a software that runs without an operating system but can make room for multiple operating systems and can also manage their resources. That's the beauty of computer science!

The virtualization market has a variety of Type 1 hypervisors to offer. For example, if you're looking for an open-source Type 1 hypervisor, there is Kernel-based Virtual Machine (KVM). If you are looking for a paid but Real Time Operating System compatible hypervisor, there is VxWorks. Such hypervisors provide better latency control due to the absence of OS layer processes. On top of that, they also provide better resource management and security. They can be costly and demand more attention while operating. So, they are mostly used for large scale deployments in Data Centers. On the other hand, if you are just a student or hobbyist who is experimenting with virtualization, you will stumble upon the other type of Hypervisors called **Type 2 Hypervisors**.

You can clearly see that figure below is quite similar to *Figure 2.3* apart from one difference, the presence of a host operating system:

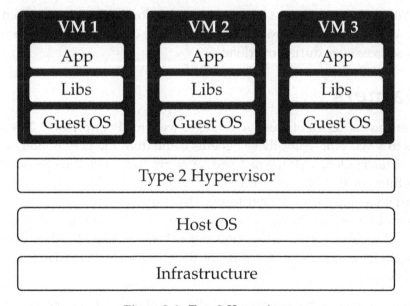

Figure 2.4: *Type 2 Hypervisors*

This is what differentiates Type 2 Hypervisors from Type 1. They are also called **Hosted Hypervisors** because they perform hardware virtualization through the host OS. Due to having to work with an additional layer of operations (OS), Type 2 Hypervisors are subjected to more latencies than Type 1. On top of that, they are also less resource efficient. But that doesn't mean they are useless. They are the go-to choice for developers who have to switch often between development and testing environments. They are also ideal for individual usage. You can do something like running a minimal OS on a VM while performing all of your other tasks on your host operating system. Oracle's Virtual Box is one of the most popular Type 2 hypervisor.

No matter which type of Hypervisor you choose, VMs offer a great deal of advantages such as:

- Allowing multiple OS environments to co-exist on the same system hardware.

- Due to logical isolation, processes running on one VM are unharmed by the corruption and/or compromises faced by the other VMs.

- Due to VMs being able to communicate among themselves and to the internet, the infrastructure can be scaled up or down horizontally instead of vertically. In other words, we can always add or remove more VMs as long as we can own or borrow sufficient infrastructure.

- Infrastructure as code can be utilized via tools like Chef or Puppet to create and/or delete VMs automatically.

- With Infrastructure as a Service on public clouds like Amazon Web Services (AWS) or **Google Cloud Platform** (**GCP**) we can practically never run out of resources even during overloads.

Containers

So, VMs are amazing. All of those advantages were really impressive, but were they exclusive to VMs? Not really, those benefits come from the very notion of isolation through virtualization. VMs are just one set of products following those principles. Come to think of it, VMs are really bulky. Their creation and destruction is time taking and if you have your own little infrastructure, you can only keep a handful of VMs active at a time. In that case, why would anyone in their right mind spare 10 GB of RAM and roughly 100 GB of storage just to keep 5 isolated webservers running simultaneously on standard PC? But are there any better alternatives? *(Note: the author smirks…)*

Yes, there are more suitable alternatives called **Containers.** If we take the traditional route, I can just define the Containers and expect you to understand or at least vaguely remember the definition. But that would not be any fun, would it? Containers are not discoveries of absolute existence like Gravity. The containers that we use today have grown on the foundation of series of other versions which were tried, tested, rejected, or utilized in the past. We will take a quick look at the significant ones in a chronological order and then define the containers of today.

Road to Containers

Not so surprisingly enough *(Déjà vu!)*, there have been a lot of attempts over the course of computing history to find the lighter alternatives of VMs. One of them was **chroot()**. Introduced in Unix v7, **chroot()** was an OS system call that stood for "change the root directory". As the name suggested, it allowed a process to operate from a different root directory.

In other words, the location of the root directory was changed for the particular process. Moreover, the child processes also followed the same changed root directory. This way, all of these processes could not access files outside of their changed root directory. This was the first successful attempt to provide one-way isolation to processes within the OS environment. Back then, it was a welcomed and sometimes useful addition to the Unix. Little to their knowledge, it was going to be the foundation of what we call **Containers** today!

To take this discussion further, check out the chronology of container evolution provided in the following *Figure 2.5*:

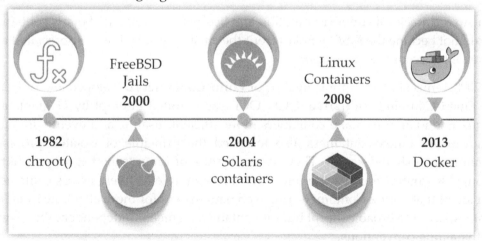

Figure 2.5: Evolution of Containers

After **chroot()**, the OS-based virtualization came to a significant standstill; not because it was not appreciated, but because it was not needed back then. The world was still fancying vertical infrastructure scaling (higher specifications on a single machine) and there were not so many hosted applications due to weak internet.

In the year 2000 though, FreeBSD (open-source OS inspired by Unix) came up with **Jails**. The `jail()` was another system call that allowed FreeBSD running systems to create sandboxed virtual user spaces. Jails had dedicated set of super user accounts, physical resources, and IP addresses while sharing the same kernel of the host OS (the FreeBSD kernel). This provided more security and isolation, and it was useful for isolating shared hosted services (similar services running on the same machine).

For example, in a VM or a normal system, if the webserver gets compromised, the attacker would get access to all of the files accessible by the webserver user account (typically **www**). In other words, just by compromising the webserver, the attacker could even access the system shell from **/etc.** directory. On the other hand, the separate super user accounts of jails would prevent host compromise and since the jails are using the shared FreeBSD kernel, they wouldn't even occupy as much resources as a VM.

In 2004, Solaris released **Solaris Containers** as well as **Solaris Zones**. This duo is a multi-stage isolation attempt on PCs with Scalable Processor ARChitecture (SPARC) architecture. Solaris Zones are virtual servers (baby VMs) on Solaris host. I used the term baby VMs because unlike traditional VMs, these zones do not have dedicated kernel and so, they do not have VM level isolation privileges like separate scheduler or separate init process. They just have resource reservations and dedicated IP address ranges. These IP addresses are then provided to the containers running on the zones. In a way, these zones attempt to host a virtual cluster of containers.

Due to architectural support limitation and less relative demand, Solaris containers could not become the MSP of Solaris, but the cluster approach was appreciated and taken into account by developers.

In 2008, Linux started supporting LXC or **Linux Containers** developed and powered by **Open Container Initiative** (OCI). OCI was a united attempt by IT giants and Linux Foundation to make containers more efficient, usable, and eventually more mainstream. Linux containers also followed the principle of isolated processes running on a shared kernel. They used a feature of Linux called **cgroups** (control groups) to control the distribution of resources more effectively across containers. On top of that, Linux Containers also used namespaces for more elaborate isolation. Namespaces is a broad concept but for containers, it meant independent filesystems with naming conventions.

In short, Linux containers were **containing** or **isolating** processes along with files and resources while sharing the kernel. It is a more promising execution of previous discoveries. Linux Containers are still supported today. In fact, we can run a basic container on Linux right now (*well, that escalated fast*)!

DIY: running a Container on Linux

Alright, time to get started with some hands-on practice. Running a container all by yourself is one of the most enlightening things to try when you are keen on learning containerization tools. If you are a fan of heist movies or crime thrillers, you can consider this part as the first impression scene where you don't understand most of the plot *(because you were not supposed to)* but the scene gets revisited over and over and every time it presents a new detail.

Similarly, the practices used in this section will be reminded multiple times while teaching Docker. This will make Docker's features more relatable and rational. On top of that, once you have seen how containers can run by using simple Linux utilities, you will not feel alienated or clueless when other tools create and/or run containers with just one command.

The prerequisites are really simple. You need a consumer Linux running on your system as the main OS or on a VM, I am running Ubuntu 18.04 and you need to perform the commands under **root privileges**. So, how do we make a Container?

Step 1: Prepare the system

Let's see what we know about the containers so far. They are isolated processes along with dedicated file systems. We can isolate the process using **chroot()** and **cgroups()**, and we can dedicate a filesystem convention using namespaces. **chroot()** is a basic Linux utility but there are chances that you might not have **cgroups()** defined, so let's add the supported library packages for it.

```
sudo su -
apt update
apt install -y libcgroup-dev
apt install -y cgroup-tools
```

Now let us make sure that none of our commands get the missing values auto-filled.

```
set -eux
```

Step 2: Obtaining the Container

As we said earlier, we need to containerize the process and the files associated with it. The process will be created by Linux itself so let us get the files. We are trying to create a containerized fish shell. Fish is another shell-like bash or korn and it stands for Friendly Interactive **Sh**ell. Let us get the tarball of the fish shell container from **git**.

```
git clone https://github.com/dsametriya/fish.git
cd fish
```

Extract this tarball in a newly created **/fish** directory.

```
tar -xf fish.tar
```

Step 3: Setup the cgroup

In this step, we will create a **cgroup**, assign it a **uuid** (Universally unique identifier) and allocate set amount of computing resources to it. The **uuid** will set it apart from other **cgroups**.

```
uuid="cgroup_$(shuf -i 1000-2000 -n 1)" // Generating a uuid
cgcreate -g "cpu,cpuacct,memory:$uuid"  // Creating a Cgroup
cgset -r cpu.shares=512 "$uuid" // Setting the CPU usage limit
cgset -r memory.limit_in_bytes=1000000000 "$uuid"//Setting the Memory limit
```

We have restricted our newly created **cgroup** to use not more than 512 mCPU (generally interpreted as half a CPU core) and 1 GB of RAM.

Step 4: Run the Container

Now, as the step itself suggests, we will run the container under the changed **/root** directory.

```
cgexec -g "cpu,cpuacct,memory:$uuid" \
unshare -fmuipn --mount-proc \
chroot "$PWD" \
/bin/sh -c "/bin/mount -t proc proc /proc && hostname linux-container
&& /usr/bin/fish"
```

Sweet ravioli, what in the world is this monstrosity of a command? Let us break it down. First of all, to avoid any confusion, the backward slashes (\) at the end of every line indicate a multi-line command.

- In the first line, we are executing the cgroup that we have created recently with the resource limits defined in the last step. In other words, we are running the container.

- Then, with **unshare** command, we are making sure that the **cgroup** does not execute in same namespace as its parent. This way, the container will be detached from the current Linux shell.

- Going forward, we are also changing the root directory for the cgroup process with **chroot()**. This is proper isolation. Separate root directory, separate namespace, and separate resource group.

- Now we have just one thing left to take care of, **/proc**. It is a **Virtual file system** that gets created every time Linux systems boot up and it is destroyed when they shut down. Proc is used to keep track of runtime stats. In the final line, we are providing a mount path for our container's **/proc**. This is important because the container's runtime status needs to be separated from host's runtime status. The container may crash while the host is running as smoothly as ever. Also, we are providing some additional information like different hostname to address the container more easily.

After you perform all of the 4 steps successfully, the output should look something like the following one:

```
root@docker:~/fish#
root@docker:~/fish# uuid="cgroup_$(shuf -i 1000-2000 -n 1)"
root@docker:~/fish#
root@docker:~/fish# cgcreate -g "cpu,cpuacct,memory:$uuid"
root@docker:~/fish#
root@docker:~/fish# cgset -r cpu.shares=512 "$uuid"
root@docker:~/fish#
root@docker:~/fish# cgset -r memory.limit_in_bytes=1000000000 "$uuid"
root@docker:~/fish#
root@docker:~/fish# cgexec -g "cpu,cpuacct,memory:$uuid" \
>      unshare -fmuipn --mount-proc \
>      chroot "$PWD" \
>      /bin/sh -c "/bin/mount -t proc proc /proc && hostname linux-container && /usr/bin/fish"
Welcome to fish, the friendly interactive shell
Type help for instructions on how to use fish
root@linux-container # 
```

Figure 2.6: Running a simple container on Linux

To make your judgment quicker, take a look at the lines beside the two white arrows. You can clearly see that you have switched from bash to fish shell in a container. This clearly means your container is running. Since we have already got it running, what comes next? Any guesses?

Basic definition of Containers

You have understood the concept of virtualization, you went through the journey of advent and evolution of Containers and you have also run a container using nothing but Linux utilities. Now, let us try to define containers using our current knowledge and the following figure:

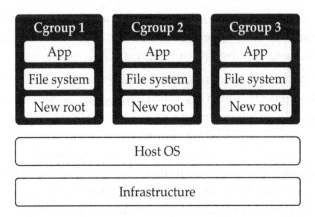

Figure 2.7: Containers on Linux

Containers are a lightweight unit of OS-Level Virtualization used to run and control isolated applications, typically scalable microservices.

What you just read is the basic idea behind raw containers. Many sources across the internet provide you market friendly definition of containers which is more attractive but less insightful. If you break down this definition, you will find two parts: an identity and a purpose. Being a lightweight unit of OS-level virtualization is the identity of the containers whereas microservice management is the purpose. Unfortunately, in Container's case, the identity is not enough to meet the purpose. For example:

- Even if we do not run these commands repetitively and create a script instead, the script will not work on all flavors of Linux.

- The resource allocation of the container was eyeballed very vaguely and that is because you are most likely going to be unaware of the proper required proportions. Plus, you have to tweak them manually based on your system configuration.

- What about the zombie process management if/when the cgroup crashes?

- If the said container is running a microservice, what about version management and regular updates?

- While these scripts might be comfortable for the developers, they are a nightmare for clients so "It worked on my machine!" issue still persists.

We can keep going, but I believe you have got the point. The kind of container we just ran did fulfill the virtualization, but it was not enough. On that stage, they could not be seen as a universally acceptable solution to enhance microservice deployment.

That is why despite of existing since decades, containers had mostly remained out of the radar of System Admins. But the tables were soon going to be turned completely upside down.

Docker: A Container Runtime Environment

Have you ever been amazed when a pro chef takes some fairly cheap street food and turns it into a popular premium restaurant recipe? Well, **Solomon Hykes** and his team did exactly that with containers when they launched **Docker** in 2013.

Figure 2.8: Docker Ecosystem

Docker is a **Container Runtime Environment (CRE)**. It means that it is a software that runs and manages Containers. It added the much-needed **Platform as a Service (PaaS)** flair to containers and eliminated the need of writing complicated commands repeatedly forever.

Apart from the CRE itself, Docker also introduced a slew of other container management products. Some of them are easy to avoid paid services while others are free to use game changers which still dominate the container user base. Out of all of these products, the most useful one is Docker itself *(I know you could guess it easily, I just had to write it)*. Docker as the CRE, can be installed on top of Host Operating system such as Linux or Windows. As you can see in the following figure, Docker acts as a bridge between the OS and the Containers:

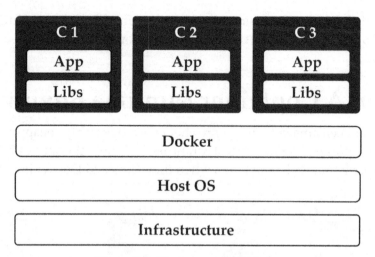

Figure 2.9: Docker and Containers

It uses the same principles of shared kernel, cgroup, and namespaces to containerize processes. While your job as a system admin might be to "serve" the microservice, Docker's job is to run the container. We will take a deeper look into its architecture in the next chapter but for now, let us just say that Docker is more meticulous about the health and performance of the containers than any average Linux user.

This by itself is a good enough reason to use Docker, but it is not what makes Docker special and revolutionary. Docker's true strength lies in its integration with its ecosystem. In the fish shell example, we cloned a container tarball from my git repository. How could you be so sure that it was not corrupted, or it was secure for your system? If we keep using such direct links for container sharing, we might end up with unmanageable amount of security compromises. That is where **Docker Registry** comes in. It maintains a global collection of downloadable container images *(we will get to them soon enough)* as well as private repositories for organizations. On top of that, it also provides verified versions of popular containers maintained by the source organization themselves.

These downloadable containers can then be imported to any system running Docker and they will perform more or less the same! Till now, Linux Containers were taking lightweight isolation as their main objective. Docker has taken it as a default asset and developed their CRE while keeping the deployment experience of containerized application in focus.

On top of that, Docker also provides its own version of container clustering. They call it **Docker Swarm**. The Docker ecosystem also consists of a convenient application development tool called **Docker Compose** and a Container building format like **Dockerfile**.

All of these offerings work almost effortlessly together, and they create a containerization-friendly environment for the application developers as well as the system admins. Containers and specially Docker are major players behind the success of the DevOps movement. With all of this, the current and most relevant definition of the Containers goes something like this:

Containers are an abstraction of the application layer, which packages codes and dependencies together.

The previous and the current definitions lead to the same concept but previously the focus was virtualization whereas now the focus is **Containerizing** the executable application (of course in a virtualized space) along with its unique dependencies while borrowing common resources from the shared kernel. You can containerize anything from webservers to OS itself to the smallest scripts. So, let us address the million-dollar question.

Virtual Machines or Containers?

It is easy to jump on the bandwagon and choose Containers but to be honest, none is universally better than the other. Both are extremely relevant and useful in today's practices and they offer a different set of advantages, albeit when it comes to microservices, Containers are the key.

From the employment perspective, containers are more beneficial since they are relatively new and the migration phase is still years away from saturation. On top of that, containers also offer a lot of certification opportunities to make your resume shine. But all of these aspects are not that important for you right now. You have just entered the world of containers and it is going to get a lot more exciting from here on. In the next chapter, we will take a deeper look into Docker's architecture and start playing hands on with it. Till then, enjoy the quiz questions!

Note - Q: Which container definition to use during interviews and other judgmental stages?

A: You can use both of these definitions whenever and whichever feels appropriate.

Conclusion

In this chapter, you entered the world of virtualization. After learning about VMs and what makes them less suitable for the deployment of microservices, you got a conceptual introduction to Containers. Now, no container creation-based product will be a mystery for you since you know the last mile implementation of containers. This chapter has also kick started our journey of learning Docker. Look forward to wonderful concepts and skills to learn in the next chapters.

Multiple choice questions

1. Which of the following is used as a bridge between OS and the host system to create Virtual Machines?

    A. PCI bus

    B. Hypervisor

    C. Switch

    D. Supervisor

    Answer: B

2. Which of the following type of hypervisor is installed without any OS on a computer system?

    A. Type 1 hypervisors

    B. Type 2 hypervisors

    C. Hosted hypervisors

    D. None of these

    Answer: A

3. What is the functionality of chroot() system call?

    A. To change the priority of the current running user process.

    B. To change the scope of the current running user process and its child processes.

    C. To change the PID of the current running user process and its child processes.

    D. To change the root directory for the current running user process and its child processes.

    Answer: D

4. Which of the following is not a type of virtualization?

    A. Emulation

    B. Virtual Machines

    C. Application Package

    D. Container

    Answer: C

5. Which of the following is not a feature of containers?

    A. Isolation

    B. Virtualization

    C. Dedicated Kernel

    D. Small footprint

    Answer: C

Questions

1. What is virtualization in a Computer Science? Have you come across virtualization in practice? Expand upon your experience.

2. What is a Hypervisor and why are they important? Explain briefly about the types of hypervisor.

3. Give a crisp definition of containers in your words. Elaborate your definition.

4. What are the fundamental differences between a Virtual Machine and a container? Which one is more suitable for microservices? Why?

5. What differentiates Docker from other container technologies?

CHAPTER 3
Introduction to Docker

Introduction

In the previous chapter, we became familiar with the concept and growth of containers and how they are different from the Virtual Machines (VM). The efforts that developers need to put to containerize the application were overwhelming, which makes them pretty much impractical to use. That is where Docker shines as a solution and this chapter explores it further. Get ready for some in-depth architectural understanding and a lot of installations!

Structure

This chapter covers:

- Docker: A deeper look
- Docker architecture
- Installing Docker on Linux
- Installing Docker Desktop on Windows
- Installing Docker Desktop on Mac
- Running fish shell as your first Docker Container

Objective

If the previous chapter was like a brochure, this one is like a welcome kit along with the joining form of an institution. As stated in the structure, it provides a detailed look into the architecture of Docker and its components. By the end of this chapter, you and your system will be ready to go wild with Docker!

Docker: A deeper look

Docker is not the only Container Runtime Environment (CRE) in the market. The Linux Containers have their own variant of CRE called **LXD** and there are other significant players like **CRI-O** and **Containerd** as well. While others are emerging CREs, Docker is a wholesome platform that provides an end-to-end containerization experience (*sounds like sales pitch, doesn't it?*). If you randomly search the term "application containers" on Google, you will see that majority of results are about Docker in one way or another. Docker has almost become synonymous to the containers. The reason is not just the first-mover advantage. As I have said earlier, what makes Docker special is its **Build-Ship-Run** model. To know more about it, check out *Figure 3.1*:

| Build your App | Pack it for Shipping | Host or Run the App |

Figure 3.1: *The Build-Ship-Run Model*

This model treats three important phases of a containerized microservice's lifecycle individually and provides three different objects to address them. These objects are called **Dockerfiles, Docker Images,** and **Containers** (*or Docker Containers… but let's just go with Containers*). We will play with them a lot in this book, but before that, let's demystify how Docker works!

Docker architecture

Compared to whatever container implementation we have seen earlier, Docker's architecture is really intriguing. It follows a client–server-ish model (*I will justify the 'ish' part soon enough*). Just like every other software, Docker is also built on the foundation of a bunch of strong APIs and a few processes that exchange, process, and shape the information using those APIs. Sounds complicatedly simple enough, right? All we have to do is understand the working of the APIs and the purpose of the processes, that's it! It is not exclusive to Docker, this trick works on any software architecture.

Docker follows the same concept of containers. In other words, it also runs an isolated process under different root directories and supports it with a cgroup and namespace. Whatever it does additionally is to enhance the performance of the containers and to make your life easier. We had mentioned this in the previous chapter and we will see it in theory in this chapter. Moreover, we will see a lot of those enhancements in action in further chapters. *Figure 3.2* is a conceptual graphical representation of Docker's operational architecture:

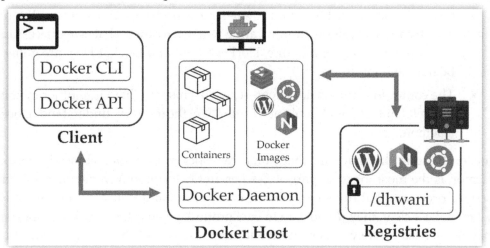

Figure 3.2: Docker architecture

The product we all commonly known as Docker is a software package written in Golang (go language). It is offered in both community (free) and enterprise (paid) editions. For learning purpose, the community edition is more than enough but we will sprinkle the references of enterprise edition wherever they are relevant.

There are three main components of Docker's architecture namely Docker Client, Docker Host, and Docker Registries. First, we will see the individual functionality of each component and then we will understand how they work with one another.

Docker Client

It is the Client end of the *Client-Server-ish* analogy we mentioned earlier. Typically, any machine or application console that runs **Docker API** (docker) is called **Docker**

Client. When you perform standard Docker installation on your system, Docker API will be installed on it as well and thus your system will turn into Docker Client. The primary way to interact with Docker API is through the `Docker` command line.

The reason why it is called a client is that Docker API by itself is just a communication link between users and Docker Daemon. The Docker API cannot create containers by itself. But that does not mean the client is not important. It carries out the essential task of validating the user requests.

Docker Host

This is the server end of the *Client–Server-ish* analogy. I called it *Client–Server-ish* because of two reasons:

- Generally, when we talk about client–server model, we think of two different and distant machines communicating with each other. That is not necessarily the case here. Most of the time, Docker Client and Docker Host are going to be the same machines.

- The communication is not client–server exclusive. There is another member as well. But we will look at it after we thoroughly understand Docker Daemon.

Docker Host is the machine that runs the Docker Daemon. Honestly, Docker Daemon is the most intricate part of Docker. In OS terminology, daemon is a term used for processes that run silently in the background and thus are non-interactive. Just to make it clear, they do not run in background because they are less important. They do so because they are essential and they don't want their performance to be obstructed by our inputs *(ouch)*! Generally, identifying daemon processes on Linux is pretty simple. All you have to do is look for processes that have names ending with small **d**. For example, **systemd**, **syslogd** or **sshd**. Our point of focus is **dockerd** (Docker Daemon).

Docker Daemon does everything that you can think about containers. It creates them, runs them, loads them, tags them, switches their network context, etc. It runs on root privileges and has the right to access kernel resources. The only way to give it any instruction is to pass it via Docker Client. In other words, when we run some commands using Docker's Command Line (docker CLI), they get translated into Application Program Interface.

(API) requests and get passed on to Docker Daemon. Docker Daemon executes the said operation and returns the response to Docker Client which gets reflected on our terminals. Client itself doesn't perform resource-sensitive tasks. There can be one or more clients talking to the same daemon and in the worst case, even if the client is compromised, daemon can just break the connection and keep going till it gets a repaired and valid client connection request.

The client–server communication between Docker Client and Docker Host is actually Inter-Process Communication (IPC) carried out via **socket()** APIs between **dockerd** (Docker Daemon APIs) and **docker** (Docker Client APIs). Sockets are communication endpoints between processes on the same or different machines. They were introduced in Unix network stack and are still widely used as transport layer backbone and are abstracted away by higher layer protocols like HTTP. If they are on the same machine, they communicate through local host and if they are on different machines, they communicate via IPs. The requests and responses are communicated in HTTP REST format like GET, POST, PUSH , and so on.

Note: Run ps -aux to get the list of all running processes to find daemon processes on your Linux system.

Since Docker Daemon runs on Docker Host, the containers and Docker Images are also created there (because **dockerd** will have access to the host's kernel). Apart from Docker Client, the Daemon also communicates with one more entity, let's check it out.

The Registries

They are the third and most unique component of Docker's architecture. Earlier calling them Docker Registries was also fine but now since many players (like Google and Amazon) have joined in, they are not exclusive to Docker. **Registries** are used to store Docker images. For now, you can say Docker Images are transportable (over internet) packaged collection of files and programs to be containerized. The registries can also be used to make the images accessible to the intended users. This makes shipping containers ever so easy, secure, and reliable. There are two types of registries, public and private ones.

Docker Hub is the most popular and easiest to use public repository. It is valuable because of the enormous amount of contributions made to it. You can find almost any Docker Image in its latest version on Docker Hub. It is managed by Docker and Docker Daemon is programmed to communicate with it directly. Utilities like image search and pull will use Docker Hub as their source unless mentioned otherwise. By the end of this chapter, we will run a container pulled from Docker Hub and we will explore most of its utilities in upcoming chapters.

Organizations or individual users can create their own public repositories on Docker Hub for better arrangement of images. Public cloud providers like Google and Amazon have their own container registries which are useful for quick container deployment on that particular cloud but that has not challenged the throne of Docker Hub as the go-to solution for any container enthusiast.

Apart from public repositories, Docker also allows you to create private repositories where unauthorized users cannot access your Docker Images. Of course, such provisions are paid and fall under enterprise-grade support. On top of that, Docker also offers **Docker Datacenters (DDC) - Their own servers and Docker Trusted Registry (DTR) - Their dedicated image verification** as other enterprise features. Added security and trustworthy infrastructure management is their way of making money, which makes sense.

Just to avoid any confusion, the registry and repository are different for Docker. Registry (generally managed by massive organizations like Docker or Google) is a collection of hundreds of thousands (if not millions) of repositories created by individual users (like you or me) or smaller organizations (like Redis).

In a nutshell, if we want to run a publicly available container, we ask Docker Client to pass the instruction to Docker Daemon. Docker Daemon then searches Docker Hub for the container image and downloads it. It unpacks the image and runs it as an isolated container. At the end, it sends us the container's running status via Docker Client. We want to see all of this in action but before that, we need to install Docker!

Installing Docker on Linux

Docker is supported across multiple Linux variants, hardware infrastructures, and ISAs. Here, I will be using Ubuntu 18.04 LTS (Bionic Beaver) on ×86_64 architecture (Intel ×86 Instruction Set for 64-bit hardware). If you are also curious about knowing your infrastructure, you can run the following command:

```
arch
```

Now let's begin Docker Installation.

Step 1: Setting up repository

As usual, first of all, we will update the system repos and install some of the pre-requisites. If you have them pre-installed, this will either update them or will let you know that you are good to go.

```
sudo apt-get update
```

```
sudo apt-get install \
apt-transport-https \
ca-certificates \
curl \
gnupg-agent \
software-properties-common
```

To briefly state the purpose of each package. HTTPS is used for exchanging REST requests and responses, ca-certificates to validate client–server communication, Client URL (curl), and GPG (more about GPG in the notes) for assisting the installation. Before setting up the repo, let's add the GPG key from Docker. This will enable public-key encryption between Docker and us to make sure we never receive a fraud package under Docker's disguise.

```
curl -fsSL https://download.docker.com/linux/ubuntu/gpg | sudo apt-key
add -
```

Note: GNU Privacy Guard (GPG) is a cryptography package used to sign documents, files, or software packages to maintain their legitimacy. It is an open-source implementation of PGP (Pretty Good Privacy) as the latter eventually got commercialized by McAfee (you might have heard of their virus scan and removal tools).

Finally, we will add the stable repository. Most of the software have multiple versions of their releases working simultaneously. You might also be a part of some of the beta-testing programs of a few games or applications. Thus, by adding the stable repository, we will make sure that whenever we run apt-get updates, Docker only sends stable updates to our system. That way, we will avoid unnecessary encounters with bugs and unstable features. Just for your information, apart from stable, docker has Test (beta) and Nightly (alpha) versions of its releases.

```
sudo add-apt-repository \
"deb [arch=arm64] https://download.docker.com/linux/ubuntu \
$(lsb_release -cs) \
stable"
```

The Docker release for **arm64** and **x86_64** is the same. So, even though my architecture is **x86_64**, I will be downloading arm64 version for Debian, which is the parent OS of Ubuntu. The `lsb_release -cs` sub-command will return the name of the Linux distribution with the codename of the distribution release. For me, this command will return Ubuntu distributor with release "18.04" and codename "Bionic".

Step 2: Installing components

Let us check if the repository is set properly. And to do so, we need to run a generic update command and see if it returns any Docker packages.

```
sudo apt-get update
```

Note the arrows in the following figure. The package list on our system has these new entries of Docker packages:

```
Hit:1 http://us-central1.gce.archive.ubuntu.com/ubuntu bionic InRelease
Get:2 http://us-central1.gce.archive.ubuntu.com/ubuntu bionic-updates InRelease [88.7 kB]
Get:3 http://us-central1.gce.archive.ubuntu.com/ubuntu bionic-backports InRelease [74.6 kB]
Get:4 https://download.docker.com/linux/ubuntu bionic InRelease [64.4 kB]
Hit:5 http://security.ubuntu.com/ubuntu bionic-security InRelease
Hit:6 http://archive.canonical.com/ubuntu bionic InRelease
Get:7 https://download.docker.com/linux/ubuntu bionic/stable amd64 Packages [11.0 kB]
Fetched 239 kB in 1s (379 kB/s)
Reading package lists... Done
```

Figure 3.3: Docker packages

Now let us install the Docker components. We are installing Docker CLI, Docker Engine Community Edition (which includes daemon), and containerd.

```
sudo apt-get install docker-ce docker-ce-cli containerd
```

Since our machine is both Docker Client and Docker Host, we are installing both Docker CLI and CE. After Docker version 18.09, **containerd** is used as a layer between docker daemon and kernel system calls.

The installation should look something like the following:

```
Setting up aufs-tools (1:4.9+20170918-1ubuntu1) ...
Setting up containerd.io (1.2.13-1) ...
Created symlink /etc/systemd/system/multi-user.target.wants/containerd.service → /lib/systemd/system/containerd.s
ervice.
Setting up cgroupfs-mount (1.4) ...
Setting up libltdl7:amd64 (2.4.6-2) ...
Setting up docker-ce-cli (5:19.03.8~3-0~ubuntu-bionic) ...
Setting up pigz (2.4-1) ...
Setting up docker-ce (5:19.03.8~3-0~ubuntu-bionic) ...
Created symlink /etc/systemd/system/multi-user.target.wants/docker.service → /lib/systemd/system/docker.service.
Created symlink /etc/systemd/system/sockets.target.wants/docker.socket → /lib/systemd/system/docker.socket.
Processing triggers for libc-bin (2.27-3ubuntu1) ...
Processing triggers for systemd (237-3ubuntu10.39) ...
Processing triggers for man-db (2.8.3-2ubuntu0.1) ...
Processing triggers for ureadahead (0.100.0-21) ...
```

Figure 3.4: Docker Engine Installation

Step 3: Are we good to go?

We are done with the installation process. Now, it is time to verify the installation. And to do so, we are going to use the traditional way of testing, Hello-World! Docker has provided an image called **hello-world** to test the installation. Let us run a container using this image and see if the installation is successful. Type the following command in your terminal.

```
sudo docker run hello-world
```

If you are able to get the output of **docker run** command like the one below, Congratulations!! You have successfully installed Docker Community Edition on your host.

```
dhwani@docker:~$ sudo docker run hello-world
Unable to find image 'hello-world:latest' locally
latest: Pulling from library/hello-world
0e03bdcc26d7: Pull complete
Digest: sha256:8e3114318a995a1ee497790535e7b88365222a21771ae7e53687ad76563e8e76
Status: Downloaded newer image for hello-world:latest

Hello from Docker!
This message shows that your installation appears to be working correctly.

To generate this message, Docker took the following steps:
 1. The Docker client contacted the Docker daemon.
 2. The Docker daemon pulled the "hello-world" image from the Docker Hub.
    (amd64)
 3. The Docker daemon created a new container from that image which runs the
    executable that produces the output you are currently reading.
 4. The Docker daemon streamed that output to the Docker client, which sent it
    to your terminal.

To try something more ambitious, you can run an Ubuntu container with:
 $ docker run -it ubuntu bash

Share images, automate workflows, and more with a free Docker ID:
 https://hub.docker.com/

For more examples and ideas, visit:
 https://docs.docker.com/get-started/
```

Figure 3.5: hello-world container (with root privileges)

Step 4: Improvement of quality of life

Did you notice the **sudo** before **docker run** command? This is because by default, Docker Daemon is bound to UNIX socket which is owned by the root user. So, non-root users can only communicate to Docker daemon if they use **sudo** before sending any Docker command. To avoid this hassle, Docker daemon creates an UNIX group called **docker** with read/write privileges and you can add non-root users in this group. This way, you can run **docker** command without remembering **sudo**, that's one less thing to worry about; hence improvement of quality of life.

```
sudo groupadd docker
```

```
sudo usermod -aG docker $USER
```

Here, **usermod** command takes the name of the currently logged in user ($USER) and adds it to the docker group. Since **usermod** command modifies the system files with the latest changes, we need to reboot the system to allow these changes to reflect. When we hit the **docker run** command again without **sudo**, this should be the expected output.

```
dhwani@docker:~$ docker run hello-world

Hello from Docker!
This message shows that your installation appears to be working correctly.

To generate this message, Docker took the following steps:
 1. The Docker client contacted the Docker daemon.
 2. The Docker daemon pulled the "hello-world" image from the Docker Hub.
    (amd64)
 3. The Docker daemon created a new container from that image which runs the
    executable that produces the output you are currently reading.
 4. The Docker daemon streamed that output to the Docker client, which sent it
    to your terminal.

To try something more ambitious, you can run an Ubuntu container with:
 $ docker run -it ubuntu bash

Share images, automate workflows, and more with a free Docker ID:
 https://hub.docker.com/

For more examples and ideas, visit:
 https://docs.docker.com/get-started/
```

Figure 3.6: hello-world container (non-root user)

Installing Docker Desktop on Windows

Before you start spinning shuriken out of spring roll sheets, let me assure you. I understand that you have some serious questions just by looking at the subtopic.

"But Nisarg, didn't you mention in Chapter 2 that containers were all about sharing Linux kernel and isolating processes? Then, how could we do that on a Windows Machine and that too without a VM?"

Do not worry. There is nothing ground breaking here. Earlier, Docker did use to install a dedicated Linux VM on Windows to make containers. Nowadays, it is using the latest feature of Windows 10 called LCOW (Linux Containers on Windows) which uses Hyper-V and a minimal Linux variant to bring Linux Kernel capabilities on Windows. So, there is no shared kernel. There are individual microkernels for Windows Containers.

Does that even carry the advantages of Docker and Containers in general? No. This is more like a testing environment. LCOW is not even supported by Windows Server 2016, so there are no scopes for datacenter deployment of containers. Just because Windows exists, Docker Desktop for Windows exists. And just because Docker Desktop for Windows exists, we are going to look at its installation.

Before installing Docker Desktop on Windows host, there are a few prerequisites that must be fulfilled:

- You need to have Windows version 10 (Pro, Enterprise, or Education) and 64-bit architecture with at least 4 GB RAM. To verify the version of your Windows OS, press ⊞ + R, which will open up the **Run** utility. Type `winver` and you will get details about your currently installed Windows OS version and build.

Hyper-V and Containers Windows features should be enabled.

Now, let us download the setup of Docker Desktop for Windows:

Step 1: Downloading the setup

And to do so, visit the link https://hub.docker.com/editions/community/docker-ce-desktop-windows and you will land on Docker Desktop webpage. The setup gets, in general cases, downloaded in **Downloads** folder on your system and the name of the setup file should be `Docker Desktop Installer.exe`.

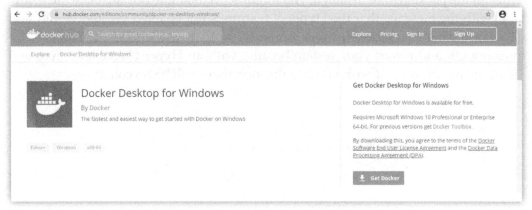

Figure 3.7: Docker Desktop for Windows

Step 2: A few clicks

After downloading the setup, double-click on it. This will open up a Windows Installer dialogue box asking for the permission to run this setup on your system. Grant all the necessary permissions and you will be redirected to the installation process. Then, another window will pop-up offering some configuration setups before the installation. We can leave the defaults configuration checked and proceed further.

At this stage, as you can see in *Figure 3.8*, Windows installer unpacks different packages of various Docker utilities and dependencies:

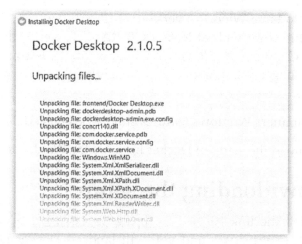

Figure 3.8: Docker Desktop for Windows – Installation

After all the packages are installed, you might see a dialogue box (just like the below one) with the message that the Hyper-V feature is not enabled yet and would you like to enable it for Docker to work properly? In that case, enable the Hyper-V by pressing OK and restart your system because without Hyper-V enabled, there will be no virtualization and without virtualization there will be no containers.

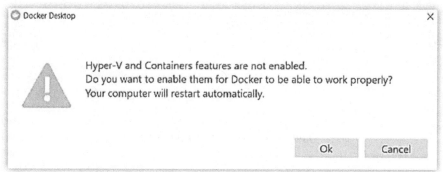

Figure 3.9: Docker Desktop for Windows – Hyper-V

Step 3: Testing the installation

After successfully installing Docker Desktop for Windows, it is time to test the installation. On the bottom right corner of the task bar, a whale icon should have been added and when you click on that icon, a list of Docker utilities will be available to you. Now, let us go to the command prompt and use the same **docker run** command to run the hello-world container on Windows. As you can see, we got the **hello-world** container, running on the Windows! Now you can go back to spinning shuriken:

```
Select Command Prompt                                                                    _  □  ×
Hello from Docker!
This message shows that your installation appears to be working correctly.

To generate this message, Docker took the following steps:
 1. The Docker client contacted the Docker daemon.
 2. The Docker daemon pulled the "hello-world" image from the Docker Hub.
    (amd64)
 3. The Docker daemon created a new container from that image which runs the
    executable that produces the output you are currently reading.
 4. The Docker daemon streamed that output to the Docker client, which sent it
    to your terminal.

To try something more ambitious, you can run an Ubuntu container with:
 $ docker run -it ubuntu bash

Share images, automate workflows, and more with a free Docker ID:
 https://hub.docker.com/

For more examples and ideas, visit:
 https://docs.docker.com/get-started/
```

Figure 3.10: *Docker Desktop for Windows – hello-world container*

Installing Docker Desktop on Mac

Just like Docker Desktop for Windows, this one is also created solely for the purpose of testing and development, not deployment. Even though both of them are called **Docker Desktop**, the Mac version is quite different from Windows. It uses a virtualization utility called **LinuxKit**, which is exclusive to **High Sierra and later Mac versions (Mojave and Catalina)**. The system should also have at least 4 GB of RAM and hardware newer than 2010.

Since Mac OS kernel has closer resemblance to Linux, many features of Docker like symlink, cgroup, and namespaces work natively. Thus, the footprints of microkernels used for bringing containers to life are much smaller than their Windows counterpart. We do not even need to break the installation down into steps here. Docker Desktop for Mac is installed as a native Mac application right in the **/Applications** folder, which means the drag and drop feature will work just fine.

Visit Docker Hub on https://hub.docker.com/editions/community/docker-ce-desktop-mac and download Docker Desktop for Mac setup file:

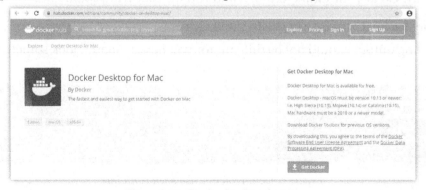

Figure 3.11: *Docker Desktop for Mac*

You will find the **docker.dmg** which is Docker's Disk Image file in the **Downloads** folder on your Mac system. Now, double-click on it to decompress and verify its content inside it. This will mount the **docker.dmg** file to your Mac system and you can find it in the list of mounted devices.

Here comes the favorite part, drag the **Docker.app** icon and drop it inside the **Applications** folder:

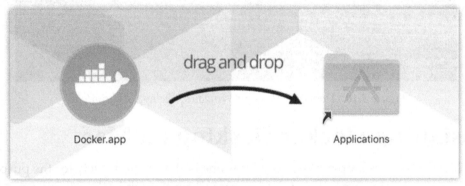

Figure 3.12: *Docker Desktop for Mac – Drag and Drop*

Now, to run Docker Desktop, double-click on the Docker app icon in the **Applications** folder and you will be directed to a couple of dialog boxes asking to acknowledge that you trust the source and to give it privileged access. Enter your system log in password to authorize Docker to make changes to your filesystem. Just like Linux and Windows, you can run the hello-world container on Docker Desktop on Mac as well.

Running fish shell as a Docker Container

As you remember, in *Chapter 2, Hello Containers!*, we ran a DIY container of fish shell on Linux with the help of the chroot(), cgroups, and namespace. The process almost took a whole page full of commands, and we had promised that Docker will simplify it. Most of you might have even guessed the solution but we are going to do it anyway. Go to your Linux terminal and run the following command:

```
docker run -it csametriya/fish-shell:latest
```

Identifying output should not be difficult for you now. It should look something like this.

```
dhwani@docker:~$ docker run -it csametriya/fish-shell:latest
Welcome to fish, the friendly interactive shell
root@02e9fa638bcb / > echo "My current directory is $PWD"
My current directory is /
root@02e9fa638bcb / >
```

Figure 3.13: Interactive fish shell container

In this one command, you indirectly used a Dockerfile, whereas you directly interacted with Docker Client, passed your request to Docker Daemon, pulled an image from Docker Hub, and ran it as an interactive container. This is the beauty of Docker. To elaborate further, since our host system did not have the fish shell Docker image, Docker daemon pulled it from my public repository on Docker Hub. The image itself does not pop out of nowhere. Someone must have built it from a Dockerfile. So, your action became a community attempt. Wonderful, right?

Conclusion

This was Docker's Build, Ship, Run model in its full glory. You not only understood Docker's architecture; but also learned how to install it on different environments and how to run your container with it. I am sure you enjoyed the simplification of the container running process using Docker. To appreciate it even further, in the next chapter, we will one-up your skillset by learning how to write Dockerfiles and we will also understand how the Docker image building process works. Till then, Good luck for the quiz and Happy reading!

Multiple choice questions

1. Which of the following is not a Container Runtime Environment?

    A. Docker

    B. Containerd

    C. CRI-O

    D. Kubernetes

    Answer: D

2. Which of the following programming languages is used for writing Docker?

    A. Python

    B. JAVA

    C. golang

    D. C

    Answer: C

3. What is the use of Docker Client?

    A. To monitor the resource usage of Docker objects.

    B. To send the user requests to Docker daemon.

    C. To create and manage Docker image repositories locally.

      D. To schedule the boot order of Docker objects and services.

Answer: B

4. Which of the following is a non-interactive process by default?

      A. Docker Registry

      B. Docker Client

      C. Docker Daemon

      D. Container

Answer: C

5. Which of the following is used to store and access Docker Images?

      A. Docker Storage

      B. Docker Volume

      C. Docker Shelf

      D. Docker Hub

Answer: D

Questions

1. Explain Docker's Build-Ship-Run model.

2. Break down Docker's architecture with a suitable diagram.

3. What is the role of Docker Daemon in Docker?

4. Run a hello-world container on your Docker Host using `docker run` command.

CHAPTER 4
Writing Dockerfiles

Introduction

In the previous chapter, we prepared our machine to work with Docker Containers. So, in a natural flow of progression, now is the time to start making your own containers. This chapter will make a casual visit to Docker Hub and then it will shift to learning how to write Dockerfiles. You will explore all of the important Dockerfile instructions and their impact on the consecutive stages of building a container image. As an author, I would like to recommend that you perform the practical tasks and read the chapter simultaneously as it will enhance your learning experience drastically.

Structure

This chapter covers:

- Exploring Docker Hub!
- Introducing Dockerfile and its instructions
- Writing your first Dockerfile
- Your Docker Image on Docker Hub

Objective

The objective of this chapter is to immerse you into Docker's treatment of containers by writing them yourself. To do so, we will go through each Dockerfile instruction explicitly and understand how and why each one of them should be used. In this chapter, you will get a mix of discussion and tutorial approaches to look at each instruction thoroughly and objectively. Till now, you have been thinking about containers, after this chapter, you will think in terms of Docker Containers. You will also have your own Docker Hub repository populated with your handwritten Docker image!

Let us explore Docker Hub!

Starting the chapter with something refreshing is always fun. Let us revisit and broaden up the context and concept of Docker Hub a little. The Docker architecture figure from the previous chapter is a perfect reference for it:

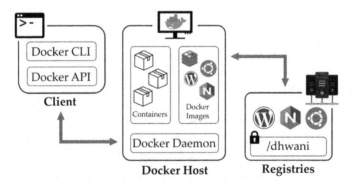

Figure 4.1: *Docker architecture*

Registries are used to store and ship container images and Docker Hub is essentially a public Docker Image Registry. We had already defined Docker Images prematurely and considered them as a packaged collection of applications and their dependencies. Further in this chapter, we will properly define Docker Images and learn about their internals. For now, you can say that Docker Images represent containerized applications. Since containers are **running processes**, shipping them is practically impossible *(unless you are motivated enough to transport running computers or servers for the sake of #YOLO)*. So, Docker Images are shipped as **ready-to-run** versions of containers. With that out of the way, let us go to Docker Hub!

Open your preferred web browser and go to **https://hub.docker.com/**. You should land on Docker Hub's landing page that looks something like the following screenshot:

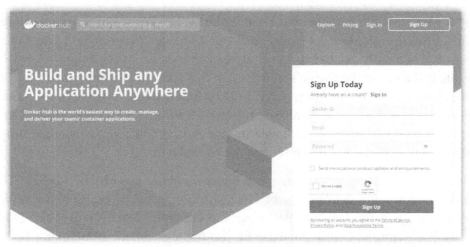

Figure 4.2: *Docker Hub landing page*

Even though signing up seems like the most natural action to perform, we are here for a different purpose. On the top right side of the page, click on **Explore** and you will be redirected to a page that should look something like the following screenshot:

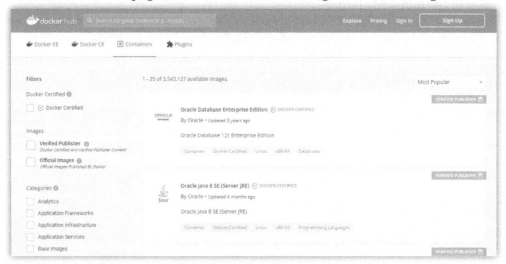

Figure 4.3: *List of Docker Images*

On the top panel, you can see four tabs among which the currently selected tab is **Containers**. But if you look at the search query in the address bar of the browser, the type field is equated by **Image**. This supports what we just mentioned recently about the containers being shipped as the compressed images. As you might have guessed, what we see here is a huge list of Docker Images available on Docker hub. To be precise, at the time of writing this book, there are over 3 million Docker Images from various contributors.

The currently visible list is sorted by popularity. Docker is not much vocal about their definition or criteria of popularity but from my experience, I can say that popularity is mostly related to the number of times an image is pulled with the possible influence of the image's ratings. Just like GitHub repositories or Play Store applications, the rankings may vary time-to-time but the current most popular Docker Image is the Oracle database Enterprise Edition. If you click on that Docker Image title, you will see a curated product-like description along with some support links. We will explore that when we upload our own image.

For now, let us focus on the left pane which is stacked with checkboxes. These checkboxes are contextual filters of Docker Images and to perform the filtering process, they use the tags visible below the one-liner description of the Docker Images. For example, Oracle database EE has the tags called "Container", "Docker Certified", "Linux", and so on. The "Container" tags are used to separate plugins and binaries from Docker Images. Since most of the tags are self-explanatory, we will focus on the important ones.

When we apply the **Docker Certified** filter, the output gets reduced to what is shown in the following figure:

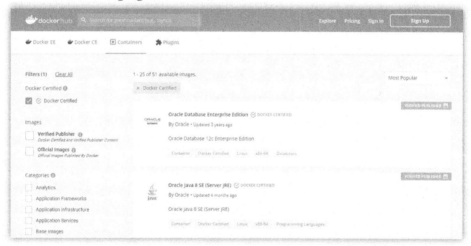

Figure 4.4: *Docker Certified Docker Images on Docker Hub*

The Docker Certified tag is applied by Docker to the scrutinized images that are built using best practices suggested by Docker. Such images are also tested and validated against Docker Enterprise Edition (EE). In other words, they are capable of leveraging features of Docker EE via APIs and they also pass its security standards. In some cases, Docker might even have collaborated with the developers of the images (for example, Oracle for JAVA) to enhance it and bring it to such standards. We will learn more about EE features and security standards in further chapters.

In a nutshell, Docker-Certified images are developed by third-party vendors (such as Oracle) but recognized and sometimes even enhanced by Docker. As you can see, there are only a handful of them (around 50 by the time of writing the book). Notice one thing though, these images were updated long ago. That is because the update rollout strategy is decided and carried out by the publishers of the image, not Docker.

This brings us to our second filter, the **Verified Publisher**. Instead of scrutinizing individual images, this tag is associated with publishers that are verified by Docker. All of the images published by such publishers are visible when this filter is applied. With so many web apps being containerized, this particular tag is going through diminishing importance. Its only use is to help you avoid fraud or fake Images in some cases.

The next filter is **Official Images**. When we turn it on, the list changes to something like the following screenshot:

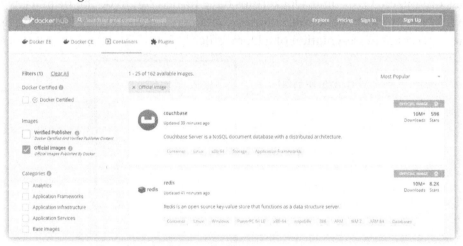

Figure 4.5: Official Docker Images

Official Images are published and maintained by Docker. They are a set of images that Docker thought were important for containerization to pick up the pace. Since they are maintained by Docker as well, if you notice below the title, most of them are updated more frequently than Docker-Certified images. Even though the list only comprises of ~160 images by the time of writing the book, the list is really diverse. It covers a lot of categories like databases, webservers, coding environments or minimal OS themselves. Fun fact, the hello-world image that we pulled in the last chapter was also a Docker Official image.

But, why are these images important? You can say they set an unofficial benchmark for containerized application performance. Since these images are mostly stable, they are good for practicing containerization. Just imagine, bugged containers on top of your operational errors when you don't even understand the technology properly, *that* is a nightmare. But this raises another important question, how did they (developers) create these images?

Introduction to Dockerfiles and its instructions

Dockerfiles are sequential sets of special instructions intended to be parsed and processed by Docker daemon for building Docker Image. In other words, they are text documents. They can be written using any text editor and they are generally easy to write and understand. Do you remember those tiresome Linux commands for manually creating containers from *Chapter 2*? Dockerfiles replace that process and make it more standard and developer friendly. They also help with keeping things organized. Over time, Dockerfiles have turned out to be the primary way of interacting with Docker and migrating to containers in general. The following figure is the conceptual representation of a Dockerfile:

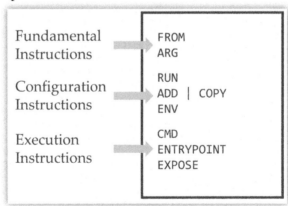

Figure 4.6: Common Dockerfile Structure

The figure shows different types of instruction keywords (without arguments) in a sequence. The categorization is not absolute or official but it will be useful while understanding the image building process.

Since Docker Images are collection of files, they are perceived as a **logical stack of layers** by Docker where each layer represents one or more files. These layers are created from Dockerfile instructions and each instance of an instruction contributes to one layer in the stack.

Before understanding these instructions, we need to understand how Docker accepts the request to build a Docker Image from a Dockerfile. Such a request is sent to Docker Daemon via Docker Client. One such example of doing so is using the **docker build** command. The command is followed by its arguments which at least include the name of the Dockerfile, the name of the resultant Docker Image and the path from which the Dockerfile and the support files can be obtained. Such a path is called the **Build Context.** In other words, Docker Image building process will be carried out keeping the content of the build context into consideration.

With that out of the way, let us explore all of the instructions of Dockerfile along with their uses one-by-one.

FROM

Considering the top-down **Left aligned left-to-right** (**LALR**) parsing of Dockerfiles, this is the first (top most) instruction (*well, mostly*). This instruction also creates the first and bottom most user-created layer of Docker Image. Docker daemon uses **FROM** to initialize a new **build stage** (Docker Image building instance) and for setting up the base image. Base images are pre-existing Docker Images (on Docker Hub if not mentioned otherwise) that you can use to build your particular application.

For example, if you want to host a customized Nginx webserver on an Ubuntu Linux container, you should not have to reinvent the wheel by trying to unnecessarily create another Ubuntu environment. You should just use the existing Ubuntu Docker Image as the base image and setup your webserver on top of it. This is one of the major reasons why Docker got personally involved into creation and maintenance of official Docker Images. Here is the syntax of **FROM** instruction:

```
FROM [--platform=<platform>] <image>[:<tag>] [AS <name>]
```

The text enclosed inside square brackets are flags and the ones inside angular brackets are values. Flags are optional, values are mandatory, and if the optional flags are used, then their values are also mandatory.

FROM itself is the keyword and **--platform** represents the infrastructure. You can mention the OS and ISA (Instruction Set Architecture) as the arguments. For example, linux/arm64. It is followed by **image:tag** combination. Image should be replaced by the name of your intended base image and tag generally represents the version of the image. The version can be product release specific (numerical) or user group specific (like canary or dev or beta). Since the value of tag is optional, if no tag is provided, Dockerfile takes "latest" as default. The latest tag is provided to images by Docker hub based on their release timestamp. Finally, we have another optional flag called **AS**. It is used to name the build stage. Such convention is useful when the image is built under multiple stages. We will look into them with practical examples later in this book. To wrap things up, let's take a look at an example of **FROM** instruction.

```
FROM ubuntu:latest
```

The above instruction is a classic example of how beginners would use **FROM**. It will simply initiate a build and set Ubuntu 16.04 as its base image. It will take the host's infrastructure specs as default values for the platform flag and will skip naming the build stage. If the build stage is not named, docker uses integer values to identify them. The first build stage receives the value 0 and the others (in a multi-stage image building) carry the streak forward.

There is a lot to cover in terms of what each instruction in Dockerfiles means and how it changes the resultant Docker Images, so we will go slowly and step by step as usual.

ARG

This is the only instruction that can precede FROM, but it is a bit special. We had mentioned earlier that each instruction results in a stacked layer of the Docker Image, ARG is not such. **ARG** is treated outside of the build context of the Docker Image (so FROM still remains the first or bottom most layer). ARG is used to declare variables that can be used by other instructions. You can say ARG is surface level similar to the Macros of C programming. **ARG** has a self-explanatory following syntax:

```
ARG <VARIABLE_NAME>=<value>
```

Along with syntax, ARG also follows a set of rules as listed:

- ARG must be written before the first FROM of the Dockerfile.
- Multiple ARGs can be used to declare multiple variables but all of them should be declared before first FROM.
- Variables defined by ARG can be referred by any other instruction but the scope of reference is limited to a single build phase, in other words, if the variable has been used once, you should write ARG followed by the used variable once more without the value. This will carry on its value from the previous declaration. In this sense, the scope of variables declared by ARG is global to the Dockerfile.

After the first **FROM**, any value declared with ARG will be ignored and any re-declaration will not be able to overwrite the already existing previous declaration.

Following these rules, the instruction from the previous example can be written as follows:

```
ARG VERSION=latest
FROM ubuntu:${VERSION}
```

The result of such instructions will be the same as setting up ubuntu:latest base image using **FROM** instruction. Here is one more sample with multiple ARGs.

```
ARG VERSION=16.04

ARG PLATFORM=linux/amd64

FROM --platform=${PLATFORM} ubuntu:${VERSION}
```

In this case, both **PLATFORM** and **VERSION** values will be passed to **FROM** and Ubuntu 16.04 for 64-bit AMD will be set as the base image. We can still spice things up a little (*because... why not?!*). Check out the following instructions:

```
ARG VERSION=latest

FROM ubuntu:$VERSION

ARG VERSION

RUN echo $VERSION > image_version
```

Here, we have used ARG by more than one instructions and to do so, we re-declared it without the value. Don't bother about the **RUN** instruction for now, we will take a deeper look at it soon. So, the latest version of Ubuntu will be set as the base image and the string "latest" will be printed in a file called **image_version**.

One realistic example of ARG would be when a Dockerfile is too long and is shared among multiple developers to commit. In such a case, declaring important variable values at the beginning makes it easier for other developers to follow. In a nutshell, ARG is an optional luxury instruction that can be used to enhance developer experience.

COPY

We have set the stage with FROM, now is the time to own it. We have seen earlier that FROM or the base image is the bottom most instruction layer in the file system of a newly built image. Every instruction that we cover from now on, will stack itself on top of the previous instruction. Unlike FROM, these instructions don't have a particular order to be stacked. Their position depends on how we write the Dockerfile.

COPY as its name suggests copies files or directories from source to destination. The source can be the build context, previous build stage or another Docker Image altogether. The destination is a path under the file system of the Docker Image. The path can be absolute or w.r.t present working directory (**pwd**) as set by the base image. This instruction can copy one or more files or directories. Let's take a look at its syntax:

```
COPY [--chown=<user>:<group>] <src>... <dest>
```

The source and destination are of course the mandatory values but an optional addition is **--chown**. This allows **COPY** to change the permission of the files being copied. In other words, you can turn a natively writable file read-only while copying it to the Docker Image file system. There are conditions of using **--chown** though. The flag is only applicable to proper Linux containers. The term proper may sound a bit vague so to expand upon it, the container file_system must recognize the user IDs (UID) and the group IDs (GID). This is possible if the Linux container file_system contains **passwd** and **group** files in the **/etc** directory.

Another variation is adding **--from** flag to the source which allows us to copy files from previously named build stages (using AS along with FROM) or images from Docker Hub. If the image or stage name does not exist, the build process will encounter an error. This instruction is widely useful from customizing webservers to building applications. Here, are some of the sample command uses:

```
COPY test.txt /home/ctest/new
```

This is the most basic application with source from the build context and a full-fledged destination path. The file **test.txt** from the host's directory containing Dockerfile will be copied to **/home/ctest/new** in docker image's environment.

```
COPY test.txt /new
```

Here is a similar application. This time, the destination path is incomplete. The daemon will create the **/new** directory under the default **pwd** of the base image. The default **pwd** can be changed by an instruction called **WORKDIR** but we will get to that later.

```
COPY --chown=777:mygroup test.txt /home/ctest/new
```

This instruction performs the same copy operation while granting the read-write-execute (octal **777**) permission to the user group named **mygroup**. It is worth noting that the user group is established in the containerized Linux environment, not the host.

```
COPY my* /newdir/
```

This variant is using a Golang wildcard (*****) which selects all of the files and directories starting with **my** initials and copies them to **/newdir** under Docker image's working directory.

```
# first build stage
FROM ubuntu:latest AS dev
COPY mydata /newdata
# second build stage
FROM centos:latest AS canary
COPY --from=dev my* /newdir/
```

Finally, this variant does the same copy operation but this time, the source is not the build context of the host. The source is previously created build stage called **dev**. We are fetching files from **dev** version (built on Ubuntu) and copying them to the canary version (built on CentOS). Now, let's take a look at a similar instruction.

ADD

This instruction also copies files from source to the destination where the destination is the Docker Image file system. It is similar to COPY in many ways, so let us focus on the differences.

- ADD allows fetching files from remote URLs and adds them to the Docker Image environment without adding them to the build context. It means uncorrupted, updated, authentic files without the host having to act as a mediator.

- Most of the times, the Dockerfile developer is not the author of such files. Thus, metadata also becomes important. ADD uses HTTP headers to fill in the metadata (like mtime aka timestamp of last modification) of the files fetched from the web.

- ADD also treats archived files with more attention. If the source file is a recognizable archive (like **.zip**, **.tar**, and so on), ADD unpacks them before copying to the Docker Image file system. This may seem insignificant but when we think about thousands of containers having to run the unpacking operation redundantly, it suddenly becomes critical. On top of that, it also consumes unnecessary storage due to duplication (both archive and unpacked versions) or another redundant clean-up operation. *(Here is a tip, whenever something seems pointless in DevOps, think of it at scale and it will change your point-of-view.)*

- ADD does not support copying files from previous build stages or from other Docker Images.

- On the other hand, COPY treats archives just like any other file and copies them without unpacking. It doesn't mean one is inferior to the other, they just have different uses.

Apart from unavailability of `--from` flag and provision of URLs as destination, the syntax of ADD is similar to COPY. We will leverage them better during Dockerfile examples.

RUN

This instruction executes commands (or programs) as a new layer on top of all of the previous layers. As you might have guessed, this is one of the most used and most important instructions of all. Unlike ADD, COPY, or FROM, which mostly keep the files unchanged, RUN makes subtle changes to the files and the Docker Image environment. As a result, the changes are committed with different caching and changelog policies while keeping layer modularity and reverting back commits in focus. For example, the most recent ADD or COPY invalidates the cache created by all of the preceding ADDs and COPYs whereas each RUN layer maintains its own cache.

RUN has two forms: `shell form` and `exec form`. Let us take a look at both of them:

1. **Shell Form**: It allows passing and executing commands directly in the shell of the container. The syntax is as following:

   ```
   RUN <command>
   ```

   The default shell for running the command is **/bin/sh** on Linux and command prompt or cmd on Windows. Let's take a look at an example that we have already seen earlier:

   ```
   ARG VERSION=latest

   FROM ubuntu:${VERSION}

   ARG VERSION

   RUN echo $VERSION
   ```

   We are using the **echo** command to print the value of **VERSION** variable to the **STDOUT** of Ubuntu. Similarly, you can run any command supported by the respective shell and execute it using **RUN**. Just like a regular Linux shell, you can also use backslashes (\) to provide multi-line commands.

2. **Exec Form**: First of all, the **exec** form is useful when the base image does not contain a proper executable shell. Here is the syntax:

   ```
   RUN ["executable", "param1", "param2"]
   ```

   This form does not involve any shell processing, so the commands and the parameters that you enter are parsed as JSON array. This also means that the double quotation marks (") are necessary. On the other hand, exec form can be used to invoke the shell and run commands as parameters. You can say that shell form is a use case of exec form. We can take the same example as earlier and run it in the exec form.

```
ARG VERSION=latest

FROM ubuntu:${VERSION}

ARG VERSION

RUN ["/bin/bash", "-c", "echo $VERSION"]
```

Here, the executable is **/bin/bash** and echo is just a parameter. We are invoking the shell for **echo** command via **RUN** instruction. You could have expanded the command further by adding the output to a file and the number of parameters would have remained the same because the parameters are for bash and not for echo. While it is necessary to invoke shell for variable replacement, many programs can be executed without shell. For such applications, exec form is lighter and more optimized.

Since both shell and exec forms have their distinct uses, none is clearly better than the other. Apart from RUN, there are a couple of other instructions that follow the two-form representation.

CMD

Dear System Admin,

*This is a microservice-specific container image. When you run the container, you should take a proper look into the product usage documentation and provide the command that we have recommended alongside **docker run**. If you don't do so, the application will not work as expected. Well, at least that is how it was supposed to be. But we have added a cure for this as well! We realize that your life could be busy with maintenances and rollouts, so we have added a default command that will execute when you run the container without any specific instruction. So, even if you have no clue about what you are doing at all, you will end up doing things right. We hope you appreciate this kind gesture of ours and give us positive feedback.*

Yours caringly,

Application Developers.

The letter above is a fictional representation of the thought process that could have gone behind the advent of CMD. On the surface, it looks similar to RUN but its purpose and execution are entirely different. The syntax of CMD is similar to RUN and it also has shell and exec form as it accepts commands or executables along with parameters (or flags), but it does not get committed during image build-time. The command provided with CMD stays reserved until the user invokes **docker run** without any executable command. Thus, CMD's accompanying command becomes the default executable if nothing is mentioned by the user.

Due to such reserved operation, there should only be one CMD per docker image (per Dockerfile). If there is more than one CMDs, the latest CMD overwrites all of the previous ones. If the user mentions a particular executable command while running the container, the CMD's command remains unused. Since, the syntax is similar to **RUN**, let's take a look at an example instead.

```
ARG VERSION=latest

FROM ubuntu:${VERSION}

ARG VERSION

RUN echo $VERSION > image_version

CMD echo "Hello User!"
```

The image will have just as many active layers committed as earlier but when we run the container from this image, **"Hello User!"** will get printed on the **STDOUT** of the Ubuntu container. From printing a welcome message to kick-starting daemon processes, you can get as creative with CMD as you want.

ENTRYPOINT

So far, we have used the Dockerfile instructions to turn an empty file system into the isolated processing environments called containers. **ENTRYPOINT** is used to turn these containers into executable instructions. The working of ENTRYPOINT is the same as CMD but its treatment (by Docker Daemon) varies significantly. ENTRYPOINT also executes commands when the container starts running and it also has shell and exec form but unlike CMD, it is difficult to avoid.

Generally, ENTRYPOINT is the process with PID 1, and it is capable of receiving UNIX system calls like SIGSTOP, SIGTERM, and so on for graceful shut down of the container. Even after defining ENTRYPOINT in the Dockerfile, you can pass additional runtime command-line arguments via docker run or additional CMD instruction without executable (just parameters). Such arguments may include decisions like running the process in foreground or daemon, attaching it to the terminal or not, and so on.

As for the selection between shell and exec forms, this one is a special case. Generally, you want ENTRYPOINT to be the startup process of your container (with PID 1) which is not possible with shell form as the shell itself will be invoked before the respective executable. In many cases, it is not even logical to do so. For example, if you are writing an OS base image, there is no way you can invoke the shell before everything else. We had also mentioned that ENTRYPOINT can be avoided. To do so, you need to mention a replacement while using **docker run** command.

The final remaining question is, **CMD or ENTRYPOINT?** As always, there is no competition, but *one of them is a must*. Both of these instructions actively co-exist because their nature complements each other. With CMD's ability to pass parameters to ENTRYPOINT and the provision of writing multi-line commands, you can invoke a bunch of processes at the start of the container and setup an efficient virtual environment. We will take a look at its practical application when we write a full-fledged Dockerfile, till then, let's take care of some nice-to-have features.

WORKDIR

This instruction changes the working directory of all of the subsequent executable instructions (like RUN, CMD, and so on) in the Dockerfile. Even though instructions like CMD are executed at container runtime, they follow the working directory setup by WORKDIR if they are written after WORKDIR. You can also say that WORKDIR is a variant of RUN in a sense that it executes **RUN cd** followed by the respective path. The syntax is simple:

```
WORKDIR <path>
```

Here is an example of **WORKDIR**:

```
ARG VERSION=latest
FROM ubuntu:${VERSION}
ARG VERSION
WORKDIR /new
WORKDIR path
RUN echo $VERSION > image_version
CMD /bin/bash
```

In the example above, the **VERSION** variable's value will be printed to a file called **image_version** under **/new/path** directory. If there is more than one **WORKDIR** instructions, the latest one appends the previous ones. (Unless initiated with **/**).

STOPSIGNAL

Just like how ENTRYPOINT or CMD determines how the container will start, **STOPSIGNAL** determines how it will terminate. The syntax is simple, the keyword

STOPSIGNAL followed by the number of the system call (like 6 or 9) or the name of the system call. Here is an example.

```
ARG VERSION=latest
FROM ubuntu:${VERSION}
ARG VERSION
RUN echo $VERSION > image_version
CMD echo "Hello User!"
STOPSIGNAL SIGTERM
```

In this example, the container will be terminated gracefully before existing. In other words, the process with PID 1 inside the container will receive **SIGTERM** system call (which is different from the default **SIGKILL**) and will exit with exit code 1. So, the container's process with PID 1 will not be a zombie child of the Docker's process which is responsible of running this container. This will ensure the proper release and redistribution of virtualized compute resources.

USER

As you might have guessed and as the name suggests, this instruction is used to set the user and group ID for the operations following it. The syntax is as following:

```
USER <user>[:<group>]
```

The values of user and group can be replaced with either the names or the numeric IDs. Here is an example:

```
ARG VERSION=latest
FROM ubuntu:${ VERSION}
ARG VERSION
USER dhwani:authors
RUN echo $VERSION > image_version
CMD echo "Hello User!"
STOPSIGNAL SIGTERM
```

The example has just one update compared to the last iteration, the CMD and RUN instructions will be carried out by user **dhwani** under the user group called **authors**. This instruction can be useful to manage resource access and to avoid direct root privileges being leveraged.

LABEL

This is a metadata instruction. It does not make any logical difference to your application but allows you to add more information about the Docker Image. **LABEL** follows a **Key-Value pair** format for adding information to the image. They can be extremely specific or completely random depending on the person writing them. The labels do not show up when we run the container but one can view them by asking for container or image description using **docker inspect** command *(more on docker inspect in the next chapter)*. Here is the syntax for LABEL instruction:

```
LABEL <key>=<value> <key>=<value>...
```

We can add more than one labels via single instruction or use one instruction for each LABEL, the choice makes no difference to the build size or stages of the Docker Image. Here is an example of **LABEL**:

```
ARG VERSION=latest
FROM ubuntu:${VERSION}
ARG VERSION
USER dhwani:authors
LABEL "MAINTAINED BY"="Cerulean Canvas"
RUN echo $VERSION > image_version
CMD echo "Hello User!"
STOPSIGNAL SIGTERM
```

The container run from this image will behave exactly the same as earlier. The only difference is an addition of metadata pointing out the maintainer of the image. Fun part is, you can put LABEL anywhere apart from the top (which is reserved for FROM or ARG) and it will work well because the commits are not logical. When your label strings have space characters or special characters, it is important to put them under double quotations. Let us take a look at another instruction with a similar syntax.

ENV

Since we are virtualizing the OS environment using shared kernel resources, we can also set individual environment variables for each container. In other words, one container's **$HOME** does not have to do anything with another container's or host's **$HOME** and vice-versa. After all, that is the beauty of virtualization. To perform this, we have the **ENV** instruction. As you might have guessed, it is used to set the environment variables of a docker image. This instruction basically overwrites the environment variables. If your base image already has some environment variables set *(in most of the cases, it will have them set)*, this instruction alters them.

Its scope is throughout the Dockerfile after its iteration. You can call one environment variable to set another one as well. Its syntax matches LABEL's with a little variation.

```
ENV <key> <value>

ENV <key>=<value>...
```

The environment variables are set as key-value pairs. If you want to set just one variable, you can separate them using space characters but, if you want to store multiple variables in a single instruction, you need to follow the same syntax as **LABEL** that is key-value separated by equality sign. Here is an example:

```
ARG VERSION=latest

FROM ubuntu:$ {VERSION}

ARG VERSION

USER dhwani:authors

ENV HOME="/usr/bin/new"

LABEL "MAINTAINED BY"="Cerulean Canvas"

CMD echo $HOME is the $VERSION version of HOME.

STOPSIGNAL SIGTERM
```

The container run by the resultant Docker Image of this Dockerfile will echo the newly set path of the **$HOME** variable using **ENV** along with the value of **$VERSION** set by **ARG**.

EXPOSE

As we have mentioned multiple times by now, containers are ideally designed to aid microservice architecture. Microservices are hosted by servers to clients and to run them successfully, we need a robust and efficient network architecture. Docker networks are a topic worthy of their own chapter (so, we will give them a dedicated chapter) but its surface is scratched by the **EXPOSE** instruction. With multiple containers running on the same host, the host (Docker) needs to know which container will listen on which port and via which protocol. Such documentation is provided via EXPOSE. Keep in mind, **EXPOSE does not publish the aforementioned port. It just lets docker know about the port that the container is supposed to listen to. The information is not absolute and the actually published port can be different from the one used with EXPOSE. Doing so will not make ANY difference to the container's performance. This is just for the sake of networking guidance.** The syntax is as follows:

```
EXPOSE <port>[/<protocol>]
```

The **EXPOSE** instruction assumes TCP by default unless mentioned otherwise. You can view the port suggested by **EXPOSE** via applying **docker inspect** command on the image. We will look at its example when we go through the **docker inspect** command.

These were the basic Dockerfile instructions. Now, we will write an actual Dockerfile and build an image out of it.

Writing your first Dockerfile

Writing a Dockerfile is a skill and the instructions are a toolbox to perform it. There are some ground rules, some commonly followed practices and some pro tips to follow. Just stating the rules and common practices is boring and counter-productive so let us take a real Dockerfile example to study those:

```
# setting the base image
ARG VERSION=18.04
FROM ubuntu:${VERSION}


# customizations
RUN apt-get update && apt-get install -y curl nginx \
    && apt-get clean \
    && rm -rf /var/lib/apt/lists/*
RUN mkdir /test-dir
ENV USER Dhwani
ENV SHELL /bin/bash
EXPOSE 80


# providing a default command
CMD ["nginx", "-g", "daemon off;"]
```

Since we have already seen the uses of all of the instructions used in this file, comprehending their roles should be fairly easy.

- First of all, we are using ARG to set the VERSION which is then used by FROM to set Ubuntu 18.04 as the base image.

- Then, we are using RUN to add dependencies and to clean up afterwards. We are also installing Nginx webserver on Ubuntu base image.

- ENV is used to add the user and to set bash as the default shell.

- EXPOSE is used to notify the user of the image which port the webserver will listen to.

- Finally, CMD is used in exec form where Nginx is the executable, **-g** is parameter 1 to set the global directives for parameter 2 which brings the process to foreground. If we had not put these parameters along with executable, we would have had to modify the nginx.conf during runtime.

This is what we get. Reading almost a dozen pages about Dockerfile instructions makes you capable enough to describe a Dockerfile in half a page! Now that we are done with it, time to address the lingering elephant in the room *(try imagining the metaphor… it is wild)* called **building the docker image using docker build command.**

Docker build invokes an image building process that takes two inputs into account; the Dockerfile and the build context. None of the terms are new here, we have just written our Dockerfile and we have seen that the build context is the set of support files for the Docker Image along with their path (on the host or remote URL). Since we do not have any support files to add, we will just provide the pwd as the build context. Also, it is advisable to put your Dockerfiles in different directories and name them **Dockerfile** without any extensions. Doing so allows Docker daemon to request auto-build trigger. So, provided that you have saved the above written code as Dockerfile (*I repeat, no extensions*) in a new directory, run the following command:

```
docker build -t nginx .
```

Once the build process is triggered, it will be carried out step-by-step. The beginning of the output will look something like the following:

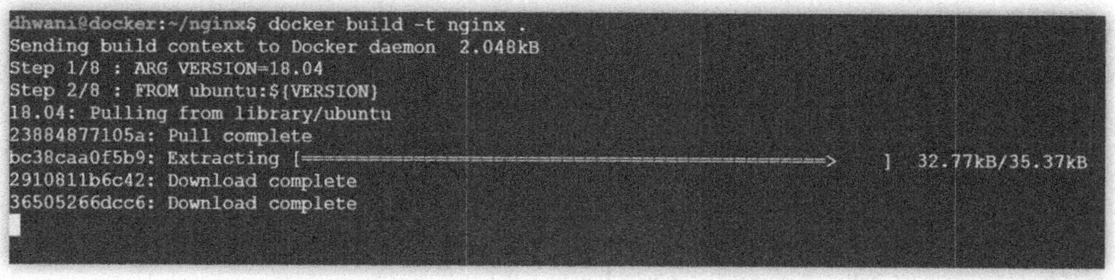

Figure 4.7: Beginning of image building process

Since the build context did not contain support files, it is as small as 2 KB. The first step was about setting the value of ARG. The layers will start being stacked up step 2 onwards which is pulling the base image. The base image is also being pulled in multiple layers. This allows optimized caching and file sharing between different builds. Let's move on to the next stages, look at the following screenshot:

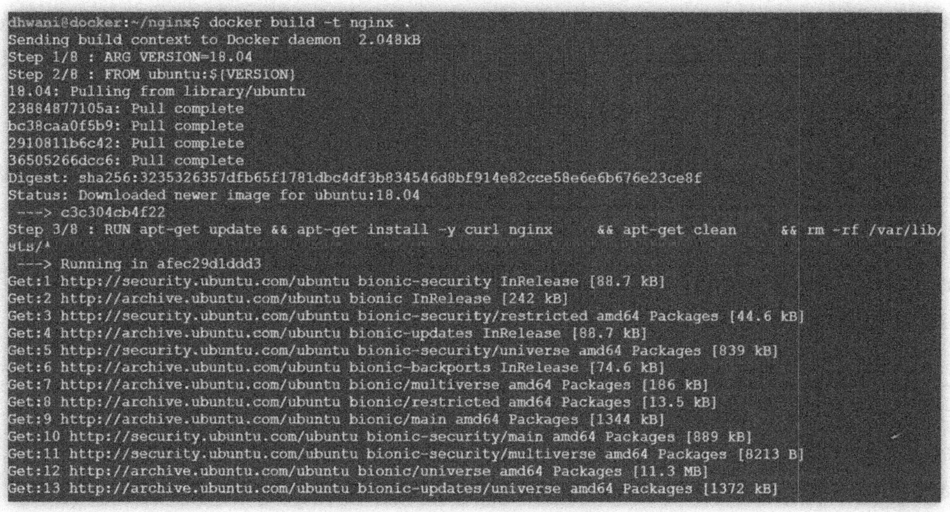

```
dhwani@docker:~/nginx$ docker build -t nginx .
Sending build context to Docker daemon  2.048kB
Step 1/8 : ARG VERSION=18.04
Step 2/8 : FROM ubuntu:${VERSION}
18.04: Pulling from library/ubuntu
23884877105a: Pull complete
bc38caa0f5b9: Pull complete
2910811b6c42: Pull complete
36505266dcc6: Pull complete
Digest: sha256:3235326357dfb65f1781dbc4df3b834546d8bf914e82cce58e6e6b676e23ce8f
Status: Downloaded newer image for ubuntu:18.04
 ---> c3c304cb4f22
Step 3/8 : RUN apt-get update && apt-get install -y curl nginx      && apt-get clean      && rm -rf /var/lib/
ats/*
 ---> Running in afec29d1ddd3
Get:1 http://security.ubuntu.com/ubuntu bionic-security InRelease [88.7 kB]
Get:2 http://archive.ubuntu.com/ubuntu bionic InRelease [242 kB]
Get:3 http://security.ubuntu.com/ubuntu bionic-security/restricted amd64 Packages [44.6 kB]
Get:4 http://archive.ubuntu.com/ubuntu bionic-updates InRelease [88.7 kB]
Get:5 http://security.ubuntu.com/ubuntu bionic-security/universe amd64 Packages [839 kB]
Get:6 http://archive.ubuntu.com/ubuntu bionic-backports InRelease [74.6 kB]
Get:7 http://archive.ubuntu.com/ubuntu bionic/multiverse amd64 Packages [186 kB]
Get:8 http://archive.ubuntu.com/ubuntu bionic/restricted amd64 Packages [13.5 kB]
Get:9 http://archive.ubuntu.com/ubuntu bionic/main amd64 Packages [1344 kB]
Get:10 http://security.ubuntu.com/ubuntu bionic-security/main amd64 Packages [889 kB]
Get:11 http://security.ubuntu.com/ubuntu bionic-security/multiverse amd64 Packages [8213 B]
Get:12 http://archive.ubuntu.com/ubuntu bionic/universe amd64 Packages [11.3 MB]
Get:13 http://archive.ubuntu.com/ubuntu bionic-updates/universe amd64 Packages [1372 kB]
```

Figure 4.8: Build process Run stage

Before we go to step 3, notice how we got a couple of alphanumeric strings at the end of step 2. They are Image Digest and Image ID of the base image. The one with SHA-2 or sha-256 encryption is called **image digest**. Image IDs are used to identify and separate the images whereas Image Digests are used for content authentication; but more on that later.

Next is the `RUN` step which is downloading files for `apt-get update`. All of these steps (apart from the first one) are creating separate layers of images and the layers have different IDs. These IDs are mapped to their location on the host in the isolated file system. Moving on, take a look at the next snapshot:

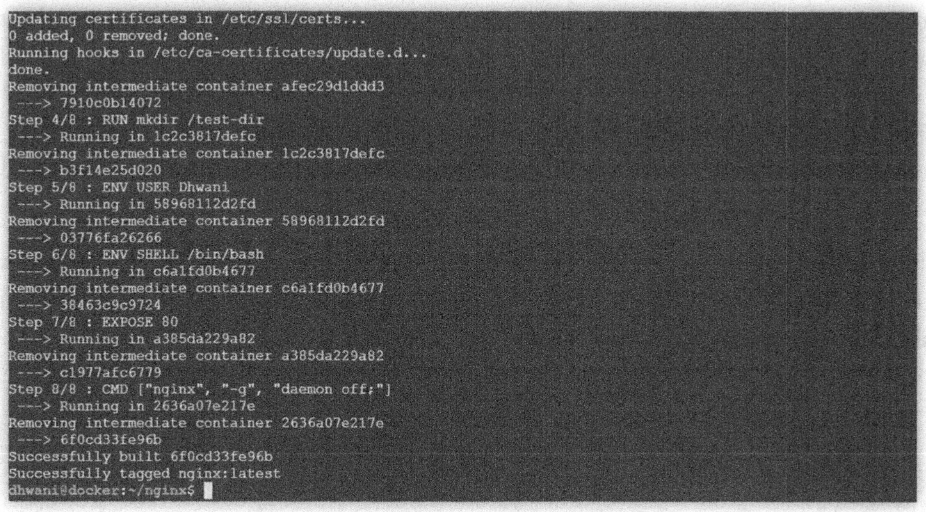

```
Updating certificates in /etc/ssl/certs...
0 added, 0 removed; done.
Running hooks in /etc/ca-certificates/update.d...
done.
Removing intermediate container afec29d1ddd3
 ---> 7910c0b14072
Step 4/8 : RUN mkdir /test-dir
 ---> Running in 1c2c3817defc
Removing intermediate container 1c2c3817defc
 ---> b3f14e25d020
Step 5/8 : ENV USER Dhwani
 ---> Running in 58968112d2fd
Removing intermediate container 58968112d2fd
 ---> 03776fa26266
Step 6/8 : ENV SHELL /bin/bash
 ---> Running in c6a1fd0b4677
Removing intermediate container c6a1fd0b4677
 ---> 38463c9c9724
Step 7/8 : EXPOSE 80
 ---> Running in a385da229a82
Removing intermediate container a385da229a82
 ---> c1977afc6779
Step 8/8 : CMD ["nginx", "-g", "daemon off;"]
 ---> Running in 2636a07e217e
Removing intermediate container 2636a07e217e
 ---> 6f0cd33fe96b
Successfully built 6f0cd33fe96b
Successfully tagged nginx:latest
dhwani@docker:~/nginx$
```

Figure 4.9: Image building completion

There is a lot going on here. First of all, notice how the RUN stage is ending with updating the CA certificates for Nginx installation. After that, we have a notification claiming to have removed intermediate containers. Such notifications are repeated after every step. What are those? As we have talked about earlier, these steps are committed as stacked layers and each layer creates its own intermediate image with different IDs. These intermediate images are run as independent processes and their cumulative results are committed into the resultant docker image after terminating the intermediate containers. Such resultant commits also have their own independent IDs.

Each RUN and ENV instruction is treated as separate layers followed by EXPOSE and CMD layers whose functions are discussed earlier. At the end, all of the intermediate images are stacked and built as a final resultant Docker Image with the Image ID ending with 96b. There is one last line to address, which suggests that the image is tagged. The tag is a result of the **-t** flag provided with the **docker build** command. We, as users, had instructed Docker Daemon to tag (name) the resulting built Docker Image as Nginx *(because naming creativity is not my strong point… or so it seems, look forward to next chapters for it)*. This was the process of building a standard docker image. But, we should not be satisfied until we have seen it in action. To run a container from this image, use the following command:

```
docker run –d --name nginx-container –p 80:80 nginx
```

This is a simple iteration of **docker run** command with a few flags. Starting from the end, we have mentioned **nginx** which is the image name to be run. This will ensure that we are creating a container out of the nginx image that we have just created. Before that, we have **-p** (port) flag followed by **80:80** (**<host_port>:<container_port>**). It will map container's port **80** to host machine's port **80** and publish it. In case your host's port **80** is already occupied, the container's webserver will not serve your requests. In that case, you can publish it to any other port on the host like **8080** or even 30000+ series. We are calling it nginx-container using **--name** flag and running it as a detached container. Detaching it means the container process will exit once its root process terminates.

There are other ways to see if the container is running but we will go with the newbie route and simply check the webserver. Since my host is a GCP VM, I will hit the combination of its external IP and the port number (in my case **80**) the container is mapped to in a web browser. Here is what the result looks like:

Figure 4.10: *Running Nginx container*

The promise is fulfilled, you just ran your own Nginx container and found it working. But this is just the beginning, we have so much variation to discuss. While doing so, we will also look at a couple of advanced Dockerfile instructions.

Building Dockerfile with HEALTHCHECK and Context

The last Dockerfile that we built did not have any support files and all of the layers were either modified files of the base image, newly created files or files fetched from web. To explore Dockerfiles and the building process further, let us take another example *(because there is no such thing like too many useful examples)*.

This time, we will write Dockerfile to containerize FLASK application for Python. Flask is a lite framework for writing web applications. To containerize it, let us create a new directory on your host called **flask**.

```
mkdir flask

cd flask
```

The flask directory will contain 3 files in total: The Dockerfile for containerization, the requirements file for customization and the application for execution. Let us take a look at the **requirements.txt** first:

```
Flask==0.12.2
```

The file contains only one line specifying the version of the Flask application. This file can be referenced in the executable application and/or the Dockerfile itself. It is a good practice to isolate aspects like version control when you're working in a team to avoid version conflicts.

The second file is **app.py** which is a simple, lightweight web app created using the FLASK library. The app isn't anything fancy, it just prints the output on a webpage.

(After all, this is a book about containers, not web application development!). Here is the code for the application.

```python
from flask import Flask
app = Flask(__name__)
@app.route('/')
def AwesomeContainers():
    return 'This is a healthy flask application.'
if __name__ == '__main__':
    app.run(host='0.0.0.0')
```

To explain briefly, this application creates a function called **AwesomeContainers** that returns the string **This is a healthy flask application** on being called. This application imports FLASK, so it expects the environment to already have the Flask framework installed before it can run. Also, it says that the application is healthy. We cannot just go bluffing around, we need to prove somehow that the application is actually healthy. Keeping that in mind, here is the code for the Dockerfile. Make sure there is nothing else apart from the Dockerfile and the support files in the directory:

```dockerfile
# Base-image
FROM ubuntu:16.04


# Prerequisites
RUN apt-get update -y && \
    apt-get install -y python-pip python-dev curl \
COPY . /app
WORKDIR /app
RUN pip install -r requirements.txt


# Health check
HEALTHCHECK --interval=10s --timeout=30s CMD curl --fail http://
localhost:5000/ || exit 1


# Making the container executable
ENTRYPOINT ["python"]
CMD ["app.py"]
```

The initial parts of the Dockerfile should be easy to interpret by now as we are just setting the base image and updating the OS environment. Then, we are using COPY instruction to copy all of the contents of the present working directory of host to the Docker Image file system. Since the source is a directory on host, you could have used ADD the same way. We are also switching the work directory to the newly copied **/app** directory and installing the components mentioned in the **requirements.txt** file.

Then, we have a new instruction called **HEALTHCHECK**. It is one of the most flexible instructions of Docker. It acts both as a setup and as a switch. You can use this instruction to define the rules of checking if the container is healthy or you can use it to turn off the health check of the base image. To do so, we have a flexible syntax:

```
HEALTHCHECK [OPTIONS] CMD command
HEALTHCHECK NONE
```

The second variant is used to disable the health check routine set-up for the base image. The base image itself does not change but its **HEALTHCHECK** instruction gets blocked from being inherited. The first variant accepts options and commands. Options are optional (*I will start reading wordplay for dummies, I promise*), whereas a command is mandatory for **HEALTHCHECK** to be any useful. Our iteration of **HEALTHCHECK** already uses two flags (options) and a command. The command is simple, if the container fails to reach localhost on port **5000**, return with exit code 1 to show that the container is not healthy. To assist it, there are two flags. Interval, which defines the period between two consecutive health checks and timeout, which determines at which point Docker Daemon will stop checking for health after consecutive unhealthy results. In this case, the Docker daemon will curl local host on the flask container every 10 s, and if the condition is not met (localhost is unreachable) for 30 s (3 health checks), the container will be flagged unhealthy.

There are two other flags apart from the ones we have used: **--start-period**, to monitor expected starting duration of the container and **--retries**, to determine how many restarts to allow before considering it unhealthy.

Finally, to make the container executable, we have ENTRYPOINT and CMD and as you might have guessed, CMD is just an argument for ENTRYPOINT. You could have written **ENTRYPOINT ["python", "app.py"]** and the result would have been the same. The only reason for detaching the parameter is the nature of application. You can add any other python file and just change the CMD's value. That way, when you rebuild the Dockerfile, ENTRYPOINT layer will not change and will be used from the cache. Let's build the Dockerfile with the following command:

```
docker build -t flask-app .
```

One thing to note here is that this time, we have used the **–t** flag to tag the resultant image. To see how the build process will start, take a look at the following image:

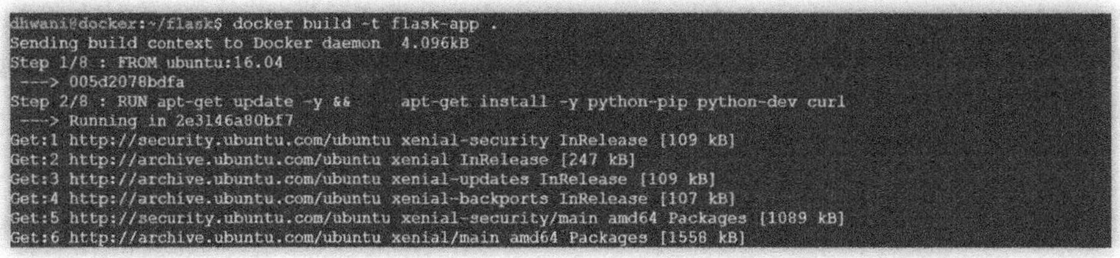

Figure 4.11: *Building flask application*

Even though the build process looks similar to the last application, there are subtle differences. For example, the size of the build context is larger than last time because of the support files. After that, we can see a new expected layer of **HEALTHCHECK** in the following image:

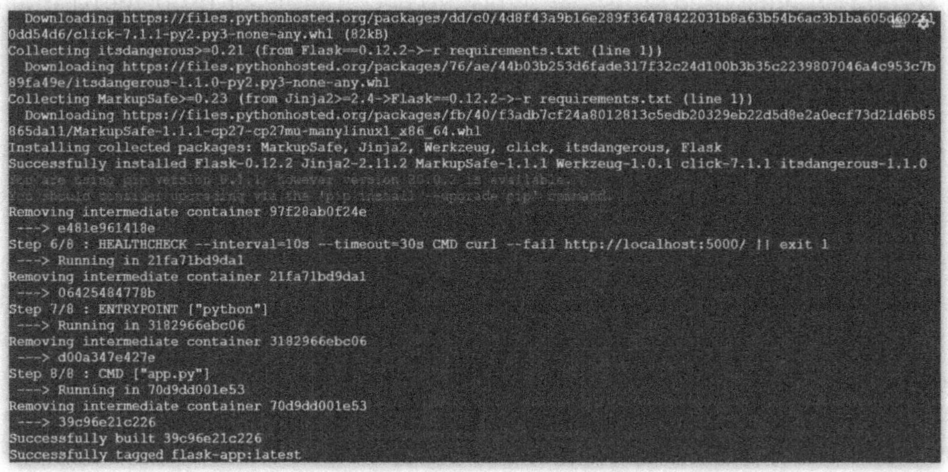

Figure 4.12: *Flask Docker Image*

Once the image is successfully built, you can use **docker run** command to spin up the container from the image as mentioned following:

```
docker run -itd --name flask -p 5000:5000 flask-app
```

The flags are the same as earlier, so there is not much to wander around. We can use the **host-IP:host-port** (host-IP remains the same, port is **5000**) combination in the web browser to see if it is serving the flask application. Here is the result of the **docker run** command in the following image:

Figure 4.13: *Running flask application*

The Flask application is running perfectly but we went out of our way to use **HEALTHCHECK** in our Dockerfile. So, we cannot just be satisfied by trivia like if we are served the application from browser, the curl should be working on local host as well. So, here is a command to list the containers:

```
docker ps -a
```

The command is similar to Linux's **ps -a** which is used to list all of the running processes. This command lists all of the containers along with their state (whether they are running or not), health status and other details. Here is the result:

```
dhwani@docker:~/flask$ docker ps -a
CONTAINER ID      IMAGE            COMMAND          CREATED          STATUS
   PORTS                  NAMES
e8528ac489ea       flask-app       "python app.py"   14 seconds ago   Up 11 seconds (health: starting)
   0.0.0.0:5000->5000/tcp    flask
dhwani@docker:~/flask$
dhwani@docker:~/flask$ docker ps -a
CONTAINER ID      IMAGE            COMMAND          CREATED          STATUS                 PORTS
              NAMES
e8528ac489ea       flask-app       "python app.py"   20 seconds ago   Up 16 seconds (healthy)   0.0.0.0
:5000->5000/tcp    flask
```

Figure 4.14: *Container's Health Status*

As you can see we have run this command twice. As the result of the first attempt, docker was unable to judge if the container is healthy or not because the HEALTHCHECK was still not complete (because curl had not finished its execution yet). In the second attempt, the health check was performed successfully and container's status was changed to **healthy**. Since we had not mentioned any particular protocol in our Dockerfile or with our **docker run** command, the FLASK container will use TCP by default. With this exercise, we practiced a few instructions and learned about health check. Let's carry this streak forward.

Setting triggers with ONBUILD

There are times when you know the solution to some problem but you are not the one to execute it. For such cases, you can set the triggers in your Dockerfile for the next user of your resultant Docker Image. In other words, you can reserve instructions while writing a Dockerfile to be committed during the build stage of another Docker

Image that uses your resultant image as the base image. This can be achieved with ONBUILD instruction. The syntax is simple, ONBUILD followed by any regular instruction.

Let us take a look at an example. We will have two Dockerfiles: mum (parent) as the base image and baby (child) as the dependent image. Let's create a directory for the Dockerfiles:

```
mkdir family

cd family
```

Here is the code for the **mum** Dockerfile:

```
FROM ubuntu:16.04

ONBUILD RUN echo "Greetings from your parent image!" > /tmp/hello.txt

CMD ["bash"]
```

FROM, RUN and CMD instructions are already familiar to you. The only variation is ONBUILD. This instruction will turn the accompanying RUN instruction into a trigger for the next image, which will treat this image as its base image. To set this image as the base image, we need to build it first using the following command:

```
docker build -f mum-Dockerfile -t mum-ubuntu .
```

Since we have multiple Dockerfiles in this directory, it is important to mention the filename along with the **–f** flag. Look at the following figure to see how the building process of **mum-Dockerfile** looks like:

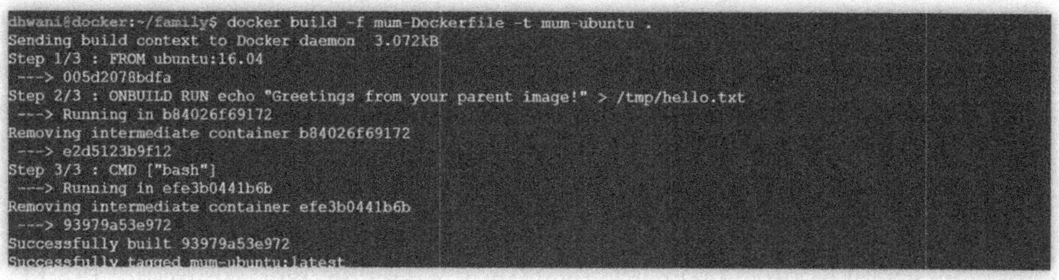

Figure 4.15: Building Dockerfile with ONBUILD instruction

As the screenshot shows, ONBUILD layer is also committed just like other layers but without getting executed. A trigger will be added to the **mum-ubuntu** image's metadata. In the case of more than one triggers (more than one ONBUILD instructions in the Dockerfile), a list of triggers is made in a sequential order and stored in the image's manifest. As for the CMD instruction for this container, we will have bash running on Ubuntu. Now, let's write the baby Dockerfile:

```
FROM mum-ubuntu:latest

CMD ["bash"]
```

This file has **mum-ubuntu:latest** as the base image. Let's build and observe it:

```
docker build -f baby-Dockerfile -t baby-ubuntu .
```

Once the build process begins, you can get a hint of what you were looking for. Take a look at the following screenshot:

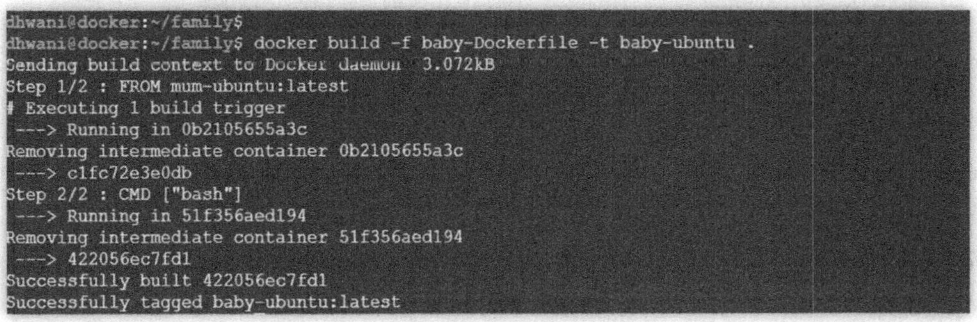

```
dhwani@docker:~/family$
dhwani@docker:~/family$ docker build -f baby-Dockerfile -t baby-ubuntu .
Sending build context to Docker daemon  3.072kB
Step 1/2 : FROM mum-ubuntu:latest
# Executing 1 build trigger
 ---> Running in 0b2105655a3c
Removing intermediate container 0b2105655a3c
 ---> c1fc72e3e0db
Step 2/2 : CMD ["bash"]
 ---> Running in 51f356aed194
Removing intermediate container 51f356aed194
 ---> 422056ec7fd1
Successfully built 422056ec7fd1
Successfully tagged baby-ubuntu:latest
```

Figure 4.16: Baby Dockerfile build process

The screenshot has a triggered RUN layer (the trigger is happening during step 1 which commits the base image using FROM instruction). As a side note, ONBUILD trigger gets executed right after FROM instruction. The trigger is the same as mentioned in the mum Dockerfile. Once the image is successfully built, we can run the container and verify the trigger:

```
docker run -itd baby-ubuntu
```

This will be an interactive container with a shell and since we have not named it, docker will return its container ID once it is ready and name the container by itself. You can verify that the container is running using **docker ps.**

Once the container is running, we need to switch to its environment. To do so, let us run **docker exec** (execute) command as follows:

```
docker exec -it inspiring_hypatia /bin/bash
```

inspiring_hypatia is the random name my container received from Docker. Yours will be different from mine. Regardless, once we have entered the virtualized container space, let us verify the trigger. Follow the sequence of commands below and execute them in your container's shell:

```
cd /tmp
```

```
ls
```

```
cat hello.txt
```

The following figure is the output when we **cat** the **hello.txt** file:

```
dhwani@docker:~/family$ docker exec -it inspiring_hypatia /bin/bash
root@de42af19b3b1:/#
root@de42af19b3b1:/# ls
bin  boot  dev  etc  home  lib  lib64  media  mnt  opt  proc  root  run  sbin  srv  sys  tmp  usr  var
root@de42af19b3b1:/#
root@de42af19b3b1:/# cd /tmp
root@de42af19b3b1:/tmp#
root@de42af19b3b1:/tmp# ls
hello.txt
root@de42af19b3b1:/tmp#
root@de42af19b3b1:/tmp# cat hello.txt
Greetings from your parent image!
root@de42af19b3b1:/tmp#
root@de42af19b3b1:/tmp#
```

Figure 4.17: ONBUILD trigger's success

As it is clearly visible, the string has been echoed properly and thus the on-build trigger has also worked well.

We have seen a lot of examples of Dockerfiles and running containers out of them. But, the resultant Docker Images are just useful for us (since they are on the host), not the world. So, let's make them available for others to use!

Your Docker Image on Docker Hub

Docker Hub is not a new concept for us now. We have talked about it a couple of times and visited it in the beginning of the chapter. We saw how there were over 3 million Docker Images by different contributors and now is the time to join their list. Before we do so, we need to set up an account. The process is simple, follow the steps given below.

- Go to Docker Hub homepage at **https://hub.docker.com**. You will be redirected to Docker Hub's home page just like the one shown below. (*The UI of Docker Hub might change over the time.*) Look for the sign-up section here and fill in the details. Docker ID is your desired username (which and rest of the fields are self-explanatory:

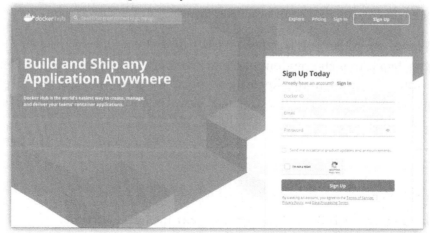

Figure 4.18: Docker Hub sign-up dialog box

- Check the required boxes (*I recommend keeping product updates and announcements box unchecked because most likely you are swimming in promotional emails*).

- Click on the most clickable part of the page, the **Sign Up** button.

- There will be an e-mail from Docker in your mailbox to verify your email ID. Once you verify it; we are good to go.

- After verifying your email, you will be redirected to the log-in page where you need to enter your Docker Hub credentials.

- When you are successfully logged in to your Docker Hub account, you can see the welcome page of your own Docker Hub account just like the following screenshot:

Figure 4.19: Docker Hub user account homepage

- As you can see in the image, there are plenty of tabs to explore. At the bottom of the page, you can see options to create a repository and to create an organization. As we read the description for the **Create a Repository** option, it is used to push container images to Docker Hub. That is what we intend to do. We will create a new repository and push a user-created docker image to that repository on our own Docker Hub registry.

- When we click on the **Create a Repository** option, we will be redirected to a page where we need to fill in some information in order to create a repository such as name, description, and visibility. Push in the following format.

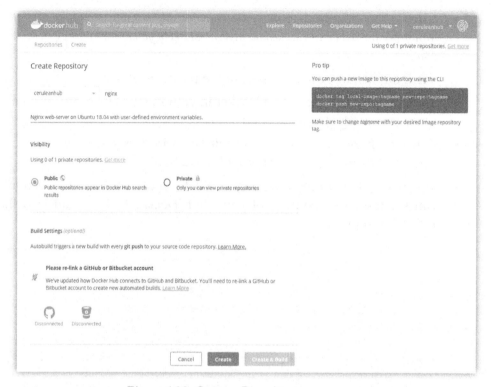

Figure 4.20: Create a Repository page

Here, we have named this repository **nginx** and added a short description for it. One thing to note here is that the repository name should be unique in the particular namespace (*In other words, two separate users can have individual nginx repositories but one user cannot have two repositories named "nginx"*). Then, we have set the visibility for this repository as **Public** (*because we do not want to waste money unnecessarily!*). By default, every Docker Hub users gets unlimited public repositories (which can be pulled by anyone on this globe) and one private repository (which can be pulled by only you or any authorized member in the organization). The **Build Setting** option lets you link GitHub or Bitbucket account to this repository in order to set autobuilding for this repository. Let us leave Build Setting as it is for now and press create to create this repository.

- After the repository is created, we will receive the page like the one below containing all the details about this repository and one command to help us push as many Docker Images as we want into it:

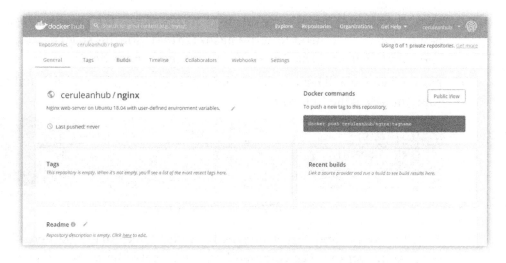

Figure 4.21: *ceruleanhub/nginx repository homepage*

As we can see in this image, the repository is empty for now (*because, you see, docker images do not pop out of imaginary fountain of eternity!!)*, so is the Readme file. If you want to add some content into this Readme file, feel free to click on the pencil symbol next to Readme. As we can see in the right side of the page, there is a **docker** command which shows us how to push a new Docker Image into this repository.

```
docker push ceruleanhub/nginx:tagname
```

Here, before pushing the image to this repository, we need to rename the image which we want to push in following format:

```
<docker hub username>/<repository name>:<tagname>
```

The reason why we are doing this is to let Docker identify and organize repositories by username. Thus, the image we are going to push will reach to the same nginx repository that is created and owned by **ceruleanhub**. It is as simple as writing a letter to someone or emailing someone. Just make sure that you do not misspell anything otherwise Docker won't be able to find the repository.

- Now, to rename the image that we want to push, we will use **docker tag** command. It is the full-fledged version of **-t** flag that we used to tag the image with **docker build** command. The syntax of this command is as follows:

```
docker tag <source_image:tag> <target_image:tag>
```

Here, the **source_image** is the one to be renamed and the **target_image** is its new name. So, we need to write **nginx:latest** for the **source_image** field and **ceruleanhub/nginx:latest** for the **target_image** field.

- Now, when we will list out docker images on our host, the result would look something like the following:

```
dhwani@docker:~$ docker images
REPOSITORY           TAG            IMAGE ID           CREATED            SIZE
ceruleanhub/nginx    latest         08deb6e4b3e1       21 minutes ago     134MB
nginx                latest         08deb6e4b3e1       21 minutes ago     134MB
ubuntu               18.04          c3c304cb4f22       3 weeks ago        64.2MB
dhwani@docker:~$
dhwani@docker:~$
```

Figure 4.22: renamed nginx image

Both the source and target images have the same Image ID here. This is because the Docker `tag` command has just created an alias (a reference) to the existing source image. It will not give any new Image ID or digest to the target image. Now, take a look at the size of both of these images. They are 134 MB of size. That is because both Docker hub and your system are running instances of Docker Daemon. Thus, there are chances that servers of Docker hub may have the layers (files) that are missing in your system. For example, your host may not have Ubuntu base image downloaded whereas Docker Hub has dozens of versions of Ubuntu. Docker hub will just reference the intermediate image IDs of the official Ubuntu image whereas your host will download it from the source to fulfill the missing dependencies and that increases its overall size.

- Before pushing any image to Docker Hub, we need to log in our Docker Hub registry through command line for more secure push process. All you need to do is use **docker login** command and provide your Docker Hub credentials.

```
docker login {OPTIONS} [SERVERS]
```

When we execute this command, you will be asked to enter your Docker Hub username or registered email and password. After you are successfully logged in, you will receive the confirmation just like the following one:

```
dhwani@docker:~$ docker login
Login with your Docker ID to push and pull images from Docker Hub. If you don't have a Docker ID, head over to h
tps://hub.docker.com to create one.
Username: ceruleanhub
Password:
WARNING! Your password will be stored unencrypted in /home/dhwani/.docker/config.json.
Configure a credential helper to remove this warning. See
https://docs.docker.com/engine/reference/commandline/login/#credentials-store

Login Succeeded
```

Figure 4.23: Docker Hub login using Docker CLI

- Now, we are ready to push our image to the **nginx** repository. And to so, use the following command:

```
docker push ceruleanhub/nginx: latest
```

- By default, Docker daemon will push five image layers at a time. Let us have a look at how the image push process looks like:

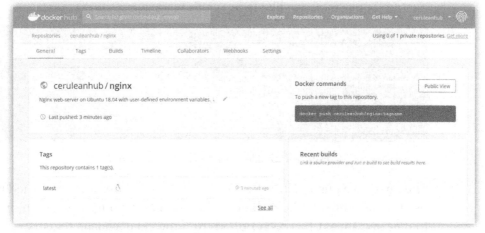

Figure 4.24: docker push command output

As shown in the image, the top two layers of the image are the ones which we have created writing the Dockerfile and the bottom four layers are of the base image Ubuntu and they are mounted from the repository where the base image is stored.

- After successfully pushing the image from the Docker host, let us check out whether the image is available on Docker hub. If the image has been successfully pushed, the change in the **nginx** repository would look like the following image:

Figure 4.25: Pushed image status on Docker Hub

As we can see, tags field states that this repository has a new tag entry. This tag has been pushed to this repository 3 min ago. It is the same latest tag that we have pushed just a while ago. Also, there has been a new entry to the counter for pushed images just below the description. It shows that a push event just happened 3 min ago. All these facts show that the image has been successfully pushed to **ceruleanhub** registry.

- Now, to complete the circle, let us pull the same image that we just pushed to **nginx** repository. For now, we only have one tag stored in **nginx** repository, so it is quite easy to guess the command to pull this image. But, when there are more tags stored in this repository, it will be easier if we can just look for the tag in a list and associated **docker pull** command at the same time. For that, just go to the **Tags** tab on the top bar as shown follows:

Figure 4.26: List of tags of nginx repository

Now, there is only one task is left to do. Copy the **docker pull** command shown in the previous image and paste it on your Docker Client's terminal screen. When you execute the command, in the most ideal case, the output should look something like this:

```
dhwani@docker:~$ docker pull ceruleanhub/nginx:latest
latest: Pulling from ceruleanhub/nginx
23884877105a: Already exists
bc38caa0f5b9: Already exists
2910811b6c42: Already exists
36505266dcc6: Already exists
e2cb04bea916: Pull complete
90bff89e70c5: Pull complete
Digest: sha256:f11b7526fd462b9f0d272465a2f1fb6e593e63e119bca966293bd6fd4f95003a
Status: Downloaded newer image for ceruleanhub/nginx:latest
docker.io/ceruleanhub/nginx:latest
dhwani@docker:~$
dhwani@docker:~$
```

Figure 4.27: Docker pull command output

The image we pushed in to the Docker hub has successfully returned back to us. The last entry of the **docker pull** command's output is one more proof that **nginx:latest** has been pulled from the **ceruleanhub** registry.

Conclusion

This felt like a long chapter, did not it? Despite of the page count not being jaw-dropping high; the progression surely was. Before this chapter, docker images seemed like a closed box that we did not understand but somehow managed to run once or twice. Now, you know how to write the Dockerfiles for them and how to build them!

This milestone is an earlier one of many, but it is extremely significant nonetheless. Writing Dockerfiles is the first and most important step toward containerization. The next chapter will enhance your containerization skills even further by teaching you the Docker Command Line.

Multiple choice questions

1. Which of the following Dockerfile instructions can precede FROM instruction in Dockerfile?

   A. RUN

   B. WORKDIR

   C. ARG

   D. SETBASE

   Answer: C

2. Which of the following Dockerfile instructions can execute a command and commit the result in a new layer on top of all existing docker image layers?

   A. ENTRYPOINT

   B. RUN

   C. FROM

   D. ONBUILD

   Answer: B

3. Which of the following Dockerfile instructions is used to run a container as an executable?

   A. ENTRYPOINT

   B. EXEC

   C. CMD

   D. RUN

   Answer: A

4. Which of the following is the exec form of CMD Dockerfile instruction?

   A. CMD ["param1","executable","param2"]

   B. CMD ['param1','executable','param2']

   C. CMD ['executable','param1','param2']

   D. CMD ["executable","param1","param2"]

   Answer: D

5. Which of the following Dockerfile instructions is used to add metadata to the Docker Image?

    A. FROM

    B. LABEL

    C. ENV

    D. RUN

    Answer: B

6. How many times can FROM instruction appear in a single Dockerfile?

    A. Only Once

    B. Three times

    C. Multiple times

    D. Five times

    Answer: C

7. Which of the following is the correct format to define HEALTHCHECK instruction in a Dockerfile?

    A. `HEALTHCHECK --interval=1m --timeout=1m \`
        `CMD curl -f http://localhost/ || exit 1`

    B. `HEALTHCHECK --start-interval=1m --timein=1m \`
        `ENTRYPOINT curl -f http://localhost/ || exit 1`

    C. `HEALTHCHECK --interval=1m --timeout=1m \`
        `ENTRYPOINT curl -f http://localhost/ || exit 1`

    D. `HEALTHCHECK --start-interval=1m --timein=1m \`
        `CMD curl -f http://localhost/ || exit 1`

    Answer: A

8. Can you find out what is wrong with this Dockerfile?

    ```
    ARG VERSION=16.04
    FROM ubuntu:${VERSION} AS build-stage
    CMD ["/bin/bash"]
    FROM ubuntu:${VERSION} AS stage-A
    RUN apt-get update && apt-get install python-pip python-dev curl \
        && apt-get clean \
        && rm -rf /var/lib/apt/lists/*
    ```

```
ENTRYPOINT ["python"]
CMD ["app.py"]
```

A. More than one FROM instruction in a single Dockerfile

B. Incorrect syntax of RUN

C. Missing ARG declaration in the stage-A

D. None of the above

Answer: C

9. Which of the following Dockerfile instructions is used to show details about the network port on which the container will listen at the run-time?

A. ENV

B. LABEL

C. PORT

D. EXPOSE

Answer: D

10. Which of the following Dockerfile instructions lets user reserve any other instruction as a trigger?

A. EXPOSE

B. ONBUILD

C. RUN

D. ARG

Answer: B

Questions

1. Explain the role of Docker Hub in Docker's Ecosystem.

2. Name the Dockerfile instructions capable of copying files from host's file system to the docker image's file system and explain their working.

3. Explain the difference between Shell form and Exec form of executable Dockerfile instructions.

4. Write a Dockerfile to host Nginx web-server on CentOS containerized environment.

CHAPTER 5
Gearing-up the Toolbox!

Introduction

Heads up, this is going to be one of the largest chapters of this book for all good reasons. Docker Command Line is versatile, exhaustive, and continuously expanding. It is the primary way of interacting with Docker. This chapter will explore a significant majority of it with suitable examples and develop a deeper understanding of how Docker perceives and presents the information regarding the containers. If you are a beginner with Docker, your life around it will not be same after it.

Structure

This chapter covers:

- Introduction to Docker Command Line
- Working with Docker Image commands
- Sharing the Docker Image
- Container life-cycle
- Working with Docker Container commands
- Sharing files with Containers using docker cp
- Miscellaneous Docker commands

Objective

If I could, I would have put a grin emoji right at the end of the title of this chapter, because that is how you will feel once the chapter ends *(or even during the chapter, if you are over-optimistic like me)*. You will feel confident and free from the shackles of inability to explore Docker by yourself. This chapter will enhance the reading experience of all of the future chapters as well as it will equip you with the toolbox to explore and experiment freely with Docker.

Introduction to Docker Command Line

As you might remember from *Chapter 3*, Docker CLI or Docker Command Line is a part of Docker Client (that is, the system or portal you will be using to operate Docker) along with Docker Application Program Interface (API). Much like most of the command lines, Docker commands are also used to invoke different Docker APIs. Since the Docker is written on the foundation of REST API, the commands invoke requests passed on to Docker daemon and serve responses provided by it. We will work with a lot of commands and understand their purpose of existence and usefulness individually. Their outputs will range from being messy to being well-formatted, being one-liner, to even being multi-page *(maybe I should not have spoiled this surprise)*.

There is a coarse classification of the commands for the sake of simplicity, but all of the following types converge back to being a part of the mammoth that is the Docker CLI.

- Docker Systems commands
- Docker Image commands
- Docker Container commands
- Docker Daemon commands

We will learn Docker Image commands before Docker Container commands, sprinkle Docker Systems commands throughout the chapter (as they seem applicable) and will address Docker Daemon commands when the time and the knowledge are sufficient. Let's start all of this with the traditional ritual of using the **version** command.

docker version

This might be one of the most predictable commands, and that is precisely why it is an excellent way to start. Version is like hello world of command lines. You mainly use this command to see if the tool is properly installed and get to know the version details. The syntax is simple:

```
docker version [OPTIONS]
```

docker version is the main command, whereas **[OPTIONS]** allows flags to tail the command. This time, we will not use any flags as we will be showcasing many of them in the further commands.

Here is what the output will look like:

```
dhwani@docker:~$ docker version
Client: Docker Engine - Community
 Version:           19.03.9
 API version:       1.40
 Go version:        go1.13.10
 Git commit:        9d988398e7
 Built:             Fri May 15 00:25:18 2020
 OS/Arch:           linux/amd64
 Experimental:      false

Server: Docker Engine - Community
 Engine:
  Version:          19.03.9
  API version:      1.40 (minimum version 1.12)
  Go version:       go1.13.10
  Git commit:       9d988398e7
  Built:            Fri May 15 00:23:50 2020
  OS/Arch:          linux/amd64
  Experimental:     false
 containerd:
  Version:          1.2.13
  GitCommit:        7ad184331fa3e55e52b890ea95e65ba581ae3429
 runc:
  Version:          1.0.0-rc10
  GitCommit:        dc9208a3303feef5b3839f4323d9beb36df0a9dd
 docker-init:
  Version:          0.18.0
  GitCommit:        fec3683
dhwani@docker:~$ █
```

Figure 5.1: Output of docker version command

This command returns the version of both client and server ends of Docker Engine (widely referred to as "Docker"); in this case, both of them are Community (free) Edition 19.03.9 with API versions 1.40. the server's Docker Engine also mentions that the minimum API version required is 1.12. This means that the versions before that are more likely to have one or more APIs deprecated. Since we have installed both client and server parts of Docker on the same machine, standard parameters like architecture, Golang version, git commit token, and building timestamp are the same. They can be different if Docker Client and Daemon are installed separately on other machines. In that case, it is in your best interest to make sure that both Client and Daemon (server) maintain identical versions.

The server end version details of Docker Engine are also paired with version numbers. Git commit tokens of **containerd** (container runtime abstraction for host's kernel system calls and other privileged resource management), **runc** (another lightweight Container Runtime Interface initially developed as a part of Docker project), and **docker-init** (tiny-init process for containers to get graceful termination and avoid zombies). The **Experimental** flag is turned off as the default setting. We can switch it manually *(we might do it at some point in the future if we feel like it, we look forward to it)*.

This was one of the Docker Systems commands. Now that we are done with the ritual let us move to the commands operating on Docker Images.

Working with docker image commands

Despite being static in nature, Docker Image has plenty of useful commands to work with. Let's start exploring them in thorough detail and with suitable examples.

docker build

This is another familiar command. We have already used **docker build** in the previous chapter to make Docker Images out of the written Docker files. We have also discussed how Docker Daemon takes build context from Docker client and stacks it as a layered file system to make a Docker Image. This summarizes the surface level working of Docker build, but we do have a variation to discuss. You might remember the syntax of this command:

```
docker build [OPTIONS] PATH | URL
```

As always, the options stand for the flag and the PATH | URL is used to describe both the Dockerfile location and build context for the target Docker Image. This time, we will use a URL instead. The URL can be anything, including your own webserver. However, we will use a GitHub repository instead as it is more accessible and generalized way to maintain the code.

To demonstrate this, we will build the same nginx Docker Image as earlier, but this time the build context will be a git repository from Cerulean Canvas's GitHub account. To do so, use the following command:

```
docker build https://github.com/cerulean-canvas/nginx.git
```

When the PATH is a local directory, all of the content of the aforementioned directory is sent to Docker Daemon as the build context. In this case, the entire GitHub repository containing the Dockerfile will be sent as the build context.

We have mentioned in the Docker architecture that the Docker client serves the purpose of verifying the requests intended for Docker Daemon along with the content of the request. To carry this role forward, the content of the GitHub repository will first be copied to the Docker Client in a temporary repository. This temporary repository will then be sent as the build context to the Docker Daemon.

In other words, whether the build context is a local directory or a URL, it makes no difference to Docker Daemon as it will receive its context from the Docker Client in both cases.

Observe the following screenshot to see how this exchange takes place effortlessly:

Figure 5.2: Output of docker build command with URL

As the response to the command is returned by Docker Daemon, it does not bother to mention the URL. The build context transfer is simply mentioned which is the size of the GitHub repository as well. Once all of the build steps are completed, we get the newly build Docker Image's ID as usual as shown in the following screenshot:

```
dhwani@docker:~$ docker build https://github.com/cerulean-canvas/nginx.git
Sending build context to Docker daemon  57.86kB
Step 1/8 : ARG VERSION=18.04
Step 2/8 : FROM ubuntu:${VERSION}
18.04: Pulling from library/ubuntu
23884877105a: Pull complete
bc38caa0f5b9: Pull complete
2910811b6c42: Pull complete
36505266dcc6: Pull complete
Digest: sha256:3235326357dfb65f1781dbc4df3b834546d8bf914e82cce58e6e6b676e23ce8f
Status: Downloaded newer image for ubuntu:18.04
 ---> c3c304cb4f22
Step 3/8 : RUN apt-get update && apt-get install -y curl nginx     && apt-get clean     && rm -rf /var/lib/apt/li
sts/*
 ---> Running in e087836452e6
Get:1 http://security.ubuntu.com/ubuntu bionic-security InRelease [88.7 kB]
Get:2 http://archive.ubuntu.com/ubuntu bionic InRelease [242 kB]
Get:3 http://security.ubuntu.com/ubuntu bionic-security/multiverse amd64 Packages [8815 B]
Get:4 http://security.ubuntu.com/ubuntu bionic-security/universe amd64 Packages [852 kB]
Get:5 http://security.ubuntu.com/ubuntu bionic-security/main amd64 Packages [930 kB]
Get:6 http://security.ubuntu.com/ubuntu bionic-security/restricted amd64 Packages [59.3 kB]
Get:7 http://archive.ubuntu.com/ubuntu bionic-updates InRelease [88.7 kB]
Get:8 http://archive.ubuntu.com/ubuntu bionic-backports InRelease [74.6 kB]
Get:9 http://archive.ubuntu.com/ubuntu bionic/universe amd64 Packages [11.3 MB]
Processing triggers for ca-certificates (20180409) ...
Updating certificates in /etc/ssl/certs...
0 added, 0 removed; done.
Running hooks in /etc/ca-certificates/update.d...
done.
Removing intermediate container e087836452e6
 ---> 905692falfc3
Step 4/8 : RUN mkdir /test-dir
 ---> Running in d2f2b1212c14
Removing intermediate container d2f2b1212c14
 ---> 33d46830fcb2
Step 5/8 : ENV USER Dhwani
 ---> Running in 23a933c2941f
Removing intermediate container 23a933c2941f
 ---> 0c7ea63e27b8
Step 6/8 : ENV SHELL /bin/bash
 ---> Running in b1d3e30a161a
Removing intermediate container b1d3e30a161a
 ---> 599a50788e14
Step 7/8 : EXPOSE 80
 ---> Running in 1f1b1ace3af6
Removing intermediate container 1f1b1ace3af6
 ---> f755c67ab94c
Step 8/8 : CMD ["nginx", "-g", "daemon off;"]
 ---> Running in 93208fa758c5
Removing intermediate container 93208fa758c5
 ---> dc6141e61976
Successfully built dc6141e61976
dhwani@docker:~$ []
```

Figure 5.3: Docker Image ID as the final result of the Docker build command

docker images/ docker image ls

Think of this command as Linux's **ls** command for files. This command returns all of the available images on the Docker host. Honestly, even I am tired of writing that **the syntax is simple**. Initially, we thought we should go with synonyms of simple but they are more likely to cause misinterpretations. So, let's try something new. We will write the same sentence in a different language every time for fun (*because... why not!*). For the fellow Indian readers, *here is Hindi* (हिन्दी)... "इसका वाक्यविन्यास सरल है" (*Read as: iska vaakya-vinyaas saral hai*).

```
docker images [OPTIONS] [REPOSITORY[:TAG]]
```

The **repository:tag** combination (even works without tag) can be used to find a particular image and see whether it exists on your host or not.

Here is a sample usage of the command followed by its output:

```
docker images
```

Figure 5.4: Default output of docker images command

Since the images are stored as repositories on Docker Hub, the names of the images can be identified under the **REPOSITORIES** column. If the same image has been built multiple times with multiple tags, it will be listed multiple times as Docker considers it different versions of the same image. Although, it does not mean the image will have multiple copies of itself. As you can see, the top two images are nginx with different tags but with the same Image ID. This means only one copy of the resultant image exists, and its metadata (tags) is stored separately.

The last **build** command that we used to create the nginx image out of the Git repository is listed as **<none>** because we did not use the **--t** (tag) flag with the **build** command. This can create confusion, so it is not a good practice. It also has a different Image ID because the build context was different, so Docker does not consider it the same image.

In this case, all of the layers were recreated, and layer caching did not help. Docker is not clever enough to assess the Dockerfile and realize that it has built something similar earlier. Its point of reference is the build context. If we provide the same build context twice, docker checks if the context has been updated, if not, it attempts to use the cached layers.

Let us try out some flags. You have a wide variety of flags to accompany **docker ls**. For example, **--filter, --format, --no-trunc** and so on. If we use the --no-trunc flag, the response will not truncate the Docker Image IDs. It will show them in full length. Here is an example:

```
docker images --no-trunc
```

To view the output, take a look at the following screenshot:

```
dhwani@docker:~$ docker images
REPOSITORY          TAG                 IMAGE ID            CREATED             SIZE
nginx               latest              5e50e9c99052        25 hours ago        144MB
nginx               v1                  5e50e9c99052        25 hours ago        144MB
test                latest              dc6141e61976        41 hours ago        134MB
<none>              <none>              ae38c179d739        42 hours ago        125MB
ubuntu              16.04               005d2078bdfa        4 weeks ago         125MB
ubuntu              latest              1d622ef86b13        4 weeks ago         73.9MB
ubuntu              18.04               c3c304cb4f22        4 weeks ago         64.2MB
dhwani@docker:~$
dhwani@docker:~$ docker images --no-trunc
REPOSITORY          TAG                 IMAGE ID
 CREATED             SIZE
nginx               latest              sha256:5e50e9c9905242ef171fe48b77b5320b84c14d6798fabc0d167432e7c41a63f6
 25 hours ago        144MB
nginx               v1                  sha256:5e50e9c9905242ef171fe48b77b5320b84c14d6798fabc0d167432e7c41a63f6
 25 hours ago        144MB
test                latest              sha256:dc6141e61976f1a4749bde834e6be0ff3c1a303ea11bbf4919f606b07df0ace5
 41 hours ago        134MB
<none>              <none>              sha256:ae38c179d739e347294756220a39d878aafefd461a4cbac6148b6e8493bec988
 42 hours ago        125MB
ubuntu              16.04               sha256:005d2078bdfab5066ae941cea93f644f5fd25521849c870f4e1496f4526d1d5b
 4 weeks ago         125MB
ubuntu              latest              sha256:1d622ef86b138c7e96d4f797bf5e4baca3249f030c575b9337638594f2b63f01
 4 weeks ago         73.9MB
ubuntu              18.04               sha256:c3c304cb4f22ceb8a6fcc29a0cd6d3e4383ba9eb9b5fb552f87de7c0ba99edac
 4 weeks ago         64.2MB
dhwani@docker:~$
```

***Figure 5.5:** Output of Docker images command with --no-trunc flag*

These are the full-length IDs of Docker Images. If you look at the bottom three images, they are all from the Ubuntu repository with different tags but they have different IDs unlike nginx ones. That is because they are different versions of Ubuntu. It means the files and builds contexts would be different and Docker would treat them as separate images. You can also see that their sizes on the host's disk are different.

Another variant is the `--format` flag used to format the output as mentioned with the command in a Go template.

```
docker images --format "table {{.ID}}\t{{.Repository}}\t{{.Tag}}"
```

Here, we have mentioned repository, Image ID, and Tag displayed in a tabular format (we have used the table directive for this purpose). `\t` is used to provide space worth of one tab as a column separator. `.ID` is the placeholders used by the Go template to fetch the value of the relevant parameter to display. The output will look like the following screenshot:

```
dhwani@docker:~$ docker images --format "table {{.ID}}\t{{.Repository}}\t{{.Tag}}"
IMAGE ID            REPOSITORY          TAG
5e50e9c99052        nginx               latest
5e50e9c99052        nginx               v1
dc6141e61976        test                latest
ae38c179d739        <none>              <none>
005d2078bdfa        ubuntu              16.04
1d622ef86b13        ubuntu              latest
c3c304cb4f22        ubuntu              18.04
dhwani@docker:~$
```

***Figure 5.6:** Formatted output of docker images command*

You can try different formatting arrangements with more or fewer columns. We will move on to the next command.

docker history

We have seen while building the containers that the Docker Daemon creates and destroys intermediate containers before building the final image. Similarly, it also creates intermediate images for each layer of the Dockerfile. These intermediate images are given separate image IDs and they can be used for caching purposes to reduce the size of the final image. For example, if your nginx and apache webserver Docker images are going to use Ubuntu Xenial (16.xx) as the base image and going to run apt-get update on it twice, they will only be downloaded and computed once. Hence, such layers will be reused and the consumed disk space will be reduced while speeding up the image building process.

The history command of Docker lists such intermediate images of the target Docker Image. There are many semantics to discuss but we will take a look at the syntax and an example first. ***In Spanish, "Su sintaxis es realmente simple."***

```
docker history [OPTIONS] IMAGE
```

The image name can be an existing image on your host or a foreign image from a registry. All of its flags are meant to format the output with various adjustments. Let us take a look at the raw output first with the following example:

```
docker history docker
```

We are looking at the history of the container image of Docker itself. It is called d-in-d or Docker-in-Docker. As we have mentioned earlier, it is useful for testing purposes. The output of the above-mentioned command will look something like the following screenshot:

```
dhwani@docker:~$ docker history docker
IMAGE          CREATED        CREATED BY                                      SIZE       COMME
NT
f038f0462ba5   4 days ago     /bin/sh -c #(nop)  CMD ["sh"]                   0B
<missing>      4 days ago     /bin/sh -c #(nop)  ENTRYPOINT ["docker-entry…   0B
<missing>      4 days ago     /bin/sh -c mkdir /certs /certs/client && chm…   0B
<missing>      4 days ago     /bin/sh -c #(nop)  ENV DOCKER_TLS_CERTDIR=/c…   0B
<missing>      4 days ago     /bin/sh -c #(nop) COPY file:5b18768029dab817…   1.85kB
<missing>      4 days ago     /bin/sh -c #(nop) COPY file:abb137d24130e7fa…   587B
<missing>      4 days ago     /bin/sh -c set -eux;   apkArch="$(apk --prin…   200MB
<missing>      4 days ago     /bin/sh -c #(nop)  ENV DOCKER_VERSION=19.03.9   0B
<missing>      4 weeks ago    /bin/sh -c #(nop)  ENV DOCKER_CHANNEL=stable    0B
<missing>      4 weeks ago    /bin/sh -c [ ! -e /etc/nsswitch.conf ] && ec…   17B
<missing>      4 weeks ago    /bin/sh -c apk add --no-cache   ca-certifica…   5.16MB
<missing>      4 weeks ago    /bin/sh -c #(nop)  CMD ["/bin/sh"]              0B
<missing>      4 weeks ago    /bin/sh -c #(nop) ADD file:b91adb67b670d3a6f…   5.61MB
dhwani@docker:~$
```

Figure 5.7: *Default output of Docker history command*

We have mentioned that there were a lot of semantics to discuss. Let us get into them. There is an interesting inter-process communication taking place. Since this is Docker-in-Docker, the common question would be: ***Are we running just the client, just the daemon or both?*** This docker container is only running docker client and using the host's Docker daemon to process its requests. In other words, the docker daemon is communicating with two different docker clients at the same time. This is definitely not an ideal scenario and should not be used in a deployment practice, but it does offer a lot of insight and we are running it on a cloud VM so if anything goes wrong, we can just dump this VM and spin-up a new one. *(I completely tarnished my expertise vibe, didn't I?!?)*

Let us explore each layer to understand its meaning:

- The bottom-most layer is the base image (Alpine Linux) which provides the environment to build the Docker application.

- Next one is the **shell** which is used by Docker to execute the **RUN** instructions. Docker runs a shell for every layer of the image it is building up from the Dockerfile. Any layer starting with **# (nop)** will be skipped by **/bin/sh**. Such non-RUN instructions will be processed by host's Docker Daemon. In fact, the second layer itself is a non-RUN (CMD) instruction thus gets a **#** (nop) comment.

- Then, it is adding packages (via apk command-line) for ca-certificates and OpenSSH client for secure communications. The Docker Client is being installed on the Docker host as a container. So, to access it, remote users will have to SSH into the Alpine container environment.

- Then, we have **nsswitch** (Name Service Switch config file), which contains the network information such as host names, passwords, groups, and so on.

- The next two layers set the environment variables **DOCKER_CHANNEL** and **DOCKER_VERSION** with the appropriate values. The channel represents stable repository, whereas the Version pulls Docker Engine 19.03.9.

- Next one is the RUN instruction which installs Docker binaries in tar file with some backup conditions if the installation fails. That is why the size of this layer is 200 MB, which is almost 98% of the total image size.

- The next couple of layers copy some Loadable Kernel Modules (LKM) into the modprobe of the base image's environment. They are used to make sure that container's Alpine can utilize (request to utilize) the Ubuntu host's system calls for resource allocation while running its containers.

- The next one sets the environment variable **DOCKER_TLS_CERTDIR** to **/cert** directory to enable the Transport Level Security. The **/cert** directory contains the ca files, the Docker Daemon certificate files, and the Docker client certificate files (**cert.pem, ca.pem, key.pem**).

- Now, in order to provide the client-level functionality to this d-in-d container, we need to share the client subdirectory of the **DOCKER_TLS_CERTDIR**. The next layer does the same. It is a RUN instruction that makes a new directory for client certificates and grants permission only to the directory owner to read, write, and execute the contents of the directory.

- The second last one layer sets the ENTRYPOINT of this image to a shell script named **docker-entrypoint.sh** which contains the code to execute Docker.

The last one is the CMD layer that initiates the shell for this container.

Since the image was not available on the host, all of the layers apart from the top have <missing> in the ID column. Let us get the history of an image available on the host. Use the following command:

```
docker history nginx:v1
```

The output would be similar to the following:

```
dhwani@docker:~$ docker history nginx:v1
IMAGE              CREATED          CREATED BY                                      SIZE       COMME
NT
5e50e9c99052       26 hours ago     /bin/sh -c #(nop)  CMD ["nginx" "-g" "daemon_   0B
fe54a464b10e       26 hours ago     /bin/sh -c #(nop)  EXPOSE 80                     0B
08f6732dc715       26 hours ago     /bin/sh -c apt-get update && apt-get install_   70.1MB
1d622ef86b13       4 weeks ago      /bin/sh -c #(nop)  CMD ["/bin/bash"]            0B
<missing>          4 weeks ago      /bin/sh -c mkdir -p /run/systemd && echo 'do_   7B
<missing>          4 weeks ago      /bin/sh -c set -xe   && echo '#!/bin/sh' > /_   811B
<missing>          4 weeks ago      /bin/sh -c [ -z "$(apt-get indextargets)" ]     1.01MB
<missing>          4 weeks ago      /bin/sh -c #(nop) ADD file:a58c8b447951f9e30_   72.8MB
dhwani@docker:~$
```

Figure 5.8: Output of docker history command for a locally built image

Starting from the bottom, the first five layers (with 4 having missing IDs) are from the Ubuntu base image *(how did I know it was Ubuntu? Because I am a magician! Just kidding, I just remembered which base image was used for nginx:v1 and also looked at apt-get. Since we have not used any other Debian variant, it had to be Ubuntu).* On the contrary, the top three intermediate images (Run, Expose and CMD) are built locally so their IDs are available. These IDs are assigned by the Docker daemon and the same IDs are published to Docker Hub if the image is pushed. When the image is pulled by another user, the intermediate image IDs are shown missing.

docker search

We do not always write the Dockerfiles for the images ourselves. Many times, we are just looking for standard solutions. One such example would be Redis database. You may want to operate a lot on a running Redis container but you would not want to write its Dockerfile yourself. When we are looking for a particular solution, search is the most useful tool. We have already seen that Docker Hub provides a sophisticated and user-friendly way to search Docker Images (inside repositories) under explore tab.

The Redis search would look something like the following screenshot:

Figure 5.9: List of Docker Images on Docker Hub

Without even typing the keywords, if we just look for official images of databases, we can find Redis sitting comfortably under PostgreSQL. But this requires us to go to the web browser and navigate through the Docker Hub, which certainly should not be the quickest way to do this. Luckily, it is not. Docker command line offers a **search** command which works as efficiently as the GUI but spares you the hassle of visiting the Docker hub. Here is in Japanese: 構文は簡単です *(Kōbun wa kantandesu)*:

```
docker search [OPTIONS] TERM
```

To search for the Redis Docker Images from the command line, use the following adaptation of the syntax:

```
docker search redis
```

The output will list available repositories containing Docker Images having names starting with **redis** in the order of popularity as shown in the following screenshot:

```
dhwani@docker:~$ docker search redis
NAME                             DESCRIPTION                               STARS     OFFICIAL
         AUTOMATED
redis                            Redis is an open source key-value store that...  8222     [OK]
bitnami/redis                    Bitnami Redis Docker Image                145
    [OK]
sameersbn/redis                                                           80
    [OK]
grokzen/redis-cluster            Redis cluster 3.0, 3.2, 4.0, 5.0, 6.0     69
rediscommander/redis-commander   Alpine image for redis-commander - Redis man...  40
    [OK]
kubeguide/redis-master           redis-master with "Hello World!"          31
redislabs/redis                  Clustered in-memory database engine compatib...  25
redislabs/redisearch             Redis With the RedisSearch module pre-loaded...  22
oliver006/redis_exporter          Prometheus Exporter for Redis Metrics. Supp...  21
arm32v7/redis                    Redis is an open source key-value store that...  21
bitnami/redis-sentinel           Bitnami Docker Image for Redis Sentinel   14
    [OK]
redislabs/redisgraph             A graph database module for Redis         11
```

Figure 5.10: Output of docker search command

We can see that there are a lot of versions of Redis available and to make our lives easier, Docker search provides (well, they tried to provide) a brief description of the images. These descriptions are the same as the ones found on Docker Hub. We also get a column dedicated to display the number of stars and a Boolean column mentioning if the image is official. The images are arranged based on the stars it has obtained, with the top image having the most stars and the bottom one having the least. These numbers are very likely to change when you run this command because of the quasi-real-time updates. Finally, we have a column called **Automated** which indicates that the image is built using the Docker auto-builder by sending the build context of the pwd. **So, what are we looking for?**

Redis (Remote Dictionary Server) is a fast, open-sourced, in-memory key-value data store that can be used as a database, cache storage, and/or a message broker. Redis allows data to stay in memory, unlike other databases (they store it on Hard Disk Drive - HDD or Solid State Drive - SSD). This makes read–write of the data blazing fast (microsecond responses, in fact, the data store will be as good as your processor and memory), making Redis a competent candidate for building real-time scalable web applications. The first result fits our description the best. It is also the Official Image.

We can reduce the number of search results by putting the **--limit** flag. Here is an example:

```
docker search redis --limit 5
```

We are only looking for the top five search results. Here is what the output will look like:

```
dhwani@docker:~$ docker search redis --limit 5
NAME                            DESCRIPTION                                 STARS       OFFICIAL
            AUTOMATED
redis                           Redis is an open source key-value store that…   8272        [OK]
bitnami/redis                   Bitnami Redis Docker Image                  148
        [OK]
rediscommander/redis-commander  Alpine image for redis-commander - Redis man…   40
        [OK]
bitnami/redis-sentinel          Bitnami Docker Image for Redis Sentinel     14
        [OK]
circleci/redis                  CircleCI images for Redis                    4
        [OK]
dhwani@docker:~$
dhwani@docker:~$
```

***Figure 5.11:** Output of docker search command with -- limit flag*

Now, what should we do with this image?

docker pull

As the name suggests, this command pulls a target Docker Image from the desired Docker registry (public or private, by default Docker Hub). In French, la syntaxe est simple:

```
docker pull [OPTIONS] NAME[:TAG|@DIGEST]
```

Docker Hub mentions the relevant pull command for a Docker Image when you visit its repository. For example, let us visit the redis's official Docker Image repository home page shown in the following screenshot:

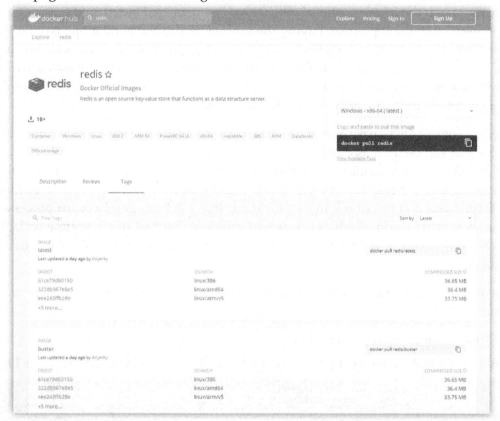

Figure 5.12: *Official redis Docker Image repository page on Docker Hub*

There are multiple versions of the Redis Docker Image identified by the tags attached to them. We can pull any image by mentioning the correct combination of image name and tag. If we want to pull the latest version, we do not need to mention the tag as Docker pulls the latest images by default if not mentioned otherwise. Since we have already pulled the latest versions of images multiple times, let us try something else:

```
docker pull redis:buster
```

We are pulling the buster version of Redis and the output of the command looks something like this screenshot:

```
dhwani@docker:~$ docker pull redis:buster
buster: Pulling from library/redis
afb6ec6fdc1c: Pull complete
608641ee4c3f: Pull complete
668ab9e1f4bc: Pull complete
78a12698914e: Pull complete
d056855f4300: Pull complete
618fdf7d0dec: Pull complete
Digest: sha256:d27740b5bd12087efc2b30ac9102fa767d6cc83611dc0fc28f0edb042e835996
Status: Downloaded newer image for redis:buster
docker.io/library/redis:buster
dhwani@docker:~$
```

Figure 5.13: docker pull command to pull redis:Buster docker image

Docker introduced content-addressable IDs in v1.10 for intermediate and final images to protect the integrity of the content of the images. The image layers are identified by a hex number obtained by applying **sha256** on the image's content. This hex number is called the **Image Digest**.

If the layer content changes, the digest also changes, avoiding unwanted substitution of layers with cached layers. This makes caching more reliable. When we pull the image, Docker Daemon also sends a configuration object along with all other layers of the image, which contains the ordered list of digests of all the layers. Docker engine verifies the content of these layers by matching their digests with the ones in that list and assembles layers in a proper sequence.

As mentioned earlier, we can also pull images from other container repositories by providing URLs instead of image names. Here is an example:

```
docker pull gcr.io/google-appengine/python
```

This command uses Google Container Registry (GCR) to pull a Python image for its App Engine Cloud service. Since, we have not mentioned explicitly, the command uses the latest version and https channels by default. Here is what the output will look like:

```
dhwani@docker:~$ docker pull gcr.io/google-appengine/python
Using default tag: latest
latest: Pulling from google-appengine/python
eb60b2c4842f: Pull complete
46a34386d3c5: Pull complete
3c2cba919283: Pull complete
cfc78cf93d8c: Pull complete
035d12fd648d: Pull complete
9803dacd25bc: Pull complete
4e423253a59b: Pull complete
022797ddaff4: Pull complete
72fa9e5ab8cb: Pull complete
03f7b4457bf9: Pull complete
a5d184ef99b4: Pull complete
Digest: sha256:10aa536017a65779b5e6c27bde4f89c7de4516152c4caf56a7379252720548d4
Status: Downloaded newer image for gcr.io/google-appengine/python:latest
gcr.io/google-appengine/python:latest
dhwani@docker:~$
dhwani@docker:~$
```

Figure 5.14: Pulling a Docker Image from Google Container Registry

These images will also have similar Image IDs and Digests since they are built on Docker Daemon despite of being pushed to a different registry. So far, we have been pulling single images from a repository. If needed, we can also go all-out by pulling the entire repository on our host. To do so, use this command:

```
docker pull redis --all-tags
```

The output will be long and redundant (to stop the pulling process, press *Ctrl + C*) but here is what the beginning of the execution will look like:

```
dhwani@docker:~$ docker pull redis --all-tags
2-32bit: Pulling from library/redis
Digest: sha256:35201a22e6690d442ec1a3fdd6e640bf4441926d9c02ecaeb3f648869594449c
2.6-32bit: Pulling from library/redis
Image docker.io/library/redis:2.6-32bit uses outdated schema1 manifest format. Please upgrade to a schema2 image
for better future compatibility. More information at https://docs.docker.com/registry/spec/deprecated-schema-v1/
d4bce7fd68df: Pull complete
a3ed95caeb02: Pull complete
f19cce48c5a8: Pull complete
564ee6d16a2e: Pull complete
a251e59b24e2: Pull complete
df7f78e810e7: Pull complete
b085a9629ef4: Pull complete
2064e34931e2: Pull complete
d56ed431390d: Pull complete
Digest: sha256:bbc7a3f61125aedfc27ffd7c679147443cf7f5fc2a591bd60fbf7bf34dc71866
2.6.17-32bit: Pulling from library/redis
Image docker.io/library/redis:2.6.17-32bit uses outdated schema1 manifest format. Please upgrade to a schema2 ima
ge for better future compatibility. More information at https://docs.docker.com/registry/spec/deprecated-schema-v
1/
d4bce7fd68df: Already exists
a3ed95caeb02: Already exists
f19cce48c5a8: Already exists
564ee6d16a2e: Already exists
a251e59b24e2: Already exists
df7f78e810e7: Already exists
b085a9629ef4: Already exists
2064e34931e2: Already exists
```

Figure 5.15: docker pull command to pull all tagged images of redis repository

There are positive and negative points in this output. As a positive point, while many might refrain from using this command with the fear of consuming too much disk space or bandwidth, they do not need to as the repeated layers will just be stacked from the cache and will not be downloaded again. You can already see this happening in the second attempt, where almost every layer is used from the cache. On the other hand, as a negative, it also means that most of the images will just be minor fixes, and many of them might even be completely outdated. Regardless, once the mass pulling is completed, you can list them out again with:

```
docker images redis
```

This command will only list the redis images on the host (like the following screenshot):

```
dhwani@docker:~$ docker images redis
REPOSITORY          TAG              IMAGE ID        CREATED         SIZE
redis               buster           235592615444    8 hours ago     104MB
redis               alpine           8e4d3b1e7f47    12 days ago     31.6MB
redis               latest           36304d3b4540    12 days ago     104MB
redis               2-32bit          19865a7ae96c    4 years ago     203MB
redis               2.8-32bit        19865a7ae96c    4 years ago     203MB
redis               2.6-32bit        62b0a5c3ea45    4 years ago     158MB
redis               2.6.17-32bit     62b0a5c3ea45    4 years ago     158MB
redis               2.6              a081f7d44c38    4 years ago     150MB
redis               2.6.17           a081f7d44c38    4 years ago     150MB
dhwani@docker:~$
dhwani@docker:~$
```

Figure 5.16: All Available tagged images pulled from redis repository

These images are sorted in reverse chronological order of creation, with the latest one on the top. It may seem natural to explore **docker push** after the pull command, but we need to learn tagging first.

docker tag

Docker Daemon uses Image IDs to primarily identify the images. Tags are used as a reference to point to the target image. This command creates such tags or references that can be used by users (*Homo sapiens*) to communicate with the daemon. Although, *its syntax is simple, (in Urdu,* اس اک وحن آساں ہے) we do need to follow a few commonly suggested practices (by Docker) for tagging an image.

- The tag name should be a valid ASCII string that can contain lowercase letters, uppercase letters, dots, dashes, and underscores.

- The length should not exceed 128 characters.

- The tag cannot start with a dot or dash.

- / is used as a separator and to represent path hierarchy among repositories

Once these practices are followed, we can tag an image in three different ways. Let us take a look at each one of them.

- **Tagging by Image ID:**

    Here we refer to an Image by its ID. You can either note it while the image is built or you can run Docker Images command and find your image out. Here is the syntax:

    `docker tag SOURCE_IMAGE[:TAG] TARGET_IMAGE[:TAG]`

    Let us run an example of this command and view the results by running Docker Images.

    `docker tag 235592615444 ceruleanhub/redis:buster-v1`

    Here is what the output will look like:

```
dhwani@docker:~$ docker images
REPOSITORY          TAG        IMAGE ID        CREATED         SIZE
ceruleanhub/redis   buster-v1  235592615444    8 hours ago     104MB
redis               buster     235592615444    8 hours ago     104MB
wordpress           latest     b301a17258fe    7 days ago      540MB
sample              latest     23cb1a2b5b4c    9 days ago      73.9MB
redis               alpine     8e4d3b1e7f47    12 days ago     31.6MB
redis               latest     36304d3b4540    12 days ago     104MB
test-3              latest     dc81f5580e56    2 weeks ago     144MB
<none>              <none>     2b418fa78e95    2 weeks ago     95.6MB
nginx               latest     5e50e9c99052    2 weeks ago     144MB
nginx               v1         5e50e9c99052    2 weeks ago     144MB
photon              latest     0135244847f5    2 weeks ago     35.3MB
test                latest     dc6141e61976    2 weeks ago     134MB
<none>              <none>     ae38c179d739    2 weeks ago     125MB
docker              latest     f038f0462ba5    3 weeks ago     211MB
python              3          659f826fabf4    3 weeks ago     934MB
python              latest     659f826fabf4    3 weeks ago     934MB
ceruleanhub/nginx   latest     08deb6e4b3e1    3 weeks ago     134MB
httpd               2.4        d4e60c8eb27a    3 weeks ago     166MB
httpd               latest     d4e60c8eb27a    3 weeks ago     166MB
nginx               alpine     89ec9da68213    6 weeks ago     19.9MB
ubuntu              16.04      005d2078bdfa    6 weeks ago     125MB
ubuntu              latest     1d622ef86b13    6 weeks ago     73.9MB
ubuntu              18.04      c3c304cb4f22    6 weeks ago     64.2MB
```

Figure 5.17: Output of docker tag command using Image ID

- **Tagging by repository-name:tag**

  When we refer to an image for tagging by its name (tag), we are essentially overwriting its previous tag with a new one. In this case, both the name and the version will be overwritten.

  Here is an example along with the output:

  ```
  docker tag redis:buster redis:buster-v2
  ```

```
dhwani@docker:~$ docker images
REPOSITORY          TAG        IMAGE ID        CREATED         SIZE
ceruleanhub/redis   buster-v1  235592615444    8 hours ago     104MB
redis               buster     235592615444    8 hours ago     104MB
redis               buster-v2  235592615444    8 hours ago     104MB
wordpress           latest     b301a17258fe    7 days ago      540MB
sample              latest     23cb1a2b5b4c    9 days ago      73.9MB
redis               alpine     8e4d3b1e7f47    12 days ago     31.6MB
redis               latest     36304d3b4540    12 days ago     104MB
test-3              latest     dc81f5580e56    2 weeks ago     144MB
<none>              <none>     2b418fa78e95    2 weeks ago     95.6MB
nginx               latest     5e50e9c99052    2 weeks ago     144MB
nginx               v1         5e50e9c99052    2 weeks ago     144MB
photon              latest     0135244847f5    2 weeks ago     35.3MB
test                latest     dc6141e61976    2 weeks ago     134MB
<none>              <none>     ae38c179d739    2 weeks ago     125MB
docker              latest     f038f0462ba5    3 weeks ago     211MB
python              3          659f826fabf4    3 weeks ago     934MB
python              latest     659f826fabf4    3 weeks ago     934MB
ceruleanhub/nginx   latest     08deb6e4b3e1    3 weeks ago     134MB
httpd               2.4        d4e60c8eb27a    3 weeks ago     166MB
httpd               latest     d4e60c8eb27a    3 weeks ago     166MB
nginx               alpine     89ec9da68213    6 weeks ago     19.9MB
ubuntu              16.04      005d2078bdfa    6 weeks ago     125MB
ubuntu              latest     1d622ef86b13    6 weeks ago     73.9MB
ubuntu              18.04      c3c304cb4f22    6 weeks ago     64.2MB
```

Figure 5.18: Output of docker tag command using repository-name:tag

- **Tagging by Repository Name**

  When we do not mention the full tag and just refer to it by the repository name, docker daemon automatically picks up the image with the latest tag and creates another tag based on our request. For example, when we use the command:

```
docker tag redis redis:v3
```

Docker daemon will create another variant of **redis:latest** (without re-downloading it since it has already been cached) and tag it **redis:v3**. Here is the result:

```
dhwani@docker:~$ docker images redis
REPOSITORY        TAG             IMAGE ID          CREATED           SIZE
redis             buster          235592615444      28 hours ago      104MB
redis             buster-v2       235592615444      28 hours ago      104MB
redis             alpine          8e4d3b1e7f47      13 days ago       31.6MB
redis             latest          36304d3b4540      13 days ago       104MB
redis             v3              36304d3b4540      13 days ago       104MB
redis             2-32bit         19865a7ae96c      4 years ago       203MB
redis             2.8-32bit       19865a7ae96c      4 years ago       203MB
redis             2.6-32bit       62b0a5c3ea45      4 years ago       158MB
redis             2.6.17-32bit    62b0a5c3ea45      4 years ago       158MB
redis             2.6             a081f7d44c38      4 years ago       150MB
redis             2.6.17          a081f7d44c38      4 years ago       150MB
dhwani@docker:~$ █
```

Figure 5.19: Output of docker tag command using only a repository name

docker push

This command is used to push the built docker images to private or public container registries like Docker Hub or GCR. The process is thorough yet simple. Docker mandates you to follow certain image tagging rules before trying to push it (as mentioned in the description of docker tag command). Simply using a Registry's URL will not allow you to push your image to that particular repository (*even if it's your private repo*); you need to manage the login credentials using docker login command. Even though its generic syntax is as simple as other commands (*looking for another language variant? Wait for it!*) I personally recommend using it with the following flags:

```
docker login [SERVER_URL [:PORT]] -u --password-stdin
```

The command takes Docker Hub as the default registry but you can mention any other public or private registry by providing the server address and the communication port combination. Following that information, we have **-u** flag to enter the username and **--password-stdin** to enter the login password via terminal. For this example, you do not need to mention the server address since we will push the image on Docker Hub itself. Once your daemon has logged in successfully with your credentials, you can push the docker image with the following command. *In German, Die Syntax ist einfach.*

```
docker push ceruleanhub/redis:buster-v1
```

This command pushes **redis:buster-v1** to **ceruleanhub** repository of the logged in Docker Hub account. This format (**repository_name / image_tag**) applies to any other registry as well. The output would look like the following screenshot:

```
dhwani@docker:~$ docker login
Login with your Docker ID to push and pull images from Docker Hub. If you don't have a Docker ID, head over to ht
tps://hub.docker.com to create one.
Username: ceruleanhub
Password:
WARNING! Your password will be stored unencrypted in /home/dhwani/.docker/config.json.
Configure a credential helper to remove this warning. See
https://docs.docker.com/engine/reference/commandline/login/#credentials-store

Login Succeeded
dhwani@docker:~$
dhwani@docker:~$ docker push ceruleanhub/redis:buster-v1
The push refers to repository [docker.io/ceruleanhub/redis]
7b9c5be81844: Mounted from library/redis
67c707dbd847: Mounted from library/redis
72d3a7e6fe02: Mounted from library/redis
cdaf0fb0082b: Mounted from library/redis
e6b49c7dcaac: Mounted from library/redis
13cb14c2acd3: Mounted from library/nginx
buster-v1: digest: sha256:76ff608805ca40008d6e0f08180d634732d8bf4728b85c18ab9bdbfa0911408d size: 1572
dhwani@docker:~$
dhwani@docker:~$ docker logout
Removing login credentials for https://index.docker.io/v1/
dhwani@docker:~$
dhwani@docker:~$ ▊
```

Figure 5.20: Output of docker push command

As mentioned in the beginning of the output, the image will be pushed to a newly created **redis** repository under the **ceruleanhub** account (which is also treated as a repository by the Docker Hub). Once the push is complete, you can try pulling it again, when you are satisfied, you can logout from the registry using **docker logout** command with the output like the following screenshot:

```
dhwani@docker:~$ docker login
Login with your Docker ID to push and pull images from Docker Hub. If you don't have a Docker ID, head over to ht
tps://hub.docker.com to create one.
Username: ceruleanhub
Password:
WARNING! Your password will be stored unencrypted in /home/dhwani/.docker/config.json.
Configure a credential helper to remove this warning. See
https://docs.docker.com/engine/reference/commandline/login/#credentials-store

Login Succeeded
dhwani@docker:~$
dhwani@docker:~$ docker push ceruleanhub/redis:buster-v1
The push refers to repository [docker.io/ceruleanhub/redis]
7b9c5be81844: Mounted from library/redis
67c707dbd847: Mounted from library/redis
72d3a7e6fe02: Mounted from library/redis
cdaf0fb0082b: Mounted from library/redis
e6b49c7dcaac: Mounted from library/redis
13cb14c2acd3: Mounted from library/nginx
buster-v1: digest: sha256:76ff608805ca40008d6e0f08180d634732d8bf4728b85c18ab9bdbfa0911408d size: 1572
dhwani@docker:~$
dhwani@docker:~$ docker logout
Removing login credentials for https://index.docker.io/v1/
dhwani@docker:~$
dhwani@docker:~$ ▊
```

Figure 5.21: docker logout command to logout from Docker Registry

docker inspect

This is another one of the most widely used commands in the docker command line. It invokes **inspect()** function of the daemon, which provides all of the data regarding the docker image in JSON array format. Docker also calls it returning low-level information about the docker objects associated with the image. *In Russian, Синтаксис прост (read as: Sintaksis prost).*

```
docker inspect [OPTIONS] NAME|ID [NAME|ID...]
```

This command is the same for Docker Images and containers. If you are going to have an image and the container by the same name (not recommended in production), it is safe to mention the object name specifically between the keywords docker and inspect. While the syntax is simple, the output can be confusing to absorb, especially for the beginners. Let us inspect the docker image of Ubuntu bionic:

```
docker inspect ubuntu:18.04
```

Since the output is too long to print in a single page, we are going to break it down into useful pieces like follows:

```
[
    {
        "Id": "sha256:c3c304cb4f22ceb8a6fcc29a0cd6d3e4383ba9eb9b5fb552f87de7c0ba99edac",
        "RepoTags": [
            "ubuntu:18.04"
        ],
        "RepoDigests": [
            "ubuntu@sha256:3235326357dfb65f1781dbc4df3b834546d8bf914e82cce58e6e6b676e23ce8f"
        ],
        "Parent": "",
        "Comment": "",
        "Created": "2020-04-24T01:07:05.743682549Z",
        "Container": "f607979929fd999f71996754275dc5058e7345748f52d58ba72b6baf449c1fb2",
        "ContainerConfig": {
            "Hostname": "f607979929fd",
            "Domainname": "",
            "User": "",
            "AttachStdin": false,
            "AttachStdout": false,
            "AttachStderr": false,
            "Tty": false,
            "OpenStdin": false,
            "StdinOnce": false,
            "Env": [
                "PATH=/usr/local/sbin:/usr/local/bin:/usr/sbin:/usr/bin:/sbin:/bin"
            ],
            "Cmd": [
                "/bin/sh",
                "-c",
```

Figure 5.22: Output of docker inspect command for Docker Image (Part I)

Starting from the top, we have Image ID, Repository Tag(s), and Repository Digest. When you pull an image and modify it, the Repository digest remains the same until you push it to your own repository. Then, we have Parent and comment field. Since, this image is built independently, there are no parent images and we did not mention any comments in the Dockerfile or during Docker Build. Next is the creation timestamp with Date and precise time.

There is a bit of container information for the image (for creating a template for running containers) that discusses basic information like host (daemon host) identifier and terminal behavior. Then, the output mentions the environment variable PATH. All of this information is mentioned in key-value format. The empty fields indicate the docker daemon taking default values.

For example, since there were no comments during the build, the default value for comments would be null, whereas the default value for the user would be root. Since the container has not started yet, **stdin**, **stdout**, **stderr** or **tty** have not been attached yet (thus, marked as false). In the bottom-most part of *Figure 5.22*, we have the command to run the shell triggered by CMD instruction.

As mentioned in the following screenshot, it is marked with the no-operation or nop tag as it will be executed during runtime:

```
        "Cmd": [
            "/bin/bash"
        ],
        "ArgsEscaped": true,
        "Image": "sha256:1102e32f7bb0a43e1b6b4e2d633afe8dd41747a5aee805a616549e26719a60e7",
        "Volumes": null,
        "WorkingDir": "",
        "Entrypoint": null,
        "OnBuild": null,
        "Labels": null
    },
    "Architecture": "amd64",
    "Os": "linux",
    "Size": 64206056,
    "VirtualSize": 64206056,
    "GraphDriver": {
        "Data": {
            "LowerDir": "/var/lib/docker/overlay2/2f9683cc7eee517bea16093e833cebd2946d04f882e28babc80e33860b5
7511d/diff:/var/lib/docker/overlay2/290ff21f48f43e7e70e70c9f7d3eacbf8223732a20d0ada713885a2d482e39d5/diff:/var/li
b/docker/overlay2/ce4192d8a58fc9ea63c2dd5102377250fb613fdfaa05341b5ccfb59022c72251/diff",
            "MergedDir": "/var/lib/docker/overlay2/f3653344853ba8df20c60263bb39970135c66d2359aab05a7bb71b02ad
66bf4b/merged",
            "UpperDir": "/var/lib/docker/overlay2/f3653344853ba8df20c60263bb39970135c66d2359aab05a7bb71b02ad6
6bf4b/diff",
            "WorkDir": "/var/lib/docker/overlay2/f3653344853ba8df20c60263bb39970135c66d2359aab05a7bb71b02ad66
bf4b/work"
        },
```

Figure 5.23: *Output of docker inspect command for Docker Image (Part II)*

The **"ArgsEscaped": true** parameter indicates the source Dockerfile having used an escape directive with RUN instruction. **** is the escape directive used to escape the process before running another one. If you have two unrelated processes in consequent RUN instructions, it is a good practice to escape first before handling second. We have certainly not mounted any volumes (storage objects for docker, topic for the next chapter), and it seems like the Dockerfile has not described any working directory or labels in particular.

The working directory will be inherited from the base image, while the ENTRYPOINT will be replaced by the CMD. Finally, it seems like we do not have any ONBUILD instruction lingering either, since the nature of Ubuntu base image is very general-purpose.

In the next bracket, we have the architectural specifications for the Docker Image and the size occupied on the host's disk. Let us move on to the next screenshot:

Figure 5.24: Output of docker inspect command for Docker Image (Part III)

First, we have the graph driver details. Graph Driver is a storage driver that allows additional plugins to map and use storage external to Docker's default storage. The type of storage driver is Overlay2. We will learn more about storage drivers soon enough. Then, we have the default storage, which is the Root file system divided into layers identified by their IDs.

At last, we have the metadata field displaying the last time the image was tagged. It is set to **00:00:00** on **01/01/0001** because the image has no tagging timestamp and the default latest tag has been granted to another updated image thus, this one loses the tag along with the timestamp.

Sharing the Docker Image

Sharing is probably the most important task you will be doing with your Docker Image; and as we know, sharing is a two-way process. It is a give-and-take situation; hence, we need two commands or two API calls to fulfill the task. Docker understands this well, and it has doubled down on the two API idea. Docker has two distinct ways of sharing Docker Images. Surprisingly (yet logically), these two ways are incompatible. Let us understand both of them and their incompatibilities with examples.

- **The Save-Load Method:**

    In this method, the Docker Image is saved as a tar file. The tar file contains individual layers of a Docker Image along with a manifest to stitch the file back into an image. Let us take a look at the syntax and an example:

    ```
    docker save [OPTIONS] IMAGE
    ```

Using this syntax, let us save the **busybox:latest** image. To control the name of the output file, we will rename it to **busybox-save.tar** using **--output** flag.

```
docker save --output busybox-save.tar busybox:latest
```

```
dhwani@docker:~$ docker images busybox
REPOSITORY          TAG          IMAGE ID          CREATED          SIZE
busybox             latest       1c35c4412082      2 weeks ago      1.22MB
dhwani@docker:~$
dhwani@docker:~$
dhwani@docker:~$ docker save --output busybox-save.tar busybox:latest
dhwani@docker:~$
dhwani@docker:~$
dhwani@docker:~$ ls -sh
total 1.4M
1.4M busybox-save.tar
dhwani@docker:~$
dhwani@docker:~$
```

Figure 5.25: Output of docker save command

The size of the original docker image was 1.22M whereas the tar file is 1.4M large. The additional space is occupied by the manifest file and the metadata. We can also view the content inside the saved tar file using tree utility as shown in the following screenshot:

```
dhwani@docker:~$ tree busybox-save
busybox-save
├── 1c35c441208254cb7c3844ba95a96485388cef9ccc0646d562c7fc026e04c807.json
├── 9719c1ce1e2335e5b108c339b9f2b2f8aae8e62f30a831c40b9d9329678fd711
│   ├── VERSION
│   ├── json
│   └── layer.tar
├── manifest.json
└── repositories

1 directory, 6 files
dhwani@docker:~$
dhwani@docker:~$
```

Figure 5.26: List of files and directories of saved Docker Image using tree command

The top JSON file contains metadata about the saved layers. The second repository contains metadata about the image itself along with another tar file with all of the layers of the docker image. This is how the top layer merges with all of the other layers without them losing their identity. Finally, we have a manifest file that has the instructions about recreating the image as it is. We can load back this image using **docker load** command. If the image already exists, it will be re-written (even with update) and if it does not exist, it will be created on the host from the tar file using the manifest. The image is re-written in the following screenshot:

```
dhwani@docker:~$ docker load --quiet < busybox-save.tar
Loaded image: busybox:latest
dhwani@docker:~$
dhwani@docker:~$ docker images busybox
REPOSITORY          TAG          IMAGE ID          CREATED          SIZE
busybox             latest       1c35c4412082      2 weeks ago      1.22MB
dhwani@docker:~$
dhwani@docker:~$
```

Figure 5.27: loading back the saved Docker Image

The quiet flag blocks docker from printing the full process of loading each intermediate image layer and providing a clean one-liner output. This method is useful when you want to share the image as itself and are confident about the compatibility of docker versions of sender and receiver's ends. The source image to be loaded can be from any file system or a URL. It means you can share a docker image just like a .exe software file from windows. But sometimes, you may not be sure about the ability of the client to use docker or about the docker version compatibility between you and your client. That is where the next method is useful.

- **The Export-Import Method:**

  While docker save packs a docker image into a tar file, docker export packs a snapshot of a running container environment (in other words, the file system of a container) into a tar file. The host exports the container as a tar file and the client imports it as a docker image. The reason behind this is quite simple. Containers are isolated file systems; resource-controlled by cgroups.

  The container host cannot have any control over the client resources, so the client has to create a container by itself from a docker image. This raises many questions like how the imported docker image is different from the loaded one or why are these sharing methods incompatible to each other? Let us go through all of them after looking at an example. Run a **busybox** container using the following command:

  ```
  docker run -itd --name busybox-cont busybox
  ```

  Then, export the container using the command as shown in the following screenshot:

  ```
  docker export --output="busybox-export.tar" busybox-cont
  ```

Figure 5.28: Output of docker export command

As we saw in the screenshot, both save and export create tar files of the same size (since we haven't done anything significant with the running container), but the internals is different.

We should view the tree structure of exported container's tar as well:

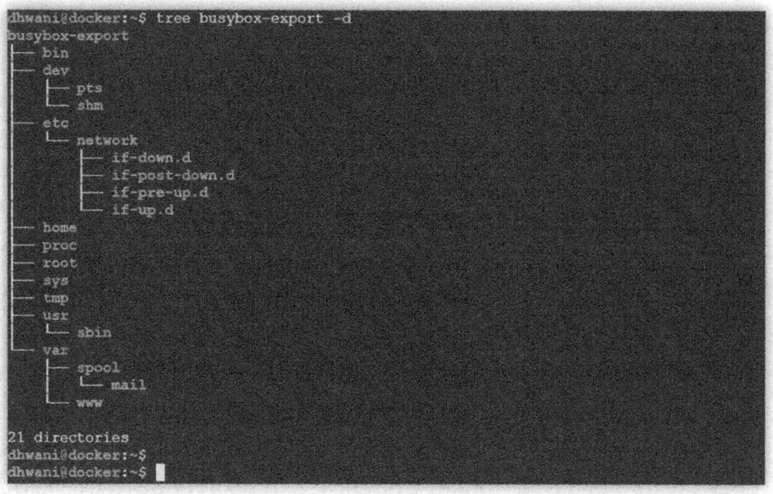

Figure 5.29: List of files and directories of exported container
file system using tree command

These ain't no layers! This is a teeny-tiny file system! Colloquial slangs aside, this is what we were expecting, the snapshot of the running container's file system. This is the file system of a busybox (Embedded Linux variant) container. When we import it, it turns into a docker image but without any CMD or ENTRYPOINT layer. This means at some point you need to specify the command to turn the image executable. Instead of leaving this task to the one running the container, it is better to do it while importing the image like the following example:

```
docker import \

--change "CMD sh" \

busybox-export.tar \

busybox:export
```

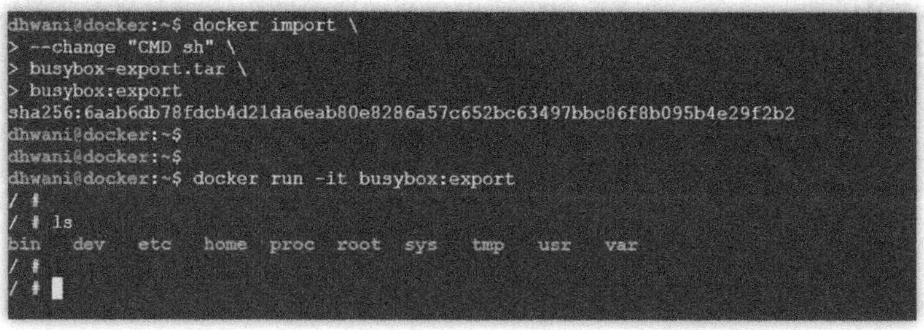

Figure 5.30: docker import command to import an exported container as Docker Image

In the multi-line command, we have used the **--change** flag to add the CMD instruction layer to the image. The source exported file is **busybox-export. tar** and the desired resultant Docker Image is **busybox:export**. The image is then run successfully as a container and the shell was the foreground program to run just as mentioned in the CMD.

These were the two Docker Image sharing methods. Let's test their incompatibilities. First of all, let's see what happens when we try to import a saved Docker Image in the following screenshot:

```
dhwani@docker:~$ docker import /home/dhwani/busybox-save.tar
sha256:402bc4a91495a648e330f564bb2f085767410ccf7b6b356c57502981227d41c3
dhwani@docker:~$
dhwani@docker:~$ docker images
REPOSITORY                           TAG               IMAGE ID        CREATED         SIZE
<none>                               <none>            402bc4a91495    8 seconds ago   1.44MB
ubuntu                               local-v1          bdbc39a4aaeb    7 days ago      66.6MB
<none>                               <none>            10a44ae92c4f    7 days ago      66.6MB
ubuntu                               local             dc71233dece8    7 days ago      66.6MB
ceruleanhub/redis                    buster-v1         235592615444    9 days ago      104MB
redis                                buster            235592615444    9 days ago      104MB
redis                                buster-v2         235592615444    9 days ago      104MB
bash                                 devel             641727efe7af    9 days ago      13.7MB
bash                                 devel-20200605    641727efe7af    9 days ago      13.7MB
ceruleanhub/nginx                    v1                2622e6cca7eb    9 days ago      132MB
nginx                                latest            2622e6cca7eb    9 days ago      132MB
wordpress                            latest            b301a17258fe    2 weeks ago     540MB
busybox                              latest            1c35c4412082    2 weeks ago     1.22MB
sample                               latest            23cb1a2b5b4c    2 weeks ago     73.9MB
ubuntu                               16.04             005d2078bdfa    8 weeks ago     125MB
gcr.io/google-appengine/python       latest            2293f8d29bbb    2 months ago    1.04GB
dhwani@docker:~$
dhwani@docker:~$
```

Figure 5.31: Failed attempt to import a saved docker image

The **Import** command did try to create an image as seen at the top of the Docker Images output, but the metadata was completely missing. While we can identify this particular image, a host full of tags and fewer images is worse than not using containers at all. On the other hand, if we try to load an exported container, the results are as shown in the following screenshot:

```
dhwani@docker:~$ docker load < busybox-export.tar
open /var/lib/docker/tmp/docker-import-617225697/bin/json: no such file or directory
dhwani@docker:~$
dhwani@docker:~$
```

Figure 5.32: Failed attempt to load an exported container

This is even better; Docker did not even want to try (*chuckles*). The files list in the manifest was unexpected and did not provide anything close to a layer (intermediate image) ID so docker just expressed its disappointment.

At the end, none is clearly better than the other. It is all about appreciating the flexibility and making the most out of them depending on the situation.

Docker Image clean-up commands

We have been playing with Docker Images a lot. From building them to exporting them, we have created and pulled a lot of variants of a lot of images, but not all of them are here to stay. As storage optimized as containers and their images may be, they still consume space on your drive and you do need to clean them up every once in a while. The first and straight forward command to do so is **docker rmi**. Here is the syntax:

```
docker rmi [OPTIONS] IMAGE [IMAGE-2 IMAGE-3 IMAGE-4...]
```

The command can be used to remove one or more Docker Images (at least one is necessary for the command to work) addressed by their repository name, tag, or ID. Here is an example with the screenshot of the output to remove a single image:

```
docker rmi nginx
```

```
dhwani@docker:~$ docker rmi nginx
Untagged: nginx:latest
dhwani@docker:~$
dhwani@docker:~$ docker images nginx
REPOSITORY          TAG               IMAGE ID          CREATED           SIZE
nginx               v1                5e50e9c99052      2 weeks ago       144MB
nginx               alpine            89ec9da68213      6 weeks ago       19.9MB
dhwani@docker:~$
dhwani@docker:~$ ▮
```

Figure 5.33: Output of docker rmi command with single image

What just happened? We asked for the removal of the image, so why did it get untagged? This ties back to the fact that the images are stored as repositories with tags. If we have multiple versions of the same image, the image does not get duplicated, it just gets multiple tags (with corresponding layers if updated any) which are displayed as different images.

When we remove such an image, it does not get deleted from the disk (otherwise, the other images would also lose the layers); just the tag gets removed from the metadata. Docker daemon (which returns the output of **docker images** command) treats this as removing that particular version of the image. On the other hand, if there is only one image from a particular repository, the **rmi** command does manage to delete it completely.

Similarly, we can remove more than one images from one or more repositories at the same time. The command remains the same with just more image names and tags like as follows:

```
docker rmi nginx:v1 nginx:alpine
```

Since, we only had two nginx variants remaining, let us remove both of them. By doing so, the layers of the image will actually be removed since there is no other nginx variant to keep these layers for, just like the output shown as follows:

```
dhwani@docker:~$ docker rmi nginx:v1 nginx:alpine
Untagged: nginx:v1
Deleted: sha256:5e50e9c9905242ef171fe48b77b5320b84c14d6798fabc0d167432e7c41a63f6
Deleted: sha256:fe54a464b10e1886395f08f9d6b3f651429e8fe480c331c737fb79ab569f28e0
Untagged: nginx:alpine
Untagged: nginx@sha256:763e7f0188e378fef0c761854552c70bbd817555dc4de029681a2e972e25e30e
Deleted: sha256:89ec9da682137d6b18ab8244ca263b6771067f251562f884c7510c8f1e5ac910
Deleted: sha256:2d4747dc369095d2106384421de7e79992c14e3031080b93a436b5ad6e359770
dhwani@docker:~$ docker images nginx
REPOSITORY             TAG                    IMAGE ID            CREATED             SIZE
dhwani@docker:~$
dhwani@docker:~$ ▮
```

Figure 5.34: Removing multiple images with docker rmi command

There are times when a container is running from a specific image. In that case, you cannot usually remove the image. This happens because the container is essentially a writable layer in the context of a process on top of the docker image's read-only layers. Another reason is the provision of a command called docker commit, which saves the changes made in the containers as a separate docker image. If the image is not deleted, all daemon has to do is saving the changes and creating a new tag instead of creating layers for a whole new image. Caching works all across docker which makes this one of the most efficient tools for deploying applications at scale. If you want to remove such an image (or an entire repository, if not mentioned any specific tag), you can force the daemon to do so by adding **--force** or **-f** flag as shown in the command and the output is as follows:

```
docker rmi ubuntu --force
```

```
dhwani@docker:~$ docker rmi ubuntu
Error response from daemon: conflict: unable to remove repository reference "ubuntu" (must force) - container ad7
c5fe69ab4 is using its referenced image 1d622ef86b13
dhwani@docker:~$
dhwani@docker:~$ docker rmi ubuntu --force
Untagged: ubuntu:latest
Untagged: ubuntu@sha256:747d2dbbaaee995098c9792d99bd333c6783ce56150d1b11e333bbceed5c54d7
dhwani@docker:~$
dhwani@docker:~$ ▮
```

Figure 5.35: Force removal of a docker image

If you do not mention the Image repository names at all, you can remove all of the images with **-a** flag. We will do that at the end of this book. Lastly, there are dangling images, in other words, the images which are not used by any running or stopped containers. When you have many images on your host, addressing each of them is tiresome and blindly using **-a** flag is dangerous. That is why we have the **docker prune** command. This command works with both images and containers, but we will look at the images variant in the example as follows:

```
docker image prune --all --force --filter "until=2020-05-31T00:00:00"
```

With the above-mentioned command, we will force prune all of the images created before 31st of May 2020 (an example timestamp) and will get an output like the following screenshot:

```
dhwani@docker:~$ docker image prune --all --force --filter "until=2020-05-31T00:00:00"
Deleted Images:
untagged: redis:2.6
untagged: redis:2.6.17
untagged: redis@sha256:6c9f9cb9a250b12c15a92d8042a44f4557ca5bc590f36e63e529d52fb15b4ddc
untagged: redis@sha256:ef3e064323c58d74ddc71426be5aefd9d397b663bc6422abacc2f37821cc04b4
deleted: sha256:a081f7d44c38b87ba89aaa5d62a6caed3b4e7e029462e7c39010e4d04aca2bb8
deleted: sha256:d16dea2286219f0a944bd033f426ce64cf9f48ea8dc3f1d990914a0af3542ad5
deleted: sha256:eea944395cf0eac4b0a53344a6d3fb5447d8efe1ab0e8e334762e3091832fc48
deleted: sha256:da2102a8bcde66f583c3f1faf8537bbd784c68f5dccff80e618e52b4a12050f4
deleted: sha256:33ba1885911edf4ead458c8414f23db26aeae0fab66f75329e10612001a84588
deleted: sha256:256adf93336173bdb4be6c7f33c6aa0c3c7e246cbd74d3f05bd5b88ea6cb5a01
deleted: sha256:4148ca3c3d71ac54a4d0fe0b141bdbf19c6b1a4508138eef9160b99a2c4a77c9
deleted: sha256:f476b42baa80f4c3666b5f1ff1a56dbb50501ccc981f90ec58ae82cb92981383
deleted: sha256:ef5343dd5d4935acb2d36db63989c10adcc9b0b14941cfde188f19f6e5ce95b5
deleted: sha256:05b9238bc48917aa4a4487111789081cba1d93c3d0ba09b2baf0f01729b1bfc8
deleted: sha256:c9e8b2e91696f7c01c9002494e4a049c00810c5d823328cc419afff9b089853b
deleted: sha256:e4cf30a83ca3cbaf438899844ee7a1c9fa9de83892f365c9f16babf1d5291b5c
deleted: sha256:903109a929adc18231715e26fe4815c56a456c4a731e34d790da14d391edc130
deleted: sha256:60c585bab6a4caee070e0337dcec1b1344ca86f4653ad311a99f19c18d75020e
deleted: sha256:824dbc7c1f71f4ba68ca8f8edc0a85a652f343f1b0b17514e83c163c74d65b50
untagged: redis:latest
untagged: redis:v3
untagged: redis@sha256:d27740b5bd12087efc2b30ac9102fa767d6cc83611dc0fc28f0edb042e835996
deleted: sha256:36304d3b4540c5143673b2cefaba583a0426b57c709b5a35363f96a3510058cd
deleted: sha256:0a0f29e43c3a5555d675d253ff51d73e4d238bd558f11ae9b63d2a2a14251b36
deleted: sha256:529a5b3d7258f27ee4d9aec07767e5bc40219f154062249445406b185a1225fb2
deleted: sha256:59c366baf28249e406a6021daba98a361b862b68c44d8a63f047d183b34db963
deleted: sha256:8c02234b86056c009036ff0c31efb9a726412392d9872dacf95103767ac3b101
deleted: sha256:ae38c179d739e347294756220a39d878aafefd461a4cbac6148b6e8493bec988
untagged: jenkins:latest
untagged: jenkins@sha256:eeb4850eb65f2d92500e421b430ed1ec58a7ac909e91f518926e02473904f668
deleted: sha256:cd14cecfdb3a657ba7d05bea026e7ac8b9abafc6e5c66253ab327c7211fa6281
deleted: sha256:9047d4817dd4203ae4d456888aa5355bc526d274713d6f168359ba61b85b6c00
deleted: sha256:b6eeb6c0e550e93a8b6293a35b2a68931a2afld21cf8fe8c53bd412369433fdc
deleted: sha256:54a9d605504efad152c1032f37f76ee95bae30607f68bd0ff48a095ebec5d820
deleted: sha256:0b5e1c633ad7fa60f5185ff00ccbff9af3608ba336dc7c01868f9cd0dd8a7137
deleted: sha256:0373335894092868f06432433f14881bd6f09d851931d6e5090601a64e0466f3
deleted: sha256:b4e8f84d7b87e7994e49a190bc35871b23f76d9cab573308fa1ae7401c50dcc6
deleted: sha256:cde912e85b12d60e9e4d056ad3c8cb35853c60291dbe4b319dcd80bcd2ef243c
deleted: sha256:8062b94ccb384de40b6777515f21b895be64218c5296bac3ee6db2ed4c5db9fe
deleted: sha256:a3411e0c109af31befac78bcbd2aba26f893717f645df8d4828bf29772417bc0
deleted: sha256:fb1cc4fe4174cb86f9614cf9ee4c6cecad4c7f0c04ca52c95fd1a7d0d79471e8
deleted: sha256:1fe73f13106502d5c58cc444a71738c518b341fd667fc26058f3e473a3cc559f
deleted: sha256:d3898f75e7b8a2a7e45bfdd351a00c4ad95b743861860635d702378fd073771d
deleted: sha256:46ddeaf1e1efd81fd6cad11c44af4e4ba71cbab32b75f60f8647f025a8874315
deleted: sha256:4e9ac8670c1ea60c504c1dc22e38a177afd782a48e17e81e06ecf60a1c8f4ef0
deleted: sha256:76dc20911db5ba40907269c70aa4ef7caf207ea4aa23818b8db2ff83ba74e1e4
deleted: sha256:b4ff564f2a75c2bc85c8eda2928ec73b13809416658f949d2b55fa24448c08b1
deleted: sha256:2d9c829ae3f7ff3e148e5c7c3a1cf378b0f90b79035e2fe9a8d78c63ccde4c89
deleted: sha256:b1ae7168c6f3e061aa3943740ec3ceaf8e582dc65feab31d2b56d464a5062d59
deleted: sha256:4a495dbc04bd205c728297a08cf203988e91caeafe4b21fcad94c893a53d96dc
deleted: sha256:3b10514a95bec77489a57d6e2fbfddb7ddfdb643907470ce5de0f1b05c603706

Total reclaimed space: 2.959GB
dhwani@docker:~$ 5-
```

Figure 5.36: Pruning dangling Docker Images

Initially, the image variants got untagged. Then, the dangling images and their intermediate images got deleted from the host file system. This is a handy command when you are working with a variety of docker images; look at the reclaimed space at the bottom! Now that we have explored the images quite a lot, let's move to its running instance, the containers!

The container life-cycle

A container goes through many phases throughout its life-cycle, and there is no better way to understand each of those phases and their implications on the host other than making it transition through those phases yourself. To get a broader picture of what we are going to do with the container, here is a state diagram of the container life-cycle:

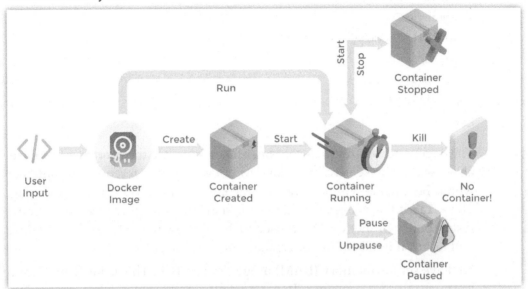

Figure 5.37: *Container Life-cycle*

As shown in the preceding diagram, the user input (from Docker Client) controls the transition between the phases whereas Docker Image is where the lifecycle actually starts from. We will go step-by-step to explore each command and each phase of the containers.

- **docker create**

    This command is applied on the Docker Images. Docker Images are a stacked sequence of read-only file system layers. This command appends a writable layer on top of them and the size of the writable layer depends on the resource limit set for the container.

    Just like the storage, it also reserves resources for the compute end of the container. This is done by creating a cgroup for the container resources. The cgroup is created by an underlying Container Runtime Environment like **containerd**. The command has a simple syntax as follows:

    ```
    docker create [OPTIONS] IMAGE [COMMAND] [ARG...]
    ```

    In case the Docker Image you have pulled does not meet your requirements to the fullest (which is most likely the case), this is one of the stages where you can make adjustments to some of its layers. You can replace the CMD, ENTRYPOINT or WORKDIR layers, trigger health-checks on/off, add metadata and even mention resource limits for the container. Here is an example:

```
docker create -it --name bob \
--label OS=Linux \
--restart=always \
--memory=1GB \
--workdir /home \
--log-driver syslog \
--no-healthcheck \
--privileged \
centos
```

The command will return a container ID to reference the container in future, as shown in the screenshot below. Another way to reference the container would be a name. We have named the container as bob using **--name** flag. The **--label** flag is used to add metadata in key-value form. We have set the restart policy to always. This is used to dictate how many times the container will restart if it fails to run or crashes due to some error.

We have set the memory (RAM) usage limit to 1GB. This is fairly high for a learning purpose container. To get a relative perspective, when we are low on resources, we limit our Virtual Machines (VMs) to use 1GB memory and assume some performance hiccups. The environment of the container itself will consume much less memory compared to VM, so the CentOS container with 1GB memory will perform much better than the CentOS VM with the same limitations.

Moving on, we have set the workdir to **/home** for convenience. Container logs are an elaborate topic and we will explore it in-depth in this book but to comprehend the next flag; processes need an agent application to store and process logs. We have set syslog as the logging agent, which is built-in the host as a daemon. Finally, we have turned off the health check and have given privileged access to the container:

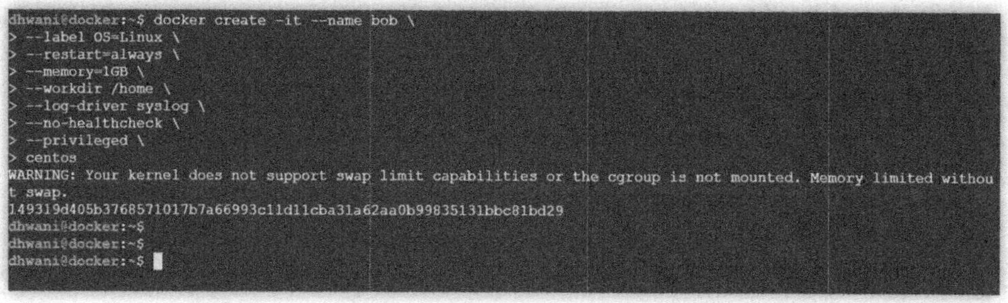

Figure 5.38: Output of docker create command

Along with the container ID, we have also received a warning. The container Id indicates that the container is created, and all of the changes (mentioned via flags) are appended. This warning has popped up because Debian variants like Ubuntu have disabled swap memory access by default (the swap limit usage is set to 0 bytes).

If we do not intend to use swap memory on the host, we can let this warning slide; but if your application infrastructure is critical about resources and swap memory is a part of your compute estimations, you can feel free to enable it by adding another flag **--memory-swap** followed by the size value (preferably after the **--memory** flag for better readability), and the warning will disappear.

Another aspect of the statement warns about **cgroups** not being mounted. This happens when **cgroups** are not enabled on your host *(or to be precise, they are disabled since they are enabled by default)*. We know this is not the case because we have already run a few containers on this host! We can verify the creation and check the state of this container with **docker ps** command as shown in the following snapshot:

```
dhwani@docker:~$ docker ps -a
CONTAINER ID     IMAGE          COMMAND             CREATED          STATUS                      PO
RTS              NAMES
149319d405b3        centos      "/bin/bash"         58 seconds ago   Created
                 bob
73504a4bddf7        centos      "/bin/bash"         44 hours ago     Exited (0) 43 hours ago
                 centos-cont
69eb5de352db        ubuntu      "/bin/bash"         45 hours ago     Exited (0) 45 hours ago
                 peaceful_shannon
2950b8da2d28        sample      "/bin/sh -c 'echo "H…"  7 days ago    Exited (0) 7 days ago
                 festive_thompson
de71ad8958d8        f91da3e9aaab  "/bin/sh -c 'echo "H…"  7 days ago    Exited (0) 7 days ago
                 amazing_curran
d2d73b4218cf        test-3      "/bin/bash"         11 days ago      Exited (0) 11 days ago
                 distracted_jepsen
dhwani@docker:~$
```

Figure 5.39: Container bob with "created" status

Though the container is definitely not running, it is ready to run. To run it, we can use the next command.

- **docker start**

This command is used to send the container from the stopped or created state to the running state. As a container is a process, a created container's process gets forked on Linux. The cgroup mounted by **docker create** command starts to act, and the resources start to get utilized. Here is the syntax:

```
docker start [OPTIONS] NAME | ID
```

You can use the container name or the container ID to refer to the container. You can use one or more containers in created or stopped state at once to start them. Let us start the **bob** container:

```
docker start bob
```

The output will be as the following screenshot:

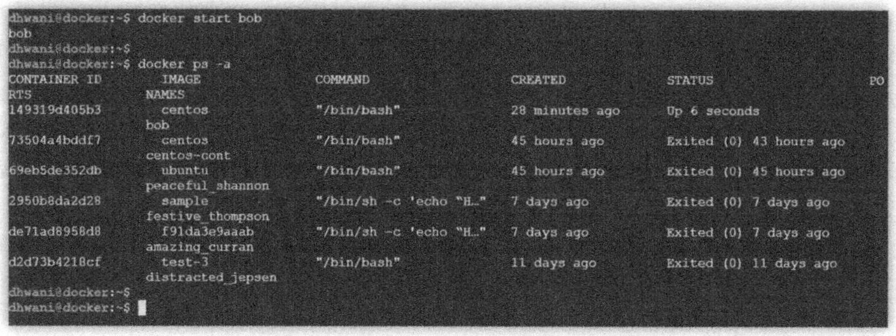

Figure 5.40: Output of docker start command

You can notice that the container was created 28 minutes ago whereas it was started just a few seconds ago. The status is described as Up which indicates that bob is running. If we want to access bob's environment, we can start it with an interactive shell instead, with the following command:

```
docker start bob --interactive
```

With this flag, we will be able to communicate to the shell of the container. The screenshot below also verifies that the WORKDIR instruction worked perfectly as the **pwd** is set to **/home**:

Figure 5.41: Output of docker start command with --interactive flag

- **docker run**

  While the combination of **docker start** and **docker create** commands provides its own set of advantages like flexibility and granular control, docker realized over time that a large majority of users would benefit if there was a single command to both create and start the container at once. This is how and when docker run came into existence. As you might have guessed, the command works directly on the docker image. It can tail flags from **docker create** command (for altering the image) and **docker start** command (for manipulating container behavior and interactions).

  From the narrative perspective, **docker run** has already been spoiled multiple times to you. We will be using it plenty of times in the book further. Let us move to the next phase of the container life-cycle. **A running container**

can have 4 possibilities. It can be stopped, paused, killed, or restarted. Let's explore each one of them one-by-one.

- **docker stop**

Starting with the cliché line, this command sends a running container to the stopped stage. To get it back up and running, we need to use the same `docker start` command that we had used on a created container; but the stopped phase is not the same as the created phase.

In this phase, the init process of the container (process with PID 1, if not init) receives a termination signal SIGTERM from the parent process of the host. The only significant flag this command has is **-t** which is an abbreviation of **--time**. The time flag indicates grace period before sending SIGKILL if SIGTERM fails to stop the container. I believe bob will have no problem stopping, so adding a grace period will not make any difference. Here is an example:

```
docker stop bob
```

The successful implementation will return the container ID or name (depending on how you addressed it in the command) as shown in the following screenshot:

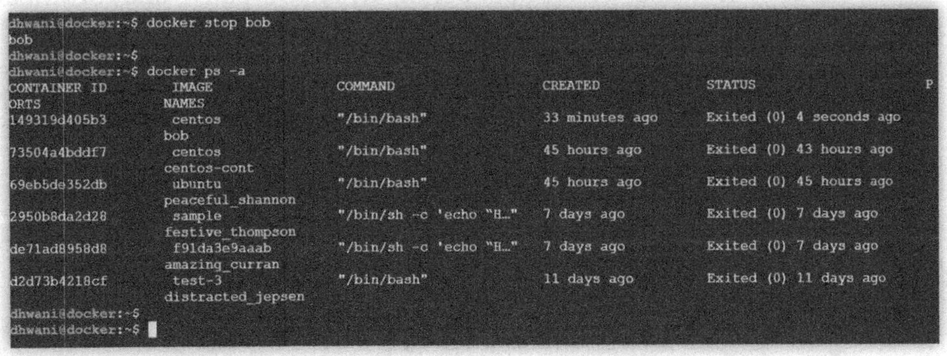

Figure 5.42: Output of docker stop command

- **docker pause and unpause**

There are times when we do not wish to stop the container, but do not want to run it either. At times like this, we can pause them. Containers use cgroups and when we run **docker pause** command, the control of the container is given to a freezer cgroup.

In simple terms, you can say freezer cgroup is SIGSTOP signal enveloped by watch utility. All of the processes of the container are suspended; and while they (processes) do not realize it, they are being watched by docker daemon.

When a process is controlled by a freezer cgroup, the cgroup itself may be in **Freezing** (during the execution of pause command), **Frozen** (after execution of the pause command) and **Thawed** (when unpaused). The following images describe what happens when we pause and unpause bob; the syntaxes are beyond simple as there are no accompanying flags available.

You can simply use one or more container references (name or ID) after the **pause** and **unpause** command, as shown in the following screenshot:

```
dhwani@docker:~$ docker pause bob
bob
dhwani@docker:~$
dhwani@docker:~$ docker ps -a
CONTAINER ID        IMAGE               COMMAND                  CREATED             STATUS
 PORTS               NAMES
149319d405b3        centos              "/bin/bash"              46 minutes ago      Up About a minute (Paused)
                     bob
73504a4bddf7        centos              "/bin/bash"              45 hours ago        Exited (0) 43 hours ago
                     centos-cont
69eb5de352db        ubuntu              "/bin/bash"              45 hours ago        Exited (0) 45 hours ago
                     peaceful_shannon
2950b8da2d28        sample              "/bin/sh -c 'echo "H…"   7 days ago          Exited (0) 7 days ago
                     festive_thompson
de71ad8958d8        f91da3e9aaab        "/bin/sh -c 'echo "H…"   7 days ago          Exited (0) 7 days ago
                     amazing_curran
d2d73b4218cf        test-3              "/bin/bash"              11 days ago         Exited (0) 11 days ago
                     distracted_jepsen
dhwani@docker:~$
dhwani@docker:~$
```

Figure 5.43: Output of docker pause command for container bob

As shown in the screenshots below, when we pause and/or unpause the container, it does not exit; it stays up the entire time.

```
dhwani@docker:~$ docker unpause bob
bob
dhwani@docker:~$
dhwani@docker:~$ docker ps -a
CONTAINER ID        IMAGE               COMMAND                  CREATED             STATUS                       PO
RTS                 NAMES
149319d405b3          centos              "/bin/bash"              47 minutes ago      Up 3 minutes
                    bob
73504a4bddf7          centos              "/bin/bash"              45 hours ago        Exited (0) 43 hours ago
                    centos-cont
69eb5de352db          ubuntu              "/bin/bash"              45 hours ago        Exited (0) 45 hours ago
                    peaceful_shannon
2950b8da2d28          sample              "/bin/sh -c 'echo "H…"   7 days ago          Exited (0) 7 days ago
                    festive_thompson
de71ad8958d8          f91da3e9aaab        "/bin/sh -c 'echo "H…"   7 days ago          Exited (0) 7 days ago
                    amazing_curran
d2d73b4218cf          test-3              "/bin/bash"              11 days ago         Exited (0) 11 days ago
                    distracted_jepsen
dhwani@docker:~$
dhwani@docker:~$
```

Figure 5.44: Output of docker unpause command for container bob

It means a cgroup is active and the resources are not freed up. After all, the processes inside the container have just received SIGSTOP, not SIGTERM or SIGKILL. Speaking of SIGKILL, here is how we kill a container by force.

- **docker kill**

  Instead of waiting for a grace period like **docker stop**, this command directly sends SIGKILL and kills the container by Out of Memory (OOM) error. In other words, this command starves the container to death! Just like many of the recent commands, this one also follows the pattern of command keywords followed by one or more containers. The only possible flag is **--signal** to change the Linux signal for killing a container like SIGKILL to SIGQUIT or SIGHUP. This process returns exit code 137, which indicates termination by SIGKILL.

Here is an example, run the following command to get the output following it:

```
docker kill bob
```

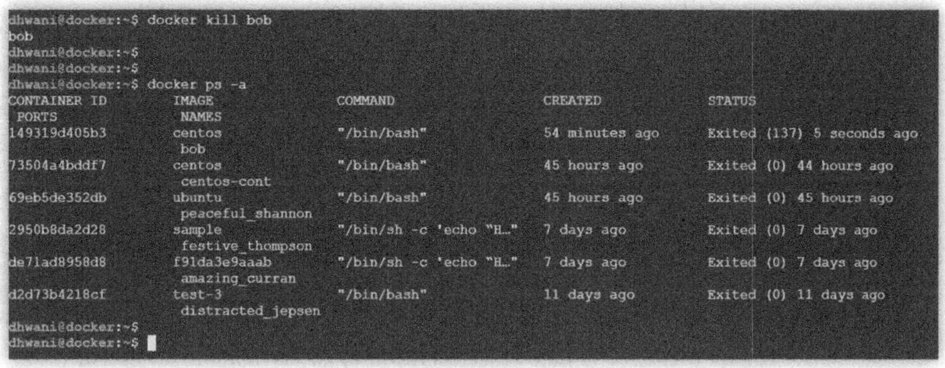

Figure 5.45: Output of docker kill command for container bob

In the list of the containers, the status of bob is still exited like stop command but the bracket explains it all. It had exited with error code 137 indicating OOM kill.

Optionally, you can also run **docker restart** command on a running, killed or stopped container to run the init process again (to get out of a crash loop situation).

Hence, we saw how a container goes from one phase to another smoothly by invoking proper APIs. In the next topic, we will cover some frequently used actions on the containers.

Working with Docker Container commands

Containers are just like a running isolated application so one can perform a lot of actions on them spanning over a spectrum of complexity. Let's start with the simple one.

docker rename

This command does exactly what its name suggests, it renames a container. The container ID remains the same, just the associated name gets overwritten by the newly input name. The word overwritten is important here as this is not a nickname.

Once you have renamed the container, you cannot address it with the previous name. Here is the syntax:

```
docker rename CONTAINER NEW_NAME
```

The container can be addressed by its name or ID as usual. You cannot use the same command to rename multiple containers at the time the book is being written. Let's rename bob.

```
docker rename bob alice
```

As shown in the output following screenshot, bob is now alice *(because, why not?!)*:

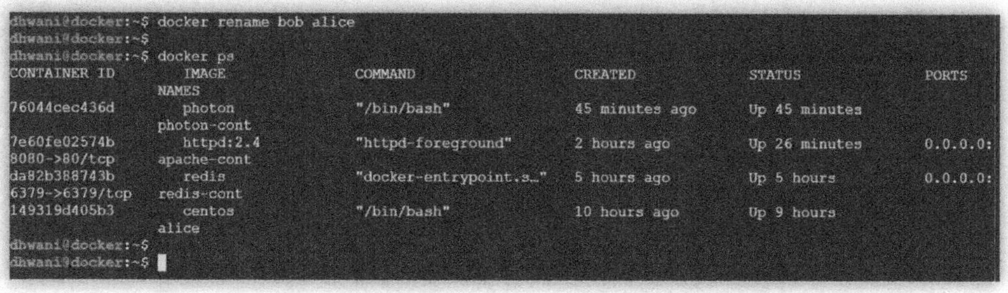

Figure 5.46: Bob is now Alice! - output of docker rename command

docker exec

This command executes the desired command *(command performs a command, love this word play)* on the running container. The initial use or the thought process behind the provision of this command was to allow developers to execute an operation (via command) on a running container environment without navigating into it. But eventually, developers started to use this command to navigate into the container itself! This happened mostly because of docker run massively, overshadowing the use of **docker create** and **docker start** combination *(I have seen t-shirts with the text printed "Dream, Plan, docker run"!).*

In any case, **docker exec** is a widely used command. It also has some limitations (and some hacks around those limitations); for example, you can only run a single command with **docker exec**. In other words, piping or commands combined with **&&** operator will not work. On the other hand, you can provide multiple commands the arguments for the single docker exec commands like **sh -c "echo nisarg && echo dhwani"**.

The command mentioned with **docker exec** runs on the PWD or defined WORKDIR of the container. This command only works if the PID 1 of the container is running. In other words, you cannot exec a stopped or killed container *(did I even need to mention that? Maybe I am underestimating my dear readers way too much!)*, but what if the container is paused? The processes are just suspended and they are going to get back up once we unpause it. It seems like Docker already knew we would try this (or maybe they got a feedback from testers) but they have made sure we do not try to do this. When we run **docker exec** on a paused container, docker daemon simply asks us to unpause it and discards our request with an error. Here is the syntax for **docker exec** command:

```
docker exec [OPTIONS] CONTAINER NAME | ID COMMAND [ARG...]
```

We have played a lot with bob and alice during the life-cycle and even after it. Let us use another docker image to try this command out. Run the following commands:

```
docker run -d --name redis-cont -p 6379:6379 redis

docker exec -it redis-cont sh
```

This will run a redis container and afterwards, open a shell in its environment. Once you have navigated to the redis terminal, you can SET a key-value pair and GET its value to verify if the SET had worked properly. To do so, follow the commands:

```
redis-cli

SET Hello World

GET Hello World
```

The entire process would look close to the following screenshot:

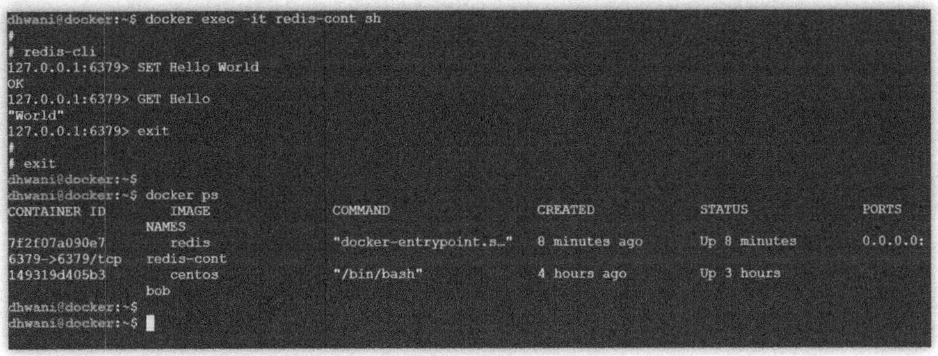

Figure 5.47: Executing docker exec command on redis container

docker attach

This command is used to attach your host's STDIN, STDOUT and STDERR to the container and interact with it. As another interpretation, it brings the CMD or ENTRYPOINT process of your container to the foreground of the host. This also means that exiting such a foreground process will result in termination of the container as, without any executable process, the container will automatically assume SIGTERM for its PID 1. Here is the syntax for **docker attach** command:

```
docker attach [OPTIONS] CONTAINER
```

The options are to be replaced by flags that grant customization like skipping integration of STDIN (**--no-stdin**) and to just watch the output or to pass signals as a proxy (**--sig-proxy**) for anonymity from the container. We do not intend any of them, so we will directly run a container and attach it to our terminal:

```
docker run -i --name busybox-cont busybox
docker attach busybox-cont
```

I have added **--i** to open the container's I/O stream. Optionally, you can also add **-d** to detach it simultaneously. This would mean that even when we exit from the CMD or ENTRYPOINT process, our container will continue to run in the background with a daemon process and will avoid PID 1 termination. Here is what the output will look like:

```
dhwani@docker:~$ docker attach busybox-cont
/ # iostat
Linux 5.3.0-1020-gcp (f12346d7bd8a)     06/08/20        _x86_64_        (1 CPU)

avg-cpu:  %user   %nice %system %iowait  %steal   %idle
           0.13    0.01    0.09    0.18    0.00   99.59

Device:            tps    Blk_read/s    Blk_wrtn/s    Blk_read    Blk_wrtn
loop0             0.00          0.01          0.00        3058           0
loop1             0.01          0.02          0.00        4340           0
loop2             0.38          0.76          0.00      171758           0
loop3             0.01          0.02          0.00        4294           0
loop4             0.00          0.01          0.00        1530           0
loop5             0.00          0.00          0.00          16           0
sda               1.28         79.90         50.20    17946934    11274762

/ # exit
dhwani@docker:~$
```

Figure 5.48: Output of docker attach command on busybox container

You can run **docker ps** to see that the container had exited with graceful termination:

```
dhwani@docker:~$ docker ps -a
CONTAINER ID        IMAGE               COMMAND                  CREATED             STATUS
PORTS                   NAMES
f12346d7bd8a        busybox             "sh"                     3 minutes ago       Exited (0) 42 seconds ago
                        busybox-cont
da82b388743b        redis               "docker-entrypoint.s…"   2 hours ago         Up 2 hours
0.0.0.0:6379->6379/tcp   redis-cont
149319d405b3        centos              "/bin/bash"              6 hours ago         Up 5 hours
                        bob
73504a4bddf7        centos              "/bin/bash"              2 days ago          Exited (0) 2 days ago
                        centos-cont
69eb5de352db        ubuntu              "/bin/bash"              2 days ago          Exited (0) 2 days ago
                        peaceful_shannon
2950b8da2d28        sample              "/bin/sh -c 'echo "H…"   8 days ago          Exited (0) 8 days ago
                        festive_thompson
de71ad8958d8        f91da3e9aaab        "/bin/sh -c 'echo "H…"   8 days ago          Exited (0) 8 days ago
                        amazing_curran
d2d73b4218cf        test-3              "/bin/bash"              12 days ago         Exited (0) 12 days ago
                        distracted_jepsen
dhwani@docker:~$
dhwani@docker:~$
```

Figure 5.49: Graceful termination of busybox container after exiting from docker attach command

After attaching the container, we have run the **iostat** utility of Linux to see the usage stats and architecture stats. An alternative to docker attach is NOT skipping **--t** while using **docker run** and performing **docker exec** with a shell invocation command afterwards.

Now that we know how to interact with the containers, let us make those interactions useful.

docker commit

This command is used to store any changes made to the containers in form of a new docker image. Though, it looks like an independent command, it is basically taking inspirations from **docker export**. The currently running container's snapshot is exported as an image and the image is then run as a container. Here is the syntax:

```
docker commit [OPTIONS] CONTAINER [REPOSITORY[:TAG]]
```

The options include provision to pause the container while committing (**-p**), making changes to the source Dockerfile (**-c**), adding an author of the changes (**-a**), and adding a change message for future reference (**-m**). Optionally (and preferably), you can provide the name of the newly created docker image as a combination of the repository name and a tag. Let's run a new Ubuntu container and modify it to demonstrate this command:

```
docker run -itd --name py-ubuntu ubuntu:18.04
```

```
docker exec -it py-ubuntu bash
```

```
/# apt install python3
```

Python3 will be installed on Ubuntu as shown in the following screenshot:

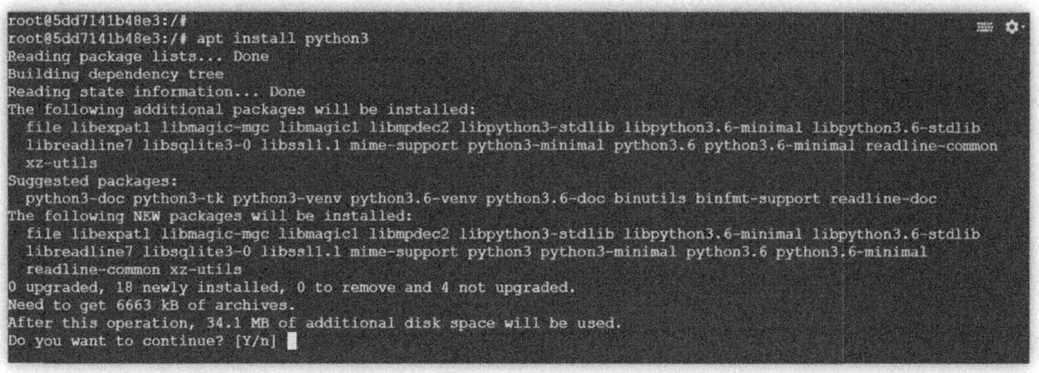

Figure 5.50: *Installing python 3 on Ubuntu container as a result of docker exec command*

The changes have been performed, now it is time to commit them using the following command:

```
docker commit --change "CMD python3" --author "Dhwani" -m "Added Python
module in Ubuntu 18.04" 5dd7141b48e3 py-ubuntu:v1
```

We have changed the CMD from running a normal shell to running python and have also added a message along with author details. The newly saved image will be named **py-ubuntu:v1**. Let's see if the image has been created:

```
dhwani@docker:~$ docker commit --change "CMD python3" --author "Dhwani" -m "Added Python module in Ubuntu 18.04"
5dd7141b48e3 py-ubuntu:v1
sha256:ccf1b8e75a8b3ac2f661e12a62182d3ebf3e21b78bfb7e0ca6a9c50c0efe6626
dhwani@docker:~$
dhwani@docker:~$ docker images
REPOSITORY          TAG        IMAGE ID        CREATED         SIZE
py-ubuntu           v1         ccf1b8e75a8b    16 seconds ago  128MB
wordpress           latest     b301a17258fe    5 days ago      540MB
busybox             latest     1c35c4412082    6 days ago      1.22MB
sample              latest     23cb1a2b5b4c    8 days ago      73.9MB
redis               alpine     8e4d3b1e7f47    10 days ago     31.6MB
redis               latest     36304d3b4540    10 days ago     104MB
test-3              latest     dc81f5580e56    12 days ago     144MB
<none>              <none>     2b418fa78e95    12 days ago     95.6MB
nginx               latest     5e50e9c99052    2 weeks ago     144MB
nginx               v1         5e50e9c99052    2 weeks ago     144MB
test                latest     dc6141e61976    2 weeks ago     134MB
<none>              <none>     ae38c179d739    2 weeks ago     125MB
docker              latest     f038f0462ba5    2 weeks ago     211MB
python              3          659f826fabf4    2 weeks ago     934MB
python              latest     659f826fabf4    2 weeks ago     934MB
ceruleanhub/nginx   latest     08deb6e4b3e1    3 weeks ago     134MB
httpd               latest     d4e60c8eb27a    3 weeks ago     166MB
nginx               alpine     89ec9da68213    6 weeks ago     19.9MB
ubuntu              16.04      005d2078bdfa    6 weeks ago     125MB
ubuntu              latest     1d622ef86b13    6 weeks ago     73.9MB
ubuntu              18.04      c3c304cb4f22    6 weeks ago     64.2MB
```

Figure 5.51: Verification of docker commit command

Look at the first and the last images in the result of the Docker images command. We had run the container from Ubuntu 18.04 (~64MB large) and the newly created py-ubuntu is 128MB large. We can also run the container to see if the CMD has been changed:

```
docker run -it --name py-ubuntu-cont py-ubuntu:v1
```

Here is what we get when we interact with the container:

```
dhwani@docker:~$ docker run -it --name py-ubuntu-cont py-ubuntu:v1
Python 3.6.9 (default, Apr 18 2020, 01:56:04)
[GCC 8.4.0] on linux
Type "help", "copyright", "credits" or "license" for more information.
>>>
```

Figure 5.52: Running a container from a committed Docker Image

This is clearly the python shell verifying that the CMD alteration worked well. Though this was exciting, all that glitters are not gold. Docker commit has very limited usability, like spontaneous testing or debugging. For any other intents of saving changes to containers, altering the docker image via Dockerfile is always a much safer option. Docker commit also does not retain any files from non-ephemeral storage (we will learn more about them in the next chapter). There is another command which is quite helpful for debugging, monitoring, or just taking a quick glance at the resource utilization of the containers.

docker stats

This command is used to stream live statistics of a target container straight into your terminal. If we do not accompany the command with a target container name, it will just stream the collective stats of all containers. While the command does not forbid you from mentioning stopped containers, they do not respond back; so it is much like knocking the door of an empty house. Optionally, you can also turn off the live stream if you want the stats of particularly current time-stamp. Here is an example:

```
docker stats apache-cont
```

We will start with a single container. Here is the output:

```
CONTAINER ID        NAME                CPU %               MEM USAGE / LIMIT     MEM %               NET I/O
        BLOCK I/O           PIDS
7e60fe02574b        apache-cont         0.01%               5.734MiB / 574.8MiB   1.00%               1.06kB / 14
2B        7.01MB / 0B         82
```

Figure 5.53: *Output of docker stats command for a single container*

The output provides us metrics like CPU usage, Memory usage, Network I/O utilized, and number of processes (PIDs). Docker does not differentiate between processes and threads, so the PIDs column will show a cumulative number of both of them.

Here is another variant:

```
docker stats --all
```

```
CONTAINER ID        NAME                CPU %               MEM USAGE / LIMIT     MEM %               NET I/O
        BLOCK I/O           PIDS
7e60fe02574b        apache-cont         0.00%               5.734MiB / 574.8MiB   1.00%               988B / 142B
        7.01MB / 0B         82
ef3a86e7da52        py-ubuntu-cont      0.00%               0B / 0B               0.00%               0B / 0B
        0B / 0B             0
5dd7141b48e3        py-ubuntu           0.00%               0B / 0B               0.00%               0B / 0B
        0B / 0B             0
f12346d7bd8a        busybox-cont        0.00%               0B / 0B               0.00%               0B / 0B
        0B / 0B             0
da82b388743b        redis-cont          0.24%               2.375MiB / 574.8MiB   0.41%               33.7kB / 24
2kB        17.3MB / 164kB       5
149319d405b3        bob                 0.00%               1.215MiB / 574.8MiB   0.21%               3.42kB / 0B
        5.41MB / 0B         1
73504a4bddf7        centos-cont         0.00%               0B / 0B               0.00%               0B / 0B
        0B / 0B             0
69eb5de352db        peaceful_shannon    0.00%               0B / 0B               0.00%               0B / 0B
        0B / 0B             0
2950b8da2d28        festive_thompson    0.00%               0B / 0B               0.00%               0B / 0B
        0B / 0B             0
de71ad8958d8        amazing_curran      0.00%               0B / 0B               0.00%               0B / 0B
        0B / 0B             0
d2d73b4218cf        distracted_jepsen   0.00%               0B / 0B               0.00%               0B / 0B
        0B / 0B             0
```

Figure 5.54: *Output of docker stats command for all containers*

(*A random adjective and a random name separated by an underscore… this is how docker names the containers by itself! Simple yet Splendid!*) While this seems informative, most of the time the system admins are looking for specific metrics. In such a case, any additional metric might just be a distraction. To avoid the distraction, we can use a formatting filter like the one mentioned in the command below:

```
docker stats --all --format "table {{.Container}}\t{{.CPUPerc}}\t{{.MemUsage}}"
```

We have already seen how this format is interpreted during the docker images section, so let us jump straight to the output:

```
CONTAINER        CPU %            MEM USAGE / LIMIT
7e60fe02574b     0.01%            5.805MiB / 574.8MiB
ef3a86e7da52     0.00%            0B / 0B
5dd7141b48e3     0.00%            0B / 0B
f12346d7bd8a     0.00%            0B / 0B
da82b388743b     0.23%            2.449MiB / 574.8MiB
149319d405b3     0.00%            1.211MiB / 574.8MiB
73504a4bddf7     0.00%            0B / 0B
69eb5de352db     0.00%            0B / 0B
2950b8da2d28     0.00%            0B / 0B
de71ad8958d8     0.00%            0B / 0B
d2d73b4218cf     0.00%            0B / 0B
```

Figure 5.55: Formatted output of docker stats command

We had just put container IDs, for an even prettier output, you can also print the container name instead. While we are on the streak of exploring commands useful for monitoring and/or debugging, (without actually debugging anything) let us explore another one of them.

docker wait

This command wraps a tiny little process around the container that catches the exit code whenever the container is stopped or killed. This is useful when you are running one or more daemon containers and you may suddenly find that some of them have exited without any notice. To be realistic, this command alone does not serve much purpose but piping its output to another metric collector with logs can turn out to be insightful. We will explore more of it when we discuss the container logs in this book. Here is the syntax:

```
docker wait CONTAINER NAME | ID [CONTAINER...]
```

Let us apply it on our **py-ubuntu** container that we had created from the committed image (no specific reason, just to make that container a little useful):

```
docker wait py-ubuntu-contl
```

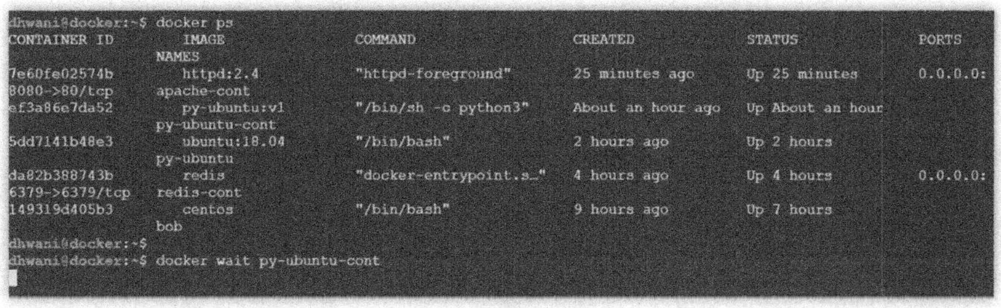

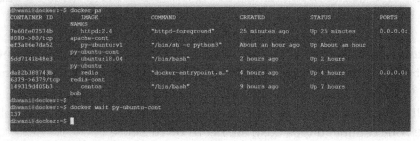

Figure 5.56: Use of docker wait command on a running container

Docker is lazy enough not to give even a single confirmation about whether the command worked successfully or not *(just print a line like "py-ubuntu is on wait" or something like that. Can we be lazy enough to uninstall you?)* But we are not lazy enough not to verify it. Open another terminal and stop **py-ubuntu** as shown in the following screenshot:

```
dhwani@docker:~$ docker stop py-ubuntu-cont
py-ubuntu-cont
dhwani@docker:~$
```

Figure 5.57: Stopping a running container

When we navigate back to the main terminal, we can see in the following screenshot that the exit code of **py-ubuntu** is printed *(why 137? because the container took longer than the grace period to shut down)* and **docker wait** command has been completed successfully:

Figure 5.58: Output of docker wait command with the exit code of a container

docker diff

Simple commands should be described simply; docker diff is one of them. It is a file system centric container change-log. Docker has allocated different codes for different kinds of changes made to a file system.

- **A**: The file or directory was added
- **D:** The file or directory was removed
- **C:** The file or directory was modified

Let us demonstrate it with another variant of minimal Linux called Photon Linux. First of all, we will run the container and make some file system level changes on it *(in other words, we will make some files and type some gibberish)* as shown in the following screenshot:

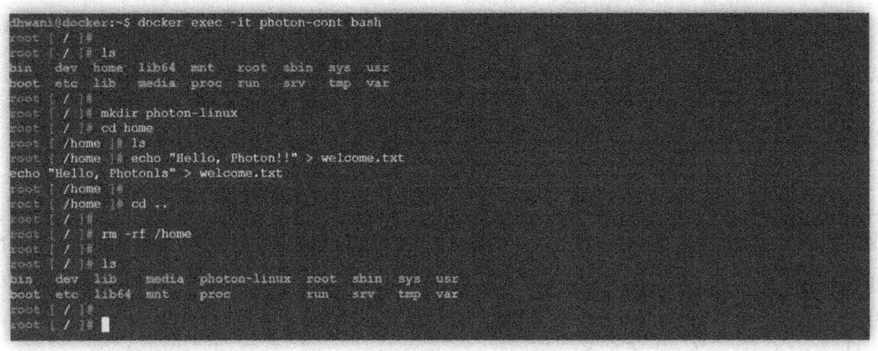

Figure 5.59: Performing file system level changes to photon container

Then, we will apply docker diff on the container expecting some changelog with above mentioned codes. The container can be referenced via its name, its ID or a truncated version of its ID.

```
docker diff photon-cont
```

Figure 5.60: Output of docker diff command for photon container

A directory called **photon-linux** was added, **/root** was changed, a temporary file called **.bash_history** was added due to running a couple of commands and **/home** was removed.

While all of these commands provide different kinds of useful information about the container, one command tops them all. Let us discuss it.

docker inspect container

We have already seen the functionality of the Docker inspect command with Docker Images and it does the same for the containers too, apart from the fact that containers return a lot more data. You do not necessarily need to mention container at the end of the Docker inspect keyword unless the Docker Image name is the same as the container name (which is not recommended at all).

It is time to inspect our helping hand while understanding the container life-cycle... bob. We already know that unfiltered inspect output will be a nightmare but since we are here to exchange knowledge, let us face the nightmare:

docker inspect bob

```
dhwani@docker:~$ docker inspect bob
[
    {
        "Id": "149319d405b3768571017b7a66993c11d11cba31a62aa0b99835131bbc81bd29",
        "Created": "2020-06-08T13:22:48.0497293722",
        "Path": "/bin/bash",
        "Args": [],
        "State": {
            "Status": "running",
            "Running": true,
            "Paused": false,
            "Restarting": false,
            "OOMKilled": false,
            "Dead": false,
            "Pid": 22896,
            "ExitCode": 0,
            "Error": "",
            "StartedAt": "2020-06-08T14:32:46.097700566Z",
            "FinishedAt": "2020-06-08T14:32:34.122901353Z"
        },
        "Image": "sha256:470671670cac686c7cf0081e0b37da2e9f4f768ddc5f6a26102ccd1c6954c1ee",
        "ResolvConfPath": "/var/lib/docker/containers/149319d405b3768571017b7a66993c11d11cba31a62aa0b99835131bbc8
1bd29/resolv.conf",
        "Image": "sha256:470671670cac686c7cf0081e0b37da2e9f4f768ddc5f6a26102ccd1c6954c1ee",
        "ResolvConfPath": "/var/lib/docker/containers/149319d405b3768571017b7a66993c11d11cba31a62aa0b99835131bbc8
1bd29/resolv.conf",
        "HostnamePath": "/var/lib/docker/containers/149319d405b3768571017b7a66993c11d11cba31a62aa0b99835131bbc81b
d29/hostname",
        "HostsPath": "/var/lib/docker/containers/149319d405b3768571017b7a66993c11d11cba31a62aa0b99835131bbc81bd29
/hosts",
        "LogPath": "",
        "Name": "/bob",
        "RestartCount": 0,
        "Driver": "overlay2",
        "Platform": "linux",
        "MountLabel": "",
        "ProcessLabel": "",
        "AppArmorProfile": "unconfined",
        "ExecIDs": null,
        "HostConfig": {
            "Binds": null,
            "ContainerIDFile": "",
            "LogConfig": {
                "Type": "syslog",
                "Config": {}
            },
            "NetworkMode": "default",
            "PortBindings": {},
            "RestartPolicy": {
                "Name": "always",
                "MaximumRetryCount": 0
            },
            "NetworkMode": "default",
            "PortBindings": {},
            "RestartPolicy": {
                "Name": "always",
                "MaximumRetryCount": 0
            },
            "AutoRemove": false,
            "VolumeDriver": "",
            "VolumesFrom": null,
            "CapAdd": null,
            "CapDrop": null,
            "Capabilities": null,
            "Dns": [],
            "DnsOptions": [],
            "DnsSearch": [],
            "ExtraHosts": null,
            "GroupAdd": null,
            "IpcMode": "private",
            "Cgroup": "",
            "Links": null,
            "OomScoreAdj": 0,
            "PidMode": "",
            "Privileged": true,
            "PublishAllPorts": false,
            "ReadonlyRootfs": false,
            "SecurityOpt": [
                "label=disable"
```

```
        "SecurityOpt": [
            "label=disable"
        ],
        "UTSMode": "",
        "UsernsMode": "",
        "ShmSize": 67108864,
        "Runtime": "runc",
        "ConsoleSize": [
            0,
            0
        ],
        "Isolation": "",
        "CpuShares": 0,
        "Memory": 1073741824,
        "NanoCpus": 0,
        "CgroupParent": "",
        "BlkioWeight": 0,
        "BlkioWeightDevice": [],
        "BlkioDeviceReadBps": null,
        "BlkioDeviceWriteBps": null,
        "BlkioDeviceReadIOps": null,
        "BlkioDeviceWriteIOps": null,
        "CpuPeriod": 0,
        "CpuQuota": 0,
        "CpuRealtimePeriod": 0,
        "CpuRealtimeRuntime": 0,
        "CpusetCpus": "",
        "CpusetMems": "",
        "Devices": [],
        "CpusetCpus": "",
        "CpusetMems": "",
        "Devices": [],
        "DeviceCgroupRules": null,
        "DeviceRequests": null,
        "KernelMemory": 0,
        "KernelMemoryTCP": 0,
        "MemoryReservation": 0,
        "MemorySwap": -1,
        "MemorySwappiness": null,
        "OomKillDisable": false,
        "PidsLimit": null,
        "Ulimits": null,
        "CpuCount": 0,
        "CpuPercent": 0,
        "IOMaximumIOps": 0,
        "IOMaximumBandwidth": 0,
        "MaskedPaths": null,
        "ReadonlyPaths": null
    },
    "GraphDriver": {
        "Data": {
            "LowerDir": "/var/lib/docker/overlay2/a9563a5b77a01750877e294a42b5ff2e560d80079da5e00b72ddc11e
18f71-init/diff:/var/lib/docker/overlay2/1f655375435d7a6c176d2ea83d18e260a84c19947e09634dc002ce989daba55dc/diff",
            "MergedDir": "/var/lib/docker/overlay2/a9563a5b77a01750877e294a42b5ff2e560d80079da5e00b72ddc11
718f71/merged",
            "UpperDir": "/var/lib/docker/overlay2/a9563a5b77a01750877e294a42b5ff2e560d80079da5e00b72ddc11e
18f71/diff",
            "WorkDir": "/var/lib/docker/overlay2/a9563a5b77a01750877e294a42b5ff2e560d80079da5e00b72ddc11ee
        "Name": "overlay2"
    },
    "Mounts": [],
    "Config": {
        "Hostname": "149319d405b3",
        "Domainname": "",
        "User": "",
        "AttachStdin": true,
        "AttachStdout": true,
        "AttachStderr": true,
        "Tty": true,
        "OpenStdin": true,
        "StdinOnce": true,
        "Env": [
            "PATH=/usr/local/sbin:/usr/local/bin:/usr/sbin:/usr/bin:/sbin:/bin"
        ],
        "Cmd": [
            "/bin/bash"
        ],
        "Healthcheck": {
            "Test": [
                "NONE"
            ]
        },
        "Image": "centos",
        "Volumes": null,
        "WorkingDir": "/home",
        "Entrypoint": null,
        "OnBuild": null,
```

```
        "WorkingDir": "/home",
        "Entrypoint": null,
        "OnBuild": null,
        "Labels": {
            "OS": "Linux",
            "org.label-schema.build-date": "20200114",
            "org.label-schema.license": "GPLv2",
            "org.label-schema.name": "CentOS Base Image",
            "org.label-schema.schema-version": "1.0",
            "org.label-schema.vendor": "CentOS",
            "org.opencontainers.image.created": "2020-01-14 00:00:00-08:00",
            "org.opencontainers.image.licenses": "GPL-2.0-only",
            "org.opencontainers.image.title": "CentOS Base Image",
            "org.opencontainers.image.vendor": "CentOS"
        }
    },
    "NetworkSettings": {
        "Bridge": "",
        "SandboxID": "0d4331ea90d799b4b70af0c9dd9fc1c625ea95af62a873e3a2b7010f4497a6a3",
        "HairpinMode": false,
        "LinkLocalIPv6Address": "",
        "LinkLocalIPv6PrefixLen": 0,
        "Ports": {},
        "SandboxKey": "/var/run/docker/netns/0d4331ea90d7",
        "SecondaryIPAddresses": null,
        "SecondaryIPv6Addresses": null,
        "EndpointID": "bd1322e04cd38dad3e91214053a74c032e1b0132612135db31199a307e767c4b",
        "Gateway": "172.17.0.1",
        "GlobalIPv6Address": "",
        "EndpointID": "bd1322e04cd38dad3e91214053a74c032e1b0132612135db31199a307e767c4b",
        "Gateway": "172.17.0.1",
        "GlobalIPv6Address": "",
        "GlobalIPv6PrefixLen": 0,
        "IPAddress": "172.17.0.2",
        "IPPrefixLen": 16,
        "IPv6Gateway": "",
        "MacAddress": "02:42:ac:11:00:02",
        "Networks": {
            "bridge": {
                "IPAMConfig": null,
                "Links": null,
                "Aliases": null,
                "NetworkID": "0ea03a68b4a529f95770b0322dc8922cfb8ae7e99066ce31066464afd3eaa5a1",
                "EndpointID": "bd1322e04cd38dad3e91214053a74c032e1b0132612135db31199a307e767c4b",
                "Gateway": "172.17.0.1",
                "IPAddress": "172.17.0.2",
                "IPPrefixLen": 16,
                "IPv6Gateway": "",
                "GlobalIPv6Address": "",
                "GlobalIPv6PrefixLen": 0,
                "MacAddress": "02:42:ac:11:00:02",
                "DriverOpts": null
            }
        }
    }
}
]
dhwani@docker:~$
```

Figure 5.61: Unfiltered output of docker inspect command for a container

This was a long very long output; but not very difficult to understand. Let us explore each JSON key-value pair field one-by-one. The output begins with basic container information like Container ID, creation timestamp, pwd, and arguments to inherited CMD (none in this case).

Then, we get precise state information of the container. Docker goes out of its way to mention not just that the container is running but also that it is not paused, restarting, OOM, or dead. This is a conscious choice. Docker realizes that most of the users will filter the output and might specifically ask for parameters such as if the container is paused or if the container is killed.

The next set of key-value pairs provide information about the root process of the container. Its PID is **22896** and it had exited gracefully. In a normal Linux environment, the PID of initial processes would not go as high but docker sees no difference between processes and smaller kernel tasks (threads), so the number reaches relatively higher peaks. On the other hand, the number of active processes remains lower than a standard Linux environment, as most of the times, we are using minimal versions of the OS inside the containers.

Moving on, we have information about the source Docker Image (which was also available in more elaborate way when we ran inspect on Docker Images), network details, and volume details. We will discuss network and storage information separately when we inspect them in the next chapter *(otherwise, the topic would fly even faster than fighter jets over your heads due to a lot of semantics)*.

Let us move straight to the isolation field. The container does not have any pre-defined CPU sharing policy with other containers as CPU sharing policies are not meant for standalone containers. When more than one container are used by an orchestrator under the same supervisory process like a Kubernetes pod; CPU sharing comes into play. Similarly, we do not have any parent cgroups on top of the container cgroup as there is no orchestrating object watching over our container.

Then, the next set of key-value pairs indicate that we (including Docker) have not blocked any I/O (peripheral or iostream) or read/write permissions. Then, a bunch of configuration parameters is set to either null or 0, this does not mean the container is not using any resources. It just means that we have not defined any boundaries in advance, and Docker will allocate the resources dynamically.

The next set of information is about graph drivers and IO mounts which is again, similar to what we have seen with the results of running the Docker inspect command on Docker Images. Focus on the labels field. Docker considers the containers as applications themselves thus, we are provided with commercial parameters of base image OS like license type, licensed software (product) title, version, and vendor name along with the same under the context of OCI, which stands for Open Containers Initiative. The CentOS is licensed under GNU Public License 2.0 to the CentOS organization as vendors and is acknowledged by the OCI. This is important because docker used containerd as the underlying CRI (Container

Runtime Environment).

Although, the next set of information is about networking and we will see most of it in the next chapter, there are a bunch of fields that do not require any pre-introduction so let us go through them. The IP address of the container is **172.17.0.2**, whereas the same of the gateway (virtual network managing the connectivity for the containers) is **172.17.0.1**. The virtual Mac address of the container (do not confuse it with the Mac address of the host) is **02:42:ac:11:00:02** and the IPv6 prefix character length is set to 16. This information is useful because containers primarily communicate via HTTP(s) REST APIs.

The more you get to know about the containers and the object interacting with them, the more each of these fields will hold value for you. Till then, you can always filter the output for the fields you want and we can move to the next command.

Sharing files with containers using docker cp

Just like ADD and COPY are essential instructions of Dockerfile, **docker cp** is an essential command of the docker command line. Generally, the only way to share user-created files with the containers is through explicit HTTP(s) requests like **wget**. But it is not always the most easily feasible option. docker cp saves you from the trouble and provisions a REST interface for sharing files from host to container and vice-versa. There are two variants of the syntax as follows:

```
docker cp [OPTIONS] CONTAINER:SRC_PATH DEST_PATH|-
```

The above variant is useful when the source file is from the container file system. For the other way around, you can use the following variant:

```
docker cp [OPTIONS] SRC_PATH|- CONTAINER:DEST_PATH
```

Even among these two variants, there are many possibilities with conditional and contextual source and destination combinations. For example:

- **Source path is a file and Destination path is a file:**

    In this case, the destination file in the container will be overwritten by the source file of the host which is basically Docker's version of replacing file with the same name. Here is an example of apache-cont container:

    ```
    docker cp /home/dhwani/apache-server/index.html apache- cont:/
    usr/local/apache2/htdocs/index.html
    ```

    Since this is a webserver, you can either cat the file or view it directly on the webserver as shown in the following screenshots:

```
root@7e60fe02574b:/usr/local/apache2/htdocs# cat index.html
<!DOCTYPE html>

<html>
<head>
  <title>DockerContainers</title>
</head>

<body>
<h2>
  It definitly works!!!
</h2>

</body>
</html>
root@7e60fe02574b:/usr/local/apache2/htdocs#
root@7e60fe02574b:/usr/local/apache2/htdocs#
```

Figure 5.62: Output docker cp command for source path (file) and destination path (file)

Figure 5.63: Execution of the copied source file in container

- **Source path is a file and destination path does not exist and is a directory:**

  In this case, when you try to copy the source file precisely into a non-existing destination directory, the Docker daemon will return a generic error (inherited from Linux) saying the file does not exist as shown in the example below followed by the snapshot of the output of this command.

  In this example, the destination path mentioned in the command, *hldocs/*, does not exist in the file system of apache-cont container.

  ```
  docker cp /home/dhwani/apache-server/index.html apache-cont:/usr/
  local/apache2/hldocs/
  ```

Figure 5.64: Output docker cp command for source path (file) and destination path (non-existing directory)

- **Source path is a file and destination path exists and is a directory:**

  In this case, the source file is successfully copied in the destination directory with the same base name. In this example, the **index.html** file is copied with the same name in the **apache2** directory in apache-cont's file system. Here is the command to perform this action followed by the snapshot of the output:

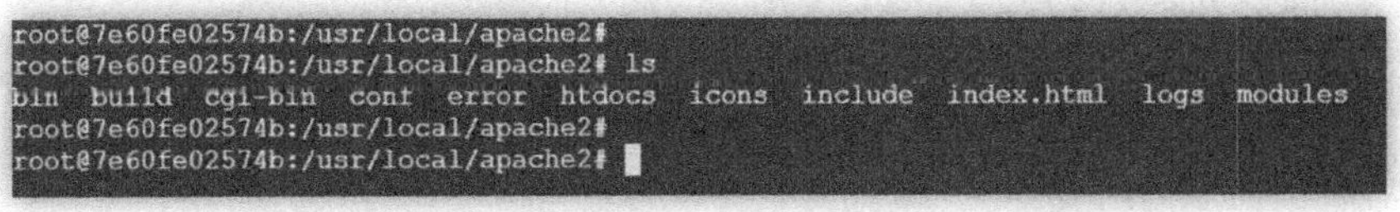

```
docker cp /home/dhwani/apache-server/index.html apache-cont:/usr/
local/apache2
```

Figure 5.65: Output docker cp command for source path (file) and destination path (existing directory)

- **Source path is a file and destination path does not exist:**

In this case, when the destination path provided in the **docker cp** command does not exist, docker daemon will create that path and copy the source file to it. If the destination path is a file, the source file will overwrite it and if the destination path is a directory, the source file will be copied in that directory with the same base name.

In this example, the destination path is a file named **home** created in **apache2** directory in apache-cont container, so now the source file, **index.html**, will overwrite the content of the **home** file. This action can be performed using the below command and the output of this command is followed by the snapshot:

```
docker cp /home/dhwani/apache-server/index.html apache-cont:/usr/
local/apache2/home
```

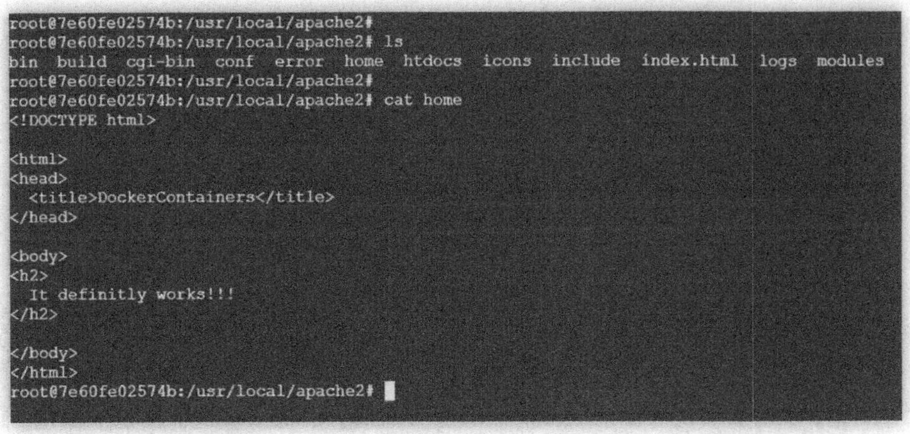

Figure 5.66: Output docker cp command for source path (file) and non-existing destination path

- **Source path is a directory and Destination Path is a file:**

Generally, when you try to copy a directory to a file, it will simply lead to an error. In this example, when we try to copy a source directory **apache-server/** to a destination file **index.html**, the Docker daemon will return an error that *it cannot copy a directory to a file*. To perform this action, use the following command and the output of this command is followed by the snapshot:

```
docker  cp  /home/dhwani/apache-server/  apache-cont:/usr/local/
apache2/htdocs/index.html
```

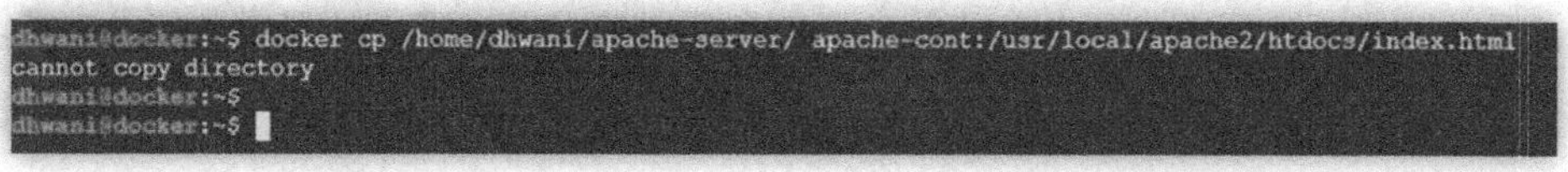

Figure 5.67: *Output docker cp command for source path
(directory) and destination path (file)*

- **Source path is a directory and destination path does not exist:**

In this case, the source path is a directory and the destination path mentioned in the command does not exist then the destination path is created and the *contents* of source directory are copied into that newly created path. Since, the source directory cannot be copied to a file, in this case, the destination path will always be a directory.

In this example, **apache-server/** is the source directory whose content will be copied to the destination directory **home** in apache-cont container. To perform this action, follow the command below and the output of the command is followed by the snapshot:

```
docker cp /home/dhwani/apache-server/ apache-cont:/usr/local/
apache2/home
```

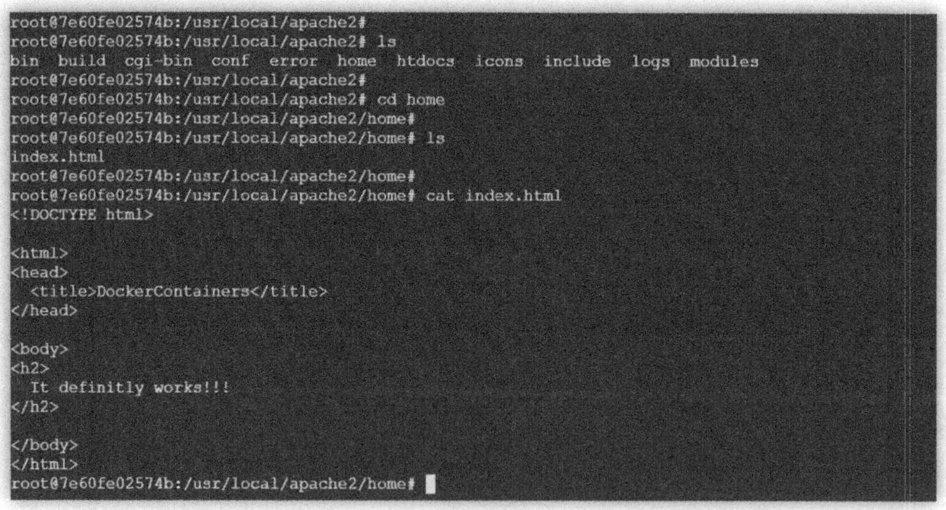

Figure 5.68: *Output docker cp command for source path (directory)
and non-existing destination path*

- **Source path is a directory and does not end with /. and destination path exists and is a directory**

  In this case, the source path is a directory and does not end with **/.** (*slashdot*) then the source directory (*along with its files and sub-directories*) will be copied as a sub-directory to the destination path directory.

  In this example, **apache-server** is the source directory which will be copied to the destination directory **htdocs** as a *sub-directory* in apache-cont container. To perform this action, follow the command and the output of the command is followed by the snapshot:

```
docker cp /home/dhwani/apache-server apache-cont:/usr/local/
apache2/htdocs/
```

```
root@7e60fe02574b:/usr/local/apache2#
root@7e60fe02574b:/usr/local/apache2# ls
bin  build  cgi-bin  conf  error  home  htdocs  icons  include  logs  modules
root@7e60fe02574b:/usr/local/apache2#
root@7e60fe02574b:/usr/local/apache2# cd htdocs
root@7e60fe02574b:/usr/local/apache2/htdocs#
root@7e60fe02574b:/usr/local/apache2/htdocs# ls
apache-server  index.html
root@7e60fe02574b:/usr/local/apache2/htdocs#
root@7e60fe02574b:/usr/local/apache2/htdocs# cd apache-server/
root@7e60fe02574b:/usr/local/apache2/htdocs/apache-server#
root@7e60fe02574b:/usr/local/apache2/htdocs/apache-server# ls
index.html
root@7e60fe02574b:/usr/local/apache2/htdocs/apache-server#
```

Figure 5.69: *Output docker cp command for source path (directory does not end with /.) and destination path (directory)*

- **Source path is a directory and ends with /. and destination path exists and is a directory**

  In this case, the source path is a directory and does end with **/.** (*slashdot*) then *only the contents (files and sub-directories)* of the source directory will be copied to the destination path directory.

  In this example, **apache-server** is the source directory, containing a file **index.html**, which will be copied to the destination directory **apache2/** in apache-cont container. To perform this action, follow the command below and the output of the command is followed by the snapshot:

```
docker cp /home/dhwani/apache-server/. apache-cont:/usr/local/
apache2/
```

```
root@7e60fe02574b:/usr/local/apache2#
root@7e60fe02574b:/usr/local/apache2# ls
bin  build  cgi-bin  conf  error  home  htdocs  icons  include  index.html  logs  modules
root@7e60fe02574b:/usr/local/apache2#
root@7e60fe02574b:/usr/local/apache2#
```

Figure 5.70: *Output docker cp command for source path (directory does end with /.) and destination path (directory)*

The action of sharing files between containers and the host is a significant asset. Type-2 hypervisors also provide the same facility for VMs. This almost marks the end of container commands. If you want to clean up your containers, you can use **docker container rm** and **docker container prune** just like you did with the images including variants like force removal. In the next topic, we will take a look at some miscellaneous commands and then, we will conclude this chapter.

Miscellaneous Docker commands

Docker Command Line is not just limited to images and containers. We had started the chapter with **docker version** command and had also hinted a twist at the end. The twist revolves around the "experimental" feature being turned off by default. There is a way to manually turn it on to leverage APIs that are currently in the experimental stage. We need to do it separately for both docker daemon and docker client. We will start with the Docker daemon. Use the following command to access the JSON config file of Docker Daemon. (you can use your preferred text editor to edit this file.)

```
sudo nano /etc/docker/daemon.json
```

Now, add the following key-value pair at the end of the file:

```
{
"experimental": true
}
```

Save and exit the file. To do the same process on the client, we need to access the json config file of the client. If the client and the daemon are on the same machines, the files are just at different locations. While the daemon file was under daemon directory, the client file in a directory called **.docker** under **$HOME**. Use the command below to access it:

```
sudo nano ~/.docker/config.json
```

Add the following key-value pair at the end of the file:

```
{
  "experimental": "enabled"
}
```

Once it is done, save and close the file and restart the docker client using the following command:

```
sudo systemctl restart docker
```

This will restart both Docker daemon and the client. Alternatively, you can start them separately as well. To see if the changes have taken any effect, rerun the **docker version** command, and the output should be like the following screenshot:

```
dhwani@docker:~$ docker version
Client: Docker Engine - Community
 Version:           19.03.9
 API version:       1.40
 Go version:        go1.13.10
 Git commit:        9d988398e7
 Built:             Fri May 15 00:25:18 2020
 OS/Arch:           linux/amd64
 Experimental:      true

Server: Docker Engine - Community
 Engine:
  Version:          19.03.9
  API version:      1.40 (minimum version 1.12)
  Go version:       go1.13.10
  Git commit:       9d988398e7
  Built:            Fri May 15 00:23:50 2020
  OS/Arch:          linux/amd64
  Experimental:     true
 containerd:
  Version:          1.2.13
  GitCommit:        7ad184331fa3e55e52b890ea95e65ba581ae3429
 runc:
  Version:          1.0.0-rc10
  GitCommit:        dc9208a3303feef5b3839f4323d9beb36df0a9dd
 docker-init:
  Version:          0.18.0
  GitCommit:        fec3683
dhwani@docker:~$
```

Figure 5.71: Experimental features on Docker Client and Server enabled

There is no point in demonstrating any experimental command. By the time you get to read the book, it might get promoted to the stable release. But, you can visit the Docker CLI documentation and search for the commands with experimental tag and play around with them.

Now, let us take a look at another informative command:

```
docker info
```

This command will provide a combined and summarized information about the docker installation, present artifacts (like unique images and containers) and kernel details of the host as shown in the following screenshot:

```
dhwani@docker:~$ docker info
Client:
 Debug Mode: false

Server:
 Containers: 9
  Running: 0
  Paused: 0
  Stopped: 9
 Images: 28
 Server Version: 19.03.9
 Storage Driver: overlay2
  Backing Filesystem: extfs
  Supports d_type: true
  Native Overlay Diff: true
 Logging Driver: json-file
 Cgroup Driver: cgroupfs
 Plugins:
  Volume: local
  Network: bridge host ipvlan macvlan null overlay
  Log: awslogs fluentd gcplogs gelf journald json-file local logentries splunk syslog
 Swarm: inactive
 Runtimes: runc
 Default Runtime: runc
 Init Binary: docker-init
 containerd version: 7ad184331fa3e55e52b890ea95e65ba581ae3429
 runc version: dc9208a3303feef5b3839f4323d9beb36df0a9dd
 init version: fec3683
 Security Options:
  apparmor
  seccomp
   Profile: default
 Kernel Version: 5.3.0-1020-gcp
 Operating System: Ubuntu 18.04.4 LTS
 OSType: linux
 Architecture: x86_64
 CPUs: 1
 Total Memory: 574.8MiB
 Name: docker
 ID: C2FT:B4GQ:TLRS:QATJ:BZ2D:ISSY:HXLE:52GC:ZRXI:BIZ6:SYCC:4GAT
 Docker Root Dir: /var/lib/docker
 Debug Mode: false
 Registry: https://index.docker.io/v1/
 Labels:
 Experimental: false
 Insecure Registries:
  127.0.0.0/8
 Live Restore Enabled: false

WARNING: No swap limit support
dhwani@docker:~$ 5~
```

Figure 5.72: Output of docker info command

Apart from the points mentioned above, we also get information like the host's cgroup driver used by docker, root directory of docker objects, versions of different docker components, and versions of host OS and its kernel. Docker considers local host an insecure registry as it does not go through its security standards. Local host is the default registry from where we push the images to docker hub. The primary registry is still docker hub indicated by its URL. This command provided static information, if we want more dynamic version of what is going on with our docker instance, we can use the following command:

```
docker pull debian

docker events
```

Figure 5.73: Output of docker events command for a Docker Image pulling event

You might be wondering, why is pulling an image the only event? That is because I had cleared up all of the images and containers before using this command. The more you work with Docker Images and containers, the more events get listed accordingly. Go ahead! Play around and expand your understanding as well as experience ☺

Conclusion

This was indeed an exhaustive chapter. But now you have so much to do with the containers and images. Even at this point, you might be excited to try lots of stuff out with maybe your personal project, with some random containers or maybe at your team's project. Containers seem handy and controllable now, but their capabilities are far from having been leveraged.

In the next chapter, we will take a deeper look into two of the most useful supportive docker objects of containers, networking, and storage.

Multiple choice questions

1. Which of the following commands is used to run a nginx web-server container as a background process?

    A. `docker run -b --name nginx-cont nginx`

    B. `docker run -d --name nginx-cont nginx`

    C. `docker run --daemon --name nginx-cont nginx`

    D. `docker run --name nginx-cont nginx`

    Answer: B

2. Which of the following commands creates a new tag for an existing Docker Image?

    A. `docker rename target_image[:TAG] source_image[:TAG]`

    B. `docker tag target_image[:TAG] source_image[:TAG]`

C. `docker rename source_image[:TAG] target_image[:TAG]`

D. `docker tag source_image[:TAG] target_image[:TAG]`

Answer: D

3. Which of the following commands will you use to inspect centos Docker Image?

A. `docker image info centos:latest`

B. `docker info centos:latest`

C. `docker inspect centos:latest`

D. `docker image describe centos:latest`

Answer: C

4. Which of the following commands can be used to pull multiple images from a single repository?

A. `docker pull <repo_name> --all`

B. `docker pull <repo_name> --all-tags`

C. `docker pull <repo_name>:<tag-1> <repo_name>:<tag-2> . . .`

D. `docker pull <repo_name> --all-images`

Answer: B

5. In the docker cp command, if the SRC_PATH is a directory and the DEST_PATH is a file, what will be the outcome of `docker cp` command?

A. Source file's contents will overwrite the contents in DEST_PATH.

B. The contents of each file of SRC_PATH will be copied into separate files into the DEST_PATH.

C. DEST_PATH will be created as a directory, and all the contents of the SRC_PATH will be copied into this directory.

D. An error will occur that it cannot copy a directory to a file.

Answer: D

6. Which of the following commands is used to display total disk space used by Docker Daemon?

A. `docker system df`

B. `docker stats`

C. `dockerd system df`

D. `dockerd info`

Answer: A

7. A container named `app-env-db` serves the application environment for your upcoming app and is ready to be deployed. You need to commit the container and push the resulting Docker Image to the organization's registry—`dbstore`. Which of the following sequence of commands will you use?

   (Note: All the prerequisites to push Docker Image to Docker hub have already been fulfilled.)

   A. `docker commit app-env-db test-env`

      `docker tag dbstore/test-env:latest  test-env`

      `docker push dbstore/test-env:latest`

   B. `docker commit app-env-db test-ENV`

      `docker tag test-ENV dbstore/test-ENV:latest`

      `docker push dbstore/test-ENV:latest`

   C. `docker commit app-env-db test-env`

      `docker tag test-env dbstore/test-env:latest`

      `docker push dbstore/test-env:latest`

   D. `docker commit app-env-db test-env`

      `docker tag test-env dbstore/test-env:latest`

      `docker push dbstore/img-env-db:latest`

   Answer: C

8. Which of the following commands can be used to remove all images associated with fd584f19954f tag?

REPOSITORY	TAG	IMAGE ID	CREATED
image-1	latest	fd584f19954f	23 seconds ago
image-2	latest	fd584f19954f	23 seconds ago
image-3	latest	ca562b85961a	40 seconds ago
image-4	latest	ba458d17824c	55 seconds ago

   A. `docker rm fd584f19954f`

   B. `docker rmi -f fd584f19954f`

   C. `docker rmi --all`

   D. `docker image prune --all`

   Answer: B

9. Which of the following commands is used to list out all the layers of a Docker Image?

A. docker image list

B. docker images

C. docker history

D. docker inspect

Answer: C

10. You need to initiate a running nginx web-server container that listens on port 80. Ensure that the container's port 80 is mapped to Docker host's port 8080 and as the final output, you should be able to access the landing page of the nginx container http://localhost:8080. Which of the following commands will you use to accomplish this task?

A. docker run -itd --name web-server -p 80:8080 nginx:latest

B. docker create --name web-server -p 8080:80 nginx:latest

C. docker run -itd --name web-server -p 8080:80 nginx:latest

D. docker create -itd --name web-server -P nginx:latest

Answer: C

CHAPTER 6
Connectivity and Storage

Introduction

In almost every previous chapter, wherever there were mentions of networking or permanent storage, you had to settle with "we will look into it soon enough". Rejoice! The **soon** is **now**. Docker does not go out of its way to create jaw-dropping novel networking innovations, but it does have a disciplined and easy way to provide communication privileges to its containers via docker network objects. The same can be said for storage. In an era of ever expanding cloud providers, Docker keeps it open-ended and simple for its storage objects to evolve and expand. This chapter is dedicated to the description and demonstration of network and storage objects.

Structure

This chapter covers:

- Container Networking Model (CNM)
- Docker Networks and their types
- Storage options with Docker

Objective

The objective of this chapter is simple. Since both networking and storage are immensely exhaustive computer science topics, this chapter focuses on taking you through a convenient route that helps you explore these topics without getting lost between curiosity and cluelessness. By the end of this chapter, you will be able to make suitable network and storage configurations and choices for your project.

Container Networking Model

The history and applications of networking are much older than virtualization. Computers could communicate from one continent to another before someone could even think about making them host their own virtualized miniature versions. This meant that every form of virtualization technology had a rich stack of Application Programming Interfaces (APIs) dedicated to networking, and containers are no different. In fact, the very reason behind their revival from being neglected as a stale Linux feature is the growth of the internet. While the physical internet is impossible to imagine without hardware components ranging from cables to servers, most of the components in a virtualized environment are actually software objects defined to emulate the behavior of their hardware counterparts.

One such software object in Linux network stack is **Linux Bridge** that emulates the functionalities of a Switch such as Learning (storing the source and destination of data packet transmission), Forwarding (sending the data to destination), Filtering (blocking unwanted access of data), and Flooding (forwarding data frame to all connections except the sender due to incomplete receiver information or due to broadcast request). Docker creates a Linux Bridge called **docker0.**

While the physical switches work around MAC addresses, docker0 uses IP addresses to identify connections. It is created by Docker Daemon when we start the Docker service using the `sysctl docker start` command. Docker daemon randomly borrows an available IP address from the host within the range defined under RFC1918 for private networks and allocates that address to `docker0` bridge. RFC1918 range is a globally agreed-upon range of IP addresses that private networks can use without clashes. To check the docker0 bridge on your host, run the following mentioned command:

```
ifconfig
```

The result of this command should be similar to the following screenshot:

```
dhwani@docker:~$ ifconfig
docker0: flags=4099<UP,BROADCAST,MULTICAST>  mtu 1500
        inet 172.17.0.1  netmask 255.255.0.0  broadcast 172.17.255.255
        ether 02:42:5e:e4:1c:32  txqueuelen 0  (Ethernet)
        RX packets 0  bytes 0 (0.0 B)
        RX errors 0  dropped 0  overruns 0  frame 0
        TX packets 0  bytes 0 (0.0 B)
        TX errors 0  dropped 0 overruns 0  carrier 0  collisions 0

ens4: flags=4163<UP,BROADCAST,RUNNING,MULTICAST>  mtu 1460
        inet 10.128.15.227  netmask 255.255.255.255  broadcast 0.0.0.0
        inet6 fe80::4001:aff:fe80:fe3  prefixlen 64  scopeid 0x20<link>
        ether 42:01:0a:80:0f:e3  txqueuelen 1000  (Ethernet)
        RX packets 112486  bytes 35880118 (35.8 MB)
        RX errors 0  dropped 0  overruns 0  frame 0
        TX packets 98744  bytes 10443944 (10.4 MB)
        TX errors 0  dropped 0 overruns 0  carrier 0  collisions 0

lo: flags=73<UP,LOOPBACK,RUNNING>  mtu 65536
        inet 127.0.0.1  netmask 255.0.0.0
        inet6 ::1  prefixlen 128  scopeid 0x10<host>
        loop  txqueuelen 1000  (Local Loopback)
        RX packets 196  bytes 18987 (18.9 KB)
        RX errors 0  dropped 0  overruns 0  frame 0
        TX packets 196  bytes 18987 (18.9 KB)
        TX errors 0  dropped 0 overruns 0  carrier 0  collisions 0
```

Figure 6.1: *Information about docker0 bridge on Linux host*

Your output can be longer or shorter *(to be honest, longer… not shorter. Even I have cropped the unnecessary portion to save some page space)* depending on the active networking utilities on your system. As we have mentioned earlier, docker0 is the virtual Linux Bridge, whereas ens4 is a veth or a Virtual Ethernet adapter. It is used as a full-duplex logical wire (way of connection) between two namespaces. Generally, one end of veth is connected to the container while the other end is connected to a Container Networking object. Take a look at the following figure to understand the position of Docker Networks:

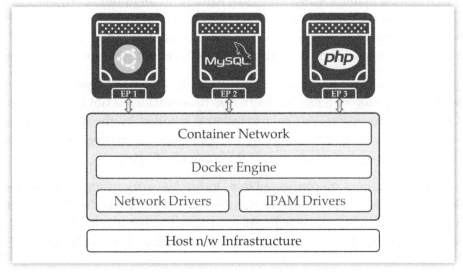

Figure 6.2: *Container Networking Model*

Any networking object intended to create a container network rests on top of the Container Runtime Environment (CRE; in this case, Docker). Above the container network, we have containers themselves, whereas below the container network, we have the host machine's network infrastructure and OS-centric network drivers. The network drivers provide an interface (API interface) to enable and configure networking on the host, while the IPAM or IP Address Management drivers provide private IPs and subnet range to Containers and Container Networks. The host's network infrastructure also includes physical components as well as utilities such as iptables. iptables is a Linux utility to create L3/L4 Firewall Rules. Rules are added as groups of **Chains,** and a bunch of chains is added to **Tables**.

Chains setup the process of allowing, rejecting, or routing the data (with the sequence of rules) and tables group up the context-specific collection of chains to address relevant target data. There are different tables like Default, Filter, NAT, and so on. Docker adds a couple of chains called **DOCKER** and **DOCKER_USER** in the NAT table to control the data coming to and going from containers. These iptables chains, along with Linux cgroups are used to create the isolated network namespaces called **Docker Networks**.

Docker Networks and their types

Docker Networks are considered the primary networking objects of Docker Containers. **Every container is connected to at least one Docker Network**. Based on this fact, we can say that all containers that we have created so far were also connected to a particular Docker Network without us mentioning anything about it whatsoever. Also, containers connected to the same Docker Network can easily talk to one another. Namespaces are used to isolate the configuration files of the Docker Networks, while cgroups are used to apply those configurations to the containers.

We already know that the containers use cgroups and namespaces of their own. While being subjected to a Docker Network, the container is not created inside the network's namespace; the container is rather controlled by the network's cgroup. The container's cgroup handles computational resource management, whereas a Docker Network's cgroup takes care of the connectivity part.

This way the containers are **connected** to a Docker Network instead of being created within one. This plug-in plug-out relationship allows much-needed flexibility to the containers with respect to their network exposure. Docker installs its own network drivers on the Docker host during the installation process. These network drivers act as templates to create various Docker Networks. Let us discuss each of those types with their applications.

Bridge network

It is the **default network** for Docker Containers. In this case, Docker takes the word *"default"* quite seriously. As mentioned earlier in this chapter *(by earlier, I mean a couple of pages ago… after all, we are not even 5 pages deep yet)*, while starting the Docker service, the Docker Daemon creates a Linux bridge called `docker0`. This bridge is used to create the bridge-type docker network called **bridge**. If we do not mention network details while creating/running the container with `docker create` or `docker run` command, Docker attaches the container to the bridge network by default.

The default bridge is not the only application of Docker Networks created by the Bridge driver. You can also create user-defined named bridge networks. While the containers connected to the default bridge can only address one another using the IP addresses, the containers connected by a named bridge network can use aliases, IP addresses or container names. This is because the names of the containers are stored as their Domain Name System (DNS) entries, and creating a user-defined bridge provides automatic DNS resolution, so the IPs and the names are linked effortlessly.

On top of that, the containers on the default bridge network share their context in the same network namespace, potentially making them fragile in terms of data security *(like a public hospital ward, you may get any random infection)*.

Containers connected to a user-defined bridge network can be disconnected and reconnected (to the same or some other network) effortlessly; this is not the case with the default network. To disconnect a container connected to the default bridge, you need to stop the container and restart it by mentioning another network's name with the `--network` flag. *(don't even think about restarting it without any network and then connecting it to some network separately. Docker never starts a container without a network attachment. Your container will once again be connected to the default network, causing instant face-palms)*. Finally, the control User-defined bridges provide scope for setting your own rules for allowing or blocking the traffic.

Let us explore these aspects practically. First of all, run the command below to get a list of Docker Networks.

```
docker network ls
```

This command returns the list of available Docker Networks on the Docker host, as shown in the following screenshot:

```
dhwani@docker:~$ docker network ls
NETWORK ID          NAME                DRIVER              SCOPE
a03d64ea7be5        bridge              bridge              local
8c8a7b6ea76e        host                host                local
9d51d7be4c3d        none                null                local
dhwani@docker:~$
dhwani@docker:~$
```

Figure 6.3: List of Docker Networks on host

The first column represents truncated **NETWORK IDs** of the network objects available on the host. Following it, we have the networks' **NAME**. Do not confuse them with the network types. Network types are shown in the **DRIVER** column showing the network driver used for creating the network. Finally, we have the **SCOPE** column. All of the networks have the scope set to **local**, which means only the containers from this host can communicate to one another if they are connected to the same network. Another variant is the **swarm** scope which allows containers on multiple hosts to connect and communicate. As always, you can use **--no-trunc** to see the complete network IDs and other formatting options to get the output in your desired format. Have a look at the following command and its results:

```
docker network ls --no-trunc
```

```
dhwani@docker:~$ docker network ls --no-trunc
NETWORK ID                                                         NAME                DRIVER              SCOPE
a03d64ea7be567775bcd58a6d6285e32be0cd022de69fc89f73b2823234f8d2c   bridge              bridge              local
8c8a7b6ea76ed63251f7cc88a9fc2a26b2275149c1f268070a85f80b03155baf   host                host                local
9d51d7be4c3d1655054b0d23ff424ed95c1816736b1236888b251f2d75f956c9   none                null                local
dhwani@docker:~$
dhwani@docker:~$
```

***Figure 6.4:** List of Docker Networks with full Network IDs*

For the context of this chapter, I have removed all of the previously created containers *(you already know how to do it, if you do not, feel free to check out Chapter 5).*

Let us create a container attached to the default bridge by doing nothing special.

```
docker run -id --name busybox-cont busybox
```

This command creates a container called **busybox-cont** and attaches it to the default bridge network. We have inspected the container in the previous chapter so let us look at it from a network's perspective by inspecting the default bridge instead with the following command:

```
docker network inspect bridge
```

The syntax is similar to inspecting a container or an image; we are just changing the object type preceded by the **docker** keyword. Here is what the output looks like:

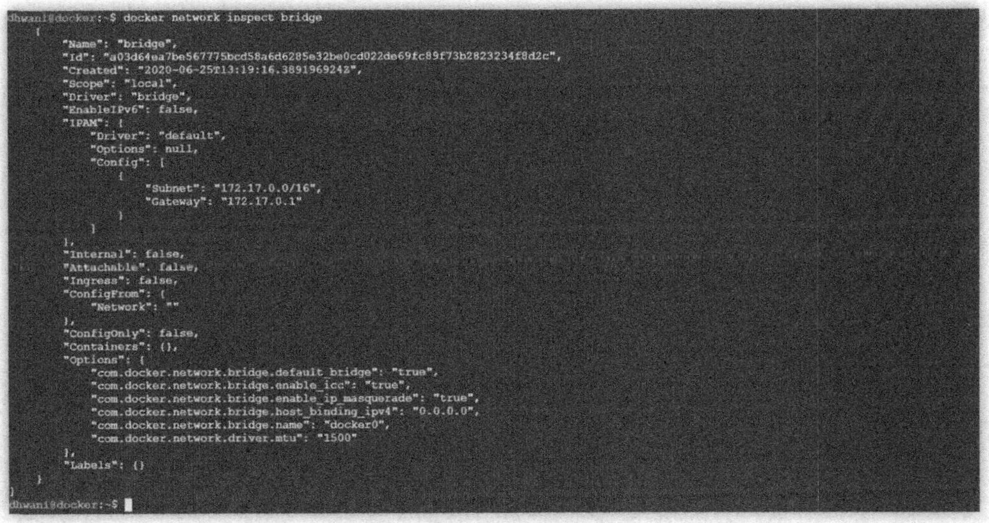

Figure 6.5: Output of docker network inspect command for default bridge network (Part I)

You, the esteemed pillars of the reader community are now familiar with the docker command line enough to skip the trivial and the already covered parts such as creation timestamp and network ID *(this also makes my life as an author a lot easier; so, thank you for reading the previous chapters and immersing yourself into the context of this book… nothing too serious, just a random act of gratitude!)*. Let us jump straight to the part which indicates that IPv6 addresses are disabled. This is the default setting of any networking software object created by Docker; but you can enable it optionally by using **--ipv6** flag while creating new networks. Even though the process of enabling IPv6 is simple from Docker's end, it may not be that simple for you. Your OS should support IPv6 (most of the modern commercial Operating Systems do) and even more importantly, your Internet Service Provider (ISP) should provide you IPv6 access.

The next section is dedicated to IPAM or IP Address Management within the network. Docker uses the **libnetwork** library from the open-source moby project for its CNM as the default solution for providing private IPs to the containers within the subnet of a Docker network. There are no specific configuration options (such as widening the IP range or choosing a particular range of IPs) enabled in the default network. We can also see the subnet IP range and the Gateway IP for the default network.

The next set of options are for a multi-host setup *(spoiler for the next chapter!)* and its overlay network. We will understand them soon enough but for now, let us say all of those parameters are set to their default values.

This was the first half of the result, let us take a look at the other half in the following screenshot:

```
        },
        "Internal": false,
        "Attachable": false,
        "Ingress": false,
        "ConfigFrom": {
            "Network": ""
        },
        "ConfigOnly": false,
        "Containers": {
            "6727094cbbe3ab53e152c0d805548db1c412f4c54b1683257c56254d95dd7e1a": {
                "Name": "busybox-cont",
                "EndpointID": "084e8e0a9336b15f6df3c591c448889de7d2dbe41eb3928991fa8acf3fc50549",
                "MacAddress": "02:42:ac:11:00:02",
                "IPv4Address": "172.17.0.2/16",
                "IPv6Address": ""
            }
        },
        "Options": {
            "com.docker.network.bridge.default_bridge": "true",
            "com.docker.network.bridge.enable_icc": "true",
            "com.docker.network.bridge.enable_ip_masquerade": "true",
            "com.docker.network.bridge.host_binding_ipv4": "0.0.0.0",
            "com.docker.network.bridge.name": "docker0",
            "com.docker.network.driver.mtu": "1500"
        },
        "Labels": {}
    }
]
dhwani@docker:~$
```

Figure 6.6: Output of docker network inspect command for default bridge network (Part II)

The topmost field ConfigOnly makes sure that the network is isolated and is not carrying anything from Docker's IPAM apart from basic configurations such as subnet range and IP mask. This sets the previously mentioned (but not explained) parameters such as ingress and internal to their default value, indicating an inactive state (which could be false, null, or disabled).

Then comes the crème de la crème, containers! This section provides the result of all of the settings we had mentioned earlier. The container has an **EndpointID**, a space (directory) in the container filesystem that stores its networking information for this particular network. If a container is connected to more than one networks, it receives multiple endpoints resulting in an extensive list of endpoint IDs. It also has a virtual mac address and an IPv4 address from the very range of the subnet of the default bridge. It does not have any IPv6 address because we had not enabled it.

Following it, we have some configuration options claiming that the Linux Bridge docker0 with a maximum Ethernet transmission rate of 1500 bytes **is** actually the default network (every other network has it set to false) with inter-container-communication (ICC) and IP masking turned on, and it is bound to the host via commonly used **0.0.0.0** *(full stop)*. Lastly, Docker does not consider it necessary to provide any labels to its default network, hence keeping the field empty.

Understanding the default bridge network was fun (and informative)! Do you know what can be even more fun? *(Drumrolls)* Creating a bridge network by yourself!

This holds more important than just trying things hands-on for the sake of learning because the default bridge is now considered legacy infrastructure and docker politely suggests us not to use it *(they could have updated it to make it more relevant… then again, who are we to judge?!).*

The following syntax is used to create a user-defined **docker network**:

```
COMMAND: docker network create [OPTIONS] NETWORK
```

Though the **OPTIONS** are kept in a square bracket indicating the flags are optional, we must use the **--driver** flag followed by the name of the network driver as its argument to create a user-defined network successfully as shown in the following example:

```
docker network create --driver bridge bridge-A
```

Whether the creation has been successful or not can be checked via listing out the networks again, which would result in output as the following screenshot:

```
dhwani@docker:~$ docker network create --driver bridge bridge-A
655b29c890d192cbf8aa647643b386713d31ee44f2a0b6b2063a90829cf88bc3
dhwani@docker:~$
dhwani@docker:~$ docker network ls
NETWORK ID      NAME        DRIVER      SCOPE
a03d64ea7be5    bridge      bridge      local
655b29c890d1    bridge-A    bridge      local
8c8a7b6ea76e    host        host        local
9d51d7be4c3d    none        null        local
dhwani@docker:~$
```

Figure 6.7: Creation of a user-defined bridge network

Having the flexibility to create user-defined networks also comes with the privilege of tuning the configurations to match our physical network architecture and project requirements. Here is an example of creating a user-defined bridge network with multiple customizations.

```
docker network create --driver bridge \
--subnet=172.10.0.0/16 \
--ip-range=172.10.1.0/24 \
--gateway=172.10.1.254 \
--label=test-bridge \
--opt com.docker.network.driver.mtu=9000 \
bridge-B
```

In this case, we have provided custom specifications for subnet, IP range, gateway address, and the largest packet size (also known as Maximum Transmission Unit or

MTU). We have also provided a label to this bridge to fill the metadata. Following is the screenshot of the result of this command:

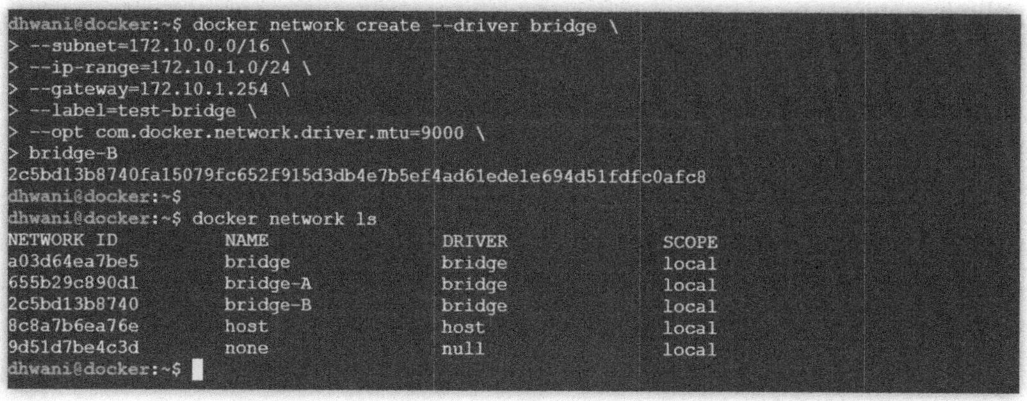

```
dhwani@docker:~$ docker network create --driver bridge \
> --subnet=172.10.0.0/16 \
> --ip-range=172.10.1.0/24 \
> --gateway=172.10.1.254 \
> --label=test-bridge \
> --opt com.docker.network.driver.mtu=9000 \
> bridge-B
2c5bd13b8740fa15079fc652f915d3db4e7b5ef4ad61edele694d51fdfc0afc8
dhwani@docker:~$
dhwani@docker:~$ docker network ls
NETWORK ID          NAME             DRIVER           SCOPE
a03d64ea7be5        bridge           bridge           local
655b29c890d1        bridge-A         bridge           local
2c5bd13b8740        bridge-B         bridge           local
8c8a7b6ea76e        host             host             local
9d51d7be4c3d        none             null             local
dhwani@docker:~$ ▮
```

Figure 6.8: Creating a custom Docker Bridge network

Whether we provide lots of customizations or we let the Docker Daemon set the values by default, the visual result of the **docker network create** command remains the same, returning the ID of the newly created network. A user-defined bridge network is not of much use if there are no containers connected to it. Let's create a busybox container and connect it to the recently created bridge-B network with the following commands:

```
docker run -id --name busybox-cont-1 busybox
```

```
docker network connect bridge-B busybox-cont-1
```

While you are already familiar with **docker run command**, **docker network connect** has just made its first appearance. The command is simple; the keywords **docker network connect** are followed by optional flags, network name, and container name. You can address the containers and networks with their IDs as well *(but you would not do that manually with a command line, would you?)*. Just like the default bridge, we can also inspect this network to verify if the container is connected.

The output of the **inspect** command will look something like the following screenshot:

```
{
    "Name": "bridge-B",
    "Id": "b63c8ff16fe3753b4238623cb68c812c0fa53d70f3f42410fdc6af91efb17a45",
    "Created": "2020-07-05T08:44:07.508133106Z",
    "Scope": "local",
    "Driver": "bridge",
    "EnableIPv6": false,
    "IPAM": {
        "Driver": "default",
        "Options": {},
        "Config": [
            {
                "Subnet": "172.10.0.0/16",
                "IPRange": "172.10.1.0/24",
                "Gateway": "172.10.1.254"
            }
        ]
    },
    "Internal": false,
    "Attachable": false,
    "Ingress": false,
    "ConfigFrom": {
        "Network": ""
    },
    "ConfigOnly": false,
    "Containers": {
        "8af278aef49f889486ed7aab95bea6ae30e33a1331f580382130f85c9d027eb8": {
            "Name": "busybox-cont-1",
            "EndpointID": "e33c1d31531c268b93492b0c3c574ac68c7dace2f79b23ad7aa3deac31ebf25a",
            "MacAddress": "02:42:ac:0a:01:00",
            "IPv4Address": "172.10.1.0/16",
            "IPv6Address": ""
        }
    },
    "Options": {
        "com.docker.network.driver.mtu": "9000"
    },
    "Labels": {
        "test-bridge": ""
    }
}
dhwani@docker:~$ 
```

Figure 6.9: Output of docker volume inspect command for user-defined network

Take a look at the flags that we had provided and the IP address of the container. Everything has been setup just the way we had instructed it to do so! Let us move another step further and try to establish some form of communication between containers. Currently, **busybox-cont-1** is the only container connected to this network. We need to connect another container, but this time, we will do it differently, as shown in the following command:

```
docker run -id --name busybox-cont-2 --network bridge-B busybox
```

This is one of the flags of docker run command that we had not discussed in the last chapter. You can connect a container to any docker network while creating it. It means that the --network flag works with docker run and docker create. By inspecting the container or the network, we can verify the success of the connection; however, we understand that you might be tired of looking at long inspect outputs.

Let us inspect the container with an accurate filter as shown in the following command:

```
docker inspect --format='{{range .NetworkSettings.Networks}}
{{.IPAddress}}{{end}}' busybox-cont-2
```

By using this filter, we are asking the daemon to provide only the container's IP address as shown in the following screenshot:

```
dhwani@docker:~$ docker run -id --name busybox-cont-2 --network bridge-B busybox
78504748596cce4204b25a9cfa96717bb9ca2bda2452a9d77fe4298be39931ed
dhwani@docker:~$
dhwani@docker:~$ docker inspect --format='{{range .NetworkSettings.Networks}}{{.IPAddress}}{{end}}' busybox-cont-
2
172.10.1.1
dhwani@docker:~$
dhwani@docker:~$
```

Figure 6.10: Fetching the container's IP address using -- format flag

The IP address **172.10.1.1** fits the range of bridge-B. Both containers (**busybox-cont-1** and **busybox-cont-2**) can communicate with each other. We can verify it by trying to ping one container from another. Let's interact with **busybox-cont-2** with the following command:

```
docker exec -it busybox-cont-2 sh
```

We can ping the other container using its IP address or its name as shown in the following screenshot:

```
dhwani@docker:~$ docker exec -it busybox-cont-2 sh
/ #
/ # ping 172.10.1.0
PING 172.10.1.0 (172.10.1.0): 56 data bytes
64 bytes from 172.10.1.0: seq=0 ttl=64 time=0.296 ms
64 bytes from 172.10.1.0: seq=1 ttl=64 time=0.085 ms
64 bytes from 172.10.1.0: seq=2 ttl=64 time=0.096 ms
64 bytes from 172.10.1.0: seq=3 ttl=64 time=0.086 ms
64 bytes from 172.10.1.0: seq=4 ttl=64 time=0.091 ms
^C
--- 172.10.1.0 ping statistics ---
5 packets transmitted, 5 packets received, 0% packet loss
round-trip min/avg/max = 0.085/0.130/0.296 ms
/ #
/ # ping busybox-cont-1
PING busybox-cont-1 (172.10.1.0): 56 data bytes
64 bytes from 172.10.1.0: seq=0 ttl=64 time=0.062 ms
64 bytes from 172.10.1.0: seq=1 ttl=64 time=0.106 ms
64 bytes from 172.10.1.0: seq=2 ttl=64 time=0.088 ms
64 bytes from 172.10.1.0: seq=3 ttl=64 time=0.085 ms
64 bytes from 172.10.1.0: seq=4 ttl=64 time=0.086 ms
^C
--- busybox-cont-1 ping statistics ---
5 packets transmitted, 5 packets received, 0% packet loss
round-trip min/avg/max = 0.062/0.085/0.106 ms
/ #
```

Figure 6.11: Inter-container communication using container IP and container name on the user-defined bridge network

The ping was successful, and there was no data loss. It is important to remember that these two containers can only communicate with each other using this particular bridge network. If you want them to communicate to other containers on the same host, you need to connect them to the other network (in this case, the default bridge network). You can also make these containers communicate with the outer world of the World Wide Web, but to do so, you need to perform the port mapping. Containers themselves cannot communicate with the internet; they need to go through the host's network infrastructure in one way or another. By performing port mapping, we map the container's desired port to one of the host's available ports so that the requests made to the host for the containers can make their way to the containers and vice versa. Here is an example of it:

```
docker run -id --name nginx -p 8080:80 nginx
```

The command above creates an nginx container, connects it to the default bridge and exposes container's port **80** to host's port **8080**, as shown in the following screenshot:

```
dhwani@docker:~$ docker run -id --name nginx -p 8080:80 nginx
Unable to find image 'nginx:latest' locally
latest: Pulling from library/nginx
8559a31e96f4: Pull complete
8d69e59170f7: Pull complete
3f9f1ec1d262: Pull complete
d1f5ff4f210d: Pull complete
1e22bfa8652e: Pull complete
Digest: sha256:21f32f6c08406306d822a0e6e8b7dc81f53f336570e852e25fbe1e3e3d0d0133
Status: Downloaded newer image for nginx:latest
9af38066e329d8744f728e37465f27bf4733900200b27d80b2caff526caf7c1e
dhwani@docker:~$
dhwani@docker:~$
```

Figure 6.12: Internal port mapping between nginx container and Docker host

If we want to access the nginx container through outside the host, we can do so by putting the host's IP and port number **8080** combination in web browser, since it would be serving the content of container's port **80** as shown in the following screenshot:

Figure 6.13: Accessing nginx container on host's port 8080

On the other hand, if we do not want to go into the pain and process of mapping the port every time, we have another option.

Host network

This network object is stored in the same networking namespace as the host itself, clearing any form of network isolation whatsoever. The containers connected to host networks will not have their own IPs. Their ports will be directly exposed to host's corresponding ports. This feature is only available on Linux and is not recommended as it almost kills the purpose of containerization or virtualization (at least in terms of network isolation).

For example, if you want to run the same nginx container as last time without mapping the container's port **80** to any host port, you can use the following command:

```
docker run -d --name nginx-1 --network host nginx
```

This command will create a new nginx container called **nginx-1** while exposing it to the host, and it can be accessed by simply using the host's IP on the browser with port **80** for nginx, as shown in the following screenshot:

Figure 6.14: *Testing of host network*

In this case, the containers do not have their own IP (you can view it by inspecting them), and therefore no DNS is maintained either. The only possible use case of this network is when you are absolutely certain about the security of your host and the traffic interacting with your container, which can tempt you to avoid mapping ports to save some time and abstraction. You can also say that it is used for quite niche purposes. Speaking of *(writing of)* niche purposes, there is another network that is not recommended as your go-to driver but does prove itself useful in certain cases.

Macvlan networks

Legacy applications can be identified as unrecognizable for millennials and a matter of pride for veterans. Jokes apart, some of the legacy applications are not compatible with the cutting edge networking infrastructure of Docker hosts and therefore need to bypass its networking stack and use the physical network directly. For such (niche) use cases, we have macvlan networks.

Before going any further with them, it is important to bear in mind that MACVLAN as a network driver only works with Linux hosts with kernel 4.0 or higher (accurate specifications suggest 3.9+, but industry practices lean toward 4.0+). For example, Ubuntu 18.04 has Linux kernel 4.15, and 16.04 uses 4.10.

With that out of the way, let us discuss MACVLAN. They provide MAC addresses instead of IP addresses to the containers, making them appear like physical network devices. To do so, it is recommended to have a physical network device in your infrastructure that can allocate multiple MAC addresses.

In this case, we are running a VM on the Google Cloud Platform. We need to use a virtual device as the source of the MAC address.

Let us list out the available networks on the Linux host.

```
ifconfig
```

The result looks like the following screenshot. You might have a couple of extra veth objects for the active bridges:

```
dhwani@docker:~$ ifconfig
docker0: flags=4163<UP,BROADCAST,RUNNING,MULTICAST>  mtu 1500
        inet 172.17.0.1  netmask 255.255.0.0  broadcast 172.17.255.255
        inet6 fe80::42:cff:fe05:c16a  prefixlen 64  scopeid 0x20<link>
        ether 02:42:0c:05:c1:6a  txqueuelen 0  (Ethernet)
        RX packets 231  bytes 29437 (29.4 KB)
        RX errors 0  dropped 0  overruns 0  frame 0
        TX packets 319  bytes 26046 (26.0 KB)
        TX errors 0  dropped 0 overruns 0  carrier 0  collisions 0

ens4: flags=4163<UP,BROADCAST,RUNNING,MULTICAST>  mtu 1460
        inet 10.128.0.2  netmask 255.255.255.255  broadcast 0.0.0.0
        inet6 fe80::4001:aff:fe80:2  prefixlen 64  scopeid 0x20<link>
        ether 42:01:0a:80:00:02  txqueuelen 1000  (Ethernet)
        RX packets 396121  bytes 347840325 (347.8 MB)
        RX errors 0  dropped 0  overruns 0  frame 0
        TX packets 185209  bytes 28960443 (28.9 MB)
        TX errors 0  dropped 0 overruns 0  carrier 0  collisions 0

lo: flags=73<UP,LOOPBACK,RUNNING>  mtu 65536
        inet 127.0.0.1  netmask 255.0.0.0
        inet6 ::1  prefixlen 128  scopeid 0x10<host>
        loop  txqueuelen 1000  (Local Loopback)
        RX packets 640  bytes 64504 (64.5 KB)
        RX errors 0  dropped 0  overruns 0  frame 0
        TX packets 640  bytes 64504 (64.5 KB)
        TX errors 0  dropped 0 overruns 0  carrier 0  collisions 0
```

Figure 6.15: *List of active network interfaces on Docker host*

This list is similar to what we had received earlier in this chapter. Let us use ens4 as the parent of our desired macvlan network, as shown in the following command:

```
docker network create -d macvlan -o parent=ens4 net-macvlan
```

The `-d` flag is used for the driver and `-o` for the options. Like the bridge networks, this command also returns the network ID, as shown in the following screenshot:

```
dhwani@docker:~$ docker network create --driver macvlan \
> -o parent=ens4 \
> net-macvlan
a629262dc2490515d8a44dc4d9aa23b880bb22372301b40f0e0a8334f2617a1b
```

Figure 6.16: *Creating a macvlan network*

To test this network out, we can create two containers, connect them to user-defined `macvlan` network and try to ping one from the other by executing the following commands:

```
docker run –itd --name mac-busybox --network net-macvlan busybox
docker run –it --name mac-busybox-1 --network net-macvlan busybox
```

The first command has created a detached container, whereas the second one lands us right into its environment. Let us ping the first container using its IP (get it by inspecting it) from the second one with the following command:

```
ping –c 5 172.22.0.2
```

The output will be successful pings with 0 data loss, as shown in the following screenshot:

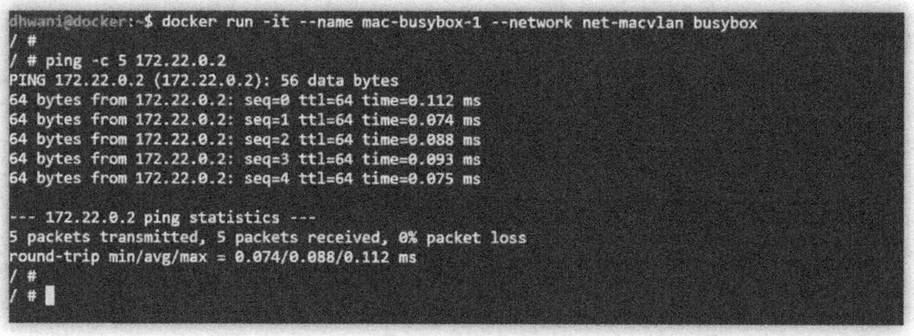

Figure 6.17: Pinging one container from another using macvlan network

These are the three native docker networking drivers for allowing standalone containers on a single host to communicate to their brethren in the same subnet or the outer Internet. If you do not have a niche profoundly defined use, the user-defined bridge should be your way to go. Things do change when we unify more than one host to create a cluster. That is where we use the following network type.

Overlay network

So far in this book, we have mentioned multiple times that more than one docker daemon can connect on a common network to create a cluster that can handle a large number of containers for an application at scale. The network used for connecting such daemon hosts is called overlay network. The name is fairly self-explanatory. The likes of Macvlan are considered underlay networks as they operate directly with the physical network of the host, whereas this network lets the underlay network play its part while operating on higher layers with protocols like TCP.

Just like bridge, docker also creates default overlay networks called **ingress** and **docker_gwbridge**. If you are wondering why you have not seen them while listing out the networks, that is because we had not initiated the **swarm** mode that creates these networks. On top of these, we can also create user-defined overlay networks just how we created user-defined bridge networks provided that we have fulfilled some necessary pre-requisites. Since the next chapter is dedicated to swarm, we will look into the functioning of overlay networks in it.

Every container of Docker is started with networking capabilities by default. If you explicitly want to isolate it and turn off all of the networking capabilities, you can connect it to **none** network. For doing so, you need to put the value **null** into the driver field while connecting the container. Let us inspect none network as shown in the command below. Based on the received outcome, you can notice that Docker has explicitly turned off all of the networking settings:

```
docker network inspect none
```

Here is the screenshot of the output:

```
dhwani@docker:~$ docker network inspect none
[
    {
        "Name": "none",
        "Id": "9d51d7be4c3d1655054b0d23ff424ed95c1816736b1236888b251f2d75f956c9",
        "Created": "2020-06-23T14:12:25.420551585Z",
        "Scope": "local",
        "Driver": "null",
        "EnableIPv6": false,
        "IPAM": {
            "Driver": "default",
            "Options": null,
            "Config": []
        },
        "Internal": false,
        "Attachable": false,
        "Ingress": false,
        "ConfigFrom": {
            "Network": ""
        },
        "ConfigOnly": false,
        "Containers": {},
        "Options": {},
        "Labels": {}
    }
]
dhwani@docker:~$
```

Figure 6.18: *Output of docker network inspect command for none network*

Despite having no driver attached, the none network does need an ID as it stores these configurations at this path to keep things clean. Just like the other networks, this one is also created when the docker service starts; thus, you do not need to do anything explicitly to enable it.

Finally, indeed, Docker networks are just another form of Docker objects, so they can be removed using **docker network rm** and pruned using **docker network prune**.

There is a little catch, though, as long as any container connected to the network exists (stopped or active), the network cannot be removed, and `docker network rm` command will generate an error *(The error will say "don't backstab your container. What will it do without the network? You meanie!" No, it will not say that but you get the point).*

These were the native networking drivers of Docker. As the phrase goes (if in any way it even exists), one solution leads to another problem. Allowing containers to communicate creates room for importing data. Since containers are running processes, they are volatile. Any data imported to the read/write layer of the container is not going to persist and the moment you kill a container; you will be sent back to square one. To avoid this situation, let us take a look at the next topic.

Storage options with Docker

Back in the early days of virtualizations, computer scientists (many of them were just called physicists) came across an inevitable phenomenon called VM sprawl which boiled down to lack of storage due to the enormous size of the VMs. While the VMs occupied a lot of storage space, they did offer a convenient userspace that allowed the operators to store quite a significant amount of data. Even while creating a Google Compute Engine Virtual Machine (GCE VM), we saw how we could occupy hundreds of GBs of storage either in terms of Hard Disk Drive (HDD) or Solid State Drive (SSD).

Unlike VMs with their own kernel space, containers are just running processes on host's kernel space monitored by a CRE. Just like networking, persistent storage is something essential but not trivially available to the containers. Without persistent storage, the changes made to the containers would fade away the moment it crashes. In theory, you can commit a container to persist its changes, but that makes only the writable layer commit, eventually making the image too large to kill the containerization's purpose altogether. So, doing it over and over is not a practical solution by any means. To solve this issue, all CREs had to figure out one way or another to add persistent storage to the containers.

Docker used the **Union File System (UFS)** that logically unifies more than one file systems by mapping their content as a record. This allowed Docker to have multiple solutions for persistent storage. The same way as network drivers, Docker also created a storage driver *(because… consistency)* to provide different storage options. In this chapter, we will explore different storage options offered by Docker and also, the other ones (3rd party plug-ins) when we discuss the docker daemon in (even more) detail. For now, let's explore the first storage option by Docker, Volumes.

Volumes

Volumes are just directories on the host file system outside the scope of the container and its writable layer *(why just writable layer? Because others are read-only anyway!)*. By default, they are the storage sandboxes created on the filesystem of the host for the containers. This means that the nature of storage will follow the configurations of the host. If the host has SSD, volumes will be SSD, and if the host has HDD, the volumes will be HDD. What if the host is a hybrid of HDD and SSD? Well, then it depends on the type of storage occupied by Docker installation because the volumes are created in **/var/lib/docker/volumes** by default. This path might have given you a hint that volumes are within the scope of Docker and thus are managed by it in terms of permissions and content.

A single volume can be mount to one or more containers and more than one volumes can be mount to a single container as well *(One for all, all for one! My Hero Academia fans can thank me later)*. To do any of it, we need to create the volume first with the following syntax:

```
docker volume create [OPTIONS] VOLUME
```

The options include flags such as **--label** for providing meta label, **--name** for providing a unique volume name across the host, **--driver** for specifying the volume driver (3ʳd party volume plug-ins) and **--opt** or options for triggering driver-specific options. There are no other native volume drivers like bridge and host network drivers. There is only single, default volume driver, which creates named and unnamed volume on the Docker host. To create a volume, execute the following command:

```
docker volume create
```

This command creates an unnamed volume. Docker decided the name of this unnamed volume. Let us say that Docker is not the best judge for naming objects. Have a look by yourself at the following screenshot:

```
dhwani@docker:~$ docker volume create
68a1cd3cceb96119c4e9e0754785237506b38598724eb0f51bd9becd16933d9b
dhwani@docker:~$
dhwani@docker:~$ docker volume ls
DRIVER              VOLUME NAME
local               68a1cd3cceb96119c4e9e0754785237506b38598724eb0f51bd9becd16933d9b
local               vol-centos
dhwani@docker:~$
```

Figure 6.19: Creating an unnamed volume

While this volume ID is **unique**, it is inconvenient, to say the least. Thus even people working at Docker recommend using a named (user-named) volume instead *(source: Docker documentation)*. Execute the following command to create a named volume:

```
docker volume create --name vol-centos
```
This volume also has a volume ID, but the command returns the volume's name instead, as shown in the following screenshot:

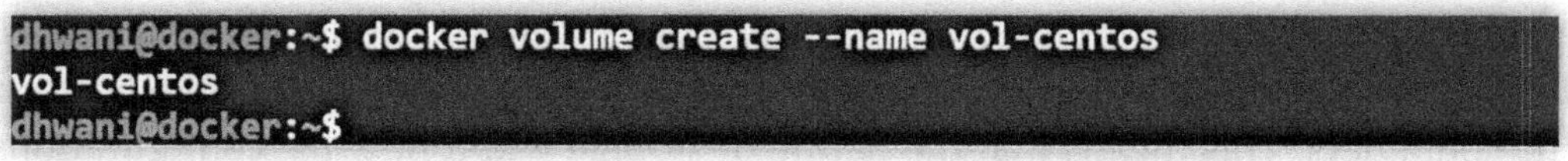

Figure 6.20: Creating a named volume

These created volumes can be listed using **docker volume ls** command with the output as the following screenshot:

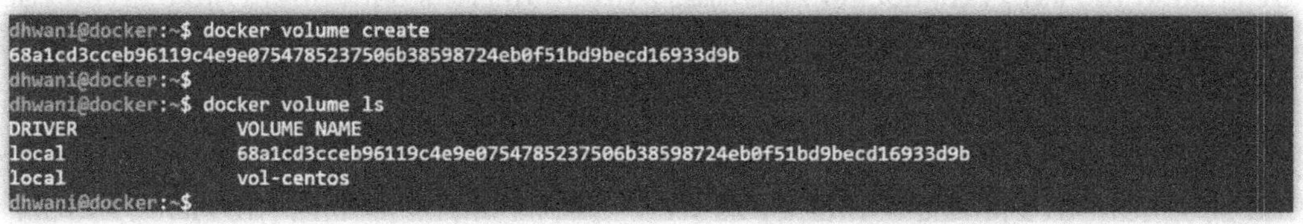

Figure 6.21: Listing out volumes on Docker host

Just like the other objects, volumes can also be inspected. For example, we can use the following command to inspect the **vol-centos** volume:

```
docker volume inspect vol-centos
```
Since volumes are just directories with managed permissions, their inspection results are smaller than most objects, as shown in the following screenshot:

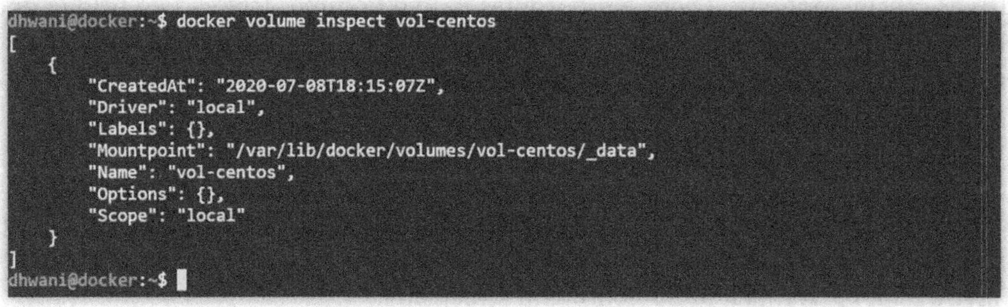

Figure 6.22: Output of docker volume inspect command for a named volume

Since we are already familiar with the fields like creation timestamp (CreatedAt), driver, labels, name, options, and scope, let us focus on the mountpoint. mountpoint is the directory created on the host filesystem that represents the named volume. If we are not naming the volume, the name in the path will be replaced by the volume ID. We can also check the contents of this named volume on the host as shown in the following commands and their result:

```
sudo su -
cd /var/lib/docker/volumes
cd vol-centos
```

```
root@docker:~#
root@docker:~# cd /var/lib/docker/volumes
root@docker:/var/lib/docker/volumes#
root@docker:/var/lib/docker/volumes# ls
68a1cd3cceb96119c4e9e0754785237506b38598724eb0f51bd9becd16933d9b   metadata.db   vol-centos
root@docker:/var/lib/docker/volumes#
root@docker:/var/lib/docker/volumes# cd vol-centos/
root@docker:/var/lib/docker/volumes/vol-centos#
root@docker:/var/lib/docker/volumes/vol-centos# ls -la
total 12
drwxr-xr-x 3 root root 4096 Jul  8 18:15 .
drwx------ 4 root root 4096 Jul  8 19:17 ..
drwxr-xr-x 2 root root 4096 Jul  8 18:15 _data
```

Figure 6.23: Exploring content in named volume on Docker host

We had to switch to superuser because regular users are not authorized to access them. First of all, in the volumes directory, we have both of the volumes as individual directories. When we navigate to the **/vol-centos**, we can see that it contains another directory called **_data** which serves as the **Mountpoint**. Only the root can read, write, or execute it and currently, the directory is empty (from our perspective). We can use the following command to **mount** this volume to a container:

```
docker run -it --rm --name centos-cont -v vol-centos:/home centos:latest
```

This is another variant of **docker run** command with **-v** flag. It indicates that we are mounting CentOS container's **/home** to **vol-centos**. Any changes made to the home directory of CentOS container will reflect on the Mountpoint of the volume. This is called mounting storage to a container. We have deliberately used the **--rm** flag with the docker run command to ensure that the container gets removed from the host after its execution ends. It is time to make some changes to the **/home** of the container. An easy to demonstrate change is the creation of a file. Let us create a file called foo. txt and exit the container, as shown in the following screenshot:

```
dhwani@docker:~$ docker run -it --rm --name centos-cont -v vol-centos:/home centos:latest
[root@fd46502c3ecd /]#
[root@fd46502c3ecd /]# cd home
[root@fd46502c3ecd home]# ls
[root@fd46502c3ecd home]#
[root@fd46502c3ecd home]# touch foo.txt
[root@fd46502c3ecd home]#
[root@fd46502c3ecd home]# exit
exit
dhwani@docker:~$
dhwani@docker:~$
```

Figure 6.24: Add data in the mounted directory of the container

From what we have seen so far, the file should reflect on the Mountpoint. Let's see if that is the case with the following commands:

```
sudo su -

cd /var/lib/docker/volumes/vol-centos/_data
```

We can see that the foo.txt is also present in the **/_data** on Docker host, as shown in the following screenshot:

```
root@docker:~#
root@docker:~# cd /var/lib/docker/volumes/vol-centos/_data
root@docker:/var/lib/docker/volumes/vol-centos/_data#
root@docker:/var/lib/docker/volumes/vol-centos/_data# ls -la
total 8
drwxr-xr-x 2 root root 4096 Jul  8 20:25 .
drwxr-xr-x 3 root root 4096 Jul  8 18:15 ..
-rw-r--r-- 1 root root    0 Jul  8 20:25 foo.txt  ←
root@docker:/var/lib/docker/volumes/vol-centos/_data#
root@docker:/var/lib/docker/volumes/vol-centos/_data# █
```

***Figure 6.25:** Reflecting the changes in the named volume on Docker host*

We can also perform the reverse task. In other words, we can prepopulate the volume and then mount it to the container. The container will be able to carry the data added to the volume as well. Let us create another file called **foo-1.txt**, as shown in the following screenshot:

```
root@docker:/var/lib/docker/volumes/vol-centos/_data#
root@docker:/var/lib/docker/volumes/vol-centos/_data# touch foo-1.txt
root@docker:/var/lib/docker/volumes/vol-centos/_data#
root@docker:/var/lib/docker/volumes/vol-centos/_data# ls -la
total 8
drwxr-xr-x 2 root root 4096 Jul  8 20:40 .
drwxr-xr-x 3 root root 4096 Jul  8 18:15 ..
-rw-r--r-- 1 root root    0 Jul  8 20:40 foo-1.txt
-rw-r--r-- 1 root root    0 Jul  8 20:25 foo.txt
root@docker:/var/lib/docker/volumes/vol-centos/_data# █
```

***Figure 6.26:** Populate named volume on Docker host*

Let us rerun the same centos container and mount the volume again with the command below, but this time, without the **--rm** flag because we do not want it to get accidentally deleted:

```
docker run -it --name centos-cont -v vol-centos:/home centos:latest
```

Navigate to the container's **/home** and verify if it contains the files from the mounted volume. The outcome of this action looks like the following screenshot:

```
dhwani@docker:~$ docker run -it --name centos-cont -v vol-centos:/home centos:latest
[root@ed564713d24e /]#
[root@ed564713d24e /]# cd /home
[root@ed564713d24e home]#
[root@ed564713d24e home]# ls -la
total 8
drwxr-xr-x 2 root root 4096 Jul  8 20:40 .
drwxr-xr-x 1 root root 4096 Jul  8 20:48 ..
-rw-r--r-- 1 root root    0 Jul  8 20:40 foo-1.txt
-rw-r--r-- 1 root root    0 Jul  8 20:25 foo.txt
[root@ed564713d24e home]#
[root@ed564713d24e home]# █
```

***Figure 6.27:** Container carrying files prepopulated on a Volume*

Both **foo.txt** and **foo-1.txt** are present. To get more information about this integration, we can inspect the container and look at the mounts section, which looks like the following screenshot:

```
"Mounts": [
    {
        "Type": "volume",
        "Name": "vol-centos",
        "Source": "/var/lib/docker/volumes/vol-centos/_data",
        "Destination": "/home",
        "Driver": "local",
        "Mode": "z",
        "RW": true,
        "Propagation": ""
    }
],
```

Figure 6.28: Inspecting mounts of a container

The **Mounts** field in the **docker volume inspect** command output shows precise information about the source location of volume, the destination location of the volume mount inside the container, and some other necessary fields.

The **Mode** key contains a value **z.** This is a response to an SELinux feature for making the files in the volume private or public. Since we are not using an SELinux host, this does not concern us. **RW** field shows the content reading and writing permissions. It is set to true, which means that this container can read content from this mounted volume and write new content to it. The default value of this field is set to **true,** but we can change it while mounting the volume on a container.

We can also create a container and a volume simultaneously while providing some customizations to both. Here is an example:

```
docker run -it --name ubuntu-backup -v vol-ubuntu:/home:ro ubuntu:latest
```

You should get an output like the following screenshot:

```
dhwani@docker:~$ docker run -id --name ubuntu-cont \
> -v vol-ubuntu:/etc:ro \
> ubuntu:latest
4a8ba90695536da6a4049cbab85d1d566ebcb21b76c214de8a78bf956e35472a
dhwani@docker:~$
dhwani@docker:~$ docker volume ls
DRIVER          VOLUME NAME
local           68a1cd3cceb96119c4e9e0754785237506b38598724eb0f51bd9becd16933d9b
local           2938775fc0afc1b1f1da500ffdfda412b1ff80189cfbd68fb1327647fd042da9
local           vol-centos
local           vol-ubuntu
dhwani@docker:~$
```

Figure 6.29: Creating a Container and a volume simultaneously

The command returns the container ID because it is a container-centric command, and the volume is just a flag (**-v**). A colon separates the parameters such as the name, the mount path, and the permissions of **--v** flag. Since this volume is of type read only, it does not allow any changes to it, as shown in the following screenshot:

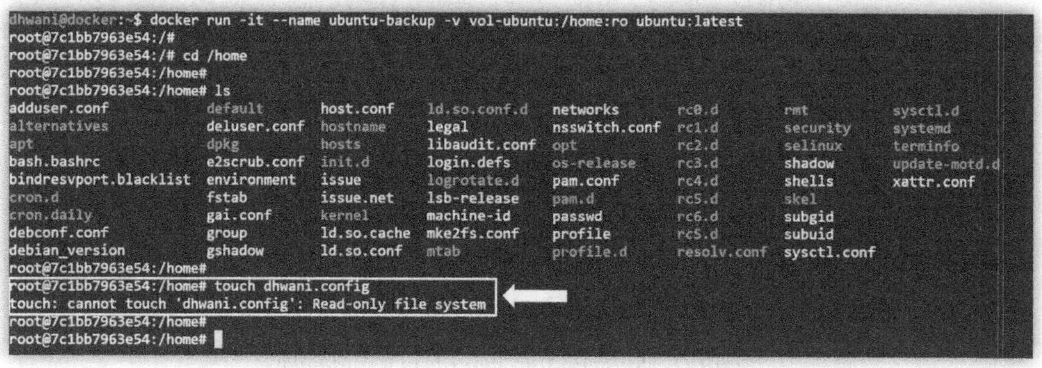

Figure 6.30: Response to changes made in a read-only volume

One interesting thing to note here is that a single volume can be mount to multiple containers. To mount the same volume as any container, we can use the flag **--volumes-from** followed by the container's name with container creation Docker commands. However, this is highly situational since the deployment environment may not have the aforementioned container to get the volume details from in the first place.

Bind mounts

Bind mounts are new enough not to be called a legacy feature and old enough to be incapable of being operated by the ever-popular Docker Command Line (CLI). Unlike Volumes that are created within the scope of Docker installation of the host, Bind mounts are free birds that can be created literally anywhere on the host storage. It does sound fancy but everything that glitters is not gold *(good old words of wisdom)*. In exchange of getting a wider storage scope to play around with, users have to sacrifice the security and privacy of their host since docker also operates as the root user, so most of the directories on your host's file system are potentially Bind mount candidates.

Just like Volumes, Bind mounts are also accessible by the containers they are mounted on. This statement should be enough to send some chills down your spine. Think of an insecure microservice container with a Bind Mount located in your **/etc** or **/bin** directory. This can also affect the other containers since, at the end of the day, they are as safe as their host. Security risks aside *(like you can ever set them aside after reading this)*, Bind mounts are useful if you want to use your container as a temporary FTP server and intend to allow access to a large chunk of data from your host. *The bottom line is simple, if you don't know what you are doing, choose named volumes; if you know what you are doing, you would not be referring to this book for the "advise".*

To create a Bind mount, you need to provide the complete path on your host along with **--v** flag. Let us create a new directory and mount it to a container using the following commands:

```
mkdir bind-centos

cd bind-centos

docker run -it --name centos-cont -v "$(pwd)":/home centos
```

Being another variant of persistent storage, Bind Mount also performs the same as Volumes in terms of reflecting data between the host and the container. To differentiate it from the volumes, let us use the **docker container inspect** command:

```
docker container inspect centos-cont
```

The outcome of the **inspect** command looks like the following screenshot. We are only interested in the mounts, so we have removed the rest of the information from the output:

```
"Mounts": [
    {
        "Type": "bind",
        "Source": "/home/dhwani/bind-centos",
        "Destination": "/home",
        "Mode": "",
        "RW": true,
        "Propagation": "rprivate"
    }
],
```

Figure 6.31: Output of docker container inspect command for bind mount details

But Nisarg! This is so simple! Why do we even have to inspect the container for this? First of all, why don't we just inspect the mount itself; second, if this is the only information to worry about, why don't we just list it out with some variant of **ls** *command?*

As I mentioned earlier, bind mounts cannot be controlled through the Docker command line, so there is no listing, inspection, or removal. Bind Mounts are like stray dogs. They do not have a name or a numerical tag. You need to remember them by their vague descriptions like, "Oh, there was a cute little white puppy with some brown spots on his tummy!" Of course, not this vague, but all we have as a reference is the absolute path on the host. The common point of intrigue is… **WHY??**

A simple reason is the starting point of this topic. They are really old, older than the time they became ambitious about storage. From a more logical point of view, Bind Mounts are a direct feature of Linux Kernel created to provide flexibility to treat directories as storage objects or storage partitions. Volumes require some form of the underlying file system on the host for UFS to work properly. Bind mounts do not require it; they can operate simply with the kernel data structure of the source.

Mount is a subtree of the large file-system tree. In the case of Docker's implementation, it simply uses Linux Kernel's bind mount feature and mounts a directory from the host to the container's file-system without adding docker daemon's operatory or observatory wrappers around it (as I said before docker became ambitious about storage). The mount is recorded as a separate process and it dies when the container is removed.

Coming back to the result of inspection, there are many trivial fields like `type, source, destination, mode` and so on but one of them draws the most attention; `propagation`. There are times when you have to clone your namespace (replicated containers, this will happen A LOT in future content of this book), and while you are at it, it is essential to control what type and amount of data get copied along with the namespace.

While the volumes have a modular identity as objects, replicated bind mounts act as shared subtrees of Linux. The shared subtrees in Linux have different propagation schemes that control how deep the data will be copied in case multiple directories of the same subtree are used as mounts. While Docker has fixed the propagation scheme to `rprivate` for Volumes, it can still be changed with Bind Mounts and we can create entities like slave sub-mounts (only allowing one-way data sharing with deeper directories of the subtree) or shared sub-mounts (open-ended data sharing).

On the other hand, rprivate keeps the subtree private and does not propagate the changes made to sub-mounts to its parent copies. Just like other aspects of bind mounts, shared sub-mounts also brought many security and privacy implications. For example, a container with no context may start receiving files from another shared mount just because it has the parent directory of the sub-mount mount to itself. Over time, it is evident and evident that Bind mount can be used for niche applications but should not be aimed for mainstream production-grade deployment.

Tmpfs

First things first, this is not a persistent storage option. This is a lightning-fast data access option. How fast? As fast as your RAM and your R/W speed, because tmpfs is a temporary file-system provisioned by Linux to exist on your RAM. This is not meant to store your data. It is meant to load a relatively smaller quantity of data onto your RAM and then provide it to an application that can process it fast.

One of the classic examples would be the input data of Redis (which is an in-memory datastore). You can think of this as a layer between persistent storage and your application to optimize its performance. You might have guessed it, but these cannot be shared with the containers, and since it is a direct Linux utility, it only works for Linux hosts. The windows alternative is called named **pipes**.

Creating **tmpfs** is simple. You just have to use tmpfs followed by the path while running a container as shown in the following command:

```
docker run -it --name tmpfs-busybox --tmpfs /tmp busybox
```

The output logs us straight into the container, as shown in the following screenshot:

```
dhwani@docker:~$ docker run -it --name tmpfs-busybox --tmpfs /tmp busybox
/ #
/ # cd /tmp
/tmp #
/tmp # touch foo.txt
/tmp #
/tmp # ls
foo.txt
/tmp #
/tmp #
```

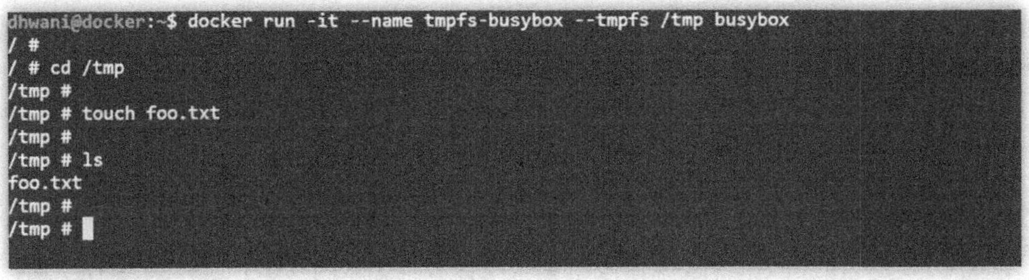

Figure 6.32: Running a container with tmpfs

We have created a busybox container and mounted tmpfs on the directory **/tmp** inside container's filesystem. To demonstrate the volatility of tmpfs, we have created a file inside **/tmp** directory called **foo.txt**. Now when we exit the container, the container will eventually stop running. Then Again, start the container using **docker start** command and exec into it using **docker exec** command and open up the shell of busybox. Let us see if the **foo.txt** exists in the following screenshot:

```
dhwani@docker:~$ docker start tmpfs-busybox
tmpfs-busybox
dhwani@docker:~$
dhwani@docker:~$ docker ps -a
CONTAINER ID    IMAGE      COMMAND       CREATED          STATUS                 PORTS
 NAMES
60ecc89c731e    busybox    "sh"          20 minutes ago   Up 9 seconds
 tmpfs-busybox
5c84f8786aef    ubuntu     "/bin/bash"   2 hours ago      Exited (0) 2 hours ago
 ubuntu
dhwani@docker:~$
dhwani@docker:~$ docker exec -it tmpfs-busybox sh
/ #
/ # ls
bin    dev    etc    home    proc    root    sys    tmp    usr    var
/ #
/ # cd tmp
/tmp # ls
/tmp #
/tmp #
```

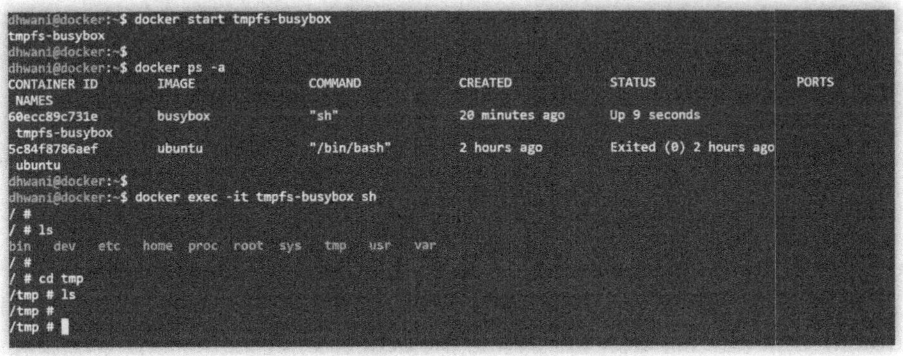

Figure 6.33: Volatility of data in tmpfs

The **foo.txt** does not exist because it got refreshed (and erased) by the time our slow fingers wrote the commands. In fact, unlike persistent storage, the blocks of

RAM allocated for tmpfs were also different both the times (by the grace of stack management), so we were operating on entirely different tmpfs. This was the basic version. You can use **--mount** flag to create a customized tmpfs, as shown in the following command:

```
docker run -it --name tmpfs-busybox \
--mount type=tmpfs,destination=/tmp-data,tmpfs-size=500m,tmpfs-mode=700 \
busybox
```

In this command, the type of the mount is set to tmpfs. The **tmpfs-size** is used to control the amount of memory this tmpfs can utilize. It is important because, unlike HDD or SSD, the RAM is smaller in size. Tmpfs block can occupy a maximum of 50% of system RAM by default. This is a convenient limit for the container but not for the host. The host may go into Out of **Memory (OOM)**, which may affect the container's performance in question along with other containers and other applications. We have set its limit to 500 MB. Finally, we have **tmpfs-mode** used to set the initial permission of the destination directory under the root user. We have set it to octal 700, indicating read/write/execute privileges for the root user.

The outcome of the command looks like the following screenshot:

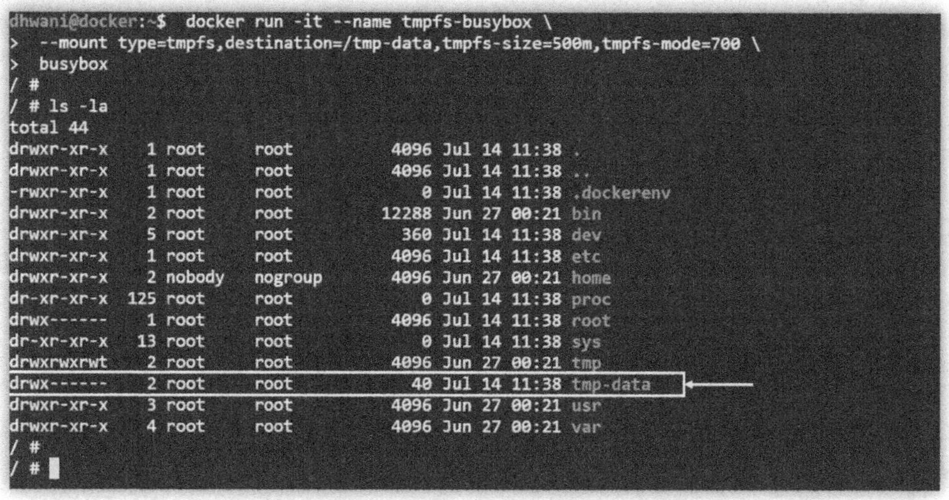

Figure 6.34: *Customized tmpfs for a container*

These were the native storage options of Docker. All of them have their niche uses and if you are confused about your own use case, try using named volumes and then experiment with others. After all, that is the beauty of containers. It gives room for experimentation even under limited hardware infrastructure. In the case of network and storage, there are also third-party plugins available on the Docker hub, but we will look into them when we extend this conversation with the advanced uses of docker after a couple of chapters. Till then, keep experimenting!

Conclusion

This chapter introduced two of the most potent support object types; **Networks** and **Storage objects**, with their native offerings. They also expanded your understanding and scope of using containers beyond just local miniature foreign OS environments. Here and now, you can make your own mini web applications and make them go live, collect some data from them, and store it on your host! It is not an exaggeration to say that now you are ready to work with containers at scale.

In the next chapter, we will study the versatile and powerful swarm mode!

Multiple choice questions

1. Which of the following is not a valid Docker Network?

    A. Null

    B. Bridge

    C. Overlay

    D. Macvlan

    Answer: A

2. In which of the following Docker Networks, there is no isolation between container network namespace and Docker host's network namespace?

    A. Bridge

    B. Macvlan

    C. None

    D. Host

    Answer: D

3. Which of the following commands is used to create a user-defined bridge network, my-net, with the sub-net range 192.168.10.0/25?

    A. `docker network create -d bridge --subnetwork 192.168.10.0/25 my-net`

    B. `docker network create --net 192.168.10.0/25 my-net`

    C. `docker network create -d bridge --subnet 192.168.10.0/25 my-net`

    D. `docker network create -d bridge --net 192.168.10.0/25 my-net`

    Answer: C

4. Which of the following is the default network driver for Docker Networks?

    A. Local

    B. Bridge

    C. Host

    D. None

    Answer: B

5. Which of the following commands is used to connect an existing Docker network to a running Docker container?

    A. `docker network attach <network-name> <container-name>`

    B. `docker container connect <network-name> <container-name>`

    C. `docker network connect --network <network-name> <container-name>`

    D. `docker network connect <network-name> <container-name>`

    Answer: D

6. What is the scope of volumes created by the default volume driver in Docker?

    A. Docker host

    B. Container storage namespace

    C. Docker host cluster

    D. Docker hub

    Answer: A

7. Which of the following Docker storage solutions cannot be managed by Docker CLI?

    A. Named Volumes

    B. Bind mounts

    C. tmpfs

    D. Unnamed Volumes

    Answer: B

8. Which of the following is the fastest storage solution provided by Docker?

    A. Named Volume

    B. Prehistoric File Storage

    C. tmpfs

    D. Bind mount

    Answer: C

9. Which of the following flags cannot be used with the docker volume create command?

A. --opt

B. --label

C. --name

D. --tag

Answer: D

10. What is the default location to store Docker Volumes on Docker host's file system?

A. /var/lib/storage/docker/volumes

B. /var/libs/docker/volumes/

C. /var/lib/docker/volumes/

D. /var/lib/volumes/

Answer: C

Questions

1. Explain the Container Networking Model (CNM) in detail.

2. Explain functionalities and use of bridge, host, macvlan, and none networks in Docker.

3. Explain the importance of data storage in Docker.

4. Explain Volumes, bind mounts, and tmpfs storage in Docker.

5. Create a user-defined bridge network and demonstrate the connection between the containers connected to it.

## CHAPTER 7

Multi-Container Applications with Docker Compose

Introduction

Containerized microservices provide the advantage of separating small units for finer scalability and operations. It also means that most applications with even a little bit of complexity are likely to have different containers for different purposes. Such applications are called Multi-container applications. Docker also provides tools to make the process of containerizing such applications easier. In this chapter, we will cover Docker Compose.

Structure

This chapter covers:

- Prominence of multiple containers
- Hello, Docker Compose!
- First Compose file
- Multi-container Compose Service (Finally!)

Objective

The objective of this chapter is simple *(this line is getting redundant)*. We will understand where Docker Compose fits in the Docker infrastructure abstraction setup. We will perform the tasks that we could perform on Docker CLI using Docker Compose, and we will also see how it simplifies the tedious Docker CLI tasks. Meanwhile, we will understand the working of Docker Compose and practice it by containerizing a multi-tier WordPress application using Docker Compose.

Prominence of multiple containers

So far, all our operations were centered around single containers. It is an excellent approach for learning, but production is a different story. It would not be an exaggeration to say that the whole purpose of containers is to handle multiple instances of isolated pieces of software broken into modular logical blocks. The multiple containers can be replicas run from the same docker image or different containers from different images altogether. Replicas can be used to load balance network traffic, whereas different containers can be used to run and manage a multi-tier application simultaneously. In both cases, the interactions (data exchange) between the containers and their resource requirements can be significantly diverse due to the applications' nature and Docker's capabilities.

One of the reasons why Docker is hailed as the go-to containerization platform is its approach toward handling multi-container applications. It is fun and games writing individual Dockerfiles for single containers and spending your day running a wide range of docker commands on your terminal, but with such practices under production-level applications, you might not even be able to keep track of the commands you had run and the reason behind using them in the first place. This problem is not uncommon.

Every development platform develops a tool to keep different parts of applications in One Piece *(I'm going to be the Pirate King! Just a fun reference for the fans)* during and after development. Most of the times, what we get is an Integrated Development Environment (IDE) to build and integrate the application, but we already have a docker daemon to build the docker images *(we even spent a few pages explaining how it builds the images)*.

On top of that, Docker being an important member of the DevOps tools family, it would be a lost opportunity if it did not utilize the ever wonderful YAML (YAML Ain't Markup Language) to tie all of the containers of the target application declaratively. Following this train of thoughts, Docker has provided a separate tool that runs on top of Docker Daemon. It is called **Docker Compose.**

Hello, Docker Compose!

There is not much to say about what Docker Compose is; it is a tool for defining (declaring) and running multi-container applications. It needs to be installed separately on top of docker as shown in the following figure and it also has its own little dedicated command line:

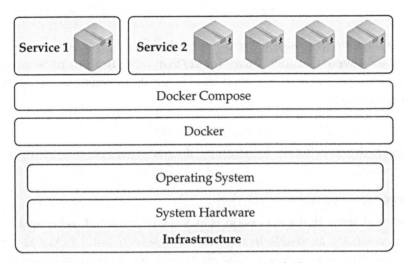

Figure 7.1: *Infrastructure abstraction with docker compose*

As per the preceding figure, Docker Compose wraps containers under objects called *services*. A service may wrap one or more containers, and it can be defined in a curated file (a similar approach to Dockerfile) called *Compose Files*. Compose files are written in YAML, and the values to different container parameters are provided as *key: value* pairs and we will learn more about the compose file soon enough but before that, let us install Docker Compose on Ubuntu environment. We recommend creating a new VM with more resources for this chapter since resource limits of the f1-micro compute instance on GCP may not be enough if you intend to do multiple trials and errors.

We are using a standard VM with 4GB of RAM, 100GB HDD storage (standard persistent storage) having Ubuntu 20.04 installed. Needless to say *(write)*, We have also installed Docker on this VM following the practices shown in the 2nd chapter. First, we will get the current stable version (1.26.2 as recommended by Docker Documentation) of Docker Compose from its git repository using `curl` as shown in the command below. Here, the **-L** flag is used to redirect the request if the target repository has been moved to a new address.

```
sudo curl -L "https://github.com/docker/compose/releases/download/1.26.2/
docker- compose-$(uname -s)-$(uname -m)" -o /usr/local/bin/docker-compose
```

The output will be like any other curl request showing download stats, as shown in the following screenshot:

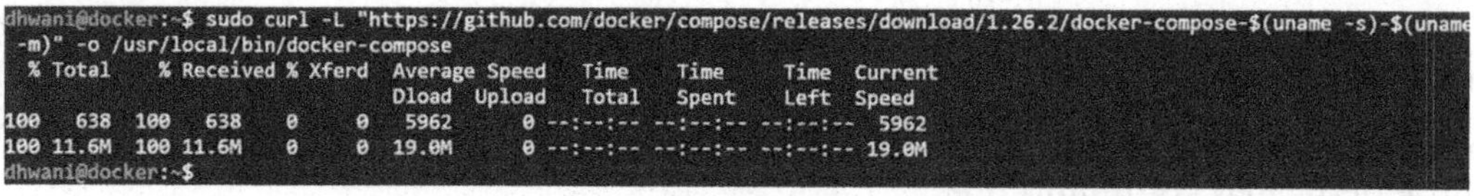

Figure 7.2: Downloading process of the stable version of Docker Compose

With the **-o** flag, we have saved the downloaded files to a newly created directory called **docker-compose** under **/usr/local/bin**. Compose runs (executes) as an independent package, so we need to change its permissions as shown in the following command:

```
sudo chmod +x /usr/local/bin/docker-compose
```

We can check the installation by running **docker-compose** and tailing it with the version keyword.

```
docker-compose --version
```

The output will show that the version is as we had intended to be, and compose is running successfully, as visible in the following screenshot. Docker also prints the build number (string) to appreciate the contribution of their developers (☺):

Figure 7.3: Successful installation of Docker Compose

First Compose file

After having Docker Compose installed on our system, we can start writing compose files to deploy containerized applications. Writing compose files involves taking care of indentations, case sensitivity and parameter values. Just describing them lexically will be a daunting task for me to write and for you to comprehend so, let us learn them by following a couple of examples! We will start with a single container example and use busybox container image. Create a new directory called busybox and navigate into it, as shown in the following commands. As beginners, it is highly recommended to store one **docker-compose** file per directory/repository.

```
mkdir busybox

cd busybox
```

Open your preferred text editor (We have used nano here) and write the following file content provided and save it as **docker-compose.yaml** (unlike the Dockerfile with has no extension):

```
1.  version: '3.8'
2.  services:
3.      os:
4.         image: busybox
5.         container_name: busybox-os
6.         cap_add:
7.           - ALL
8.         command: echo ‹WELCOME TO BUSYBOX, THE SWISS ARMY KNIFE OF
           EMBEDDED LINUX.›
9.         devices:
10.          - "/dev/sda:/dev/sda"
11.        environment:
12.           LOGNAME: cerulean_canvas
13.           HOME: /cerulean_canvas
14.        init: true
15.        labels:
16.           Creator: «Cerulean Canvas»
17.        logging:
18.           driver: «journald»
19.        pid: host
20.        restart: on-failure
21.        stop_signal: SIGUSR1
22.        volumes:
23.           - busybox_data:/etc
24.
25.  volumes:
26.     busybox_data:
```

There are a lot of things that do not necessarily change your skill level or your expertise but just knowing them turns your overall experience toward a technology or tool more coherent. If you are like me, scratching your head over wondering the reason behind two different file formats, the following paragraphs might throw some insight about it.

Chronologically, Dockerfile was the original document format used by Docker to provide image details to Docker Daemon. The intention of Dockerfile format was to remain independent from other formats and provide as much versatility as possible in the context of the docker image. While it may not always be the case, many times, succeeding in making developers get used to a new file format for a new platform helps to avoid immediate competition. Docker Compose was introduced at a later stage, and its intent was not to establish Docker as something mainstream in the DevOps toolchain, but to smoothen the experience of developers using Docker for large scale or multi-tier applications.

With the rise in Infrastructure as Code *(and Kubernetes, but more on that later)*, YAML was getting ample positive attention as a human-readable and less complex representation for JSON objects for streaming infrastructure data, and it was exactly what Docker was looking for. Therefore, compose files are written in YAML. Dockerfiles are still the primary way to interact with Docker Daemon but Compose files are a convenient way to Dockerize multi-container applications.

Compose files are written in YAML. **YAML** is a data serialization language. It translates complex data structures from other programming languages to platform-neutral small-sized objects recreated on other machines. YAML is extensively used in Infrastructure as Code tools, and Docker Compose uses it to make the containerized application design more human-readable. YAML uses whitespace indentation without "tab". You can learn more about YAML at **www.yaml.org**. Compose files use scalars (integers, strings, and so on) to declare variable parameters such as the first line that sores the version number. It also uses objects like service and volume to enclose multiple parameter declarations under their limited (to object) scope. The first declaration is of the version. This is not the Docker Compose version; it is the version of the Compose File. This is important because Compose is not an independent tool. It depends on Docker Engine, so it is important for Docker Engine to be updated enough to process the request streamed by composing. To make this compatibility match easy, the Compose file version is written at the top of the file. The table below informs which Compose file versions are compatible with which Docker Engine versions.

The Docker Engine versions are regardless of community or enterprise editions. We are using Compose file version 3.8 (latest while writing the book) compatible with the latest version of Docker Engine.

Sr. No	Compose File Version	Minimum Docker Engine Release Version
1	3.8	19.03.0+
2	3.7	18.06.0+
3	3.6	18.02.0+
4	3.5	17.12.0+
5	3.4	17.09.0+
6	3.3	17.06.0+
7	3.2	17.04.0+
8	3.1	1.13.1+
9	3.0	1.13.0+
10	2.4	17.12.0+
11	2.3	17.06.0+
12	2.2	1.13.0+
13	2.1	1.12.0+
14	2.0	1.10.0+
15	1.0	1.9.1+

Table 7.1: Compose file versions supported by Docker releases

Now, continuing with the **docker-compose** file, we have two objects, Services and Volumes. In most cases, you will also find Networks accompanying services and volumes, but since this is our first attempt on Compose, we are keeping things grounded.

Services can be considered as wrappers around one or more (generally more) containers that pass the container configurations to the Docker Daemon on behalf of the developer. You can provide every parameter of docker create, docker network create, docker volume create, or docker run to your compose file via services and other objects. Services focus on APIs requested by docker create and docker run. The one and only service we have in this file is named **os**. Of course, you can name it anything you desire.

Next, we have provided the image name. Docker will search for this string in the registry and fetch the first image with the most stars (and verified one if possible). Since the request is being passed on to Docker Daemon, the default registry will be Docker Hub unless configured manually for the respective daemon. The name of the container will be set to **busybox-os**. Optionally, you can also provide the build context as a path on host or a URL.

The next attribute, `cap_add` is used to provide Linux Capabilities to containers. Capabilities are evolved version of Linux's formal permission granting approach. Instead of keeping things binary, with processes either being privileged or unprivileged with a lot of wanted or unwanted permissions granted or taken away by default, capabilities provide more refined control overgranting permission to processes. By mentioning `ALL` to `cap_add`, we are essentially turning the container into a privileged process in terms of the old approach.

Just like `cap_add`, compose also provides `cap_drop` to exclude specific permissions. Linux Capabilities is a vast topic, and explaining all of them in detail may take a pretty long chapter in a book of OS fundamentals. So, a common practice is looking them up on **https://man7.org/linux/man-pages/man7/capabilities.7.html** whenever you need to know more about them.

Command provides the value of CMD to the Docker image. We are simply echoing a string. **Devices** map the storage device (or block of storage device addressed by path) on the host to container's file system. We are mapping host's `/dev/sda` to Container's `/dev/sda`.

Environment field passes the ENV or `--env` value to container to set its environment variables. Switching **init** to true sets up an init process inside the container that takes over the role of sending system calls and other interrupts to the processes running inside the container.

Labels add metadata as usual. We are adding the creator's name, you can add whatever you wish to.

Next field provides the **Logging** configurations for the container. This can be considered as the abstraction of docker container logs command. You can specify the logging driver, log streaming destination and number of logs to be streamed. Docker supports many logging drivers like splunk, fluentd, syslog, and so on. We have set the driver to journald. Docker also supports public cloud platform-specific logging drivers like gcplogs and awslogs.

Next is the `pid` (PID) mode. Setting it to host allows containers to share pid namespaces of its host system. As a result, the container can pass PIDs to host and can also access host's PIDs. A good use case for this would be docker-in-docker. Next is the `stop_signal` field. It is used to pass the STOPSIG to container (to replace container's default stop signal).

Volumes field under services is used to mount the volume to the path inside container filesystem separated by a colon. On the other hand, Volumes is also an independent object used to create named volume on the host. We are creating a volume called `busybox_data`, and we are mounting our container to the same.

Though not as vast as the docker command line itself, docker-compose command line also boasts a good variety of commands. With the following command, you can figure out which command is useful for you:

```
docker-compose help
```

The outcome of the preceding command is shown in the following screenshot:

```
dhwani@docker:~/wordpress$ docker-compose help
Define and run multi-container applications with Docker.

Usage:
  docker-compose [-f <arg>...] [options] [COMMAND] [ARGS...]
  docker-compose -h|--help

Options:
  -f, --file FILE             Specify an alternate compose file
                              (default: docker-compose.yml)
  -p, --project-name NAME     Specify an alternate project name
                              (default: directory name)
  -c, --context NAME          Specify a context name
  --verbose                   Show more output
  --log-level LEVEL           Set log level (DEBUG, INFO, WARNING, ERROR, CRITICAL)
  --no-ansi                   Do not print ANSI control characters
  -v, --version               Print version and exit
  -H, --host HOST             Daemon socket to connect to

  --tls                       Use TLS; implied by --tlsverify
  --tlscacert CA_PATH         Trust certs signed only by this CA
  --tlscert CLIENT_CERT_PATH  Path to TLS certificate file
  --tlskey TLS_KEY_PATH       Path to TLS key file
  --tlsverify                 Use TLS and verify the remote
  --skip-hostname-check       Don't check the daemon's hostname against the
                              name specified in the client certificate
  --project-directory PATH    Specify an alternate working directory
                              (default: the path of the Compose file)
  --compatibility             If set, Compose will attempt to convert keys
  --env-file PATH             Specify an alternate environment file

Commands:
  build       Build or rebuild services
  config      Validate and view the Compose file
  create      Create services
  down        Stop and remove containers, networks, images, and volumes
  events      Receive real time events from containers
  exec        Execute a command in a running container
  help        Get help on a command
  images      List images
  kill        Kill containers
  logs        View output from containers
  pause       Pause services
  port        Print the public port for a port binding
  ps          List containers
  pull        Pull service images
  push        Push service images
  restart     Restart services
  rm          Remove stopped containers
  run         Run a one-off command
  scale       Set number of containers for a service
  start       Start services
  stop        Stop services
  top         Display the running processes
  unpause     Unpause services
  up          Create and start containers
```

Figure 7.4: Docker Compose man page

Since we are done with understanding the compose file, it is time to run it with the following command:

```
docker-compose up
```

This command will create all the objects mentioned in the compose file. *Is not that fun? Now there is no need to keep writing redundant commands to create single objects tediously.*

The output of the command will provide confirmation of every object being created, as shown in the following screenshot:

```
dhwani@docker:~/busybox$ docker-compose up
Creating network "busybox_default" with the default driver
Creating volume "busybox_busybox_data" with default driver
Pulling os (busybox:)...
latest: Pulling from library/busybox
61c5ed1cbdf8: Pull complete
Digest: sha256:4f47c01fa91355af2865ac10fef5bf6ec9c7f42ad2321377c21e844427972977
Status: Downloaded newer image for busybox:latest
Creating busybox-os ... done
Attaching to busybox-os
busybox-os  | WELCOME TO BUSYBOX, THE SWISS ARMY KNIFE OF EMBEDDED LINUX.
busybox-os exited with code 0
dhwani@docker:~/busybox$
```

Figure 7.5: Output of docker-compose up command

Docker behaved just as we had expected it to. It created a bridge network and a named volume; it also created a busybox container by pulling the appropriate image. Just how docker ps is used to list out containers, **docker-compose ps** is used to list out services, as shown in the following screenshot:

```
dhwani@docker:~/busybox$ docker-compose ps
    Name                    Command             State   Ports
--------------------------------------------------------------
busybox-os    echo WELCOME TO BUSYBOX, T ...    Exit 0
dhwani@docker:~/busybox$
dhwani@docker:~/busybox$
```

Figure 7.6: Output of docker-compose ps command

Since we had explicitly mentioned the logging driver, let us check out the container logs of busybox-os with the following command:

```
docker-compose logs
```

```
dhwani@docker:~/busybox$ docker-compose logs
Attaching to busybox-os
busybox-os  | WELCOME TO BUSYBOX, THE SWISS ARMY KNIFE OF EMBEDDED LINUX.
dhwani@docker:~/busybox$
dhwani@docker:~/busybox$
```

Figure 7.7: Output of docker-compose logs command

The logs indicate that there were no warnings or exceptions and the container echoed the string to its stdout perfectly. Compose does not bother about managing volumes or networks too much. It just acts as a mediator and passes their creation request to the daemon. If you want to list volumes or networks, you can always use docker's CLI with **docker network ls** and **docker volume ls**. The same goes for their removal. As shown in the screenshot below, docker-compose rm only removes all the services it had created.

You need to remove the networks and volumes separately by using the regular Docker command line:

```
dhwani@docker:~/busybox$ docker-compose rm
Going to remove busybox-os
Are you sure? [yN] y
Removing busybox-os ... done
dhwani@docker:~/busybox$
dhwani@docker:~/busybox$ docker volume ls
DRIVER              VOLUME NAME
local               busybox_busybox_data
dhwani@docker:~/busybox$
dhwani@docker:~/busybox$ docker network ls
NETWORK ID      NAME              DRIVER      SCOPE
acda5295cc54    bridge            bridge      local
25d923b1894a    busybox_default   bridge      local
b215195e9fec    host              host        local
81248d8cb3c6    none              null        local
```

Figure 7.8: Consequences of docker-compose rm command (consequences sound totally out of place, right?!)

Multi-container Compose Service (Finally!)

Docker compose can execute multiple services from a single compose file which gives opportunities to tie multi-tier application containers. One classic example would be a hosted WordPress application built on top of LAMP (Linux, Apache, MySQL, PHP) stack. To get started, create an empty directory called **WordPress** and navigate into it. Due to Developer's intuition, you would be tempted to name this file something contextual like **wordpress-compose.yaml**, not a good idea!

Unlike Dockerfiles, where the Docker Daemon recommends only to use the filename "Dockerfile" for the sake of auto-builder but it would build any other file without extension anyway. But the same is not with Docker Compose. It does not accept filenames other than **docker-compose.yaml** or **docker-compose.yml**. Compose eliminates the requirements of multiple files; thus, having one compose file per project is feasible. If you are wondering, what will happen if you try to use any other filename, you should look at the following screenshot:

```
dhwani@docker:~/wordpress$ nano wordpress-compose.yaml
dhwani@docker:~/wordpress$
dhwani@docker:~/wordpress$
dhwani@docker:~/wordpress$ docker-compose up
ERROR:
        Can't find a suitable configuration file in this directory or any
        parent. Are you in the right directory?

        Supported filenames: docker-compose.yml, docker-compose.yaml

dhwani@docker:~/wordpress$ 
```

Figure 7.9: Invalid configuration filename error

Create a file called **docker-compose.yaml** and populate it with the following content:

```
1.  version: '3.3'
2.  services:
3.    db:
4.      image: mysql:5.7
5.      volumes:
6.        - db_data:/var/lib/mysql
7.      restart: always
8.      environment:
9.        MYSQL_ROOT_PASSWORD: somewordpress
10.       MYSQL_DATABASE: wordpress
11.       MYSQL_USER: wordpress
12.       MYSQL_PASSWORD: wordpress
13.   wordpress:
14.     depends_on:
15.       - db
16.     image: wordpress:latest
17.     ports:
18.       - "8000:80"
19.     restart: always
20.     environment:
21.       WORDPRESS_DB_HOST: db:3306
22.       WORDPRESS_DB_USER: wordpress
23.       WORDPRESS_DB_PASSWORD: wordpress
24.       WORDPRESS_DB_NAME: wordpress
25. volumes:
26.   db_data: {}
```

Since we have already seen the basics of a compose file, let us see how this file is different from the previous one. First, it has two services named db and wordpress. The service **db** is a MySQL 5.7 container with a volume **db_data** mount on **/var/lib/mysql**. It has some environment variables set for the credentials of the database server.

On the other hand, we have the second service called wordpress which is dependent on the **db** service. This is a relation unique to compose that allows establishing dependencies between different services. MySQL **db** is the backend service while **wordpress** is the frontend service. Both services have set the restart policy of the containers to **always**. **wordpress** has mentioned the port mapping instruction and has also provided some environment variables. These variables are for the credentials of the **db** service. This relationship implies that the **wordpress** service will start only after the successful start of **db** service.

We can verify it by running **docker-compose up** command as shown in the following screenshots:

```
dhwani@docker:~/wordpress$ docker-compose up
Creating network "wordpress_default" with the default driver
Creating volume "wordpress_db_data" with default driver
Pulling db (mysql:5.7)...
5.7: Pulling from library/mysql
bf5952930446: Pull complete
8254623a9871: Pull complete
938e3e06dac4: Pull complete
ea28ebf28884: Pull complete
f3cef38785c2: Pull complete
894f9792565a: Pull complete
1d8a57523420: Pull complete
5f09bf1d31c1: Pull complete
1b6ff254abe7: Pull complete
74310a0bf42d: Pull complete
d398726627fd: Pull complete
Digest: sha256:da58f943b94721d46e87d5de208dc07302a8b13e638cd1d24285d222376d6d84
Status: Downloaded newer image for mysql:5.7
```

Figure 7.10: Pulling MySQL:5.7 docker image

After successfully pulling **mysql:5.7**, docker daemon will start pulling the latest wordpress image:

```
Pulling wordpress (wordpress:latest)...
latest: Pulling from library/wordpress
bf5952930446: Already exists
a409b57eb464: Pull complete
3192e6c84ad0: Pull complete
43553740162b: Pull complete
d8b8bba42dea: Pull complete
eb10907c0110: Pull complete
10568906f34e: Pull complete
03fe17709781: Pull complete
98171b7166c8: Pull complete
3978c2fb05b8: Pull complete
71bf21524fa8: Pull complete
24fe81782f1c: Pull complete
7a2dfd067aa5: Pull complete
a04586f4f8fe: Pull complete
b8059b10e448: Pull complete
e5b4db4a14b4: Pull complete
48018c17c4e9: Pull complete
d09f106f9e16: Pull complete
289a459a6137: Pull complete
c4e8f9c90fda: Pull complete
Digest: sha256:6da8f886b20632dd05eeb22462f850a38e30600cedd894d2c6b1eb1a58e9763c
Status: Downloaded newer image for wordpress:latest
```

Figure 7.11: Pulling WordPress docker image

Since there were no MySQL or WordPress images on our host, these images have been pulled from the docker hub. You might have noticed that we have not provided any names for the containers to be created. In such case, compose will name them in this format: **<<PROJECT-NAME_SERVICE-NAME_NUMBER>>**.

For example, the MySQL container of the db service will be named **wordpress_db_1** as shown in the following screenshot:

Figure 7.12: Creating both containers

You can read the "Done" confirmation beside both the containers at the top of the screenshot. Below that, we can see the entrypoint process logs of both services. Since we had not explicitly provided any entrypoint replacements, Docker Daemon has executed the entrypoint mentioned in the original Dockerfiles of the images pulled.

Just like the previous compose project, we can use **docker-compose ps** to list the number of running containers as shown in the following screenshot:

Figure 7.13: Containers of the wordpress service

We can see that both containers are up and running. Their default CMDs are running custom **docker-entrypoint** scripts, which explains why there were so many log entries right after the attaching docker client terminal to containers. By default, database container is not exposed on the internet, while the wordpress container's port **80** is exposed to host's port **8080**. To test it out, go to your web browser and hit the combination of **<host-IP>:8080**.

In my case, we will hit the external IP of VM on port **8080**. It is important to know that the wordpress service will only be able to work properly if there are no processes serving on port **8080**. If port **8080** is busy, you need to free up the port for wordpress. *(To be on a safe side, you can change the port mapping configuration in docker-compose file* *and map container's port **80** to apart from host's port **8080** or **80**).*

WordPress is working! You can continue to experiment with WordPress and can also create a dummy blog page! It should work well with the current resources provided by docker daemon:

***Figure 7.14:** WordPress Home Page*

While we are smoothly viewing the webpage on the browser, Docker Compose is also keeping a record of the events regarding the service. To be honest, events were first introduced by Kubernetes, but we are at least a couple of chapters away from it, so let's view the compose events with the following command:

```
docker-compose events
```

The output will be something like the following screenshot. Notice the container name at the end of the events to identify which events are related to which container:

```
dhwani@docker:~/wordpress$ docker-compose events
2020-08-16 09:12:32.203337 container create ac5cb6a6d6638411156ca3ab4011b20e67949b4b8700b0d77bd092e2ec406541 (image=mysql:5.
7, name=wordpress_db_1)
2020-08-16 09:12:32.212599 container attach ac5cb6a6d6638411156ca3ab4011b20e67949b4b8700b0d77bd092e2ec406541 (image=mysql:5.
7, name=wordpress_db_1)
2020-08-16 09:12:32.711665 container start ac5cb6a6d6638411156ca3ab4011b20e67949b4b8700b0d77bd092e2ec406541 (image=mysql:5.7
, name=wordpress_db_1)
2020-08-16 09:12:32.829772 container create 009227d7ddf94d064a664d32a7b4497c0c82ba481be08912e5e4b37f2a20abed (image=wordpres
s:latest, name=wordpress_wordpress_1)
2020-08-16 09:12:32.846740 container attach 009227d7ddf94d064a664d32a7b4497c0c82ba481be08912e5e4b37f2a20abed (image=wordpres
s:latest, name=wordpress_wordpress_1)
2020-08-16 09:12:34.922047 container start 009227d7ddf94d064a664d32a7b4497c0c82ba481be08912e5e4b37f2a20abed (image=wordpress
:latest, name=wordpress_wordpress_1)
```

***Figure 7.15:** Streaming events of the wordpress service containers*

Events are an abstraction of the APIs invoked behind the scenes of docker-compose up. Both containers of the **wordpress** service did not have much complex configurations, so the only events we received are **create, attach** and **start** sequentially. These events also reinforce the dependence relationship between **wordpress** and **db** services. Services are not just about containers. They are a full package of containers, storage, and configurations. Let's find out about storage and networks related to this service.

```
docker volume ls

docker network ls
```

The volume is once again created just as expected as shown in the following screenshot:

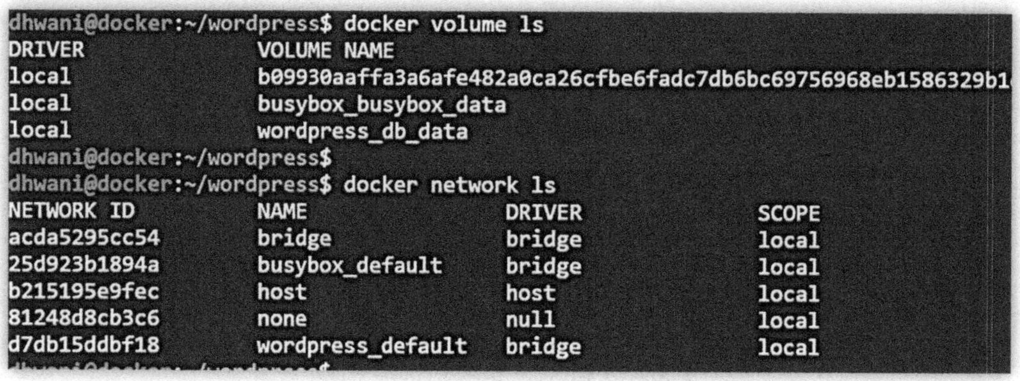

Figure 7.16: Networks and Volumes on the docker host

The objects that arise many questions are the networks. We did not ask for any of them, so why did they get created? Let's remember the basics of docker networks.

- If we do not connect the container to any network, it automatically gets connected to the default bridge network.

- The containers in the same network can communicate with one another (there are other basics but these two are enough to make the point).

If Docker Compose would not create any network object for this service, containers would be connected to the default bridge. This would make your application vulnerable as any present or future containers would be able to communicate to it. To prevent such vulnerabilities, Docker Compose creates a new network for each application.

Furthermore, the following command lists the processes running inside the containers of the current service in context.

```
docker-compose top
```

```
dhwani@docker:~/wordpress$ docker-compose top
wordpress_db_1
  UID      PID     PPID    C    STIME   TTY     TIME       CMD
---------------------------------------------------------------
systemd+   4757    4725    0    09:21   ?       00:00:01   mysqld

wordpress_wordpress_1
  UID      PID     PPID    C    STIME   TTY     TIME        CMD
----------------------------------------------------------------
root       4889    4866    0    09:21   ?       00:00:00    apache2 -DFOREGROUND
www-data   5159    4889    0    09:21   ?       00:00:00    apache2 -DFOREGROUND
www-data   5160    4889    0    09:21   ?       00:00:00    apache2 -DFOREGROUND
www-data   5161    4889    0    09:21   ?       00:00:00    apache2 -DFOREGROUND
www-data   5162    4889    0    09:21   ?       00:00:00    apache2 -DFOREGROUND
www-data   5163    4889    0    09:21   ?       00:00:00    apache2 -DFOREGROUND
```

Figure 7.17: Running processes inside wordpress service containers

This is a well-arranged output. We get every detail starting from the user, Process ID, Parent Process' ID, number of crashes (none have crashed), system time when the process was executed, time taken to complete the process and finally, the command used to execute the process.

We can view the logs of the compose services with a single command and the output will differentiate the logs of both containers by itself. This time, we will limit the number of logs with the following command:

```
docker-compose logs --tail 10
```

```
dhwani@docker:~/wordpress$ docker-compose logs --tail 10
Attaching to wordpress_wordpress_1, wordpress_db_1
db_1        | 2020-08-16T09:21:34.938522Z 0 [Warning] CA certificate ca.pem is self signed.
db_1        | 2020-08-16T09:21:34.939439Z 0 [Note] Skipping generation of RSA key pair as key files are present in data dir
ectory.
db_1        | 2020-08-16T09:21:34.940360Z 0 [Note] Server hostname (bind-address): '*'; port: 3306
db_1        | 2020-08-16T09:21:34.942014Z 0 [Note] IPv6 is available.
db_1        | 2020-08-16T09:21:34.942377Z 0 [Note]   - '::' resolves to '::';
db_1        | 2020-08-16T09:21:34.942786Z 0 [Note] Server socket created on IP: '::'.
db_1        | 2020-08-16T09:21:34.946881Z 0 [Warning] Insecure configuration for --pid-file: Location '/var/run/mysqld' in
the path is accessible to all OS users. Consider choosing a different directory.
db_1        | 2020-08-16T09:21:34.961084Z 0 [Note] Event Scheduler: Loaded 0 events
db_1        | 2020-08-16T09:21:34.962378Z 0 [Note] mysqld: ready for connections.
db_1        | Version: '5.7.31'  socket: '/var/run/mysqld/mysqld.sock'  port: 3306  MySQL Community Server (GPL)
wordpress_1 | WordPress not found in /var/www/html - copying now...
wordpress_1 | Complete! WordPress has been successfully copied to /var/www/html
wordpress_1 | AH00558: apache2: Could not reliably determine the server's fully qualified domain name, using 172.21.0.3. Se
t the 'ServerName' directive globally to suppress this message
wordpress_1 | AH00558: apache2: Could not reliably determine the server's fully qualified domain name, using 172.21.0.3. Se
t the 'ServerName' directive globally to suppress this message
wordpress_1 | [Sun Aug 16 09:21:35.831801 2020] [mpm_prefork:notice] [pid 1] AH00163: Apache/2.4.38 (Debian) PHP/7.4.9 conf
igured -- resuming normal operations
wordpress_1 | [Sun Aug 16 09:21:35.832506 2020] [core:notice] [pid 1] AH00094: Command line: 'apache2 -D FOREGROUND'
dhwani@docker:~/wordpress$
dhwani@docker:~/wordpress$
```

Figure 7.18: Container logs of wordpress service

Docker Compose can also trigger the container life-cycle stages other than create and start. For example, use the command below to pause the containers.

```
docker-compose pause
docker-compose ps
```

The **pause** command is followed by **ps** command to verify if the containers are paused. The output will look like the following screenshot:

```
dhwani@docker:~/wordpress$ docker-compose pause db
Pausing wordpress_db_1 ... done
dhwani@docker:~/wordpress$
dhwani@docker:~/wordpress$ docker-compose ps
        Name                    Command              State           Ports
-----------------------------------------------------------------------------
wordpress_db_1          docker-entrypoint.sh mysqld    Paused    3306/tcp, 33060/tcp
wordpress_wordpress_1   docker-entrypoint.sh apach ... Up        0.0.0.0:8000->80/tcp
dhwani@docker:~/wordpress$
```

Figure 7.19: Pausing the database container of wordpress service

Similarly, you can also unpause the container and verify its state using the following commands:

```
docker-compose unpause
docker-compose ps
```

```
dhwani@docker:~/wordpress$ docker-compose unpause db
Unpausing wordpress_db_1 ... done
dhwani@docker:~/wordpress$
dhwani@docker:~/wordpress$ docker-compose ps
        Name                    Command              State           Ports
-----------------------------------------------------------------------------
wordpress_db_1          docker-entrypoint.sh mysqld    Up        3306/tcp, 33060/tcp
wordpress_wordpress_1   docker-entrypoint.sh apach ... Up        0.0.0.0:8000->80/tcp
dhwani@docker:~/wordpress$
```

Figure 7.20: Unpausing the database container of wordpress service

We can play around with the service containers a little more by trying to stop and start the containers with the following commands:

```
docker-compose stop
docker-compose ps
docker-compose start
docker-compose ps
```

The output of these commands will look like the previous ones, so focus on the state of the containers:

```
dhwani@docker:~/wordpress$ docker-compose stop db
Stopping wordpress_db_1 ... done
dhwani@docker:~/wordpress$
dhwani@docker:~/wordpress$ docker-compose ps
        Name                    Command              State           Ports
-----------------------------------------------------------------------------
wordpress_db_1          docker-entrypoint.sh mysqld    Exit 0
wordpress_wordpress_1   docker-entrypoint.sh apach ... Up        0.0.0.0:8000->80/tcp
dhwani@docker:~/wordpress$
dhwani@docker:~/wordpress$ docker-compose start db
Starting db ... done
dhwani@docker:~/wordpress$
dhwani@docker:~/wordpress$ docker-compose ps
        Name                    Command              State           Ports
-----------------------------------------------------------------------------
wordpress_db_1          docker-entrypoint.sh mysqld    Up        3306/tcp, 33060/tcp
wordpress_wordpress_1   docker-entrypoint.sh apach ... Up        0.0.0.0:8000->80/tcp
```

Figure 7.21: Stopping and starting of the database container of wordpress service

Mentioning individual services followed by **docker-compose** allows us to operate on individual containers even within the scope of compose. To extend this utility further, let's execute the wordpress container like Docker **exec** with the following command:

```
docker-compose exec wordpress sh
```

The syntax is simple, **docker-compose exec** command is followed by the service name and the command to be run while executing the container. This command should open a shell of wordpress container as shown in the following screenshot. I am also interacting with the shell to see if it is working properly:

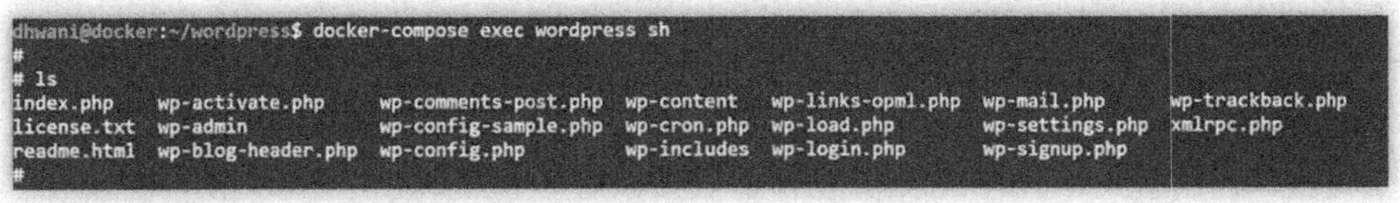

Figure 7.22: *Executing wordpress container using docker-compose exec command*

The terminal navigated to the root of wordpress container and listed files stored in its environment successfully. Furthermore, we can continue staying in the container and play a bit more like opening a familiar file as shown in the following screenshot:

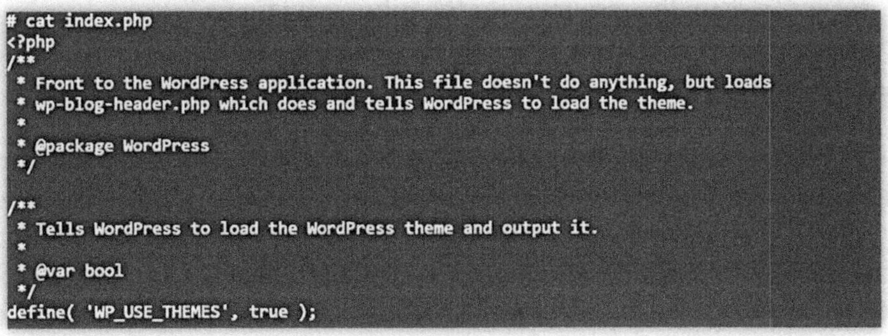

Figure 7.23: *Opening index.php inside a wordpress service container*

Finally, just how we can **docker-compose up** to start multiple containers as services, we can also use **docker-compose down** to stop and remove all the running containers of a docker compose service as shown in the following screenshot:

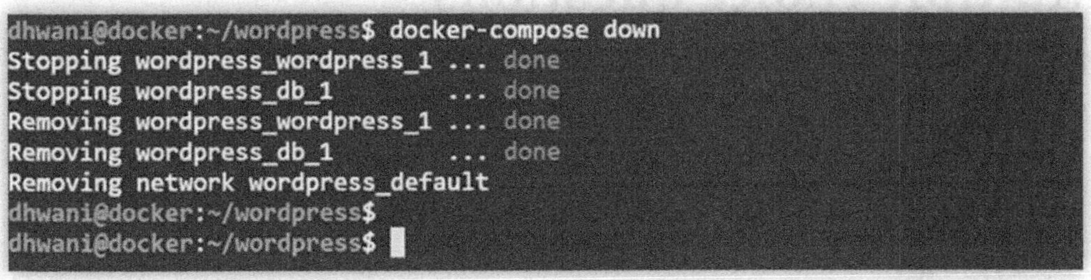

Figure 7.24: *Taking down multiple containers with docker-compose down command*

This command is a combination of **docker kill** and **docker rm**. It also removes all networks created with docker compose service but not volumes. You must remove any volume created by the docker compose service manually. In fact, looking at the events, when taking down services gives an interesting perspective as shown in the following screenshot:

```
2020-08-16 10:05:38.382784 container kill fd931db7007e53ebf4d40e98cf8ca5ba0a99f32af8bf21eebf869476af5973be (image=wordpress:
latest, name=wordpress_wordpress_1, signal=28)
2020-08-16 10:05:39.518226 container die fd931db7007e53ebf4d40e98cf8ca5ba0a99f32af8bf21eebf869476af5973be (exitCode=0, image
=wordpress:latest, name=wordpress_wordpress_1)
2020-08-16 10:05:40.057277 container stop fd931db7007e53ebf4d40e98cf8ca5ba0a99f32af8bf21eebf869476af5973be (image=wordpress:
latest, name=wordpress_wordpress_1)
2020-08-16 10:05:40.088380 container kill 2ccfac25659ddfa4957bdefeb393365a16089bf6b370896a0ec95896c2b622c1 (image=mysql:5.7,
 name=wordpress_db_1, signal=15)
2020-08-16 10:05:41.792283 container die 2ccfac25659ddfa4957bdefeb393365a16089bf6b370896a0ec95896c2b622c1 (exitCode=0, image
=mysql:5.7, name=wordpress_db_1)
2020-08-16 10:05:41.881926 container stop 2ccfac25659ddfa4957bdefeb393365a16089bf6b370896a0ec95896c2b622c1 (image=mysql:5.7,
 name=wordpress_db_1)
2020-08-16 10:05:41.954998 container destroy 2ccfac25659ddfa4957bdefeb393365a16089bf6b370896a0ec95896c2b622c1 (image=mysql:5
.7, name=wordpress_db_1)
2020-08-16 10:05:41.975553 container destroy fd931db7007e53ebf4d40e98cf8ca5ba0a99f32af8bf21eebf869476af5973be (image=wordpre
ss:latest, name=wordpress_wordpress_1)
```

Figure 7.25: Container events while shutting down docker compose project

The events give details about the exit code of the containers (indicating their graceful shutdowns) and the whole takedown process, including the final stage of destruction where docker frees up the resources for the future containers.

Conclusion

Docker Compose is an all-rounder utility tool that provides much-needed abstraction of containerization process while maintaining the necessary granularity of control. Being part of the native Docker ecosystem and being managed by docker helps Docker Compose to stay relevant and up to date with the growth of Docker. In this chapter, we explored its usefulness to a significant extent, and we also simplified the process of containerizing complex multi-tier applications. Docker compose will appear again during orchestration and we will continue to leverage its simplicity. In the next chapter, we will learn about container orchestration.

Multiple choice questions

1. Which of the following format is used to write docker-compose configuration file?

    A. Go

    B. Python

    C. YAML

    D Java

    Answer: C

2. From the following choices, what is the correct extension of docker-compose file?

   A. .yml

   B. .ymal

   C. .compose

   D. none

   Answer: A

3. Which of the following docker-compose file configurations options is used to provide Linux capabilities to containers?

   A. cap_mount

   B. cap_add

   C. cap_insert

   D. cap_merge

   Answer: B

4. Which of the following docker-compose file configurations is used to establish inter-service dependencies?

   A. inter-service

   B. mount-service

   C. depends_on

   D. service_seq

   Answer: C

5. Which of the following docker-compose commands is used to build, create, and start docker compose service containers?

   A. docker-compose attach

   B. docker-compose start

   C. docker-compose build

   D. docker-compose up

   Answer: D

6. Which of the following docker-compose commands is used to stream events of all containers of a compose project?

   A. docker-compose events

   B. docker-compose stream

   C. docker-compose status

   D. docker-compose live

   Answer: A

7. Which of the following docker-compose commands is used to display running processes inside compose service containers?

   A. docker-compose ps

   B. docker-compose top

   C. docker-compose ls

   D. docker-compose rs

   Answer: B

8. Which of the following docker-compose commands is the equivalent of docker exec command?

   A. docker-compose attach

   B. docker-compose connect

   C. docker-compose execute

   D. docker-compose exec

   Answer: D

9. Which of the following docker-compose file configurations is used to forward system calls and interrupts to the other running processes inside containers?

   A. sys-forward

   B. init

   C. set-init

   D. none

   Answer: B

10. Which of the following is the supported compose configuration filename?

    A. compose.yaml

    B. doc-compose.yaml

    C. docker-compose.yaml

    D. docker.compose.yaml

    Answer: C

CHAPTER 8

Container Orchestration with Docker Swarm

Introduction

Container orchestration is all about controlling the behavior of many related or unrelated containers. Understanding and practicing container orchestration is as (if not more) important as writing Dockerfiles or managing individual containers. This chapter introduces the concept of orchestration in-depth and covers Docker Swarm, a container orchestration tool offered by Docker.

Structure

This chapter covers:

- Facing the inevitable - the orchestration
- Understanding Docker Swarm
- Getting started with Docker Swarm
- Working with Docker Swarm
- Understanding networking in Docker Swarm
- Container orchestration
- Working with Docker Stack
- Cleaning up Docker Swarm

Objective

The objective of this chapter is to make you comfortable with container orchestration. While the basics remain the same, the mindset of a system admin needs to change a little when dealing with a swarm of containers (pun intended). Docker Swarm is a good starting point for learning container orchestration as its terminology is built on top of Docker's own objects, and it has a steeper learning curve compared to others. By the end of this chapter, you will be able to perform simple orchestration tasks and will be ready to learn more elaborate orchestration.

Facing the inevitable - the orchestration

Do you remember *Chapters 1* and *2*, where we considered containers as the small footprint solution for hosting web applications instead of VMs? We had also talked about containers being an insignificant feature of Linux operating systems for decades and Google being the early bird to realize their true potential. None of this was done keeping a single container or even a few small containers in mind. Just think about it, setting up a VM on the cloud, installing Docker on it and creating another layer of isolation (with containers) just for running one instance of a Nginx webserver is not even practical. Instead, you would run it on your system if you want isolation, security, and better control; a VM would also be sufficient. Containers are meant to serve isolated microservices **at scale**. They are meant to be in the range of at least dozens to show the financial benefits of migration.

Multiple containers also bring multiple issues. First of all, handling these containers individually becomes impractically tedious and messy *(remember Steve Jobs' iPhone introduction speech when he showed his discontentment toward styluses? You will have a similar negative bias for containers if you have to manage a lot of them individually).* Second, just look at the following image:

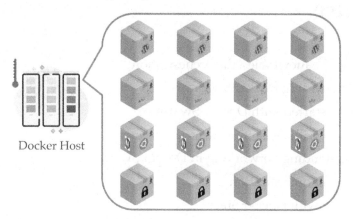

Figure 8.1: A Docker Host with too many containers

Notice a cute, little thermometer besides the Docker Host. It indicates overload on the system. After all, the containers are isolated processes managed by the Docker daemon on the host. Too many concurrent processes will take a toll on the machine. One way to solve this issue is vertical scaling which means increasing RAM, storage, and/or processing capacity, but that would concentrate the point of errors and failures to a single (physical or virtual) machine.

In the era of distributed computing, it is the most common and efficient solution to have multiple, relatively small instances of the software communicating seamlessly to divide a larger task into smaller, easy-to-monitor threads of operation. Taking this approach to containers introduces us to the concept of **container orchestration**. Just like Containers, the **Concept** of Container Orchestration is more important than a stringent definition. To understand it, look at the following figure:

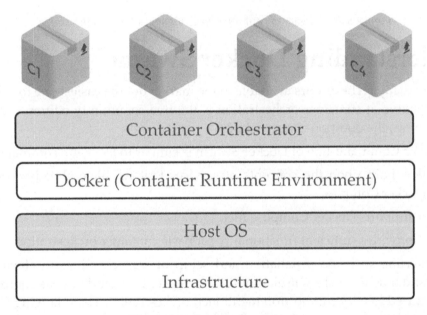

Figure 8.2: *Container orchestrator*

The container orchestrator is a tool (set of integrated programs) running on top of the Container Runtime Environment to manage the deployment, life cycle, and behavior of multiple containers across several hosts. If We had to highlight the most important part of this flexible definition, We would stress on ***multiple containers across the several hosts***. As shown in the following figure, the orchestrator runs all or some of its processes on a number of containers hosts and creates a cluster to deploy a large number of containers without overloading any instance:

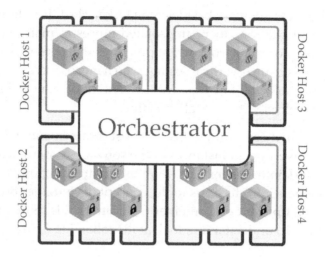

Figure 8.3: A cluster of container hosts managed by an orchestrator

Understanding Docker Swarm

There are many orchestrators available in the market but the easiest one to begin the learning curve of container orchestration is the free community edition of Docker Swarm. Now, the question comes, why?

- The Command-line of Docker Swarm is similar to Docker's command line.
- It is built upon the concepts of services that we have already seen with Docker Compose.
- It supports Docker Compose files.
- It provides sufficient functionality for basic container orchestration.

Before starting with the installation and setup of a Docker Swarm cluster, let's understand how it envelops itself around the Docker hosts and how its components are structured to perform the aforementioned orchestration. The following figure is a good reference:

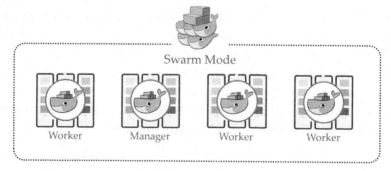

Figure 8.4: Docker Swarm Nodes

Docker Swarm is generally packed alongside Docker in the standard community edition installations (like the one we had followed). We do not have to install separate components (unlike compose). Swarm is inactive by default, so we have to initiate the *"Swarm mode"* to activate it. Since swarm connects Docker hosts into a cluster, there needs to be a hierarchy among the hosts to pass down user requests efficiently. One or more hosts are turned into managers, and the rest are called workers.

The hosts are connected via an overlay network and can be considered nodes of quasi-mesh network topology. Depending on their role (manager or worker), different processes of swarm installation packages are active on these nodes. For example, Managers have Components like Orchestrator, Allocator, Dispatcher, Scheduler, and an API endpoint active, as shown in the following figure:

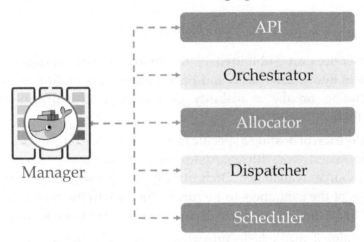

Figure 8.5: *Components of Docker Swarm's Manager*

Each of these components has distinct roles to play in the grand scheme of orchestration.

- **API Endpoint:** This works like the receptionist at an admin office. It listens to the HTTP API requests passed by the client(s) and provided by users and gets back to them with appropriate responses. It also passes the API requests to the corresponding component. As you might have guessed, with every updated version of the swarm; if there are new commands or new flags to the previous commands, API endpoint's definition will also be updated to process or forward the requests.

- **Orchestrator:** Just like Docker Compose, Swarm also deploys containers as services:

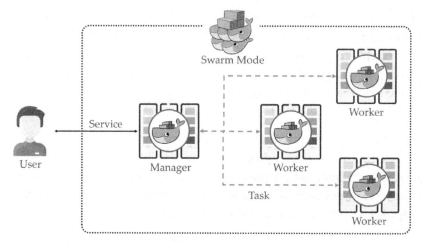

Figure 8.6: Docker Swarm Orchestration Model

The services are submitted to the manager. The manager divides these services into smaller tasks and passes these tasks to different worker nodes depending on the availability of resources to maintain quasi-uniform distribution of load.

The decision of hosting a specific task of the service on a specific node is made by the orchestrator with regards to or regardless of user preferences depending on resource availability. Orchestrator also passes the configurations and details of the containers to be run by the task to the nodes. It does it using **the Dispatcher**. These are well-defined idle tasks waiting to be executed.

- **Scheduler:** The idle tasks provided by the orchestrator receive signals from scheduler to finally get executed. In simple words, the **Orchestrator** decides **where** the containers will run, whereas the **Scheduler** decides **when** they will run. This may sound like an inessential role just added for the simplicity, but when we think of applications at scale, the Scheduler's role becomes even more crucial than the orchestrator as it manages the availability of resources by not allowing tasks to overload the workers during large scale update rollouts or shifting the load from one set of containers to another.

- **Allocator:** We have seen earlier that Docker uses IPs for communication among containers and DNS to tag them. Like how an independent Docker daemon installation creates a default **bridge** network (as seen in *Chapter 6*), swarm installation creates a default bridge network called **docker_gwbridge** on every swarm node and connects them via a default overlay network called **ingress**. To understand this further, look at the following figure:

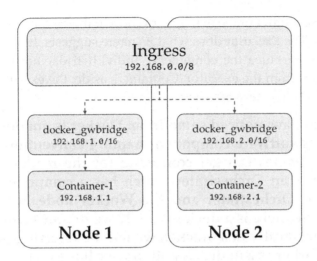

Figure 8.7: Docker Swarm Network Allocation

The **docker_gwbridge** provides IP addresses to containers for communication, while the ingress network provides rules for subnet and allows communication between the containers of the same service on different nodes. To keep things simple, containers of a swarm cluster also communicate (if they need to) via IP addresses; these IP addresses are provided by the Allocator, which keeps the activities of networks in check.

With the components mentions above, the manager handles most of the heavy lifting of orchestration. While not being as heavy, the worker's role is equally essential. It runs containers (tasks) and communicates the status to the manager. To do so, it needs two components, as shown in the following figure:

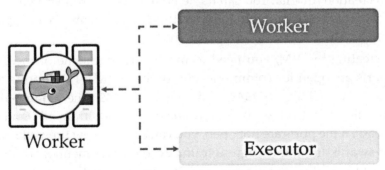

Figure 8.8: Components of Docker Swarm Worker node

The first software component of the Worker node is **the Worker** (*it is just like saying you need apples to make apple pie… trivial but important*). It communicates to the

Dispatcher and **Scheduler** of the manager to check if there is any task to be obtained and/or to be run. The **Executor** does what its name suggests. It runs the tasks (thus creates, runs, and executes the containers). Individual daemons of Docker hosts receive instructions from the executor. Containers aside, the executor also manages other Docker objects like networks and volumes.

Note: You might have noticed something. Docker is not the most creative firm as far as its software component naming convention is concerned; the component names can get confusing for the readers and/or users. Docker Swarm is an Orchestrator which has a component running on managers called Orchestrator and the Worker node has a component called Worker. So, here is a declaration. If we do not mention "software component" specifically in a bracket, we will be referring to Orchestrator as a tool and Worker as a node. As authors, we hope it clears out potential misunderstandings.

Getting started with Docker Swarm

We know, after reading seven beautifully written chapters, you can easily guess that the first step toward getting started with Docker Swarm is… **Installation!**

Unlike Docker installation, this time, we need to fulfill a bunch of pre-requisites as follows:

- We want to make a 3-node swarm cluster with 2 workers and a manager. All of them need to be individual machines or VMs. Make 3 n1-standard Ubuntu VMs on your Google Cloud Platform account. You can refer to chapter 1 for the VM creation tutorial. You can name your VMs according to your naming convention preferences, but to replicate this tutorial, name them "manager", "worker-1", and "worker-2", respectively.

- While creating the VM, you need to make sure that some of the TCP and UDP ports are open for communication (in each VM). These ports are TCP port **2377**, TCP-UDP port **7946**, and UDP port **4789**. The **default-allow-all** firewall rule of GCP allows ingress traffic on all ports from all IP addresses. In any case, if the ports are not open, you can create a new firewall rule called **docker-swarm** and allow ingress traffic on the ports mentioned above. Do not forget to mention the network tag name while creating the VM.

- Install Docker Engine version 1.12 (community) or newer on all the VMs. You can refer to *Chapter 2* for Docker installation Tutorial.

Your GCE VMs page should look something like the following screenshot:

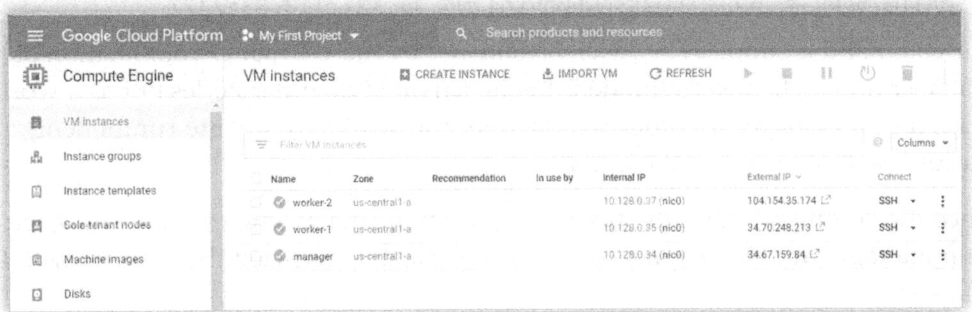

Figure 8.9: A list of VMs ready for Docker Swarm Cluster setup

Once these pre-requisites are fulfilled, you are ready to turn these unrelated VMs into a fully functional Docker Swarm Cluster. As mentioned earlier, Swarm mode already exists in a standard Docker installation; you just have to activate it. One of the VMs voluntarily (in reality, by your command) needs to declare itself as the manager of the cluster, and the other ones can **join** its cluster as the workers.

To create a smooth interface for allowing workers to be able to join, the manager needs to **advertise** its IP address along with a token. This is done using the following command on the manager:

```
docker swarm init --advertise-addr <manager-IP>
```

The part enclosed in angular brackets needs to be replaced by the IP of your desired manager. This command initiates the swarm mode and creates a unique token that remains valid for 24 h. The worker nodes can use this token to create an authentic connection with the manager. The output will be similar to the following screenshot:

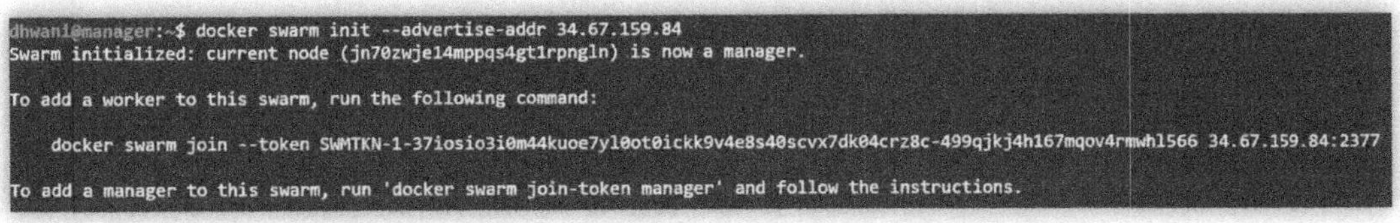

Figure 8.10: Creating a joining token on the manager

The result of the **docker swarm init** command has given us another command. The token generated on your system will be different from mine (that is the whole purpose of the token); just copy the command provided to you on your screen and run it on both of your workers. Again, ensure that the Docker community edition is adequately installed on both worker nodes, just like the manager node.

```
docker swarm join --token SWMTKN-1-2qjiyk37z2mdgy3lyr5aiz6jaisvcser6yu7r
bf50n1lm7mgkk-4jqv8ikcnw2sshw60hvthl2wd 34.121.110.83:2377
```

The command is simple. The token is followed by the **<IP:port>** combination of the manager node. The Swarm mode is being activated on other nodes but as a worker instead of a manager. In other words, only the worker (software component) and executor will be active on these machines.

Once the command has run successfully on both the machines, **navigate back to your manager node's terminal** to check if the cluster has listed the workers with the following command:

```
docker node ls
```

This command lists out available nodes on the swarm cluster with their availability, status, and other important information such as ID (used by Docker to identify the nodes) and numerical version of Docker installation. The outcome of the above command looks like the following screenshot:

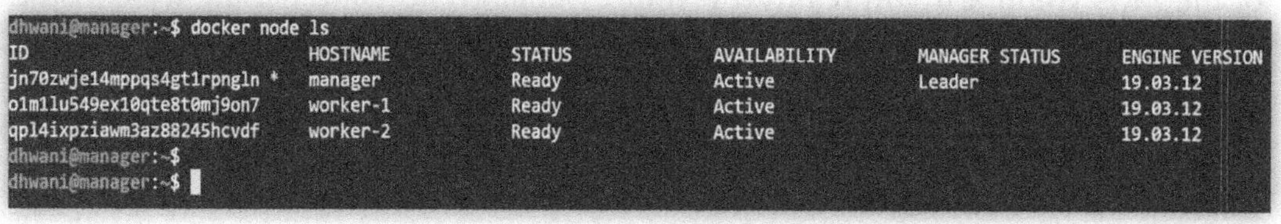

Figure 8.11: Listing out nodes on the swarm cluster

The asterisk adjacent to the manager's ID is to indicate the current node or the node you are operating from. The **STATUS** indicates successful enrollment of the nodes in the cluster, while the availability is a stat for the scheduler of the manager. **Active** indicates that the nodes are available to accept scheduled containers. Situationally, it can also be **Pause** indicating an unwillingness to accept new tasks but maintaining the running of current containers or **Drain,** which means it has shut down the existing tasks and is not accepting new ones either. We will encounter them later in this chapter.

MANAGER STATUS is a special column. It represents the role of every node in the cluster. **No value** indicates **workers** that don't participate in the cluster management. These nodes serve the simple yet essential purpose of running the container tasks (*that is why you have a cluster in the first place, right!?*). The possible values are Leader, Reachable and Unavailable. The leader is, as its name suggests, the primary manager of the cluster (the one who initiated it). It handles most of the orchestration management tasks for the cluster.

Apart from the Manager, both of our nodes are workers so they cannot attain the Reachable or Unavailable values. We can promote one or more of them as managers for fault tolerance. There are possibilities of a leader node going down, if there are no backup managers, the cluster is as good as gone.

On the other hand, if you are using cloud VMs with ephemeral IPs, your Manager's IP will have changed within 24 h or so, which makes adding new nodes difficult. It is recommended to give permanent (static) IPs to the managers when using Swarm for production *(it is okay to stick to ephemeral IPs for learning purpose; save money/credits)*. If the leader goes down, the rest of the managers perform a mini election to pick a new leader. This process of obtaining majority votes is called **Quorum.** To make sure managers do not end up having a tie, it is recommended to maintain odd numbers of managers in the cluster.

Orchestration itself is a resource-consuming process. It is important for the manager to have enough resources (aside from the containers it might already be managing) to replace the leader efficiently. If enough resources are available, the manager's status becomes reachable, and it can advertise its token and get requests from other workers. In an otherwise scenario, the manager would be Unavailable. It means it cannot communicate with other managers and thus cannot put his vote of acceptance.

Let us rephrase the requirements. It is recommended to have an odd number of reachable managers to perform a successful quorum if the leader goes down. Based on first come first serve, one of the reachable managers advertises its willingness and availability to become the leader if the current leader is out of communication. The other reachable leaders send their confirmation and take back the backup position.

If the leader stops sending heartbeat signals to other managers, backup managers perform another election to choose a new leader. On a large-scale cluster, this process keeps going if multiple leaders go down over time. The algorithm used to perform such a quorum is called the **Raft Consensus** *(to put it simply, Raft Consensus is Democracy meets Meritocracy)*. If we want to inspect the cluster in-depth, we can use the command below on the leader node.

```
docker node inspect --pretty self
```

This is another variant of the **docker node** command that lists information about the mentioned node at the end. You can ask for information about one or more nodes by providing their hostname or IDs and you will have a result like the following screenshot:

```
dhwani@manager:~$ docker node inspect --pretty self
ID:                     jn70zwje14mppqs4gt1rpngln
Hostname:               manager
Joined at:              2020-09-08 10:53:09.664287722 +0000 utc
Status:
 State:                 Ready
 Availability:          Active
 Address:               34.67.159.84
Manager Status:
 Address:               34.67.159.84:2377
 Raft Status:           Reachable
 Leader:                Yes
Platform:
 Operating System:      linux
 Architecture:          x86_64
Resources:
 CPUs:                  1
 Memory:                3.597GiB
Plugins:
 Log:           awslogs, fluentd, gcplogs, gelf, journald, json-file, local, logentries, splunk, syslog
 Network:               bridge, host, ipvlan, macvlan, null, overlay
 Volume:                local
Engine Version:         19.03.12
TLS Info:
 TrustRoot:
-----BEGIN CERTIFICATE-----
MIIBajCCARCgAwIBAgIUWJdxvJaVjxZ5w8/MFJRlCcHh4FEwCgYIKoZIzj0EAwIw
EzERMA8GA1UEAxMIc3dhcm0tY2EwHhcNMjAwOTA4MTA0ODAwWhcNNDAwOTAzMTA0
ODAwWjATMREwDwYDVQQDEwhzd2FybS1jYTBZMBMGByqGSM49AgEGCCqGSM49AwEH
A0IABMbsGK+cEggVhQx5u1dfUnN4z3OefU3uiqlPAUHT5ReOeq8ErSQEAG1RQas/
TbrloQjf1U4+3J57N7P9gGBwKzqjQjBAMA4GA1UdDwEB/wQEAwIBBjAPBgNVHRMB
Af8EBTADAQH/MB0GA1UdDgQWBBSu/3BO7TZkjaDxqe/wETvRWzg9VTAKBggqhkjO
PQQDAgNIADBFAiArMJUmWZuKKx3d6L5me2GAMrJ6b3sp64/DJtqjJOQMdAIhAPez
JvSZm/RNlHdcjTH42RxpGWwGda3pkl7iHKQgEaO5
-----END CERTIFICATE-----
```

***Figure 8.12:** Output of manager node inspection*

The output is pretty printed as we had requested in the command. Apart from the information that we already know or have looked into earlier, it gives a reference to Raft consensus by expanding the status to **Raft Status**. We have been also provided with the system infrastructure followed by a supported logging agent, network-volume objects, and TLS certificate. At the bottom of the output, we get information about the issuer of the TLS certificate.

Working with Docker Swarm

What could possibly be better than getting hands-on with a newly created fresh juicy swarm cluster? Nothing.

Let us start by deploying a service on the cluster. Services can only be deployed through the managers so, make sure you are on one. To deploy a redis container service, run the following command:

```
docker service create --name redis-swarm redis
```

Unlike interacting with Docker Daemon directly, the swarm interface skips printing a lot of details on the terminal and focuses on results much like a higher abstraction tool should. With a unique service ID below the command, the output should look something like the following screenshot:

```
dhwani@manager:~$ docker service create --name redis-swarm redis
o2go7hr6v6f8muhrqaf3dqjjd
overall progress: 1 out of 1 tasks
1/1: running   [==================================================>]
verify: Service converged
dhwani@manager:~$
dhwani@manager:~$ ▮
```

Figure 8.13: Creating a swarm service

In any case, if you are wondering what happens if you run this command on one of the workers, you might encounter the following error:

Error response from daemon: This node is not a swarm manager. Worker nodes can't be used to view or modify cluster state. Please run this command on a manager node or promote the current node to a manager.

(But why did the author type out the response? Wouldn't putting a screenshot have been more authentic? Yes, it would have been. This is what happens when you add content during proofreading :p)

We can also list out the services with the following command, just how we used to list images and containers previously:

```
docker service ls
```

The output of this command will list the services and its other parameters like a truncated service ID, service name, mode, number of replicas, utilized Docker Image, and ports if exposed any as shown in the following screenshot:

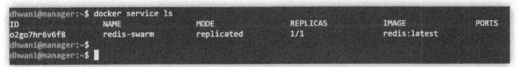

Figure 8.14: Listing out the Swarm services

The **MODE** column shows the value called **replicated**. Another possible value is **global**. Replicated services create desired (user-defined) replicas of each container, while global services run one replica of the container on each node. Global services are useful for daemon processes like logging agents, while replicated services are used to deploy workloads.

We can go a step deeper to list out the tasks running inside services with the following command:

```
docker service ps redis-swarm
```

The result of the above command is a well-arranged list of running tasks of the target service, as shown in the following screenshot:

Figure 8.15: Listing out tasks of a Swarm Service

The output begins with a truncated task ID. Docker takes care of task naming by simply putting a numeric identifier preceded by a dot following the service name. Then, we have the image used, the node on which the task is scheduled, states of the task (*what does the user desire vs what swarm is doing, which is the same thing in this case*). There are two more columns listing errors during the execution of the task and the port exposed. Both are empty for this task.

We can go another layer deeper and list the containers running by the task with the same old **docker ps** command as shown follows:

```
docker service ps redis-swarm
```

Since these are newly created VMs, we do not have any containers running prior to the redis service as shown in the following screenshot:

Figure 8.16: Listing out containers

Moving further, we can also inspect the service using the following command, just like the container and other objects of the Docker toolchain:

```
docker service inspect redis-swarm
```

Much like other inspect commands, this one also returns a lot of information (unless demanded some specific parameters using the format flag), and we are going to interpret all of them.

The entire output is encapsulated in a closed bracket, and individual parameters are grouped by relevance under curly brackets.

The first information is the service ID, the expanded version of the truncated ID we received from **docker services ps** command, as shown in the following screenshot:

```
dhwani@manager:~$ docker service inspect redis-swarm
[
    {
        "ID": "o2go7hr6v6f8muhrqaf3dqjjd",
        "Version": {
            "Index": 21
        },
        "CreatedAt": "2020-09-08T12:38:55.291410323Z",
        "UpdatedAt": "2020-09-08T12:38:55.291410323Z",
        "Spec": {
            "Name": "redis-swarm",
            "Labels": {},
            "TaskTemplate": {
                "ContainerSpec": {
                    "Image": "redis:latest@sha256:933c6c01829165885ea8468d87f71127b1cb76a711311e6c63708097e92ee3d1",
                    "Init": false,
                    "StopGracePeriod": 10000000000,
                    "DNSConfig": {},
                    "Isolation": "default"
                },
                "Resources": {
                    "Limits": {},
                    "Reservations": {}
                },
                "RestartPolicy": {
                    "Condition": "any",
                    "Delay": 5000000000,
                    "MaxAttempts": 0
                },
```

Figure 8.17: *Inspecting a Swarm Service (Part 1)*

The ID is followed by the version index of Docker and the timestamps of service creation and update. We also get a service specification that contains service metadata and container details. The container details, resource limitations, and restart policies are encapsulated under a task template since the containers are controlled by a task.

The task template is followed by orderly Placement preference displaying combinations of architecture and OS as shown in the following screenshot:

```
                "Placement": {
                    "Platforms": [
                        {
                            "Architecture": "amd64",
                            "OS": "linux"
                        },
                        {
                            "Architecture": "amd64",
                            "OS": "linux"
                        },
                        {
                            "OS": "linux"
                        },
                        {
                            "OS": "linux"
                        },
                        {
                            "Architecture": "arm64",
                            "OS": "linux"
                        },
                        {
                            "Architecture": "386",
                            "OS": "linux"
                        },
                        {
                            "Architecture": "mips64le",
                            "OS": "linux"
                        },
                        {
                            "Architecture": "ppc64le",
                            "OS": "linux"
                        },
                        {
                            "Architecture": "s390x",
                            "OS": "linux"
                        }
                    ]
                },
```

Figure 8.18: *Inspecting a Swarm Service (Part 2)*

The service has not been forcefully updated anytime and is being performed by a CRE. Then, we have the service mode as replicated with one replica as we had seen earlier with the **docker services ls** command.

Next are the service update and rollback configurations. Think of them as the controller of your gaming console. The controller remains the same, but the results change depending on the game. Similarly, the same set of configuration's different values define the behavior of service update and rollback process.

Parallelism defines how many tasks will be updated or rolled back simultaneously; value 1 indicates the service containers will be updated or rolled back one by one. If the process gets interrupted or fails for some reason, the pause value of **FailureAction** field indicates that update or rollback will be paused till the issue is solved.

Both processes also have a monitor field that indicates a timer before swarm starts to monitor the update or rollback for the failure. Typically, it is set to **5000000000**. Before you lose faith in me as an author, let me clarify that 5000000000 is denoted in ns or nanoseconds which basically means 5 s (*Why didn't they mention it so? All they had to print was ns right?*).

The next one, **MaxFailureRatio,** indicates the failure of updates or rollbacks to tolerate.

Finally, **Order** can have one of the two values. If it is set to "stop first" (default), it will stop the service first before updating it or rolling back. But if it is set to "start first", it will start the updated service before stopping the previous one. These fields and their value can be seen in the following figure:

```
"Mode": {
    "Replicated": {
        "Replicas": 1
    }
},
"UpdateConfig": {
    "Parallelism": 1,
    "FailureAction": "pause",
    "Monitor": 5000000000,
    "MaxFailureRatio": 0,
    "Order": "stop-first"
},
"RollbackConfig": {
    "Parallelism": 1,
    "FailureAction": "pause",
    "Monitor": 5000000000,
    "MaxFailureRatio": 0,
    "Order": "stop-first"
},
"EndpointSpec": {
    "Mode": "vip"
}
},
"Endpoint": {
    "Spec": {}
}
}
```

Figure 8.19: Inspecting a Swarm Service (Part 3)

We have seen in a couple of results that the service we created has only one instance of redis container running. Let us scale it up to 4 using the following command:

```
docker service scale redis-swarm=4
```

This command works on one or more services. If you want to scale more services, just use **service-name=number-of-replicas** following the **docker service scale** command. The output of the above command, along with listing the service tasks, is shown in the following screenshot:

```
dhwani@manager:~$ docker service scale redis-swarm=4
redis-swarm scaled to 4
overall progress: 4 out of 4 tasks
1/4: running   [==================================================>]
2/4: running   [==================================================>]
3/4: running   [==================================================>]
4/4: running   [==================================================>]
verify: Service converged
dhwani@manager:~$
dhwani@manager:~$ docker service ps redis-swarm
ID             NAME            IMAGE           NODE       DESIRED STATE   CURRENT STATE            ERROR
1bvnu7hss9v8   redis-swarm.1   redis:latest    manager    Running         Running 32 minutes ago
d2k7tmkoqf2u   redis-swarm.2   redis:latest    worker-2   Running         Running 11 seconds ago
7i0s16aqwg5u   redis-swarm.3   redis:latest    worker-1   Running         Running 11 seconds ago
oen5fks1agtl   redis-swarm.4   redis:latest    worker-2   Running         Running 11 seconds ago
```

Figure 8.20: Scaling a Swarm Service

We will play with more services and perform other orchestration tasks but before that, it is important to understand the binding element of nodes under swarm mode.

Understanding networking in Docker Swarm

We have seen earlier that an overlay network named ingress and bridge networks called **docker_gwbridge** are created when we activate swarm mode. If we do not connect a container to any user-defined overlay network, Swarm connects it to the ingress network by default to provide configurations for control and data traffic.

Just like other network objects, we can list these networks to get a better picture *(no pun intended)* and you can witness the result in the following screenshot:

```
docker network ls
```

```
dhwani@manager:~$ docker network ls
NETWORK ID     NAME              DRIVER    SCOPE
f794395f0003   bridge            bridge    local
3989bbd425e7   docker_gwbridge   bridge    local
9b097fb52a4c   host              host      local
2y01hqaxey9b   ingress           overlay   swarm
80db484cf2f3   none              null      local
dhwani@manager:~$
dhwani@manager:~$
```

Figure 8.21: Listing out networks on a swarm node

This screenshot indicates that the Docker community edition installation created to host, none, and bridge (default) networks, whereas the swarm mode activation created another couple of networks named ingress and **docker_gwbridge**.

The redis service container (which we have created a bit earlier) is connected to the default overlay network, whereas the nodes in swarm mode communicate via **docker_gwbridge** network. You will get the same stack of networks on worker-1 and worker-2 as well. Let's create a new user-defined overlay network on the manager using the following command:

```
docker network create \
 --driver overlay \
 --subnet=10.15.0.0/16 \
 --gateway=10.15.0.2 \
 --opt encrypted \
 --attachable \
 my-swarm-net
```

This will create an encrypted and attachable overlay network named **my-swarm-net** using the subnet and the aforementioned subnet range and gateway IP. The attachable flag allows services and standalone containers to connect to this network.

Yes, you can also connect containers outside the scope of the swarm cluster to this network, but it is not recommended for genuine security concerns *(reminder: containers on the same network can communicate with one another)*. The output will look something like the following screenshot *(getting a dollar for every time we write this line should get you some decent wireless earbuds)*:

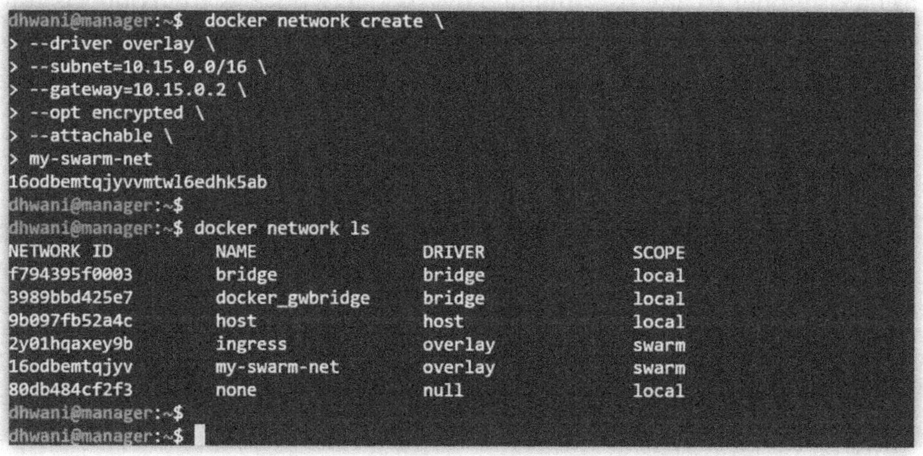

Figure 8.22: Creating a user-defined swarm network

The output of the above command returns the network ID and the newly created overlay network, which can be viewed by listing the available networks again. Since we have created this network, it is time to make it useful. We can create a service and connect it to the my-swarm-net overlay network to see if it gets the port exposure required to serve the client request.

For this example, we are choosing the Nginx webserver which can be deployed using the following command. This could feel a bit redundant but make sure you run the command on the manager.

```
docker service create --name nginx-swarm \
--constraint node.role!=manager \
--label testGroup=A1 \
--mount type=volume,source=nginx-vol-swarm,destination=/etc/nginx \
--network my-swarm-net \
--replicas 3 \
--replicas-max-per-node 2 \
--restart-max-attempts 3 \
--publish 8080:80 \
--update-parallelism 2 \
nginx
```

Notice that we are doing a lot with this command. Apart from deploying a service connected to a user-defined overlay network; we are also requesting a volume for storage and providing its mounting details. On top of that, we have also passed the preferences on how many maximum containers do we intend to be scheduled on a single node. This is with respect to this particular service. If any node already has an existing container, the service can still schedule 2 Nginx replicas on it since the replicas-max-per-node is set to 2 (*Why is it not max-replicas-per-node? we guess we will never know… development decisions*).

We are instructing to expose the container's port **80** to host's port **8080** on each task, respectively. We have seen the meaning of update parallelism while inspecting the redis service, and in this case, it is set to 2. If the containers fail for some reason, the service will restart after 3 unsuccessful recovery attempts (*this is where the volume is useful*).

We have added a metadata label (*testGroup=A1 doesn't mean anything in this context, we just wanted it to look legitimate, you can put any key=value pair of your choice*) for future orchestration purposes. Most importantly, this service has a constraint. In other words, the scheduler cannot put the containers on whichever node it wants to because we have specifically instructed it not to schedule the service tasks on the manager.

The direct question is, what if placing the tasks on the manager is the only choice? Different orchestrators can have different approaches on how to handle such a situation (*ahem, foreshadowing something… keep reading the book, and you will find out in a few chapters*); swarm chooses to let the user preference take utmost priority and fails the service if the other two nodes are not available.

The command will behave similarly to the **redis service** command despite of all of the configurations. It will return the service ID and the status of the service having converged successfully. It will not return any information about the port or the volume so you will have to inspect it yourself.

The output of the command will resemble the following screenshot:

```
dhwani@manager:~$ docker service create --name nginx-swarm \
> --constraint node.role!=manager \
> --label testGroup=A1 \
> --mount type=volume,source=nginx-vol-swarm,destination=/etc/nginx \
> --network my-swarm-net \
> --replicas 3 \
> --replicas-max-per-node 2 \
> --restart-max-attempts 3 \
> --publish 8080:80 \
> --update-parallelism 2 \
> nginx
jgovgivfqayizxamt2obvbxhz
overall progress: 3 out of 3 tasks
1/3: running   [==============================================>]
2/3: running   [==============================================>]
3/3: running   [==============================================>]
verify: Service converged
dhwani@manager:~$
dhwani@manager:~$
```

Figure 8.23: Connecting service to the user-defined overlay

List the service using the same command as earlier, as shown in the following screenshot:

```
dhwani@manager:~$ docker service ls
ID              NAME            MODE          REPLICAS              IMAGE            PORTS
jgovgivfqayi    nginx-swarm     replicated    3/3 (max 2 per node)  nginx:latest     *:8080->80/tcp
o2go7hr6v6f8    redis-swarm     replicated    4/4                   redis:latest
dhwani@manager:~$
```

Figure 8.24: Listing the new replicated service

The replicas column also shows the other instruction of having a maximum of 2 tasks per node. Unlike the last service, the port column does show an exposure value. Let's list out the tasks of this service as shown in the screenshot below to observe the container scheduling choices made by the swarm under our constraints:

```
dhwani@manager:~$ docker service ps nginx-swarm
ID              NAME             IMAGE            NODE        DESIRED STATE    CURRENT STATE                    ERROR
4kug1v8qmiq2    nginx-swarm.1    nginx:latest     worker-1    Running          Running about a minute ago
0zaax1wewmhu    nginx-swarm.2    nginx:latest     worker-2    Running          Running about a minute ago
pn15jcf347hk    nginx-swarm.3    nginx:latest     worker-1    Running          Running about a minute ago
dhwani@manager:~$
dhwani@manager:~$
```

Figure 8.25: Observing nginx replica scheduling

There are no replicas scheduled on the manager node. Also, neither worker-1 nor worker-2 can have more than 2 replicas, and this looks perfect! You can also inspect the IP addresses, subnet, network, and volume details. Since we have come this far, let's not see off the topic without looking at the ever so familiar nginx welcome page!

Since the containers are scheduled on worker-1 and worker-2, copy either of their external IP address and hit the `<IP>:<port>` combination in your browser to get the output as shown in the following screenshot:

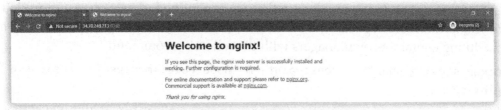

Figure 8.26: nginx default welcome page

Container orchestration

While there are many tightly and loosely written "technical" definitions of orchestration, the word itself comes from orchestras… multiple musicians playing instruments of different groups (woodwind, brass, percussion, and so on) to create relatively more impactful harmony. When we take this concept to computer science, the fundamentals remain the same with adjusted context.

In this case, containers from different functional groups of applications such as front-end, back-end, or daemon are **orchestrated** to achieve cost-efficient and smooth overall application performance. But you already know this, even if you didn't; the definition did not feel surprised at all… did it?

At this point in your learning curve, the important part is witnessing and practicing container orchestration. Deploying a service is just a tiny part of the entire orchestration spectrum. Citing a popular phrase, making something work is not as difficult as making sure it keeps working. The same logic applies to software too. Deploying or shipping software is not as prone to glitches as performing server-wide bug fixes, update rollouts, load balancing, scaling, etc. Gladly, the container orchestrators are designed and built to take away most of the burden from your shoulders. All you have to do is, learn how to call simple APIs (in this case via commands) to perform your desired operations.

Updating services

Take update rollouts and rollbacks for an instance. They are a pervasive part of a system admin's work routine. Rollbacks are not just used if the update is critically unstable; they can also be used to shift back from an environment for testing a new feature or architecture to the regular one. In traditional admin workflow, rolling out updates or rolling them back requires setting up VMs of target configurations, routing the load (traffic) to them, turning off the current configuration VMs and eventually clean them up. With Docker Swarm, you can do all of this with just one simple command.

Let us try it out on the nginx service that we ran in the last section. As an update, we will add 3 more replicas and remove the constraint that stops the swarm from scheduling containers on managers with the following command:

```
docker service update --constraint-rm 'node.role!=manager' --repicas=6
nginx-swarm
```

This command should increase the number of nginx replicas to 6, with some of them even scheduled on the manager. To view the results, run:

```
docker service ps nginx-swarm
```

The outcome of the preceding commands mentioned is shown in the following screenshot:

```
dhwani@manager:~$ docker service update --constraint-rm 'node.role!=manager' --replicas=6 nginx-swarm
nginx-swarm
overall progress: 6 out of 6 tasks
1/6: running   [==================================================>]
2/6: running   [==================================================>]
3/6: running   [==================================================>]
4/6: running   [==================================================>]
5/6: running   [==================================================>]
6/6: running   [==================================================>]
verify: Service converged
dhwani@manager:~$
dhwani@manager:~$ docker service ps nginx-swarm
ID             NAME            IMAGE          NODE       DESIRED STATE   CURRENT STATE            ERROR
4kug1v8qmiq2   nginx-swarm.1   nginx:latest   worker-1   Running        Running 16 minutes ago
0zaaxlwewmhu   nginx-swarm.2   nginx:latest   worker-2   Running        Running 16 minutes ago
pn15jcf347hk   nginx-swarm.3   nginx:latest   worker-1   Running        Running 16 minutes ago
uy3haf5v3ym4   nginx-swarm.4   nginx:latest   worker-2   Running        Running 36 seconds ago
av7ta3y1is7z   nginx-swarm.5   nginx:latest   manager    Running        Running 32 seconds ago
wokvio5b5ite   nginx-swarm.6   nginx:latest   manager    Running        Running 32 seconds ago
dhwani@manager:~$
dhwani@manager:~$
```

Figure 8.27: Updating the service

In this example, we have performed two orchestration tasks simultaneously: scaling service and updating a cluster. Now, let us try rolling back the newly created replicas with the following command:

```
docker service update --rollback nginx-swarm
```

Execution of the preceding command restores the service to 3 replicas, and the result is as shown in the following screenshot:

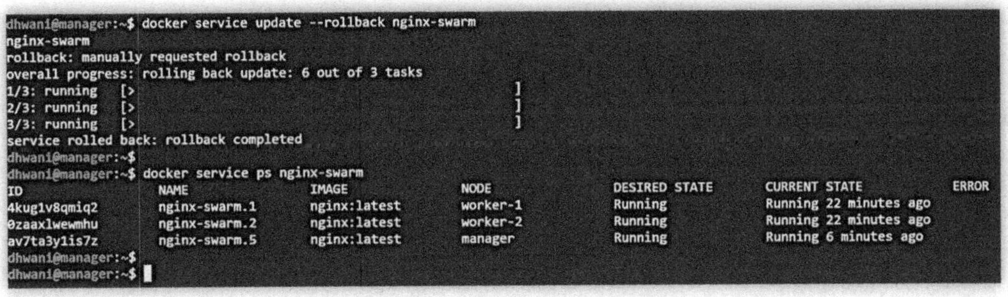

Figure 8.28: rolling the service back

If you pay close attention, you will realize that the rollback is not absolute. All the command did was to adjust the number of replicas. The task **nginx-swarm.5** is still here, and **nginx-swarm.3** is gone. Different orchestrators have different behavior under such circumstances, but this is how swarm operates.

On top of that, the constraint on the manager has also not returned. This is because the constraint is a cluster-level API whereas rollback is a service-level API. If you want the service to be more "like before" you can put the constraint on the manager and manually remove the container from it. The new container will be scheduled on either of the two workers.

Node management

Let us test more of the cluster-level orchestration. Currently, our cluster has one Manager and two workers. The workers can be promoted to managers with the following command:

```
docker node promote worker-1
```

This command will promote **worker-1** as can be seen in the following output screenshot when we get a list of nodes:

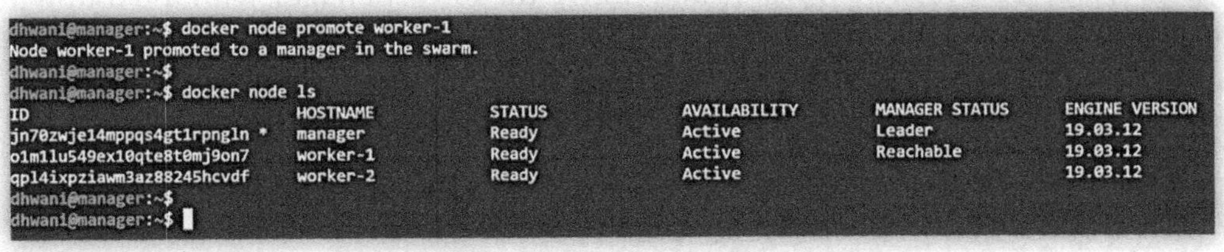

Figure 8.29: Promoting worker-1 to manager

Now, we have two nodes with the role of manager with **worker-1** gaining the reachable manager status. It means it is available to participate in the quorum if the leader goes down. Another case where **worker-1** will automatically become the leader is if the manager is demoted with the following command:

```
docker node demote manager
```

The manager will be demoted and apart from the text confirmation, we can also verify it by calling a manager API (such as listing nodes) as shown in the following screenshot:

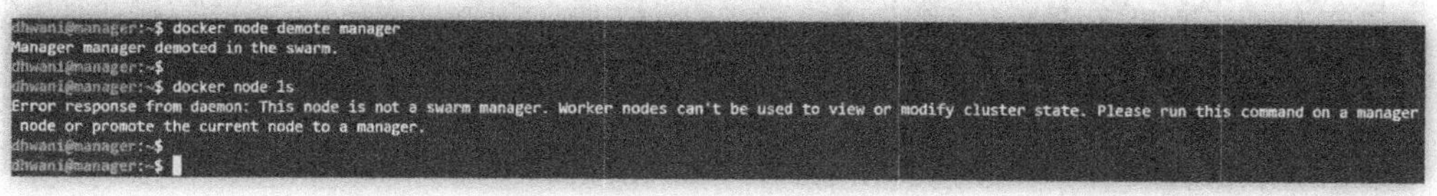

Figure 8.30: Demoting Manager

Since the manager node has now turned into a worker, we cannot perform any orchestration-related tasks from it. For now, SSH into the VM named **worker-1** and run the same command to list the nodes to see it working. Execute **docker node ls** commands, and its outcome should look like the following screenshot:

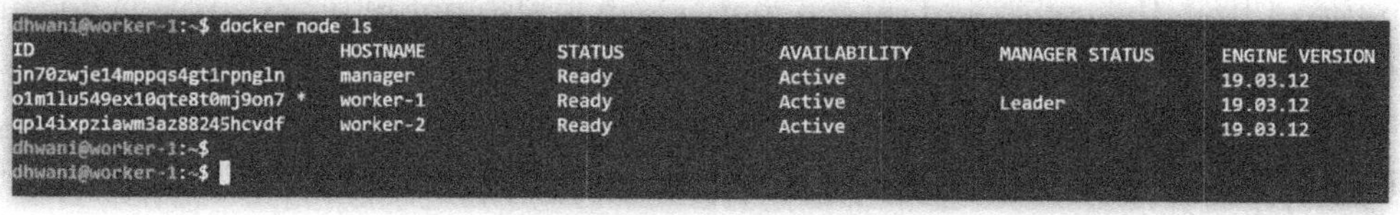

Figure 8.31: The new leader

You might be wondering, what happens if we try to demote the current leader (since there is no reachable manager to take its place)? The best way to find out is to try it hands-on as shown in the following screenshot:

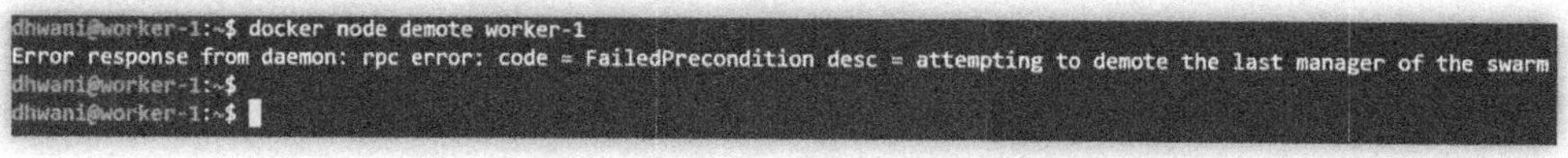

Figure 8.32: Trying to demote the only manager

As expected, swarm cluster is not irresponsible enough to demote the only manager. We get a similar error when we try to remove the only manager with the following command as well! Let us try to remove this node using the following command and see the result in the following screenshot:

```
docker node rm worker-1
```

Figure 8.33: Trying to remove the only manager

We are getting an error response here: "The node is a cluster manager and is a member of the raft cluster. It must be demoted to the worker before removal."

Great, we cannot demote the only manager, neither can we remove it from the cluster. This means the cluster does not get compromised unless there is an overloading or infrastructure level glitch, right? No. Though the only remaining manager cannot kick itself or demote itself, it can leave the cluster by user instruction. Just like **docker swarm join**, use **docker swarm leave** followed by the node name to leave the cluster as shown in the following screenshot:

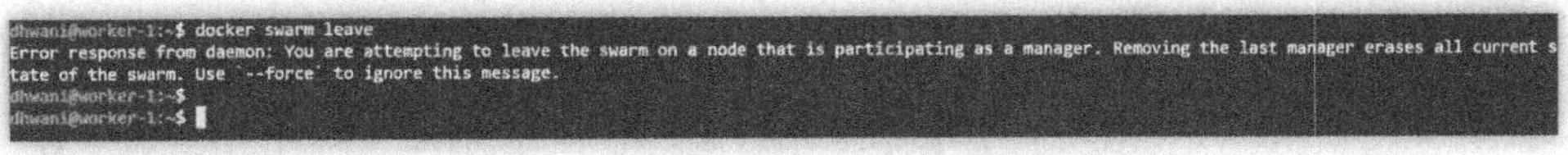

Figure 8.34: Making the only manager leave the cluster

Docker does not fulfill the request, but it gives a hint to use **--force flag**. So, why not?

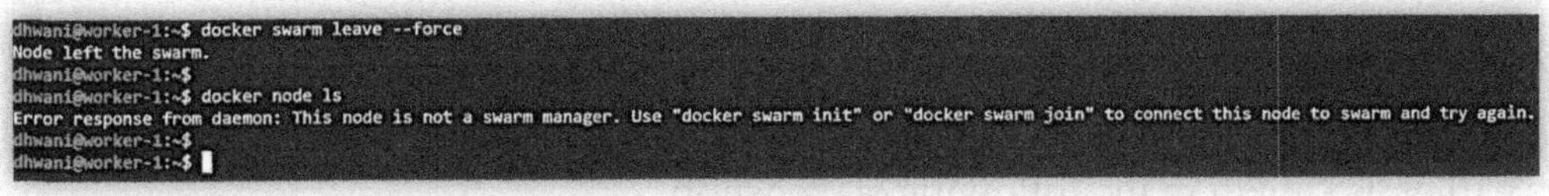

Figure 8.35: Making the only manager leave by force

The cluster is as good as non-existent. The worker nodes are trying to reach out to the manager, but there is no manager node available in the cluster. As a user, you cannot promote any worker nodes due to a lack of administrative privileges of the cluster. This is nothing short of a disaster; let us see how to manage it. There are two ways to handling such situations. We will learn the straightforward one first.

Reinitializing the cluster

You need to initiate a new swarm cluster. But it is not that simple. Using the **init** command with the Docker Swarm invokes the manager components. Force leaving a node does not invalidate the previously active components. The nodes are not missing the objects; just some of the objects are missing the required privileges. This situation is called the quorum failure (inability to elect a new leader) which we need to address while re-initiating the cluster.

Since most of the readers are likely to be on worker-1, let us use that as the leader of our new Swarm cluster and make the other nodes join using the following command. This will remove all of the data from the previous cluster from all of the nodes:

```
docker swarm init --force-new-cluster --advertise-addr <node-IP>
```

```
dhwani@worker-1:~$ docker swarm init --force-new-cluster --advertise-addr 34.70.248.213
Swarm initialized: current node (mmqxgnfzs72tmkkfdznqqacbt) is now a manager.

To add a worker to this swarm, run the following command:

    docker swarm join --token SWMTKN-1-12ih1awax62sbl92ut4zc7olf1xmapvzlhy2nvl6z2ruo42toq-coai24ydsf03acoxqyd8bs4vy 34.70.248.213:2377

To add a manager to this swarm, run 'docker swarm join-token manager' and follow the instructions.
```

Figure 8.36: Reinitializing the swarm cluster

The `--force-new-cluster` flag removes the user-defined services and other objects and starts a fresh cluster with previously attached nodes. Thus, the other two nodes have joined automatically. You can verify it by listing the nodes from the leader, as shown in the following screenshot:

```
dhwani@worker-1:~$ docker node ls
ID                            HOSTNAME    STATUS    AVAILABILITY    MANAGER STATUS    ENGINE VERSION
bj25nlyuc1ml2szdvdug9owyx     manager     Ready     Active                            19.03.12
mmqxgnfzs72tmkkfdznqqacbt *   worker-1    Ready     Active          Leader            19.03.12
y8g9918gk99nlc6x9ge20dil7     worker-2    Ready     Active                            19.03.12
dhwani@worker-1:~$
```

Figure 8.37: Listing out the nodes of the new cluster

You are free to use the join command to add new nodes to the cluster. We can also test the cluster by trying to run a new redis replicated service with the same commands as earlier as shown in the following screenshot:

```
dhwani@worker-1:~$ docker service create --name redis-swarm --mode global redis:latest
zm9sx94e1acam6zs35gijxd1s
overall progress: 3 out of 3 tasks
y8g9918gk99n: running   [==================================================>]
bj25nlyuc1ml: running   [==================================================>]
mmqxgnfzs72t: running   [==================================================>]
verify: Service converged
dhwani@worker-1:~$
dhwani@worker-1:~$ docker service ps redis-swarm
ID              NAME                                              IMAGE           NODE        DESIRED STATE    CURRENT STATE
                PORTS
v2wonlt2zthc    redis-swarm.y8g9918gk99nlc6x9ge20dil7             redis:latest    worker-2    Running          Running 53 seconds ago

zi0sz5yeodqg    redis-swarm.bj25nlyuc1ml2szdvdug9owyx             redis:latest    manager     Running          Running 53 seconds ago

swka0he76a63    redis-swarm.mmqxgnfzs72tmkkfdznqqacbt             redis:latest    worker-1    Running          Running 53 seconds ago
```

Figure 8.38: Testing the cluster with a redis service

This definitely "worked" but deep down, we all know that you cannot afford to lose all your services and their data and other objects in production settings. That is why there are two ways to deal with quorum failure disaster. Let us take a look at the other one.

Back-up and recovery of the cluster

To ensure we don't lose an abundance of progress, we can back-up the cluster at a specific timestamp and recover it under a critical situation. This is a pretty common practice with database servers or just VMs in general. The question is, what does swarm back up?

We have seen earlier that most of the decisions taken by the manager components of swarm *(such as scheduler, allocator, dispatcher, orchestrator)* intend to match the current state of the cluster to the desired state. The term state is broadly inclusive as it covers configurations, objects, and data. Swarm saves the **cluster state** at the time the backup API is invoked.

The only condition for the backup process to work is that the cluster should have recommended amount of nodes as managers to perform the quorum *(more than half of the total nodes should be managers; just one remaining manager voting itself doesn't make quorum useful)*.

In our cluster of 3 nodes, we need to have at least two managers. Let us promote the old manager with the following command:

```
docker node promote manager
```

Once the manager is promoted as the manager *(ouch… terrible naming conventions are infectious)*, as shown in the following screenshot, we can move forward with the backup process:

Figure 8.39: Maintaining Quorum requirements

Let us back up the cluster following the below process step-by-step:

1. The first step is not mandatory, but it is recommended. We need to stop the Docker service before taking the backup to make sure the state of the cluster does not change while we are backing it up. In case you do not stop the service, it is called a "hot backup".

   Make sure you are on the leader and run the following command:

   ```
   sudo systemctl stop docker
   ```

   Gain root privileges using sudo su *(or su -i or su -s depending on your faith)*, as shown in the following screenshot:

Figure 8.40: Swarm cluster backup step 1 and 2

2. As wise developers say, ***Everything in Linux is a File***. Your intended backup is also present in arranged files under **/var/lib/Docker/swarm** directory. Just perform **ls** command to list out the contents of **swarm** directory, as shown in the following screenshot:

```
root@worker-1:/var/lib/docker# ls swarm/
certificates  docker-state.json  raft  state.json  worker
root@worker-1:/var/lib/docker#
root@worker-1:/var/lib/docker#
```

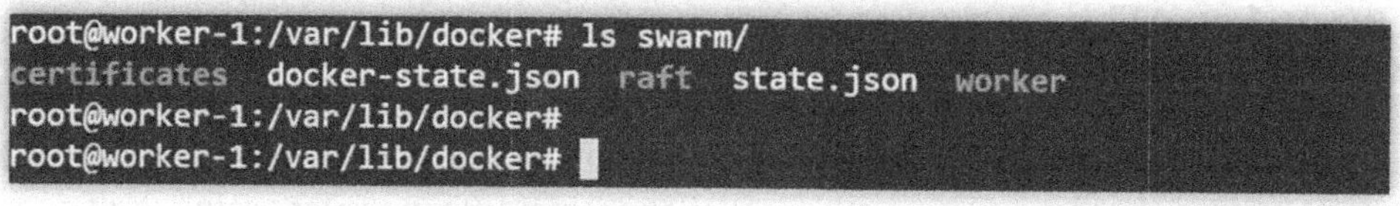

Figure 8.41: Content under swarm directory

The **/swarm** directory has certificates, state variables in JSON format, quorum information under **/raft** directory and worker nodes' information under **/worker** directory. The question is, what do we want to back up? Simple, all of it!

3. The previous navigation was just for the learning purpose. You can head back to the home directory (still under root privileges) and make a new directory called **swarm-backup** for saving the backup. Copy the content of /var/lib/docker/swarm into this directory with the following commands:

```
mkdir swarm-backup

cp -r /var/lib/docker/swarm/  /home/<user>/swarm-backup
```

As always, you can verify the contents of the copied directory with ls as shown in the following screenshot:

```
root@worker-1:/home/dhwani# cp -r /var/lib/docker/swarm/  /home/dhwani/swarm-backup
root@worker-1:/home/dhwani#
root@worker-1:/home/dhwani# ls swarm-backup/
swarm
root@worker-1:/home/dhwani#
```

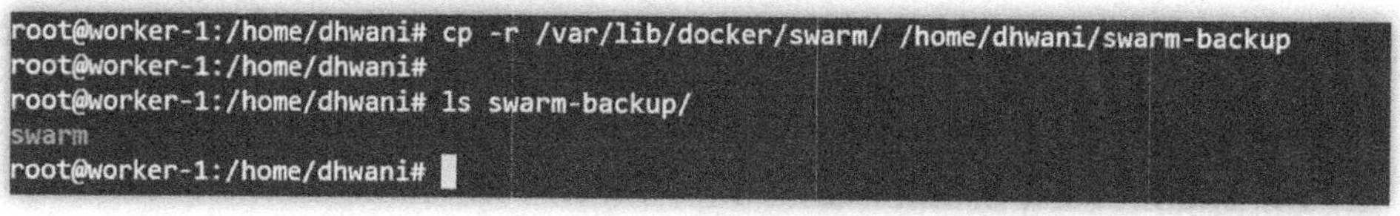

Figure 8.42: Backing up is just copying

Technically, the process of backing up the cluster is over. You can literally do anything with the swarm-backup directory; make copies of it, archive it, save it somewhere on the cloud, provide its path to a higher abstraction tool that would automate the entire backup and restore process in one click or something the choice is yours. Now we will restore it.

4. We will manually create an artificial disaster on the cluster (like mock drills in multiple industrial and administration sectors). Let us start the stopped Docker service and check its status to ensure we do not try the next steps too early.

```
sudo systemctl start docker

sudo systemctl status docker
```

The status of Docker service should be active as shown in the following screenshot:

```
dhwani@worker-1:~$ sudo systemctl start docker
dhwani@worker-1:~$
dhwani@worker-1:~$ sudo systemctl status docker
● docker.service - Docker Application Container Engine
     Loaded: loaded (/lib/systemd/system/docker.service; enabled; vendor preset: enabled)
     Active: active (running) since Tue 2020-09-08 14:58:47 UTC; 11s ago
TriggeredBy: ● docker.socket
       Docs: https://docs.docker.com
   Main PID: 14770 (dockerd)
      Tasks: 10
     Memory: 43.7M
     CGroup: /system.slice/docker.service
             └─14770 /usr/bin/dockerd -H fd:// --containerd=/run/containerd/containerd.sock
```

Figure 8.43: Restarting Docker service

Now, we will make all the nodes leave the cluster using the following command (**MAKE SURE TO RUN THIS COMMAND ON ALL NODES**):

```
docker swarm leave --force
```

Return to **worker-1** (the leader when we backed the cluster up) and stop the Docker service again. Navigate to **/var/lib/docker** and remove **/swarm** by force. This will remove all the traces of the previous cluster.

We are doing this because, in a practical scenario, you would use a backup point to restore your cluster when some or all of your managers are facing the kind of issues that make taking a U-turn easier than fixing them. Here are the commands to do the above mentioned (make sure your root privileges are intact):

```
cd /var/lib/docker
```

```
rm -rf swarm
```

5. The cluster and its data are successfully removed. To restore the cluster, copy the backed up **/swarm** to **/var/lib/docker** as shown in the following screenshot:

```
root@worker-1:/home/dhwani# cp -r /home/dhwani/swarm-backup/swarm /var/lib/docker/
root@worker-1:/home/dhwani#
root@worker-1:/home/dhwani# ls /var/lib/docker
builder  buildkit  containers  image  network  overlay2  plugins  runtimes  swarm  tmp  trust  volumes
root@worker-1:/home/dhwani#
root@worker-1:/home/dhwani# █
```

Figure 8.44: Copying the backed up state of the cluster

6. Restart the Docker service and fore-initialize the swarm cluster using the following commands, and check out the snapshot below for the result.

```
sudo systemctl start docker
sudo systemctl status docker
docker swarm init --force-new-cluster
```

```
dhwani@worker-1:~$ docker swarm init --force-new-cluster
Swarm initialized: current node (mmqxgnfzs72tmkkfdznqqacbt) is now a manager.

To add a worker to this swarm, run the following command:

    docker swarm join --token SWMTKN-1-12ih1awax62sb192ut4zc7olf1xmapvz1hy2nvl6z2ruo42toq-coai24ydsf03acoxqyd8bs4vy 34.70.248.213:2377

To add a manager to this swarm, run 'docker swarm join-token manager' and follow the instructions.
dhwani@worker-1:~$
```

Figure 8.45: Restarting the cluster

Use the **joining** command along with the token on the rest of the workers and navigate back to the leader (worker-1). We went through all of this to see if we can retain the data after a cluster gets re-initialized. Now it is time for the litmus test.

List out the services and take a breath of relief with the output similar to the following screenshot:

```
dhwani@worker-1:~$
dhwani@worker-1:~$ docker service ls
ID              NAME            MODE        REPLICAS    IMAGE           PORTS
zm9sx94e1aca    redis-swarm     global      3/3         redis:latest
dhwani@worker-1:~$
dhwani@worker-1:~$ docker service ps redis-swarm
ID              NAME                                                IMAGE           NODE        DESIRED STATE    CURRENT STATE
                PORTS
vo0u43wyag04    redis-swarm.mmqxgnfzs72tmkkfdznqqacbt               redis:latest    worker-1    Running          Running 46 seconds ago
v2won1t2zthc    redis-swarm.y8g9918gk99nlc6x9ge20di17               redis:latest    worker-2    Shutdown         Running 43 minutes ago
zi0sz5yeodqg    redis-swarm.bj25nlyuc1ml2szdvdug9owyx               redis:latest    manager     Shutdown         Running 43 minutes ago
swka0he76a63    redis-swarm.mmqxgnfzs72tmkkfdznqqacbt               redis:latest    worker-1    Shutdown         Failed 52 seconds ago
ainer: redis-swar.."
dhwani@worker-1:~$
```

Figure 8.46: Cluster restored without data loss

The cluster is active except for one detail. When we joined the rest of the nodes to the cluster, they received new node IDs with the new token. When you list the nodes out, you will get 5 nodes instead of 3, as shown in the following screenshot:

```
dhwani@worker-1:~$ docker node ls
ID                              HOSTNAME    STATUS    AVAILABILITY    MANAGER STATUS    ENGINE VERSION
bj25nlyuc1ml2szdvdug9owyx       manager     Down      Active                            19.03.12
v5s0ve9tjm9vtombrtbw2bhr7       manager     Ready     Active                            19.03.12
mmqxgnfzs72tmkkfdznqqacbt *     worker-1    Ready     Active          Leader            19.03.12
v48yn1cyhle7t95ovneldbau0       worker-2    Ready     Active                            19.03.12
y8g9918gk99nlc6x9ge20di17       worker-2    Down      Active                            19.03.12
```

Figure 8.47: Node list of the recovered cluster

We know you have A LOT of questions. If the re-initialized cluster could not get the nodes back, why did we back up the data from **/worker** in the first place? What is the point of keeping the IDs of **down** nodes? Why did we not get two managers like we had when we backed it up? Does that not violate the quorum recommendations?

While all these questions are legitimate, swarm cannot overthrow the importance of user input and cluster security. With new token and certificates, the swarm reinforces the cluster security, which could have been compromised while losing the original cluster. You can always promote another node as the manager to maintain the quorum recommendations again. As for the IDs of the nodes in the down state, they can be useful for log keeping and disaster analysis. With the clearly accessible IDs, you can filter out the relevant logs to find why did the node face any issue. Let's increase the security of the cluster even further.

Locking the Swarm cluster

Swarm clusters have a feature called **Auto Lock** which remains **OFF (value false)** by default. We can turn it on using the following command:

```
docker swarm update --autolock=true
```

Running this command will return an unlock key as shown in the following screenshot:

```
dhwani@worker-1:~$ docker swarm update --autolock=true
Swarm updated.
To unlock a swarm manager after it restarts, run the `docker swarm unlock`
command and provide the following key:

    SWMKEY-1-j4DOdR7sDtPPx6rVFA6aM7cjhRNDCAz4LpuCVnjifM0

Please remember to store this key in a password manager, since without it you
will not be able to restart the manager.
```

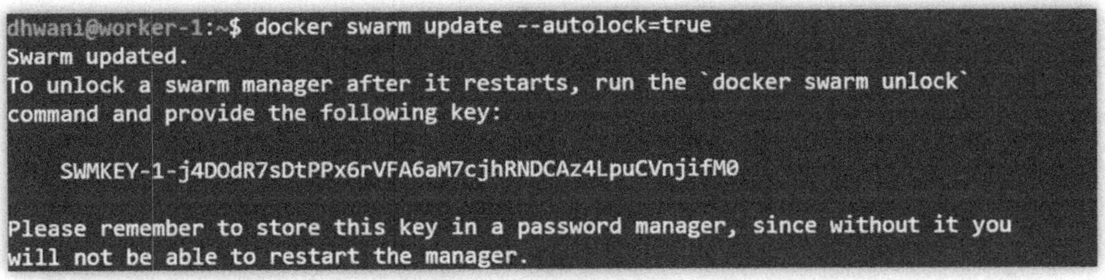

Figure 8.48: Locking the swarm cluster

SAVE THIS KEY. This key will be necessary to access your swarm cluster since you will have to unlock it using this key.

After updating the autolock value to true for this swarm cluster, we need to restart the Docker service using **sudo systemctl restart docker** to apply these new autolock settings. Anyone who tries to access the cluster without unlocking it gets an error like the following screenshot:

```
dhwani@worker-1:~$ sudo systemctl restart docker
dhwani@worker-1:~$
dhwani@worker-1:~$ docker node ls
Error response from daemon: Swarm is encrypted and needs to be unlocked before it can be used. Please use "docker swarm unlock" to unlock it.
dhwani@worker-1:~$
dhwani@worker-1:~$ 
```

Figure 8.49: Accessing a locked cluster

To unlock the cluster, use the following command and enter the key when prompted, as shown in the following screenshot:

```
dhwani@worker-1:~$ docker swarm unlock
Please enter unlock key:
dhwani@worker-1:~$
dhwani@worker-1:~$ docker node ls
ID                            HOSTNAME    STATUS    AVAILABILITY    MANAGER STATUS    ENGINE VERSION
bj25nlyuc1ml2szdvdug9owyx     manager     Down      Active                            19.03.12
v5s0ve9tjm9vtombrtbw2bhr7     manager     Ready     Active                            19.03.12
mmqxgnfzs72tmkkfdznqqacbt *   worker-1    Ready     Active          Leader            19.03.12
v48ynlcyhle7t95ovneldbau0     worker-2    Ready     Active                            19.03.12
y8g9918gk99nlc6x9ge20di17     worker-2    Down      Active                            19.03.12
dhwani@worker-1:~$
dhwani@worker-1:~$ █
```

Figure 8.50: Unlocking the cluster

In case you have lost the key (while the cluster is unlocked) you can fetch it use Docker **swarm unlock-key** command. You can also rotate the key (change it) to make the cluster even more secure.

You can use the Docker **swarm unlock-key** command followed by the **--rotate** flag, as shown in the following screenshot:

```
dhwani@worker-1:~$ docker swarm unlock-key
To unlock a swarm manager after it restarts, run the `docker swarm unlock`
command and provide the following key:

    SWMKEY-1-j4DOdR7sDtPPx6rVFA6aM7cjhRNDCAz4LpuCVnjifM0

Please remember to store this key in a password manager, since without it you
will not be able to restart the manager.
dhwani@worker-1:~$
dhwani@worker-1:~$ docker swarm unlock-key --rotate
Successfully rotated manager unlock key.

To unlock a swarm manager after it restarts, run the `docker swarm unlock`
command and provide the following key:

    SWMKEY-1-EgYyraUslkXIZeSYjuYBS0cnTU6j6kfhMYFPYB+yNag

Please remember to store this key in a password manager, since without it you
will not be able to restart the manager.
```

Figure 8.51: Rotating the key

We performed many orchestration tasks ranging from deploying a simple service to disaster management and cluster access security. Now let us learn an exciting function of Docker CLI to integrate Compose and Swarm.

Working with Docker Stack

Docker Stack is a command-line utility used to create one or more services on a swarm cluster using compose file. There are a few fundamental differences, though. Docker composes talks directly to Docker Daemon, whereas Docker Stack passes the information to daemon via swarm. Also, the node where we run Docker Stack might be different from the node where the tasks of the service will be deployed. So, even though the Docker stack command works much like Docker compose, it does not support the following flags.

- build
- cgroup_parent
- container_name
- devices
- tmpfs
- external_links
- links
- network_mode
- restart
- security_opt
- userns_mode

Let us try to run a **wordpress-mysql** service on swarm. It has different types of containers, so Swarm's behavior should be interesting. First, create a new directory and navigate into it using the following command:

```
mkdir wordpress-stack && cd wordpress-stack
```

Use your favorite text editor to create a YAML file called **docker-compose. yaml** and populate it with the following content:

```
1. version: '3.3'
2.
3. services:
4.    db:
5.      image: mysql:5.7
6.      environment:
7.        MYSQL_ROOT_PASSWORD: somewordpress
8.        MYSQL_DATABASE: wordpress
9.        MYSQL_USER: wordpress
10.       MYSQL_PASSWORD: wordpress
11.     volumes:
12.       - db_data:/var/lib/mysql
13.     deploy:
14.       mode: global
15.     networks:
```

```
16.       WP-stack:
17.
18.    wordpress:
19.      depends_on:
20.        - db
21.      image: wordpress:latest
22.      environment:
23.       WORDPRESS_DB_HOST: db:3306
24.        WORDPRESS_DB_USER: wordpress
25.        WORDPRESS_DB_PASSWORD: wordpress
26.        WORDPRESS_DB_NAME: wordpress
27.      ports:
28.        - "8000:80"
29.      deploy:
30.       mode: global
31.      networks:
32.          WP-stack:
33.
34.    volumes:
35.    db_data: {}
36.
37.    networks:
38.    WP-stack:
39.      driver: overlay
```

The file is like the compose file we had written in the last chapter except two major changes. We have mentioned the service mode to global (one background replica on each node) and we have set the network driver to Overlay. Use the following command to deploy the stack of Docker services:

```
docker stack deploy --compose-file docker-compose.yaml wordpress-mysql
```

The command will return the text status of the objects being created as shown in the following screenshot:

```
dhwani@worker-1:~/wordpress-stack$ docker stack deploy --compose-file docker-compose.yaml wordpress-mysql
Creating network wordpress-mysql_WP-stack
Creating service wordpress-mysql_wordpress
Creating service wordpress-mysql_db
```

Figure 8.52: Deploying a stack of services

To clear out any confusion, we are creating two global services with this stack. This can be verified using the Docker **stack ls** command, as shown in the following screenshot:

```
dhwani@worker-1:~/wordpress-stack$ docker stack ls
NAME              SERVICES        ORCHESTRATOR
wordpress-mysql   2               Swarm
dhwani@worker-1:~/wordpress-stack$
dhwani@worker-1:~/wordpress-stack$ docker stack services wordpress-mysql
ID            NAME                        MODE      REPLICAS   IMAGE              PORTS
bpvcilza8vpe  wordpress-mysql_wordpress   global    3/3        wordpress:latest   *:8000->80/tcp
qjcvj5nj4dbx  wordpress-mysql_db          global    3/3        mysql:5.7
dhwani@worker-1:~/wordpress-stack$
dhwani@worker-1:~/wordpress-stack$
```

Figure 8.53: Listing the stack of services

Even though stack does not build the images, it can always pull them. Both of the services are active in global mode. This automatically scales their replicas to 3 since we have 3 active nodes, and none of them has a constraint that would block the scheduling of the daemon service.

To list the tasks running under these services use **docker stack ps** followed by the stack name as shown in the following screenshot:

```
dhwani@worker-1:~/wordpress-stack$ docker stack ps wordpress-mysql
ID            NAME                                                        IMAGE              NODE       DESIRED STATE
ERROR         PORTS
y93ahc144abb  wordpress-mysql_db.mmqxgnfzs72tmkkfdznqqacbt                mysql:5.7          worker-1   Running

o1m0kmww40fp  wordpress-mysql_db.v5s0ve9tjm9vtombrtbw2bhr7                mysql:5.7          manager    Running

2w1cda4h7kt1  wordpress-mysql_db.v48ynlcyhle7t95ovneldbau0                mysql:5.7          worker-2   Running

hplncp70x69z  wordpress-mysql_wordpress.v5s0ve9tjm9vtombrtbw2bhr7         wordpress:latest   manager    Running

7c254r369zsc  wordpress-mysql_wordpress.v48ynlcyhle7t95ovneldbau0         wordpress:latest   worker-2   Running

pvob82t8aynq  wordpress-mysql_wordpress.mmqxgnfzs72tmkkfdznqqacbt         wordpress:latest   worker-1   Running
```

Figure 8.54: Listing tasks of a Docker stack

There are two containers on each node, just as expected. Let's verify if the service is actually serving the requests or not. Use the external IP of the leader (in this case, worker -1) in the **<IP:port>** combination in the web browser.

If the service is running correctly, it should show the following WordPress welcome page as displayed:

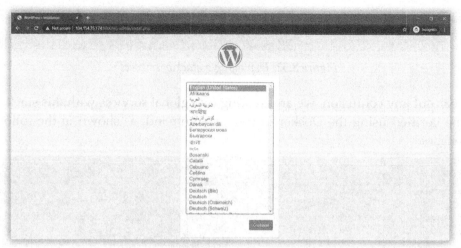

Figure 8.55: WordPress running on swarm

Furthermore, you can also utilize the features of Docker service commands on the stack services individually. For example, to obtain the cluster-wide logs of the wordpress service, you can use the Docker **service logs** command followed by the service name as demonstrated in the following screenshot:

```
dhwani@worker-1:~/wordpress-stack$ docker service logs wordpress-mysql_wordpress
wordpress-mysql_wordpress.0.hplncp70x69z@manager    | WordPress not found in /var/www/html - copying now...
wordpress-mysql_wordpress.0.hplncp70x69z@manager    | Complete! WordPress has been successfully copied to /var/www/html
wordpress-mysql_wordpress.0.hplncp70x69z@manager    | [08-Sep-2020 15:23:21 UTC] PHP Warning:  mysqli::__construct(): (HY000/2002): Conne
dard input code on line 22
wordpress-mysql_wordpress.0.hplncp70x69z@manager    |
wordpress-mysql_wordpress.0.hplncp70x69z@manager    | MySQL Connection Error: (2002) Connection refused
wordpress-mysql_wordpress.0.hplncp70x69z@manager    |
wordpress-mysql_wordpress.0.hplncp70x69z@manager    | MySQL Connection Error: (2002) Connection refused
wordpress-mysql_wordpress.0.hplncp70x69z@manager    |
wordpress-mysql_wordpress.0.hplncp70x69z@manager    | MySQL Connection Error: (2002) Connection refused
wordpress-mysql_wordpress.0.hplncp70x69z@manager    | AH00558: apache2: Could not reliably determine the server's fully qualified domain
 Set the 'ServerName' directive globally to suppress this message
wordpress-mysql_wordpress.0.hplncp70x69z@manager    | AH00558: apache2: Could not reliably determine the server's fully qualified domain
 Set the 'ServerName' directive globally to suppress this message
wordpress-mysql_wordpress.0.hplncp70x69z@manager    | [Tue Sep 08 15:23:30.536309 2020] [mpm_prefork:notice] [pid 1] AH00163: Apache/2.4.
0 configured -- resuming normal operations
wordpress-mysql_wordpress.0.hplncp70x69z@manager    | [Tue Sep 08 15:23:30.537054 2020] [core:notice] [pid 1] AH00094: Command line: 'apa
wordpress-mysql_wordpress.0.pvob82t8aynq@worker-1   | WordPress not found in /var/www/html - copying now...
wordpress-mysql_wordpress.0.pvob82t8aynq@worker-1   | Complete! WordPress has been successfully copied to /var/www/html
```

Figure 8.56: Cluster-wide logs of swarm service

Finally, just like how you could deploy all the objects via a single stack command, you can also remove them using **docker stack rm** followed by the name of the stack, as shown in the following screenshot:

```
dhwani@worker-1:~/wordpress-stack$ docker stack rm wordpress-mysql
Removing service wordpress-mysql_db
Removing service wordpress-mysql_wordpress
Removing network wordpress-mysql_WP-stack
dhwani@worker-1:~/wordpress-stack$
dhwani@worker-1:~/wordpress-stack$
```

Figure 8.57: Removing objects deployed by Docker stack

Cleaning up Docker Swarm

After learning this much, the cluster is nothing short of a mess. Cleaning it up gracefully is as important as setting it up error-free for the longevity of your infrastructure. Starting with the services, the stack is already removed, so we should have the redis and nginx services running when we run the **docker services ls** command as shown in the following screenshot:

```
dhwani@worker-1:~$ docker service ls
ID              NAME            MODE            REPLICAS        IMAGE           PORTS
tlj2it9ygb5c    nginx-swarm     replicated      3/3             nginx:latest    *:8080->80/tcp
7aa8e0dbokbo    redis-swarm     replicated      3/3             redis:latest
dhwani@worker-1:~$
```

Figure 8.58: The remaining services

Use the following command to remove a targeted service:

```
docker service rm redis-swarm
```

This will remove the redis-swarm service from the cluster, and you will be left with the nginx-swarm service as shown in the following screenshot:

```
dhwani@worker-1:~$ docker service ls
ID              NAME            MODE            REPLICAS        IMAGE           PORTS
tlj2it9ygb5c    nginx-swarm     replicated      3/3             nginx:latest    *:8080->80/tcp
dhwani@worker-1:~$
dhwani@worker-1:~$
```

Figure 8.59: Removing a swarm service

Similarly, you can also remove nginx-swarm service. Alternatively, you can remove multiple targeted services at the same time by mentioning them separated by space in the command. Moving on, we can remove the nodes. Ideally, the workers should be removed without much trouble, but since ours is a recovered cluster, we have two entries for the workers.

Removing them using their hostname will not work, so we will have to use their node ID, as shown in the following screenshot:

```
dhwani@worker-1:~$ docker node rm worker-2
Error response from daemon: node worker-2 is ambiguous (2 matches found)
dhwani@worker-1:~$
dhwani@worker-1:~$ docker node ls
ID                          HOSTNAME        STATUS      AVAILABILITY    MANAGER STATUS
bj25nlyuc1ml2szdvdug9owyx   manager         Down        Active
v5s0ve9tjm9vtombrtbw2bhr7   manager         Ready       Active
mmqxgnfzs72tmkkfdznqqacbt * worker-1        Ready       Active          Leader
v48ynlcyhle7t95ovneldbau0   worker-2        Ready       Active
y8g9918gk99nlc6x9ge20dil7   worker-2        Down        Active
dhwani@worker-1:~$
dhwani@worker-1:~$ docker node rm y8g9918gk99nlc6x9ge20dil7
y8g9918gk99nlc6x9ge20dil7
dhwani@worker-1:~$
dhwani@worker-1:~$
```

Figure 8.60: Using Node ID to remove ambiguous nodes

As we have seen previously, managers cannot be removed simply. They need to be demoted to worker or need to be removed by force. And finally, the leader needs to leave the Swarm cluster by the user's command. Removing other managers before making the leader leave the cluster will result in a graceful clean up. Once you are done with all of it, do not forget to delete your VMs from the cloud. We have a lot more of them to make and a lot of other exciting demonstrations to perform!

Conclusion

This chapter included most of the important aspects of using Docker Swarm. While more practice will certainly make you better at swarm, we are nowhere near the end of learning container orchestration. As mentioned earlier in this chapter, Swarm is a great orchestrator to get the basic idea of container orchestration. This chapter proves it. From setting up a cluster to deploying different services, from constraining container scheduling to recovering your lost cluster... This was a powerful introduction to the world of container orchestration. But, how far can swarm take you? What are the alternatives? How far can orchestration go? What more can YOU do with the orchestrators? Answers to all these questions lie in the next section of this book. If you are immediately starting to read it, most welcome; if you are taking a strategic break, see you soon! Kubernetes and we will be waiting for you at the other end. Till then, enjoy containers!

Multiple choice questions

1. Which of the following is not a node type in Docker Swarm?

   A. Manager

   B. Worker

   C. Master

   D. None of the above

   Answer: C

2. Which of the following components of the swarm allocates IP addresses to all running tasks?

   A. Dispatcher

   B. Allocator

   C. Orchestrator

   D. Scheduler

   Answer: B

3. Which of the following triggers the initialization of a task?

A. Dispatcher

B. Allocator

C. Orchestrator

D. Scheduler

Answer: D

4. Which of the following is used to pass a task to its corresponding node using HTTP request/response?

A. Dispatcher

B. Allocator

C. Orchestrator

D. Scheduler

Answer: C

5. Which of the following networks is used to connect one or more member nodes in a swarm cluster?

A. Overlay

B. Ingress

C. Bridge

D. docker-gwbridge

Answer: D

6. Which of the following commands is used to list out tasks of one or more services in swarm?

A. `docker service ls`

B. `docker service ps`

C. `docker service task ls`

D. `docker services`

Answer: B

7. Which of the following commands is used to revoke cluster management and orchestrating privileges from the manager node?

A. `docker node down`

B. `docker node rm`

C. `docker node demote`

D. `docker node --change nodeType=worker`

Answer: C

8. Which of the following commands is used by worker nodes to leave swarm cluster gracefully?

   A. `docker node rm worker`

   B. `docker swarm rm worker`

   C. `docker swarm exit`

   D. `docker swarm leave`

   Answer: D

9. Where do manager nodes store the current swarm state and manager logs on Docker host?

   A. /var/lib/docker/swarm

   B. /etc/lib/docker/swarm

   C. /var/log/docker/swarm

   D. run/lib/docker/swarm

   Answer: A

10. Which of the following commands is used by nodes to join the swarm cluster as worker node?

    A. `docker swarm join worker`

    B. `docker swarm join --token <worker-token>`

    C. `docker swarm --join --token`

    D. `docker swarm join nodeType=worker --token <worker-token>`

    Answer: B

Questions

1. Explain the Orchestration of Containers and its significance.

2. Explain Swarm mode in Docker.

3. Explain Overlay Networking in Swarm mode.

4. Explain backup and disaster recovery of a Swarm Cluster.

5. Create a replicated swarm service of Apache webserver that should only be deployed on worker nodes and connected to a user-defined Overlay network. The swarm cluster has 3 manager nodes and 2 worker nodes.

## CHAPTER 9

Introduction to Kubernetes

Introduction

This is the first chapter of the second section of the book. This is where the journey shifts from Docker's family of tools to Kubernetes. It covers the very basics of Kubernetes as an independent tool and as a part of the container ecosystem. We will take a look at the architecture of Kubernetes cluster and the functionality of its components. We will also spin up our first Kubernetes cluster on GCP VMs (Google Cloud Platform's Virtual Machines) and will begin to discuss its operations.

Structure

This chapter covers:

- The MVP of your skillset
- Choosing between K8s and Docker Swarm
- Kubernetes architecture
- Setting up the K8s Cluster
- K8s Operations: The concept of Pods
- Namespaces

Objective

This is a lightweight and discussion-oriented chapter. We will discuss facts, perspectives, and a little bit of setup while weaving relevant explanations around them. The objective of this chapter is to familiarize you with Kubernetes as an orchestrator. By the end of this chapter, you will be able to spin up a basic Linux container on a Kubernetes cluster and will also be able to justify the output's nature.

The MVP of your skillset

Building any suspense is futile. Chances are pretty high that you picked this book up because you saw the word "Kubernetes" on the cover, or because you are excited about the impressive pay-scale provided to the certified and/or experienced Kubernetes skill holders, or you want to scope the ceiling of microservice architecture's robustness at scale.

In any case, it is an undeniable fact that Kubernetes **(or K8s in short, because there are 8 letters between K and s)** has soared in popularity and adoption in the past few years, its role is pivotal in the success of containers and your journey as a container enthusiast is incomplete without **at least** knowing K8s.

The story of Kubernetes begins at one of the most exciting places in the IT industry, Google. It is one of the biggest tech giants with billions of users as its target consumers. With ever-expanding services, billions of petabytes worth of Data, and thousands of investors' money at stake, Google was one of the first companies to encounter the **Forests of Servers** problem.

They had adopted the concept of Linux Containers for cost and performance-efficient resource utilization. Back then, there were no e-learning platforms. One of the authors of this book had not even started his college. There was no container runtime environment (CRE) like Docker either. They had to build everything by learning and learn everything by trying. This is how Borg, the predecessor of Kubernetes, was born. Google built and used Borg for almost a decade before giving it to **Cloud Native Computing Foundation (CNCF)** to incubate, develop, and manage it further as an open-source container orchestrator. Since then, K8s has grown significantly in terms of features and user base. Like any other open-source technology, one of the critical factors behind the rapid success of K8s is its vibrant community of contributors and well-maintained documentation.

Choosing between K8s and Docker Swarm

Back when we started playing around with containers, this was the hottest debate. Simplicity (Swarm) or Scale (K8s)? Shorter learning curve (Swarm) or Granular control (K8s)? Depending on your needs, you would fall on either of the sides. The decisive parameters are still the same, but the metaphorical clouds of judgment seem to have cleared up. If you do not aim for massive scale or fine control, Swarm could be your easy-to-adapt choice. For everyone else, we have Kubernetes.

Note:

Kubernetes Documentation:

https://kubernetes.io/docs/home/

Large-scale cluster management at Google with Borg (White Paper): https://static. googleusercontent.com/media/research.google.com/en//pubs/archive/43438.pdf

These tools coexist for a good reason. Many Public Cloud providers (Google, Amazon, Microsoft, and Digital Ocean, to name a few) offer their managed K8s solutions, whereas Mirantis enjoys the privilege of providing premium features on Docker Swarm. Moreover, both Swarm and K8s have implemented each other's features as they grew (with one of them taking more from the other but we are not here to judge, are we?), and both have become feature-rich.

While K8s uses Docker Hub as the default registry to find Container images, Docker UCP (*now known as Mirantis Kubernetes Engine*) offers both Swarm and Kubernetes as orchestrator options (*We would have also mentioned the fact that Docker is the default CRE used by K8s but that has changed, and both are switching to containerd in 2021*). While one can have more usefulness than the other in the eyes of its user base, there is no clear winner. For learners, Docker Swarm is a great tool for understanding container orchestration, whereas K8s is a great tool for understanding **container orchestration in depth.** Naturally, this book has also been structured using the same principles. Since we have already understood how container orchestration works, understanding how K8s handles it differently will give you a broader and clearer perspective toward its actions themselves. Before any of that, we need to look at the building blocks of K8s by understanding its architecture.

Kubernetes architecture

Kubernetes is a Greek word meaning the helmsman of a ship. The name is fitting since the entire container ecosystem is following the shipping naming convention.

A **container cluster** is like a ship full of cargos, and K8s holds the steering wheel of that ship as the orchestrator.

From a bird's eye view. The architecture of a K8s cluster would look pretty simple. There are two types of machine instances — **Control Plane (many times referred to as Master) and Nodes,** as shown in the following figure:

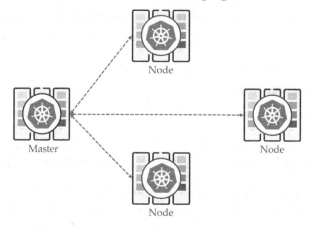

Figure 9.1: Types of machines/nodes in Kubernetes

They both run the same K8s stack but serve different purposes. Depending on which components are active on a machine, it becomes Control Plane or node. Let us take a look at the master first through the following figure:

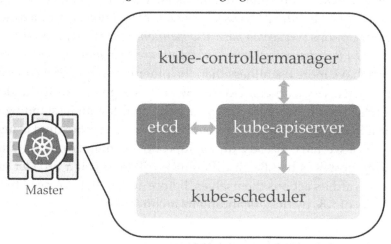

Figure 9.2: Control Plane components in Kubernetes

This is the kind of figure you can find on the internet if you search about K8s Control Plane *(although this particular figure is drawn by the authors themselves… genuine content!).* This group of components or processes are called the **control plane of Kubernetes**.

As a tool, K8s follows microservice architecture. All of its processes are containerized, and they communicate to one another via APIs written using HTTP REST requests. Let's look at each of the components one by one as follows:

- **kube-API server:** It exposes the APIs of other components and serves as the attentive front-end of the Control Plane. It also validates the requests made by users regarding K8s objects. You can draw some parallels between Swarm's API Endpoint and K8s' kube-apiserver. The figure above shows that it is the only component directly communicating to all other control plane components.

- **kube-controller-manager:** It serves as a parent or managing process for several controller processes (such as node controller, replication controller, jobs controller, service accounts and token controller, deployments controller, etc. We are going to explore the relevant objects as we go further in the book). You can consider the controller as a watch loop and wrapper processes around the container for contextual tasks such as scaling (replication). Each controller is an individual process, but all of them are monitored by a single process called kube-controller-manager.

  This process itself is scalable. In other words, if there are too many workloads, the Control Plane can have replicas of kube-controller-manager for handling them, and all of them will work in sync. Alternatively, we can also have multi-Control Plane clusters which naturally mean multiple instances of these processes. K8s does not have a lead role of nodes like Swarm, so all Control Planes work in sync to maintain a **Desired State** of events, objects and variables requested by the user *(aka you, the special one!)*.

- **kube-scheduler:** It does what its name suggests, scheduling (deciding on which node and when the container will be scheduled). kube-apiserver validates the user requests and passes them on to kube-controller-manager, creating the definition and configurations of objects to be scheduled. These definitions are provided to the kube-scheduler, which analyses the resource requirements and allots available node to it (or puts it on a temporary halt to avoid overload). Much like apiserver and controller-manager, this is also a scalable process.

- **etcd:** This smallest-looking block is arguably the biggest differentiator between Swarm and K8s. Etcd is another CNCF graduated project. It is a key-value store (a database that stores information in key-value pairs), and K8s uses it to store every detail. Object definitions, object behavior, container state, cluster state, container and cluster configurations, service configurations, ingress-egress rules, environment variables, object IDs, user inputs, event logs and everything else is modeled as key-value pairs, and etcd keeps track of it.

It can only be accessed via kube-apiserver, and no internal process (such as controllers) can order its automatic scaling. For high availability or simply for avoiding loss of Control Plane's configurations, etcd needs to be backed up manually *(paid services like hosted K8s on the cloud can take care of that for you, but that is an entirely different discussion for another chapter)*. Of course, you will be demonstrated how to do that when the book's narrative reaches the appropriate point.

As a tool, etcd grows independently and individually. This means that with each version update, K8s can decide which features of then updated etcd to incorporate and which ones to skip. etcd makes things fast and simple because it is a distributed database *(it is cluster friendly)*. It can take direct inputs from HTTP requests (which is exactly what K8s uses) to store them as key-value pairs.

It also runs watch loops on the values of the keys and can create alerts when the value changes, which is an ideal behavior for a tool like Kubernetes that strives to maintain the user desired state. In short, every change in the cluster and every decisive action or observation performed under kube-apiserver will be recorded by etcd and backed up if appropriately configured. It means you can restore cluster Control Plane to its safer state snapshot and spin up the failed containers under the worst-case scenario; this leads to fault tolerance.

While this architecture looks impressive, you might be wondering why none of them explains how the containers will run? That is because what we have seen so far is just the **control plane** part of K8s (aka the orchestration logic); next are the components outside the control plane, as shown in the following figure:

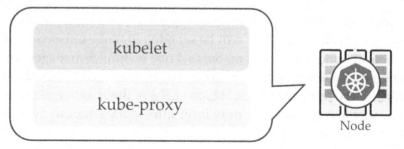

Figure 9.3: Node components in Kubernetes

- Every K8s machine runs a set of kubelet and kube-proxy. **kube-proxy** is a network proxy for the containers running under K8s. If the host OS has a network stack that includes packet filtering rules, in that case, kube-proxy utilizes them to perform packet filtering and routing. In the absence of these rules, it relies on itself to accomplish filtering and routing of packets. This is an important component as it manages container-container, node-node, node-container, container-internet communication.

- **kubelet** is an agent process running on each node to make sure the desired containers are running. kube-controller-manager of the control plane forwards user request to the appropriate controller and interprets it by creating an object definition for k8s. This object definition is provided to kube-scheduler, which assigns a node and a running timestamp to it. kube-apiserver acts as a validator of all of these requests and stores data in etcd. The definition data and execution instructions are exchanged using kube-proxy to the respective node. kubelet creates the object on the respective node, which is why kubelet always runs on top of a CRE.

An overarching misunderstanding among beginners is that Control Planes do not have or do not run K8s components such as kubelet and kube-proxy. That is not true; control plane components are a subset of the entire K8s installation stack. Apart from a few user-controlled configurations, the K8s stack installation stays the same on all nodes irrespective of their role.

The number of active components and their authority over other nodes decides their roles. To understand this further, the K8s stack on a typical Control Plane (control plane) looks something like the following figure:

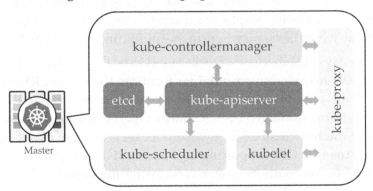

Figure 9.4: *All Control Plane components in Kubernetes*

Conversely, a typical node would have active components, as shown in the following figure:

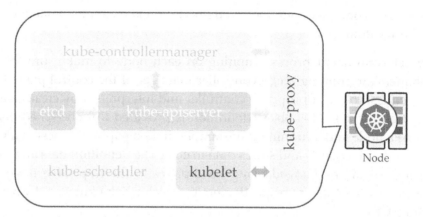

Figure 9.5: All node components in Kubernetes

The components washed out in the figure above (control plane components) are not active when a node joins the cluster as a node. They become active either when promoted to being a Control Plane or initiates a new cluster. To understand these things better, let us take a look at a typical K8s cluster setup as the topic below.

Setting up the K8s cluster

There are multiple ways to setup a K8s cluster ranging from running individual binaries bare-metal to 1-click deployment on the cloud. We will focus on the most widely used way which lies somewhere in the middle in terms of effort requirements.

In the caveman days of Kubernetes, Docker used to be the default and the most used **CRE**, offering K8s an underlying **Container Runtime Interface** (**CRI**) adapter called dockershim. It was a proprietary part of the Docker Engine. Eventually, in 2015, the Linux Foundation open-sourced the CRI under **Open Container Initiative** (**OCI**) to make containers more accessible. Today, even Docker is a part of the OCI Compliance and uses `containerd` (a CRI supporting OCI standards). K8s has announced to stop supporting dockershim with its newer versions by the end of 2021. It means that you can still run Docker to create Container images (since they are OCI compliant). Docker remains the most widely used containerization tool, but k8s will not need it as a dependency to run on a Linux host.

If you are reading this book, by the time `dockershim` as a CRE adapter is not supported, you can use `containerd` as a CRI instead. For everyone else, we have seen how to install Docker in *Chapter 2*. You can follow the same installation process for Docker and install K8s on top of it.

To create a 3-node cluster with 1 Control Plane and 2 nodes, we need 3 separate VMs like Docker Swarm, as shown in the following screenshot:

Figure 9.6: *A list of VMs ready for Kubernetes Cluster setup*

If you want to install Docker as the container runtime, you can follow the Docker installation process mentioned in *Chapter 2*. If you want to work with `containerd`, perform the installation steps mentioned below on all cluster nodes depending on the circumstances discussed previously.

- **Prerequisites:** Ensure the nodes have at least 2 GB of RAM with 2 or more CPU cores, and Control Plane has 4 GB of RAM (K8s requires 2 GB, but 4 GB is a safer choice for the Control Plane). Also, ensure that TCP ports 6443, 2379-2380, 10250-10252, and 30000+ are open and available on all VMs. To allow bridging the physical network stack into VLAN, make sure the bridge `netfilter` module is enabled.

  You can use the command below to do so.

  ```
  sudo modprobe br_netfilter
  ```

  To ensure that your Linux Node's iptables can access the bridge traffic correctly, you should ensure **net.bridge.bridge-nf-call-iptables** is set to **1** in your **sysctl** config with the following commands:

```
cat <<EOF | sudo tee /etc/modules-load.d/k8s.conf
br_netfilter
EOF
cat <<EOF | sudo tee /etc/sysctl.d/k8s.conf
net.bridge.bridge-nf-call-ip6tables = 1
net.bridge.bridge-nf-call-iptables = 1
EOF
sudo sysctl --system
```

- **Container runtime:** The following commands are used to install and configure containerd. Execute these commands in the mentioned order on all cluster nodes.

```
sudo apt-get update && sudo apt-get install -y containerd
sudo mkdir -p /etc/containerd
containerd config default | sudo tee /etc/containerd/config.toml
```

Restart the **containerd** service to let the changes take effect using the following command:

```
sudo systemctl restart containerd
```

- **Kubernetes components:** We will install most of the K8s components using a tool called kubeadm. The reason why we said most of the components is because even kubeadm doesn't install kubelet (we have already discussed its significance in the architecture section) and kubectl (the K8s client command line) because of version compatibility semantics. Even if we mention the compatibility table here, it will be updated by the time you read this book. The best way to be future proof is to check out the link mentioned in the note at the bottom of the page to make sure you are using compatible versions of kubelet, kubectl, and other components of K8s installed using kubeadm.
With that out of the way, run the commands below on all VMs to install the components. If you choose to run Docker as CRE, you already have https and curl installed on your system. If you are starting fresh and using **containerd**, install them using the following command:

```
sudo apt-get update && sudo apt-get install -y apt-transport-https curl
```

Like Docker installation, download the Google Cloud public signing GPG key and your key manager.

```
sudo curl -fsSLo /usr/share/keyrings/kubernetes-archive-keyring.gpg
https://packages.cloud.google.com/apt/doc/apt-key.gpg | apt-key add -
```

Note:

https://kubernetes.io/releases/version-skew-policy/

Finally, execute the following commands to setup the Kubernetes repository and to install K8s components.

```
echo "deb [signed-by=/usr/share/keyrings/kubernetes-archive-
keyring.gpg] https://apt.kubernetes.io/ kubernetes-xenial main" |
sudo tee /etc/apt/sources.list.d/kubernetes.list

sudo apt-get update
sudo apt-get install -y kubelet kubeadm kubectl
sudo apt-mark hold kubelet kubeadm kubectl
```

- **Contextually Optional:** This part is just a safety net. Most likely, you will never have to use it. K8s automatically detects Docker at the time of writing the book. It has promised to configure auto-detection for containerd and CRI-O by the time Docker's support as the runtime is discontinued. If the promise is delivered a little later than expected, add the following lines in **/var/lib/kubelet/config.yaml** to configure cgroup driver for K8s (which is cgroupfs by default if installed using Docker).

  ```
  apiVersion: kubelet.config.k8s.io/v1beta1

  kind: KubeletConfiguration

  cgroupDriver: kubeadm init
  ```

  Restart kubelet to make the changes effective using the following commands:

  ```
  sudo systemctl daemon-reload

  sudo systemctl restart kubelet
  ```

- **Initiating the Control Plane and Joining the Nodes:** The installation commands mentioned so far were meant to be executed on all VMs. We need to execute a few commands on the Control Plane (control plane) node to grant it the privileges to create and configure a Kubernetes cluster. To initialize the Control Plane (control plane) node, execute the following command on it:

  ```
  kubeadm init <args>
  ```

  Several arguments such as **--apiserver-advertise-address, --pod-network-cidr** are available with the kubeadm init command to provide additional support in the cluster creation process. We will look at them while discussing advanced cluster configurations. **kubeadm init** command runs a series of prechecks to check the availability of the VM. You might witness a few warnings during the precheck process, but they are safe to be ignored.

  After downloading the K8s components, we can see a list of post-installation instructions shown in the following screenshot:

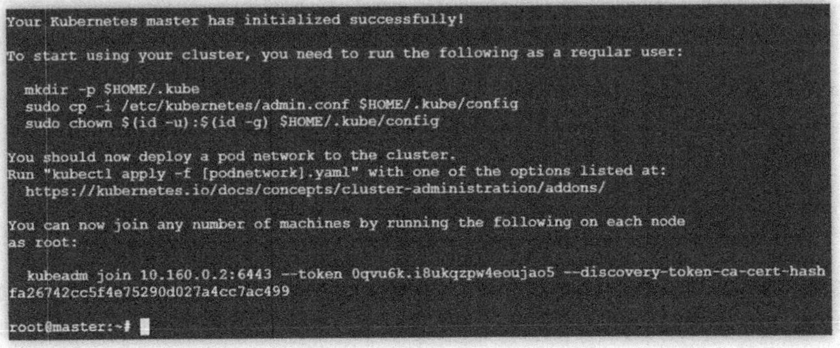

Figure 9.7: Kubernetes cluster join token for nodes

Copy and save the entire **kubectl join** command along with advertised IP and tokens. These tokens are valid for 24 h. You can use this command as it gets displayed on your screen and run it on other nodes to make them join the cluster initialized by the Control Plane. After 24 h, you need to run **kubectl token** `create` to get another token and use it with the **kubectl join** command.

To access the cluster as a regular user, run the following commands as a regular user on the Control Plane:

```
mkdir -p $HOME/.kube

sudo cp -i /etc/kubernetes/admin.conf $HOME/.kube/config

sudo chown $(id -u):$(id -g) $HOME/.kube/config
```

- **Pod network:** These are add-on network configurations to allow the pods (wrappers encapsulating containers, A LOT more on them soon) to communicate with one another. We can set them up by providing a pre-written YAML configuration file provided by respective vendors. K8s supports a group of Pod Networks (Calico, Romana, Flannel, AWS VPC CNI, Azure CNI, GCE and many others). To appreciate the simplicity and to keep things vendor-neutral, we will use Weavenet created by Weaveworks. Use the following command to initialize it:

```
kubectl apply -f https://cloud.weave.works/k8s/net?k8s-
version=$(kubectl version | base64 | tr -d '\n')
```

Finally, to see if your cluster is listing the nodes we have joined so far, run kubectl get nodes to receive output as shown in the following screenshot:

```
dhwani@master:~$ kubectl get nodes
NAME     STATUS   ROLES                  AGE   VERSION
master   Ready    control-plane,master   92s   v1.20.2
node-1   Ready    <none>                 76s   v1.20.2
node-2   Ready    <none>                 73s   v1.20.2
```

***Figure 9.8:** List of nodes in a Kubernetes Cluster*

All of the nodes are visible, and the control plane has been initiated. The cluster is ready to run user-defined containers next topic onwards.

K8s operations: the concept of pods

Let's dive into how to operate K8s. You, as a reader, are already ahead of a significantly large crowd of learners since this is not the first container orchestrator for you to use. Instead of understanding container orchestration, you can focus on how K8s has implemented different orchestration techniques.

For starters, apart from joining the node to a cluster or viewing machine-specific logs, we will not be touching the nodes. Most of our operations will be performed on the Control Plane. There are different ways (like dashboards) to provide user requests, but we will stick to the fastest and the most efficient user-friendly tool called **kubectl** command line. Regardless of which user input method you lean toward, K8s does not run plain containers. It wraps them around another layer of orchestration called **Pods**.

Pods, We have been avoiding using this term till now *(even while explaining the K8s architecture)* as much as possible. But trust us, K8s is ALL about pods. So, what are pods? They are the smallest unit of orchestration in K8s and the only way to interact with containers. Their creation and operations are handled by kubelet.

A Pod can have one or more containers inside it, but mostly you will find one pod per container, as shown in the following figure:

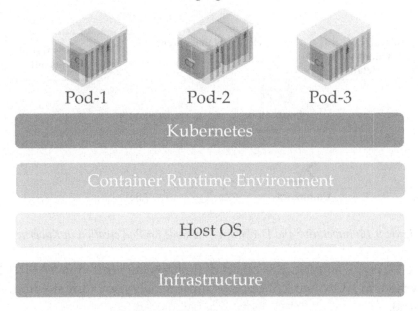

Figure 9.9: Pods in Kubernetes

K8s is designed with the fact in mind that containers die. Their failure is natural, and thus the restart policy of containers hosted by pods is set to "always" by default. This allows you to persist the data of a container if it crashes since the pod will spin it up again and provide it with the lost data. Pods come with many concepts that demonstrate the strength of k8s as an orchestrator and allow you to make your migration to containers more reliable. We will look at all of them as the book progresses but let's focus on creating a pod for the time being.

There are two ways to create pods (or any object) in K8s: Imperative and Declarative. Just like programming, while creating objects imperatively, you have to mention every configuration and what to do with them, while in the case of declarative object creation, K8s will take the object definition and create it using its object templates. Imperative object creation provides greater performance and behavior control, while declarative creation provides simplicity and speed while working at scale.

You can use direct commands or object definitions in the case of the Imperative method. Commands are not as mature, and you lose a lot of control (which is the very reason why you would use imperative methods), so it is recommended to stick to providing object definitions via files.

To get a better understanding of the object creation options, take a look at the following figure:

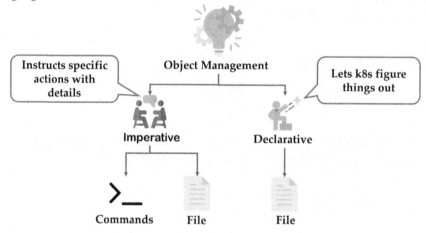

Figure 9.10: Imperative and Declarative methods for Pod creation in Kubernetes

Much like Docker Compose, K8s object definitions are written in YAML (they can also be written in JSON, but YAML is the most widely used format within the user community).

Here is a simple definition of a K8s pod running busybox container. You can write this using any available text editor in a file called **imperative-pod.yaml** (*of course, you can name it anything; just make sure to provide the **.yaml** extension*):

```
1. apiVersion: v1
2. kind: Pod
3. metadata:
4.   name: imp-pod
```

```
5.    labels:
6.       app: imp
7.  spec:
8.    containers:
9.      - name: imp-container
10.        image: busybox
11.        command:
12.          - sh
13.          - '-c'
14.          - echo This pod is created imperatively && sleep 3600
```

Let us have a good look at this YAML. As we can see, there are 4 main fields or keys here: **apiVersion**, **kind**, **metadata**, and **spec**. Some of these keys are specified as a key-value map using the colon (:) as a separator. Each member of the map should be placed on a new line.

Let's begin with the **apiVersion** field. It is used to define the version schema of the target object. The value of this field represents the API group and the version of K8s objects. **v1** was the first stable release of K8s, and here it represents that the pods are a part of apiVersion v1 under the core API group. As K8s keeps growing, newer API version groups keep getting introduced, which contain newer object types. This signifies that pods have existed since the beginning of K8s (CNCF's K8s).

Next is the **kind** field. This field is used to define the type of object we want to create. We want to create a pod; hence the value of the field is set to **Pod**.

Next up is a pretty familiar term, **metadata**. This field contains meta information such as name, labels, annotations, and so on which sets 2 of the same kind of objects apart *(names are useful for users, whereas for internal uses like Docker, K8s also provide unique names and IDs to its objects)*. We have named this pod as **imp-pod** and labeled it with **app: imp**. We are going to know more about labels in the upcoming chapters but for now, remember that labels are used to organize and categorize K8s objects.

The last one is the **spec** field. It is used to describe the desired behavior of this object. Regardless of the object type, this is the field where most of the important configurations take place. We want this pod to run a **busybox** container. We need to create a template that contains all of the necessary details for it.

As you can see, the **name** of the container is **imp-container**. The **image** to be executed inside the container is **busybox(:latest)**. The default **command** for this container will execute the SHELL, echo the string. **This pod is created imperatively** and will sleep after 120 s. Both of these statements are clubbed with a logical AND operator, so If any of them fails to execute, the castle of cards will collapse.

This is the user-provided object definition; in other words, the user desired state for this particular object (pod). It is time to create a pod using the imperative method. Execute the **kubectl create** command and provide the pod object YAML file using the **-f** flag.

The outcome of this command looks like the following screenshot:

```
dhwani@master:~$
dhwani@master:~$
dhwani@master:~$ nano imperative-pod.yaml
dhwani@master:~$
dhwani@master:~$ kubectl create -f imperative-pod.yaml
pod/imp-pod created
dhwani@master:~$
dhwani@master:~$ 
```

Figure 9.11: Imperative method to create a Pod

The **create** instruction is provided explicitly to the kube-apiserver. Other such explicit instructions could be **delete**, **run**, **taint**, **drain** and so on. *(We will look at them as the book progresses)*. Therefore, this method is called **imperative**.

On the contrary, **kubectl apply** command also creates the pod, but using the declarative method. Think of it like this: With **kubectl create** command, you provide the object definition and instruction as your desired state of the cluster, whereas with the **kubectl apply** command, you are providing the object definition as the desired state. K8s tries itself to match the current state with your desired state. In other words, if the object doesn't exist, it will be created.

When we run the **kubectl get pods** command, you can see the **imp-pod** listed as running (along with another pod created outside the relevance of the book for practice), as shown in the following screenshot:

```
dhwani@master:~$
dhwani@master:~$
dhwani@master:~$ kubectl get pods
NAME        READY    STATUS      RESTARTS    AGE
dec-pod     1/1      Running     0           101s
imp-pod     1/1      Running     0           15m
dhwani@master:~$
dhwani@master:~$ 
```

Figure 9.12: List of Pods

So, what is the difference? Well, it is about thought processes and practices. It is helpful to use imperative object configuration files (**kubectl create -f**) while learning K8s to clearly understand what you wanted to achieve and what you ended up doing.

On the other hand, when you move to more advanced workflows like creating a CI/CD pipeline and automating updates, declarative object configurations prove to be more useful as the objects (such as pods) created declaratively carry a bunch of annotations provided by K8s to help users and third-party tools (if integrated) keep track of activities.

To get more details about pods, we can use K8s's **describe** command (similar to docker **inspect**). We can write this command by providing the object type and object name along with the following command:

```
kubectl describe pods <pod-name>
```

```
dhwani@master:~$
dhwani@master:~$
dhwani@master:~$ kubectl describe pods imp-pod
Name:           imp-pod
Namespace:      default
Priority:       0
Node:           gke-gke-cluster-001-default-pool-e47f218a-tkdm/10.128.0.52
Start Time:     Tue, 25 May 2021 11:19:17 +0000
Labels:         app=imp
Annotations:    <none>
Status:         Running
IP:             10.52.2.6
IPs:
  IP:   10.52.2.6
Containers:
  imp-container:
    Container ID:   docker://7519644bd0b24c793ccb710b7b6993d2da2a6abf4ef964c01098bb62694bb696
    Image:          busybox
    Image ID:       docker-pullable://busybox@sha256:b5fc1d7b2e4ea86a06b0cf88de915a2c43a99a00b6b3c0af731e5f4c07ae8eff
    Port:           <none>
    Host Port:      <none>
    Command:
      sh
      -c
      echo This pod is created imperatively && sleep 3600
    State:          Running
```

Figure 9.13: Description of imp-pod

The results consist of helpful details that can be divided into two categories.

1. They are container configurations similar to the output of docker inspect.

2. They are about topics we have not touched upon yet.

To keep things simple, we will learn about all of the aspects of K8s and then perform a thorough analysis of kubectl describe results.

The pods we created are not the sole residents of this cluster. As we had mentioned earlier, K8s components are also spun up as containers. To view them, we have to understand the concept of namespaces.

Namespaces

Containers and K8s are built for scale. Even though Infrastructure as Code reduces IT manpower requirements drastically, assuming that one DevOps Engineer will be handling an entire cluster hosting hundreds of containers is unrealistic. This means a cluster will be accessed by an entire team (or more than one teams).

In such situations, namespaces play a critical role by providing logical separation of resources running across the cluster as well as indirect access control with the help of other authorization and access control mechanisms discussed in later chapters. They act as a scope of naming and operations; in other words, you cannot have two same resources with the same name under one namespace. If you want to have two pods with the same name, you need to put them in different namespaces. It also means that most object-specific commands will operate on your present namespace unless mentioned otherwise.

For example, when we write **kubectl get pods**, we get pods on the present namespace *(that is why you haven't seen any other pods so far)*:

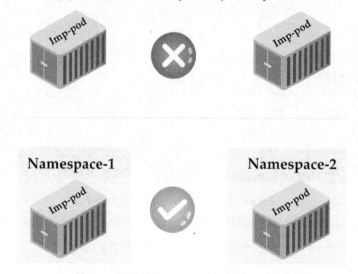

Figure 9.14: Namespaces in Kubernetes

This brings another bunch of questions. How do I know which namespace am I working on? How many namespaces are there? Can I create my own namespaces? How? Let us address them.

K8s spins a cluster up with four namespaces with the following uses:

- **default:** If you do not specify any namespace, this is where your objects will land.

- **kube-public:** As the name suggests, K8s or users may use this namespace to host add-on objects which are safe to be accessed by the public (non-authorized users or guests). This namespace may be absent in the clusters not bootstrapped by kubeadm.

- **kube-system:** A namespace reserved for internal components of K8s. This may not be accessible to the guest users. When **you** spin up a cluster, your user account is not a guest, so you will view it soon enough.

- **kube-node-lease:** This is another namespace for internal components, but instead of hosting trivial components like kube-system, it stores node-specific information such as availability status, heartbeat (node health-check heartbeat), and so on. This is useful for third-party monitoring tools to manage the cluster.

You can verify how many of these namespaces are available on your cluster by running **kubectl get namespaces** as shown in the following screenshot:

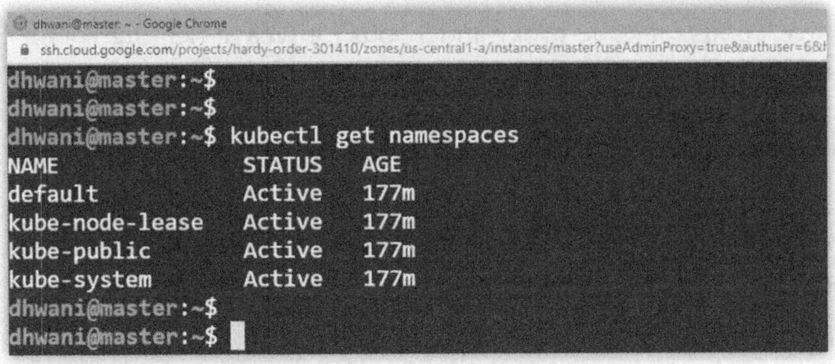

Figure 9.15: List of default namespaces in Kubernetes

You might feel familiar with the received list of namespaces in Kubernetes. Likewise, you might have already figured out that the **imp-pod** and **dec-pod** are created in the **default** namespace.

We can recall the K8s architecture when we list pods from all namespaces with **kubectl get pods --all-namespaces** command, as shown in the following screenshot:

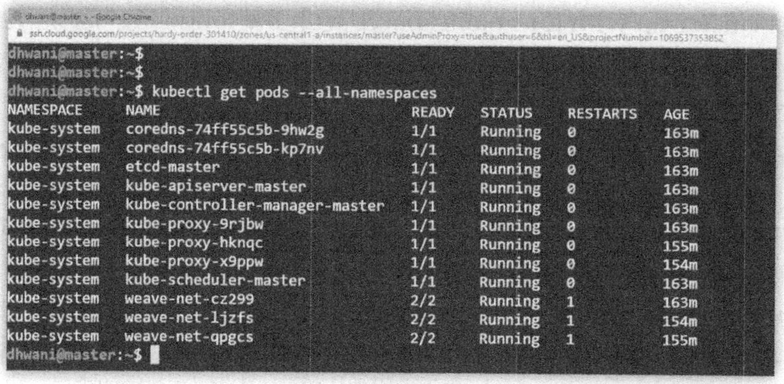

```
dhwani@master:~$
dhwani@master:~$
dhwani@master:~$ kubectl get pods --all-namespaces
NAMESPACE     NAME                              READY   STATUS    RESTARTS   AGE
kube-system   coredns-74ff55c5b-9hw2g           1/1     Running   0          163m
kube-system   coredns-74ff55c5b-kp7nv           1/1     Running   0          163m
kube-system   etcd-master                       1/1     Running   0          163m
kube-system   kube-apiserver-master             1/1     Running   0          163m
kube-system   kube-controller-manager-master    1/1     Running   0          163m
kube-system   kube-proxy-9rjbw                  1/1     Running   0          163m
kube-system   kube-proxy-hknqc                  1/1     Running   0          155m
kube-system   kube-proxy-x9ppw                  1/1     Running   0          154m
kube-system   kube-scheduler-master             1/1     Running   0          163m
kube-system   weave-net-cz299                   2/2     Running   1          163m
kube-system   weave-net-ljzfs                   2/2     Running   1          154m
kube-system   weave-net-qpgcs                   2/2     Running   1          155m
dhwani@master:~$
```

Figure 9.16: *List of pods running in all namespaces in Kubernetes*

The preceding snapshot was clicked before deploying any workloads on the cluster; therefore, you cannot see imp-pod and dec-pod on the list. We have a significant number of pods from **kube-system** namespace. In typical situations, most Control Plane and node components are deployed under the **kube-system** namespace. (*we better not mess with this one*) Since we have a cluster with one Control Plane and two nodes, we have one set of Control Plane components like kube-apiserver, kube-controller-manager, kube-scheduler, kube-proxy, and etcd.

We also have 3 pods for kube-proxy and 3 pods for weave-net (one set for each VM). As you might have guessed, there are no kubelet pods. The reason for this is that kubelet is a Linux process responsible for creating pods and running the containers inside them using CRE (*after all, we have used apt-get install kubelet, not docker run kubelet or kubectl run kubelet*).

If you want to have a broader perspective on the scheduling of the pods, you can use **`-o wide`** flag with the previous command, as shown in the following screenshot:

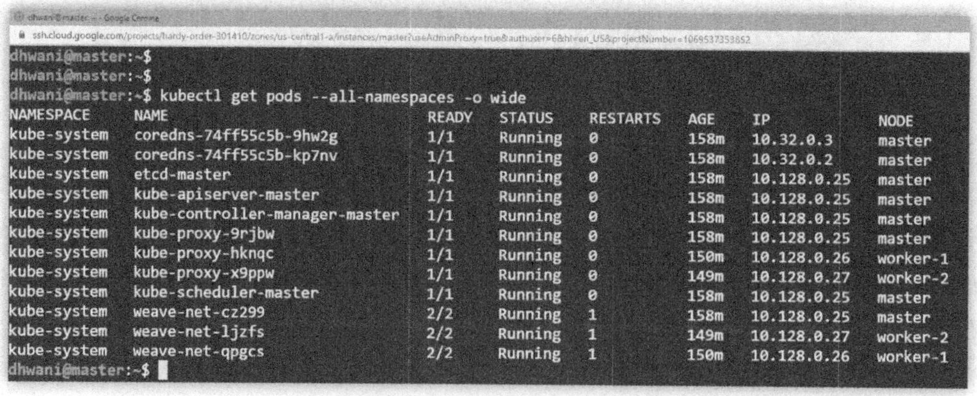

```
dhwani@master:~$
dhwani@master:~$
dhwani@master:~$ kubectl get pods --all-namespaces -o wide
NAMESPACE     NAME                              READY   STATUS    RESTARTS   AGE    IP            NODE
kube-system   coredns-74ff55c5b-9hw2g           1/1     Running   0          158m   10.32.0.3     master
kube-system   coredns-74ff55c5b-kp7nv           1/1     Running   0          158m   10.32.0.2     master
kube-system   etcd-master                       1/1     Running   0          158m   10.128.0.25   master
kube-system   kube-apiserver-master             1/1     Running   0          158m   10.128.0.25   master
kube-system   kube-controller-manager-master    1/1     Running   0          158m   10.128.0.25   master
kube-system   kube-proxy-9rjbw                  1/1     Running   0          158m   10.128.0.25   master
kube-system   kube-proxy-hknqc                  1/1     Running   0          150m   10.128.0.26   worker-1
kube-system   kube-proxy-x9ppw                  1/1     Running   0          149m   10.128.0.27   worker-2
kube-system   kube-scheduler-master             1/1     Running   0          158m   10.128.0.25   master
kube-system   weave-net-cz299                   2/2     Running   1          158m   10.128.0.25   master
kube-system   weave-net-ljzfs                   2/2     Running   1          149m   10.128.0.27   worker-2
kube-system   weave-net-qpgcs                   2/2     Running   1          150m   10.128.0.26   worker-1
dhwani@master:~$
```

Figure 9.17: *List of pods running in all namespaces with additional details*

In this result, you can also verify which pods are on **worker-1** and which are on **worker-2**. As for the **coredns**, it is a DNS-based service discovery tool used to identify objects from their IPs. It is another graduated project by CNCF, much like containerd or K8s. As for creating new namespaces, we believe you would appreciate it learning with other orchestration techniques. So, we will briefly revisit and continue the namespaces in the very next chapter.

This is our primary playground. A fully functional K8s cluster with a couple of nodes and an economical Control Plane. It is the setup we will use for most topics to learn and practice a lot of K8s concepts. As we move further, we will upgrade the cluster as per requirements.

Conclusion

This chapter covered the introduction and setup of Kubernetes. You got familiarized with the architecture and components of a K8s cluster. You also understood K8s' position in the container market and busted a few myths about when to choose K8s over Swarm, and how control plane components are not the only ones running inside the Control Plane node. The cluster setup was easy to understand because you had followed a similar procedure in the very last chapter.

In the following chapters, we will understand the different workloads and how K8s handles them. We will also look at networking and storage objects of K8s before moving to advanced cluster orchestration.

Multiple choice questions

1. Which of the following organizations is responsible for hosting, managing, and maintaining the Kubernetes project?

   A. Cloud Network Computing Foundation

   B. Cloud Native Computing Foundation

   C. Cloud Native Container Foundation

   D. Cloud Network Container Foundation

   Answer: B

2. How are non-Control Plane machines identified as in Kubernetes?

   A. Nodes

   B. Minions

   C. Managers

   D. Droplets

Answer: A

3. Which of the following Kubernetes components can directly communicate to the distributed key-value store "etcd"?

    A. `kube-controller-manager`

    B. `kube-apiserver`

    C. `kube-scheduler`

    D. `cloud-controller-manager`

    Answer: B

4. Which of the following Kubernetes components is used to store all the cluster data?

    A. `etcd`

    B. `kube-scheduler`

    C. `kubelet`

    D. `kube-proxy`

    Answer: A

5. Which of the following is the smallest deployable unit in Kubernetes?

    A. `Pod`

    B. `Container`

    C. `Service`

    D. `Image`

    Answer: A

6. Which of the following is the most used pod implementation?

    A. One container per Pod

    B. One service per Pod

    C. One volume per Pod

    D. One role per Pod

    Answer: A

7. What is the significance of apiVersion in Kubernetes objects?

    A. They are Kubernetes' way to determine the kind of object.

    B. They are Kubernetes' way to determine the hierarchy of the object to make sure controllers monitor the basic objects.

    C. They are Kubernetes' way of grouping objects to manage them without affecting the objects of other groups.

D. They make navigating documentation easier.

Answer: C

8. What is the default validity of cluster join tokens in Kubernetes?

   A. 5 min

   B. 24 h

   C. 2 h

   D. 30 min

   Answer: B

9. Which of the following apiVersion applies to pods?

   A. `apps/v1`

   B. `v1`

   C. `apps/v1beta1`

   D. `v1beta1`

   Answer: B

10. Which of the following ports is NOT reserved in the inbound direction on non-Control Plane nodes in a Kubernetes cluster?

    A. 10250

    B. 30001

    C. 32766

    D. 10251

    Answer: D

Questions

1. Explain Kubernetes architecture and its components.

2. State the differences between Kubernetes and Swarm.

3. Write a YAML pod definition file to create an ubuntu 18.04 pod on a Kubernetes Cluster.

4. Write down a step-by-step procedure of bootstrapping a Kubernetes cluster of 3 nodes and 1 Control Plane using kubeadm.

5. How many namespaces will you get after bootstrapping a K8s cluster using kubeadm. State their names and uses, respectively.

## CHAPTER 10

Workload Orchestration with Kubernetes

Introduction

The previous chapter introduced you to Kubernetes; this chapter will help you see it in action. Kubernetes has different controllers for different types of workload objects. Mastering them enables you to orchestrate your containerized microservices better. This chapter will treat each workload type as a separate topic and will dive deep into it. We will also look at some core Kubernetes concepts while playing with these workloads.

Structure

This chapter covers:

- Playing with namespaces
- Labels and selectors
- K8s wheel of objects
- Back to pods (Liveness and Readiness Probes, Resource Limits)
- Init containers

Objective

This is a practice-heavy chapter. We will begin exactly where we had completed the previous chapter. You will get to write and understand more Kubernetes object definition YAMLs. By the end of this chapter, you shall be used to the structure of a Kubernetes object YAML and what to look out for. You will also understand the purpose and operations of different workload objects and their controllers. You will have your base built up to begin practicing basic workload definitions.

Playing with namespaces

This chapter will cover a lot of basic orchestration using K8s. Before we move to the workloads, it is important to cover namespaces, labels, and selectors. We have seen the concept of namespaces in the previous chapter. They are the logical division of the cluster across the nodes in the context of resource allocation and access. A standard K8s cluster bootstrapped using Kubeadm will have four pre-configured namespaces. If you do not specify any particular namespace, your workloads (such as pods) will be scheduled on the default namespace.

To create a user-defined namespace, use **kubectl create** command followed by the keyword namespace and the namespace's name. Technically ~~speaking~~ writing, you can use the YAML file for this purpose, but it does not provide any more control or customization than command, so there is no reason to go that far. However, if you are using K8s on production systems, you want the configuration (in YAML or JSON) declaratively defined and under version control.

```
kubectl create namespace my-namespace
```

As the command succeeds, we get a confirmation, as shown in the following screenshot:

Figure 10.1: Create a user-defined namespace

You can verify this further by listing the namespaces, as shown in the following screenshot. The user-defined namespace is added along with its age.

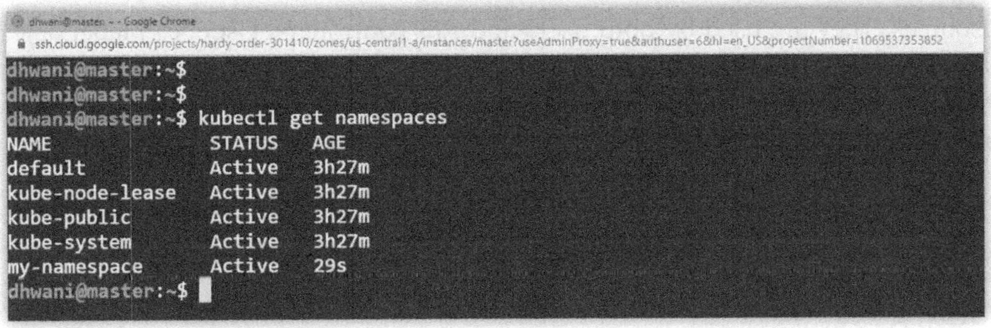

Figure 10.2: *List of all namespaces available in K8s cluster*

To schedule a pod (or any workload) in a particular namespace, you can mention the namespace's name with **-n** flag. For example:

```
kubectl create -f imperative-pod.yaml -n my-namespace
```

It creates another pod called **imp-pod** but in **my-namespace**. We can view it using **kubectl get pods** with **--all-namespaces** flag:

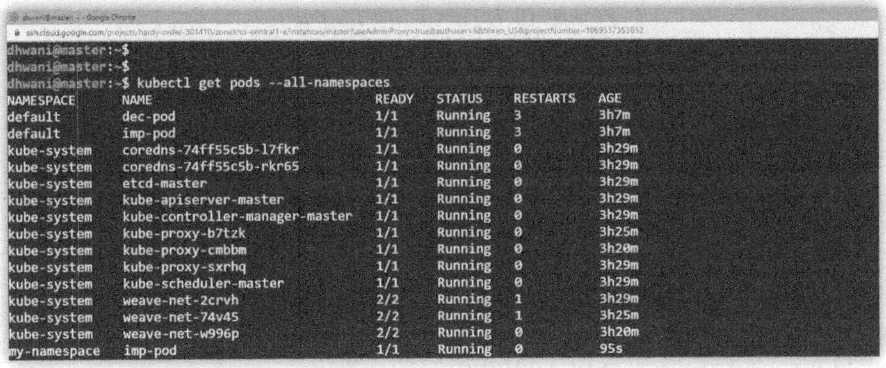

Figure 10.3: *A complete list of running pods in all namespaces*

This brings another conclusion: **the name of an object of a particular type is unique across the namespace in a K8s cluster** (however, resources that don't fall under any namespace's scope like namespaces themselves or nodes need to have absolutely unique names across the cluster). If you want to have a more precise output, you can use **-n** flag with **kubectl get pods** and provide the namespace instead of **--all-namespaces**. This also works as an object sorting mechanism. Writing of object sorting, let's talk about an even more efficient way in the next topic.

Labels and selectors

Labels are key-value paired indexed metadata associated with K8s objects. They are used for attribute-based quick and efficient identification and arrangement of resources. They are used by both users and K8s controllers. Users can label objects according to their use cases, while controllers use labels to determine which objects will be controlled by them. The following figure is a conceptual representation of labels:

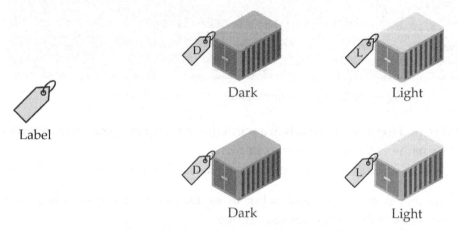

Figure 10.4: Labels in Kubernetes

Any K8s object can have one or more labels at any point in time (in most natural use cases, the objects will have more than one labels). Adding or removing a label does not affect the performance of an object since label is just a form of metadata (though it may alter its behavior if the label imposes a controller on the object, more on that later).

Labels become more significant when they are used with **Selectors**. As a quick analogy, you can think of labels as tags and selectors as finders or magnifying glasses. Here is a graphical representation:

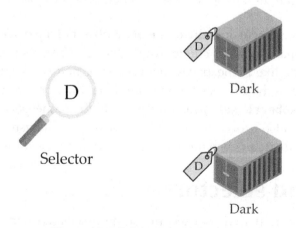

Figure 10.5: Selectors in Kubernetes

There are some syntax and search guidelines to follow while using labels and selectors:

- The labels have **two parts: keys and values**. Keys can be words, domain names, or sub-domain names followed by a keyword separated by a slash (**/**). The domains or subdomains are called **prefixes**. They are optional but, if added, must not be longer than 253 characters. The keywords are called **names**. They can contain alphabets, numbers, dashes, underscores and/or dots and must not exceed 63 characters. They are case sensitive.

- The value part of the labels also follows the same rules as the names of the keys. To put it in simple terms, prefixes can be subdomains separated by dots, and names are keywords added using a slash after subdomain. The values are also keywords having the same liberties and limitations as the names of the keys. For example, `app:nginx, environment:dev, ceruleancanvas.com/author:Nisarg`, and so on.

- You cannot use `kubernetes.io/` and `k8s.io/` prefixes since they are reserved for K8s itself.

- There are two types of selectors based on label requirements: **Set-based selectors and Equality-based selectors**.

- **Set-based selectors** are used for filtering out multiple labels. They have three operators: `in, notin` and identifier of existence. For example, `app in (nginx, redis)` lists pods with label key **app** and values `nginx or redis`. Similarly, if we put a `notin` like `app notin (nginx)`, K8s lists all pods with key app excluding value **nginx**. The identifier of existence is generally used to disregard values and only focus on keys. Simply writing **app** lists all the objects with label key **app** regardless of their value and writing `!app` excludes objects with label key **app**.

- Equality-based selectors are used to single out particular key-value pairs using equality operator (`=` or `==`) or inequality operator (`!=`). As you might have guessed, writing `app=nginx` or `app==nginx` only lists objects with **app: nginx** key-value paired label (they may have other labels though), whereas writing `app!=nginx` discounts them.

- One or more **equality** or **set-based selection** rules can be applied in a single statement using comma separation. For example, `environment (dev, prod), app!=redis` is a valid search and returns objects which satisfy both rules.

We will look at heavy use of labels and selectors throughout this and further chapters when we play with workloads, services, and other mechanisms of K8s orchestration.

K8s wheel of objects

Apart from trivial resources like memory (RAM) or third-party resources like Docker Images, everything native to K8s is created and managed in the form of independent or integrated objects. These objects can be classified into four broad categories, as shown in the following infographic:

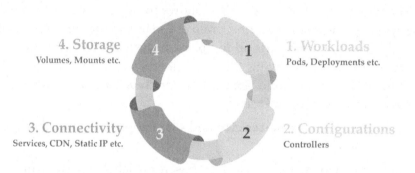

Figure 10.6: Infographic representation of different Objects in Kubernetes

Let us talk about them one-by-one:

- **Workloads:** Traditionally, a workload is an application running on a set of resources. In terms of K8s, workloads are objects encompassing independent or groups of containers under contextual conditions. Pods are the most basic examples of Workloads. There are a bunch of other workloads to discuss in this chapter. Generally, these workloads are created and supervised by controllers.

- **Configurations:** There are many aspects of an application that do not require containers. For example, controllers. Other candidates are toggles and variable values. They are written as key: value pairs and stored in etcd. We have already seen that controllers are watch loop processes designed to create, supervise, and control relevant workloads. The number of workload controllers is limited in a standard K8s installation stack, but one can always add user-defined controller definitions for typical use cases.

- **Connectivity:** Networking in K8s is a vast topic, but all of its significant tasks are defined as objects such as services or ingress controllers. An advantage of having a loose model of objects to define everything is to have ease of tallying the current state and meeting the end goal to match the current state with the desired state. A stack of container networking utilities also run as containers and are wrapped under workloads (such as weave-net pods, which we had seen earlier in kube-system namespace).

- **Storage:** This is one of the most fascinating and well-developed areas of K8s (compared to its contemporaries). From ephemeral storage to managed backup configured cloud storage, K8s has provisions for everything. The field is still open for custom storage objects. If nothing else is defined, every workload is provided with a standard volume *(We are avoiding specific names to maintain a comfortable ambiguity and focus on the broader picture. We will explore networking and storage objects in the next chapter in great detail. After all, I want you to have a mind-blowing experience, not to have your minds blown by info-dump).*

We will take at least three chapters to cover all types of objects mentioned in this wheel. For now, it is time to get started with Workloads. This is where K8s starts to become fun. We have already seen pods and one of their basic YAML definitions. Let us make replicas of such pods.

Replicasets

Replicasets are a higher unit of orchestration compared to pod, which means they will supervise the pods. Their purpose is pretty obvious to scale and manage the number of pod replicas. We can increase or decrease the number of replicas of a pod using a Replicaset. Replicasets are controlled by Replicaset Controller. Pods are given labels, and Replicasets use selectors to keep track of which pods to include under its umbrella. This is useful when we do not want to write multiple YAML files for similar pods, as shown in the conceptual following figure:

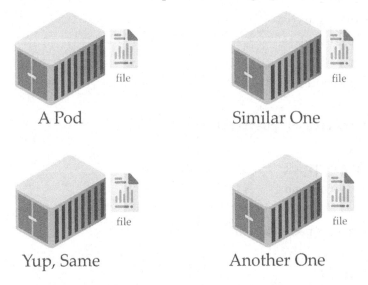

Figure 10.7: Multiple configuration files for similar pods

It is also possible to provide a pod definition along with Replicasets. It would mean that the creation of those pods will also be managed by Replicasets (Replicaset controller will request the trigger of the Pod Controller). While doing so, you need to provide pod specs as a pod template to the YAML file of Replicasets. Let us take an example:

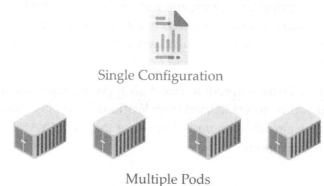

Single Configuration

Multiple Pods

Figure 10.8: *Concept of Replicaset*

We will write a YAML file to create a replicated PHP **guest-book** application. You do not need to worry even if you have never run any PHP code since everything is abstracted inside the container. The focus is exclusively on K8s Replicasets. Create a YAML file called **replicaset.yaml** (or a name of your choice) and populate it with the following content written:

```
1.  # Object Setup
2.  apiVersion: apps/v1
3.  kind: ReplicaSet
4.
5.  # Meta Information
6.  metadata:
7.    name: replicaset-guestbook
8.    labels:
9.      app: guestbook
10.     tier: frontend
11.
12. # Replicaset Specification
13. spec:
14.   replicas: 3
15.   selector:
16.     matchLabels:
```

```
17.      tier: frontend
18.
19. # Pod Metadata and Specifications
20.   template:
21.     metadata:
22.       labels:
23.         app: guestbook
24.         tier: frontend
25.
26. # Container Specification
27.     spec:
28.       containers:
29.       - name: php-redis
30.         image: gcr.io/google_samples/gb-frontend:v3
31.         ports:
32.         - containerPort: 80
```

Let us break this YAML file down from *"Oh! This seems different"* to *"Ah, I see!"*. The API version for the Replicaset object is different from Pods. Pods are a part of the core K8s API group (**v1**). In other words, they exist since the beginning of K8s. Replicasets are relatively new (earlier, there was a legacy mechanism called Replication Controller) hence, they fall under a newer API group called **app/v1**.

Next, we have the kind of object we want to create, which is Replicaset. The metadata field contains the name of the Replicaset (**replicaset-guestbook**) and labels. Unlike the previous YAMLs, this one has two labels. The first is **app**, with value **guestbook** and the second is **tier** with value **frontend**.

Next is the **Spec** field *(this is the last "main" field of this YAML, everything below is the subfield)*. The first thing to mention here is the number of replicas (simple as that, no rocket science). In this case, we will have 3 replicas of the target pod, but you are free to change this number as per your own will or requirements while keeping the availability of your system's resources in mind. The next up is the selector. As we have discussed in **Labels and Selectors**, selectors can identify a set of objects having a particular label. Here, the selector of this Replicaset will look for pods having the label **tier: frontend,** and those pods will directly be managed by this Replicaset.

WAIT! Mind the indentation. Okay, let us take a look at the pod template. The Replicaset will use the pod template to create a homogeneous set of pods. There is one important thing to notice here. For the **selector** to perform the **selection** successfully *(love the wordplay, just love the wordplay)*, we need to make sure that each pod created using this template must have a label `tier: frontend`. To do so, we need to add that label under the metadata field of this Pod template. There is another spec field dedicated to the pod template. It contains the information regarding the container to be running inside pod. We are going to create a php extension for Redis based on an image gb-frontend of version 3 stored in Google's container registry (since this is not docker hub, we need to mention the URL). The port **80** of the container will be open for communications.

Time to create the object. Type the command **kubectl create** followed by the **-f** flag and the name of the YAML file, **replicaset.yaml**. We get the confirmation as indicated in the following screenshot:

```
dhwani@master:~$
dhwani@master:~$ kubectl create -f replicaset.yaml
replicaset.apps/replicaset-guestbook created
dhwani@master:~$
```

Figure 10.9: Create Replicaset object

As we list the pods, we get to know that 3 new guestbook pods are ready and running as you can see in the following screenshot:

```
dhwani@master:~$
dhwani@master:~$ kubectl get pods
NAME                        READY   STATUS    RESTARTS   AGE
dec-pod                     1/1     Running   5          5h58m
imp-pod                     1/1     Running   5          5h58m
replicaset-guestbook-g9wv8  1/1     Running   0          47s
replicaset-guestbook-rrrn2  1/1     Running   0          47s
replicaset-guestbook-tcvnj  1/1     Running   0          47s
```

Figure 10.10: List out pods to verify the creation of Replicaset pods

To view more details about the pods, like where are they scheduled and what are their IPs, you can run the same command with **-o wide** flag.

```
dhwani@master:~$
dhwani@master:~$
dhwani@master:~$ kubectl get pods -o wide
NAME                        READY   STATUS    RESTARTS   AGE     IP          NODE     NOMINATED NODE
dec-pod                     1/1     Running   5          5h58m   10.44.0.1   node-1   <none>
imp-pod                     1/1     Running   5          5h59m   10.36.0.1   node-2   <none>
replicaset-guestbook-g9wv8  1/1     Running   0          62s     10.44.0.3   node-1   <none>
replicaset-guestbook-rrrn2  1/1     Running   0          62s     10.44.0.2   node-1   <none>
replicaset-guestbook-tcvnj  1/1     Running   0          62s     10.36.0.3   node-2   <none>
dhwani@master:~$
dhwani@master:~$
```

Figure 10.11: Networking and Scheduling information of Replicaset pods

You can copy the name of either of the three pods and type **kubectl describe pod** followed by pasting that pod's name. Press *Enter* to view the pod description:

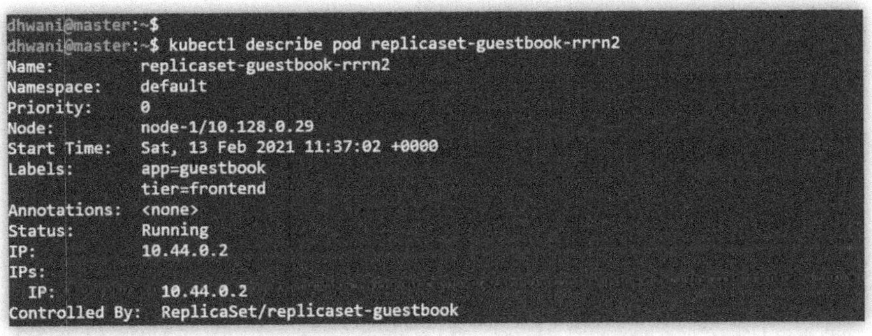

```
dhwani@master:~$
dhwani@master:~$ kubectl describe pod replicaset-guestbook-rrrn2
Name:           replicaset-guestbook-rrrn2
Namespace:      default
Priority:       0
Node:           node-1/10.128.0.29
Start Time:     Sat, 13 Feb 2021 11:37:02 +0000
Labels:         app=guestbook
                tier=frontend
Annotations:    <none>
Status:         Running
IP:             10.44.0.2
IPs:
  IP:           10.44.0.2
Controlled By:  ReplicaSet/replicaset-guestbook
```

Figure 10.12: Describe a Replicaset pod

Most of this pod's description details are similar to what we have seen with the imperative pod. Still, there are a couple of key points to notice.

- The pod received the labels mentioned in the meta of the pod template and is reflecting them properly.

- A new field called **Controlled By** indicates that this pod is created and managed by the guestbook Replicaset.

The primary purpose of having a higher level of orchestration object is to abstract away the pod. **kubectl** command-line treats Replicasets the same way it treats pods or any other objects. In other words, you can also list out the available Replicaset using the same command to list out pods or any other K8s object.

Execute **kubectl get rs** command and mention the name of the replicaset to get the details specific to it. The outcome looks like the following screenshot:

```
dhwani@master: ~ - Google Chrome
ssh.cloud.google.com/projects/hardy-order-301410/zones/us-central1-a/instances/master?useAdminProxy=true&authuser=6&hl=en_US&projectNum
dhwani@master:~$
dhwani@master:~$
dhwani@master:~$ kubectl get rs replicaset-guestbook
NAME                     DESIRED   CURRENT   READY   AGE
replicaset-guestbook     3         3         3       7m8s
dhwani@master:~$
```

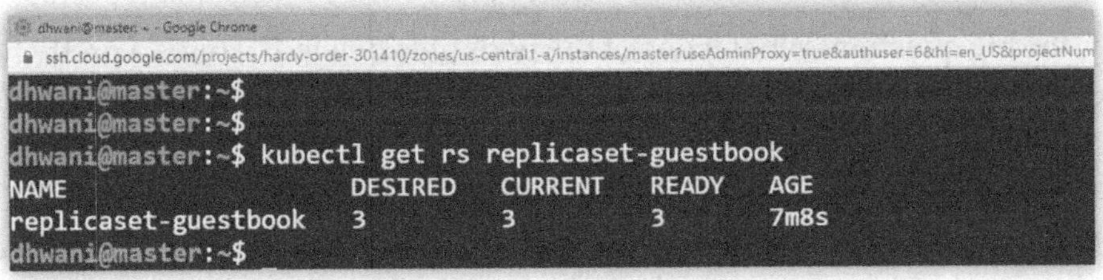

Figure 10.13: List out Replicasets (rs)

The output is a little different from pods' list. We do not get columns like status or restarts because ReplicaSet itself does not have any restarts. The containers inside the pods controlled by ReplicaSets perform restarts, and this can be checked by listing specific pods. On the other hand, we get new columns like **DESIRED** and **CURRENT,** which reflect the watch loop nature of Replicaset and how it continuously attempts to match the number of current replicas with the number of desired replicas.

We can also get more details about a Replicaset by executing the command **kubectl describe** followed by the Replicaset's name. The outcome of this command looks like the following screenshot:

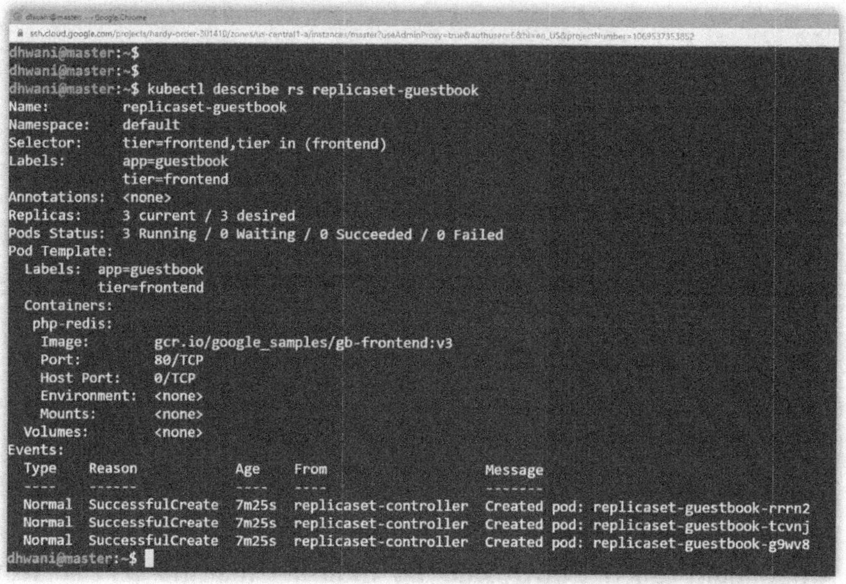

Figure 10.14: *Detailed information about Replicaset guestbook*

This Replicaset resides in the `default` namespace, and the selector is set for the label **`tier: frontend`**. There are no annotations. The Pod template is the same as mentioned in its object definition YAML file. The **Pods STATUS** field shows the statuses for the pods controlled by this Replicaset. All 3 of them are running successfully. Replicaset events are listed at the bottom. They are less exhaustive than pod events because these events are monitored by Replicaset Controller. Once the pod creation has been scheduled, the responsibility shifts to pod controller, which keeps track of subsequent events.

Finally, the big question. What if one of the pods gets deleted? This is a pretty healthy Replicaset on a contextually resourceful cluster; so, none of the pods will get deleted by themselves.

So, we need to delete one of the pods controlled by this replicaset manually. To do so, execute the command **`kubectl delete pod`** command followed by the name of any of the three pods. The outcome of this command looks like the following screenshot:

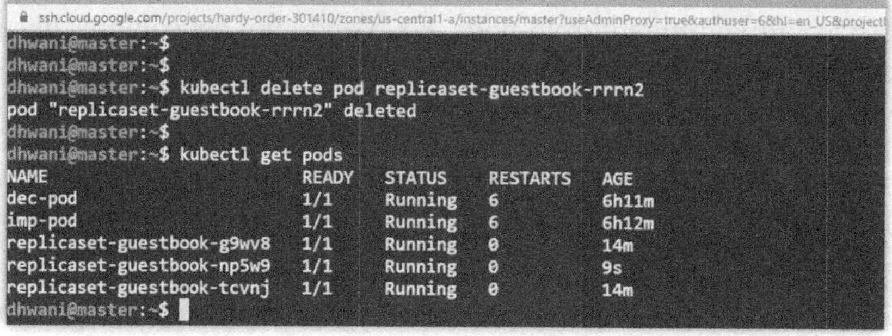

Figure 10.15: *Replicaset maintains desired state (no. of replicas)*

The pod did get deleted, but we are back to having the same number of pods when we list the pods out again. This is because the Replicaset controller made sure that the number of current pods meets the desired number. It spun up a new pod that can be noticed since one of the three Replicaset pods has a younger age! This brings another question; what if we do intend to delete a pod? You can change the YAML and decrease the number of desired replicas. Just use **kubectl apply** command, and you will have one less pod. Of course, if you delete the entire Replicaset, none of the pods will be spun up again.

Replicasets are a great way to use containers at scale, but they are not the top of the object chain. Most of the times, they are used under deployments.

Deployments

Deployments stand even higher than Replicasets in terms of supervisory nature. They are capable of creating their own Replicasets, which in turn can create pods accordingly. They are the most widely used workload object for stateless applications. Just like Replicasets, they also use Labels and selectors for pod identification. Deployments are used as all-rounder objects for various purposes like creating containers, scaling containers, clubbing containers together, exposing them to the internet, and so on. Their more intelligent and more configurable watch-loop makes them more user-friendly choice compared to something like a ReplicaSet.

How smart? Let us understand via an example. Create a file called **deployment.yaml** and populate it with the following code:

```
1.  apiVersion: apps/v1
2.  kind: Deployment
3.  metadata:
4.    name: deploy-nginx
5.  spec:
6.    selector:
7.      matchLabels:
8.        app: nginx
9.    replicas: 3
10.   template:
11.     metadata:
12.       labels:
13.         app: nginx
```

```
14.    spec:

15.      containers:

16.      - name: deploy-container

17.        image: nginx:1.7.9

18.        ports:

19.        - containerPort: 80
```

Take a close look at this file. You will realize that it is remarkably similar to Replicaset (including the API version). You can precisely tell what each field in the file represents. Despite that, there are performance differences; let us create the deployment to examine them.

The creation process is also the same as earlier, **kubectl create** command followed by **-f** flag and the file name. The result would resemble the following screenshot:

Figure 10.16: Create a deployment from object configuration YAML file

You can play around by listing pods and Replicsets again, but we will stick to listing out the deployment directly using **kubectl get** command followed by the type of object, which in this particular case is deployments to get the output as shown in the following screenshot:

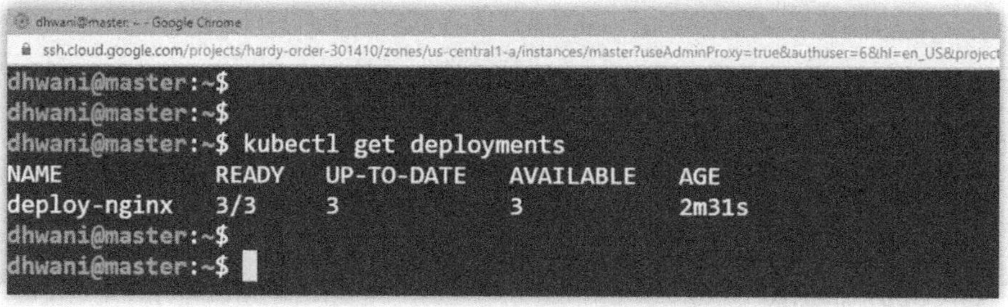

Figure 10.17: List out deployments in Kubernetes

Just as the list of Replicasets was represented differently from the list of pods, the list of deployments has its own share of uniqueness. Apart from **READY** and **AVAILABLE** columns, we have **UP-TO-DATE** column as well. This is useful while rolling out updates using deployments. Unlike the Waterfall software development model, agile microservices update very frequently. The capacity and ease of rolling out updates without disrupting the app performance are crucial.

Take a use case, if you are updating your software once every 6 months or once a year, you might be comfortable with keeping it down under maintenance for a few hours; but if you are updating it every alternate day or sometimes multiple times a day (updating recommendation engine settings by continuously learning from user behavior and so on), you cannot afford to keep your app down every now and then. In that case, you need to update rollouts without downtimes.

Kubernetes deployments are designed to perform such smooth rollouts. We can understand it better by running **kubectl describe** command followed by the deployment's name.

The outcome of this command looks like the following screenshot:

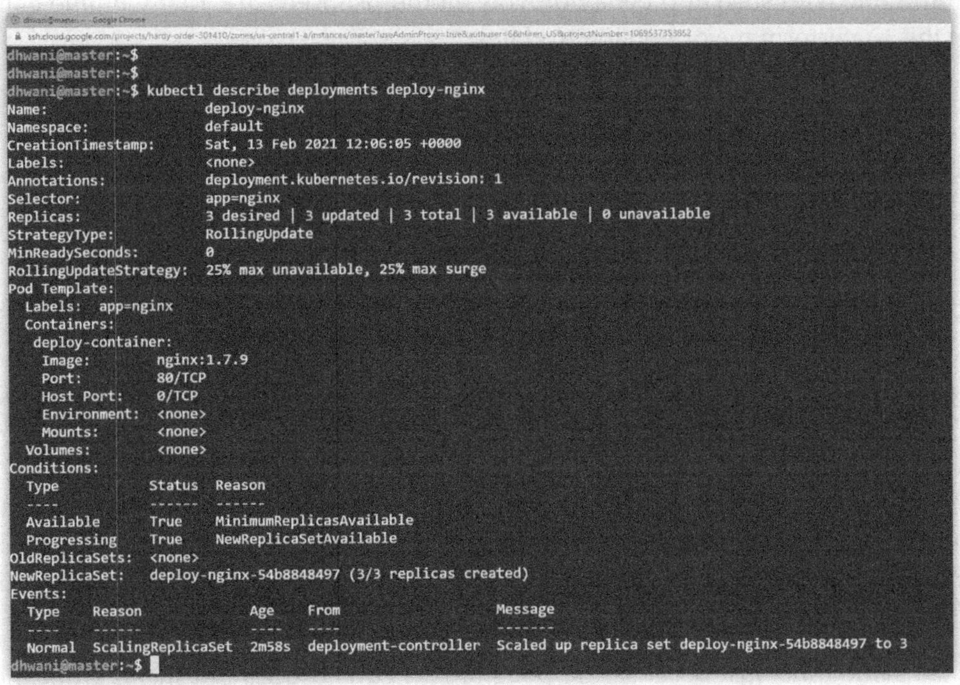

Figure 10.18: Describe deployment for detailed information

Just like every other description, this one also has metadata, user-provided information, and container information. They are pretty similar to pods or Replicasets. The unique fields are related to the update strategy. Deployments are updated **if and only if** there is some change in the pod template. These changes can include changing the container image, limiting resources, changing access, adding or altering metadata, changing storage options, and so on.

If the pod template remains the same and just the number of replicas is subjected to change, it is called scaling, not updating. We have already seen how scaling works with Replicasets. It is the same with deployments. You can change the number of replicas by modifying the deployment's YAML file or using the `kubectl scale` command with the `--replicas` flag and the number of replicas you want to create.

In the case of update strategies (involving a change in pod template), there are two possible values: **Recreate** and **Rolling Update.** The Recreate strategy kills all of the pods before creating any new ones. This means intentional downtime and is useful when you don't want to confuse client-side applications with the collision between different session data generated during usage.

A practical example would be blocking someone on Twitter but viewing their posts until refreshing or restarting the app (thus triggering a new session). If you are not comfortable with such app behavior, you should use **Recreate**. Many online games use this to perform major version updates.

If you do not want to cause any downtime, K8s deployments provide an update strategy called **Rolling Update**. This opens plenty of possibilities. There are two controlling parameters of the Rolling Update Strategy.

1. **MaxSurge:** Maximum number of extra pods (surplus pods after desired replicas) allowed while rolling out the update.

2. **MaxUnavailable:** Maximum number of pods that can be discounted from serving the application while rolling out the update.

The rolling update strategy does not kill all of the pods before creating new ones. It kills pods as it creates new ones and routes the load toward the newly created pods. As the process goes on, all of the old pods are replaced by new ones. For example, let us say you have a database server deployment about to receive the rolling updates. Your desired number of replicas is 4. If the Max surge is set to 25%, the deployment controller will create 1 updated pod first; at one point, there will be 5 pods in total (which is 1 more than desired replicas).

At the same time, just because the pods are scheduled does not mean all of them are serving the application. While the traffic is being routed from old to new pods, there could be a small timeframe when both old and new pods are not serving. Max Unavailable will define this; setting it to 25% means there needs to be at least 3 out of 4 serving pods at any given time. Together, this means in the deployment of 4 pods, a rolling update strategy with 25% Max surge and 25% Max Unavailable setting will update and replace one pod at a time. This can be 2 pods at a time if both values are set to 50%. This can also be 2 new pods created at a time while one replaced at a time if Max surge is set to 50%, but Max unavailable is set to 25%.

The next concern is how to decide the values of Max Surge and Max Unavailable? The answer is simple: it depends on your application. The better you know your application, the more informed and comprehensive decision you are likely to make. Let us say the update involves using a different Docker Image. If the image is just an updated version of your current image, the chances are high that most of the underlying layers would be the same, that is, they would be reused from the cache. This is a resource-efficient scenario. You can let loose a little on the surge and make it 50% since the cloud usage wouldn't break your bank.

Moreover, suppose the rollout is happening during less app traffic. In that case, you can also use more max unavailable and get done with the rollout quickly rather than allowing it to stall for long. You may have noticed; many web portals of essential services (for example Railways, Airlines, Healthcare, Banks, and so on) update themselves during the late night of respective time zones. Similarly, university websites should also prefer quick rollouts with the higher surge to ensure that many students can access exam results as they are declared.

Conversely, when a social media giant like Facebook wants to roll out Year-end videos, the rollout might take weeks to cover all users, which indicates relatively safer surge and almost 0 unavailabilities. In a no-compromise scenario like handling the Black Friday sale on Amazon, the deals need to be updated to every user on the same day. The only leeway is the time zone difference between users of different countries. This becomes a matter of investment. You might want to resort to more efficient deployment topologies like Blue-Green, where you would pre-spin-up the entirety of your updated workload and only focus on shifting the load gradually on the big day. This is a high-risk, high-return use case where rolling updates are not the best bet. It is also recommended to run beta tests on separate canary deployments in a production environment before rolling out the updates.

We can have a better look at this by performing a sample rolling update. Looking back at the code, we can see that the nginx version is 1.7.9. The following command will set it to 1.16.1 with a rolling update strategy.

```
kubectl set image deployment/deploy-nginx deploy-container=nginx:1.16.1
--record
```

The base command is **kubectl set**, the attribute is **image**, the target object is **deployment/deploy-nginx**, and the target image is **nginx:1.16.1**. The **--record** flag will help us print and view the change-cause to track what changes our deployment has been through imperative commands (because declarative commands are recorded by default). The output looks like the following screenshot:

Figure 10.19: *Rollout update in deployment*

This was quick! Usually, it can take anywhere between a few minutes to even a few hours with dozens or more pods. In that case, you can view the status of rollout using **kubectl rollout status** command followed by object type and name.

```
kubectl rollout status deployment deploy-nginx
```

The output looks like the following screenshot:

Figure 10.20: *Status of update rollout in deployment*

3 new pods are created, and 3 old ones are terminated. This was not a patch on the previous Replicaset. It is a new Replicaset definition, with the previous one having been scaled down to 0 pods. We can verify this by listing replicasets using **kubectl get rs** command. The outcome looks like the following screenshot:

Figure 10.21: *List of Replicasets*

Furthermore, if we perform more than one updates over time, we can even view the history of rollouts by running the following command along with the target object's name:

```
kubectl rollout history deployment.apps/deploy-nginx
```

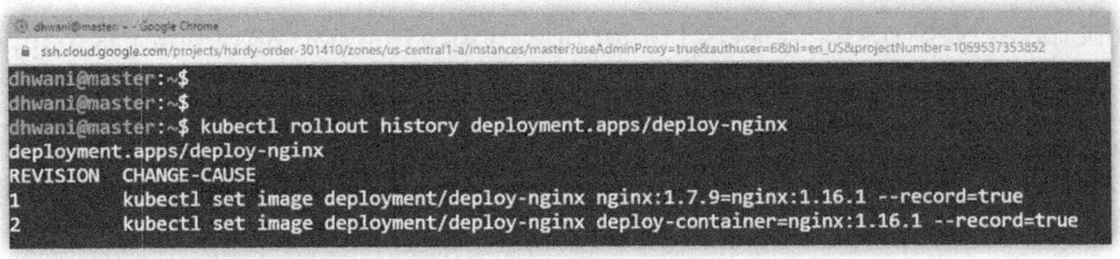

Figure 10.22: History of rolled out updates of a deployment

The revisions are listed in chronological order, and since we had used the **--record** flag earlier, we also get to see the appropriate change cause. This may not sound important for an individual cluster operator but becomes critical when working in a team. Transparency can mitigate more than half of the teamwork conflicts. You can also restore the deployment to its original state by using **kubectl rollout undo** command.

Finally, how can we even call it an Nginx container if we don't open the Nginx standard homepage on the browser?! Deployments or any other workloads with labels can be exposed using K8s networking objects called **Services**. The next chapter explores them in-depth, thus, for the time being, think of them as private, little antenna for our deployment. We can expose the deployment using **kubectl expose** command. This command creates a service called **my-nginx-service** and maps nginx's port **80** to the host's available port:

```
kubectl expose deployment deploy-nginx --type=NodePort --port=8080
--target-port=80 --name=my-service
```

Execute the following command to list out K8s services:

```
 kubectl get svc
```

svc is the abbreviation of Service, just as **rs** is the abbreviation of replicaset, or **p** is the abbreviation of pods:

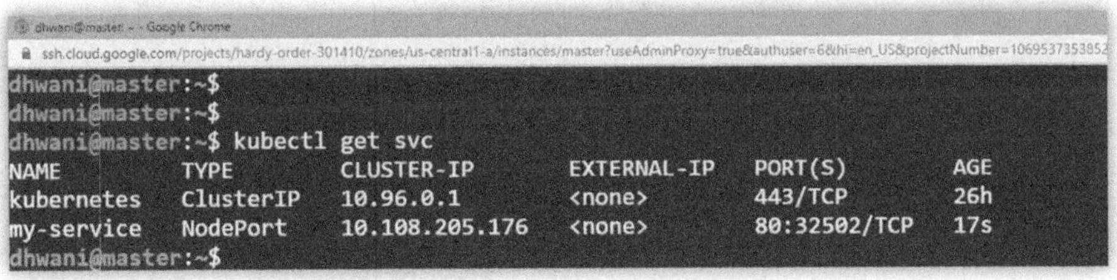

Figure 10.23: List of services in K8s cluster

A default service called Kubernetes is active since we bootstrapped the cluster and below that is the user-defined service. We will describe the service when we cover

Kubernetes Networking objects, but for now, notice that port **80** of nginx is mapped to host (node)'s port **32502**.

To successfully run the **<IP>:<port>** combo on the browser, we need to create a firewall rule to allow external connections. Go to **GCP Dashboard** | **VPC Networks** | **Firewall Rules** and click on **Create New Firewall Rule**.

Once the **New Rule** page pops up, fill in the title and the configuration options as shown in the following screenshot:

Figure 10.24: Firewall rule creation in Google Cloud Platform (GCP)

Once the rule is set up, hit the combination of external IP and your mapped VM port on a new browser window to witness the deployment working perfectly well.

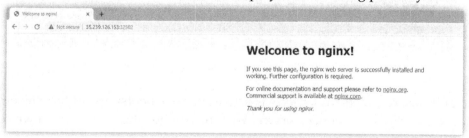

Figure 10.25: Landing page of NGINX web server deployed on K8s

Jobs and Cron Jobs

Moving on from deployments, we have jobs. They are handled by Jobs-Controllers. To define them simply, jobs mean objects that don't keep the container inside the pod running for eternity. Once the containers' purpose is fulfilled, they exit. In more technical terms, the commands provided to the containers are time and iteration limited. Once they get executed, the container gracefully stops and gives the resources back to the host! This makes them resource and scheduling efficient. This also means that they may have to be re-run multiple times, but it is better than keeping resources occupied permanently.

Jobs are come in handy when the nature of the application is not "always on" or "always serving". Naturally, applications like webservers or database servers are not good fits for jobs. You can call containers to create an ad-hoc environment for specific calculations and store the value for further use even after the container is dead. Here is an example. Create a file called **job.yaml** and populate it with the following code:

```
1.  apiVersion: batch/v1
2.  kind: Job
3.  metadata:
4.    name: job-pi
5.  spec:
6.    template:
7.      spec:
8.        containers:
9.        - name: job-container
10.          image: perl
11.          command: [«perl», «-Mbignum=bpi», «-wle», «print bpi(2000)»]
12.        restartPolicy: Never
13.    backoffLimit: 4
```

The **apiVersion** is **batch/v1** as jobs belong to the batch group of APIs. This is suitable because jobs are beneficial for conclusive batch processes. The name of the Job is **job-pi,** and it is configured to run a PERL container that calculates and prints the value of **pi** up to **2000** digits.

Do pay attention to the **Restart Policy**, which is set to **Never**. This is completely in line with the nature of Job. Furthermore, what if the job fails to execute? The container will not be able to shut down gracefully and will have to restart. This behavior contradicts jobs' primary purpose: to free up the resources once the job is done. To counter this phenomenon, the **Back off Limit** is set to 4. This means that after 4 unsuccessful iterations, the job will stop trying, and its resources will be freed up.

Create the job object using the imperative command from the Job's objects configuration YAML file, **`job.yaml (kubectl create -f <filename>)`** and list the pods as shown in the following screenshot:

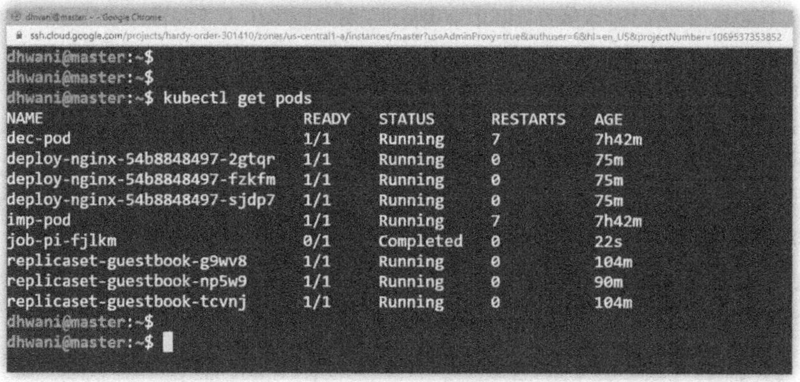

```
dhwani@master:~$
dhwani@master:~$
dhwani@master:~$ kubectl get pods
NAME                              READY   STATUS      RESTARTS   AGE
dec-pod                           1/1     Running     7          7h42m
deploy-nginx-54b8848497-2gtqr     1/1     Running     0          75m
deploy-nginx-54b8848497-fzkfm     1/1     Running     0          75m
deploy-nginx-54b8848497-sjdp7     1/1     Running     0          75m
imp-pod                           1/1     Running     7          7h42m
job-pi-fjlkm                      0/1     Completed   0          22s
replicaset-guestbook-g9wv8        1/1     Running     0          104m
replicaset-guestbook-np5w9        1/1     Running     0          90m
replicaset-guestbook-tcvnj        1/1     Running     0          104m
dhwani@master:~$
dhwani@master:~$
```

Figure 10.26: *Verification of creation of job-pi pod*

As expected, the pod created by Job-pi is in the completed state. This means the job was executed successfully (*K8s should have written "Good Job!"*). We can get more information about the job as we describe it as shown in the following screenshot:

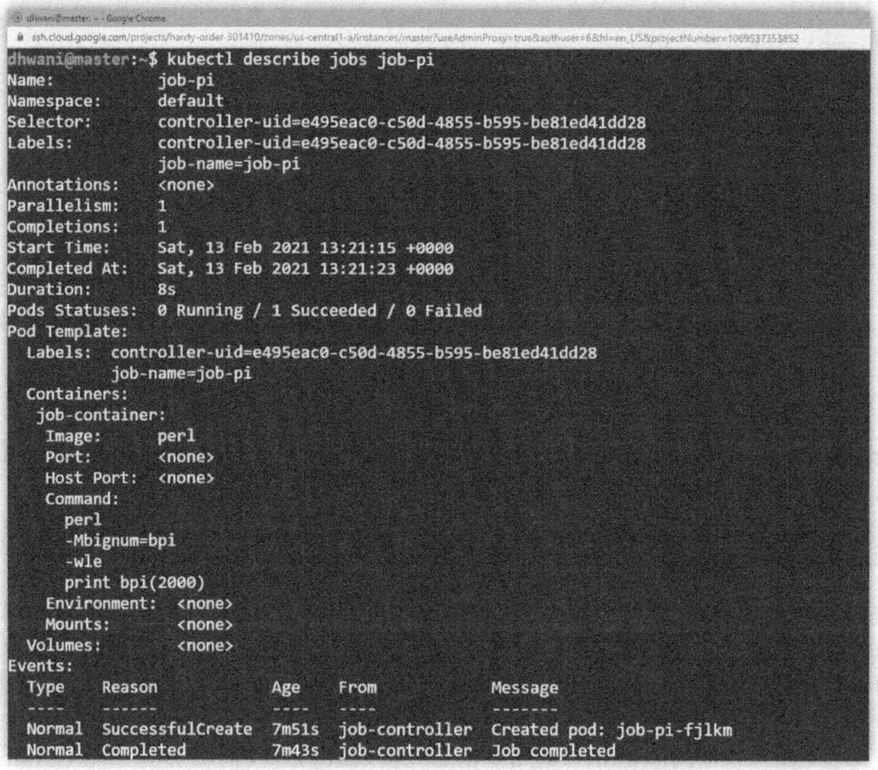

```
dhwani@master:~$ kubectl describe jobs job-pi
Name:           job-pi
Namespace:      default
Selector:       controller-uid=e495eac0-c50d-4855-b595-be81ed41dd28
Labels:         controller-uid=e495eac0-c50d-4855-b595-be81ed41dd28
                job-name=job-pi
Annotations:    <none>
Parallelism:    1
Completions:    1
Start Time:     Sat, 13 Feb 2021 13:21:15 +0000
Completed At:   Sat, 13 Feb 2021 13:21:23 +0000
Duration:       8s
Pods Statuses:  0 Running / 1 Succeeded / 0 Failed
Pod Template:
  Labels:  controller-uid=e495eac0-c50d-4855-b595-be81ed41dd28
           job-name=job-pi
  Containers:
   job-container:
    Image:      perl
    Port:       <none>
    Host Port:  <none>
    Command:
      perl
      -Mbignum=bpi
      -wle
      print bpi(2000)
    Environment:  <none>
    Mounts:       <none>
  Volumes:        <none>
Events:
  Type    Reason            Age    From            Message
  ----    ------            ----   ----            -------
  Normal  SuccessfulCreate  7m51s  job-controller  Created pod: job-pi-fjlkm
  Normal  Completed         7m43s  job-controller  Job completed
```

Figure 10.27: *Description of the job object*

If you look at events, you get the age of the job, which is 7+ min old; compared to that, the duration of the job completion is just 8s. This means the job saved the resources for over 400s after being created *(Good Job)*! Other noticeable parameters are **Parallelism** and **Completion**.

This was a single iteration job, so we had not mentioned the field in YAML, but you can mention them directly under the spec field. If you increase the completion counts, you can provide parallelism to choose how many pods you intend to create and execute in parallel. These features add to the fact that jobs are ideal for conclusive batch processing.

Another million-dollar question is, where is the value of Pi? To retrieve it, you can check out the job logs using **kubectl logs** command followed by the object name. The outcome of this command returns the value of **Pi** up to **2000** digits, as shown in the following screenshot:

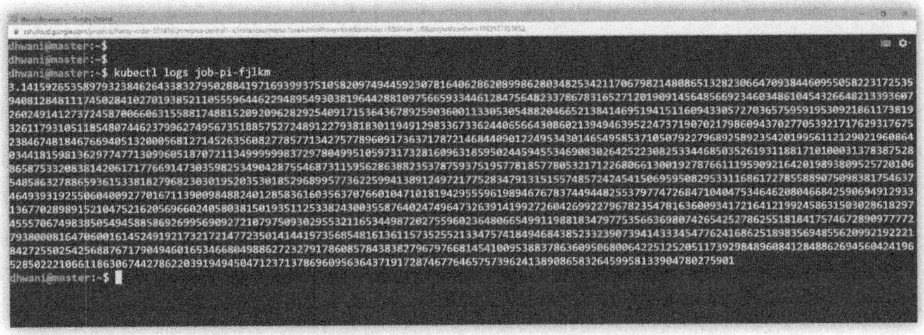

Figure 10.28: Result of Job pod after its completion

This value log was collected by the default logging driver of K8s called **json-file**. There are more useful alternatives scheduled to be discussed in further chapters in greater depth.

Another similar but interesting object is called **Cron Job**. They are wrappers around Jobs. Just how Jobs have Pod Templates, Cron Jobs have Job templates. They are used for the periodic scheduling of jobs. The schedules are defined using **Cron Schedule Expression**. Here is an example. Create a file called **cronjob.yaml** and populate it with the following code:

```
1.  apiVersion: batch/v1beta1
2.  kind: CronJob
3.  metadata:
4.    name: hello
5.  spec:
```

```
6.    schedule: «*/1 * * * *»
7.    jobTemplate:
8.      spec:
9.        template:
10.             spec:
11.               containers:
12.                 - name: hello
13.                   image: busybox
14.                   args:
15.        - /bin/sh
16.        - -c
17.        - echo You, yes you can make this book best-seller!
18.        restartPolicy: OnFailure
```

One of the main specs of this cronjob is **schedule**. ***/1 * * * *** indicates that the job will run once every minute. The next one is the meta and the job template. The job runs a simple busybox pod that prints the ultimate fact *(yes, you…, you can turn this book into a bestseller. Share it with your loved ones, your colleagues, your boss, and your juniors. They call this a shameless plug these days… Light comments aside; we genuinely hope that you're enjoying this book so far!)*.

After saving the file, create the **cronjob** object using **kubectl create -f** followed by object name and file name. You can list the **cronjob** like the following screenshot:

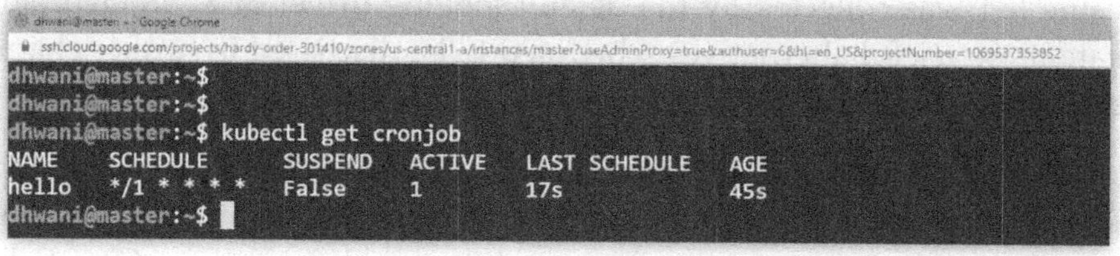

Figure 10.29: List of Cronjobs

The list displays the schedule, last scheduling instance, and several active job instances. The age of the job at the time of screenshotting was 45 s. You will see the last scheduled column updating as you let it age (semantic pun intended).

To dig deeper into this cronjob object, describe it using the **kubectl describe cronjobs** command. The outcome of this command looks like the following screenshot:

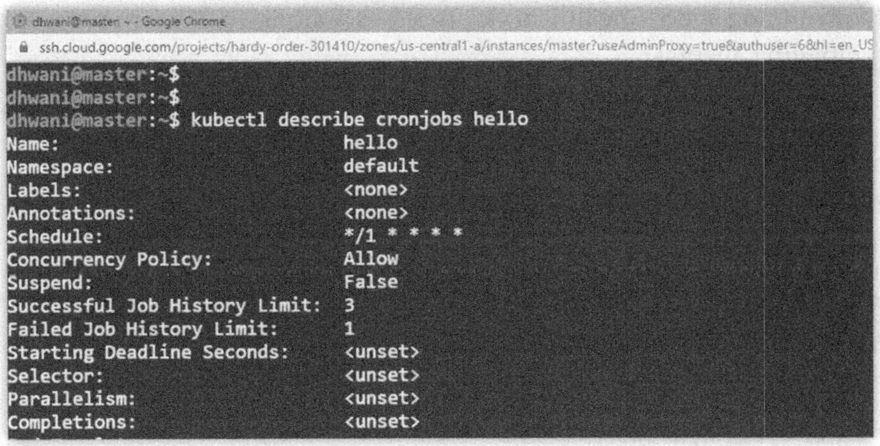

Figure 10.30: Description of a Cronjob

All right, let us begin dissecting it! The cronjob itself has no labels or annotations. It doesn't have any selector that may seem absurd at first, but cronjob does not control any pods. It is just controlling a single job object which in turn is using the pod template.

On top of parallelism, we also have a concurrency policy. This means that not only can job pods run processes in parallel, but multiple jobs can also run in parallel, sharing node resources (like vCPU cores and memory). This is important because the job will be scheduled every minute. What if it takes more than a minute to complete it? As you might have guessed, whether to keep the concurrency ON or not is up to the user *(yes, you, the one who knows the cluster resources and the application behavior the best)*. You can maximize the concurrency by limiting pod resources (this part is just a couple of topics away). We want to ensure that the cron job is doing well; the limit of recording the history of successful jobs is set to 3, whereas the history of unsuccessful jobs is set to 1. This is like the digital manifestation of the wise words do not indulge too much in success but be wary of every failure!

Jobs are significant objects to have time and resource-controlled pods run smoothly. Not all pods are at the forefront, though; the next topic explores the background process pods!

Daemonset

We discussed the concept of daemon (or background) processes in *Chapter 2*. K8s has provisioned a dedicated controller and object type for such process containers. The object is called **Daemonset**. To maintain consistency across the cluster, DaemonSet runs one container of the said process on each node in the background. This is useful for running special healthcheck processes, garbage collector processes, or for running logging agents.

To create a sample DaemonSet, create a YAML file called **daemonset.yaml** and populate it with the following code:

```
1.  apiVersion: apps/v1
2.  kind: DaemonSet
3.  metadata:
4.    name: test-daemonset-1
5.    labels:
6.      app: test-daemon-1
7.  spec:
8.    selector:
9.      matchLabels:
10.       app: test-daemon-1
11.   template:
12.     metadata:
13.       labels:
14.         app: test-daemon-1
15.     spec:
16.       containers:
17.       - name: busybox
18.         image: busybox
19.         args:
20.         - sleep
21.         - "10000"
```

Most of the fields in this YAML are similar to what we have seen earlier. The selector again plays a huge role in the operations of the Daemonset. As long as pods have the label used with the selector, the Daemonset ensures that a copy of that pod runs on each node. Play around with labels (remove the selector label from one of the pods or give some random pod the selector's label). Daemonset will ensure that a copy of the new pod is always available on all nodes. This makes it crucial to differentiate the mnemonics of Daemonset labels from other labels.

After creating the object using standard object creation methods (imperative or declarative), we can get more clarification by listing the pods out, as shown in the following screenshot:

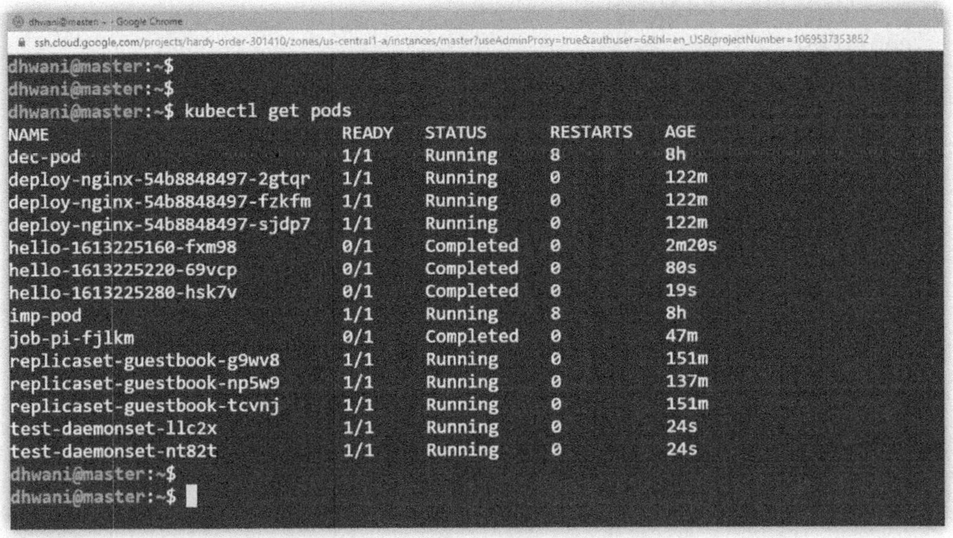

Figure 10.31: Verification of creation of Daemon pods

The bottom-most pods are controlled by the Daemonset. They are scheduled on each node (if you are wondering why just two of them and not three, the master does not allow scheduling workload unless configured otherwise explicitly). We will look at the Daemonset application's actual example a couple of chapters later while discussing logging agents.

Back to pods (liveness and readiness probes, resource limits)

It is time to come full circle. Previously, we had discussed the fundamental fields of a pod definition, but the pods are more flexible and configurable than you think. Here is an example, create a file called **prob.yaml:**

```
1. apiVersion: apps/v1
2. kind: Deployment
3. metadata:
4.   name: prob-busybox
5. spec:
```

```
6.    selector:
7.      matchLabels:
8.        run: prob-busybox
9.    replicas: 2
10.   template:
11.     metadata:
12.       labels:
13.         run: prob-busybox
14.     spec:
15.       containers:
16.       - name: prob-busybox
17.         image: busybox
18.         args:
19.         - /bin/sh
20.         - -c
21.         - touch /tmp/prob-check; sleep 30; rm -rf /tmp/prob-check;
           sleep 600
22.         resources:
23.           requests:
24.             memory: «64Mi»
25.             cpu: «250m»
26.           limits:
27.             memory: «128Mi»
28.             cpu: «500m»
29.         readinessProbe:
30.           exec:
31.             command:
32.             - cat
33.             - /tmp/prob-check
34.           initialDelaySeconds: 5
35.           periodSeconds: 5
36.         livenessProbe:
```

```
37.            exec:
38.              command:
39.                - cat
40.                - /tmp/prob-check
41.            initialDelaySeconds: 7
42.            periodSeconds: 5
```

This is yet another deployment with 2 replicas and a pod template. This pod template is a lot more exhaustive than the ones we have used so far. Let us understand the newer fields:

- **Liveness Probe:** K8s uses this probing routine to verify if the pod is live. If the pod has encountered any deadlock or any crash loop, it is recommended to restart the container. The liveness probe is performed automatically at a fixed time interval defined under **periodSeconds** field. One natural exception to this would be the time when the container is starting. To avoid an unintentional container restart loop, the liveness probe is halted for the duration mentioned in the **initialDelay** field. In the example used above, the liveness probe runs cat on the probe-check file under **/tmp** directory. It returns a success code for the first 30 s and fails soon after removing the file and its directory after 30 s delay. This gives us a chance to witness the success and failure of liveness probe.

- **Readiness Probe:** K8s uses this probe to see if the container is ready to serve the incoming traffic requests. Even when a container is live, its desired communication port could be occupied, or it could be waiting for an external trigger before serving the traffic. Readiness probes can be different for TCP or HTTP requests. Ideally, you would want to run an HTTP GET request on the specified port to see if the container is serving the request; to keep things simple, we are using cat for readiness probe.

- **Resource Limits:** No pod can have (or needs) unlimited resources. Depending on which node the pod is to be scheduled, it is helpful to keep track of how many resources the pod will consume. There are two key terms: **Request** and **Limit**. Request is the number of resources a pod can ask from the node. Sometimes, the node has spare resources available. In that case, it can allow pod to use more resources than it had requested. Timing them right can allow pods to use different processes like periodic junk clean-up or pre-rendered calculations. The maximum of this luxury resource amount is called **Limit.** In this example, the pod has requested 64 MB RAM and 256 mCPU, whereas it can have a maximum of 128 MB RAM and 512 mCPU.

We can view all of this information by describing the deployment pod using the **kubectl describe pod** command. You can find the details about the **Limits** field in the description, as shown in the following screenshot:

```
Limits:
    cpu:        500m
    memory:     128Mi
Requests:
    cpu:        250m
    memory:     64Mi
Liveness:       exec [cat /tmp/prob-check] delay=7s timeout=1s period=5s #success=1 #failure=3
Readiness:      exec [cat /tmp/prob-check] delay=5s timeout=1s period=5s #success=1 #failure=3
Environment:    <none>
```

Figure 10.32: CPU and memory request data for a pod

Furthermore, description events can also tell you if the liveness probe had succeeded or failed. We can see the failed (after succeeding for 30 seconds) liveness probe in the following screenshot:

```
Events:
  Type      Reason      Age                 From                Message
  ----      ------      ----                ----                -------
  Normal    Scheduled   72s                 default-scheduler   Successfully assigned default/prob-busybox-79fb767b77-s7tk6 to node-2
  Normal    Pulling     71s                 kubelet             Pulling image "busybox"
  Normal    Pulled      70s                 kubelet             Successfully pulled image "busybox" in 1.155181016s
  Normal    Created     70s                 kubelet             Created container prob-busybox
  Normal    Started     70s                 kubelet             Started container prob-busybox
  Warning   Unhealthy   26s (x3 over 36s)   kubelet             Liveness probe failed: cat: can't open '/tmp/prob-check': No such file or directory
  Normal    Killing     26s                 kubelet             Container prob-busybox failed liveness probe, will be restarted
  Warning   Unhealthy   5s (x7 over 35s)    kubelet             Readiness probe failed: cat: can't open '/tmp/prob-check': No such file or directory
dhwani@master:~$
```

Figure 10.33: Events for Liveness and Readiness probe

Init Containers

The most significant advantage of containers is their lightweight package, making them easy to ship, update, restart, and backup. Being lightweight comes with a caveat though, the containers are supposed to be ready-to-run in ideal scenarios, but practically, it may not always be the case. Applications may need some additional setup for a particular architecture and having different docker images for a hundred different architectures is not efficient. It becomes tiresome to keep all of them updated, and the software delivery flow gets compromised (*agile loses its agility*).

This is where **init containers** are useful. They are subroutines executed before running the default command of the primary pod(s). They follow the run-to-completion scheduling model. If there are more than one init containers, they will be executed in the sequence they are mentioned in the YAML file. The pod controller ensures that init containers run successfully before the primary pod starts. If they (one or more of them) fail, the pod controller restarts them until they succeed. Init containers do not have any dedicated restart policy (*dear K8s devs, maybe this is something to work on?*). If the pod's restart policy is set to Never, the failing init container will result in failure of the pod itself (*a well-written pod with no problems in and by itself will never get a chance to prove its worthiness... dark times*).

Another advantage of having init containers is client security. We already know that there are private and public images. If the client wishes to keep the details regarding their architecture setup private, it is not a wise choice to make their entire Docker Image public. You can break it down into two or more parts instead and provide a private Docker Image for init containers, whereas the public Docker Image for regular pod containers.

By now, you have created enough pods to take standard pod fields for granted; bring your focus straight into the **initContainers** field. This pod object definition file contains two init containers, **init-busyservice** and **init-mydb,** for our busybox application pod.

1. apiVersion: v1

2. kind: Pod

3. metadata:

4.   name: init-pod

5.   labels:

6.   app: myapp

7. spec:

8.   containers:

9.   - name: init-container

10.   image: busybox:1.28

11.   command: [‹sh›, ‹-c›, ‹echo Hey, there!!! && sleep 3600›]

12.   initContainers:

13.   - name: init-busyservice

14.   image: busybox:1.28

15.   command: [‹sh›, ‹-c›, «until nslookup myservice.$(cat /var/run/secrets/kubernetes.io/serviceaccount/namespace).svc.cluster.local; do echo waiting for busyservice; sleep 2; done»]

16.   - name: init-mydb

17.   image: busybox:1.28

18.   command: [‹sh›, ‹-c›, «until nslookup mydb.$(cat /var/run/secrets/kubernetes.io/serviceaccount/namespace).svc.cluster.local;   do echo waiting for mydb; sleep 2; done»]

If you look at the commands for these containers, both of them are configured to wait for the service objects, **myservice** and **mydb,** in the default namespace. Once these containers receive acknowledgment of these services' existence, they will execute their default command and make way for the app container (init-container) to start its execution.

Use **kubectl apply** command with **-f** flag to create this pod. After creating the pod, we can check the status of init-pod using **kubectl get pods** command, and the output should look like the following screenshot:

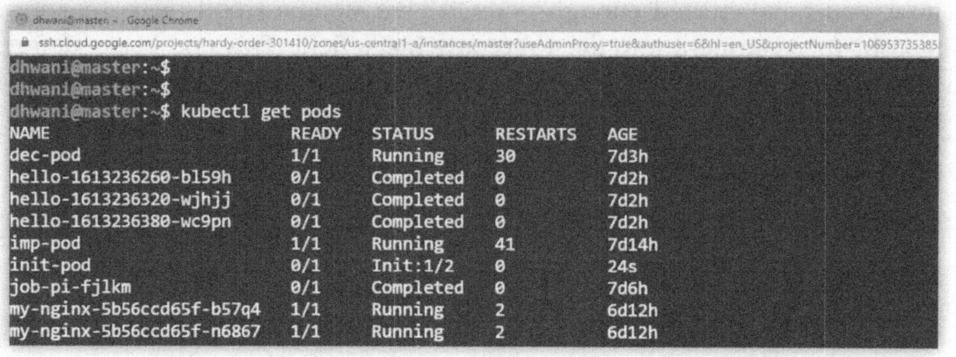

Figure 10.34: List of pods to verify the creation of init-pod

As you can see, the status of init-pod is not the usual **RUNNING** or **COMPLETED**. It is **Init:1/2** which suggests that one of the init containers has successfully completed its execution while the other is still running to complete its task. Now, to look more into this, we need to describe the init pod using **kubectl describe pod** command followed by the pod's name, which is **init-pod**.

The output of this command should return useful information, as shown in the following screenshot:

Figure 10.35: Detailed information for init containers

You can notice in the above screenshot that there are 2 init containers for this pod. One of them is in **TERMINATED** state because the service object, **init-busyservice**, that container was looking for already exists in the default namespace. The condition was successfully completed for this init container. For the remaining one, we need to create a service object **mydb** in the default namespace. There is another way to verify that the init container is still looking for the DNS of **mydb** service object. You can print the logs of **init-mydb** container using the following command:

```
kubectl logs init-pod -c init-mydb
```

The output of this command should look something like this:

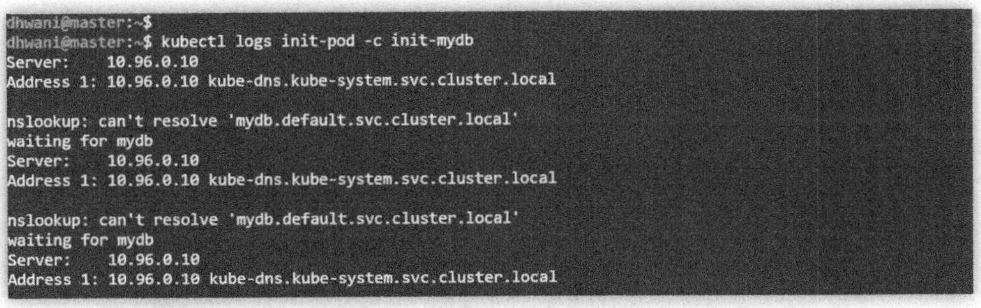

Figure 10.36: Logs of init-mydb container

The **init-mydb** container is actively looking for an object with the DNS **mydb.default. svc.cluster.local** in the default namespace, and the absence of that object restricts it to process further. If you have noticed in the screenshot, it has printed a string that the container is **"waiting for mydb"**. This is the response we get as per the command we have written in the YAML file. When the container is done looking for the service object's DNS, it echoes this string and sleep for 2 s and starts looking for it again until it can successfully get a response from the service object.

Now, to help this init container succeed in its job, we need to create a service object called **mydb** in the default namespace. You need to write an object configuration file as always for service and use the **kubectl apply** command to create that service declaratively. You can find the YAML for **mydb** service as follows:

1. apiVersion: v1
2. kind: Service
3. metadata:
4.   name: mydb
5. spec:
6.   ports:
7.   - protocol: TCP

```
8.    port: 80
9.    targetPort: 9377
```

It is a simple service object definition file. Do not worry about the specifics of this file for the moment; we will learn them in the next chapter. To make it easier to understand, we have mentioned the **apiVersion** and kind of object, same as pod definition or deployment definition file. The metadata consists of the name of the service object; make sure that you use the exact name of the service object that is mentioned in command of **init-mydb** container or else, the container will keep looking for this service for its eternity! Spec field in this file consists of the necessary details about ports that should expose the service and the pod container.

Create this YAML using **kubectl apply** and list out the pods to check the status of **init-pod** once again:

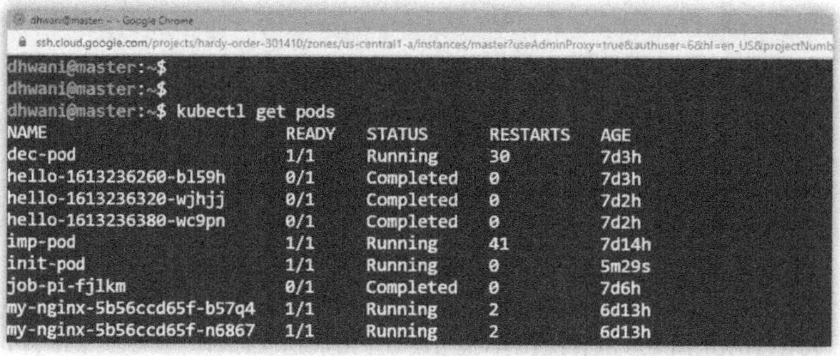

Figure 10.37: Successfully completion of init containers

As expected, the status of **init-pod** has changed to **RUNNING** which means that both init containers have successfully fulfilled their conditions and have made way for the application container of the pod. Let's check out the logs of **init-mydb** container using **kubectl logs** command. The output should look something like the following screenshot:

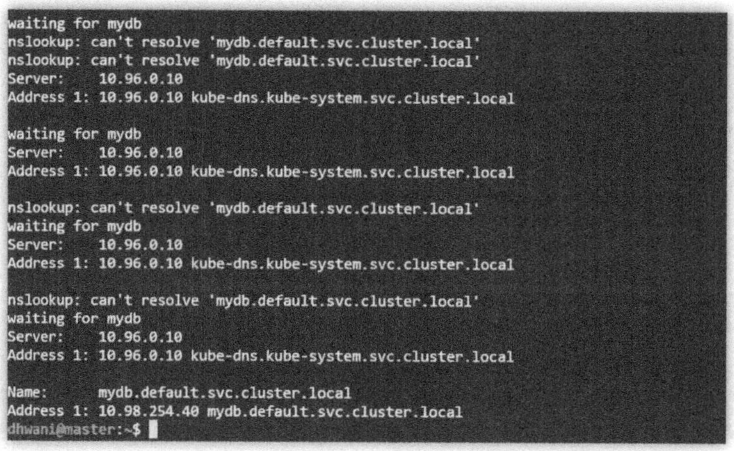

Figure 10.38: Log entry for DNS of service object init-mydb container logs

If you notice the last entry of the container log, it has successfully logged the DNS of **mydb** service object, which made the init container complete its job successfully. If we describe the init pod again, the status of **init-mydb** container should be changed from **RUNNING** to **TERMINATED** after completion of its command.

You can refer to the following screenshot to see this change in **init-mydb** container:

```
init-mydb:
  Container ID:  docker://62b9adfcb17c2793225f2be3ce55a723fcda8df673f649e82867103d90e8d3a0
  Image:         busybox:1.28
  Image ID:      docker-pullable://busybox@sha256:141c253bc4c3fd0a201d32dc1f493bcf3fff003b6df416dea4f41046e0f37d47
  Port:          <none>
  Host Port:     <none>
  Command:
    sh
    -c
    until nslookup mydb.$(cat /var/run/secrets/kubernetes.io/serviceaccount/namespace).svc.cluster.local; do echo waiting for mydb; sleep 2; done
  State:          Terminated
    Reason:       Completed
    Exit Code:    0
    Started:      Sat, 20 Feb 2021 20:06:02 +0000
    Finished:     Sat, 20 Feb 2021 20:11:15 +0000
  Ready:          True
  Restart Count:  0
  Environment:    <none>
  Mounts:
    /var/run/secrets/kubernetes.io/serviceaccount from default-token-glsmx (ro)
```

Figure 10.39: init-mydb container status change

If you notice the events for init pod, the creation of the application container is a few seconds ago, which also proves that the app container was created and started only after both init containers completed their execution:

```
Events:
  Type    Reason     Age    From               Message
  ----    ------     ----   ----               -------
  Normal  Scheduled  6m21s  default-scheduler  Successfully assigned default/init-pod to node-2
  Normal  Pulled     6m21s  kubelet            Container image "busybox:1.28" already present on machine
  Normal  Created    6m21s  kubelet            Created container init-busyservice
  Normal  Started    6m20s  kubelet            Started container init-busyservice
  Normal  Pulled     6m20s  kubelet            Container image "busybox:1.28" already present on machine
  Normal  Created    6m20s  kubelet            Created container init-mydb
  Normal  Started    6m20s  kubelet            Started container init-mydb
  Normal  Pulled     67s    kubelet            Container image "busybox:1.28" already present on machine
  Normal  Created    67s    kubelet            Created container init-cont
  Normal  Started    67s    kubelet            Started container init-cont
dhwani@master:~$
```

Figure 10.40: Events of init pod

To sum it up, a pod is a sequential combination of multiple containerized processes and supervisory probes. The event timeline of components of a pod from its initiation to termination looks like the following figure:

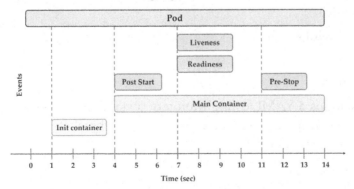

Figure 10.41: Pod components' timeline

This might make you believe that the pods are much more than simple wrappers around the containers. We are not even thoroughly done with the pods yet. It has another couple of tricks up its sleeve, but they are within the scope of another chapter *(that is, Chapter 12)*.

Conclusion

This chapter was a demonstration of the diverse range of treatments K8s can provide to its containers. We started with simple pods and looked at many important tasks such as sorting, scaling, and exposing containers. We also ran them as always-on and run-to-completion foreground processes or silent background processes. We made their resource utilization efficient and made them more competent and self-reliant with probes and init containers. All of these were possible with different workloads and their controllers. In the next chapter, we will explore the networking and storage objects of Kubernetes. Till then, practice hard!

Multiple choice questions

1. Which of the following is the correct hierarchy of administration within Kubernetes objects?

    A. Container < Pod < Deployment < Replicaset

    B. Container < Pod < Replicaset < Deployment

    C. Deployment < Replicaset < Pod < Container

    D. Replicaset < Deployment < Pod < Container

    Answer: B

2. Which of the following objects is a part of the apps API group in Kubernetes?

    A. Deployment

    B. Service

    C. Endpoint

    D. Pod

    Answer: A

3. Following is a YAML configuration of a standard Kubernetes pod. Choose the correct response to fill between the square brackets of the command sub-field under containers.

```
apiVersion: v1
kind: Pod
```

```
metadata:
name: test
spec:
containers:
name: test-container
image: ubuntu
command: [    ]
```
A. 'sh', '-c', 'echo Correct Answer!'

B. sh, -c, echo Correct Answer!

C. 'sh, -c, echo Correct Answer!'

D. "sh, -c, echo Correct Answer!"

Answer: A

4. Which of the following kubectl commands is used to list out all running Replicasets in a K8s cluster?

A. kubectl get replicasets

B. kubectl list replicasets

C. kubectl get rs

D. kubectl list rs

Answer: C

5. Which of the following Kubernetes objects manages Replicasets?

A. kubelet

B. kube-scheduler

C. Deployment

D. kube-controller-manager

Answer: C

6. What does Job object do in Kubernetes?

A. Creates one or more deployments to complete the assigned task(s).

B. Creates one or more pods to successfully complete assigned task(s).

C. Creates maintenance pods to perform periodic maintenance of K8s cluster.

D. Creates daemon pods to perform software testing for target containerized applications.

Answer: B

7. What will be the status of the Pod after a Job has been successfully completed?

   A. Terminated

   B. Completed

   C. Finished

   D. Succeeded

   Answer: B

8. Which of the following Kubernetes objects is used to create Jobs on a repeating schedule?

   A. Job

   B. Cron Job

   C. Daemon Set

   D. Deployment

   Answer: B

9. Which of the following Kubernetes objects will you use to create a copy of a log collection daemon pod on each node of your K8 cluster?

   A. Job

   B. Cron Job

   C. Deployment

   D. DaemonSet

   Answer: D

10. Which of the following kubectl commands is used to create a pod declaratively?

    A. `kubectl create -f <pod-definination.yaml>`

    B. `kubectl create <pod-definination.yaml>`

    C. `kubectl apply -f <pod-definination.yaml>`

    D. `kubectl apply <pod-definination.yaml>`

    Answer: C

Questions

1. Create a namespace called "awesome" and populate it with the pod named "awesome-ubuntu" using docker image of Ubuntu:latest.

2. Create three more Ubuntu:latest pods in the awesome namespace using a single YAML file.

3. What are the types of objects in Kubernetes? Describe each one of them in brief.

4. Write a YAML file for a CentOS deployment with 3 replicas. Make sure none of the replicas claims more than 200MB of RAM.

5. What is the difference between container probes and init containers? Give an example of each.

## CHAPTER 11

Networking and Storage with Kubernetes

Introduction

The previous chapters familiarized you with the architecture and workload structure of Kubernetes. The workloads communicate among themselves or to the internet. They also generate data; some of that data are disposable while the rest might need to be persisted. Kubernetes is equipped with an efficient and diverse set of Networking and Storage objects; this chapter explains them in-depth and demonstrates their applicability.

Structure

This chapter covers:

- Understanding networking in a K8s cluster
- Types of Kubernetes services
- Writing your first service
- Exposing the service externally
- Understanding storage in Kubernetes
- Types of storage objects in K8s

Objective

This chapter will explain how K8s manages to keep everything in one place through networking and how it provides a range of flexible and scalable storage solutions. This means we will have a good balance of theory and practical topics. By the end of this chapter, you will be able to expose your containerized applications to the internet and will also be able to persist your data in case of container failure.

Understanding networking in a K8s cluster

Kubernetes is a continuously evolving orchestrator. If we only look at it from a consumer's perspective, our reasoning may not resonate with some of their offering choices and implementation details. Thus, it is important to shift the perspective a little while trying to understand something as integral as networking. Albeit all of the objects we have learned so far are important, if they do not get to talk to one another, the entire microservice model crumbles down to error 404. Think about what the primary goals of a tool like K8s should be, to offer seamless networking to its objects:

- Container to Pod communication,
- Pod to Pod communication,
- Pod to Host node communication,
- Pod to other node (including Master) communication,
- Node to Node communication,
- Providing reasonable (if not cutting edge) sophistication and security standards to containerized applications,
- Be cloud-friendly

Even though a diverse set of networking objects can be created with **Infrastructure as Code (IaC)** privileges, the overarching networking model of K8s as a tool should unmistakably solve all of the above-mentioned challenges while keeping its implementation **Easy and Scalable**. The following figure is the most abstracted version of how K8s components communicate:

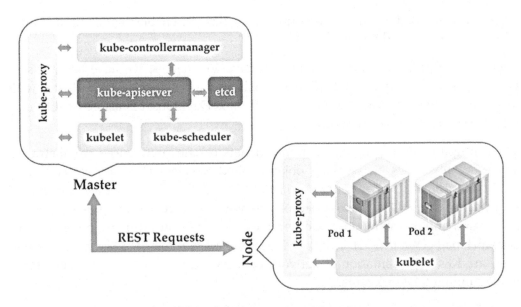

Figure 11.1: *Communication between different K8s components*

I used the words "most abstracted" because the figure only highlights one important Networking component, **Kube-proxy**. In *Chapter 9, Introduction to Kubernetes*, it was introduced as a Network Proxy for the containers. Pods and containers are ephemeral, as they die, their DNS records change.

Proxies are used to evade unnecessary DNS record caching by clients, which could lead to slower data refreshes (in case of updated pod DNS on the server) and compromised application performance. Kube-proxy provides monitoring and adding/removal of iptables rules, TCP-UDP-SCTP forwarding for load balancing, Virtual IPs for Kubernetes objects, and Endpoints for objects to enable their communication.

As you might have noticed, many of these responsibilities overlap with what Docker can already do and so far, we have been relying on K8s cluster setup on top of full-fledged Docker Engine. Does Kube-proxy use Docker's underlying architecture to enable these features? Yes, **if** it is installed on top of Docker. Just memorizing what Kube-proxy does is... futile. It's better to understand **why** it does so.

We have already seen in *Chapter 2* and *3* how iptables rules enable or block incoming requests for physical or virtual workload. This helps to define a pod's behavior. A standalone standard pod will generally be able to communicate to other pods on the same node in the same namespace (much like a little private network) and with kube-apiserver via Kube-proxy. On the other hand, if the pod is a part of a larger orchestration object like a deployment, it is quite possible that some of its *brothers and sisters* are scheduled on other nodes. Iptables will easily enable their communication while blocking everything else.

Even though pods and other K8s objects have Virtual IPs, we have already seen that we name them quite meticulously. Such naming is enabled by a cluster-wide local DNS server that runs as a Daemonset. This Daemonset is also useful to map workloads to actual web domains.

The configurations caused by customized networking preferences are abstracted away as Kubernetes Networking objects called **Services** *(No, they are not micro-services; they are not Swarm Services... they are K8s services. Yes, they could not come up with another name)*. Unlike workload objects which get created by kubelet, Services are created and maintained by kube-proxies. Services don't **run** any pods; they are not workloads *(You will not see any pod templates when you write K8s service YAMLs)*. They are K8s' representation of network configuration records to refer and utilize while running the workloads.

The following picture is a graphical representation of K8s services:

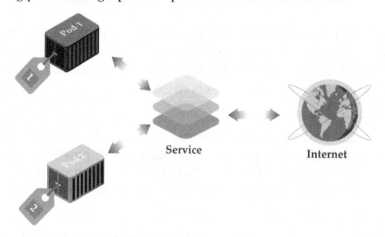

Figure 11.2: Kubernetes Service

Services create a separate endpoint for whichever pods they connect to and pods can connect to multiple services ending up with as many endpoints. Services have their Virtual IP and a Virtual IP range (to pass on to workloads), since the incoming traffic proxied by kube-proxy is routed to services before reaching respective workloads. This behavior is similar to docker networks except services are more elaborate and flexible. They can target any level of workload object and simplify the network configuration of larger workloads like deployments. They do it by using labels and selectors. The selectors on services search for workloads with appropriate labels to create respective endpoints.

Service Endpoints are combination of Virtual IP provided to the pod by the service and the port the pod will listen to. As a drawback, even if a pod has more than one container, they do not get individual IPs which can lead to performance lag. Hence it is recommended to use one container per pod unless facing strict requirements. Every pod that we have created so far has received its name from kube-dns Daemonset. You can view it by running **kubectl get svc --all-namespaces** as shown in the following screenshot:

Figure 11.3: List of default running services in a Kubernetes cluster

Apart from kube-dns, we also have a service called Kubernetes. It is a ClusterIP type of service which allows objects to make requests to kube-apiserver. Both of these services limit their scope within the cluster. To expose the pods to external internet, there are other service types available. In fact, let us make them the focus of next topic!

Types of Kubernetes services

Services are REST objects just like Pods or Replicasets. They can be created imperatively or declaratively, and their definition can be provided to kube-apiserver using HTTP POST request. While pod networks are sufficient to make pods communicate with one another using default Kubernetes Service, there are times when you have to expose your service to the internet. It is also called publishing a service. Depending on how you publish the service (whom do you allow to communicate to the service), the services can be categorized into the following types:

- **ClusterIP:** This leads to internal exposure *(ah, an oxymoron!)*. The endpoints provide a cluster-internal IP. This is the default service type unless mentioned otherwise. Here is a graphical conceptualization of this service type:

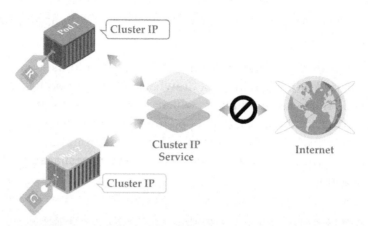

Figure 11.4: ClusterIP service

All of the K8s components we have seen so far (and we will likely see in future chapters) communicate to one another using ClusterIP. This allows HTTP REST APIs to function without interference from other internet elements. It is a simple and secure way to make the orchestration play out smoothly at scale. Even if the workloads are exposed using other service types, they will have ClusterIP as their backbone.

- **NodePort:** This type of service exposes the connected workloads to internet through each Node's IP on a static port across the cluster. When an external request tries to access the workload through NodePort, the NodePort service routes the request to the ClusterIP service which routes the request to respective workload. Check out the figure below for graphical representation of NodePort service:

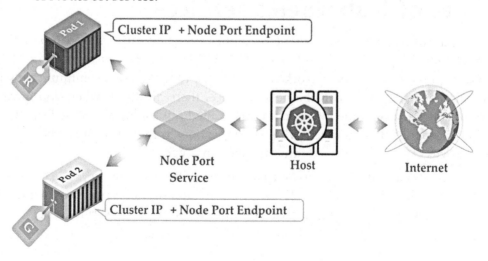

Figure 11.5: NodePort service

As shown in the preceding figure, the endpoints created by NodePort service will not have an IP address. The objects connected to the service will have a backend Cluster IP created by the cluster IP service and an endpoint to exchange requests and data through NodePort service. Unless you mention a specific port (subjected to port's availability), the port will not be decided by kube-proxy. It will be determined by the control plane components (in this case, kube-apiserver and kube-scheduler) keeping the desired state of the cluster in consideration. Generally, you are likely to get a random port between 30,000 and 32,767.

- **Load Balancer:** This is a special service mainly designed for K8s clusters running on Cloud (not necessarily public clouds). If your cloud provider supports the creation of HTTP or TCP load balancers, this service can be used to expose your workloads to that load balancer. Just how NodePort automatically creates a backend ClusterIP service, Load Balancer service automatically creates NodePort and ClusterIP services.

Take a look at the following figure:

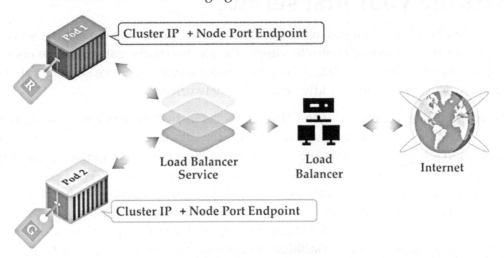

Figure 11.6: Load balancer service

Depending on whether your cloud provider supports reservation of static IPs and static IP ranges, you can provide load balancer IP under your service's desired state; otherwise, your workloads will get ephemeral IP addresses which will be updated if changed by the service itself. We will explore more about this when we run hosted K8s on cloud in further chapters.

- **External Name:** This is used to map your existing service to a domain name. It returns a CNAME record for your service which can be provided to the domain name to map it to the respective service. There is no creation of backend services or proxying or routing involved. You can even go as far as calling it an aliasing method.

This categorization was based on how a service would "expose" the workload. They use labels and selectors to determine which workloads to expose and/or load balance. In some cases, you do not desire any proxying or load balancing. You can provide it **None** service type and create an entity called a **Headless Service**. This essentially means there will be no ClusterIP for this service and requests made to it will not be attended by kube-Proxy. Headless services can be created with or without selectors. If created with selectors, the endpoints created by the service consist of IP addresses. They work like a normal NodePort service just not handled by kube-proxy. If created without selectors, the K8s control plane returns a CNAME record for this service which can be used to map it to other service or an external load balancing mechanism. Let's create the services and witness them in action!

Writing your first service

Creating a service is a cluster-wide operation. kube-apiserver validates the service definition and the service controllers apply the service configurations on the nodes. Depending on which workloads are exposed by the service, a service's configurations can play active role or just sit idly on a node's network stack.

When we create a container using Docker, it gets its own network namespace that enables it to have a dedicated virtual IP and `eth0` interface. Kubernetes creates one network namespace per pod. The containers on the same pod can have their `eth0` but get shared IP. They can even talk to each other on localhost. When we create a Kubernetes service, we create an interface that enables bridge communication between pods' `eth0` and node's root `veth`. Based on the service types you have seen in the previous topic; you can deduce that different service types impose different traffic routing and exposure conditions to determine when the bridge will be open and when it would not be.

The simplest implementation example would be a ClusterIP service. We can create a sample deployment and allow its pods to communicate with one another using a ClusterIP service. Follow the definition below for an nginx deployment with 2 replicas.

```
1. apiVersion: apps/v1
2. kind: Deployment
3. metadata:
```

```
4.    name: my-nginx
5.  spec:
6.    selector:
7.      matchLabels:
8.        run: my-nginx
9.    replicas: 2
10.   template:
11.     metadata:
12.       labels:
13.         run: my-nginx
14.     spec:
15.       containers:
16.       - name: my-nginx
17.         image: nginx
18.         ports:
19.         - containerPort: 80
```

Let us write another YAML to define the service. Once we are done writing it, we will break it down to its last syntax:

```
1.  apiVersion: v1
2.  kind: Service
3.  metadata:
4.    name: serve-nginx
5.    labels:
6.      run: my-nginx
7.  spec:
8.    ports:
9.    - port: 80
10.     protocol: TCP
11.   selector:
12.     run: my-nginx
```

The object kind Service falls under the **core** API group of version **v1** - just like pods. This is not much of a surprise since they are integral to the very functioning of K8s components. Metadata consists the name of the service and its label. Selectors help the service to filter out the target workloads *(for example, we want to target pods of nginx deployment that we have run earlier, so we need to configure the service's selector to look for pods having the label run: my-nginx).*

The spec field is your service's crème-de-la-crème. It contains information related to ports, communication protocols, type of service, selector, etc. Since the default type of any service created in K8s is ClusterIP, we do not need to mention it. Even though services are not workloads, they have their own endpoints which are used to route requests to appropriate workloads. This Service's endpoint will use TCP port **80**. You can call it the service port. Summing up the spec field, it will create a service of type ClusterIP which will connect to only those pods who have been labeled as run: nginx on port **80**. Just like any other object, you can use kubectl apply or kubectl create command followed by **-f** flag and the name of the file to create the service object:

```
kubectl apply -f serve-clusterIP.yaml
```

The output of the above command should look something like this:

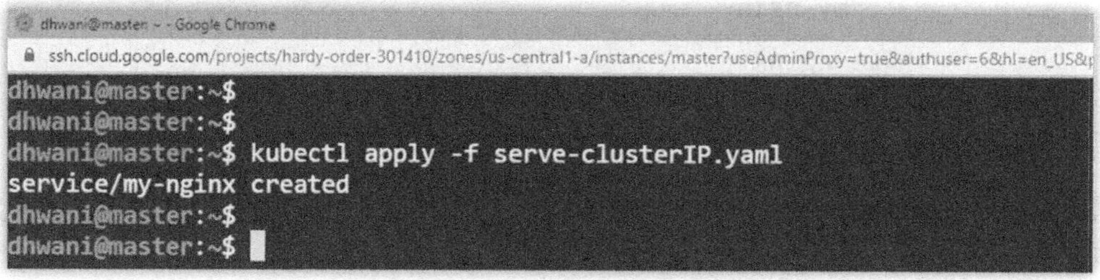

Figure 11.7: ClusterIP service creation process

After creating this service, let us list out services in the default namespace using the following command:

```
kubectl get svc
```

You can list out any Kubernetes object using **kubectl get** command, all you need to know is how to spell that object correctly.

The list of services should look something like this:

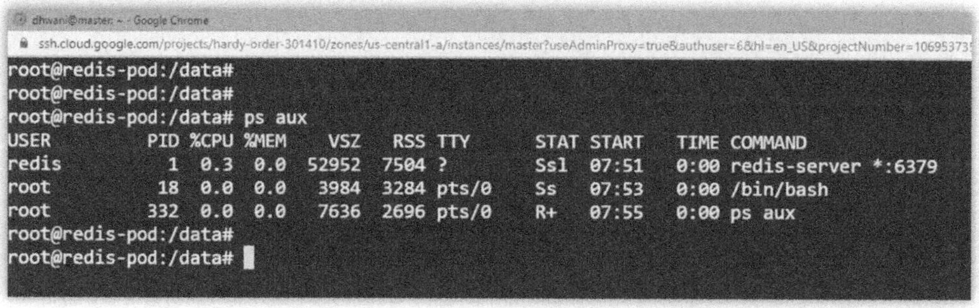

Figure 11.8: List of Cluster IP services in the default namespace

As you can see in the screenshot, we have two running services at the moment and both of them are of type ClusterIP. We also got a new cluster IP for our service. Since this a cluster exclusive service, we have not received any external IP address for this service. Our service is exposed on port **80** which means any pod with the valid label can connect to our service on port **80**/TCP. To know more details about the service such as endpoints, you can describe it with the following command:

```
kubectl describe svc serve-nginx
```

We should get the detailed information about our service similar to the following screenshot:

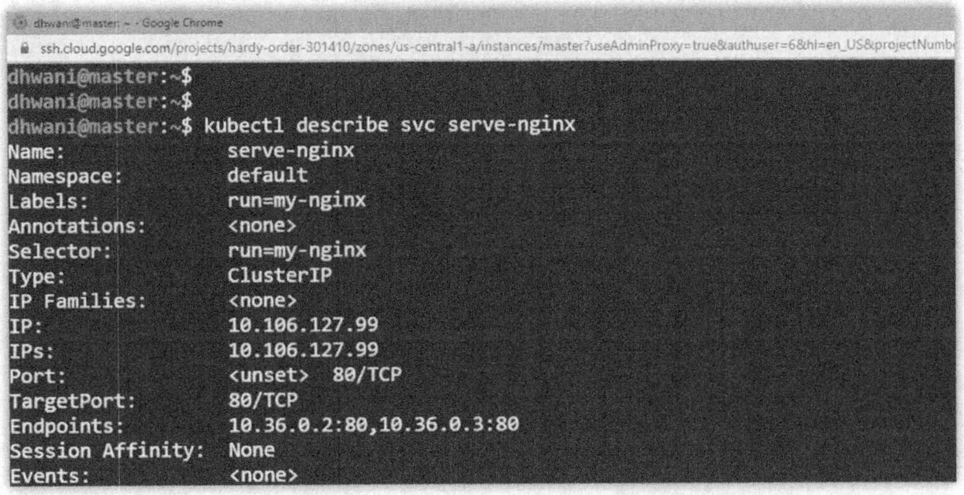

Figure 11.9: Description of a ClusterIP service

Most of the information is familiar so let's address the new fields. We have not provided any desired IP family (IPV4 or IPV6) to our kube-apiserver, so it is set to default (IPV4) which is also reflected in the very next field that shows the virtual service IP. The service port is **80** for TCP communication and the <unset> indicates absence of a dedicated name given to the port while defining the service. It does not create any performance difference (specially at such a small scale) but naming ports might be helpful for better readability when you expose multiple ports for different purposes. While the service will be listening on port **80**, it will also be routing the requests to the pods connected to it. The target port defines the port used by the pods connected to the service. Since our service is connected to two pods, it has two dedicated endpoints to route requests to. We do not have any routing priorities for this couple of pods, so the session affinity is set to none. None is the default session affinity, but you can set it to Client IP to forward a particular client's requests to a particular pod.

The service is exposed to the cluster. It means we cannot access it through a new browser tab from our machine since it would be an external request. Currently, we are SSHed to Master and the Master is very well a part of the cluster so we should get a positive response by using curl on service's virtual IP and service port combination.

```
curl http://10.106.127.99:80
```

We do get the nginx welcome page but in HTML format as shown in the following screenshot:

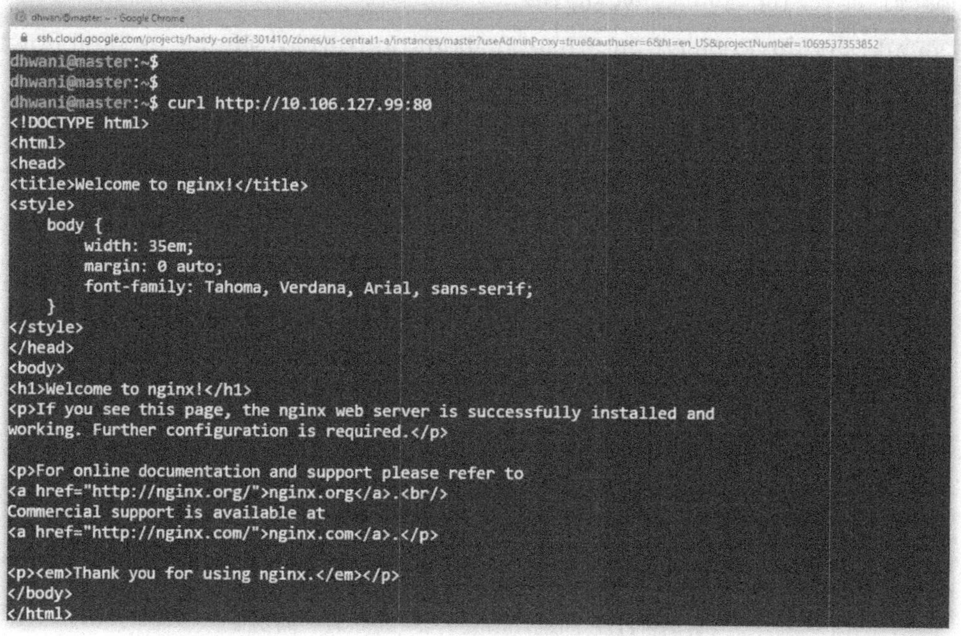

Figure 11.10: ClusterIP serving the Pod internal to K8s cluster

Exposing the service externally

A NodePort service's definition is quite similar to ClusterIP except the type field. Let us keep the deployment the same as previous topic and create a NodePort service for it using the YAML definition written as follows:

```
1.  apiVersion: v1
2.  kind: Service
3.  metadata:
4.    name: serve-nginx-nodeport
5.    labels:
6.      run: my-nginx
7.  spec:
```

```
8.    type: NodePort
9.  ports:
10.   - port: 8080
11.     targetPort: 80
12.     protocol: TCP
13.     name: http
14.   - port: 443
15.     protocol: TCP
16.     name: https
17.  selector:
18.     run: my-nginx
```

The object kind, selector, labels, and apiVersion are exactly the same as ClusterIP service; the spec field makes all of the difference. To avoid the default value, the service type is set to NodePort. It is followed by a bunch of protocols and ports. These are the ports the service will be listening to. They will externally be mapped to host's ports ranging from **30000 to 32676**. This time the ports are named so we will ideally avoid the <unset> indication in the service description.

Let's create the service using **kubectl create** command as shown in the following screenshot:

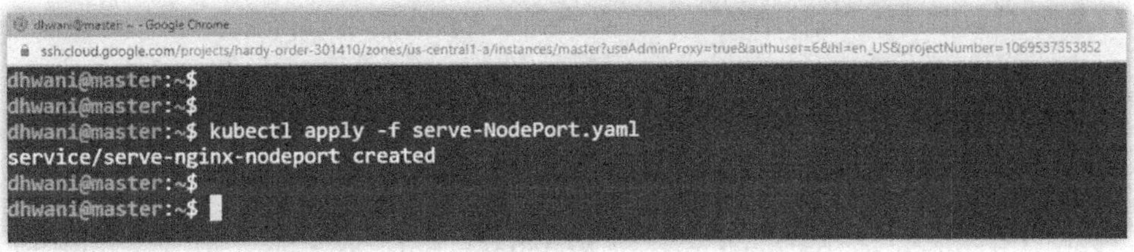

Figure 11.11: NodePort service creation process

After successfully creating the service, let us list out all services in the default namespace using **kubectl get svc** command and the outcome should look something like the following screenshot:

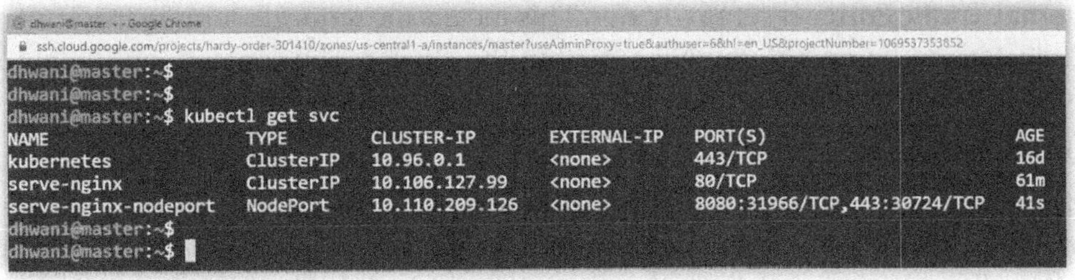

Figure 11.12: List of NodePort services in the default namespace

We now have three running services out of which two are of ClusterIP (old ones) type and one is NodePort (new) type. If you have noticed, the PORT(S) column has a different entry for NodePort service. We can see port **8080** and port **443** as we had mentioned in the YAML file but there are two more ports here: **31966** and **30724**. Let's gather some more information about them. Describe this NodePort service using kubectl describe command:

```
kubectl describe svc serve-nginx-nodeport
```

Let us understand the information about this service shown in the following screenshot:

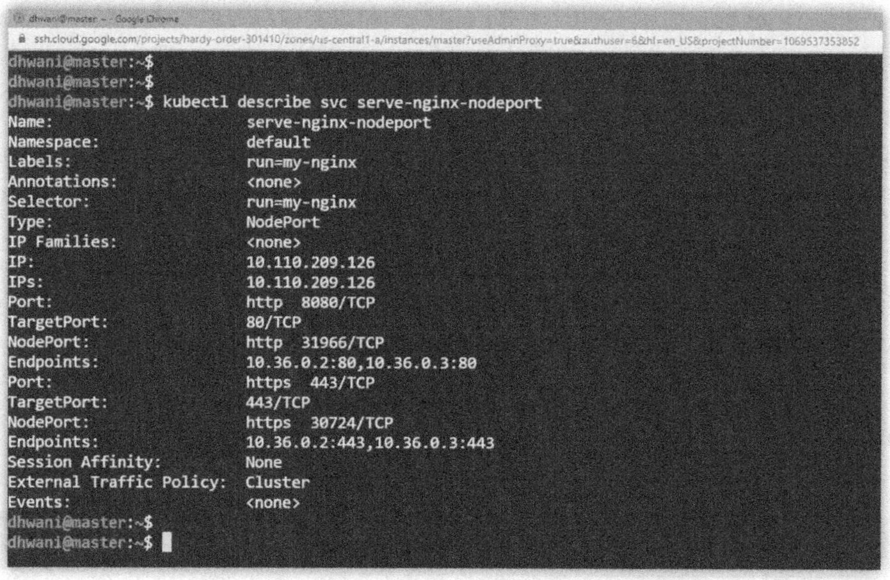

Figure 11.13: Description of a NodePort service

The key difference is the existence of **NodePort** field and the service type being NodePort. The ports are named so there is no **<unset>** indicator and all of these ports from K8s' network namespace are mapped to respective ports of host's network namespace (**8080** to **31966** and **443** to **30724**).

For both NodePorts, there are two ClusterIP endpoints (one for each pod). The **External Traffic Policy** is set to **Cluster**. This means the requests coming from outside the cluster can be routed anywhere within the cluster. The contrary option is **local** which only routes the requests to the workloads available on the same node as the request having been made.

Finally, it is time to access this service from outside the cluster. Provided that the cloud firewall is not blocking your request (*in GCE's case you might have to create a rule to allow all connections, link to the documentation can be found in the tip-box at the bottom of the page)*, all you have to do is hit the External-IP:NodePort (any node's IP and port are fine since the external traffic policy is set to cluster) combination in the browser and the result should resemble the following screenshot:

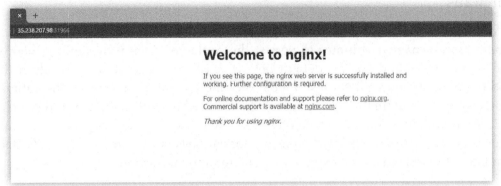

Figure 11.14: Exposing nginx pod to the external world through NodePort service

The service is working as expected! You can finally expose your service to the internet using K8s. We will also take a look at the load balancer service and ingress resources when we explore Hosted K8s on Cloud. They will allow external IPs dedicated to services and configuration of custom ingress (incoming) traffic forwarding rules. For now, let us move to another core functional pillar of K8s as an orchestrator, storage objects.

Understanding storage in Kubernetes

Just how networking objects play an important role in creating the individuality of the objects by enabling communication endpoints, Storage objects keep the context of objects relevant by preserving the data if/when the containers crash or get terminated. We have already seen the Docker Storage objects in *Chapter 6* and K8s just ups the game with its own version of them.

To understand the storage objects most comprehensively, you need to look at them from not only one but two points of view. The **Host**'s point of view and the **K8s as a tool**'s point of view. From the host's point of view, any storage object is just a folder/ directory and its content (including subfolders/subdirectory and files) paired up with permissions about who can read, write, or execute the content. From K8s' point of view, Storage objects are data persistence entities that need to be accessible by the pods effortlessly. Just how services are **connected** to the pods, storage objects are **mounted** to them (the pods). This is where the pod philosophy of having a wrapper process that outlives the containers shines the brightest.

Note:

Using firewall rules on GCP: https://cloud.google.com/vpc/docs/using-firewalls

Containers are designed to and supposed to die. While Docker does provide the option of named volumes to persist the container data, provisioning them is an active choice and not the default behavior. K8s pods act differently, all of the pods are mount with a default storage object and all storage objects of K8s outlives the containers' lifetime. This means container crashes will never cause data loss. Moreover, the functionality scope of K8s storage objects is not just limited to data persistence. There are different types of storage objects for different types of data and target workloads. Let's explore all of them in the next topic.

Types of storage objects in K8s

Just like workloads or networking objects, storage objects are also created by their respective controllers and their definitions are validated by Kube-apiserver. K8s offers a vast variety of storage objects and their list is continuously increasing with releases of new updates. The simplest way to categorize them is by focusing on their target data and purpose. Here is a list of storage objects in K8s code tree:

- **Volumes:** This is probably the simplest type of storage object available. Volumes are used for persisting container data and to allow data sharing between containers of the same pod. They can be ephemeral or persistent. **Ephemeral** volumes have lifetime equal to pods mounted to them, whereas **persistent** volumes outlive even the pods. Different cloud providers and file systems need different configurations to enable persistent volumes and that's why their allocation is decoupled from the pod creation process. **Persistent Volumes** are created as large chunk of storage blocks and smaller units are mounted to pods using objects called **Persistent Volume Claims** or PVCs.

- **Storage Class:** Provisioning a storage block on a third-party infrastructure requires permissions, precision, and policies to follow. For example, let us assume that you want to reserve a block of storage on Amazon Web Service's Elastic Block Storage. Even if you have installed K8s with admin rights, the AWS will not trust it. On top of that, your AWS data centers may offer both SSD and HDD storage options with different file systems. Which kind of storage will you reserve? Most importantly, everything on cloud is billed based on the usage duration. When (or under which conditions) will you release the provisioned storage? Storage classes answer all of these questions. To avoid the authorization issue, AWS (and many other infrastructure providers) have worked with K8s to give it Read/Write/Execute permissions under specified conditions. You can use this integration by creating a storage class of the provider type AWS and enable an interface to allow you to provision persistent volumes based on the nature described under the storage class. We will look at how persistent volumes use storage class while exploring hosted K8s on cloud.

- **Secrets:** They are used to pass sensitive information (CA certificates, passwords, authentication tokens, and so on) to containers inside the pods. This avoids the need to use an encryption mechanism in the pod environment while assuring data safety. Secrets store the data as unencrypted base-64 encoded strings (*more about base-64 encoding in the tip box*). Alternatively, you can encrypt the data inside your secrets using **Encryption configuration** objects. The encryption options such as KMS provide 16 and 32-bit encryption key support. The secrets are created as K8s API objects, but their data is not stored under etcd. When you describe a workload with a secret mounted to it, the description only shows name of the secret and not the data inside it. Furthermore, you can also restrict who can view the secrets by using different identity and access management methods discussed in the next chapter.

- **Downward API:** There are times when a pod needs metadata about itself. To avoid delays and unnecessary request routings to and from K8s service to kube-apiserver, Downward APIs provide pod (or pod template) fields and container field information to the pod. They can be streamed as files inside a mounted volume or as container environment variables. You can call them one of the most niche storage objects with limited but subtle functionality.

- **ConfigMaps:** Just how secrets are used to provide sensitive information and Downward APIs are used to provide pod's own information, ConfigMaps are used to inject container configurations to the pods. What type of configurations and why? The configuration can be application or platform-specific data in key value form, logs in form of files or something as trivial as installation path. This helps keeping the container image portable. The same image can be shipped to multiple clients with different software and/or hardware infrastructures and specific configurations can be sent separately using ConfigMaps. This also allows faster testing and subsequent application rollout to different groups of users.

- **Volume Snapshots:** They are volume backups at the time of snapshot creation used for creating another safety net for data persistence. Volume snapshots are created using **Volume Snapshot Classes** that define the conditions for snapshot provision and deletion.

- **CSI:** As we mentioned earlier, the volume creation mechanisms are defined in the code tree of K8s. It means that with every update; they have to cater to newer infrastructure provider requests and comply to changes made by pre-existing infra providers. This increases testing burden on the team and delays the release cycle. In any case, if the release cycle time is not compromised, the subsequent releases might lose focus from the core features and Quality of Life upgrades. To avoid this, CSI (Container Storage Interface) is created as baseline rules for third party infrastructure vendors to create out of the tree storage solutions in terms of plugins. This is not a new concept; pod networks, service discovery, and network mesh were already decoupled from the code tree earlier and it just signifies K8s' growth as a mature tool to cater more 3rd party vendors.

`base-64 encoding: https://developer.mozilla.org/en-US/docs/ Glossary/Base64`

We can learn more about storage objects as we test them out in practice in the upcoming topic.

Working with Kubernetes storage

So far in our journey with Kubernetes, we have created a significant number of pods for different purposes, but we never really got into the nitty-gritty of how and where containers store information about their identity, their tokens to access different APIs, and the app configuration data. Let us call back a few details from our human persistent storage aka brain-memory! Earlier in *Chapter 9, Introduction to Kubernetes*, we had created a pod using imperative method called imp-pod. We had not provided any storage object to the pod but K8s was kind enough to mount one by itself!

Let us check it out using the standard pod description (`kubectl describe pod`). The command provides information about every aspect, but I have cropped the output to direct the focus on the topic of discussion as visible in the following screenshot:

```
Containers:
  imp-container:
    Container ID:   docker://73f6612f1113064f7182fe401e8da151fb9ed3750810dbf976c75c95bc2d204b
    Image:          busybox
    Image ID:       docker-pullable://busybox@sha256:e1488cb900233d035575f0a7787448cb1fa93bed0cc
    Port:           <none>
    Host Port:      <none>
    Command:
      sh
      -c
      echo This pod is created imperatively && sleep 3600
    State:          Running
      Started:      Sat, 13 Feb 2021 05:39:00 +0000
    Ready:          True
    Restart Count:  0
    Environment:    <none>
    Mounts:
      /var/run/secrets/kubernetes.io/serviceaccount from default-token-glsmx (ro)
```

Figure 11.15: mounts details of a container

This container has a field called **Mounts** which is used to list out all storage objects mounted to it. When a pod is created, a read-only (ro) ephemeral projected volume of type **secret (default-token-xxxx)** is mounted inside the container at **/var/ run/secrets/kubernetes.io/serviceaccount.** It contains a token that is used by the container to make API requests to kube-apiserver through kube-proxy using Kubernetes service endpoint as seen in the previous topics. This token helps kube-apiserver validate the request of the container *(we have always mentioned that kube-apiserver validates the REST requests; now it has come full circle at least in terms of pods).* You can see the details about the volume at the bottom part of the pod description as shown in the following screenshot:

```
Volumes:
  default-token-glsmx:
    Type:        Secret (a volume populated by a Secret)
    SecretName:  default-token-glsmx
    Optional:    false
QoS Class:       BestEffort
Node-Selectors:  <none>
Tolerations:     node.kubernetes.io/not-ready:NoExecute op=Exists for 300s
                 node.kubernetes.io/unreachable:NoExecute op=Exists for 300s
Events:
  Type    Reason     Age    From               Message
  ----    ------     ---    ----               -------
  Normal  Scheduled  5m38s  default-scheduler  Successfully assigned default/imp-pod to node-2
  Normal  Pulling    5m37s  kubelet            Pulling image "busybox"
  Normal  Pulled     5m36s  kubelet            Successfully pulled image "busybox" in 668.376333ms
  Normal  Created    5m36s  kubelet            Created container imp-container
  Normal  Started    5m36s  kubelet            Started container imp-container
dhwani@master:~$
```

Figure 11.16: Volumes details of pod

This secret is NOT OPTIONAL. In other words, you should find it in every pod (of course it is not optional, otherwise how would kube-apiserver validate a pod request; poor pod would be like a lonely employee who forgot his RFID attendance tag at his company). This makes it an integral part of the pod design. No matter how many times the containers die and restart, their API requests will always be validated by the token as long as the pod exists. Moving further, let's talk about a generic data volume that persists the data generated by or populated inside a container.

Persisting data after container crash using emptyDir

Before going deep in emptydir type of storage, let us understand how a pod behaves when it does not have a storage to back up its container data. Have a look at the following YAML file. It is a pod definition file that will create a redis container. The **spec** field of this redis pod has only two fields for the container: **name** and **image**.

```
1. apiVersion: v1
2. kind: Pod
3. metadata:
4.    name: redis-pod
5. spec:
6.    containers:
7.    - name: redis-container
8.      image: redis
```

We have not mentioned anything about volumes which means that this container will rely only on the on-disk storage during its execution. Create the pod using **kubectl apply** or **kubectl create** command and observe its description which will only have a secret token as seen with the imp-pod in the last page. We do not have any other volumes mounted on redis pod yet. Next step should be doing something with this container to generate some form of data. Execute the container using the following command:

```
kubectl exec -it redis-pod -- /bin/bash
```

We have successfully navigated to the redis container environment's terminal. Create a text file named redis-intro and populate it with a text string. Then, save the file to data directory. This operation should look something like the following screenshot:

Figure 11.17: Populate container with data

The data is stored inside the container but what if the container dies? Since it is extremely inefficient to wait for a container to die by itself, let us crash it manually. Crashing a container is not rocket science. At the end of the day, containers are just micro virtualization of Linux environment; killing the process with PID (process ID) 1 should do the job. First, let us list the processes using the following command:

```
ps aux
```

This command will list out all running processing of this container regardless of their scope. The output of this command should look like the following screenshot:

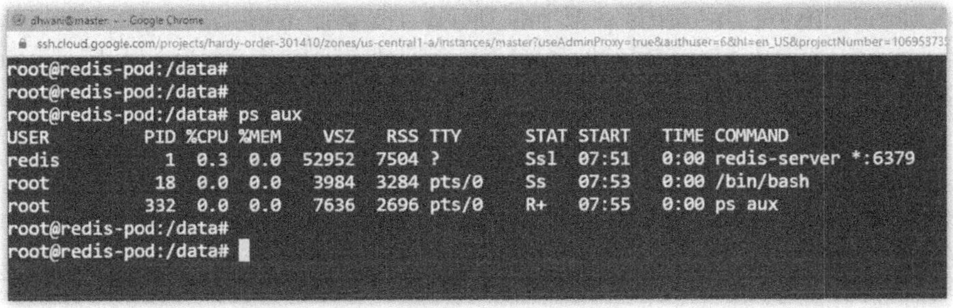

Figure 11.18: List of running processes inside a redis container

We have 3 running processes: **redis**, **root**, and **ps aux**. In order to kill the container, the easiest way is to use the **kill** command with the PID of the process you want to kill:

```
kill 1
```

After killing redis process, we should receive a termination message with an appropriate exit code as shown follows:

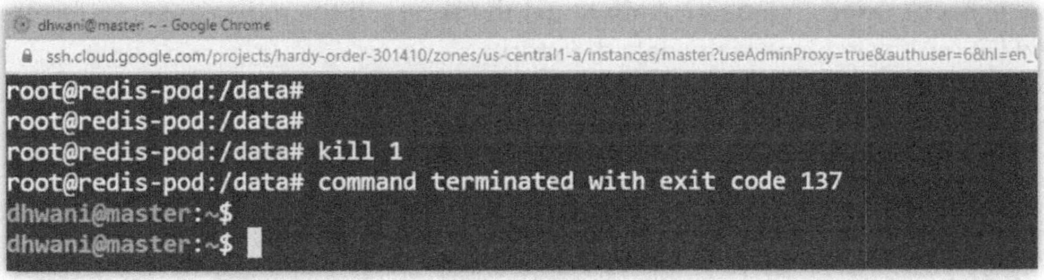

Figure 11.19: Kill redis container with SIGKILL signal

If we introspect a little here, the **exit code 137** shows that the container has failed since it has received a SIGKILL signal. It can be a manual intervention, or the container is simply out-of-memory. In this case, it was manual intervention *(for more details about Linux exit codes, follow the link in the tip box)*.

After successfully killing the container, let's list out pods again using the same, old **kubectl get pods** command and the list of should look something like the following screenshot:

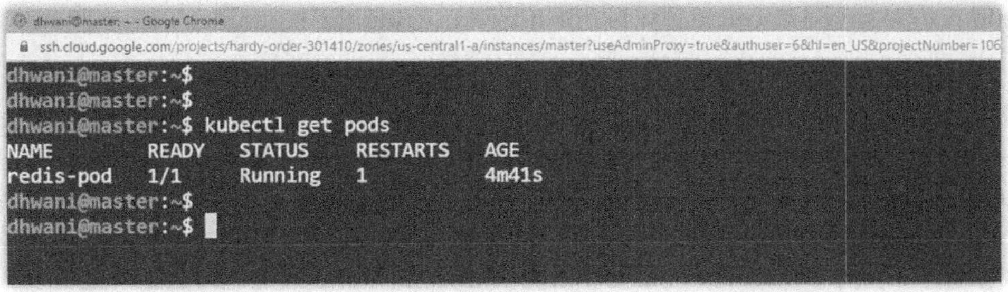

Figure 11.20: Redis pod restarted after receiving SIGKILL

The container inside the redis pod has faced a restart *(caused by yours truly)*. Let's exec the container and look for the text file which we had created earlier inside the container.

Note:

> **Overview of signals in Linux: https://man7.org/linux/man-pages/man7/ signal.7.html**

Note:

> **Overview of kill signal in Linux: https://man7.org/linux/man-pages/ man1/kill.1.html**

Note:

> **Exit codes with special meaning: https://tldp.org/LDP/abs/html/ exitcodes.html#AEN23549**

Use **kubectl exec** command again to get the access of the redis container terminal and list out the content of the data directory:

Figure 11.21: No data persisted after Pod restart

The text file that we had created earlier has vanished. When we killed the container, kubelet respawned another container from scratch to meet the pod's desired state. This means a new file system was initialized for the new container and all of the layers were loaded into it. Think about it as removing a folder and recreating it. The folder with the similar name might be recreated but the data will not come back *(use this analogy to explain volumes to a 10 years old)*. The data from the previous container could not be saved because it was not stored outside the container's filesystem.

To overcome this problem, the simplest solution that Kubernetes provides is ephemeral volumes. They are useful when the application needs additional storage to support some services to store data locally as long as the session is active. For example, the data collected by the caching services of your application can be stored in an ephemeral volume to keep the performance of your application consistent. Kubernetes supports several different kinds of ephemeral volumes such as emptyDir, ConfigMap, secrets, and so on. We will start with the simplest one: emptyDir.

emptyDir is created and managed by kubelet on the node where the pod is scheduled. It uses storage locally available to the node (RAM for ephemeral purposes, HDD/SSD for persistent purposes) with the help of Kubelet. When you create a pod, kube-scheduler selects a node with sufficient local ephemeral storage to schedule the pod and kubelet will be responsible to assign and the required storage for volumes mounted to pods. If the pod uses more than the allocated ephemeral storage, kubelet will kick it out of the Node to be rescheduled on another node (*this does not happen frequently though*).

The emptyDir volume is initialized as an empty directory on the node where the pod is scheduled. This volume can be read, modified, and shared by all containers of the pod. One important thing to note here is the lifetime of emptyDir volume. It depends on the lifetime of Pod. Once the pod is deleted or removed, the contents of emptydir will also be removed. But mind well, I said POD, not CONTAINER.

Let us understand the working of emptydir by using the same redis pod example. If you remember, earlier we had created redis pod without any volume mounts. This time let's mount emptydir to redis pod. Open a new YAML file and write the new pod definition as shown in the following file:

```
1.  apiVersion: v1
2.  kind: Pod
3.  metadata:
4.    name: redis-vol
5.  spec:
6.    containers:
7.    - name: redisvol-container
8.      image: redis
9.      volumeMounts:
10.     - name: redis-volume
11.       mountPath: /data
12.   volumes:
13.   - name: redis-volume
14.     emptyDir: {}
```

We have made a few changes in the metadata of pod and container. There is a new entry for **volumeMounts** in the **spec** field of pod. **volumeMount** key has two values: **volume name** and **mount path**. Let us keep them aside for a while and jump to the last section of the file.

Volumes field is the place where we have defined all volumes used by the pod. It is mandatory to define all volumes used by the pod at the end of the object definition file. We have defined an emptydir volume named **redis-volume**. **{}** in the emptyDir key shows that we do not intend to provide any further configuration details for this.

Optionally, you can specify details such as where would you like your emptyDir to reside *(in-memory which is the default option or local disks; if you want faster read-writes for this container, RAM is the way to go otherwise, you can spare the RAM for other processes including but not limited to the containers running on the node and schedule your volume on a local disk)*. It will be mounted on **/data** in all containers running inside this pod.

Create this pod by using **kubectl apply** command followed by **-f** flag and the new pod definition file name. After creating the pod, describe it and observe the information about the volume mounts as shown in the following command:

```
kubectl describe pod redis-vol
```

When you receive the information about redis-vol pod, the volume mounts section should look something like this:

```
    Mounts:
      /data from redis-volume (rw)
      /var/run/secrets/kubernetes.io/serviceaccount from default-token-q72b4 (ro)
Conditions:
  Type              Status
  Initialized       True
  Ready             True
  ContainersReady   True
  PodScheduled      True
Volumes:
  redis-volume:
    Type:       EmptyDir (a temporary directory that shares a pod's lifetime)
    Medium:
    SizeLimit:  <unset>
  default-token-q72b4:
    Type:       Secret (a volume populated by a Secret)
    SecretName: default-token-q72b4
    Optional:   false
```

Figure 11.22: EmptyDir volume mounted on redis pod

As expected, there are two mount location inside the container and two-volume entries inside the volumes section of pod description. One of them is the default-token volume for the API access token and the other one is the emptydir volume. As we have studied earlier in Docker Volumes, tmpfs is fast in terms of operational activities but it can persist data only till the container is running. In Kubernetes, tmpfs can persist data until the node reboot. The SizeLimit is unset for this volume so kubelet will allow this pod to use the ephemeral storage of node until it reaches its limit.

After creating the volume, let's test it by populating it with some data first. Get the access of redisvol-container using the **kubectl exec** command:

```
kubectl exec -it redis-vol -- /bin/bash
```

As we have done earlier, let's create a text file in **/data** directory and populate the volume. After that, kill the redis process by using the **kill** command and PID of the redis process. After performing all these steps, the outcome should look something like this:

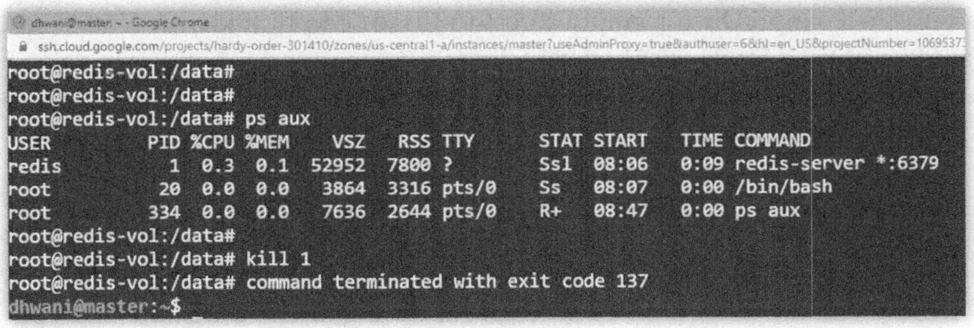

Figure 11.23: Kill redis process using SIGKILL after populating data in container

After killing the redisvol-container, we should be a container restart inside redis-vol pod as shown in the following screenshot:

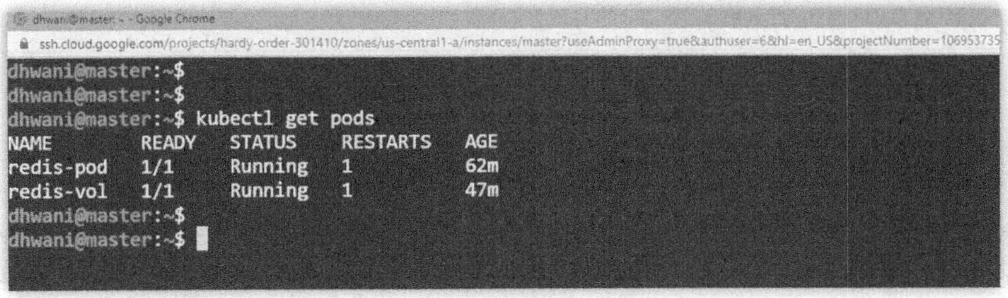

Figure 11.24: redis-vol pod in RUNNING state after a restart

After getting a fresh restart, redis-vol pod got a new container spun up by kubelet. Let's quickly access this new container and verify the contents of **/data** directory. If everything has gone in the right direction, we should be able to see something like this:

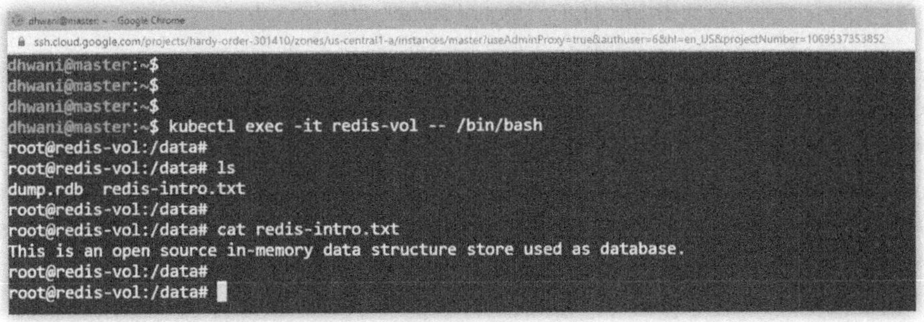

Figure 11.25: Data inside the container persists in Emptydir volume

The text file that we created persisted in the **/data** directory of the newly created container. When we killed the container, kubelet used the same pod template to spin up a new container which mounted the emptydir volume on the **/data** directory of the new container. As we said earlier, the contents of emptydir volume do not vanish when the container dies.

In a nutshell, emptyDir (or empty directory) is an empty folder dedicated to the pod to be utilized by its eventual containers. This is useful for arbitrary data such as the text string used in the example. For something more private, we have secrets explained in the next topic.

Supplying sensitive information using secrets

Secrets encode (and encrypt, if configured) sensitive information and pass it to workloads without other users or processes accessing it. There are different types of built-in secrets for different types of data in Kubernetes code tree. The default type of secrets is **Opaque** that is used to store unstructured, arbitrary user data. Another secret type that we have already encountered while describing imp-pod was the **Service-account** secret. The following table sheds more light on types of secrets for respective sensitive data:

Type of secret	Usage
Opaque	unstructured user data
kubernetes.io/service-account	service account token
kubernetes.io/dockercfg	serialized ~/.dockercfg file
kubernetes.io/dockerconfigjson	serialized ~/.docker/config.json file
kubernetes.io/basic-auth	credentials for basic authentication
kubernetes.io/ssh-auth	credentials for SSH authentication
kubernetes.io/tls	data for a TLS client or server
bootstrap.kubernetes.io/token	bootstrap token data

Table 11.1: Types of Kubernetes Secrets

There are two ways to create a secret in Kubernetes. First, using the object definition YAML file (just like every other object we created so far). Second, using the **kubectl** command. We will go with the second method for this example.

To create secrets using **kubectl** command line, we first need to create two text files (*sensitive information!!!*) which contain the username and password details. You can use **echo** command to populate these files with the desired data:

```
echo -n "admin_001" > ./username.txt
```

```
echo -n "21ssa3adhpn" > ./password.txt
```

Use **kubectl create** command followed by the type of object (a generic secret), object name and the source of data:

```
kubectl create secret generic user --from-file=./username.txt
```

```
kubectl create secret generic pswd --from-file=./password.txt
```

The outcome of these command should be like the following screenshot:

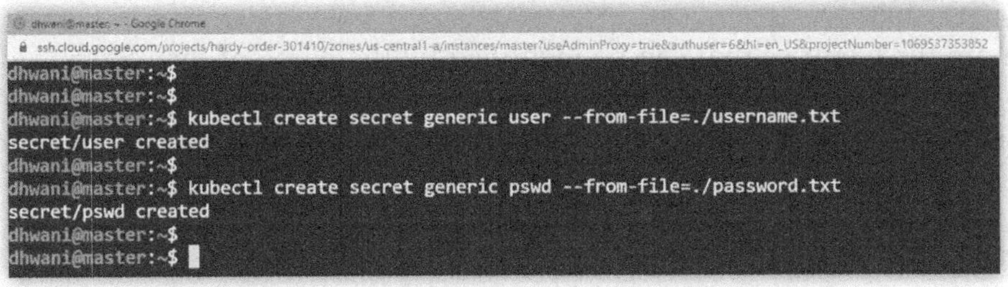

Figure 11.26: Secrets creation using kubectl command line

The command worked successfully, and the secrets are created. Other possible sources of data could be a directory, an environment variable, or a URL. A single secret can package one or more key-value pair of the input data. When a secret is created from a file, if not mentioned, the filename of the file will be taken as the key and the data of that file will be taken as the value to that key. Although in this case, we have explicitly instructed the secrets to be identified as **user** and **pswd**, so the keys for these secrets are **user** and **pswd**, while the values are the data available inside those text files.

The command **kubectl create secret** is supposed to be followed by the **source type and the secret type**. The source type in this example is **generic** which indicates secret creation from a **file or a directory**. Alternatively, the sources can also be of type **tls** or **docker-registry** which create TLS secrets with public and private keys or dockercfg (docker config) secrets for authenticating images against a docker registry (e.g Docker Hub) respectively. The secret type can be anyone mentioned in the table above; when it is left blank, the default type is Opaque.

Both of these secrets are created in the default namespace. If you want to create a secret in another namespace apart from default, you need to mention it while writing the **kubectl create secret** command. Let us list out the secrets of default namespace by using the following command:

```
kubectl get secrets
```

The outcome of the command should look something like this:

Figure 11.27: List of secrets in default namespace

There are three entries that can be identified by the name of the secrets and their types. DATA column shows the number of key-value pairs packaged by the secrets. The user and pswd secrets each have one pair which means single data entry per each secret. Let us describe one of the of secrets (user) to understand it better.

```
kubectl describe secrets user
```

The description of user secret should look something like the following screenshot:

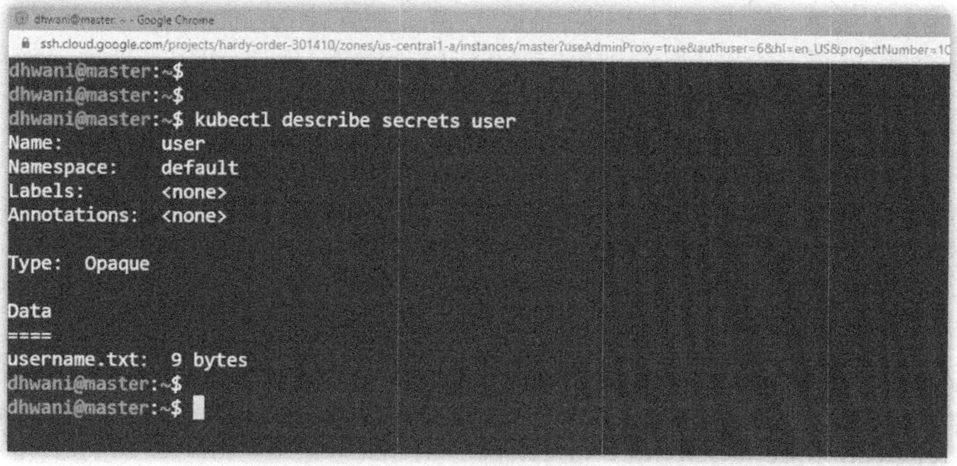

Figure 11.28: Description of a secret (user)

The type is **Opaque** and **Data** field shows the name of the file which we have provided while creating the secret. The description only shows the name and disk size of the file, not the content inside it *(otherwise the secret wouldn't be so opaque, would it?)*. We can access the data once we navigate inside the container of the pod.

Create a busybox pod using the object definition file and mount the secrets created above to a specific location inside the container. You can follow the code to achieve our goal:

```
1. apiVersion: v1

2. kind: Pod
```

```
3.  metadata:
4.    name: projected-volume
5.  spec:
6.    containers:
7.    - name: pv-container
8.      image: busybox
9.      args:
10.     - sleep
11.     - "3600"
12.     volumeMounts:
13.     - name: busybox-pv-volume
14.       mountPath: "/projected-volume"
15.       readOnly: true
16.   volumes:
17.   - name: busybox-pv-volume
18.     projected:
19.       sources:
20.       - secret:
21.           name: user
22.       - secret:
23.           name: pswd
```

The **pv-busybox** container is programmed to sleep after 3600 s of its execution. A new mount path **/projected-volume** will be created at runtime with only read-only permission inside the container and a volume busybox-pv-volume will be mounted on this newly created path. The volume is defined at the bottom of the pod template. Unlike emptyDir volume, we do have some information about the type the of volume that should be projected on this pod. In order to let the secrets (user and pswd) be consumed by the pod, we need to refer them under the volumes field of pod's specification.

When the pod definition is expanded by the kube-apiserver, it does not verify the existence of the secret referred in the volumes field. Once the pod gets scheduled on a cluster node, kubelet of that node identifies the secret and requests for the value of that secrets to kube-apiserver (which fetches it from etcd). If the secret already exists, kubelet will get its value and populate it on the pod. In the otherwise case, kubelet will keep on trying to fetch the secret's value which will result into `container creating` state of pod. Only after mounting the volume successfully, containers of a pod can achieve `running` state.

Let's create our pod called **projected-volume** by using either **kubectl apply** or **kubectl create** command. The outcome should look something like this:

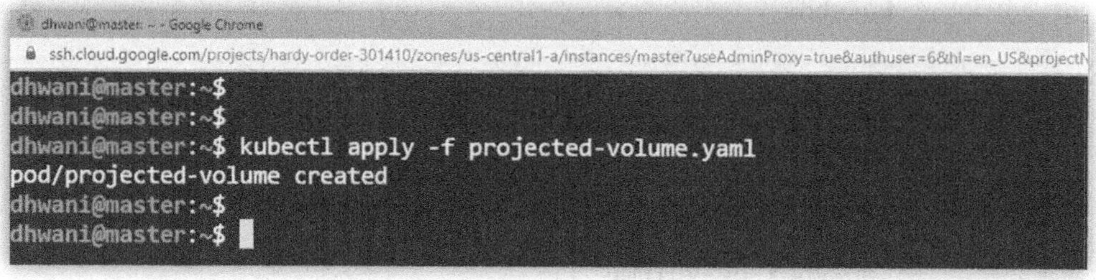

Figure 11.29: Pod with a projected volume (secret) creation process

Let us see if we were able to mount the projected volume, busybox-pv-volume successfully on the pod. List out all running pods using **kubectl get pods** command and you should receive the outcome similar to the following one:

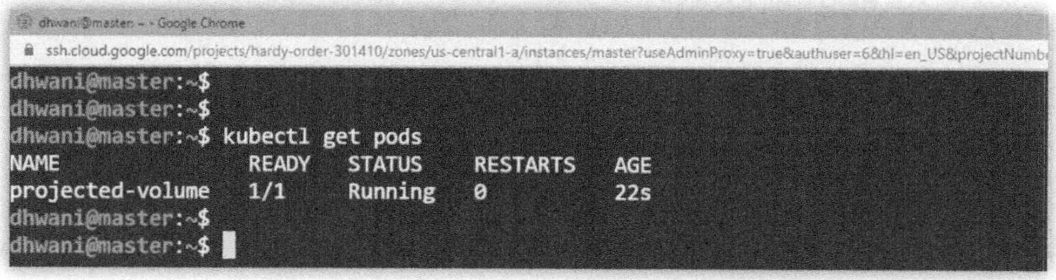

Figure 11.30: Status of projected-volume pod

The pod's status is **RUNNING** which means that the volume has been successfully mounted on the pod and kubelet was able to successfully fetch the data of both the secrets. To have a concrete proof-of-observation, we can exec into the busybox container and look for the contents of secrets. To do so, we need to attach our client terminal to container's SHELL, and we can do that by executing the following command:

```
kubectl exec -it projected-volume -- /bin/sh
```

After getting the access of busybox container, let's verify if the **projected-volume** directory exists. If the directory is created, you should be able to witness something similar like this on your client terminal:

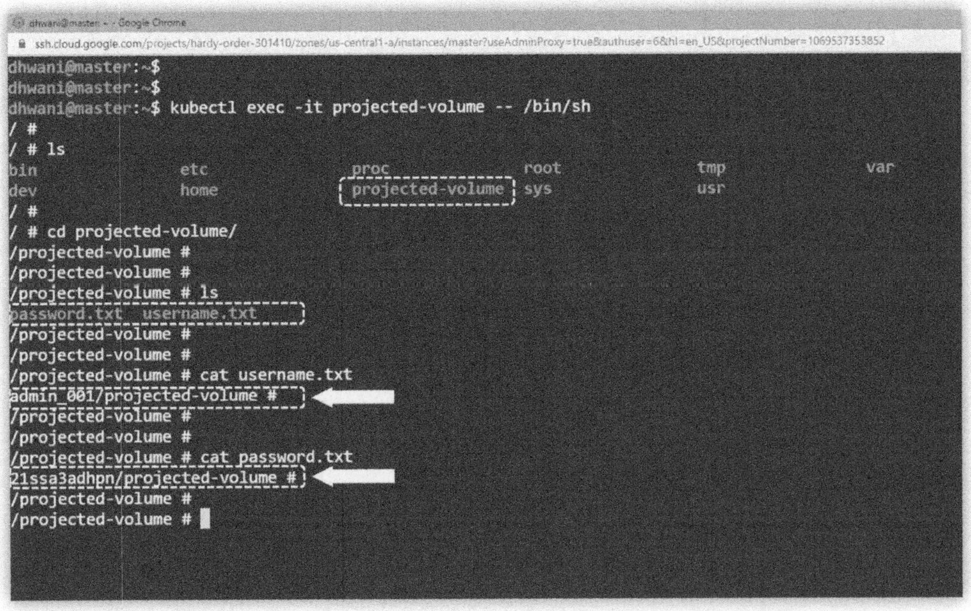

Figure 11.31: Pod consumes data from the mounted projected volume (secret)

We were able to create a **projected-volume** directory in busybox container and it does contain both the files, **username.txt** and **password.txt**. When a secret is consumed by a pod, each key inside the secret is mounted as a file under the **mountPath**. Here, both the secrets are consumed as these text files by the pod. When we view the contents of the file, we receive the data we had stored in the original text files.

If you decide to experiment more with secrets and you want to define your secret just like we did with pods, deployments, replicasets and other Kubernetes objects, you can look the object definition file created by Kubernetes for the user secret. By using the following command, we can get object definition file for any object in any format:

```
kubectl get secrets user -o yaml
```

This is the YAML equivalent of the secret that we had created using **kubectl create secret** command:

1. apiVersion: **v1**

2. data:

3.   username.txt: **YWRtaW5fMDAx**

4. kind: **Secret**

5. metadata:

6.   creationTimestamp: "2021-03-23T13:24:13Z"

7.   managedFields:

```
8.   - apiVersion: v1
9.     fieldsType: FieldsV1
10.    fieldsV1:
11.      f:data:
12.        .: {}
13.          f:username.txt: {}
14.        f:type: {}
15.      manager: kubectl-create
16.      operation: Update
17.      time: "2021-03-12T13:24:13Z"
18.    name: user
19.    namespace: default
20.    resourceVersion: "4330"
21.    uid: 53e88111-efea-4557-bc34-15f35acd0309
22. type: Opaque
```

The secret object's configurations contain **apiVersion**, **data**, **kind**, **metadata**, and **type** fields. Data field consists of the encoded data as base64 string. Any addition to this string is not valid so you cannot temper with the encoded data. metadata field has a lot of new entries than other k8s objects such as **operation: Update**. When a secret is being consumed by a pod, kubelet keeps a track of its updated values and reflects the changes accordingly in the mounted volume inside the **0pod**. This way we can always update the data in a secret.

When you create a secret using its configuration file, all you need to consider is the type of the secret and data you want to package inside that secret. You can take the following sample file as the reference for the secret's object definition in YAML file format:

```
1. apiVersion: v1
2. kind: Secret
3. metadata:
4.   name: user
5. type: Opaque
6. data:
7.   username: admin_001
```

Just like the API access token secret, we can look for the other default secrets used by Kubernetes and its components when we bootstrap a cluster. You can use the following command and list out all available secrets in all namespaces:

```
kubectl get secrets --all-namespaces
```

The outcome of this command will list a lot of different type of secrets available in the cluster:

Figure 11.32: List of default secrets available in all namespaces in a Kubernetes cluster

It is a long list of secrets with majority of them being service account tokens used by different services. For example, there is a deployment controller token, endpoint controller token, weave-net token, generic-garbage-collector token, kube-proxy token, and many more. All of these tokens are used by K8s objects to make authorized API calls to perform their tasks.

The takeaway from the secrets is the preservation of sensitivity and passing the data to appropriate target (process or path). But not all data is sensitive, some information can be out-in-open yet decoupled from the container image to create a smooth app shipping experience. The next topic solves this issue by exploring a ConfigMap example.

Working with ConfigMaps

Let us start with listing out every available ConfigMaps in the cluster. Use the usual **kubectl get** command with **–all-namespaces** flag to get an output looking like the following screenshot:

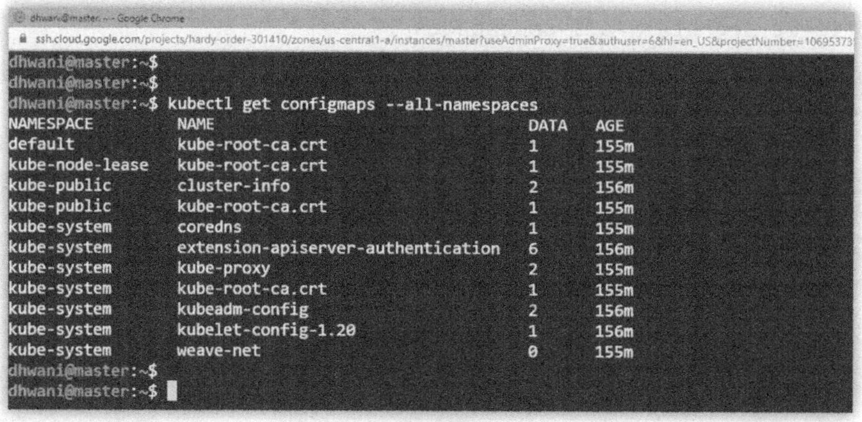

Figure 11.33: List of default ConfigMaps in a Kubernetes cluster

When we had bootstrapped the cluster, the dynamic configurations (configurations that change according to cluster state and user input) for Kubernetes components (nodes, cluster, objects) and authentication information is stored inside the ConfigMaps.

Let us describe one of these ConfigMaps in detail by using **kubectl describe configmap** command. The outcome should look something like the following screenshot:

Figure 11.34: Description of default kubelet ConfigMap for version 1.20

This is the description of the ConfigMap for the kubelet of the master node. It contains information such as authorization and authentication details, connectivity details, logging details, healthcheck details, and so on. Each Kubelet stores its configurations in a file. The configurations are derived from the ConfigMap described above.

The ConfigMaps are updated depending on the desired state or change in the current state of the cluster. As the ConfigMap gets updated, kubelet streams new configurations to the file by overriding the previous one. Further operations performed by the kubelet follow the newer configurations. The watch loop runs with small intervals which enables kubelet to spin up new containers in pods when the old ones die or new pods in Replicaset when the old ones are removed to maintain a desired state. After all, kubelet can make requests to respective workload controllers to get updated workload definition through kube-proxy and kube-apiserver.

We can also create custom ConfigMaps for our application pods. In order to create ConfigMaps, we first need to prepare data that we want to package under them. For this example, we will populate a busybox container with some dummy game layout and game-play data. For the convenience's sake, we will create a new directory and a couple of files inside it as mentioned in the following part:

Details of file 1:

```
nano gameplay.beta1
enemies=fireSlimes
lives=1
enemies.cheat=true
enemies.cheat.level=noGoodRotten
secret.code.passphrase=BOODUUDUDUD
secret.code.allowed=false
```

Details of file 2:

```
nano gameLayout.beta1
android:layout_width="wrap_content"
android:layout_height="match_parent"
android:orientation="vertical"
android:text="Hello, I am a Button"
color.good=purple
color.bad=yellow
allow.textmode=true
how.nice.to.look=fairlyNice
```

Both of these files are populated with dummy data for an android smartphone game. They contain data for the game layout and game play. To create ConfigMap containing these two files, we can use the following **kubectl** command:

```
kubectl create configmap game-config --from-file=./game-config-beta1/
```

Just like Secrets, ConfigMap can be created from a configuration file/directory, environment variable, or some command-line arguments. For this example, we are going take the **game-config-beta1** directory as the input source which contains both configuration files. After executing the command, the output should look something like the following screenshot:

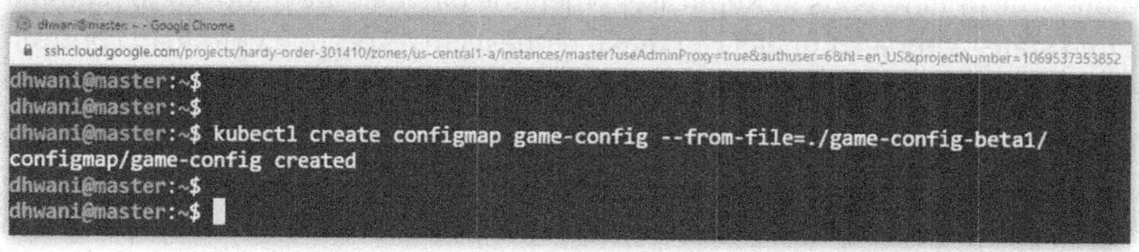

Figure 11.35: ConfigMap creation using kubectl command line

After the ConfigMap has been created, we can list them out in the default namespace by using **kubectl get configmaps** command. The outcome should look something like the following screenshot:

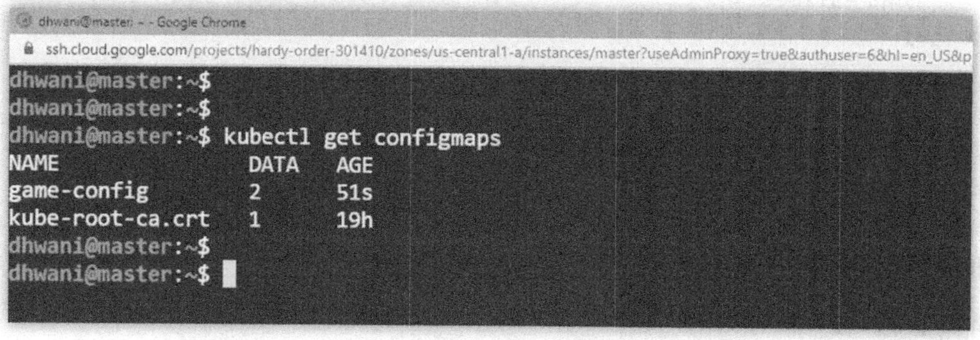

Figure 11.36: List of ConfigMaps in default namespace

The ConfigMap called **game-config** has been created in the default namespace so we need to make sure that the pod consuming it is created under the same namespace as well. The **DATA** field shows the number of key entries packaged inside the ConfigMap. Just like Secrets, files under the target reference directory (mentioned after **-f** flag) are stored as the keys and their content as the values of the keys inside the ConfigMaps. These objects are not designed to store large chunks of data. You can only store up to 1 MiB data per ConfigMap.

In order to get more information about the ConfigMap, we can use the same **kubectl describe** command and define the type of object as configmap and mention the name of the object.

```
kubectl describe configmaps game-config
```

The outcome should look something like this:

Figure 11.37: Description of game-config (user-defined) ConfigMap

The ConfigMap is populated with the configuration data provided by us in form of the content inside the files. Unlike Secrets, we can actually see the contents of the packaged config files since ConfigMaps are not designed to store sensitive data *(nothing opaque here, all crystal clear).*

At this stage, we can finally create and configure a busybox container using the ConfigMap. You can take the reference of the following pod object definition YAML. As you might have guessed, the definition is pretty similar to the one used with secrets since the only difference is the volume type. To better understand the working of the ConfigMaps, the CMD will just open a terminal and display the content of the config file populated by the ConfigMap as shown in the following code:

```
1. apiVersion: v1
2. kind: Pod
3. metadata:
4.     name: config-test-pod
5. spec:
```

```
6.    containers:
7.      - name: test-container
8.        image: k8s.gcr.io/busybox
9.        command: [ "/bin/sh", "-c", "cat /etc/config/gameplay.beta1" ]
10.       volumeMounts:
11.         - name: config-volume
12.           mountPath: /etc/config
13.     volumes:
14.       - name: config-volume
15.         configMap:
16.           name: game-config
17.     restartPolicy: Never
```

We have defined a configmap called config-volume, and mounted it to **/etc/config** file inside the busybox container environment. After having observed the pod definition YAML, create the pod using **kubectl <apply/create>** command and describe the pod using **kubectl describe pod** command. The outcome should look something like the following screenshot:

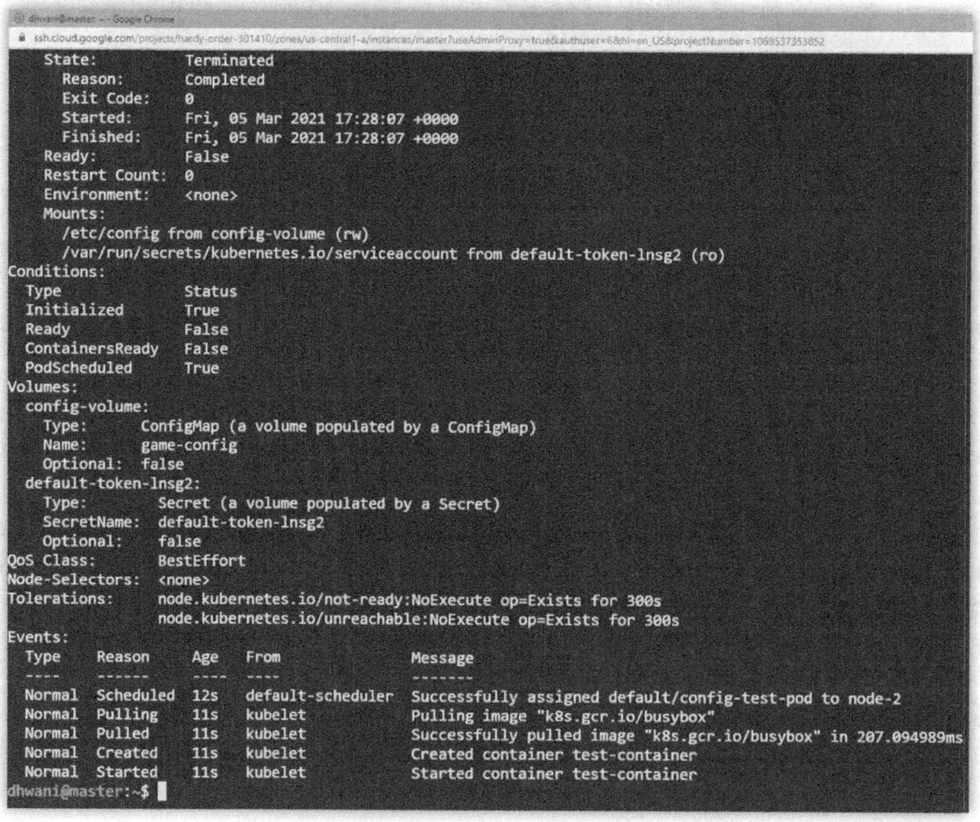

Figure 11.38: ConfigMap mount details of a pod

The **Volume** field enlists a ConfigMap named **game-config** and a default-token secret as expected. The **Events** field also shows the successful creation and running of the container which means that the volume was successfully mounted on pod, and the container has consumed the values of the ConfigMap. We had configured the container to display the contents of the **gameplay.beta1** file. As we had set the restart policy to never and the container has successfully finished its task, the pod is in the COMPLETED state which means it is not possible to attach to container's shell *(come to think of it, we could have also created a job! There are always multiple ways to do the same task and the most important factors are simplicity and achieving the desired output)*. We can list out logs of the pod. To so do, run the following command:

```
kubectl logs config-test-pod
```

The outcome of this command should be something like this:

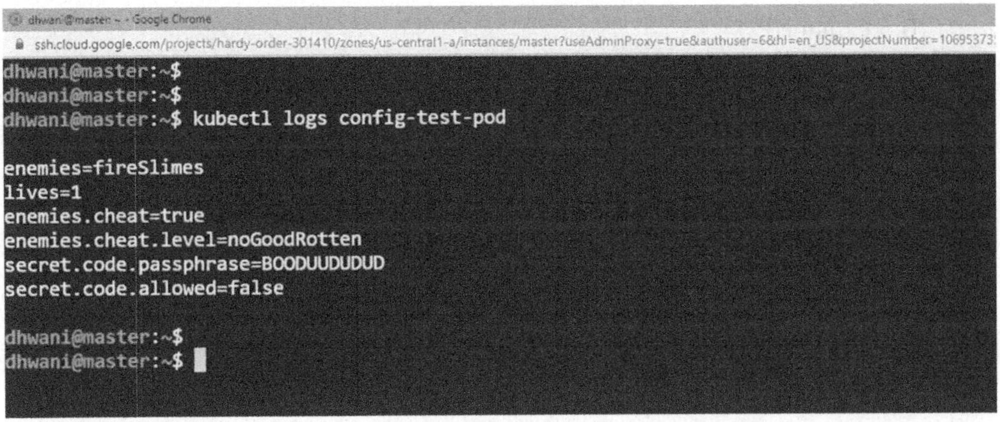

Figure 11.39: Pod consumes data from user-defined ConfigMap (game-config)

Log entry of config-test-pod clearly states that the container did consume the data from ConfigMap, saved it under **/etc/config** directory, and displayed the contents of **gameplay.beta1**.

There are many other different types of volumes. Most of them are cloud-provider specific. We will explore the persistent options while working with hosted K8s on Cloud in *Chapter 13, Hosted Kubernetes on Cloud*. For now, you can rest assure that your containers will not be clueless after every restart as long as the wrapper of pod is healthy.

Conclusion

This chapter covered two extremely important aspects of Network and Storage objects in K8s. You can expose your containers within and outside the cluster. You can store arbitrary data or pass sensitive information while maintaining the reliability and security. Most importantly, you understand the networking and storage models of Kubernetes. Even if the offerings grow in future, the strong base will help you grasp them faster. There is still a little more to explore in these directions but what you have seen so far should undoubtedly enable you to try a bunch of live containerized web applications that generate temporary data. In the next chapter, we will cover advanced orchestration with Kubernetes.

Multiple choice questions

1. Which of the following services does not allow you to access your containers outside the cluster?

    A. NodePort

    B. ClusterIP

    C. Load Balancer

    D. External Name

    Answer: B

2. Which of the following is not a service type in Kubernetes?

    A. NodePort

    B. ClusterIP

    C. Load Balancer

    D. Host

    Answer: D

3. Which of the following options add/remove iptable rules of the host?

    A. kube-proxy

    B. kubelet

    C. service-controller

    D. kube-apiserver

    Answer: A

4. Which of the following namespaces contain a service named **kubernetes** to communicate with kube-apiserver via kube-proxy?

    A. default

    B. kube-system

    C. kube-public

    D. All namespaces

    Answer: D

5. A pod can have only one _____ but multiple _____ .

   A. container, service

   B. ClusterIP, service endpoints

   C. service endpoint, ClusterIP

   D. service endpoint, containers

   Answer: B

6. Which of the following volume is not a projected volume in Kubernetes?

   A. Secret

   B. ConfigMap

   C. Downward API

   D. EmptyDir

   Answer: D

7. Which of the following volume types provide metadata to the pod about itself?

   A. ConfigMap

   B. Secret

   C. Storage Class

   D. Downward API

   Answer: D

8. Which of the following secret types are used to store arbitrary, sensitive data?

   A. Hollow

   B. Generic

   C. Opaque

   D. Top Secret

   Answer: C

9. Which of the following class of storage objects decouple support and development of storage APIs from K8s code tree?

   A. CSI

   B. CNI

   C. CBI

   D. FBI

   Answer: A

10. How do you feel about the book so far?

    A. Love it!

    B. It is the best book I have ever read!

    C. I am happy to have borrowed/bought this book.

    D. All of the above.

    Answer: D

Questions

1. Explain the role of kube-proxy in the Kubernetes architecture.

2. List the types of Kubernetes services and explain them briefly.

3. Write YAML files to create an Apache2 deployment with two replicas and a service to expose it outside the cluster.

4. Explain the role of storage classes in Kubernetes Storage Model.

5. Explain the difference between service account token, tls, and Opaque type of secrets. Create a YAML file of a pod which has any two of these mounted to itself.

6. Write a pod with two different containers and expose it using a ClusterIP service. How will the containers of the pod communicate to one another?

## CHAPTER 12

Advanced Orchestration with Kubernetes

Introduction

The previous chapters focused on making things work, this chapter will focus on having more granular control over the definitions and behavior of the objects. We will explore authorization and security mechanisms offered and supported by Kubernetes. We will also look at advanced pod scheduling options. This is an important chapter as it covers many topics that are required to understand the behavior of hosted K8s services on the Cloud, which are discussed in further chapters.

Structure

This chapter covers:

- Advanced container orchestration
- Kubernetes authorization
- Working with Kubernetes authorization
- Establishing Kubernetes cluster security
- Pod priority classes
- Controlling pod scheduling

Objective

At this point, you are already familiar with the architecture, components, workloads, and other objects of K8s. This chapter acknowledges the fact and builds some advanced concepts on the top of it. We will discuss why and how specific configurations are helpful to make us spend less time writing redundant pod manifests. To make a decent balance between theory, demonstration, and application, we will combine a bunch of settings in a single pod manifest and explore their behavioral implications while understanding the topics of advanced orchestration.

Advanced container orchestration

When Kubernetes and containers make their way to the majority of the University Curricula, this will be one of the ambiguous viva examination questions that can have infinite possible answers, and mostly all of them will be correct (by the way, the term viva comes from Latin phrase viva voce which means orally). You can have your own judgment and interpretation of what counts as "advanced" container orchestration and what doesn't. This chapter presents the authors' view of it and expands upon the same with conceptual explanations and examples.

The previous chapters focused on making things work. We didn't care about what if a deployment gets scheduled on a heavily loaded node or what if someone hacks into our services. This is where advanced orchestration comes in. It largely relates to making the cluster more robust and secure. This can be achieved by implementing layers of security tools and configurations, having precise control over workload scheduling, setting up contextually systematic access control, etc. We will look at these topics individually and will also link them as the explanation takes its course. Let's start with authorization.

Kubernetes authorization

Do you remember the time when you realized that you have always had more rights and privileges in your country than a tourist or an immigrant because you were born there? This topic gives you a similar feeling. Having bootstrapped the K8s cluster as an admin user gives you many privileges that you are likely to have taken for granted. This is important because whatever API requests you have made to the Kube-apiserver so far, had always been authorized for your Linux user account. K8s' authorization works hands-in-hands with Linux's (or Cloud Provider's) identity management system.

When we make requests to the Kube-apiserver (for validation, since that is the job of the Kube-apiserver) through the Kubectl command line (or directly using the K8s APIs), it checks for the following details:

- Who is making the request (**user**)?

- Is he authorized (**permission**) to make such a request?

- Which **group** does the user belong to?

- Which **resource** is this request targeting?

- Which **namespace** does the target resource belong to?

- Which **lower resource** is this request targeting (e.g. pods through deployments)?

- Which **API** does it want to get served from?

- What is the HTTP **request verb** (k8s APIs like get, create, describe, update, delete, and so on)?

Once the request is analyzed, Kube-apiserver can decide whether to authorize it to access or act upon the resource mentioned in the request. There are multiple ways of authorization for different sources of requests.

- **Node authorization:** This is used to give a metaphorical VIP pass to node essential resources, specially Kubelets. A program called **node authorizer** from K8s control plane grants read, write, and certificate signing privileges to requests originated from Kubelets. To make sure that no other source is impersonating as a Kubelet, the Kubelet must add the node-name with the request that would match the list of available nodes in the records of Kube-apiserver. In short, every legit request from the nodes within the cluster will always get a green signal.

- **Attribute-Based Access Control (ABAC):** Neither every user is an admin nor every process making a request to the k8s control plane is a Kubelet. ABAC policies determine whether a request can be authorized or not based on the attributes carried by the request. Anything including but not limited to user details, object version details, annotations, specs, or resource requirements can be considered the attributes of a request. Policies are pre-defined documented JSON lists of objects, and the permissions or access granted to them. The policy keeps updating with K8s versions. Due to their inconvenient format *(even though this is an opinion, it is as strong as a fact)* and the number of K8s objects increasing with every update, ABAC is losing its popularity and usage over RBAC.

- **Role-Based Access Control (RBAC):** RBAC puts a decoupled layer of simplicity between the attributes and the access, the layer is called **Roles.** In terms of K8s, Roles are a group of API objects just like workloads or services, whereas for users, they are an access sorting and management tool. Their logic works similar to the access control offerings provided by the Cloud providers (such as GCP IAM) and working with them is as simple as working with any other K8s object.

RBAC provides Roles for node-level access and ClusterRoles for cluster-wide access provision. It also offers **Binding** objects to associate roles with workloads. Binding objects like RoleBindings or ClusterRoleBinding help keeping Roles and Cluster Roles independent from workloads just how PVCs keep Persistent Volumes independent from them. We will have an in-depth look at RBAC in the next topic.

- **Webhooks:** For starters, webhooks are HTTP callbacks POSTed (*generally*) to notify a web application event (success, failure, alert... anything). As a K8s authorization mode, webhooks detach the function of authorization from the cluster and its control plane (*outsourcing of a kind*). This mode establishes a communication channel between the cluster and an external REST service (*via webhooks, of course*) that authorizes the requests for your server. You need to create a YAML configuration file to denote the webhook URL and the remote service URL (along with their CA keys, if applicable). This approach is beneficial for programs intending to act as third-party access management solutions.

The trade-off between an additional layer of security versus complexity can swing on any side depending on your use case and workforce, but webhooks are definitely not as ubiquitously applicable as RBAC.

All of these authorization modes can be triggered while bootstrapping your K8s cluster. The current version of kubeadm triggers at least RBAC by default. You can use `--authorization-mode` flag followed by an equal sign and value (ABAC, Webhook, RBAC) to choose your preferred mode.

Working with Kubernetes authorization

The best way to observe the implementation of topics like authorization is by looking at a full-fledged containerized application. Luckily, we don't have to look too far to find such a use case as Kubernetes itself is one of the most significant examples of containerized distributed microservice-based applications. We have mentioned earlier in this chapter that your admin account is already privileged. Let's see how K8s provided you with these privileges.

We can start by listing out the available roles. Run **kubectl get roles** for all namespaces to get a list of them as shown in the following screenshot:

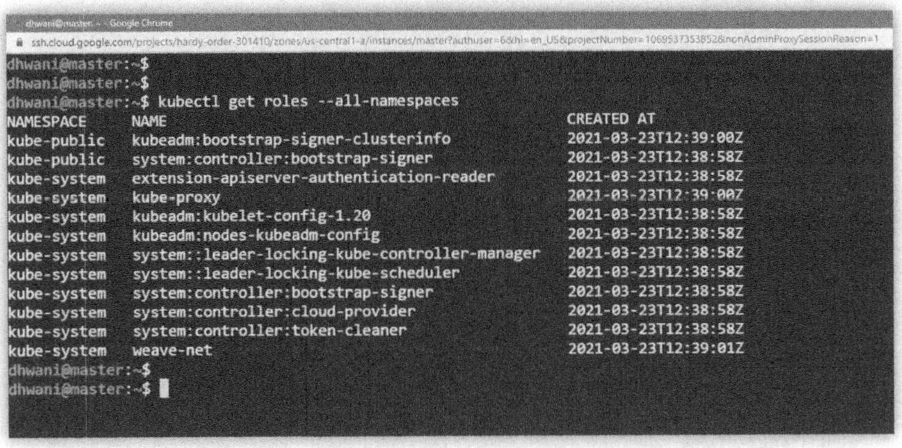

Figure 12.1: Built-in Kubernetes roles

There are different roles targeted toward different objects, and most of them are created within Kube-system namespace. Expanding upon a familiar-looking role should give further insight. Describe Kube-proxy role using **kubectl describe** command as shown in the following screenshot:

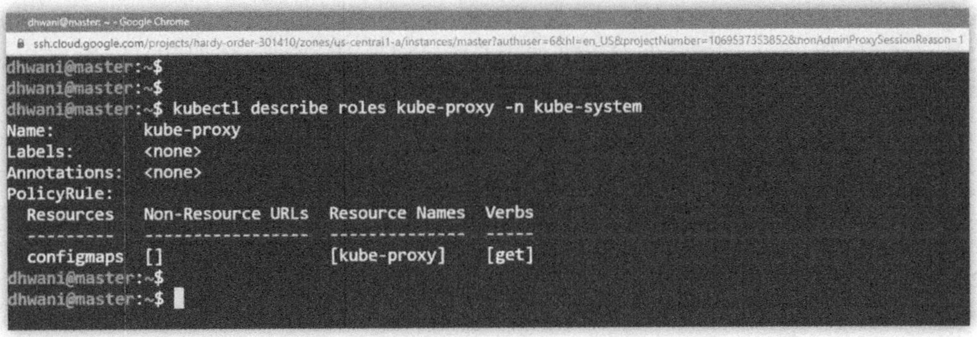

Figure 12.2: Description of Kube-proxy role

This is one of the simplest roles as it doesn't have any significant meta information and has only one Policy Rule. It grants the reading right (using get verb) of a configmap called **kube-proxy** to the Kube-proxy daemonset. Albeit the role is independent of Daemonset but this is precisely why we chose Kube-proxy to get described. We already knew the target workload since we had studied Kube-proxy in depth in *Chapter 11, Networking and Storage with K8s*. Even though the role is fairly simple, K8s auto-fills many details from its own object template. We can take a look at it by expanding the role in YAML format as shown in the following screenshot:

```
dhwani@master:~$
dhwani@master:~$ kubectl get role kube-proxy -n kube-system -o yaml
apiVersion: rbac.authorization.k8s.io/v1
kind: Role
metadata:
  creationTimestamp: "2021-03-23T12:39:00Z"
  managedFields:
  - apiVersion: rbac.authorization.k8s.io/v1
    fieldsType: FieldsV1
    fieldsV1:
      f:rules: {}
    manager: kubeadm
    operation: Update
    time: "2021-03-23T12:39:00Z"
  name: kube-proxy
  namespace: kube-system
  resourceVersion: "243"
  uid: 89d34945-24d4-4903-86a8-bb2ed9b36eea
rules:
- apiGroups:
  - ""
  resourceNames:
  - kube-proxy
  resources:
  - configmaps
  verbs:
  - get
```

Figure 12.3: YAML manifest of Kube-proxy role with auto-filled details by K8s

Roles fall under authorization group of K8s APIs. The updates of the fields of this object (Role) are handled by Kubeadm as we update the k8s version or a specific API using **kubeadm update** or **kubeadm upgrade** command. The authority is granted to Kubeadm since it is the process requesting for this role by bootstrapping the K8s cluster. Apart from **apiVersion**, each K8s resource also registers a **resourceVersion** number to help setup a watch utility on it (as used with commands like **kubectl get** pods). This number also helps in K8s' own API level version control.

Moving on to the access grant rules, we can see that all three parameters are mentioned in different fields. The accessible resource type is mentioned under **resources**, the name of the resource to be accessed is mentioned under **resourceNames**, and the grant verb is mentioned under **verbs**. For successful access to the Kube-proxy daemon, this role needs to be **bound** to the user, group of users, or service account that created Kube-proxy. This is done using **RoleBindings**. You can list out available role bindings of your cluster using **kubectl get** command as shown in the following screenshot:

```
dhwani@master:~$
dhwani@master:~$
dhwani@master:~$ kubectl get rolebindings --all-namespaces
NAMESPACE     NAME                                              ROLE                                                      AGE
kube-public   kubeadm:bootstrap-signer-clusterinfo              Role/kubeadm:bootstrap-signer-clusterinfo                5d1h
kube-public   system:controller:bootstrap-signer                Role/system:controller:bootstrap-signer                  5d1h
kube-system   kube-proxy                                        Role/kube-proxy                                          5d1h
kube-system   kubeadm:kubelet-config-1.20                       Role/kubeadm:kubelet-config-1.20                         5d1h
kube-system   kubeadm:nodes-kubeadm-config                      Role/kubeadm:nodes-kubeadm-config                        5d1h
kube-system   system:extension-apiserver-authentication-reader  Role/extension-apiserver-authentication-reader           5d1h
kube-system   system::leader-locking-kube-controller-manager    Role/system::leader-locking-kube-controller-manager      5d1h
kube-system   system::leader-locking-kube-scheduler             Role/system::leader-locking-kube-scheduler               5d1h
kube-system   system:controller:bootstrap-signer                Role/system:controller:bootstrap-signer                  5d1h
kube-system   system:controller:cloud-provider                  Role/system:controller:cloud-provider                    5d1h
kube-system   system:controller:token-cleaner                   Role/system:controller:token-cleaner                     5d1h
kube-system   weave-net                                         Role/weave-net                                           5d1h
dhwani@master:~$
dhwani@master:~$
```

Figure 12.4: List of default role bindings

You may notice a dedicated binding for the Kube-proxy role. Upon expanding it further using the description API (using **kubectl describe** command), it shows that the role is bound to the **Kubeadm Bootstrapper Group** as shown in the following screenshot:

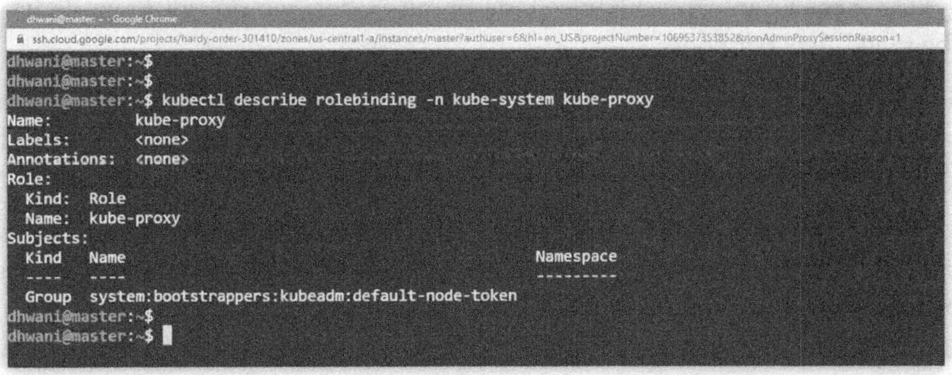

Figure 12.5: Kube-system role binding description

You can observe the YAML outputs of the role-binding as well as the target configmap to get a better understanding of which configurations are exactly covered under the policy served by the Kube-proxy role. Roles are Node-level resources. K8s also offers authorization objects with the scope covering the entire cluster. They are called **Cluster Roles** and **Cluster Role Bindings**. They operate exactly the same way except for their scope being cluster wide. Here is a list of default-created cluster roles while bootstrapping a K8s cluster using Kubeadm:

Figure 12.6: Default cluster roles

The screen had its size limits, so this screenshot does not even cover half of the available cluster roles. This cluster has so many cluster roles because most of the control plane components work with the entire cluster, not just a particular node. The **kube-scheduler** can schedule pods on all nodes, we do not have dedicated Kube-schedulers per node.

This also applies to cluster-wide add-ons such as logging agents or third-party garbage collectors. Cluster roles can be ridiculously simple or meticulous enough to make us appreciate the attention to details.

Take the **cluster-admin** cluster role for an example. You can describe it using **kubectl describe** command followed by the object type, object name, and the namespace as shown in the following screenshot:

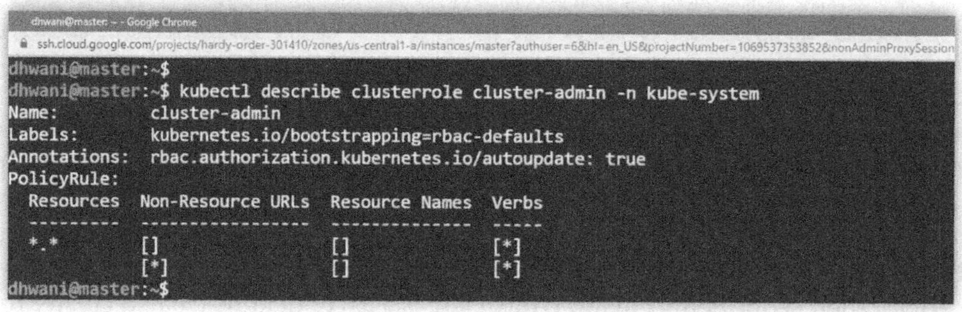

Figure 12.7: Description of cluster-admin cluster role

This cluster role grants all verbs of permissions for all objects to the user *(it is equivalent to having all six infinity stones in the world of K8s)*. On top of that, the cluster role also has an auto-update policy (indicated by the annotation), so whenever we get newer objects or object types, the user having the privileges of this role can control them. Conversely, control plane objects like deployment controllers have specific permissions for specific objects. Check it out in the following screenshot:

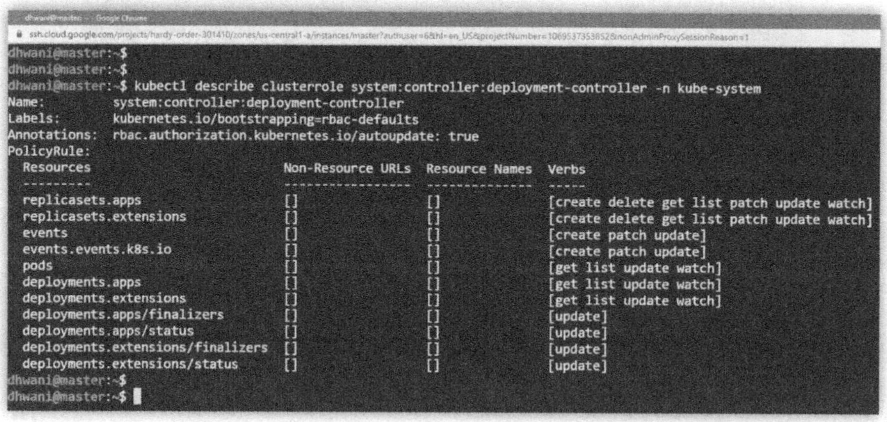

Figure 12.8: Description of deployment-controller cluster role

This cluster role allows deployment controllers to **create, delete, list, patch, update,** or **watch** the replicasets, but only lets them view (**get, list, watch**) and update podSpec. Creation, deletion, and patching pod privileges are granted to replicasets instead. This maintains a proper hierarchy of operations between the objects. On top of that, the deployment controller can also create events (visible through object descriptions) and update indicator object values. You can observe more controllers and their respective cluster roles to get a better idea of how to create your own role and access granting strategies using Role-Based Access Control. RBAC works best under the assumption that nobody violates these access policies, but the reality is quite undisciplined and often requires layers of measures to keep the access policies in check. The tools and techniques used to do so fall under a broad area of security practices.

Establishing Kubernetes cluster security

One doesn't need to elaborate the importance of infrastructure security in this day and age, and K8s can't escape from the responsibility of being secure either. If your cluster is not secure, your application is not secure. K8s can be configured on a diverse set of infrastructural components; there is no textbook use case to consider while trying to make the cluster secure. Therefore, the security of a K8s cluster is addressed in four different layers, and coincidentally, all four layers' names start with C *(if we can have four Ps of marketing, why can't we have 4 Cs of cluster security?!)*. You can find them in *Figure 12.9*:

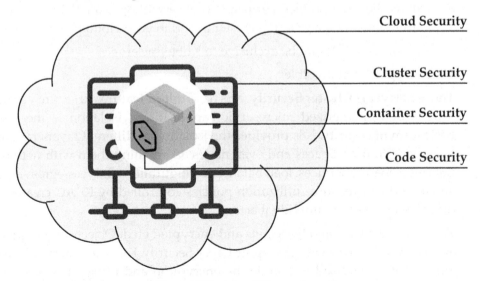

Figure 12.9: 4Cs of Cluster Security

1. **Cloud Security** or infrastructure security is the outermost layer of the K8s security model. The term cloud is used because a majority of K8s clusters are deployed on the cloud (for more information, refer to the note* below). Every cloud provider has its own implementation of security features, and the state of security across mainstream public cloud providers is efficiently competitive.

   Note:

   A big picture of how and where people choose to deploy Kubernetes https://containerjournal.com/features/findings-from-the-2021-kubernetes-adoption-report/

   Most of them provide encryption of data during transit (sending and receiving requests and responses) and rest (static stored data), and they maintain a robust physical infrastructure with fault tolerance and backup management. All of these are enveloped under strict access management policies, firewall rules, and optional features such as IP shuffling and masking. In case you are deploying your cluster on-premises (*yes, it is on-premises... not on-premises*), your team also needs to look for a similar level of custom security implementations while mandating the following practices:

   - Restrict public access to control plane components.

   - Configure the nodes not to accept requests from other nodes if they come from ports not mentioned in the ClusterIP service.

   - Follow the least privilege principle (not providing more than necessary permissions) while granting cluster access to your cloud provider.

   - Access to etcd should be exclusive to Kube-apiserver.

   - Encrypt etcd, if possible.

2. The next layer is **Cluster Security**. K8s has built-in features to secure various aspects of containerized microservice applications. Isolation is the most basic form of security. K8s provides the isolation at different layers ranging from pods to namespaces and even nodes. Combining them with network policies (separate services, load balancer configurations, ingress-egress rules, and so on) and resource utilization policies controlled by RBAC creates an organized fortress of individual actors.

   The data can be secured by secrets and encrypted etcd. Objects and requests are secured by TLS keys (Transport Layer Security Keys are Pairs of Public and Private keys used to handle the encryption and decryption of secure data exchange sessions between two or more parties) and `service-account-token` secrets.

3. The third layer, **Container Security,** is very loosely coupled with K8s. The term loosely coupled is used to the indicate lack of control that K8s have over the choices that determine the Container Security.

- It is essential to use a CRE (Container Runtime Environment) that provides strong isolation between the containers. **Docker** and **Containerd** are good choices for this purpose.

- Use official third-party images wherever possible and make sure to pull signed images from trustworthy registries like Docker Hub or Google Container Registry.

- If your organization makes its own images, make sure to sign them and host them on private or public registries. Do not indulge in direct image exchange.

- Restrict unnecessary privileged users inside the containerized environment.

- Consult professionals for container vulnerability scanning and cluster security auditing.

4. **Code Security,** the fourth and final layer, is something entirely dependent on the developer of the application *(aka you, the ever-priceless reader!)*. It is also the most likely layer to introduce vulnerabilities. While there is no specific way of writing a secure application code, you can keep the following points in mind.

- When your microservice needs to communicate to the client using TCP, make sure to perform a mutual TLS handshake. You can also encrypt your data in transit or let your cloud provider handle it.

- Don't expose your service on ports other than necessary and planned. Consult your network specialist to keep your port exposure to a minimum, using efficient load balancing without compromising the performance.

- If your application design involves the uses of 3rd party libraries, make sure to check their privacy and data handling policy periodically. Keep an eye on the updates of such libraries and the potential vulnerabilities introduced by them.

- Scan your code for potential code security flaws using **Static Application Security Testing Tools** like Brakeman, Bandit, Deepscan, Fortify, GitLab, SonarQube, or Seeker. Make sure to choose the tool that supports your development language and follows OWASP (Open Web Application Security Project) benchmark. You can find the exhaustive list of tools in the note* at the end of the page.

Note: A comprehensive list of Static Application Security Testing (SAST) tools

https://owasp.org/www-community/Source_Code_Analysis_Tools

But what about Kubernetes? What built-in **security** settings does it offer, and how do we tweak them? Saying that K8s provides tools to enhance security would be hyperbolic. What it does provide, though, are interfaces to utilize Linux Kernel's own security features that have evolved over decades of research and improvements by the continuous contributions of countless open-source developers.

- **RunAs:** Containers use `cgroups()` and `namespaces()` to create isolation. While it ideally is a robust isolation practice, we do need to keep in mind that the container processes are run by the host.

  If they run with root privileges, they can exploit system calls on the host to impact processes outside the container (this happens because containers do not have their own kernel modules, they share Linux's kernel modules and implement them in their own namespace scope). This makes the host vulnerable.

  To avoid such unintended exploitations, containers or pods can be configured to run as a user other than root by adding the `runAsUser` or `runAsGroup` field followed by the User ID or the Group ID. This brings another question: If not as the root user, which user ID to choose?

  This can be figured out in multiple ways. The easiest option is to go through the README documentation provided by the developer of the Dockerfile. If such a doc does not exist, you can scold the team and go a layer deeper. Use a user created by the base image *(most of the verified base images have a non-root user created to make it more secure for the clients, for example, nodejs image has a non-root user called node with UID 1000)*. In case you don't have any details of such a User ID, you can create your own user by adding a simple RUN instruction in the Dockerfile as shown below and configure your pods accordingly.

  ```
  RUN useradd -u 9995 non-root
  ```

- **SELinux:** Linux kernel has a security framework called LSM (Linux Security Modules) that contains multiple security implementation models. One of them is SE or **Security Enhanced Linux**. It applies labels *(like user, role, type, level; not to be confused with K8s meta labels; lack of naming-convention innovation is a recurring theme for containers)* on processes and objects for virtual sorting. The objects with similar labels are applied to similar access policies.

Both RBAC and SELinux use **explicit access control policy** (only granting access if asked for it explicitly), contrary to default access provided by tools like Docker. **RBAC** blocks attempts of the unauthorized cluster (objects, configurations, and allotted resources) access from malicious clients and processes within the cluster, whereas SELinux acts as a barrier between the host and the cluster objects to blocks attempts of bilateral unauthorized access and activity. This way malicious processes on the cluster can't harm the host.

Such an implementation is important because K8s is not a single file compiled and run locally. It is built on the top of many blocks, and RBAC can't save you when underlying Linux utilities or third-party tools like Docker get corrupted. Kubeadm enables SELinux labels and policies while starting a K8s cluster. These policies are passed on to lower-level objects like pods when they are created. You can overwrite them by mentioning your own or a preconfigured SELinux policy under `securityContext` field and `seLinuxOptions` subfield of the pod YAML manifest. You can list out available policies under `kubectl get selinuxpolicies` or create your own.

- **SecComp Profile:** Secure Computing (SecComp) is a Linux Kernel inclusion that acts as a checkpoint between userspace requests and kernel space resources. Users can provide JSON profiles that have descriptions about what **actions** to take when certain system calls are used by the container. Just like SELinux policies, SecComp profiles are also provided under `securityContext` field under spec field in a YAML manifest. The `seccompProfile` field has two subfields. The `type` subfield indicates whether to use a default profile (with value `RuntimeDefault`) or a user-defined profile (with value `localhost`) followed by the profile path.

- **Privilege Escalations:** Normally, a child process does not get more privileges than its parent process. This means the CRE disallows processes created by the containers to use `chroot`. This is good because it stops attackers from exploiting bugs and vulnerabilities and making unexpected processes gain access to kernel resources and system calls to compromise the system security. Docker does it by setting `no_new_privs` flag on Linux processes to true. In case you want to allow your container and its children processes to escalate privileges or you are unsure of your CRE's behavior, K8s allows you to configure this flag within the YAML manifest itself by mentioning `allowPrivilegeEscalations` to true or false under the same `securityContext` field.

- **Linux Capabilities:** Earlier, the privileges of processes were binary. Either they had privileges similar to the root process, or they had no privileges at all. This was an under-evolved approach waiting for its well-deserved overhaul. The overhaul is Linux capabilities. There are over 100 Linux capabilities. Find more information about them in the note*. It provides granular control over what processes can do and what they can't. Different privileges are divided into capabilities that act as ON/OFF switches for the particular context.

Note:

An exhaustive list of Linux capabilities

https://man7.org/linux/man-pages/man7/capabilities.7.html

Most normal processes need 0 capabilities *(their file-system default privileges are enough to make them work smoothly)*. Processes like ping require additional capability like CAP_NET_RAW. This capability object allows TCP binding between **physical or virtual devices**. Most of the K8s objects act as virtual network-enabled devices since the entire premise of containerization revolves around virtualization. You can run **getcaps <PID>** command on any process to see which capabilities they need. Understanding their significance is a matter of practice and use cases. *(You don't need to remember each and every one of them, just get accustomed to referring to the man page efficiently.)*

You can add Linux capabilities to your container by adding capabilities subfield under **securityContext** followed by add key and an array of capabilities in **["CAP_1","CAP_2"]** format. As you might have noticed, all of these configurations are to be mentioned under the **securityContext** field in a YAML manifest. That is because all of them together form the **Security Context** of the pod.

Here is an example YAML file of a pod with a security context.

```
1. apiVersion: v1
2. kind: Pod
3. metadata:
4.   name: security-context-demo
5. spec:
6.   securityContext:
7.     runAsUser: 1000
8.     runAsGroup: 3000
```

```
9.          capabilities:
10.         add: ["NET_ADMIN", "SYS_TIME"]
11.      seccompProfile:
12.        type: Localhost
13.        localhostProfile: <path of the file>
14.      seLinuxOptions:
15.        level: "<value>"
16.        role: "<value>"
17.        type: "<value>"
18.        user: "<value>"
19.    volumes:
20.    - name: sec-ctx-vol
21.      emptyDir: {}
22.    containers:
23.    - name: sec-ctx-demo
24.      image: busybox
25.      command: ["sh", "-c", "sleep 1h"]
26.      volumeMounts:
27.      - name: sec-ctx-vol
28.        mountPath: /data/demo
29.      securityContext:
30.        allowPrivilegeEscalation: false
```

The key takeaway from this file is that you don't have to be a master of all trades. You should use whichever security configurations you are comfortable with. Pods and containers can have separate security contexts (although in case of contradictions, container security context overrides pods' values). This is done to provide customizations for multi-container pods. As K8s grow further, they might introduce new security provisions with possibly new steps to implement them, but the basics boil down to the 4Cs of Cluster Security mentioned at the beginning of the topic. With that in mind, we can move on to other aspects of advanced orchestration.

Pod priority classes

The Kube-scheduler from the cluster's control plane decides which pod to schedule at a particular time depending on resource status provided by the Kubelets of the respective nodes, but are its decisions always reliable? What if a critical pod is held back because of a superfluous one? If you deploy a website on a K8s cluster, which pod should be scheduled first, the ads or the customer support bot? Kube-scheduler can't judge the importance of a pod with respect to other ones by itself.

To ensure that this situation does not compromise the application performance (and eventually the client or user experience), K8s has provisioned an object to quantify the relative priority of workloads. This object is called the Pod Priority Class. If K8s objects could emote, *Figure 12.10* shows how pods and a priority class would interact:

Figure 12.10: Goofy K8s objects living their life

This is a unique resource as it does not fall into any namespace. You can say it is a key-value-based meaningful meta of the pods. Using this object, pods can be given any integer value of priority below 1 billion (1000000000). The largest numbers (close to a billion) are reserved for system critical pods, but you are free to use all of the other ones. This makes a few things clear.

- You should not be surprised if a pod has a priority value of a million but is still in a pending stage since there can always be pods with a much higher priority value.

- Before setting up the priority value of your own class, it is important to analyze which values are given to other classes since Pod Priority Classes operate on relative priority.

- This feature by itself is kind of a vulnerability. Since it is non-namespaced, any user with object creation rights can create spam pods of high priority and block your essential pods. To avoid that, make sure to have strict RBAC policies. Logging and Monitoring can help to ease out this situation, but they will be addressed in the next chapter. As an alternative solution, you can limit the priority of the pods by using Resource Quotas.

When we bootstrap a K8s cluster, we get a couple of built-in priority classes, which can be listed with a simple **kubectl get** command, as shown in the following screenshot:

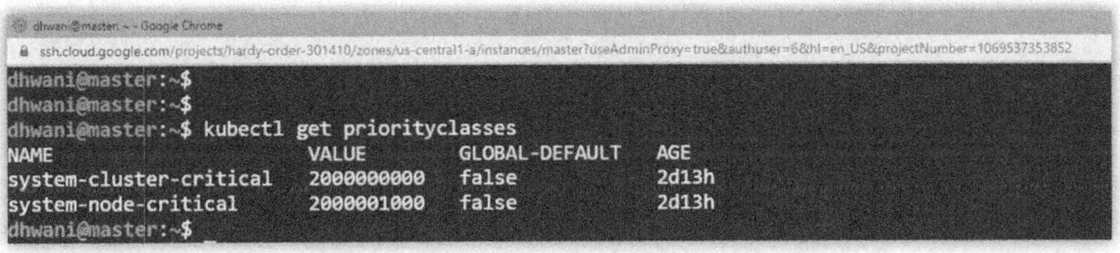

Figure 12.11: Default Pod Priority Classes

Their values already spoil their relative priority (which is higher than most of the pods you will ever create). To understand this priority assignment, we need to look at the pods running with these priority classes. Let's run a **kubectl get pods** to command with a formatted output that asks explicitly for Priority classes, as shown in the following screenshot:

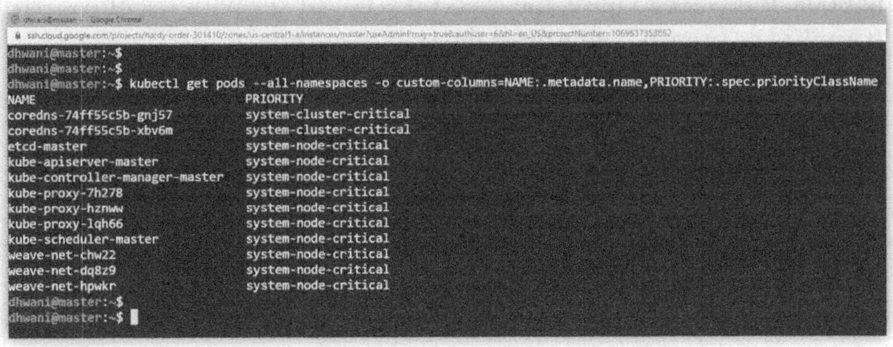

Figure 12.12: Pods with their priority classes

While the naming doesn't give away the inspiration behind making these classes with such priority, the pods scheduled with them clear the picture out. There are times when third-party software development teams are making add-on versions of their product specifically for K8s. This is healthy for both parties since it offers growth to K8s and consumer reach to third-party tools.

To make sure their performance is uninterrupted, K8s needs to offer a Quality-of-Service guarantee. To walk their talk, they need to offer a pod priority class above most user-defined workloads. Such a priority class is system-cluster-critical. K8s' DNS server CoreDNS uses this. On the other hand, to make sure nothing kicks out the essential components of the K8s architecture, we have a class with an even higher priority called system-node-critical.

Needless to say, don't try to schedule your pods with these classes. Let your workloads run on default priority or create your own class. To make your own priority class, you need to create a simple YAML object as shown in the following screenshot:

```
GNU nano 4.8                                                    priorityClass.yaml

apiVersion: scheduling.k8s.io/v1
kind: PriorityClass
metadata:
  name: high-priority
value: 1000000
globalDefault: false
description: "This is a high priority class."
```

Figure 12.13: Example of a pod priority class manifest

It is an object of **PriorityClass** kind under the scheduling API group. Name and Description are meta information and it does not have any dedicated spec field. This class has priority value of a million *(it is high but not even close to critical, just how it should be)*. Setting **globalDefault** to true enables the class to change the priorities of existing pods. If it is set to false, the class does not tinker with the already running pods. It applies its priority value **after** the class is created.

Another optional field is **preemptionPolicy**. This allows the priority class to replace (preempt) lower priority pods with higher ones and reschedules lower ones depending on resource availability. Its default value is `preemptLower` that does exactly as we explained in the last line. Another value is Never, which blocks pre-existing pods from getting pre-empted. Once you create a pod using the priority class, it can be viewed as shown in the following screenshot:

```
dhwani@master ~ - Google Chrome
  ssh.cloud.google.com/projects/hardy-order-301410/zones/us-central1-a/instances/master?useAdminProxy=true&authuser=6&hl=en_US&projectNumber=1069537353852
dhwani@master:~$
dhwani@master:~$
dhwani@master:~$ kubectl get priorityclasses
NAME                     VALUE         GLOBAL-DEFAULT    AGE
high-priority            1000000       false             83s
system-cluster-critical  2000000000    false             2d19h
system-node-critical     2000001000    false             2d19h
dhwani@master:~$
dhwani@master:~$
```

Figure 12.14: Pod with a user-defined priority class

This priority class can be used to create a pod with higher priority than other user-defined pods. If a pod has not been given any priority class, it does not have any default priority. It gets scheduled or pre-empted depending on resource availability at the time of scheduling request.

You can find the pod priority details in its description, as shown in the following screenshot:

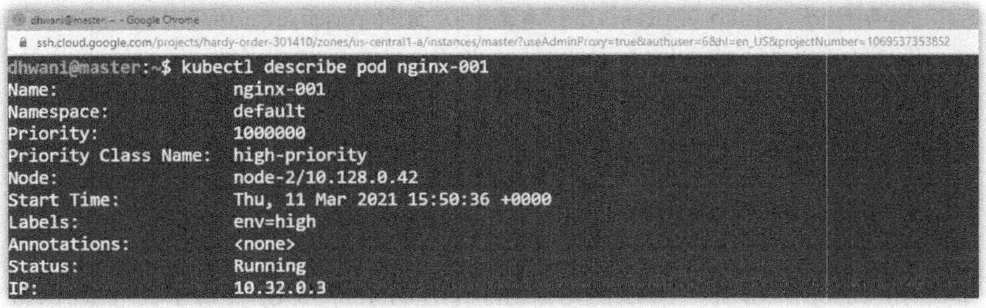

Figure 12.15: *Pod Priority information in pod description*

Controlling pod scheduling

Aside from controlling which pods will be prioritized over others, we can also control **where (on which node)** the pods are scheduled. This is useful when some pods require special resources such as GPU or faster storage. It is financially efficient to analyze the resource requirements of your application and divide the pod deployment based on it. It is also useful when you want to provide additional security or isolation to some decoupled microservice portion of your application. K8s provides both pod attraction and pod repelling mechanisms to control these aspects. Let's take a look at them one-by-one.

- **Node Selector:** This is another practical use-case of ever flexible Labels and Selectors. Label your nodes with the desired pairs of keys: values and provide the same pairs to the pods in the **nodeSelector** field under spec field. This becomes a part of the pod definition and gets processed by the Kube-scheduler while looking for a node to schedule the pod. Keep in mind, this just narrows down the list of possible nodes where the pod can be scheduled. If the node carrying the desired labels is already occupied, the new pod with node selector can't preempt any other pods. The pod remains unscheduled and waits for its turn.

- **Node Affinity:** This is similar to nodeSelector but more flexible *(In a fictional parallel universe, you can also call it Node Selector Pro Max… Ultra)*. Node Affinity draws a line between what are extremely important labels and what are nice-to-have labels. Four lines ago, we saw how a pod remains unscheduled if the node with desired labels is unavailable for scheduling. What if the desired labels were not essential but just the best-case scenario? This is where the behavior of Node Affinity is more relevant.

  Node Affinity divides nodeSelector labels into two categories: `requiredDuringSchedulingIgnoredDuringExecution` and `preferredDuring SchedulingIgnoredDuringExecution`. The keywords are **Required** and

Preferred, which represent **Hard** and **Soft** requirements, respectively *(and that is how we will refer to them to make the conversation less alienating)*. Yes, the field names are ridiculous. They could have gone for something simpler like "must have" and "should have", but in K8s' defense, they plan to release two more variants of these fields for scenarios where the labels are removed during the pods runtime.

Regardless, Node Affinity is a powerful tool. You can choose to fill either one or both of the values and this will dictate how your pod will behave. If you choose to fill only the hard requirement field, it will result in scheduling performance similar to Node Selector. If you decide to fill only soft requirements, your pod will be scheduled on some other node even if the target node is occupied. You can do a mix and match of both if you want a precise performance.

For example, if your application **needs** GPU (hard requirement) and would work optimally with SSD (soft requirement), you can label nodes that have respective features and provide GPU under hard requirements while putting SSD in soft requirements. The snippet of the pod manifest would look like the following code:

```
1. spec:
2.   affinity:
3.     nodeAffinity:
4.
5.     #Hard Requirement
6.       requiredDuringSchedulingIgnoredDuringExecution:
7.         nodeSelectorTerms:
8.         - matchExpressions:
9.           - key: gpu
10.             operator: In
11.             values:
12.             - available
13.
14.     #Soft Requirement
15.       preferredDuringSchedulingIgnoredDuringExecution:
16.       - weight: 1
17.         preference:
```

```
18.            matchExpressions:
19.            - key: ssd
20.              operator: In
21.              values:
22.              - available
```

In the hard requirement section, the **nodeSelectorTerms** is a non-compulsive unit whereas **matchExpressions** is a compulsive unit of operation. In other words, if you provide multiple Node Selector Terms, Kube-scheduler looks for at least one of them to be satisfied. On the other hand, for any Node Selector Term to be satisfied, all of the Match Expressions terms need to be fulfilled.

The **weight** in the soft required section can range from numerical value 1 to 100, with 1 being the lightest and 100 being the heaviest. In case multiple available nodes fulfill the soft and hard requirements, the one with the most weight will be given the scheduling priority. This is the weight of the preference. Kube-scheduler considers multiple factors like resource availability, hard requirement terms fulfilment, and so on. If the soft preference has a higher weight, a node fulfilling just one hard preference, but multiple soft references may become more eligible for scheduling the pod. Since these are soft preferences, it is better to keep the preference weight low.

- **Inter-pod affinity and anti-affinity:** This is similar to Node affinity except it considers pods' labels to define the affinity instead of nodes' labels. This allows you to schedule your new pods on nodes that are already running your other desired pods. Inter-pod affinity also supports notions of soft and hard affinity with the same field options as Node affinity that is, **requiredDuringSchedulingIgnoredDuringExecution** and **preferredDuringSchedulingIgnoredDuringExecution**. In the case of inter-pod affinity, K8s also allows you to choose nodes that are **not running** specific pods. This feature is called **Pod anti-affinity**. Similar to both the affinities discussed so far, this can also be defined as a soft or hard preference. Here is what a pod manifest snippet with inter-pod affinity looks like:

```
1.  affinity:
2.  #Hard Requirement
3.    podAffinity:
4.      requiredDuringSchedulingIgnoredDuringExecution:
5.      - labelSelector:
6.          matchExpressions:
```

```
7.             - key: tier
8.               operator: In
9.               values:
10.                - backend
11.             topologyKey: topology.kubernetes.io/zone=us-central-1a
12.
13.   #Soft Requirement
14.     podAntiAffinity:
15.       preferredDuringSchedulingIgnoredDuringExecution:
16.       - weight: 20
17.         podAffinityTerm:
18.           labelSelector:
19.             matchExpressions:
20,.           - key: group
21.               operator: In
22.               values:
23.                - canary
24.             topologyKey: topology.kubernetes.io/zone=us-central-1a
```

In this example, the pods must be scheduled on nodes that have pods running with label **tier:backend**. A soft priority with more weight than the last example is given to nodes with pods running with label **group:canary**. There is another field called **Topology Key**. The topology key is used to filter out nodes based on their physical location or their topology context on-premises. In this case, we want to limit our pods to nodes running on GCP's US Central 1A zone. These labels can be applied manually if you're bootstrapping the cluster, or they are provided by default if you are using a Hosted K8s as a service platform (*soon to be explored in the next chapter*). To establish the **anti-affinity**, switch the **operator** from **In** to **NotIn**.

- **Taints and Tolerations:** Taints allow Nodes to decide which pods to accept or reject. A node can be tainted not to schedule particular pods or any pod at all. Taints are applied in the form of key-value pairs with the **kubectl taint** command, as shown in the following code.

```
kubectl taint nodes node-1 type=test:NoSchedule
```

This taint will block every incoming pod on node-1 in any namespace. In this case, **type** is the key, **test** is the value, and **NoSchedule** is the effect. It will not evict the existing pods. You can verify the taint by describing the node using **kubectl describe** as shown in the following screenshot:

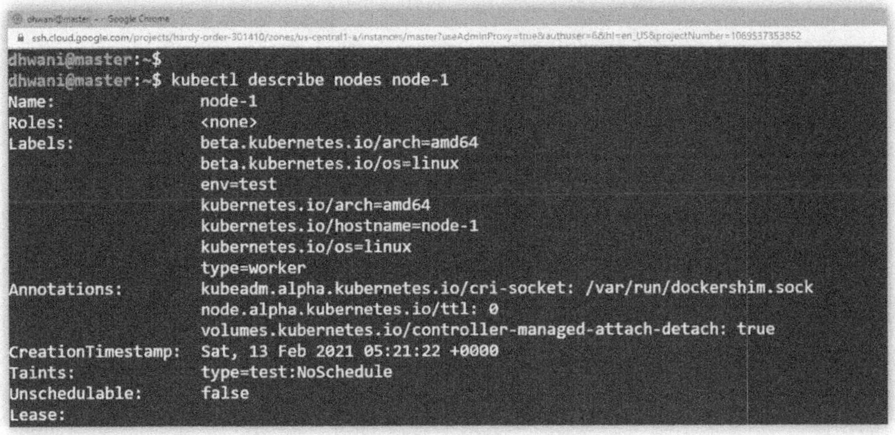

```
dhwani@master:~$
dhwani@master:~$ kubectl describe nodes node-1
Name:               node-1
Roles:              <none>
Labels:             beta.kubernetes.io/arch=amd64
                    beta.kubernetes.io/os=linux
                    env=test
                    kubernetes.io/arch=amd64
                    kubernetes.io/hostname=node-1
                    kubernetes.io/os=linux
                    type=worker
Annotations:        kubeadm.alpha.kubernetes.io/cri-socket: /var/run/dockershim.sock
                    node.alpha.kubernetes.io/ttl: 0
                    volumes.kubernetes.io/controller-managed-attach-detach: true
CreationTimestamp:  Sat, 13 Feb 2021 05:21:22 +0000
Taints:             type=test:NoSchedule
Unschedulable:      false
Lease:
```

Figure 12.16: A tainted Node

The taint remains functional as long as it is not manually removed. This can be troublesome as operators might forget to remove the taints even after they don't need them *(it is reassuring yet amusing how developers of such tools never rely on the operators' punctuality and precision)*. If you think of taints as a no-entry board for pods, we also need a VIP pass that allows us to breach the no-entry condition.

Tolerations are the metaphorical VIP pass. They are specifically designed to counter the taints. Since taints are key: value pairs provided to the nodes, tolerations are key: value pair conditions provided to pods. For example, if we intend to counter the taint **type: test:NoSchedule**, the pod with the toleration should have its manifest look like the following code:

```
1. apiVersion: apps/v1

2. kind: Deployment

3.metadata:

4.   name: toleration-busybox

5.spec:

6.   selector:

7.     matchLabels:

8.       run: toleration-busybox

9.   replicas: 3

10.  template:

11.    metadata:
```

```
12.       labels:
13.         run: toleration-busybox
14.     spec:
15.       containers:
16.       - name: toleration-busybox
17.         image: busybox
18.         command: ['sh', '-c', 'echo Hey, there!!! && sleep 120']
19.       tolerations:
20.       - key: "type"
21.         operator: "Equal"
22.         value: "test"
23.         effect: "NoSchedule"
```

The PodSpec has a toleration with key **type**, value **test,** and effect **NoSchedule**. This is the same as the taint applied. This means that this pod will negate the taint and will be scheduled on node-1 if the scheduler finds other parameters appropriate. Operator **equal** indicates the equation between key and value.

If you do not want to specify the value, you can skip the value field and provide **Exists** in the operator section. This taint and toleration combination works as a hard scheduling condition. To opt for a soft condition, you can replace the effect's value with **PreferNoSchedule**.

Once you create the deployment, you can list the pods with a wider output to see which pods are scheduled on which nodes as shown in the following screenshot:

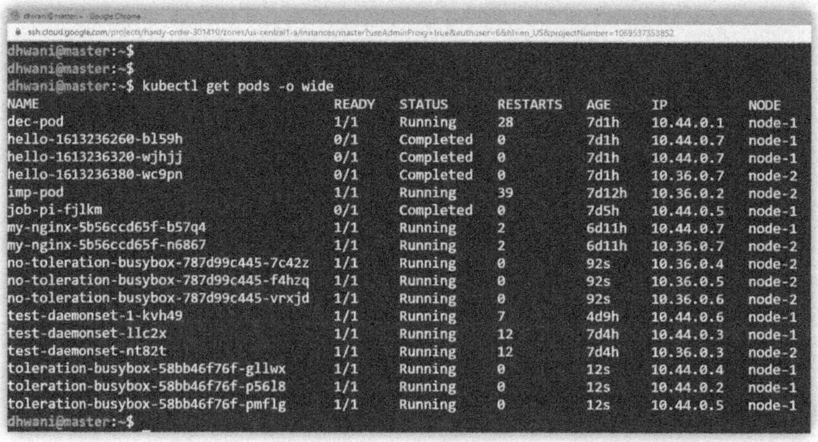

Figure 12.17: Pods with tolerations scheduled on a tainted node

You can see that the busybox pods with tolerations are scheduled on Node-1. When you bootstrap a K8s cluster using Kubeadm, masters are tainted to block all user-defined pods by default. This is to maintain the performance and resource availability of the master. You can define your own taints and tolerations to control the precise scheduling of pods depending on your application's use case.

Conclusion

This chapter introduced you to various intricate mechanisms of Kubernetes that allow you to configure and control authorization, access, security, and scheduling of your cluster resources and workloads to achieve advanced level or orchestration. These advantages can be taken to a higher stage when you work with solutions that are tailor made to enhance your K8s application deployment experience. In the next chapter, we will introduce you to the basics of hosted K8s services on the Cloud.

Multiple choice questions

1. Which of the following is not a part of the 4Cs of K8s Security Model?

    A. Cloud Security

    B. Cluster Security

    C. Class Security

    D. Code Security

    Answer: C

2. Which of the following options is used in K8s security context?

    A. SELinux labels

    B. Load Balancers

    C. Privilege escalations

    D. Seccomp profiles

    Answer: B

3. Which of the following features addresses pod scheduling?

    A. Tolerations

    B. RBAC

    C. ABAC

    D. Webhooks

    Answer: B

4. Which of the following is not an affinity option?

   A. requiredDuringExecutionIgnoredDuringScheduling

   B. IgnoredDuringSchedulingRequiredDuringExecution

   C. preferredDuringSchedulingIgnoredDuringExecution

   D. None of the above

   Answer: C

5. Which of the following is a bad security practice?

   A. Unencrypted etcd

   B. Unnecessary exposed ports

   C. Too many admins

   D. All the above

   Answer: D

Questions

1. Explain the 4Cs of the K8s security Model.

2. State the differences between RBAC and ABAC.

3. Write a YAML pod manifest file to schedule an ubuntu 18.04 pod on a node with GPU.

4. Explain the pod security context.

5. Explain the difference between a node and inter-pod affinity.

CHAPTER 13
Managed Kubernetes on Cloud

Introduction

This chapter introduces a new type of Kubernetes offering called managed K8s on Cloud. With web applications moving toward being cloud-native or hybrid cloud users, the demand for skills with Kubernetes offerings on the Cloud has skyrocketed over the past couple of years. This chapter introduces the concept of managed K8s as a service and explores subtle differences compared to locally bootstrapped Kubernetes. Keeping the reading experience fresh also explores the practical implementation of previously untouched topics like stateful sets or Ingress.

Structure

This chapter covers:

- Managed Kubernetes on cloud
- Google Kubernetes engine: architecture and setup
- Deploying Kubernetes workloads on GKE
- Understanding and working with StatefulSet
- Working with the load balancer service

- Working with the ingress
- Persistent volume

Objective

This chapter aims to smoothen up the transition from locally bootstrapped Kubernetes to Cloud Managed Kubernetes. It also covers demonstrations of topics that are easy to access on a cloud-native environment, such as Load Balancer service or Persistent Volume. By the end of this chapter, you will be comfortable with the Cloud-managed K8s of your choice.

Managed Kubernetes on Cloud

We have understood and practiced the power of Kubernetes in previous chapters. Although K8s can handle the complexities and scale of a microservice-based containerized application efficiently, the ship may not sail equally smoothly for everyone. Let us ask some questions to ourselves:

- Do you have flexibly scalable server infrastructure at your disposal, or are you using Cloud to deploy your applications?
- What if you don't have enough time and/or skills to consider every intricate detail of your app deployment? Is handling K8s by yourself is still a great idea?
- Do you have a team skilled enough to translate your application's traffic, growth, and performance into K8s deployments?
- If you recruit a new team of K8s experts, will the investment pay off?
- Do you have a work culture mature enough to take the blame on failures and perform immediate fixes?
- Even with a skilled workforce, you may not decide to deploy your application on-premises; in that case, can your team handle both K8s and Cloud?

A part of your brain might discard these doubts thinking of them as "Inadvertent business risks", but the answer to these questions can make or break the execution of your business ideas. If you are positively confident about these questions, all you have to do is move forward (***Go Beyond… Plus Ultra!*** *Hope it made My Hero*

Academia fans' eyes sparkly like Izuku's). In an otherwise case, leaving the intricacies in the hands of experienced professionals and deploying your application on a managed Kubernetes Solution on Public Cloud platforms with a flexible payment model might be the option you were looking for!

The Sannin of the world of cloud computing *(Naruto fans!!!!)* Amazon Web Services, Google Cloud Platform, and Microsoft Azure (along with many other ninjas), provide a feature rich, generally available (GA), pay-as-you-go managed Kubernetes Cluster services. Amazon Web Service (AWS) offers Amazon EKS to run and scale K8s services on AWS cloud infrastructure, on the other hand, Azure offers Azure Kubernetes Service (AKS) along with Visual Studio code K8s tools for faster development experience. While all three of them offer more or less equally decent quality of service and performance statistics, Google was the first to invest and market heavily in the research and implementation of managed K8s service. Since then, Google has stayed slightly ahead of the curve with their thriving community and ever minimalistic user-friendly graphical interface.

All of them use their respective VM services to install tailored Kubernetes with additional components and plugins like storage, network, and logging drivers to suit their product ecosystem. In this chapter, we are using Google's GKE (Google Kubernetes Engine) to explore the operations of the managed K8s services on a public Cloud Platform.

GKE: architecture and setup

It offers a custom K8s cluster of the desired number of nodes with desired configurations to valid Google Cloud Platform account owners. It uses pre-existing GCP services like Google Cloud VMs (Google Compute Engine), Google Persistent Storage disks, Google Cloud IAM (Identity and Access Management APIs), Google Cloud VPC (Virtual Private Cloud), along with third-party supported services like Stackdriver logging and Monitoring to offer a robust functional cluster setup. Before digging deep into them, let's know a bit more about how GKE operates.

Since we are already comfortable with the basic architecture of K8s, understanding the GKE architecture is not a difficult challenge. The following figure represents how the components of a GKE cluster communicate to one another and the user:

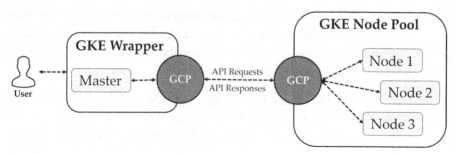

Figure 13.1: GKE components interaction model

The master and the nodes are enclosed under Google Cloud's APIs, acting as watch loops, control loops, error handlers, and request validators (you can call them wrappers to make the discussions concise). These wrappers observe and authenticate the requests made to and processed by the cluster on its resources to optimize their performance and calculate billing *(we will talk more about billing once we are done discussing important aspects of GKE)*. They communicate to the cluster using the **Cloud Controller Manager** of the K8s control plane.

Let us understand the architecture better by creating a GKE cluster. Check out the following screenshot:

Figure 13.2: GKE Cluster Creation Prompt

Just like the GCE VMs, we have used so far, the process of creating your first GKE cluster starts at the Google Cloud Platform Dashboard. Go to the Hamburger menu icon, navigate to **Kubernetes Engine | Clusters** tab, and you should find yourself redirected to the cluster creation page with a cluster creation prompt shown in the figure above.

Click on the **CREATE** button and find yourself landed on the cluster configuration page looking similar to the following screenshot:

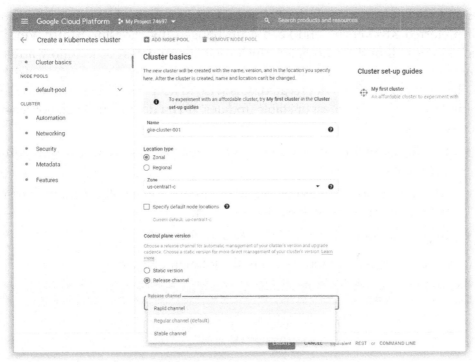

Figure 13.3: Basic cluster configuration page

Once you are done naming the cluster *(in our case, gke-cluster-001, because lack of naming creativity is infectious)*, you can decide where you intend to schedule the cluster. Public cloud providers have data centers across the globe. **Regions** are geographical areas representing the location of the data center(s). For example, Los Angeles is the us-west2 region, whereas Mumbai is the asia-south1 region. In these regions, GCP has **Zones** called us-west2-a, us-west2-b, us-west2-c or asia-south1-a, asia-south1-b, and asia-south1-c. The zones can represent a section of the region, such as a building on the data center with close coupled network connections or a floor on a large data center building.

To avoid a single point of failure, you can choose either a zonal or regional cluster. The zonal cluster distributes your nodes across the zones, whereas regional clusters distribute your nodes across multiple regions. You can consider potential lag and cost to estimate your requirements. In this example, we have chosen the **Zonal** cluster at `us-central1-c` (Iowa).

The next configuration option is the **Release Channel**. The performance and behavior of the cluster are determined by the type and amount of resources you offer and the version of the control plane. GKE gives users the flexibility to choose their preferred K8s version and keep it unchanged (by choosing **Static Version**, which ignores all of the automated cluster version updates) or to follow a release channel of their convenience. If your application deployment strategy consists of K8s objects that have been deprecated, it is wise to keep the version static for some time and catch up to the latest or stable updates. If you do not face such bottlenecks, you can choose:

- **Stable channel** to receive updates of versions that are tested well and are supported,

- **Regular channel** to receive regular updates (generally 2 minor versions behind the latest available K8s version) or

- **Rapid channel** to leverage latest K8s updates.

Let us move to the next section shown in the following figure:

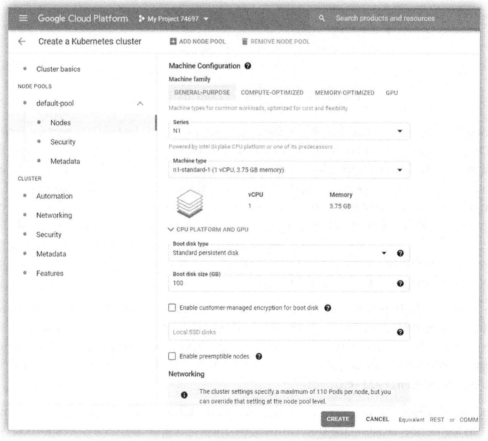

Figure 13.4: Configuration of the node pool

The node-pool defines the number of available nodes with identical configurations. Their resource offerings categorize the machines in terms of specific use cases (Memory optimized for more RAM, Compute-optimized for more CPU cores, and so on). We have chosen general-purpose n1-standard type machines with 1vCPU (1 thread on 1 core of a processor) and 3.75GB of memory. We have also used 100GB of unencrypted standard persistent disk (GCP's term for optical hard drive, another option is SSD which is faster and costlier).

We have disabled the automatic preemption, allowing GKE to preempt (scale down, turn off or reschedule) one or more of our nodes for maintenance or handle the overload. After this, click on the **Node Security** tab to land on the page looking like the following screenshot:

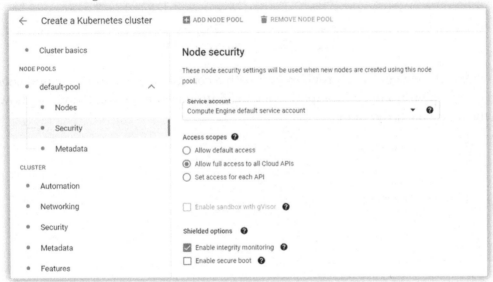

Figure 13.5: Node Security Settings

The node security is different from the cluster security explored in detail in the last chapter. This section only deals with who can access the nodes and how much access are they granted. Just how K8s grants RBAC access to Linux users accounts, GKE grants node access to GCP service accounts.

Service accounts are created to provide different IAM roles to a GCP user in your organization. Service accounts are also given to objects to automate processes. In this case, Compute Engine is given full access to edit the nodes. Enabling the node integrity monitoring protects it from potentially harmful malware and rootkits by checking the source of every application installed on the Node level or trying to access root privileges.

The other two features that have been left disabled are gVisor sandboxes that add an extra layer of isolation on containers and secure boot to keep the driver integrity in check. Once you are done with node security, you can move to the metadata section and fill in the details like taints, labels, and so on.

Click on the **CREATE** button, and your cluster should be enlisted as ready, as shown in the following screenshot:

Figure 13.6: The cluster is ready.

To access the cluster, GKE provides you with a command to run on the cloud shell. You can copy it from the prompt or click the button to run the command, as shown in the following screenshot:

Figure 13.7: GKE cluster access command

We need to use the gcloud container cluster get-credentials because the cloud shell runs on a different VM (possibly even a different region) than the cluster and is just connected via SSH.

As always, a simple way to check the running cluster for yourself is to see the pods running on the kube-systems namespace, as shown in the following screenshot:

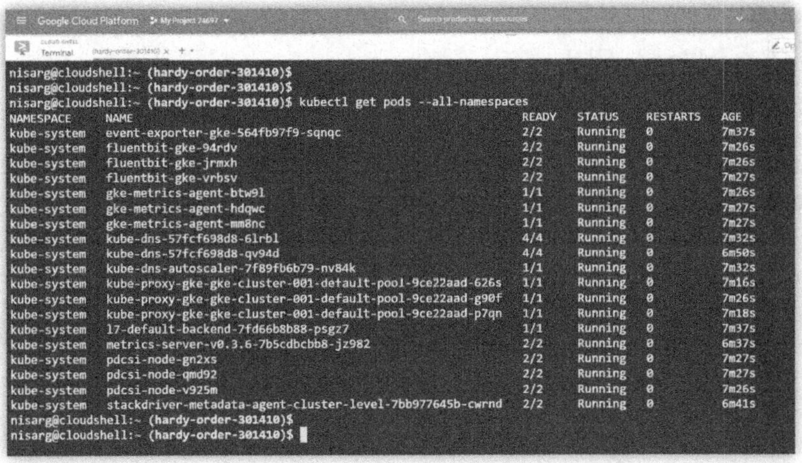

Figure 13.8: Pods running on the GKE Cluster

Two immediate things to notice are the absence of control plane components and two sets of most components. We have fluent-bit for logging (little brother of fluentd, explained later in this chapter), persistent disk CSI driver for storage, metrics agent for collecting states, stackdriver for collecting metadata logs, kube-DNS for recording services and `IP:DNS` mapping and a bunch of other add-on pods for smoothening out the performance. Control plane components are not visible since they are managed on master, and users cannot access master by default. You need to authorize your VPC to access control plane components (more on that later in the chapter). Since we are done with setting up the cluster, now it is time to test it.

Deploying Kubernetes workloads on GKE

After creating the K8s cluster on GKE, the next step should be to deploy K8s workloads. We have learned and worked with different K8s workloads (deployment, batch job, cron job, and so on) in previous chapters, so you should be aware of their functioning. To optimize the process of working with them in GKE, they are divided into categories based on the applications they are deploying. Some of the most widely used categories are:

- Stateless applications,
- Stateful applications,
- Batch Job, and
- Daemon.

On GKE, we can create, manage, monitor, and delete objects using its intuitive GUI and a handful of kubectl commands. There are three methods to create an object in GKE:

- kubectl command line
- GKE workloads GUI
- GKE REST API and Kubernetes API

We will use a combination of the first and second methods to create workloads in GKE. We first need to navigate to the list of clusters available in the current GCP project. The list should look something like the snapshot below after following the procedure of cluster creation as mentioned in the previous topic:

Figure 13.9: A List of clusters in GKE

We have our cluster `gke-cluster-001` in the running and healthy state (you can see the green tick mark before the cluster's name). To deploy a workload in this cluster, we have to click on the option deploy above the cluster list.

The next window we should encounter should look like the following screenshot:

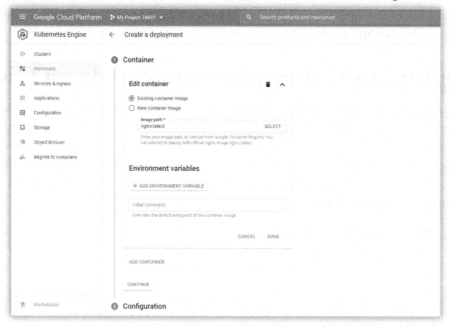

Figure 13.10: GKE workload creation webpage

The workload creation process in GKE is divided into two parts: Container and Configuration. The container section is used to define the container image of the application you want to deploy and define environment variables and custom commands to run during the execution of an application container. There are two ways to define the container image:

- First, by using the existing container image stored in the Google Container registry or Google Artifact Registry,
- Second, by creating a new container image from a repository (containing Dockerfile and app config files) provided by Google Cloud Source Repository, GitHub, and Bitbucket.

We will use the first method to edit the container of our workload. We will build the container image for the nginx web server using Google Cloud build service and push the resulting image to Google Container Registry. The first step is to enable the Google Container Registry API.

In the GCP console window, navigate to the hamburger icon (*located at the top left corner of the window*) and go to **Products | API and Services | Library.** In the search box, type `Google Container Registry`, and it navigates you to the homepage of this API which should look like the following screenshot:

Figure 13.11: *Homepage of Google Container Registry API*

After enabling it, the next step is to build our container image. To keep things simple, create a new directory to save the Dockerfile for the nginx webserver. You can find the contents of this Dockerfile as follows:

```
1. FROM ubuntu:16.04
2. RUN apt-get update && apt-get install nginx -y \
3.      && apt-get clean \
4.      && rm -rf /var/lib/apt/lists/*
5. EXPOSE 80
6. CMD ["nginx", "-g", "daemon off;"]
```

After creating this Dockerfile, we can use the **gcloud** command to build the container image and tag it to push it to a new repository called **gke-nginx** under the current project.

```
gcloud builds submit --tag gcr.io/<GCP-project-ID>/gke-nginx
```

The **gcr.io** is the default container registry in GCP, and it stores images in data centers in the United States. Also, the image pushing process creates a corresponding Google Cloud Storage bucket to store the data on the registry. When you initiate the building process, the initial phase should look like the following screenshot:

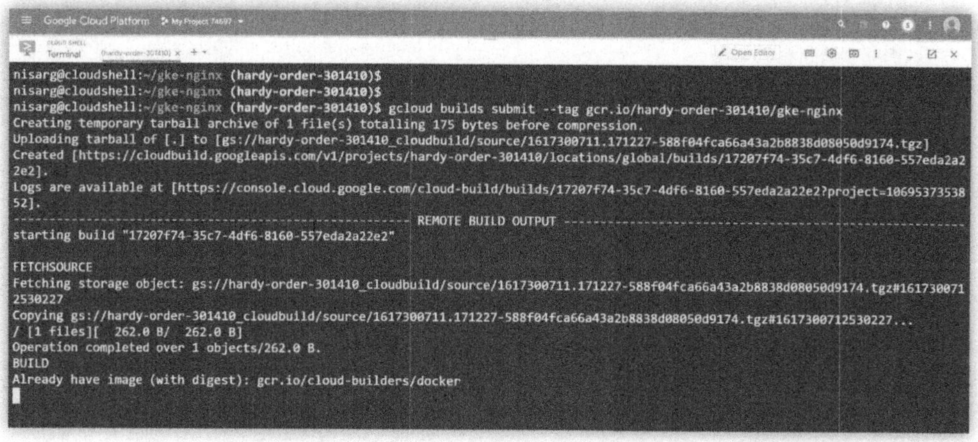

Figure 13.12: Building a container image using Google Cloud build

As the process begins, the current directory's (nginx Dockerfile) content is packed in a temporary tarball file and stored in the Cloud Storage bucket created for the container registry. Cloud build imports the contents from the Storage bucket and executes it as a series of build steps. Each build step is run inside a Docker container. The building process should resemble the following screenshot:

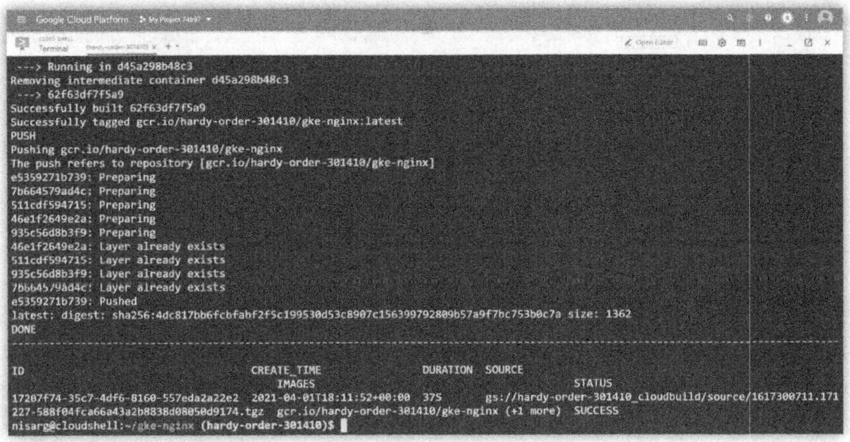

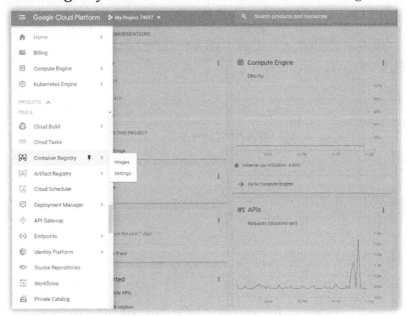

Figure 13.13: *Finishing the container build*

At the end of the building process, Cloud Build tags as mentioned in the command and push it to the specified repository on Google Container Registry.

We can look for this pushed image in **Container Registry** by navigating through the GCP dashboard the same way we did with API and Services. You can look for the **Container Registry** service in GCP as shown in the following screenshot:

Figure 13.14: *Container Registry in the list of Google Products*

List out the stored image in the container registry, and you should witness similar to the following screenshot:

Figure 13.15: nginx container image in Google Container Registry

The visibility or the scope of this repository is set to **Private**, making it exclusive to this project. You should have sufficient permissions to pull and push images to this repository.

After getting the container image ready, let us go back to the workloads page and provide the repository location of gke-nginx in our container registry. The outcome should look like the following screenshot:

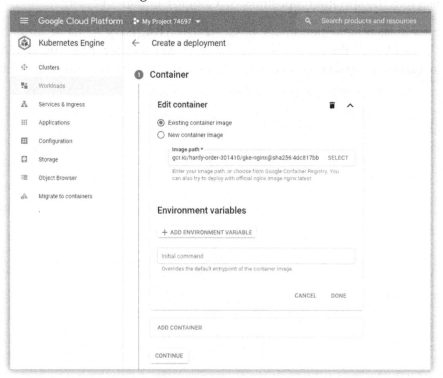

Figure 13.16: Container configuration editing page

You can add multiple containers in this deployment by clicking on **ADD CONTAINER** option before **CONTINUE**, but such practice is not recommended in production unless the application demands so. After editing the container details, we need to mention a few configuration details about the deployment, such as name, target namespace, and labels. If you do not specify any other namespace, it is set to the default namespace.

After filling the relevant container details, the outcome looks like the following screenshot:

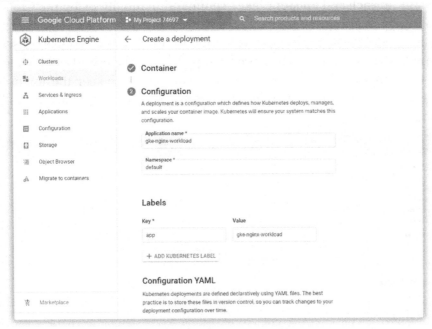

Figure 13.17: Namespace configuration

At the end of the process, a configuration YAML is created based on the information we provided about the deployment earlier. This YAML is similar to what we used to write to create a deployment using the kubectl command line. All deployments in GKE are created declaratively. When we deploy this workload, and the outcome looks like the following screenshot:

Figure 13.18: The deployment details of the Workload - Part I

This is the description page of the workload we just created. Aside from the name, we can notice multiple options on the top row besides deployment details. Edit option allows us to update the deployment configurations. You can use kubectl commands to attach the client terminal to the application pod container and execute a command inside that container. Both of these actions can also be performed using the **kubectl attach** and **kubectl exec** command manually using the Cloud Shell. There are graphical representations of the CPU, memory, and Disk usage by the application pod. These graphs help us to monitor the overall resource consumption by the application pod on different timestamps. This is one useful asset when we are dealing with a heavy production workload. It can help us to keep the app optimized technically and financially. The other part of the deployment details looks like the following screenshot:

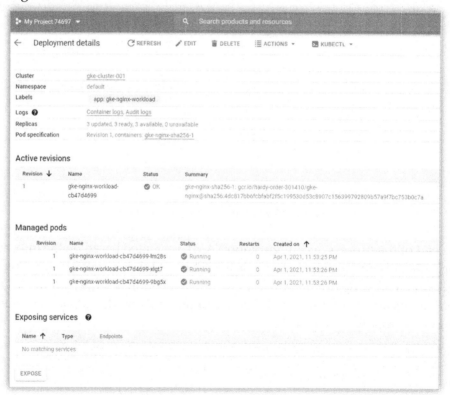

Figure 13.19: *The deployment details of the workload - Part II*

You can find many familiar details here but presented differently. There are details about the cluster on which the workload is deployed, namespace and labels, replica details, and pod specification. There are logs about container and audit logs, but we will look deeper into them in the next chapter.

This workload is managing three different nginx pods and all running without any restarts. The active revisions field has only one entry which is the current revision. Any update provided to this workload will be treated as another revision of the original application and will be mentioned under the active revision field if it will be the one serving the application at that time. When the need arises, you can easily scale this workload with a single click. Such a feature is handy when the amount of traffic your application received exceeds and you are short on resources. With a single click, GKE can spin up as many as nodes you required (In the GCP trial version, we can only create up to 8 nodes at a time).

To scale up the application, go to **Actions** | **Scale**. It asks you about the number of replicas you want to create, we keep the number of replicas to 6 (keeping Google's free tier limitations in mind), and after confirming our choice, the outcome looks like the following screenshot:

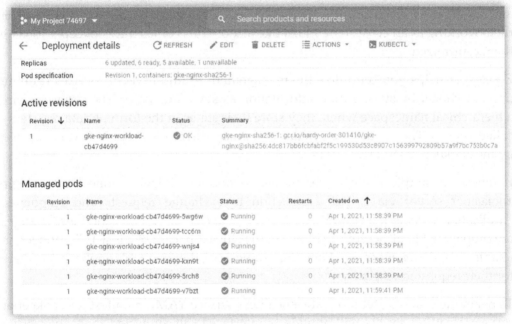

Figure 13.20: Scaled-up Deployment

After scaling up the workload, there are 3 more replicas of revision 1 is running.

Understanding and working with StatefulSet

We have been working with stateless workloads so far. In other words, in multi-tier application deployment, the order of pod creation and termination did not matter. There are microservice-based applications where the inception of one service may act as a dependency for another. In such cases, the service must be in the desired state before its dependent service can start off. While the decoupled nature of the microservices does reduce the state dependency a lot, there are cases where states are inevitable. Such applications are called **stateful applications**. K8s has a dedicated workload type of handling stateful applications called **stateful sets**. As an operator, you can control the order of creating and removing pods using the stateful sets.

To demonstrate the functionality of the Stateful Sets in Kubernetes, we are going to containerize and deploy the Apache Zookeeper on GKE. This demonstration will also use the Pod Disruption Budget *(a new topic in a new topic!)* and Kubernetes services.

The prime focus of this demonstration, Apache zookeeper, is an open-sourced centralized server used to host distributed applications *(to make it simple, it is the etcd equivalent of Apache ecosystem)*. Unlike CNCF, Apache is pretty creative when it comes to naming its offerings. They already have Hadoop having an icon of an elephant. They also have the Pig, the Mahaut *(the dudes riding and breeding elephants)*, and the Hive (derived from beehives). Things were getting quite wild with all of them working as an ecosystem, much like a zoo. Thus comes the Zookeeper to keep them centralized.

Zookeeper helps you centralize the management of hundreds of services running on your cluster by storing their information as key-value pairs. The services share a hierarchical namespace where they store their states in the form of data registers - called znodes. The znodes are similar to files and directories kept in RAM occupied by the zookeeper servers.

It follows a simple client-server model to operate. Clients connect to a single zookeeper server via a TCP connection to exchange requests and responses. Application services periodically update their states in the znode, and these changes are propagated to all servers available in the cluster. In case of a lost TCP connection to a single zookeeper server, clients can connect to other available zookeeper servers for their requested responses.

To begin the example, let us create a headless service YAML manifest for zookeeper servers. Headless service will provide an interface to all connected zookeeper server pods to communicate with one another simply by using the service name.

```
1.  apiVersion: v1
2.  kind: Service
3.  metadata:
4.    name: zk-hs
5.    labels:
6.      app: zk
```

```
7.  spec:
8.    ports:
9.    - port: 2888
10.      name: server
11.    - port: 3888
12.      name: leader-election
13.    clusterIP: None
14.    selector:
15.      app: zk
```

Pods connected to this headless service will receive **Endpoints** that will point directly toward zookeeper Pods having the label **app: zk**. The headless service must have two ports, one for exchanging states and the other for performing the leader election.

To load balance client connections, we will create a ClusterIP service by following the YAML following file:

```
1.  apiVersion: v1
2.  kind: Service
3.  metadata:
4.    name: zk-cs
5.    labels:
6.      app: zk
7.  spec:
8.    ports:
9.    - port: 2181
10.      name: client
11.    selector:
12.      app: zk
```

Ports mentioned in both service objects' YAML files must correspond to the container port that we will specify in the **.spec.template** field of StatefulSet's YAML.

The next object is the Pod Disruption Budget. In Kubernetes, PDB can be used to keep a certain number of pods running after hitting a disruption. There are two kinds of disruptions: voluntary and non-voluntary. **Voluntary disruptions** include the manual removal of pods from the running workload. **Non-voluntary disruption** is performed by the system in response to a hardware or software error. To keep our Zookeeper safe from any such accidental hazard, we want to create a disruption budget for all zookeeper pods.

Follow the below object definition YAML to create a Pod Disruption Budget:

```
1.  apiVersion: policy/v1beta1
2.  kind: PodDisruptionBudget
3.  metadata:
4.    name: zk-pdb
5.  spec:
6.    selector:
7.      matchLabels:
8.        app: zk
9.    maxUnavailable: 1
```

According to the YAML above, whenever any disruption occurs for this workload, the maximum number of pods that can be unavailable is **1**. It restricts the removal of any more pods before restoring the removed Pod. By setting up the PDB for this workload, we made sure that the application would not stop serving clients even after facing the unavailability of a particular pod. It will redirect the traffic from the affected Pod to another Pod and will try to recreate it to match the desired state of the application.

The last step is to create a StatefulSet for Apache Zookeeper. Follow the object definition YAML to create it:

```
1.  apiVersion: apps/v1
2.  kind: StatefulSet
3.  metadata:
4.    name: zk
5.  spec:
6.    selector:
7.      matchLabels:
8.        app: zk
9.    serviceName: zk-hs
10.   replicas: 3
11.   template:
12.     metadata:
13.       labels:
14.         app: zk
15.     spec:
16.       containers:
```

```
17.        - name: kubernetes-zookeeper
18.          imagePullPolicy: Always
19.          image: «k8s.gcr.io/kubernetes-zookeeper:1.0-3.4.10»
20.          ports:
21.          - containerPort: 2181
22.            name: client
23.          - containerPort: 2888
24.            name: server
25.          - containerPort: 3888
26.            name: leader-election
27.          command:
28.          - sh
29.          - -c
30.          - "start-zookeeper \
31.            --servers=3 \
32.            --data_dir=/var/lib/zookeeper/data \
33.            --data_log_dir=/var/lib/zookeeper/data/log \
34.            --conf_dir=/opt/zookeeper/conf \
35.            --client_port=2181 \
36.            --election_port=3888 \
37.            --server_port=2888 \
38.            --tick_time=2000 \
39.            --init_limit=10 \
40.            --sync_limit=5 \
41.            --heap=512M \
42.            --max_client_cnxns=60 \
43.            --snap_retain_count=3 \
44.            --purge_interval=12 \
45.            --max_session_timeout=40000 \
46.            --min_session_timeout=4000 \
47.            --log_level=INFO"
48.          volumeMounts:
49.          - name: zoo-volume
```

```
50.            mountPath: /var/lib/zookeeper
51.        volumes:
52.        - name: zoo-volume
53.          emptyDir: {}
```

It is the longest one we have seen so far! But we can go on to understand it by breaking it down. The object type is **StatefulSet** belongs to the apiVersion **apps/v1**. This StatefulSet will manage pods with label **app: zk**. The **serviceName** shows the name of the service (**headless service: zk-hs**) which will govern this StatefulSet. This governing service must be created before creating the StatefulSet because it is responsible for providing network identity to this StatefulSet and to provide hostnames to the created pods. The pod template contains a lot of configuration details for zookeeper pods. The container of this kubernetes-zookeeper Pod exposes 3 different ports for server, client, and leader-election.

The default command for this container contains a startup script called start-zookeeper, containing a list of parameters to be run. These parameters are as following: number of servers to be initiated, the locations of data directory (where Zookeeper stores its snapshots), log directory (where Zookeeper stores its logs) and configuration data directory, declaration of server, client, and leader election ports, session timeout details, sync time details, memory details, and logging details. Zookeeper uses **emptyDir** type of storage to back up the data stored at **/var/lib/ zookeeper** inside the container.

This sums up the writing of the object definition files required for different Kubernetes objects to create a StatefulSet for Apache Zookeeper. The list of these files must be similar to the following screenshot:

Figure 13.21: Contents of gke-statefulset directory

To keep things clean, you can create all these files under a separate directory. When you are dealing with an application that requires creating multiple objects, the standard practice is to keep them under separate directories. To save us some time, let us leverage this opportunity and create these objects with a single command. Earlier, we used **kubectl apply** and **-f** flag to mention the file's name present in the current directory. But, in this case, we will provide the entire directory as an input to **kubectl apply** command:

```
kubectl apply -f ./
```

The outcome of this command should look like the following screenshot:

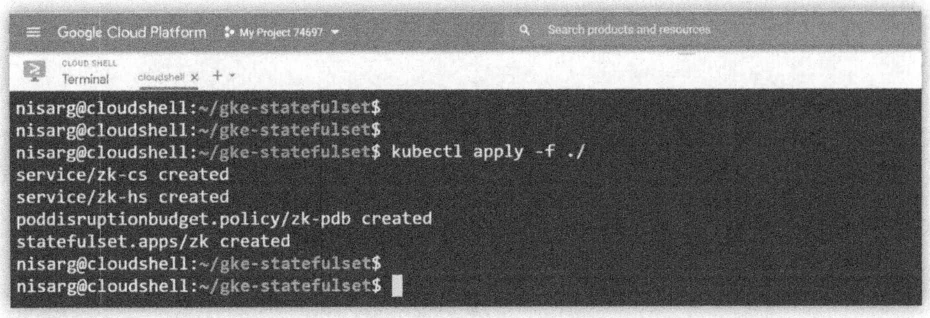

Figure 13.22: Object creation confirmation

The objects were created in the sequence of the stored YAML files, and the headless service was created before the StatefulSet, which means that this StatefulSet will be governed by the headless service nonetheless. Meanwhile, we can keep a watch on the sequence of pods created by the StatefulSet controller and, to do so, execute the following command:

```
kubectl get pods -w -l app=zk
```

-w or **--watch** flag watches for changes after listing out any object. The flag **-l** or **--label** selects objects among the list based on the provided label (**key=value** pair). The outcome of this command should look like the following screenshot:

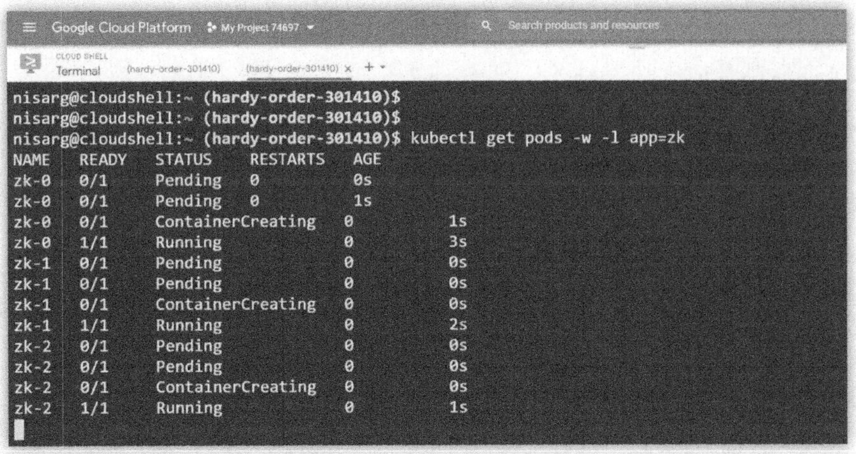

Figure 13.23: Zookeeper Pods

From the preceeding screenshot, we can watch these containers from the creation stage to the running stage. Once all of the three pods reach the running state, press *Ctrl + C* to terminate the watch process. It is an efficient way to swiftly identify if any pod in the creation stage is facing any troubles.

After running pods, let us verify the states of headless service and ClusterIP service we created earlier. Execute **kubectl get svc** command, and you shall receive the outcome of it as follows:

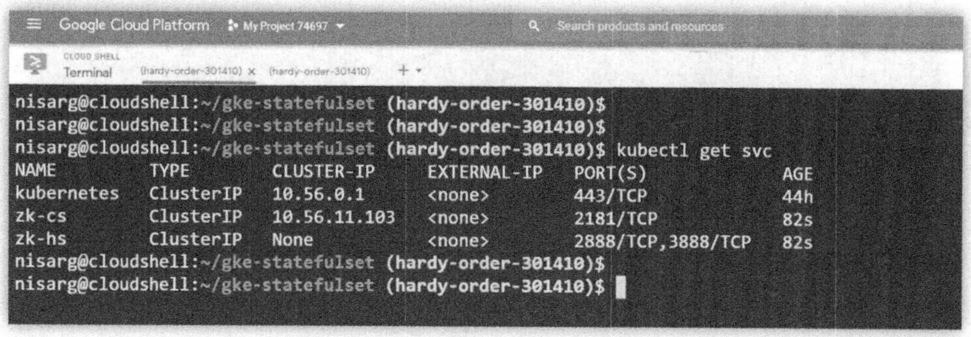

Figure 13.24: Zookeeper Services

Headless service does not have any sort of ClusterIP address which makes it out of the scope of kube-proxy. The zk-cs client service has received the ClusterIP. The StatefulSet controller provides these pods with a unique hostname based on its ordinal index. Hostnames of servers are useful when we need to perform leader election. The hostname is defined in the format **<statefulset name>-<ordinal index>**. Zookeeper servers use natural numbers as unique identifiers and non-integer values as ordinal indices. Identifiers are stored in servers as a file called **myid** at the location **/var/lib/zookeeper/data**. Let us get a list of the hostnames of all 3 replicas of the zookeeper pod by executing the following command:

```
for i in 0 1 2; do kubectl exec zk-$i -- hostname; done
```

This command runs **kubectl exec** command in all 3 zookeeper pods at once and delivers the result like the following screenshot:

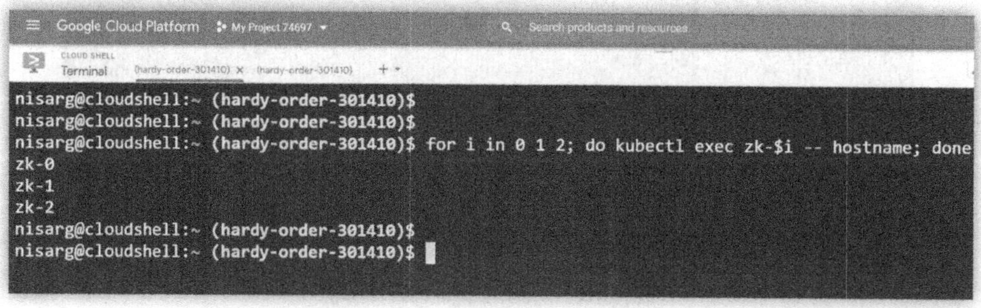

Figure 13.25: Zookeeper Execution

It might be difficult to communicate with these server pods only by their hostnames. The Fully Qualified Domain Name (FDQN) of these servers helps us resolve their domain names into a pod IP address. Headless service has already created their FQDNs following this format: **<hostname>.zk-hs.default.svc.cluster.local** and kube-DNS keeps A records of all these FDQNs to resolve them to Pod's IP address. Let's find out FDQN for all three zookeeper server pods by following this command:

```
for i in 0 1 2; do kubectl exec zk-$i -- hostname -f; done
```

The outcome of the above command should look like the following screenshot:

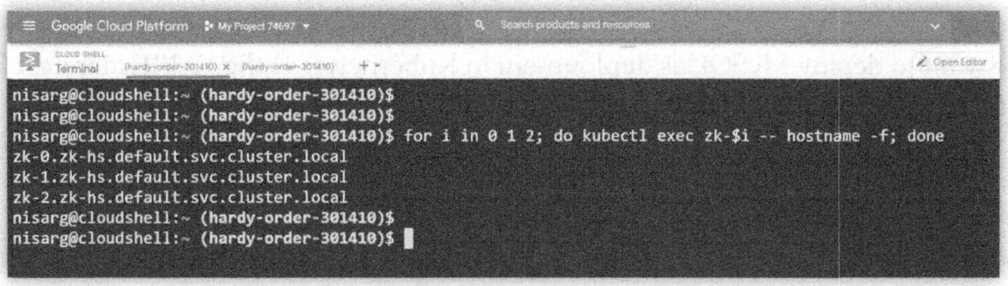

Figure 13.26: Zookeeper Service Domain names

This was an example of a stateful application. You can play with it further by executing one or more pods using **kubectl exec** command. The way how pods under the Stateful sets get created in order, they also get removed in order. You can run the **kubectl delete** command with a watch flag to see this phenomenon in action. While you are at it, we will play with one of the easily accessible offerings of the Google Cloud Platform, Load balancers!

Working with the Load Balancer service

As we have seen in *Chapter 11*, the Load Balancer service uses the system's load balancer (for example, GCP's HTTP Load Balancer) to create endpoints for the workloads. The endpoints can be provided with static or dynamic IPs depending on resource availability. The load Balancer service also creates a NodePort and ClusterIP service to function smoother. It is time to test it in practice.

We will take an example of our good old WordPress and MySQL. This example is divided into two parts: frontend and backend. The frontend of this example is deployed as WordPress and the backend as MySQL database. Let us start with the backend. First, open the cloud shell in your GCP project and create a password for MySQL database and package it as a secret object using the following command:

```
kubectl create secret generic mysql-pswd --from-literal=password=abc@123
```

After executing the command, you shall receive the outcome something like the following screenshot:

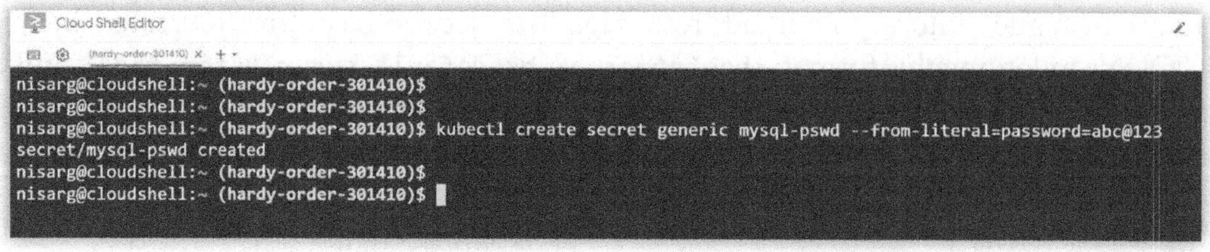

Figure 13.27: MySQL password secret

We want to deploy MySQL as deployment in Kubernetes, so the YAML manifest file for it has many familiar terms, as shown in the following code:

```
1.  apiVersion: apps/v1
2.  kind: Deployment
3.  metadata:
4.    name: mysql-db
5.    labels:
6.      app: wordpress
7.  spec:
8.    selector:
9.      matchLabels:
10.       app: wordpress
11.       tier: mysql
12.   strategy:
13.     type: Recreate
14.   template:
15.     metadata:
16.       labels:
17.         app: wordpress
18.         tier: mysql
19.     spec:
20.       containers:
21.       - name: mysql-container
22.         image: mysql:5.6
```

```
23.        env:
24.        - name: MYSQL_ROOT_PASSWORD
25.          valueFrom:
26.            secretKeyRef:
27.              name: mysql-pswd
28.              key: password
29.        ports:
30.        - containerPort: 3306
31.          name: mysql-container
32.        volumeMounts:
33.        - name: mysql-volume
34.          mountPath: /var/lib/mysql
35.      volumes:
36.      - name: mysql-volume
37.        emptyDir: {}
```

We have set the deployment strategy to replace the old version with the new one whenever the deployment receives an update. The secret we created earlier is fed as an environment variable in the mysql container. Then an emptyDir storage is mounted on the container to backup the data of the MySQL database. To make database pods talk with each other, we need to create a headless service with no ClusterIP. Doing so keeps the backend isolated from the external traffic. To create this service, follow the service object definition YAML as follows:

```
1.  apiVersion: v1
2.  kind: Service
3.  metadata:
4.    name: mysql-db
5.    labels:
6.      app: wordpress
7.  spec:
8.    ports:
9.    - port: 3306
10.   selector:
11.     app: wordpress
```

```
12.    tier: mysql
```

```
13.    clusterIP: None
```

This is all we need for our backend part of the application. For the front end, we have a WordPress deployment and a Load Balancer service using Google's external HTTP(s) Load Balancer.

To create a WordPress deployment, follow the YAML file:

```
1. apiVersion: apps/v1
```

```
2. kind: Deployment
```

```
3. metadata:
```

```
4.   name: wp-frontend
```

```
5.   labels:
```

```
6.     app: wordpress
```

```
7. spec:
```

```
8.   selector:
```

```
9.     matchLabels:
```

```
10.      app: wordpress
```

```
11.      tier: frontend
```

```
12.   strategy:
```

```
13.     type: Recreate
```

```
14.   template:
```

```
15.     metadata:
```

```
16.       labels:
```

```
17.         app: wordpress
```

```
18.         tier: frontend
```

```
19.     spec:
```

```
20.       containers:
```

```
21.       - name: wp-container
```

```
22.         image: wordpress:4.8-apache
```

```
23.         env:
```

```
24.         - name: WORDPRESS_DB_HOST
```

```
25.           value: mysql-db
```

```
26.         - name: WORDPRESS_DB_PASSWORD
```

```
27.           valueFrom:
```

```
28.             secretKeyRef:
```

```
29.               name: mysql-pswd
```

```
30.                key: password
31.           ports:
32.           - containerPort: 80
33.             name: wp-container
34.           volumeMounts:
35.           - name: wp-volume
36.             mountPath: /var/www/html
37.         volumes:
38.         - name: wp-volume
39.           emptyDir: {}
```

For this deployment, the deployment strategy is also set to recreate. There are two passwords set for this deployment: the frontend host and the other one for the MySQL database. These passwords are necessary to grant the authorized access to the frontend as well as the backend deployment. To create the Load Balancer service, follow the object definition YAML:

```
1.  apiVersion: v1
2.  kind: Service
3.  metadata:
4.    name: wp-frontend
5.    labels:
6.      app: wordpress
7.  spec:
8.    ports:
9.      - port: 80
10.   selector:
11.     app: wordpress
12.     tier: frontend
13.   type: LoadBalancer
```

The type of service is set to LoadBalancer. This is the only change we need to make (apart from the container port declaration) in the standard service object definition YAML. When working on any cloud infrastructure, the LoadBalancer service object is configured using the native network load balancer. GCP offers four types of Load Balancers: External HTTP(s), Internal HTTP(s), External TCP/UDP, and Internal TCP/UDP. All of them are divided based on the type of traffic and the direction of the traffic they load balance.

In GCP, External HTTP(s) Load balancing is implemented on GFE (Google Front Ends). It is an infrastructure service used as the reverse-proxy solution for the incoming requests on GCP. Requests forwarded by GFE are received by External HTTP(s) Load Balancer whose scope is set to Global. It distributes the received traffic to the different parent instance groups located in different regions. Internal HTTP(s) Load Balancer located in these regions receives this traffic and forward it to the middleware instance groups.

We can create these objects simultaneously by giving the entire directory containing object definition files as the input in the following command:

```
kubectl apply -f ./
```

The outcome of the above command should look like the following screenshot:

```
nisarg@cloudshell:~/mysql_wordpress (hardy-order-301410)$
nisarg@cloudshell:~/mysql_wordpress (hardy-order-301410)$
nisarg@cloudshell:~/mysql_wordpress (hardy-order-301410)$ kubectl apply -f ./
service/mysql-db created
deployment.apps/mysql-db created
service/wp-frontend created
deployment.apps/wp-frontend created
nisarg@cloudshell:~/mysql_wordpress (hardy-order-301410)$ 
```

Figure 13.28: Creation of WordPress-MySQL objects

When the LoadBalancer service gets created, Google Cloud Controller wakes up and provision a network load balancer with a static IP accessible outside the scope of your GCP project. We can fetch this IP from the home page of Services and Ingress in the GKE dashboard. Click on it, and you should be able to get the external IP of your Load Balancer service shown in the following screenshot:

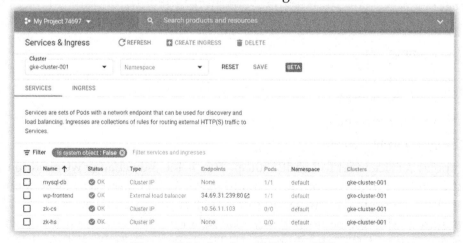

Figure 13.29: Service and Ingress GUI

When we describe the wp-frontend service, we get the details about the provisioned Load Balancer, its External and Internal Ips, and details about the external endpoint as shown in the following screenshot:

Figure 13.30: Details of the wp-frontend load balancer service

After receiving the Load Balancer IP and port combination, the only task to do is ping that IP address. Open up the web browser and hit the Load Balancer IP on port **80**, and the outcome you receiver should look like the following screenshot:

Figure 13.31: WordPress launched

Let us understand what happened here. We (the external clients) sent the HTTP GET request to the Load Balancer service using the IP address and the TCP port. The

GET request was forwarded to one of the WordPress pods on port **80**. The container fetches the requested data and sends it to the client as a POST request.

Working with the Ingress

Ingress is a Kubernetes networking object that manages external access of workloads (HTTP and HTTPS) by setting up a set of traffic rules for the services connected to them. Ingress object does not expose any arbitrary ports or protocols of services associated with it. It also gives externally accessible URLs, HTTP and HTTP(s) traffic load balancing, name-based virtual hosting, and SSL/TSL certificates for request termination.

To create an ingress object, you first need to deploy an ingress controller. Ingress controller is responsible for creating and configuring external or internal HTTP(s) Load balancer based on the configurations provided by the ingress object. Unlike other objects, ingress controllers are not initiated by kube-controller-manager when we bootstrap the cluster, but GKE already has a default ingress controller. Kubernetes support various kind of third-party ingress controllers.

Before creating the ingress object, we need to have an operational deployment to which we can send requests to access it. For this example, we are going to use the standard example of hello-app provided by Google. This Docker Image contains the HTTP server implementation, which responds to all HTTP requests with a standard response of **"Hello, World!"**. Following is the YAML file for hello-app version 1.0:

```
1.  apiVersion: apps/v1
2.  kind: Deployment
3.  metadata:
4.    name: web
5.    namespace: default
6.  spec:
7.    replicas: 3
8.    selector:
9.      matchLabels:
10.       run: web
11.   template:
```

```
12.    metadata:
13.      labels:
14.        run: web
15.    spec:
16.      containers:
17.      - image: gcr.io/google-samples/hello-app:1.0
18.        imagePullPolicy: IfNotPresent
19.        name: web
20.        ports:
21.        - containerPort: 8080
22.          protocol: TCP
```

It is the standard YAML file to create a deployment object. We have configured the container's port **8080** for communication purposes. This deployment deploys version 1.0 of hello-app. Create the deployment using **kubectl apply** command and verify it by navigating to the home page of Workloads as shown in the following screenshot:

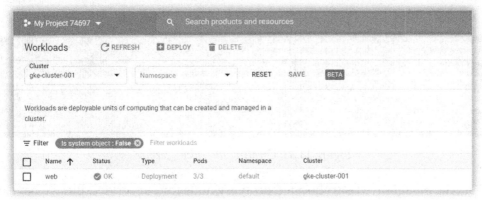

Figure 13.32: *Operational deployment*

The default ingress controller of GKE only supports either NodePort or LoadBalancer services as the one EndPoint for the application pods to create a NodePort service. Following is the YAML file for the NodePort service:

```
1. apiVersion: v1
2. kind: Service
```

```
3. metadata:
4.    name: web
5.    namespace: default
6. spec:
7.    ports:
8.    - port: 8080
9.       protocol: TCP
10.      targetPort: 8080
11.   selector:
12.      run: web
13.   type: NodePort
```

Use the **kubectl apply** command with **-f** flag and the name of the NodePort service object's YAML to create this service. Since it is a NodePort service and we have not mentioned any NodePort, GKE will randomly select a port between **30000** and **32676** to be assigned as the NodePort to make the service available on every node of the cluster.

To find out NodePort, list out the services running on GKE with **kubectl get svc** command, and the outcome should look like the following screenshot:

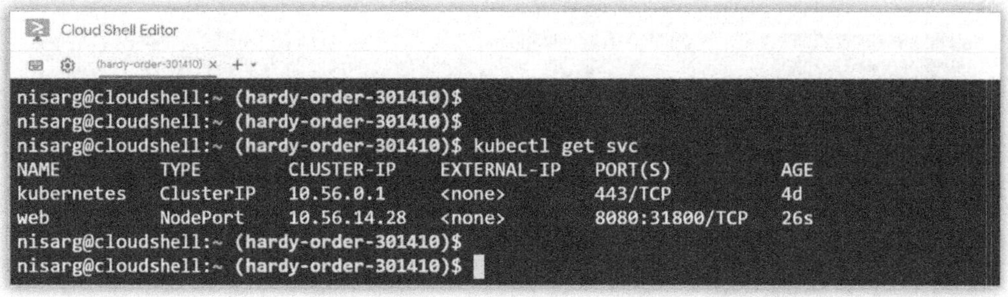

Figure 13.33: Creating the "web" service

We got the NodePort **31800** allocated on every node for our service. But we have not received any external IP, which means that simply creating a NodePort service will not help us expose our application outside of the GKE cluster. We still need to create an ingress object.

There are two ways to create Ingress in GKE: creating the object definition YAML file (just like the other Kubernetes objects) and using the Google Kubernetes Engine GUI. To make this process easy and fun, we will opt for the second way.

To create an ingress object in GKE, go to the **Services and Ingress** page, select the service and click on the **Create Ingress** option on top of the web page. Once you click on it, you should be able to see the webpage shown in the following screenshot:

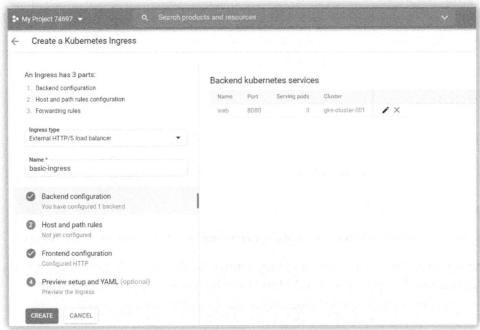

Figure 13.34: Creating a K8s ingress

The process of ingress creation has three steps: Back-end configuration, Host and Path rules configuration, and Forwarding rules. Backend configuration consists of a list of backend services to which the ingress object will forward all the received request. The host and path rules are used to determine the direction of your traffic. You need to mention the paths associated with your backend services where you want to direct the HTTP requests in this step. There are three `pathTypes` supported in GKE:

- **Prefix:** Matched based on a URL path prefix split by / with case sensitivity.

- **Exact:** Matches the URL path with case sensitivity.

- **ImplementationSpecific:** Matches the pathType defined in the IngressClass. It can be a separate pathType, Prefix, or Exact pathType.

If there are any hostnames configured for the received IP address, we need to explicitly mention each host with its relevant path for its respected backend service.

If the requested host and path combination does not exist, all requests are directed to the `defaultBackend` service (*when we receive a 404 error page!*).

In this example, we do not have any other backend services to configure, so the **defaultBackend** service is set to the same backend service we have configured. The webpage to configure host and paths looks like the following screenshot:

Figure 13.35: Host and path rule configuration

Note:

https://kubernetes.io/docs/concepts/services-networking/ingress/#path-types

After finishing two steps, the final step shows us the preview of the ingress object configuration. The preview should look like the following screenshot:

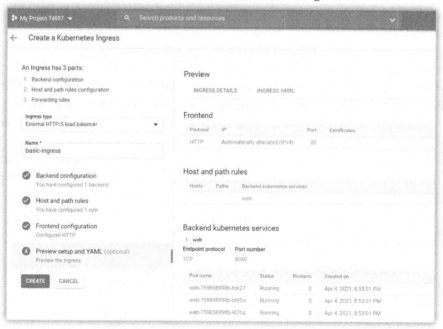

Figure 13.36: Final ingress configuration

The frontend is the external HTTP Load Balancer which receives the IPv4 address once created and configured with the ingress object. We only have a single host and path rules that allow us to send requests to all the possible paths of the service. The backend service has 3 running pods connected to it via port **8080**. These are the steps you need to perform to create an ingress object for a deployment running on a GKE cluster. Press the create button to create the basic-ingress object, and the outcome of it should look like the following screenshot:

Figure 13.37: Basic ingress created

The basic-ingress object for our GKE cluster gke-cluster-001 is in the creation process because the GKE ingress controller creates and configures an external HTTP(s) Load Balancer to route the external traffic received on its port **80** to the NodePort service (web) on its port **8080**. After the successful completion of the creation and configuration of the load balancer, we can check out the details of the basic-ingress object, and they should look like the following screenshot:

Figure 13.38: Inspecting ingress object

In normal situations, we can send a GET request to the application using the external IP address and can receive the server's response as the POST request on our web browser. The response from the **hello-app** deployment should look like the following screenshot:

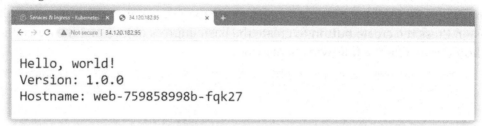

Figure 13.39: Service version 1.0.0

We got a string, version number, and the Pod's hostname who has responded to our GET request as a response to our request. Ingress controllers are bootstrapped with standard load balancing policies such as load balancing algorithms, backend weighing schemes, etc. Whenever there are many requests, the ingress object tries to load balance to the nearest instance from the origin of the client request to provide the fastest response possible. GKE also performs periodic healthchecks based on a set of healthcheck parameters for the backend services. Each backend service can have different healthchecks designed based on the most standard way to test the health of a backend service is by sending the GET requests to the **/** (root) location to the serving application pod. If the application is running normally, it will send HTTP 200 response and if it is not, you shall receive the error message shown in the following screenshot:

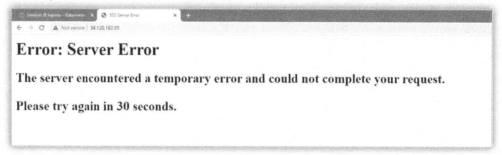

Figure 13.40: Encountering 502 Server Error

This was a simple ingress object configured to direct traffic from a single IP address to a single backend service. But when we deal with a multi-tier application having multiple microservices running different tasks, we would want to keep things simple by having a single IP address to direct and load balance the external traffic received by the applications to these services. The simple fanout feature of Ingress can help us out.

A fanout configuration in ingress routes traffic received from a single IP address to more than one backend services based on the requested HTTP URI. We can understand this better using an example. Earlier, we deployed a sample hello-app of version 1.0 as deployment and created a NodePort service to expose it. Let us create another deployment to deploy hello-app version 2.0 and expose it by creating a new NodePort service. Follow the YAML files for the deployment web-2 below:

```
1.  apiVersion: apps/v1
2.  kind: Deployment
3.  metadata:
4.    name: web-2
5.    namespace: default
6.  spec:
7.    replicas: 3
8.    selector:
9.      matchLabels:
10.       run: web-2
11.   template:
12.     metadata:
13.       labels:
14.         run: web-2
15.     spec:
16.       containers:
17.       - image: gcr.io/google-samples/hello-app:2.0
18.         imagePullPolicy: IfNotPresent
19.         name: web-2
20.         ports:
21.         - containerPort: 8080
22.           protocol: TCP
```

We have replaced the name of the deployment (**web-2**), Labels (**run: web-2**), image name (**hello-app:2.0**), and the container name (**web-2**). Follow the NodePort service object definition YAML:

```
1.  apiVersion: v1
```

```
2. kind: Service
3. metadata:
4.   name: web-svc-2
5.   namespace: default
6. spec:
7.   ports:
8.   - port: 8080
9.       protocol: TCP
10.      targetPort: 8080
11.   selector:
12.      run: web-2
13.   type: NodePort
```

Use **kubectl apply** command to create both of these objects. To create the ingress object for web and web-svc-2 services, go to **Services and Ingress page**, select both service objects, and press the create button. Since there are two backend services, we have mentioned the host and path rules for them individually. Have a look at the following screenshot:

Figure 13.41: Host and Path configuration for the Multi-path Ingress

We have set up the target path for web service as **/***. Using wildcard ***** shows that we can send requests to all sub-paths under the root path, whereas for **web-svc-2**, we can send requests to all sub-paths under **/v2** directory. Fill in other details as we have done in the previous example and create the ingress object. The result should look like the following screenshot:

Figure 13.42: Listing out the Multi-path Ingress

We have received 2 entries in the Frontend column for our two backend services. The IP address to access both backend services is the same, but the paths are different. When we hit both URLs in the web browser, the outcome of `http://34.120.182.95` should look like the following screenshot:

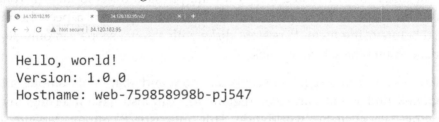

Figure 13.43: Version 1.0.0 on the regular path

To access the other backend service, hit `http://34.120.182.95/v2/` in a new browser window, and the outcome should look like the following screenshot:

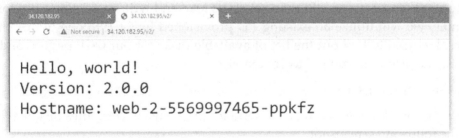

Figure 13.44: Service version 2.0.0 on the nested path

We got the server response from the web-2 deployment, which runs version 2.0 of the sample `hello-app`.

Persistent Volume

A **Persistent Volume** is a storage object used to provide persistent data storage in a Kubernetes cluster. It is considered the cluster resource, which means it exists outside Pods' scope, making them independent of Pods. This way, even if the Pod is deleted or recreated, the pod data stored in the mounted PV does not get affected and can easily retrieve it back to the Pod. Persistent Volume Claims can dynamically provision persistent Volume or manually provisioned by a cluster manager. Earlier in *Chapter 11*, we had made the data persist even after the container crash using emptyDir Volume. This time, we will make the data persist even after the Pod crashes using Google's persistent disk. The interface to access it is already available in GKE via the Container Storage Interface (CSI) module pods we had encountered at the beginning of the chapter.

In GKE, the default storage option used for PV is Persistent Disk (PD). They are independent network storage devices used by VM instances to accommodate the need of the physical disks for VMs on cloud infrastructure. The data stored on persistent disks are distributed across several physical disks located in zones and regions. The scope of these persistent disks is an important aspect the must be declared before using them. Persistent disks with a zonal scope can only store and share data among the selected zones.

In contrast, PDs with a regional scope can store and share data among all zones accumulated under that particular region. You can also have inter-regions PD to make your data available worldwide. Still, this aspect entirely depends on the storage requirements and the amount of exposure you want your application to face.

You can either create a new non-bootable PD to attach to your node, or you can mount an existing disk provisioned to any of your nodes in the cluster. The recommended approach is to create a new PD and set up its read and write restrictions. But for this example, we will utilize an existing PD provisioned by GCP to one of our cluster nodes. We need to find out the list of available disks for our GCP project, and you can use the gcloud command to get that list:

```
gcloud compute disks list
```

The execution of the preceding command gives us a list of computes disk that looks like the following screenshot:

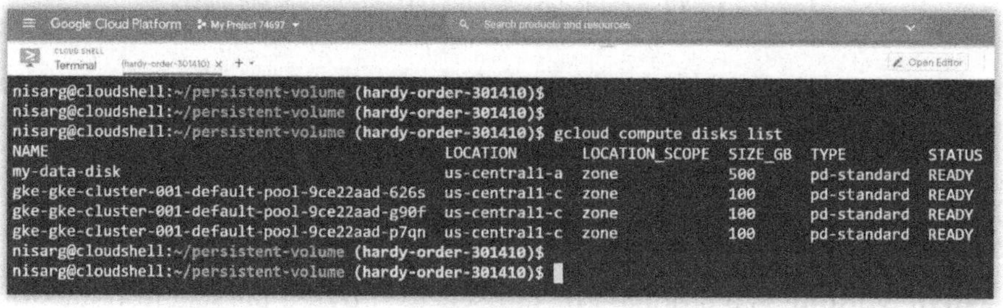

Figure 13.45: List of available persistent disks on GKE cluster

There are three types of storage disks available in GCP, and you can select any one of them while creating the new PD:

- Standard Persistent Disk (pd-standard)
- Balanced Persistent Disk (pd-balanced)
- SSD Persistent Disk (pd-ssd)

All nodes in our GKE cluster have standard persistent disks of 100GB attached storage capacity. These PDs are zonal persistent disks; the data stored on these disks cannot be accessed by any other instances apart from those deployed in the us-central zone. We will use one of these PD to create a persistent volume.

There is a default Storage Class available in GCP, which uses the standard PD as the storage option. This default class is used when there is no Storage Class mentioned in the Persistent Volume Claim (PVC). You can list out storage classes using the following command:

```
kubectl get storageclass
```

The outcome of the preceding command should look like the following screenshot:

Figure 13.46: GKE storage classes

There are three storage classes available in this GKE cluster, along with the default storage class. The **Provisioner** column suggests the type of storage provisioner for the particular storage class. The default storage class has been provisioned by **gce-pd** Volume. **Reclaim policy** is used to show what to do with the provisioned persistent storage after using, and the default is **DELETE**. **VolumeBindingMode** shows how PVC should be provisioned and bound. The default action is **Immediate.** **Volume Expansion** field is set to true, which means that storage classes allow volume expansion.

To create a Persistent Volume Claim, follow the YAML file:

1. kind: PersistentVolumeClaim

2. apiVersion: v1

3. metadata:

4.   name: pv-claim

5. spec:

6.   accessModes:

7.   - ReadWriteOnce

8.   volumeMode: Filesystem

9.   resources:

10.   requests:

11.   storage: 1Gi

12.   storageClassName: standard

According to this claim, we want the standard storage class to provision 1Gi of persistent storage. The next step must be to create a persistent Volume to claim. Following is the object definition file for the Persistent Volume object:

1. apiVersion: v1

2. kind: PersistentVolume

3. metadata:

4.   name: my-volume

5.   labels:

6.   failure-domain.beta.kubernetes.io/zone: us-central1-c

7. spec:

8.   capacity:

9.   storage: 10Gi

10. accessModes:

11. - ReadWriteOnce

12. storageClassName: standard

13. gcePersistentDisk:

14.   pdName: gke-gke-cluster-001-default-pool-9ce22aad-626s

We have used PD attached to node 1 of our cluster to provision a 10Gi persistent volume. Ensure that the persistent Volume you are creating is in the same zone as your instances are in. Use the **kubectl apply** command to create PV and PVC objects, and the outcome should look like the following screenshot:

Figure 13.47: Listing out available persistent volumes

To make a use of PV that we created, we will create a redis pod and mount this volume inside the redis container. The YAML file to create a redis pod with PV is as following:

```
1.  apiVersion: v1
2.  kind: Pod
3.  metadata:
4.    name: redispv-pod
5.  spec:
6.    containers:
7.      - name: redispv-container
8.        image: redis
9.        volumeMounts:
10.       - mountPath: «/data»
11.         name: my-pd
12.   volumes:
13.     - name: my-pd
14.       persistentVolumeClaim:
15.         claimName: pv-claim
```

We mention the name of the PVC that we created earlier to create a volume for this redis pod. Kubelet on the node where the Pod has been scheduled looks for the Volume associated with PVC mentioned in the YAML file. The storage class associated with this PV provisions the demanded storage from the provided persistent disk (aka GKE cluster node's PD). Create the Pod using **kubectl apply** command, and you shall receive the confirmation message as shown in the following screenshot:

Figure 13.48: Creating Redis Pods

We can also find the location of the PV directory created on the GKE cluster node whose PD has been used as the storage option for redis pod. You need to go to **Compute Engine | VM Instances** page and SSH into the **gke-gke-cluster-001-default-pool-9ce22aad-626s** node. We will use the Linux command to list out all block storage devices connected to this particular node (VM instance), and the outcome should look like the following screenshot:

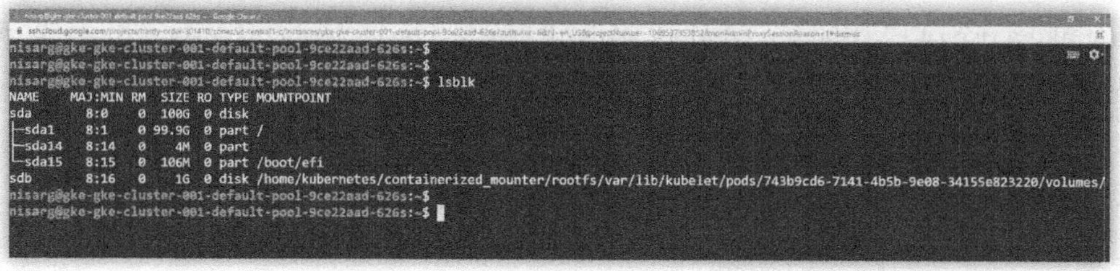

Figure 13.49: Locating volume on the persistent disk

The last entry of this disk list gives us information about the provisioned storage (PV) location for the Redis pod. In other words, the data inside **/data** directory of the Redis container will be stored at this location on this GKE node. We can populate the **/volumes** directory with some data to see it getting propagated to the Redis container. Enter into the superuser mode to navigate to this location using the **cd** command and find the target directory as shown in the following screenshot:

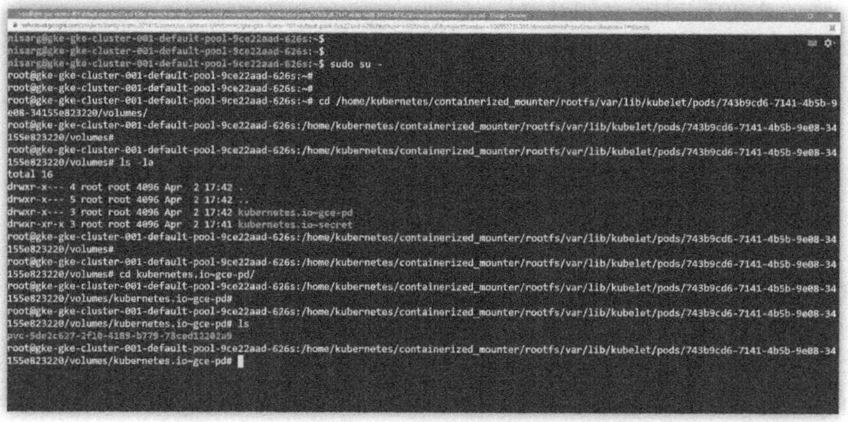

Figure 13.50: Populating the /volumes directory

We will populate the PV by creating 3 files using the touch command: **foo.txt, foo_1.txt,** and **foo_2.txt.** And the outcome should look like the following screenshot:

Figure 13.51: Populating the persistent volume

We have successfully added some data to provisioned PV directory on the GKE cluster node. Close the SSH connection on the node and return to Cloud Shell to list the Redis container's contents of **/data** directory. When you click on the exec option on the Workload homepage for Redis-pod, you should receive a Cloud Shell command to exec the container. Follow the modified command as shown:

```
gcloud container clusters get-credentials <gke-cluster-name> --zone <zone-name> --project <project-ID> && kubectl exec redispv-pod -c redispv-container -- ls /data
```

Replace the details about the cluster name, zone, and the project ID with your details and use the **kubectl exec** command to list contents of **/data** directory of **redispv-container**.

The outcome of this command should look like the following screenshot:

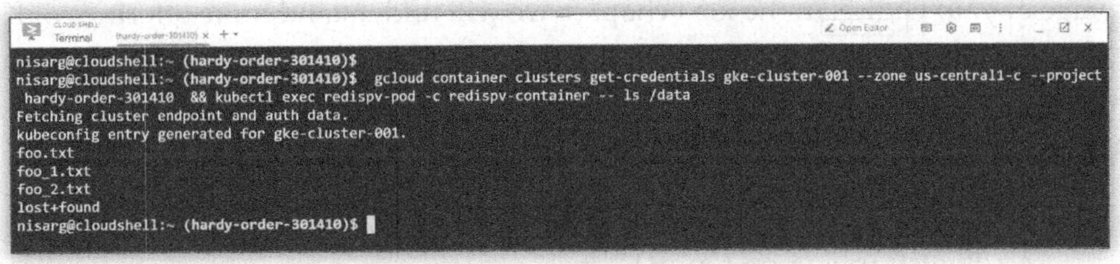

Figure 13.52: Verifying the PV mount

redispv-container contains the data we created on the GKE node. PV has been successfully mounted on the target location inside the container. It will be interesting to verify whether it can persist the data after removing the container. To do so, We will delete the present Pod (use **kubectl delete pod <pod-name>** command) and create a new Redis pod using the same pod object definition file and will change the name of the Pod from **redispv-pod** to **redispv-pod-001**. Make these change in the pod object YAML file and use the **kubectl apply** command to create this new Pod.

After creating the new Redis pod, list out the contents of its data directory using the following command:

```
kubectl exec redispv-pod-001 -c redispv-container -- ls /data
```

The outcome of this command should look like the following screenshot:

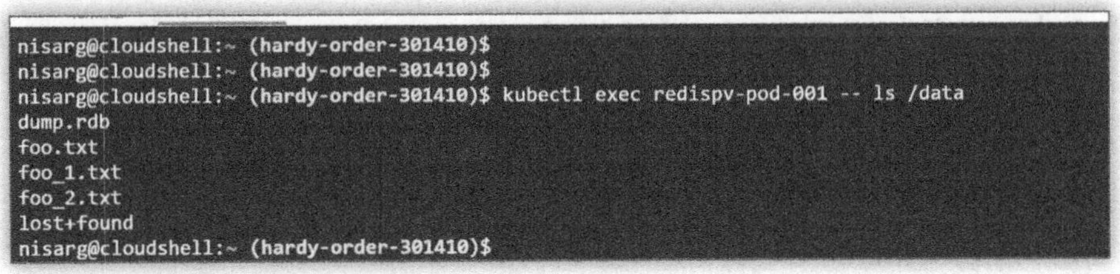

Figure 13.53: Verifying the data persistence after volume removal

The data is safe and sound. The same steps can also be performed on a locally bootstrapped K8s cluster with a few additional steps of writing a custom storage class for your storage type. You can also write a load balancer service on local K8s if you have your load balancer setup. But that is the beauty of the Cloud. It grants you the leisure of focusing on the application performance by taking care of mundane setups for you (or making them as easy as one click).

Conclusion

In this chapter, we set up our first managed K8s cluster on GKE and explored its operations. We saw how intuitive it is to use the GUI to observe the workloads or how easy it is to set up complex objects like load balancer services, Ingress or persistent storage of your choice. In the next chapter, we will understand more offerings of K8s on Cloud and discuss its pricing.

Multiple choice questions

1. Which of the following is not a method of using Kubernetes?

    A. Bootstrapping on Linux Kernel

    B. Managed Kubernetes on Cloud

    C. Minikube with Linux Virtual Machine

    D. Running as a native windows application

    Answer: D

2. Which of the following Cloud Providers offer managed Kubernetes on Cloud as a service?

    A. Google Cloud Platform

    B. Amazon Web Services

    C. Microsoft Azure

    D. All of the above

    Answer: D

3. Which of the following workload objects is helpful to schedule ordered creation and destruction of pods?

    A. Replica Sets

    B. Stateful Sets

    C. Deployments

    D. Cron Jobs

    Answer: B

4. Which of the following objects on a managed Kubernetes environment provides an interface to occupy SSD and HDD outside the scope of pods?

   A. Volumes

   B. Secrets

   C. CSI

   D. CNI

   Answer: C

5. Which of the following load balancers are not offered by GKE?

   A. TCP

   B. HTTP

   C. TELNET

   D. All of the above

   Answer: C

Questions

1. Explain the Google Kubernetes Engine Architecture in detail.

2. Write the YAML manifests for an nginx deployment and its load balancer service.

3. Explain the difference between Node Security and Cluster Security.

4. Explain the difference between Deployments and Stateful sets with example YAML manifests.

5. Configure a hostpath ingress to serve Nginx and Apache webserver welcome pages on respective paths following a common load balancer IP.

CHAPTER 14
Containers in Production with GKE

Introduction

This chapter continues to explore the **Google Kubernetes Engine (GKE)** and takes its uses to a production-friendly environment. We start by understanding how the production environment differs from the development or testing environment and what are the general expectations from a production-ready container cluster. We move to tools and technologies, simplifying the execution of expectations from such clusters. By the end of this chapter, you will have matured your thinking as a K8s Cluster operator.

Structure

This chapter covers:

- Kubernetes in production environments
- High availability cluster in GKE
- Logging in GKE
- Monitoring in GKE
- Prometheus

- Understanding and working with Service Mesh
- Helm
- Continuous delivery using Spinnaker on GKE
- The bling-bling of billing

Objective

This chapter covers a lot of third-party tools and services. The objective of this chapter is not to make you the master of all trades but to provide enough introduction with examples that you can decide whether the tool is useful to you and if you should invest your time and/or resources in it.

Kubernetes in production environments

After successful development and testing, every application needs to be moved to the production environment to be available to the clients for monetization. While creating the application production environment, the following aspects are important to consider:

- The infrastructure should be secure and dynamically scalable
- The cluster should be highly available to avoid potential downtime
- The cluster should have sufficient logging and monitoring capabilities
- The cluster should have robust traffic management and service-to-service communication
- The cluster operations and application deployments should be easy to carry out
- The cluster should support a pipeline to integrate development and production

Even though Kubernetes is a highly efficient tool, it may not be sufficient to achieve all of the goals mentioned above at once. This is where third-party tools and services find their usefulness. Over time, K8s and cloud-native software have developed an ecosystem to enhance one another's applicability and mitigate their flaws. This chapter will cover the significant players of the ecosystem, but before that, let's discuss high availability for clusters.

High availability cluster in GKE

To understand the notion of **high availability**, it becomes crucial to understand when a cluster becomes **unavailable**. The cluster becomes unavailable in two cases:

- The workloads are overloaded
- The master components are not available

To avoid the master's unavailability, GKE allows us to choose between **regional** and **zonal** clusters. So far, we have seen zonal clusters. Our previous zonal GKE cluster had 3 nodes and 1 master. While GKE does handle the scaling of K8s master resources, highly available clusters don't wait for potential overload to occur. Regional clusters have at least one master in each zone (in the case of the asia-south1 region, the cluster would have one control plane in asia-south1-a, asia-south1-b, and asia-south1-c each). To determine which master would serve the request first, the masters perform a quorum (leader election similar to swarm managers). As the load increases, it scales the masters up. Once the control plane availability is taken care of, the focus can be shifted to workload availability. To prepare our workloads to meet any accidental or induced surges, we need to focus on a few design aspects while setting up the GKE environment.

- **Types of the cluster**: Whether your GKE cluster is spread across a zone (**zonal cluster**) or replicated across multiple zones in a region (**regional cluster**).

- **Types of autoscaling:** Whether your cluster scales up its resources like RAM, CPU, or Storage in the set amount of node instances (**vertical scaling**) or increases the number of node instance replicas (**horizontal scaling**).

- **Healthcheck policy:** What parameters and their values mark your cluster as healthy to operate. This is application specific. A mission-critical service may have a more stringent definition of calling itself healthy than a casual application.

The job of resizing the number of nodes in a node pool of a GKE cluster belongs to the cluster autoscaler. Based on the demands of the workloads, cluster autoscaler adds and optimizes nodes for your cluster. If the demand is high, it adds nodes to the node pool based on the defined machine template for VM instances in GCP, and if the request is low, it scales down the cluster to the minimum node count defined. When you create a new GKE cluster, you can enable the auto-scaling feature as shown in the following screenshot:

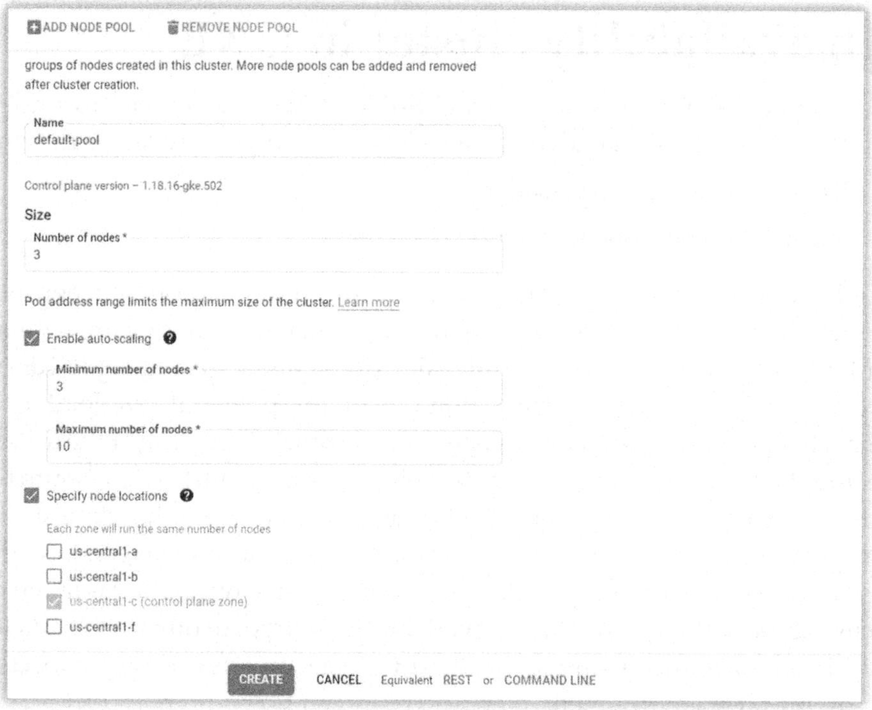

Figure 14.1: *Auto-scaling configurations for GKE cluster*

The default number of nodes created for a GKE cluster is **3**. Suppose you have calculated your resource requirements before deploying the workload. In that case, you can manually change the value of this field accordingly. Cluster autoscaler works on a per-node basis, which means that we need to specify the number of nodes (minimum and maximum nodes) for the target node pool. We can configure the cluster autoscaler for any node pool by selecting the **Enable auto-scaling** option in the **Node pool details** page during GKE cluster creation.

After getting configured for the given node pool, the cluster autoscaler continuously monitors the actual resource utilization of pods running on the nodes and nodes' health to make decisions for making changes to the size of the node pool. If there are not enough resources to schedule pods on any of the nodes, the cluster autoscaler creates and adds new nodes based on the node configuration of the pool.

In the other scenario, if nodes are underutilized, the cluster autoscaler removes the unwanted nodes and brings the cluster back with the minimum size of the node pool. We can also configure the location for these new nodes by enabling the **Specify node locations** option. We can schedule the new nodes in other zones of the same region where the original zone is located. Zone availability is a vital parameter for cluster auto-scaling.

Nodes located at an unavailable zone are deleted and recreated in other zones until they reach the specified maximum number of nodes, which means that if we hit the max limit in all available zones, we cannot have any more nodes in that region. It sometimes becomes the reason for a failed scaling process.

It is equally important to take actions against underutilized resources. Any node with underutilized resources can be removed from the cluster to optimize the overall resource utilization. Cluster autoscaler uses profiles to strike a balance between what to remove and what to keep. Based on these profiles, it can save up the number of resources required to handle future deployments while handling the underutilized resources. There are two autoscaling profiles available in GKE:

- **Balanced:** This is the default profile.
- **Optimize-utilization**: This is a resource optimization-centric profile.

You can select any of the profiles based on requirements. You can select the type of profile under the **Automation** option as shown in the following screenshot:

Figure 14.2: Auto-scaling profile selection for GKE cluster

For existing GKE clusters, you can edit these properties, such as autoscaling profiles and many more, by clicking on the pencil icon located in line with their respective names. Click on the name of the cluster that you want to edit, and you should be able to land on a webpage shown in the following screenshot:

Figure 14.3: Enable Vertical Pod auto-scaling for existing GKE cluster

When we enable the **Vertical Pod Auto-scaling**, it leads us to a message window stating that the cluster autoscaler is taking charge to analyze and adjust the CPU and memory resource requests of running containers on our target node pool. When we save these changes, it leads us to a panel describing node auto-provisioning for this target node pool.

The panel looks like the following screenshot:

Figure 14.4: Setup for node auto-provisioning for GKE cluster

Logging with GKE

Logs are an essential aspect of any kind of application. They are generally the go-to source for finding the root cause of any unexpected behavior. On top of that, logs can also be used to set up alerting and automated actions. While logs have their advantages, they also come with their fair share of challenges. Storing and sorting the logs and collecting the logs from simultaneously running distributed microservices can be troublesome, and this is where third-party tools come into the picture.

As the default logging solution for GKE, we have Cloud logging. It is a part of the Cloud Operation suite (formerly known as StackDriver), which is helpful to collect application and Kubernetes cluster logs for debugging and troubleshooting. **Cloud logging** is a fully managed service that provides real-time management of different log data from Kubernetes workloads, GKE environment (VMs), and other in-use GCP services.

For the latest, stable versions, the default logging solution for GKE clusters is Cloud logging of the Cloud Operations suite. Legacy logging service for Kubernetes clusters and workloads is deprecated, so it is highly advisable to keep Cloud Logging as the default logging solution for GKE clusters. While creating a GKE cluster, you can configure logging and monitoring on the `Features` page as shown in the following screenshot:

Figure 14.5: Enable Cloud Logging for a GKE cluster

Container runtimes come with the native logging drivers to fetch logs from running containers and services. For example, Docker uses JSON-file logging driver as the default solution to fetch logs from containers and services and store them on the nodes on which they are running. When Docker is used as the container runtime for Kubernetes, unless modified, it uses the default JSON-file logging drivers to keep the log of containers running inside Kubernetes Pods.

The disadvantage of using a "local" logging driver is that it stores system and container logs in the disk memory of the respective node on which they are running, which makes them centrally inaccessible. As time goes on, the log entries keep increasing, which eventually consumes more node resources, leading to the lack of node resources for future deployments. Another thing to keep in mind is that if a pod is removed from the node, its container logs will also be deleted from the node's memory.

When we use the Cloud Logging default logging solution, the GKE cluster creates the cluster-level logging by deploying a per-node logging agent to read container and system logs. These logging agents can read stdout and stderr container logs and forward them to Log routers for further processing. Log router checks each log entry that it receives against the rules to determine whether to discard or forward logs to Cloud Logging API.

After receiving different log entries, Cloud logging filters them out based on their parent resources and exports them to their respective destinations such as Cloud storage, BigQuery, Pub/Sub, and Log buckets using the **LogSink** object. LogSink has information about the parent resource of the log, its destination with the location, writer's identity, and log exclusion filter details. If there are no other storage facilities configured to the GKE cluster, Cloud logging uses log buckets as containers in the GCP project to store and organize the logs. These logs are indexed and optimized in a way that we can quickly analyze them in real-time.

By default, GKE collects logs for the workloads deployed on it, but sometimes such application logs are not needed for analysis. For such reason, we can control the type of logs collected by Cloud logging by changing the type of logging for the cluster. We can either set it while creating the cluster or edit it for the existing cluster. There are mainly four and in total five types of logging and monitoring services of Cloud operation:

- System and workload logging and monitoring (default selection)
- System and workload logging only (Monitoring disabled)
- System monitoring only (Logging disabled)

- System logging and monitoring only
- Legacy logging and monitoring

There are various third-party logging agents available in Google's marketplace, which we can use for a better logging experience. One of them is fluentd. It is an open-source data collector tool that unifies all facets of log data processing (such as collection, filtering, and exporting) across the cluster. Fluentd adds a unifying logging layer between the log data source and the backend systems, which puts these systems at lower risk of getting any direct lousy log data entries.

In this section, we are going to install a customized fluentd logging agent for our GKE cluster. We will deploy fluentd as a daemonset on every node of the GKE cluster, which collects different log data (system and workload logs) and sends it to the cloud logging service.

The first step to install fluentd would be cloning its repository from Google Cloud platforms official Github account. Clone the GitHub repository for fluentd by executing the following command in your Cloud Shell window:

git clone https://github.com/GoogleCloudPlatform/kubernetes-engine-customize-fluentd

After cloning the repository to our GKE cluster, we should be able to find **/kubernetes** directory containing fluentd configurations YAMLs and a test application YAML on our system as shown in the following screenshot:

```
$ ls
CONTRIBUTING.md   create-cluster.sh   kubernetes   LICENSE   README.md   test-logger
$
$ cd kubernetes/
$
$ ls
fluentd-configmap.yaml   fluentd-daemonset.yaml   test-logger.yaml
$
```

Figure 14.6: Fluentd configuration files

The configurations that fluentd uses to watch and collect container logs are all defined in the **fluentd-configmap.yaml** file. Container runtime is responsible for fetching and storing container log data at a particular location on the node machine. For example, if the container runtime for the GKE cluster is set as Docker, the container logs are stored at **/var/lib/docker/containers** directory as log files.

For a standard Kubernetes cluster (bootstrapped by kubeadm), the node's kubelet creates a symbolic link to these log files to a different location on the same node under the **/var/log/containers** directory. Every symbolic link is created in a particular format **<POD_NAME>_<NAMESPACE>_<CONTAINER_NAME>.log** to make the log data collection process smoother. This **/var/log/containers** directory on the cluster node is mapped to the **/var/log** directory in the container running Fluentd instance, thus, we end up collecting logs of containers running on that particular node.

The logs in fluentd containers are tagged in a particular format for the record reformer to extract essential details like pod names, namespace names, and container names and map in a format: **k8s_container.<NAMESPACE_NAME>.<POD_NAME>.<CONTAINER_ NAME>** which are known to Cloud Logging API. Also, Fluentd instances must be running on each available node of the cluster. To do that, we deploy them as a daemonset whose object definition file is defined as **fluentd-daemonset.yaml.**

We are also going to create a test deployment workload that emits random logging statements. The source code for this deployment is located at **test-logger.yaml** file, which is presented in the following code:

```
1.  apiVersion: apps/v1
2.  kind: Deployment
3.  metadata:
4.    name: test-logger
5.  spec:
6.    replicas: 3
7.    selector:
8.      matchLabels:
9.        component: test-logger
10.   template:
11.     metadata:
12.       labels:
13.         component: test-logger
14.     spec:
15.       containers:
16.         - name: test-logger
17.           image: gcr.io/cloud-solutions-images/test-logger
```

We will create all of these Kubernetes objects at once by using the following command:

```
kubectl apply -f kubernetes/.
```

The output of the above command should look like the following screenshot:

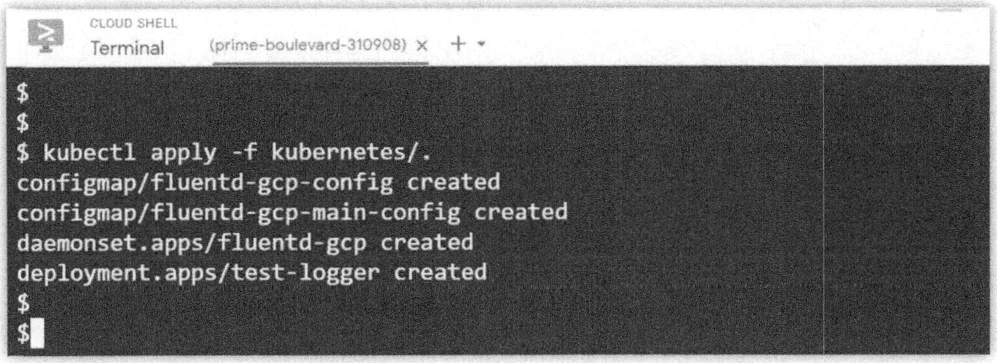

```
CLOUD SHELL
Terminal      (prime-boulevard-310908) ×  + ▾

$
$
$ kubectl apply -f kubernetes/.
configmap/fluentd-gcp-config created
configmap/fluentd-gcp-main-config created
daemonset.apps/fluentd-gcp created
deployment.apps/test-logger created
$
$
```

Figure 14.7: Fluentd Kubernetes object creation

After creating fluentd configmap, daemonset, and the test deployment, when we list out pods of all namespaces, we should witness the result as shown in the following screenshot:

```
Cloud Shell Editor

      (prime-boulevard-310908) ×  + ▾
$
$
$ kubectl get pods --all-namespaces
NAMESPACE     NAME                                         READY   STATUS    RESTARTS   AGE
default       test-logger-66b545cb9f-cqbrm                 1/1     Running   0          2m29s
default       test-logger-66b545cb9f-jjdwn                 1/1     Running   0          2m29s
default       test-logger-66b545cb9f-rsggb                 1/1     Running   0          2m29s
kube-system   event-exporter-gke-564fb97f9-hzgpm           2/2     Running   0          73m
kube-system   fluentbit-gke-grtqs                          2/2     Running   0          73m
kube-system   fluentbit-gke-ts85n                          2/2     Running   0          73m
kube-system   fluentbit-gke-xzpfl                          2/2     Running   0          73m
kube-system   fluentd-gcp-kcwjh                            2/2     Running   0          2m29s
kube-system   fluentd-gcp-pc7z2                            2/2     Running   0          2m29s
kube-system   fluentd-gcp-xfzsr                            2/2     Running   0          2m29s
kube-system   gke-metrics-agent-h9b6d                      1/1     Running   0          73m
kube-system   gke-metrics-agent-qzmvh                      1/1     Running   1          73m
kube-system   gke-metrics-agent-vrg6h                      1/1     Running   0          73m
kube-system   kube-dns-6465f78586-fnfd5                    4/4     Running   0          73m
kube-system   kube-dns-6465f78586-xz4bv                    4/4     Running   0          72m
kube-system   kube-dns-autoscaler-7f89fb6b79-18txs         1/1     Running   0          73m
```

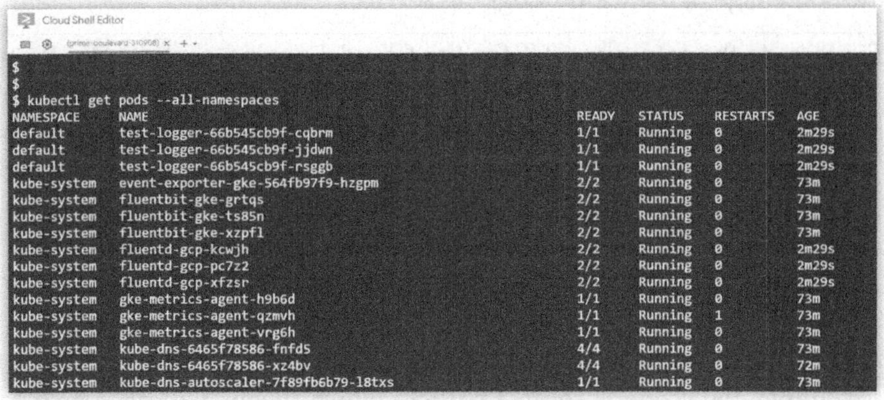

Figure 14.8: List of Fluentd object pods

Based on the age of the pods, we can filter out 3 Fluentd pods running in the kube-system namespace and 3 test-logger deployment pods running in the default namespace. Kubernetes clusters created on GKE come with a Fluent Bit logging collector and processer. It is a light-weighted log collector that collects container and system logs from different nodes in the GKE cluster and forwards the data to Fluentd for aggregation, processing, and routing to the supported destinations. Some of the features of Fluent Bit, such as small footprint, unstructured data formatting, aggregation from multiple data sources, security, are the suitable reasons to use it with the combination of Fluentd to achieve high performance in K8s clusters.

Since the test-logger deployment is running successfully for some time, it might have generated a few log entries to analyze. We can check out the logs for the GKE cluster by accessing the logs option for the cluster as shown in the following screenshot:

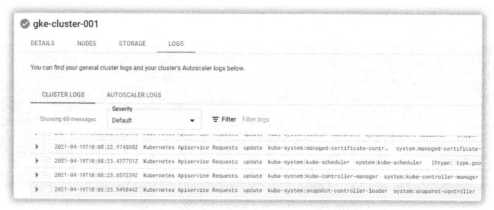

Figure 14.9: General logs of the GKE cluster

We got a long list of general cluster logs. To get a detailed view of these logs, click on the expand window option on the top right side of the log window. It will redirect us to the homepage of the Cloud Logging service.

Logs Explorer is the intuitive GUI for the Cloud Logging service. We can watch, parse, retrieve, analyze different kinds of log data here. The entire window of Logs explorer is divided into multiples sections delivering different functionalities. They are as following:

- **Action Bar:** This section consists of features to manage and control the appearances of log entries. **OPTIONS** tab consists of the information about the legacy Logs Viewer, a summary of the new logging features, and a way to send feedback to Google Cloud Platform. **REFINE SCOPE** is used to refine the scope of logs within the Cloud project or the storage views. In this example, the scope is set to **Projects** which means we can search for logs only within the current Cloud project.

  We can create a short URL of the current query by using **SHARE LINK** to share it with others effortlessly. We can restrict the query results within a specified time range by setting the **Time-range selector**. For this example, the Time-range selector is showing the query results of the **past 1 hour.** We can change the Log Explorer's layout by selecting the **PAGE LAYOUT** option. In the end, we have a navigate to the documentation for Cloud Logging by using the **LEARN** option.

- **Query Builder:** This is the space where we can craft our queries about the received log data. A query is a string containing an expression that is used to filter out logs based on it. Query Builder is located on the top of the window and below the Action bar, as shown in the following screenshot:

Figure 14.10: *Query Builder in Cloud Logging*

A simple example for a query is as follows:

```
[FIELD_NAME] [OP] [VALUE]
```

`resource.type = "k8s.container"`

During the query matching, a comparison takes place with the help comparison operator (=) between the entered value (**k8s.container**) and the entered pathname of a field in a pool of log entries (**resource.type**). As a result, we shall receive log entries of the **k8s.container** resource type in the Query Result window.

Let us understand query building by creating a short query to get the logs of any node of our **gke-cluster-001** cluster. Navigate to the Query Builder pane and build the following query:

`resource.type= "k8s.node"`

`resource.labels.node_name=""gke-gke-cluster-001-default-pool-2ec1979d-mh11"`

When you run this query, the outcome looks like the following screenshot:

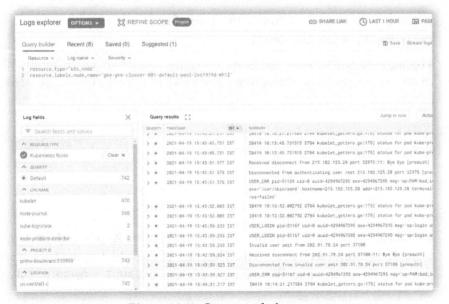

Figure 14.11: *Outcome of a log query*

- **Log fields:** It is a simple, graphical way to query logs. The queries that we build in Query Builder are populated and updated in **Log fields**. We can also add fields from Log Fields to Query Builder to narrow down the query results.

The layout of **Log fields** looks like the following screenshot:

Figure 14.12: Log Field pane in Cloud Logging

If there is no query defined, the Logs Field will display queries by the `resource.type` and `severity`.

- **Histogram:** As the name suggests, this pane lets us visualize the distribution of logs over time. The **Histogram** pane looks like the following screenshot:

Figure 14.13: Histogram pane in Cloud Logging

Each histogram bar represents a time range on the X-axis and the number of log entries received on the Y-axis. The color of these histogram bars represents the severity of the log. **Blue bars** represent `DEFAULT,  DEGUB,  INFO,  AND`

NOTICE logs. Yellow bars represent WARNING logs. **Red bars** represent ERROR, CRITICAL, ALERT, AND EMERGENCY logs. We can change the timeline by moving forward or backward by using the forward (>) and backward (<) arrows. Also, we can expand or narrow down the range of data shown between a timestamp by zooming in and out.

- **Query Results:** This is the showdown pane that we will use most of the time while working with various log entries. Query Results pane looks like the following screenshot:

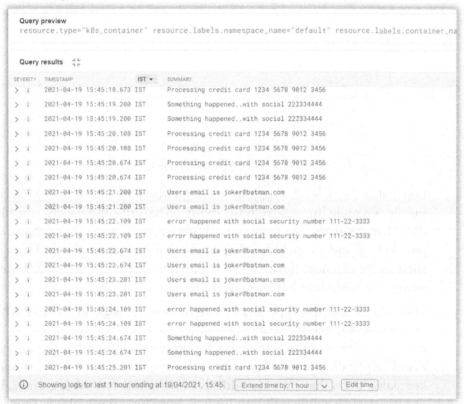

Figure 14.14: Query result pane in Cloud Logging

Query results pane is now streaming logs as a result of a matched query. According to that query, we requested for logs of containers (**resource.type**) named as test-logger (**resource.labels.container_name**) and are running in the default namespace (**resource.labels.namespace_name**) of the cluster named gke-cluster-001 (**resource.labels.cluster_name**). These are the random log entries generated by the test-logger deployment.

When we expand these log entries, the outcome looks like the following screenshot:

Figure 14.15: *Expanded Log entry in Query results*

Log entries in Cloud Logging are structured in JSON format because it provides a more human-friendly approach to write and handle multiline log data than a simple text format. Each log entry is made up of metadata and payload. Metadata includes the standard information about the log entry, such as its creation time, whereas payload is the event (represented as a string or a hash) that has been recorded.

There can be multiple types of payloads for a single log entry. The **textPayload** field shows the event (the message string) that has been recorded by this log entry. The **insertId** is a 16 character unique identifier for the log entry to avoid duplication among log entries sharing similar values. The **labels** are key:value pairs that provide additional details about the log entry. We can use these labels while building up the query for a particular **resource.type** to narrow down the query results. The severity of this entry falls under INFO, which means that it represents routine information about the process. If you want to know more about different log severities and what they represent, check out the link of its documentation in the note-box at the end of the page.

Note:

Types of Log Severities in GCP:

https://cloud.google.com/logging/docs/reference/v2/rest/v2/LogEntry#logseverity

Logs dashboard

Following the trend, we even have log dashboards to get a high-level overview of systems running on Google Cloud. It provides us with different bar charts representing the severity of each cloud resource over an interval of time. There can be occurrences where we will need to integrate various Google Cloud API to our Kubernetes workload to deploy the applications successfully. Monitoring K8s resources alongside the used Google Cloud resources can expedite the process of initial analysis. This dashboard primarily focuses on the following set of cloud resources:

- Compute Engine
- App Engine
- GKE
- Cloud Load Balancing
- Cloud SQL
- BigQuery

Following are the charts for GKE cluster logs, GKE cluster errors, GKE container logs, and GKE container errors:

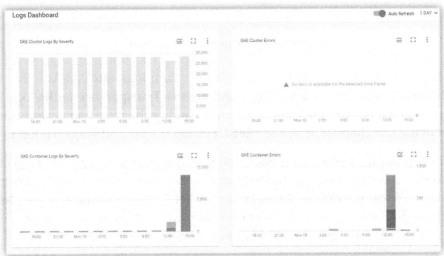

Figure 14.16: Cloud Logging Logs Dashboard

All of these charts can be downloaded in PNG format for easy shareability. In the GKE container errors chart, all running containers of the GKE cluster are represented here with unique colors. This way, we can quickly locate the resource type and its name and can further take the necessary measure.

Logs Router

As we have seen earlier, Logs router works as a gateway between the Log data source and Cloud Logging service. It performs checks on received log data against the predefined Sinks and decides on whether to forward the log entry to Cloud Logging to store.

For every Google Cloud project, Cloud Logging creates two log buckets to store logs: **_Default** and **_Required**. Also, It creates two log sinks named **_Default** and **_Required** to route logs to the respective log buckets. We can create user-defined log buckets and their corresponding sinks to get more control over logs' routing and storage process.

When we click on the Logs Router tab on the Cloud Operations Logging homepage, the home page for Logs Router looks like the following screenshot:

Figure 14.17: Homepage of Logs router

_Required log bucket is used to store critical system logs, such as Admin Activity Audit Logs, System Event audit logs, and Access Transparency audit logs. These logs are retained for 400 days, and we cannot modify the retention period. Also, we cannot make any changes or delete **_Required** log bucket and sinks related to it.

On the other hand, **_Default** log bucket ingests (stores) those log entries rejected by **_Required** log bucket. Logs in **_Default** log bucket are retained for a flexible period of 30 days. We cannot delete **_Default** log bucket, but we can modify the **_Default** sink. If we do not want to create any user-defined log buckets for our GKE cluster logs, we can configure the **_Default** log bucket as the log storage solution.

Monitoring in GKE

Monitoring may sound like a luxury when you run a single pod or two. Still, as the application scales up, the monitoring dashboards are the most comprehensive way to observe the application performance and resource status. They also help us layout a big picture that can enhance the precision of analysis and reduce the chances of misleading interpretations of the situation.

Monitoring resources of a Kubernetes cluster allows easing the management of the containerized applications by keeping track of the utilization of various cluster resources such as CPU, memory, and storage. We can set up alerts to send notifications when any resource consumption reaches the critical limit, when the resource is underutilized, or when due to any reason, pods or nodes are unavailable.

For GKE clusters, we have the Cloud Monitoring service of the Cloud Operation suite. When Cloud Monitoring is integrated into the GKE cluster, it collects various data of Kubernetes workloads, the GKE cluster, and different Google Cloud API used by the GKE cluster. Just as Cloud Logging, we can navigate to the dedicated Cloud Monitoring homepage, which looks like the following screenshot:

Figure 14.18: Homepage of Cloud Monitoring

Cloud Monitoring consists of various services and features to support and optimize the overall resource monitoring process, and they are as follows:

- Dashboards
- Services
- Metrics explorer
- Alerting
- Uptime checks
- Groups

Dashboards

Dashboards are the simplest and most optimum way nowadays to view and analyze critical metric data. Cloud Monitoring comes with a set of predefined dashboards for a few standard Google Services. Also, we can set up custom dashboards to display custom resources with the selected metrics. We can also create dashboards from configuration files. The default view for the dashboard home page looks like the following screenshot:

Figure 14.19: List of preexisting monitoring dashboards

These pre-designed dashboards are available (including the GKE dashboard) for some critical Google Cloud resources, such as VM instances, Disks, and Firewalls. What interests us the most is the GKE dashboard. When we navigate to it, it looks like the following screenshot:

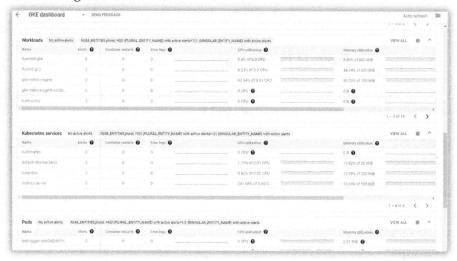

Figure 14.20: Homepage of GKE cluster dashboard

All the Kubernetes resources, such as workloads, Kubernetes services, namespaces, nodes, pods, and containers, have been listed here with the associated resource information. For example, all the running nodes in our GKE clusters are listed here with different matrics and current values. The default metrics for any resource are CPU and memory utilization, disk utilization, Error logs, Container restart count, and associated alerts. When we expand this panel, it looks like the following screenshot:

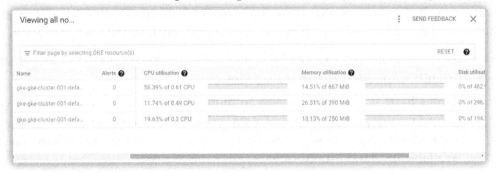

Figure 14.21: CPU and Memory utilization monitoring of GKE cluster nodes

As we expand details of any of these nodes, the outcome looks like the following screenshot:

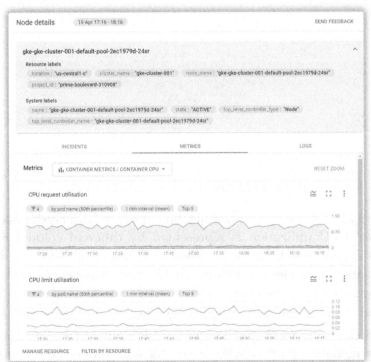

Figure 14.22: Expanded details of CPU and memory utilization of one of the GKE cluster nodes

For any Kubernetes node, the most critical aspect that needs continuous monitoring should be its CPU and memory utilization. Containers scheduled on cluster nodes request CPU and memory resources from the node's resource pool. When these requests exceed the set limit, the node might reach the OOM state, leading to the termination of many application containers to free up node resources. It may affect the performance of the application due to the removal of some essential containers. To avoid such situations, we can take the help of Cloud Monitoring to monitor the node's resources and make quick decisions to avoid any harm to the application.

Dashboards use different types of charts known as dashboard widgets to represent data. Currently, supported charts are as follows:

- **Line Chart:** A line chart is used to monitor changes in resource data over a continuous period. Different data values are plotted as points that are connected using line segments. Following is the sample line chart that is available in Cloud Monitoring:

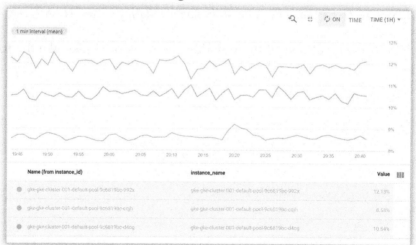

Figure 14.23: Line chart in Cloud Monitoring

Figure 14.23 shows the CPU utilization of every GKE cluster node. All three nodes' CPU utilization is represented by different colored lines against the defined period. The X-axis shows the time, and Y-axis shows the CPU utilization in numeric % values. There are multiple configurations, such as getting an x-ray version of a colored chart or displaying statistical measures of the resource available to modify this chart according to user requirements.

- **Stacked area chart:** A stacked area chart is similar to the line chart regarding how the data is plotted in the chart. The only difference is that it is used to plot quantitative data values over a period where they are represented with a different band of color.

The following screenshot shows the sample stacked area chart in Cloud Monitoring:

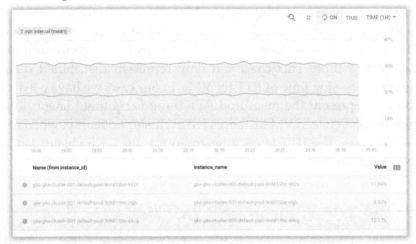

Figure 14.24: Stacked area chart in Cloud Monitoring

The stacked area chart is helpful when we want to represent the change in the volume of data over a period rather than focusing on individual data values:

- **Stacked Bar chart:** The stacked bar chart is the extension of the standard bar chart. Each bar of the standard bar chart is divided into sub-bars, stacked on top of the other sub-bar, and represents different categorical variables. The following screenshot is an example of a stacked bar chart representing the CPU utilization values of different GKE cluster nodes:

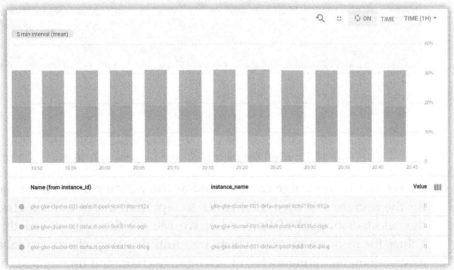

Figure 14.25: Stacked bar chart in Cloud Monitoring

Each bar in *Figure 14.25* is divided into three sub-bars (filled with different colors) representing the CPU utilization of each cluster node.

- **Heatmap chart:** The heatmap chart is a two-dimensional graphical representation to display the distribution of resource metric data over time. The color-coding method is used to represent the concentration of data values at a time. This chart can only represent distributed data such as server processing time or RTT for VMs. In our case, we have used a heatmap chart to represent the measured RTT (round-trip-time) latency over a TCP connection between VM instances (GKE cluster nodes) spawned in Google's data centers. The RTT latency heatmap for our GKE cluster looks like the following screenshot:

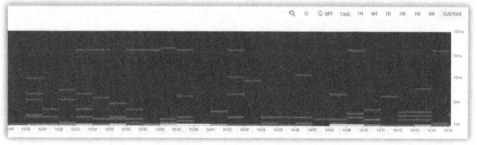

Figure 14.26: Heatmap chart in Cloud Monitoring

The heatmap chart uses different colors to represent a range of data based on the selected color theme. A white overline percentile line represents data covered under different data ranges (50th to 90th percentile).

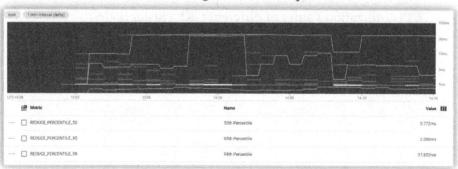

Figure 14.27: Heatmap chart with overline percentile line

- **Gauge chart:** The gauge chart is used as the warning and danger indicator for the resources. It uses color codes to represent the resource metrics over the selected interval of time. Also, we can set the color-coded threshold values for resource metrics. There are multiple gauge charts available such as speedometer, rating meter, quarter gauge chart, and liner gauge chart.

The following screenshot is an example of the speedometer gauge chart used to represent the mean value of CPU usage of all VM instances in the cloud project:

VM Instance - CPU usage [MEAN]

19.9

Figure 14.28: Gauge chart in Cloud Monitoring

There are two threshold values for the CPU usage metric in this gauge chart: warning (represented as a yellow color arc) and danger (represented as a red color arc). If the CPU usage exceeds the soft limit, its value shows in the yellow part, and if it crossed the hard limit, we get notified about it when it reaches the red part.

Services

Service monitoring is another essential aspect that helps us to keep our applications optimized and robust. In the present times, when most organizations are migrating to container-based application development and deployments to develop their products, we need an optimal solution that monitors different metrics of the services running our applications.

Cloud Monitoring's Service monitoring feature helps us monitor services through different service monitoring components such as SLI (Service-level Indicator), SLO (Service-level object), and error budget. It has been a market practice that when a company offers a service – whether it is through the cloud or traditional infrastructure, it provides its clients with a Service-level Agreement (SLA) that defines various service levels (metrics) regarding the service.

SLA is a legal agreement between the service provider and the client on mutually agreed conditions which may consist of legal consequences that both parties can face if they fail to live up to the promises. If SLA is the formal agreement between the service provider and consumer, SLO is an agreement within the SLA about a specific service metric. SLO is more of a consumer-friendly agreement that works as a guideline for the developing team to deliver the most reliable services to their consumers. The clearer the SLO is, the easier it becomes to understand for developers.

To decide the success of the SLO, we need a mechanism that can check whether the service levels are under safe limits, and this mechanism is known as the SLI. SLI shows the primary aspect that has been set as the performance goal for the service. In Cloud Monitoring, we can set SLI and define a service metric for that SLI to be monitored. There are three default metrics available: Availability measures how available the service was to users, Latency measures how quickly the service responded to the user requests, and custom metrics. After setting up these metrics, we need to set up the performance goal for the service. It ranges between 0 and 100%, and you can set up this value based on the performance restrictions you want to impose.

Most services have a loose but satisfactory value set as the performance goal based on the available service resources. As the demand increase, we can set a more strict performance goal to improve the quality of the service. *Figure 14.29* shows the custom SLO created for the kube-system service of the K8s cluster along with the monitoring data of its various resource metrics:

Figure 14.29: Service-level Object (SLO) for a Kubernetes service

Metrics explorer

When we want to monitor a specific resource and its metrics quickly at a particular time interval, we can use Metrics Explorer. It can help us create, save, share, and configure different charts for various resource metrics not mentioned in the main dashboard. The Metrics Explorer GUI is primarily divided into two parts: configuration pane and chart pane. Following is the screenshot of a Metric explorer webpage with a resource query and its representation as a line chart:

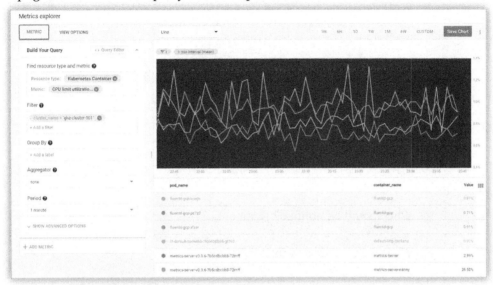

Figure 14.30: *Visualization of a resource query in Metrics Explorer*

The left pane can select the resource and its metrics and a few more configuration details. The right pane shows the Line chart created by observing the set resource metrics for the configured period. We can save this chart and make it available on our dashboard, and we can also share this chart by creating a shareable URL. We can also set a few chart-related options such as the color mode, a comparison between the past chart, and the representation of any set threshold value.

Alerting policy

Alerting policy is a combination of conditions that trigger alerts and actions (such as a notification by email) to take when such triggers occur for the concerned resource. Alerting functions perform a continuous examination of attributes, capacity, and performance of resources. An alert policy consists of a list of actions to take when alerts are received. Typically, these actions send a notification message to mobile devices, slack channels, emails, webhooks, SMS, and Cloud Pub/Sub service.

The following screenshot shows the homepage to create a new alerting policy for kubernetes containers of our K8s cluster:

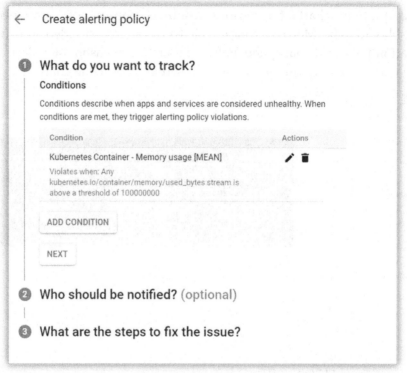

Figure 14.31: Creation page for alerting policy for Kubernetes containers

There is a four steps process that we need to follow to create an alert policy for any Kubernetes or Google Cloud resource:

- The target resource
- A set of alert conditions for the target resource
- Actions to take against the alerts
- Notifications channels

In *Figure 14.31*, we create an alert policy for the resource-type kubernetes containers to watch their memory usage. When you add an alert condition, it asks about the target resource and the metric we want to monitor (just how we mentioned it in the Metrics Explorer). For the next step, we need to set the condition trigger for this alert policy. There are four condition triggers available with the Cloud Monitoring tool:

- Percentage of the time series violation
- Number of time series violation
- All-time series violation
- Any time series violation

These condition triggers define which time series can invoke the trigger of the alert policy. The configuration for our alerting policy is defined in the following screenshot:

Figure 14.32: Alerting policy configuration setup

We can break down the condition for this alerting policy as monitor the most recent mean value of the memory usage by Kubernetes containers, if the memory usage goes above the threshold value (~100MB) at any time, invoke the trigger and send the alert. The preview chart pane shown in *Figure 14.33* represents the threshold value with a dotted red line in the line chart of memory usage by Kubernetes containers:

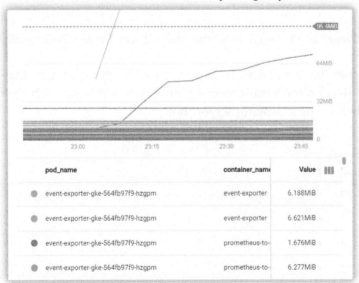

Figure 14.33: Threshold value for the alerting policy

All alert conditions are divided into two types: **metric absence** and **metric threshold**. The type of condition we created with our alert policy is the metric threshold that triggers the alert for the resource metric if its value rises above or falls down a threshold value over a specific period.

On the other hand, metric absence, as the name suggests, triggers the alert for the resource metric when the metric has no data after generating at least one data value over a specific period. After defining the notification channel and naming the alert policy, it looks like the following screenshot:

Figure 14.34: Notification setup and metadata for the alerting policy

Once the alert policy is created, it starts to monitor the configured resource metric and send an alert on the notification channel if its value goes above the threshold value, as shown in the following screenshot:

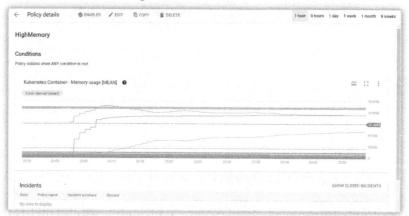

Figure 14.35: Details of the HighMemory alerting policy

When the memory usage metric violates the alert policy, it creates an incident. The alert is sent to the configured notification channel. The following screenshot shows the state of alerting policy after receiving a bunch of policy violations:

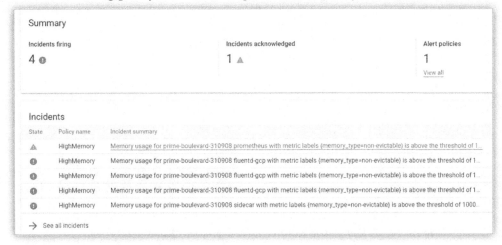

Figure 14.36: List of policy violations and their information

Uptime check

The name of this feature itself explains its functionality. Uptime check is used to send a test request to a resource to check whether it responds. In typical cases, this feature is used to determine the availability of the resource. We can also create an alert policy uptime check to monitor its operation and send alerts if it fails.

Groups

It is another helpful service of Cloud Monitoring that allows grouping a set of resources as a group. For example, we have around 50 K8s containers running on all three cluster nodes, and we want to monitor their memory usage and CPU usage. Creating charts for each container for these two entities can take an enormous amount of our precious time, and it is not a feasible solution over time.

Once we group all kubernetes containers as a single resource group, we can create various charts to monitor their resources with a single query.

The following screenshot shows the group of kubernetes containers and their memory and CPU usage charts:

Figure 14.37: Key metric monitoring of a group of Kubernetes resources

To gain more granular control over these resources, we can also create sub-groups from the parent group. We can also define standard alert policies for the group that sends us the alerts regarding some standard metrics such as over or under memory and CPU resources usage.

Prometheus

Prometheus is an open-sourced system monitoring and alerting toolkit originally built to monitor SoundCloud's (A renowned audio distribution and music sharing platform) microservice architecture-based system. Later on, it graduated from CNCF (Cloud Native Computing Foundation) and now serving as one of the most prominent monitoring solutions for Kubernetes.

Prometheus uses the multi-dimensional data model to store the data as time-series *(A series of data points listed over a period for the same resource metric)* of the resources discovered by service discovery or resource information.

As for the architecture of the Prometheus goes, Prometheus follows the **Pull model** configuration for monitoring a system. Prometheus servers (central data collectors) periodically send requests to get metrics (scrapping) of resources from an instrumented job consisting of several processes (called instances). Instrumented jobs expose resource metrics to Prometheus servers regardless of their locations.

By following the Pull model, the central collector can minimize the burden on target systems to share their metric data periodically.

There is a concept called **Instrumentation** in computer programming, which serves as the foundation of the monitoring process for any resource. Developers instrument the application by adding a few lines of code in its binaries or the source files. This code helps monitor different traits and components, such as taking samples of memory usage over time or record request and response payloads of an HTTP service. Applications getting instrumented can be managed and monitored efficiently by monitoring tools and solutions.

When it comes to Prometheus, applications need to be instrumented using the suitable **client library** from the pool of client libraries of Prometheus. We can choose a client library based on the programming language used to write the application code. The client library is responsible for sending the current state of tracked metrics to the Prometheus servers. But, in some cases where the services do not live long enough to send their metric data, an intermediatory called **Pushgateway** comes to their rescue. It allows these services to send their metric data from their short-lived service-level batch jobs to an intermediatory job and make it available for Prometheus servers for scrapping.

When the Prometheus server scrapes a target, it is labeled with the scraped time series for identification purposes and stored in a local, on-disk time-series database. The stored metric data is grouped into blocks of two hours, where each hour block consists of one or more files that contain all time-series samples for that window of time. The local storage for Prometheus is limited to a single node, but it also offers integration with third-party remote storage solutions. Prometheus also has a functional query language called **PromQL** to query and aggregate the time-series data stored in this database in real-time. The results of these queries can be presented as a graph or viewed as a tabular form in the web UI of Prometheus, known as **PromDash.**

Installing and configuring Prometheus on GKE

One of the easiest ways to install and configure Prometheus for a Kubernetes cluster created on GKE is by cloning the GitHub repository of Prometheus provided by Google Cloud Platform. This repository contains all the necessary configuration files. Execute the following command in the Cloud Shell window:

```
git clone https://github.com/GoogleCloudPlatform/prometheus-stackdriver-gke
```

Once the repository is cloned on the local system, we can navigate into that directory and list out its contents. The list should look like the following screenshot:

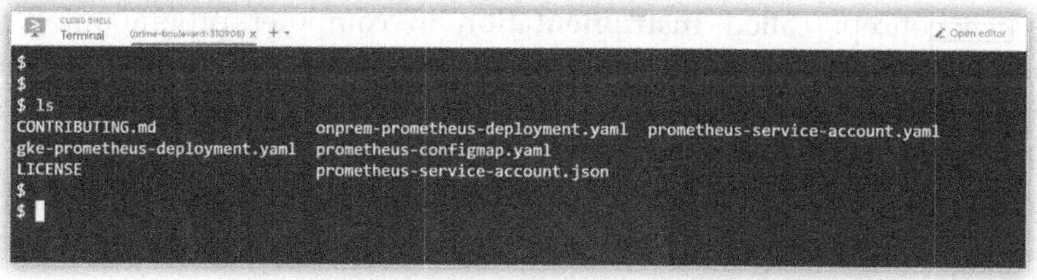

Figure 14.38: *List of configuration files for Prometheus*

As per *Figure 14.38*, we have a deployment YAML to deploy the Prometheus server, a configmap YAML containing configurations for this server, a deployment YAML for deploying the Prometheus server on-premise, and a service account YAML to create a clusterrole and clusterrolebinding for Prometheus kubernetes service.

Before installing the Prometheus on our K8s cluster, we need to create an IAM service account on GCP to grant a few permission to monitor cloud resources by Prometheus. Execute the following command to create a new service account in GCP and name it prometheus-service-account.

```
gcloud iam service-accounts create prometheus --display-name prometheus-
service-account
```

After creating the service account, execute the following commands to store the service account email address and the current GCP project ID in different environment variables for future uses.

```
export PROJECT_ID=$(gcloud info --format='value(config.project)')
```

```
export PROMETHEUS_SA_EMAIL=$(gcloud iam service-accounts list \
                    --filter="displayName:prometheus-service-account" \
                    --format='value(email)')
```

Among all the roles available in GCP, we need to bind the Prometheus with the **monitoring.metricWriter** role lets Prometheus sidecar container write, store, and manage the monitoring data for cloud resources. Execute the following command to bind Prometheus's service account with the **monitoring.metricWriter** role.

```
gcloud projects add-iam-policy-binding ${PROJECT_ID} --role roles/
monitoring.metricWriter --member serviceAccount:${PROMETHEUS_SA_EMAIL}
```

The output of the above command looks like the following screenshot:

Figure 14.39: IAM policy to bind monitoring.metricWriter to Prometheus's service account

GCP's Cloud Monitoring API needs to authenticate the Prometheus sidecar container before granting it access to use the API, and the service account key does it. We need to download the service account key of Prometheus's service account and store it in the working directory.

```
gcloud iam service-accounts keys create $WORKDIR/prometheus-service-account.json --iam-account ${PROMETHEUS_SA_EMAIL}
```

After setting up the roles and permissions for Prometheus on Google cloud, we can install the Prometheus server for our three-node K8s cluster. To keep things simple, we create a dedicated namespace for all Prometheus-related objects. Execute the following command to create a new namespace:

```
kubectl create namespace prometheus
```

We need to create a clusterrole and the clusterrolebinding for the Prometheus Kubernetes service to grant it the permissions to retrieve metrics of all the deployments running in all Kubernetes namespaces. To create this clusterrole and its binding, all we need to do is execute the following command:

```
kubectl apply -f prometheus-service-account.yaml
```

As a result of the preceding command, we get a new service account for Prometheus Kubernetes service, a clusterrole, and a clusterrolebinding for the same service account as shown in the following screenshot:

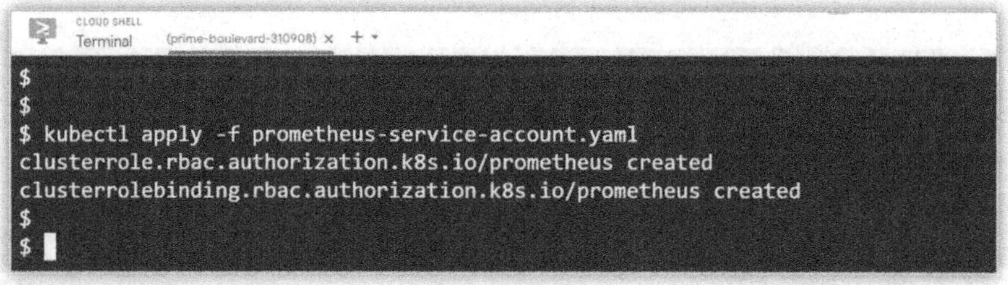

Figure 14.40: *Create clusterrole and Clusterrolebinding for Prometheus's Service account*

The next step is to create the configmap for the Prometheus server. This configmap contains the configuration details for the server's scrape configurations and instrumented job configurations for different Kubernetes objects (nodes and pods) and services (kube-apiserver and kubernetes-cadvisors). We already have cloned the object YAML file for this config, so we need to execute the following command to create this configmap.

```
kubectl apply -f prometheus-configmap.yaml
```

We need to define a few environment variables used in the Prometheus server's deployment manifest according to our requirements. Following are the environment variables and their values, which will be used while deploying the Prometheus server:

```
export KUBE_NAMESPACE=prometheus
```

```
export KUBE_CLUSTER=gke-cluster-001
```

```
export GCP_LOCATION=us-east1-c
```

```
export GCP_PROJECT=$(gcloud info --format='value(config.project)')
```

```
export DATA_DIR=/prometheus
```

```
export DATA_VOLUME=prometheus-storage-volume
```

```
export SIDECAR_IMAGE_TAG=0.8.2
```

```
export PROMETHEUS_VER_TAG=v2.19.3
```

The Prometheus deployment creates a single pod containing two containers: the Prometheus server and the monitoring sidecar. The Prometheus server container collects the metrics from pods making their metrics available for monitoring. The monitoring sidecar container is used to push the collected metrics by the server to the Cloud's Monitoring agent associated with the K8s objects.

To create the Prometheus server deployment, we need to replace the values of the environment variables defined in the object YAML file with the one we declared a while ago. Execute the following command to create a deployment for the Prometheus server with the new configurations.

```
envsubst < gke-prometheus-deployment.yaml | kubectl apply -f -
```

This command creates a Prometheus pod containing two running containers, and if we list out the pods running in the Prometheus namespace, the outcome looks like the following screenshot:

Figure 14.41: Running Prometheus deployment

The Prometheus deployment is running and serving at the container's port **9090**. To visit the PromDash, the Prometheus server's web UI, we need to forward the traffics from the container's port **9090** to the system's port **9090**. Execute the following command to retrieve the name of the Prometheus pod and store it in an environment variable:

```
export PROMETHEUS_POD_GKE=$(kubectl get pods --namespace prometheus -l "app=prometheus-server" -o jsonpath="{.items[0].metadata.name}")
```

After getting the name, execute the following command to perform the port forwarding:

```
kubectl port-forward --namespace prometheus $PROMETHEUS_POD_GKE 9090:9090 >> /dev/null &
```

The outcome looks like the following screenshot:

Figure 14.42: Forward the traffic from Prometheus's gate pod to CloudShell instance

The Cloud Shell's web preview option allows us to visit the server UI by changing the port value from **8080** to **9090**. Once we are done with it, we are navigated to a new browser window serving the PromDash like shown in the following screenshot:

Figure 14.43: Homepage of Prometheus GUI (PromDash)

Prometheus discovers the running resources of the GKE cluster that have successfully exported their metric data for monitoring. Let's check the targets of one of these instrumented jobs, such as kubernetes-apiservers, the outcome looks like the following screenshot:

Figure 14.44: List of targets of an instrumented job in Prometheus

Understanding and working with Service Mesh

In *Chapter 11*, we have seen how Kube-proxy is used to maintain service discovery, cluster IPs, endpoint allotment, and port forwarding across the workloads. For all forms of application we have seen so far, Kube-proxy was very efficient, but in this chapter, we came across a concerning fact. GKE nodes can host over a hundred workload pods!!! Imagine tens of such nodes with hundreds of pods on each one of them, and you are left with a mess of thousands of pods at the mercy of a few dozen kube-proxy instances.

From keeping tabs on crashed and restarted pods to creating or altering Iptables rules for them, Kube-proxy will have its hands full of load irrespective of its vertical scaling provisions. There is a subtle reason behind it. Just how Docker Swarm pales to cater containers at scale because of its fundamental design, Kube-proxy gets weakened with too many pods because it is written with reference to **Nodes**, not **Pods**. This is where **Service Mesh** comes in. It is a network of proxies dedicated to pods instead of nodes. In the case of **Istio** (*it's a service mesh tool for distributed services*), **Sidecar Proxies are created within the scope of pod's isolation with the help of Envoy**(*It's a proxy for distributed services*).

Service mesh is implemented by creating sidecars for each microservice. Sidecar's responsibilities include service-to-service communication, service monitoring, authentication, and authorizations regarding the service and anything that directly affects its microservice. These capabilities of Service mesh technology provide operational control and observability into the behavior of the whole network of distributed microservices of a complex application (cloud-native and on-premise).

As the network of microservices scales in size and complexity, so does its service mesh. The scaling of service mesh leads to difficulties in its operational activities. To address these issues, there are many open-sourced service mesh frameworks such as Istio, Consul Connect, and Linkerd are available for the Kubernetes ecosystem.

Istio is a collaborative project by Lyft, Google, and IBM to provide a fast and secure service mesh to establish inter-service communication for microservice-based applications. Leading Cloud providers such as Google and Microsoft rely upon Istio as their default service mesh solution for Kubernetes Cloud services. Istio makes it easy to establish a network between deployed services with load balancing, authentication, service monitoring, and service-to-service authentication.

Istio service mesh is divided into two parts: Control plane and Data pane. The control plane is responsible for configurations and management of the proxies to route the network traffic. The Data plane comprises a set of proxies deployed as sidecars to route and control the traffic between microservices over a service network. Istio uses Envoy proxy, a high-performance proxy, as a sidecar to mediate traffic in the service mesh. Envoy proxy can perform dynamic service discovery, load balancing, health checks, metrics monitoring, staged rollouts, and fault injection as sidecars.

Istio on the GKE cluster is disabled by default. We can enable it during or after the cluster creation process. When you enable the Istio on GKE, it asks us to choose between two mesh-wide security options: Strict mTLS and Permissive mTLS. If we choose Strict mTLS, Istio enforced a mutual TLS (mTLS) encryption between all services and control plane components unless we override it. Services refuse to accept unencrypted traffic.

If we choose Permmissive mTLS, Istio allows services to accept both encrypted and unencrypted traffic. Just like Strict mTLS, we can also modify the rules that allow unencrypted traffic to services. The test application that we are going to deploy to demonstrate the functionality of Istio may send unencrypted traffic, thus, we need to select the Permissive mTLS mesh security option for our K8s cluster. The selection window for mesh security options for GKE looks like the following screenshot:

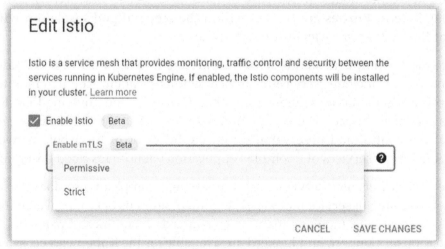

Figure 14.45: Setting up the mesh security option for the GKE cluster

Installation of Istio on GKE is an automated process. We do not need to clone any repository or apply any object configuration YAML file like any other objects seen so far. It is just one click away.

After enabling (installing) Istio on our GKE cluster, the outcome looks like the following screenshot:

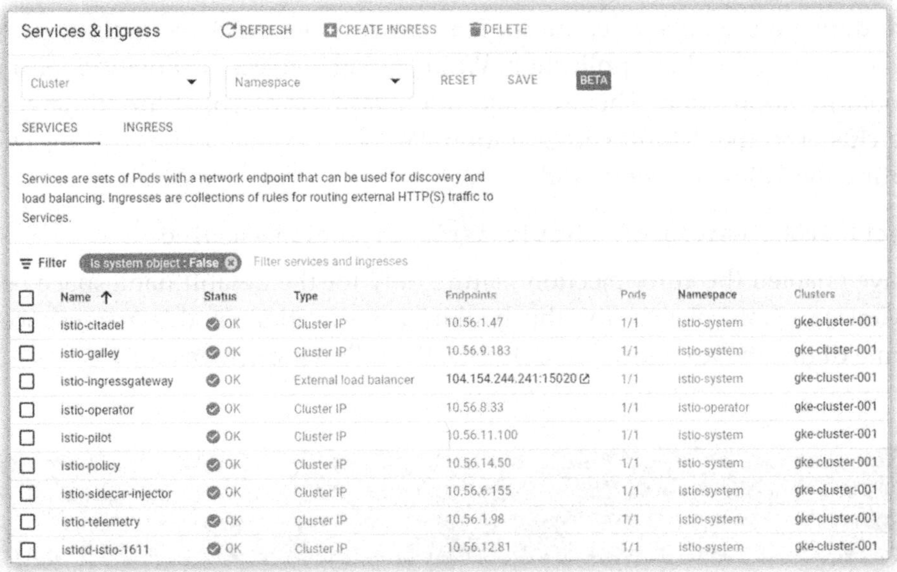

Figure 14.46: List of Istio services running on the GKE cluster

Istio itself is built as a set of microservices performing their designated tasks. When we list out the services running on our GKE cluster, we can find a few services related to Istio. All these services perform different tasks for Istio. For example, **istio-pilot** service is used for service discovery, **istio-gallery** is used for configuration, and **istio-citadel** is used for certificate generation. These microservices are part of Istio's control plane. All of their binaries are packaged in a single binary called **istiod**. For security purposes, **the istio-policy service applies custom policies to enforce rules regarding** traffic limits, access restrictions, and header rewrites and redirects.

In the Istio service mesh, the HTTP/TCP traffic to/from the cluster is managed and distributed by a load balancer called **gateway**. When Istio gets installed on any cloud infrastructure, the cloud provider assigns an external load balancer with a list of exposed ports and routing rules. For GKE clusters, **istio-ingressgateway** load balancer service associated with Kubernetes Ingress provides a flexible and efficient way to handle and distribute incoming traffic and expose the services externally.

Bookinfo Application and Istio

We will understand the functionality of Istio using an exciting example of a book info application comprised of four different microservices written in different programming languages, and they are productpage, details, ratings, and reviews. The final state of this application has a review microservice with three versions: v1, v2, and v3.

Before deploying Istio service mesh, it is essential to inject the sidecar proxy for every microservice of this application. We are going to inject the Envoy sidecar proxy for bookinfo application. The auto-injection feature is disabled for all namespaces of the cluster in the default configuration. We need to enable the auto-injection by executing the following command:

```
kubectl label namespace default istio-injection=enabled
```

We have enabled the auto-injection feature only for the default namespace because we want to create objects for the bookinfo application in this namespace. The outcome of the above command looks like the following screenshot:

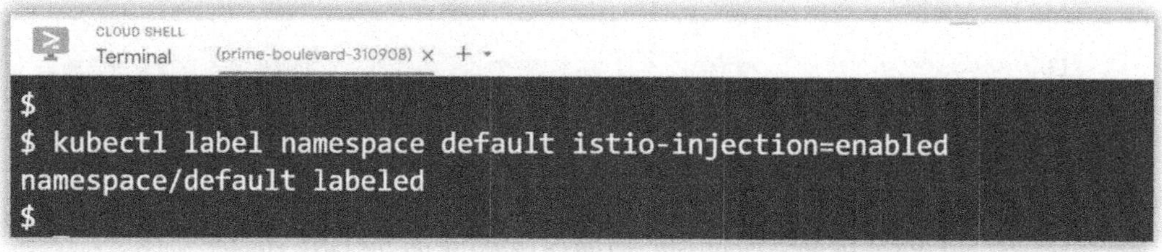

Figure 14.47: Creating a new namespace to isolate workloads for bookinfo application

When we enabled Istio for our GKE cluster, it created a samples directory that contains the YAML file to deploy the bookinfo application. Use the following command to create the Kubernetes objects mentioned in **bookinfo.yaml** file:

```
kubectl apply -f bookinfo.yaml
```

The outcome of the above command looks like the following screenshot:

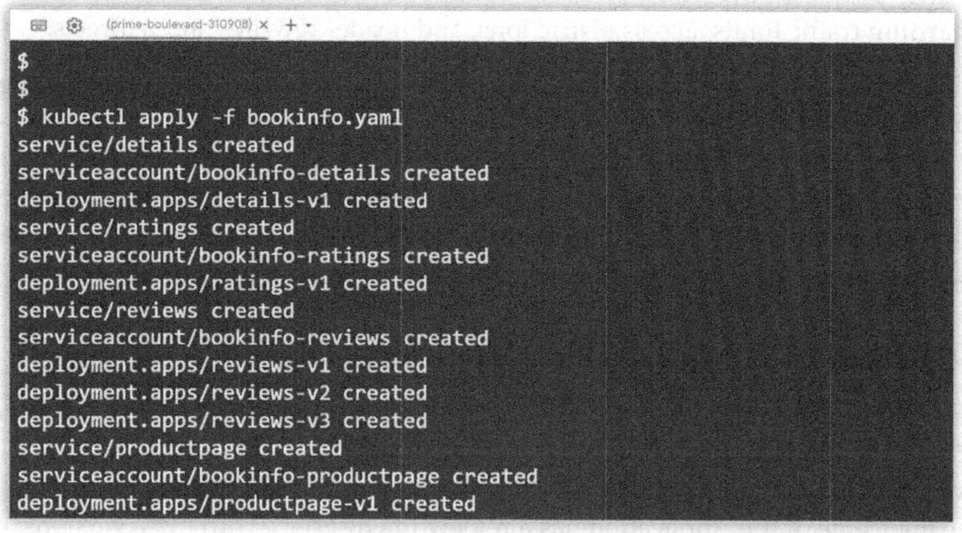

Figure 14.48: Creation of Kubernetes objects for bookinfo application

The `kubectl apply` command on single bookinfo.yaml file defines all four microservices, their service accounts, and deployments at once. If you cannot locate configuration files for the bookinfo application, follow the link mentioned in the note box at the end of this page. To verify their status, list out the services running in the default namespace using the `kubectl get svc` command, the outcome looks like the following screenshot:

```
$
$
$ kubectl get services
NAME          TYPE        CLUSTER-IP      EXTERNAL-IP   PORT(S)     AGE
details       ClusterIP   10.56.7.51      <none>        9080/TCP    59s
kubernetes    ClusterIP   10.56.0.1       <none>        443/TCP     33h
productpage   ClusterIP   10.56.10.12     <none>        9080/TCP    54s
ratings       ClusterIP   10.56.2.23      <none>        9080/TCP    58s
reviews       ClusterIP   10.56.10.137    <none>        9080/TCP    56s
```

Figure 14.49: List of services of bookinfo application

All four services are defined as the ClusterIP service, which means that the bookinfo application is yet to be exposed externally. To make this application externally accessible, we need to create an Istio Ingress Gateway object which maps the path to a route at the edge of the service mesh. Create a new gateway resource by following the YAML file as:

1. apiVersion: networking.istio.io/v1alpha3
2. kind: Gateway
3. metadata:
4.   name: user-gateway
5. spec:
6.   selector:
7.   app: istio-ingressgateway
8.   servers:
9.   - port:
10.   number: 80
11.   name: http
12.   protocol: HTTP
13.   hosts:
14.   - "*"

This Gateway object configuration sets up a proxy that acts as a load balancer exposing port **80** (HTTP) for the Kubernetes ingress. The next step is to set up the **INGRESS_HOST** and **INGRESS_PORT** variables to access this new gateway object. Verify that the istio-ingressgateway service has an external load balancer assigned by the cloud provider, working as the ingress gateway.

Note:

Source code for bookinfo application:

https://github.com/istio/istio/tree/release-1.9/samples/bookinfo/platform/kube

If your cloud provider has assigned a load balancer, there will be an external IP address and a port combination of the load balancer shown with the istio-ingressgateway service, just as shown in the following screenshot:

	Name ↑	Status	Type	Endpoints	Pods	Namespace	Clusters
☐	istio-citadel	✔ OK	Cluster IP	10.56.1.47	1/1	istio-system	gke-cluster-001
☐	istio-galley	✔ OK	Cluster IP	10.56.9.183	1/1	istio-system	gke-cluster-001
☐	istio-ingressgateway	✔ OK	External load balancer	104.154.244.241:15020 ☑	1/1	istio-system	gke-cluster-001
☐	istio-operator	✔ OK	Cluster IP	10.56.8.33	1/1	istio-operator	gke-cluster-001
☐	istio-pilot	✔ OK	Cluster IP	10.56.11.100	1/1	istio-system	gke-cluster-001
☐	istio-policy	✔ OK	Cluster IP	10.56.14.50	1/1	istio-system	gke-cluster-001

Figure 14.50: External Load balancer for Istio-ingressgateway service

Once we are done with the verification, we can set up the environment variables for ingress host and port. Execute the following command to set the variables from the values of the same from the istio-ingressgateway service.

```
export  INGRESS_HOST=$(kubectl  -n  istio-system  get  service  istio-ingressgateway -o jsonpath='{.status.loadBalancer.ingress[0].ip}')
```

```
export  INGRESS_PORT=$(kubectl  -n  istio-system  get  service  istio-ingressgateway -o jsonpath='{.spec.ports[?(@.name=="http2")].port}')
```

```
export SECURE_INGRESS_PORT=$(kubectl -n istio-system get service istio-ingressgateway -o jsonpath='{.spec.ports[?(@.name=="https")].port}')
```

The last step of this process is to create a virtual service bound to the default and the new gateway to control the forwarding arriving at particular gateway ports. Create a new virtual service YAML file to create a new virtual service object who can forward the traffic arrived at the ingress gateway load balancer to the productpage service at port **9080**.

```
1.  apiVersion: networking.istio.io/v1alpha3
2.  kind: VirtualService
3.  metadata:
4.    name: bookinfo
5.  spec:
6.    hosts:
7.    - "*"
8.    gateways:
9.      - bookinfo-gateway
10.     - user-gateway
11.   http:
12.   - match:
13.     - uri:
14.         exact: /productpage
15.     - uri:
16.         prefix: /static
17.     - uri:
18.         exact: /login
19.     - uri:
20.         exact: /logout
21.     - uri:
22.         prefix: /api/v1/products
23.     route:
24.     - destination:
25.         host: productpage
26.         port:
27.           number: 9080
```

After creating the object YAMLs for the ingress gateway object and the virtual service, we create them using the following commands:

```
kubectl apply -f istio-gateway.yaml
kubectl apply -f virtual-service.yaml
```

After receiving the confirmation of these object creations, it is time to check whether we can access the bookinfo application outside of the cluster. We already have the external load balancer IP address and the destination path/productpage. Write the IP address and the destination path combination in a new web browser window and send the request to access the application. The outcome of this process looks like the following screenshot:

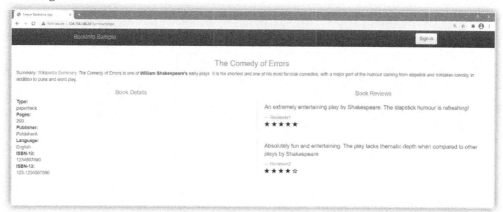

Figure 14.51: Homepage of bookinfo application

All four microservices: details, ratings, reviews, and the productpage are serving seamlessly to the request made from the outside of the cluster. For the GKE cluster with the enabled monitoring and logging support, the Istio stackdriver adapter is installed along with its other core components. The adapter is used to send resource metrics and logging data to the Google Cloud Monitoring and Cloud logging APIs, providing observability of the service mesh. We can use the Google Operation suits monitoring and logging tool such as dashboard, explorers to monitor and visualize the received service mesh data.

Helm

After observing the time-tested microservice architecture, many IT companies and tech vendors migrate from the pure monolithic approach to a hybrid approach (monolithic and microservice architectures) for app development. With this new approach, developing such heavy applications with support services becomes a tedious job for developers. Many open-sourced tools that we studied in this chapter were created with a common goal: To make working with Kubernetes hassle-free. One more open-sourced tool that makes developers' and clients' lives peaceful with its offerings is Helm.

Helm is the package manager for Kubernetes that allows developers and operators

(DevOps people) to efficiently package, deploy, and manage Kubernetes applications on the K8s cluster. Helm was developed with the combined efforts of Deis (a container tool company owned by Microsoft) and Google, and it is now a part of the CNCF family.

In Kubernetes, every object or workload used to develop the application can be created by defining the object's configurations in a YAML file. As the complexity of the application increases, the number of different objects required to develop such an application also increases, which results in lots of YAML files. If we want to make any changes in the object's configuration, such as changing the port details of a pod, we need to make modifications to that object's YAML file manually. It is indeed a tedious job to look out for that particular YAML file out of hundreds and thousands of files. This is the time where we can leverage Helm.

As we mentioned earlier, Helm is a package manager for Kubernetes. It does what it is supposed to do. It packages YAML files related to a set of Kubernetes resources in a package known as the **chart**. Helm functions like any other package managers that we know such as yum for CentOS or apt for Ubuntu. It can download Kubernetes supported software packages, install the software from the YAML files, configure the deployments, automatically update the software version, and many other tasks that other package managers can do.

Helm is mainly made up of two components: Helm Client and Helm library. Helm client is a command-line client used by the users for local chart development, repository management, communicating with the Helm library, and release management.

Helm library provides the necessary assistance to create, install, manage, and uninstall helm charts in a Kubernetes cluster by communicating with Kubernetes APIs over REST requests. Before Helm 3.0.0, another server component known as Tiller was responsible for communication between the Helm and Kubernetes APIs. When Kubernetes made RBAC the default mode for authorization, Tiller was replaced by Helm library with less focus on Helm-related authorizations tasks.

The core of the Helm package manager is Helm Chart. As we stated earlier, it is a collection of files to describe a related set of Kubernetes resources. On the host system, charts are represented by a file directory containing a set of files. For example, the chart Jenkins is represented as **/jenkins** file directory on the host system.

We are going to understand Helm's functionality by installing Jenkins on our GKE cluster using Helm and a Jenkins Helm chart. We can start by cloning the repository for the configuration files for Jenkins from Github by executing the following command in Cloud Shell:

https://github.com/GoogleCloudPlatform/continuous-deployment-on-kubernetes.git

As a result of the above command's execution, a new directory/`continuous-deployment-on-kubernetes` is created, containing files for the Jenkins setup on Kubernetes and the Jenkins chart. The list looks like the following screenshot:

Figure 14.52: List of Jenkins configuration files and sample application files

The **/sample-app** directory contains the YAML files for all the objects needed to deploy a working Jenkins deployment. You can visit the GitHub repository we cloned to get more information about the contents of these files. The next step is to install Helm on our Kubernetes cluster. We are going to install Helm from its binary file. We can do so by using a software package known as wget to retrieve set up files for Helm version 3.2.1 for Linux AMD 64 architecture by sending the HTTP GET request to Helm's servers. We can accomplish this task by the following command:

wget https://get.helm.sh/helm-v3.2.1-linux-amd64.tar.gz

The outcome of the above command gives us a tar file containing the setup file for the Helm version 3.2.1. After extracting content from this tar file using the tar zxfv command, the outcome looks like the following screenshot:

Figure 14.53: Extracted Helm installation binary file

All the contents of the **helm-v3.2.1-linux-amd64.tar.gz** are extracted and put in a new directory called **/linux-amd64**. To start using Helm, we need to copy the binary file of helm from the **/linux-amd64** to the local path where binaries for all the applications are located. Execute the following command to accomplish this task (the **pwd** is **/linux-amd64**).

```
mv helm /usr/local/bin/helm
```

After moving the binary, we should be good to go to add a chart repository. Just as Docker Hub is the one-stop solution to find Docker Images for many popular applications, Helm has an Artifact Hub with several standard charts for many popular applications such as Jenkins, Datadog. Consul, Terraform, etc. This feature is still in beta, so a few charts are available for use, but it will grow with time. The Helm chart for Jenkins is available on Artifact Hub, and we will use it to install Jenkins on Kubernetes by Helm.

We can execute helm commands by executing its binary. Execute the following command to get the version of the installed Helm:

```
./helm version
```

Figure 14.54: Helm version information

To use this chart, we need to set up a stable repository on our cluster. To do so, use the helm command line and execute the following command:

```
helm repo add jenkinsci https://charts.jenkins.io
```

After setting up the Jenkins repository, perform the update command to refresh the chart details on that particular chart repository. If there are any updates in Jenkins charts, such as version change, it gets updated by this **update** command:

```
helm repo update
```

The outcome of the above commands looks like the following screenshot:

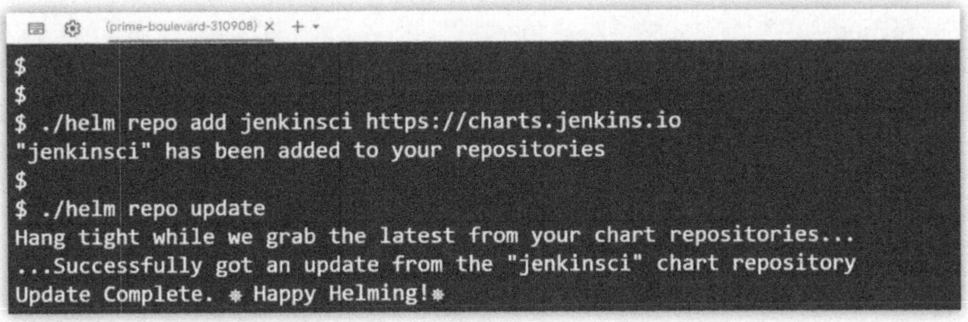

Figure 14.55: Creation of Helm repository for Jenkins chart

After setting up the Jenkins chart repository, we can see a file called **values.yaml** is added in our working directory. Values are one of the built objects in Helm, which is used to define the default configurations for the chart. We can add or override these values as per the requirements. The following screenshot shows the content of the values.html file that we got for our cluster:

```
1.  master:
2.    installPlugins:
3.      - kubernetes:latest
4.      - workflow-job:latest
5.      - workflow-aggregator:latest
6.      - credentials-binding:latest
7.      - git:latest
8.      - google-oauth-plugin:latest
9.      - google-source-plugin:latest
10.     - google-kubernetes-engine:latest
11.     - google-storage-plugin:latest
12.   resources:
13.     requests:
14.       cpu: "50m"
15.       memory: "1024Mi"
16.     limits:
17.       cpu: "1"
18.       memory: "3500Mi"
19.   javaOpts: "-Xms3500m -Xmx3500m"
20.   serviceType: ClusterIP
21. agent:
22.   resources:
23.     requests:
24.       cpu: "500m"
25.       memory: "256Mi"
```

```
26.    limits:
27.      cpu: "1"
28.      memory: "512Mi"
29. persistence:
30.  size: 100Gi
31. serviceAccount:
32.  name: cd-jenkins
```

We are using GCP as the cloud provider and GKE to create and manage our Kubernetes cluster, so we need to add a few GCP-related specifications to Jenkins's **values.yaml** file to make the installation process smoother and successful. The values that we added in this file are the requested CPU and memory details, which plugins to install, which service account to use for installation, and so on.

After setting up the chart repository and the **values.yaml** file, we can install Jenkins for the Helm chart by executing the following command:

```
./helm install cd-jenkins -f jenkins/values.yaml stable/jenkins --version
2.6.4 --wait
```

The release's name is set to cd-jenkins, and we can set up a new name for every new release. We have provided the configurations in the values.yaml file and set the version of the to be installed Jenkins container image to 2.6.4. **--wait** flag is used to display the entire installation process in detail on the terminal screen. After the Jenkins is installed, the outcome looks like the following screenshot:

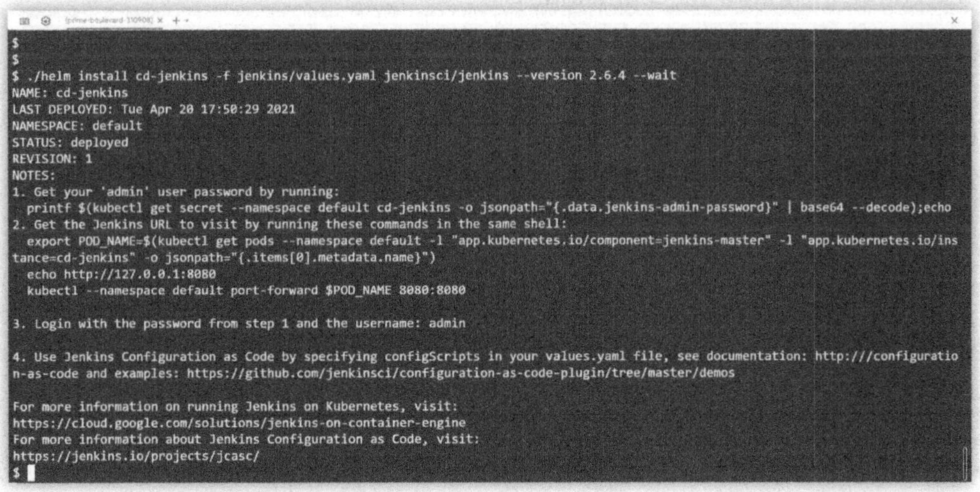

Figure 14.56: Installation of Jenkins using helm chart

At the end of the installation, we are left with a few Kubernetes workloads and a list of instructions to figure out some crucial details like Login account details, Jenkins GUI URL, and Jenkins documentation references. When we list out the Kubernetes services using **kubectl get svc** command for the default namespace, the outcome looks like the following screenshot:

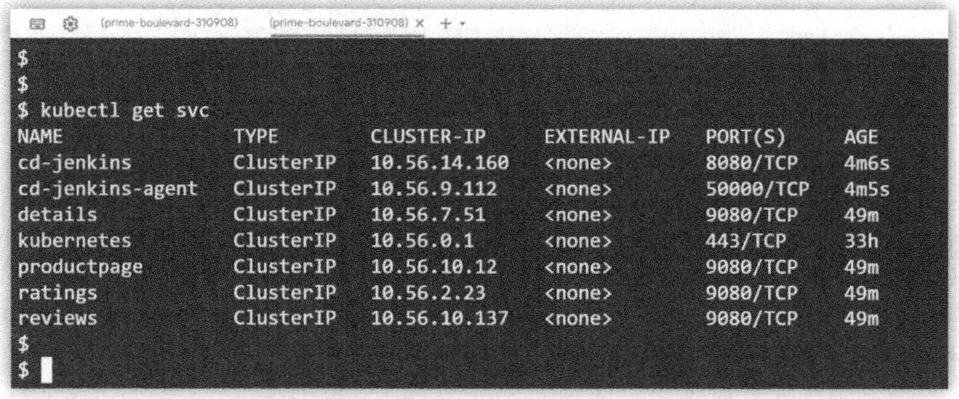

Figure 14.57: Running Jenkins and Jenkins agent services

Jenkin services (**cd-jenkins** and **cd-jenkins-agent**) exposes the Jenkin deployments on ports **8080** and **50000** within the Kubernetes cluster. So, any pods matching with the services' selector get exposed on the mentioned ports. All the Jenkins pods such as builder, agent, and UI are accessible only inside the Kubernetes cluster. To connect to the pod that can serve the Jenkin UI component, we need to forward the traffic from the UI pod to port **8080** of the instance running the Cloud Shell. Extract the details about the Jenkins URL from the pod, and store it in an environment variable by executing the following command:

export POD_NAME=$(kubectl get pods -l "app.kubernetes.io/component=jenkins-master" -o jsonpath="{.items[0].metadata.name}")

After setting the variable, use the following **kubectl port-forward** command to forward traffic from Jenkins UI pod's port 8080 to Cloud Shell's port 8080.

kubectl port-forward $POD_NAME 8080:8080 >> /dev/null &

After doing this task, we are all set to visit the Jenkins UI. All we need to do is click on the web preview button on Cloud shell and select preview on port **8080**, this leads us to a new browser window, which looks like the following screenshot:

Figure 14.58: Homepage of Jenkins

The Jenkins set-up is ready, and you can use it to set up CI/CD release flow. Jenkins was initially developed as a Continuous Integration centric tool but the community usage guided its development to become an all-rounder. Another such tool used as a complete CI/CD pipeline manager is Spinnaker. You can choose either of them depending on the preferences and requirements of your project, and we will look at CI/CD from Spinnakers's perspective to maintain the diversity in the book.

Continuous Delivery using Spinnaker on GKE

Spinnaker is an open-sourced, multi-cloud continuous delivery platform for releasing software updates. Developed by Netflix and extended by Google, Microsoft, Oracle, and Pivotal, Spinnaker was the replacement of Netflix's Asgard, a web-based cloud management and deployment tool to simplify the delivery of Netflix service on AWS. Asgard indeed helped Netflix to liberate its development and production teams from dwelling too much into AWS specifics by introducing the notion of clusters, applications, naming conventions, and various deployment options, but Asgard had a few shortcomings.

First And Foremost, it was designed to support only the AWS platform making its adoption difficult for other cloud platforms. Furthermore, people outside the Netflix organization could not leverage Asgard to its full potential due to permission issues. It led people on a spree to fork the Asgard source code and make changes in the source code suited to their development environments. Such frequent changes in the source code led to its fragmentation that caused Netflix some severe troubles. As a result of such events, the centralizing team and the Edge Center API teams joined their forces to create a more reliable, pluggable, fast, and has multi-cloud support called Spinnaker.

Spinnaker allows users to create pipelines representing the product's delivery process, starting from creating the product's deployable assets to their deployment in the production environment. The pipeline stages can be run serially or parallelly and can be triggered manually or by an event. Spinnaker also provides the capability for repeatable automated deployments, multi-cloud support, and application and cluster management services. Unlike Asgard, Spinnaker aims to make it easier to extend and enhance the cloud deployment models to eliminate the requirement of forking its source code for customization.

Before installing and configuring Spinnaker on Google Cloud Platform, a couple of requirements should be fulfilled. We need to create a new GKE cluster with the following requirements:

- minimum 4vCPU and 12 GB RAM
- Ubuntu 14.04
- Enable VPC based traffic routing (Alias IP)

To fulfill the mentioned minimum system requirement while creating the GKE cluster, we need to change the machine type for the nodes to n1-standard-4 (4vCPU, 15GB memory) as shown in the following screenshot:

Figure 14.59: GKE cluster nodes' configuration

To fulfill another system requirement, we need to navigate to the Networking page of the node pool of the GKE cluster and enable the VPC-based traffic routing as shown in the following screenshot:

Figure 14.60: Enable the VPC-native traffic for the GKE cluster

To installation process of Spinnaker on Google Cloud Platform is easy to understand and quick to perform. Google Marketplace provides a wide range of enterprise-grade applications specially curated for the Google Cloud Platform. To install Spinnaker for Google Cloud Platform, go to **Navigation Menu | Products Marketplace** and search for `Spinnaker` in the search box. The result leads us to the homepage of Spinnaker with its installation details as shown in the following screenshot:

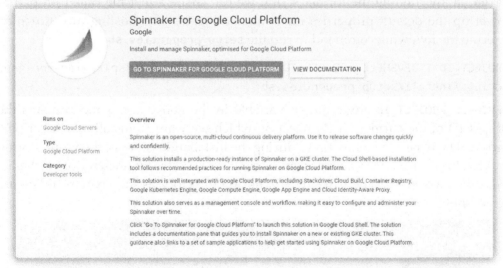

Figure 14.61: GCP's tailored version of Spinnaker available in Google's marketplace

By clicking on **Go to Spinnaker for Google Cloud Platform**, GCP provisions a Cloud Shell machine and clones a repository containing the configuration files for a production-grade Spinnaker on it. We can connect to this machine by opening up the Cloud shell terminal window shown in the following screenshot:

Figure 14.62: Cloning process of Spinnaker's configuration files to the Cloud Shell instance

This cloned repository contains source codes and shell scripts to set up GCP-related resources (GKE, Cloud Storage Buckets, Cloud Functions, Memorystore, and Service Accounts) and services (Cloud Build) to run and manage Spinnaker successfully on GCP. To proceed with the Spinnaker installation process, navigate to the directory containing the install scripts at **~/cloudshell_open/spinnaker-for-gcp/scripts/install**.

The installation directory contains two shell scripts: **setup_properties.sh** and **setup.sh**. By running the former script, we can create a text file called properties to set up the default properties for Spinnaker against the hosting infrastructure. Execute the following command to run the **setup_properties.sh**:

PROJECT_ID=${DEVSHELL_PROJECT_ID}   ~/cloudshell_open/spinnaker-for-gcp/
scripts/install/setup_properties.sh

DEVSHELL_PROJECT_ID environment variable in the above command contains the project ID of the current GCP project on which we want to install Spinnaker. The project ID will be used many times during the installation process; therefore, storing it as a value of an environment variable is convenient. Once the shell script finishes its execution, we receive a new file in the **/install** directory, as shown in the following screenshot:

```
$
$ ls
instructions.txt   provision-spinnaker.md   setup_properties.sh   spinnakerAuditLog
properties         quick-install.yml        setup.sh
```

Figure 14.63: List of Spinnaker's configuration and installation scripts

The newly created properties file contains a list of environment variables used to define the default properties that need to be considered during the installation of Spinnaker. The content of the property file looks like the following screenshot:

```
 properties

 1    #!/usr/bin/env bash
 2
 3    # This file is generated just once per Spinnaker installation, prior to running setup.sh.
 4    # You can make changes to this file before running setup.sh for the first time.
 5    # If setup.sh is interrupted, you can run it again at any point and it will finish any incomplete steps.
 6    # Do not change this file once you have run setup.sh for the first time.
 7    # If you want to provision a new Spinnaker installation, whether in the same project or a different project,
 8    #    simply wait until setup.sh completes and delete this file (or the entire cloned repo) from your
 9    #    Cloud Shell home directory. Then you can relaunch the provision-spinnaker.md tutorial and generate a new
10    #    properties file for use in provisioning a new Spinnaker installation.
11
12    export PROJECT_ID=prime-boulevard-310908
13    export DEPLOYMENT_NAME=gke-cluster-002
14
15    export SPINNAKER_VERSION=1.24.4
16    export HALYARD_VERSION=1.40.0
17
18    export ZONE=us-east1-c
19    export REGION=us-east1
20
21    # The specified network must exist, and it must not be a legacy network.
22    # More info on legacy networks can be found here: https://cloud.google.com/vpc/docs/legacy
23    export NETWORK=default
```

Figure 14.64: Spinnaker's properties file

The primary purpose of the properties file is to provide the installer with the default values of the installation environment. For example, as per the above screenshot, we need to enter our current GCP project ID to PROJECT_ID variable, the name of the cluster on which we want to install Spinnaker in DEPLOYMENT_NAME, the versions of Spinnaker and Halyard (Spinnaker's configuration service) that we want to install, the specified network details on GCP platform that Spinnaker should use, and so on.

Here is the complete properties file generated on our cluster, you can customize the content according to your host infrastructure.

```
1.  export PROJECT_ID=<project_ID>

2.  export DEPLOYMENT_NAME=<cluster_name>

3.

4.  export SPINNAKER_VERSION=1.25.4

5.  export HALYARD_VERSION=1.40.0

6.  export ZONE=us-east1-c

7.  export REGION=us-east1

8.

9.  export NETWORK=default

10. export SUBNET=default
```

```
11. export NETWORK_PROJECT=$PROJECT_ID

12. export NETWORK_REFERENCE=projects/$NETWORK_PROJECT/global/
    networks/$NETWORK

13. export SUBNET_REFERENCE=projects/$NETWORK_PROJECT/regions/$REGION/
    subnetworks/$SUBNET

14.

15. # If a cluster does not exist, it will be created.

16. export GKE_CLUSTER=$DEPLOYMENT_NAME

17.

18. # These are only considered if a new GKE cluster is being created.

19. export GKE_CLUSTER_VERSION=1.15.12

20. export GKE_MACHINE_TYPE=n1-highmem-4

21. export GKE_DISK_TYPE=pd-standard

22. export GKE_DISK_SIZE=100

23. export GKE_NUM_NODES=3

24.

25. export TIMEZONE=Etc/UTC

26.

27. # If the service account does not exist, it will be created.

28. export SERVICE_ACCOUNT_NAME="gke-user@$PROJECT_ID.iam.
    gserviceaccount.com"

29.

30. # If Cloud Memorystore Redis instance does not exist, it will be
    created.

31. export REDIS_INSTANCE=$DEPLOYMENT_NAME

32.

33. # If the bucket does not exist, it will be created.

34. export BUCKET_NAME="$DEPLOYMENT_NAME-6xn7rrpmq7d0e7khkxq8-1619031524"

35. export BUCKET_URI="gs://$BUCKET_NAME"

36.

37. # If the CSR repo does not exist, it will be created.
```

```
38. export CONFIG_CSR_REPO=$DEPLOYMENT_NAME-config
39.
40. # Used to authenticate calls to the audit log Cloud Function.
41. export AUDIT_LOG_UNAME="k6nf4fp23gdoco1p05sj-1616931524"
42. export AUDIT_LOG_PW="bm42vpxgdswfkuu5pmxo-1616931524"
43.
44. export CLOUD_FUNCTION_NAME="${DEPLOYMENT_NAME//-}AuditLog"
45.
46. export GCR_PUBSUB_SUBSCRIPTION=$DEPLOYMENT_NAME-gcr-pubsub-
    subscription
47. export GCB_PUBSUB_SUBSCRIPTION=$DEPLOYMENT_NAME-gcb-pubsub-
subscription
48.
49. export PUBSUB_NOTIFICATION_PUBLISHER=$DEPLOYMENT_NAME-publisher
50. export PUBSUB_NOTIFICATION_TOPIC=$DEPLOYMENT_NAME-notifications-topic
51.
52. # The properties following this line are only relevant if you intend
    to expose your new Spinnaker instance.
53. export STATIC_IP_NAME=$DEPLOYMENT_NAME-external-ip
54. export MANAGED_CERT=$DEPLOYMENT_NAME-managed-cert
55. export SECRET_NAME=$DEPLOYMENT_NAME-oauth-client-secret
56.
57. # If you own a domain name and want to use that instead of this
    automatically-assigned one,
58. # specify it here (you must be able to configure the DNS settings).
59. export DOMAIN_NAME=$DEPLOYMENT_NAME.endpoints.$PROJECT_ID.cloud.goog
60.
61. # This email address will be granted permissions as an IAP-Secured Web
    App User.
62. export IAP_USER=<gcp_admin_user_email_id>
```

This property file is generated once per installation, and we need to create it before running the setup script. If we need to make any changes in the Spinnaker configurations, we need to remove the existing properties file and create a new one by running the **setup_properties.sh** script.

After modifying the properties file, we are all set to initiate the installation process of Spinnaker on our GKE cluster. Execute the following command to run the setup. sh script in the Cloud Shell terminal.

```
~/cloudshell_open/spinnaker-for-gcp/scripts/install/setup.sh
```

The **~/cloudshell_open/spinnaker-for-gcp/scripts/install/** is the location where we have stored the setup.sh script, if you have placed this file on some other location on your system, you need to provide the relevant path to make this script run or navigate to the destination directory and execute **./setup.sh** command to execute the script.

The installation process for Spinnaker looks like the following screenshot:

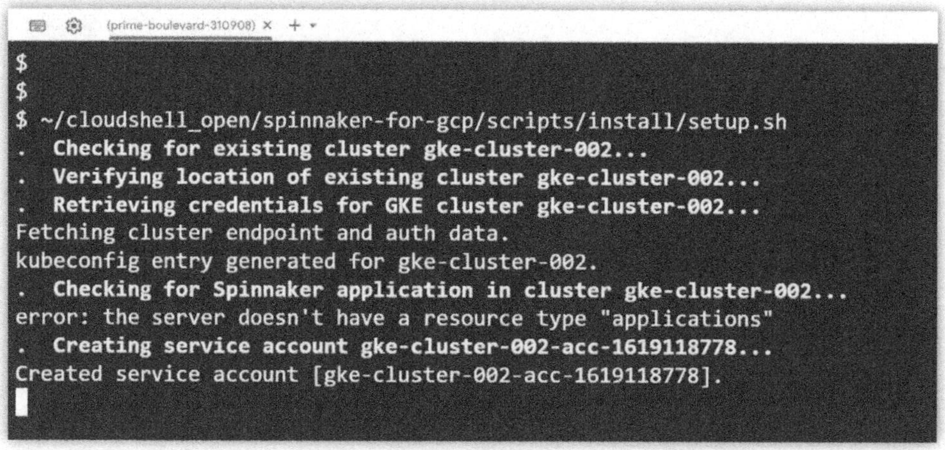

Figure 14.65: Installation of Spinnaker on GKE cluster

The installation process for Spinnaker starts by verifying the default values provided in the properties file. If the Spinnaker installer cannot find the defined cluster, it creates a new cluster based on the cluster template defined in the properties file. If the mentioned cluster exists, it creates the service account, storage buckets, PUB/SUB subscription, cloud function for audit logs, etc.

It is a bit long installation process, so we need to be patient enough to let it complete successfully. Once the installation process is completed, we receive the completion notification as shown in the following screenshot:

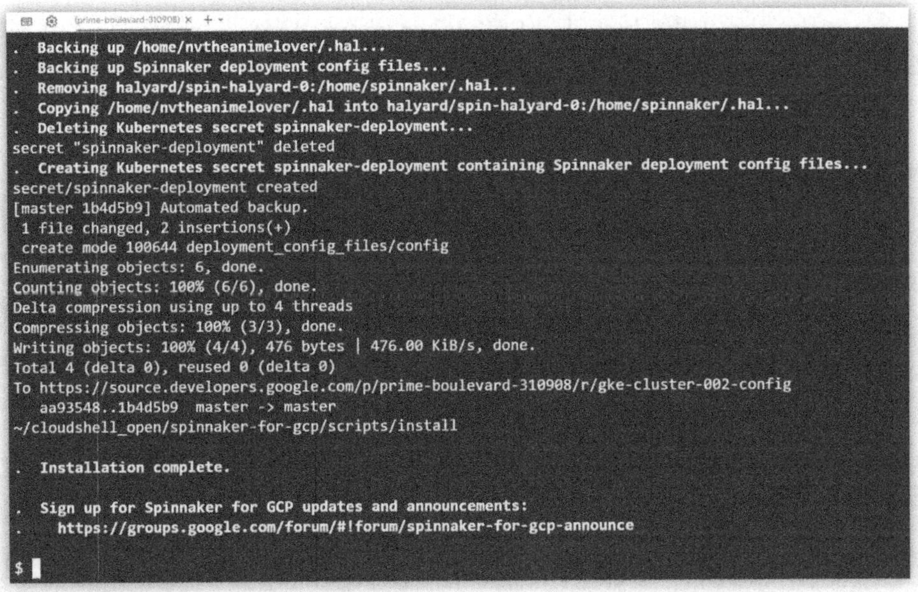

Figure 14.66: Notification of the completion of Spinnaker installation

To persist the changes made by the installation process in the host environment, we need to restart the Cloud Shell or the host system. The installation script took care of everything and created Spinnaker components as Kubernetes workloads and services. All the Spinnaker workloads are created under a separate namespace (spinnaker) to ensure that they are isolated from the rest of the workloads.

When we list out all the namespace available on the cluster, the outcome looks like the following screenshot:

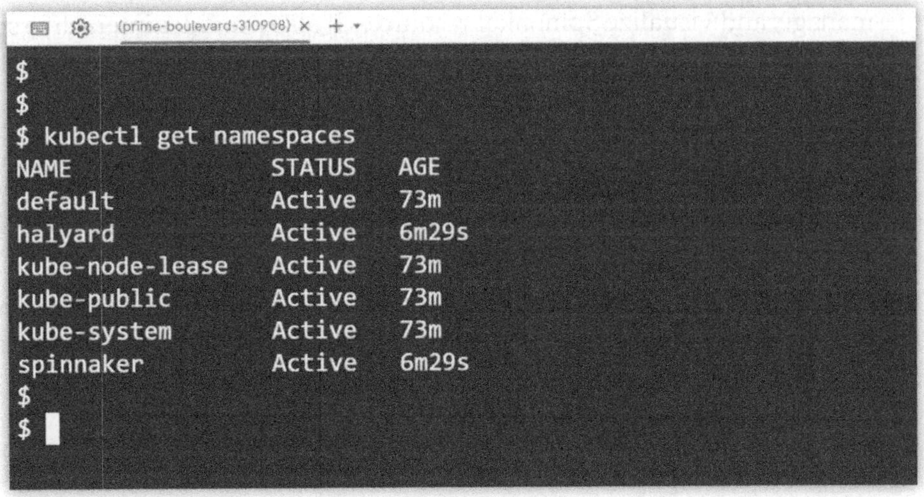

Figure 14.67: Custom namespaces created for Spinnaker objects and workloads

To know more about the installed Spinnaker components running as Kubernetes pods, execute the command **`kubectl get pod -n spinnaker`**, and the outcome looks like the following screenshot:

```
$
$
$ kubectl get pods -n spinnaker
NAME                                READY   STATUS    RESTARTS   AGE
spin-clouddriver-6f8f64dbf6-hg7v4   1/1     Running   0          5m35s
spin-deck-7756b7546d-d6p5s          1/1     Running   0          5m36s
spin-echo-859956cbb6-b8hph          1/1     Running   0          5m34s
spin-front50-5c59557847-g674m       1/1     Running   0          5m37s
spin-gate-8589d769d9-gw9nv          1/1     Running   0          5m34s
spin-igor-55f6f5c5cb-g2vxg          1/1     Running   0          5m39s
spin-kayenta-6495bb877b-rqrfc       1/1     Running   0          5m35s
spin-orca-6dbb5b96f8-hqblk          1/1     Running   0          5m32s
spin-rosco-5947cbb69f-7v6bb         1/1     Running   0          5m32s
$
$
```

Figure 14.68: *List of all running pods containing Spinnaker components*

To understand the functionality of each Spinnaker component, let's list out and understand them one by one:

- **Cloud Driver:** It is an interface to a set of virtual resources provided by cloud providers that Spinnaker has control over. All the activities performed in Spinnaker, such as deploying server groups, storing deployable artifacts, automation via pipelines, are managed and monitored by Cloud Driver.
- **Deck:** It is a web-based UI with intuitive and interactive graphics to create, manage, and visualize Spinnaker resources. It also provides interactive space to create, manage, and configure different pipelines and their templates based on the selected deployment strategies.
- **Echo:** It is a service that manages triggers, alerts, notifications, and cron jobs in Spinnaker. It also collects events from other Spinnaker services and routes them to the assigned event collector/processor. It also integrates with other services to trigger pipeline executions.
- **Front50:** It is a persistent data store to store metadata of applications, pipelines, jobs, and service accounts configurations. Various Cloud storage backends such as Google Cloud Storage, Amazon S3, Redis, and SQL are supported by Front50.

- **Gate:** It is the front-end API of Spinnaker instance that is exposed to users. It manages authentications and authorizations of sub-service APIs and resources of Spinnaker. It also acts as the *gate (as the name suggests...!)* for all the communications between the Spinnaker Deck UI and backend services.

- **Igor:** It is a wrapper API used to trigger pipelines via Continuous Integration and Source Control Management (SCM) services for Spinnaker. The supported SCMs are GitHub, Bitbucket, Gitlab, and Stash. The supported CI services are Google Cloud Build, Jenkins, Travis, Gitlab CI, Artifactory, Nexus, Wercker, and Concourse. Igor runs several pollers to monitor the new build/artifact/pipeline, cache the results into the Redis instance, and send the events to echo to invoke the pipeline triggers.

- **Kayenta:** It is Spinnaker's automatic canary analysis service. Canary release is a deployment process in which the partially rolled-out update to the current deployment gets constantly evaluated to ensure its success against the current deployment. The evaluation is done based on the key metrics describing the behavior of the old and new deployment versions.

  If there are any significant differences, the canary is aborted, and all the traffic is routed to the old deployment. Kayenta integrates with 3rd party monitoring services such as DataDog, Prometheus, New Relic, Google Operation Suits (previously known as Stackdriver), etc., to carry out canary monitoring tasks.

- **Orca:** It is the orchestration service used to orchestrate pipelines by forwarding and waiting for the status of various tasks requested in a pipeline. It is also responsible for making sure that all sub-services and their states are passed on correctly.

- **Rosco:** It is a "bakery" service used to create immutable Virtual Machine images or image templates for various Cloud Providers such as GCE Images, AWS AMIs, Azure VM images, etc. It is currently a wrapper around Harshicorp's Packer tool used to create identical machine images for multiple platforms from a single configuration source.

The internal communication between Spinnaker components is an essential part of the Spinnaker ecosystem. To establish a reliable and secure communication network for its components, Spinnaker has created a bunch of ClusterIP services shown as the following screenshot:

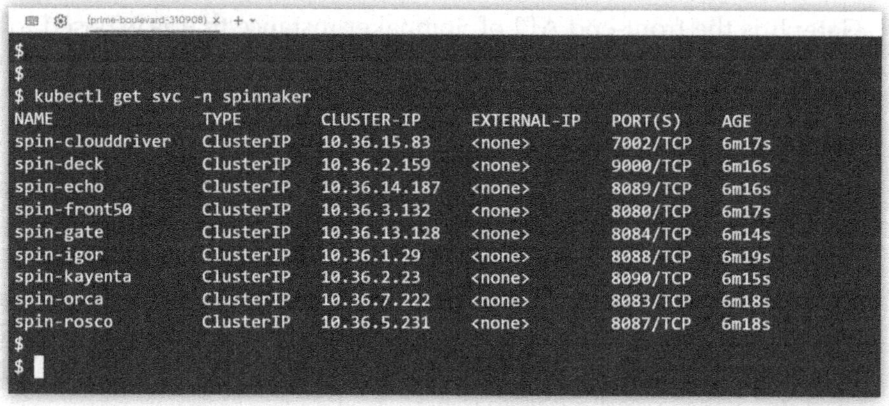

Figure 14.69: List of all running services for Spinnaker components

The spin-deck service is responsible for exposing the pod containing the Deck UI component. There are two ways to make the spin-deck externally accessible:

- Edit the spin-deck service object YAML and change the type of service from ClusterIP to LoadBalancer.

- Forward the traffic from the spin-deck service to port 8080 of the Cloud Shell machine.

To keep things simple, we will use the second method to expose Deck UI externally, but if you are looking for a more static solution, the other way is a good choice. To forward the traffic from spin-deck pod to port **8080** of Cloud shell machine, we need to run a script **connect_unsecured.sh.** This script is located in the **/manage** directory along with a few configurations scripts for Spinnaker. Execute the following command to run this script:

`~/cloudshell_open/spinnaker-for-gcp/scripts/manage/connect_unsecured.sh`

The outcome of the above command looks like the following screenshot:

Figure 14.70: Establish external access to Spinnaker

By running this single script, we located the spin-deck pod, extracted its name, saved it in an environment variable and performed the forwarding process. For now, this

Spinnaker instance is nonsecure and only accessible by us. There are a few ways to secure it, but they are out of the scope of this book.

To visit the Deck UI of Spinnaker, go to the web preview option of Cloud Shell located on the top right corner of the screen and click on the **Preview on port 8080**. It leads us to a new browser window that looks like the following screenshot:

Figure 14.71: Homepage of Spinnaker GUI (Deck UI)

Sample application on Spinnaker

First of all, before working with the sample application, we need to associate our Spinnaker instance with a version control tool. GitHub is the most commonly known option for it. For the Google Cloud platform, they have their version control offering called Cloud source repository. You can configure Git and push the sample application to your repository using the following commands:

```
git config --global user.email "<EMAIL_ADDRESS>"
git config --global user.name "<USERNAME>"
```

The next step is to download the source code and its dependencies, execute the following command in Cloud Shell and perform the untar operation on the downloaded tar file:

```
cd ~
wget https://gke-spinnaker.storage.googleapis.com/sample-app-v4.tgz
tar xfvz sample-app-v4.tgz
```

The extracted files are placed in a separate directory called **/sample-app,** and the content of this directory is as shown in the following screenshot:

```
$
$ cd sample-app/
$
$ ls
cloudbuild.yaml  CONTRIBUTING.md  docs        glide.yaml    k8s      pkg        spinnaker
cmd              Dockerfile       glide.lock  Jenkinsfile   LICENSE  README.md  tests
$
$
```

Figure 14.72: List of configuration files for the sample application

The **/k8s** directory contains the object definition files of deployments and services for the application's front-end and back-end components. Cloud Build helps us create the required Docker images for various applications components and push them to the Container Registry. The changes made in this pushed code need to be notified to Spinnaker using some mechanism. In our case, we are going to use Cloud Build's build triggers. A build trigger can be invoked by a condition, an event, or an action.

In this example, since the sample application is containerized, the most efficient way to observe the changes in the application would be to monitor the build sessions of the workload. Before configuring the build trigger, we need to create a source repository to host the source code of the sample application. Execute the following command to make the initial commit to the source code repository (**/sample-app**):

```
cd sample-app

git init

git add .

git commit -m "Initial Commit"
```

After committing to the source code repository, we need to create a new remote repository to host the code. Since we are working on Google Cloud Platform, it is feasible for us to use one of their offerings to store, manage, and track the source code: Cloud Source Repository. Execute the following commands to create a new repository on Cloud Source Repository and push the contents of **/sample-app** into its master branch.

```
gcloud source repos create sample-app

git config credential.helper gcloud.sh

export PROJECT=$(gcloud info --format='value(config.project)')

git remote add origin https://source.developers.google.com/p/$PROJECT/r/sample-app

git push origin master
```

At the end of the execution of all the above commands, navigate to the Cloud Source Repository's home page, and it should look like the following screenshot:

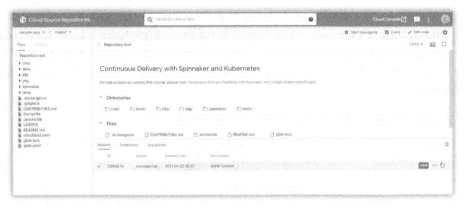

Figure 14.73: A Cloud Source Repository hosting the application source code

We can configure Cloud build trigger to initializes a new build when a specific event occurs. In other words, the trigger only reacts to those pushed Git tags that are prefixed with v.*. Once the trigger is invoked, Cloud build builds new Docker images and pushes them to the Container Registry. To configure the build trigger, go to Cloud Build and click on the create a trigger option and fill out the information regarding the trigger. Once we are done with it, the outcome looks like the following screenshot:

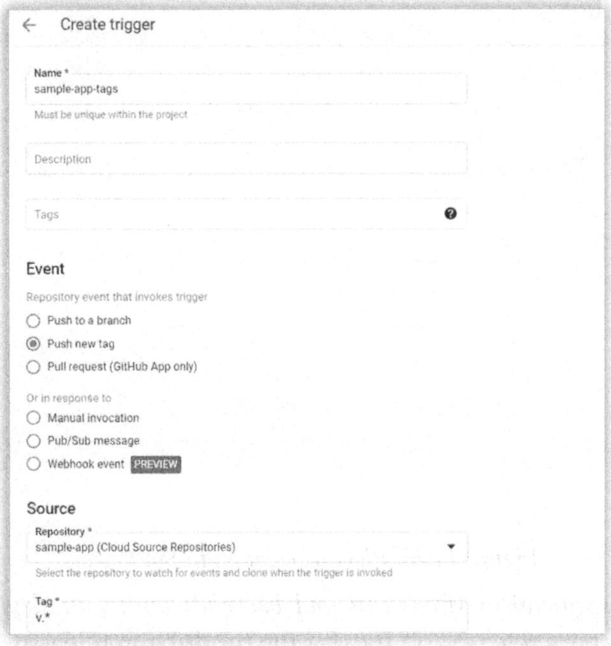

Figure 14.74: Configuring the Cloud Build Trigger

This can be considered as an updated rollout of the sample-app's workload. We can control and monitor this update rollout of the CI/CD pipeline. We already have a sample pipeline configuration in JSON format available at **/sample-app/spinnaker**.

You can understand this file and create your version of the pipeline template, but for demonstration's sake, we are going to keep the template as it is. Before creating the continuous delivery pipeline, we need to create the application that is going to leverage it. Execute the following command to create the sample application in Spinnaker:

```
spin application save --application-name sample \
                --owner-email ceruleancanvas@example.com \
                --cloud-providers kubernetes \
                --gate-endpoint http://localhost:9000/gate
```

After saving the application in Spinnaker, it is time to create its continuous delivery pipeline configured to detect the tagged Docker Image prefixed with v in the container registry. Execute the following command to create this pipeline in Spinnaker:

```
spin pipeline save --gate-endpoint http://localhost:8080/gate -f pipeline.json
```

As soon as the sample application and its continuous delivery pipeline are ready, we can open it in Spinnaker and check out the pipeline tab, which should look like the following screenshot:

Figure 14.75: *Pipeline creation in Spinnaker*

It is a two-tier application (*front-end and backend*) *with four deployments and four services (two* for canary release and two for the production release). It constitutes two delivery stages: The canary stage and the Production stage. For the readers who are unfamiliar with the terminology, Canary releases are directed toward a small set of users, generally for feedback purposes, whereas production releases are aimed toward a large user base.

Spinnaker has set up a pipeline for us. As we push the code to the git repository with a tag commit, Spinnaker deploys it to the canary release and then to the production release. It can deploy to both of them simultaneously, but we have disabled this feature to emulate the canary usefulness scenario properly. After successful canary deployment, the operator can change any configuration or push the code to the production stage.

Let's test this out by performing updates on the code. We do so by pushing a new version tag, as shown in the following screenshot:

```
$
$
$ git tag v1.0.1
$
$ git push --tags
Total 0 (delta 0), reused 0 (delta 0)
To https://source.developers.google.com/p/prime-boulevard-310908/r/sample-app
 * [new tag]          v1.0.1 -> v1.0.1
$
$
$ git tag v1.0.2
$
$ git push --tags
Total 0 (delta 0), reused 0 (delta 0)
To https://source.developers.google.com/p/prime-boulevard-310908/r/sample-app
 * [new tag]          v1.0.2 -> v1.0.2
$
$
```

Figure 14.76: Pushing new version tags to the deployment

The application has been updated from v1.0.1 to v1.0.2. This change is reflected on the pipeline if you observe the following screenshot:

Figure 14.77: Spinnaker pipeline for the canary stage

Once the canary deployment along with services for both tiers is rolled out, we are prompted to make the decision to stop or continue the pipeline. Before we continue the pipeline, let's justify the **Continuous Integration/Continuous Delivery** claim. A simple yet important question is… What is being integrated, and what is being delivered continuously? The application itself (workloads, services, and other potential supplementary objects) is being delivered continuously. As for the integration, we can understand it by looking at the following screenshot:

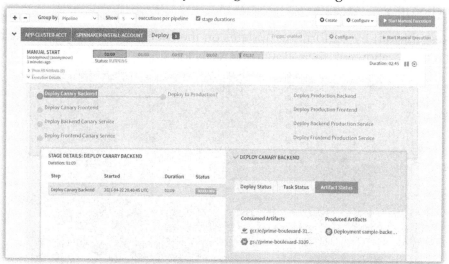

Figure 14.78: Detailed information about Canary backend stage

This screenshot has one particular deployment (canary backend) in focus. If you notice at the bottom right corner, the pipeline is taking input from the Google container registry and Google Cloud Storage and producing an output object being operated by a Kubernetes Cluster (deployment). This is just one process. Similarly, the service could also be using a load balancer or ingress.

Other workloads could also be using other offerings of Google Cloud (or even third-party tools). All of these are being integrated under the pipeline of one tool and are processed in parallel to achieve CI/CD. The next thing that we should do is to hit the continue button and watch the pipeline flow further, as shown in the following screenshot:

Figure 14.79: Spinnaker pipeline for the production stage

The production deployment and services' scheduling has also begun. As we know that, this is just a sample application. The complexity and components can scale up a lot depending on your use case. As it gets complicated with higher-level applications, you get more chances to appreciate the automation and smoothness offered by such CI/CD pipelines. But do you know something? Everything comes at a cost…!

The bling–bling of billing

Let's talk about billing on Cloud. We can address this topic in two different ways:

- You get the price of each service offered by Google, and the authors teach you school-level mathematics.

- We let the price tags stay where they are (on respective cloud provider's documentation, link in the note*) and talk about how to control them efficiently.

Analyzing cloud billing is just like making BOM (Bill of Materials) for your hardware project. Every nook and cranny counts. Your user interface might hint to you that you get each node of your cluster $24/month, and if you keep it active for more than 25 days of the month, you will get a discount of $2 per node.

If you take it on face value and estimate your application running cost for the month to approximately be $66–$70, you will be unpleasantly surprised, to say the least.

Why? Did the cloud provider lie to you? No, but a bold price tag narrowed your field of observation. It is not anyone's fault. It could have been your first time using such a service that can cloud (pun intended) your budget estimations.

In any case, now that you have read this book and got the heads up, you should keep the following things in mind to perform efficient cost estimation.

- You are not using just nodes. You could also be using blob storage, persistent storage, database storage, data warehousing, and other supplementary offerings.

- Your data transactions (requests) are processed over a set amount of bandwidth that also costs money.

- Services like Load Balancers, Ingress, non-preemptive nodes, static IPs are charged separately.

  Note:

  https://cloud.google.com/pricing/list

  https://cloud.google.com/products/calculator

- The addition of third-party ecosystem components like service mesh comes at an extra cost.

- Additional layers of security like SSL certificates are excluded from your cluster cost.

- Nodes are priced depending on their resources. A GPU heavy node may cost much higher than simply extending a few hundred gigabytes of HDD storage.

- Aiming for high availability via regional clusters can increase your total cost exponentially.

- Your cloud project could be billed on your organization's billing account. In that case, the activities of other users from your organization can also affect the bill.

- On top of all of this, you may require to bear additional costs for paid offerings like Windows Server OS, GitHub Private Repositories, or Docker Pro features.

These are a lot of additional charges. Just listing them out might bring down our motivation for using the cloud. But they are nothing to be scared of. Many of these charges are also applicable to on-premises infrastructure. On top of that, by paying your cloud provider for these services, you are essentially reducing your IT operational labor cost on-site. To make things even better, you can follow these steps to make sure your bills never break your profit ratio.

Once you are done experimenting with different features and observing the resultant performance of your software product hosted on containers, you can make an informed list of which features you necessarily require and which ones are optional.

- You can observe your bill as you go. Keep an eye on the growing bill and understand its breakdown in the early stages of your deployment to make sure you did not make a false estimate.

- Automatic scaling is a double-edged sword. While it allows your application not to show the unpleasant 404 to the clients, it can also shoot the bills higher than expected. Even if you enable horizontal and/or vertical autoscaling, make sure to set up a higher limit.

- Keep an eye on the changes of charges incurred by third-party tools.

- Set up billing alerts to receive notifications when your bill crosses certain thresholds.

- Ensure to keep your cluster sanitized (pruning zombie containers, periodic garbage collection, scheduled cache maintenance) to keep its resource consumption minimum.

- Optimize your application design over time. For example, if Alpine Linux works for you, don't stick to Ubuntu. When the containers scale horizontally, the resource quota difference makes a huge impact. Additionally, you can also replace heavy libraries with lightweight alternatives depending on your choice of programming language.

- Make sure not to run double versions of services for similar purposes.

- Make sure to have tight access control over members of your organization.

- Most importantly, when you are done with your clusters... **DELETE THEM.** Click on the cluster name on the cluster list page and hit the "DELETE" button. The cloud provider may ask you to enter the project name to verify your action, submit it and congratulate your wallet for one less burden to worry about (*The authors themselves have made the mistake of keeping a cluster unnecessarily alive and paying up unwanted charges. The authors are guilty, but they also came to realize that experience is the most prominent teacher. The authors don't want the readers to go through the same experience. The authors want your financial well-being. The authors are good people. The authors think that they should stop their typed tragic blabbery. That's it from the authors. DON'T FORGET TO DELETE YOUR RESOURCES AFTER YOUR JOB IS DONE.*)

By following these practices, you can keep your cloud bills under a pleasant and well-estimated threshold and keep your customers happy with reliable service. Just like Kubernetes on-premises, practice and experience will make your expertise over cloud resource consumption and billing optimization more refined and reliable.

Conclusion

This chapter expanded the capabilities of hosted K8s on Cloud and explored some container supportive tools like service mesh, package manager, logging and monitoring agents, CI/CD pipelining tool, etc. These are tools and technologies used to make production-grade deployments smooth and fast. The next chapter will briefly introduce the Serverless K8s offering of Google Cloud, the Cloud Run.

Multiple choice questions

1. Which of the following components does NOT need to be scaled to achieve cluster high availability?

    A. etcd

    B. Kube-apiserver

    C. Cloud-controller-manager

    D. Helm

    Answer: D

2. How does a high availability cluster decide which instance of control plane will serve the incoming API request?

    A. FCFS

B. Round Robin

C. Quorum

D. Priority-based distribution

Answer: C

3. Which of the following is not a logging agent?

A. Logstash

B. FluentD

C. Fluent-bit

D. Prometheus

Answer: D

4. How does Helm define K8s applications?

A. Sheets

B. Charts

C. Manifests

D. Objects

Answer: B

5. Which of the following deployment strategies is used to target a small group of users?

A. Blue-Green

B. Rapid Update

C. Target tracking

D. Canary

Answer: D

Questions

1. Explain the key differences between a normal and a highly available Kubernetes cluster.

2. Explain the importance of monitoring and dashboards for Kubernetes cluster management.

3. Write a Helm chart to run stateful Apache Zookeeper on Containers.

4. What is CI/CD, and how is it achieved using containers?

5. List out the steps to avoid overbilling while using hosted Kubernetes on Cloud.

CHAPTER 15
Serverless Containers

Introduction

In the previous chapter, we explored hosted or Managed Kubernetes on Cloud. In this chapter, we will cover something that has become the center of the conversations around the Kubernetes Ecosystem; Kubernetes going serverless. To put it simply, serverless means not having to worry about the underlying infrastructure at all! This has many financial and technical benefits, but it's not 100% glittering gold. This chapter will explore how to deploy your workloads on serverless K8s along with its positive and negative aspects.

Structure

This chapter covers:

- Introducing Serverless Kubernetes
- Getting Started with Cloud Run
- Hosting your first Serverless Container

Objective

We have been diving deep into every topic and every aspect of Container, Docker, and Kubernetes so far. As a result, you are equipped with a strong foundation of basic concepts. This grants me the freedom to take you on a quick stroll to explore bleeding-edge offerings in the container ecosystem without making you feel alienated. If you are jumping straight to this chapter in search of some deep dive on Serverless Kubernetes, your purpose might remain unfulfilled. This is like a reward chapter for the readers who have grated me their precious time and attention for 15 chapters. At the end of the chapter, you will have enough understanding of Serverless to decide whether you want to explore it in-depth or otherwise.

Introducing Serverless Kubernetes

As we saw in the last chapter, when we use hosted Kubernetes platforms like Google Kubernetes Engine, we as users, talk to the service-providing platform like Google Cloud instead of the master of the cluster, but we do have to manage the cluster. We are very well aware of the cluster configurations, and we also have to keep an eye on the resource utilization to see if we have to scale the cluster for better load handling. In other words, hosted Kubernetes allows us to host and manage a cluster on their resources:

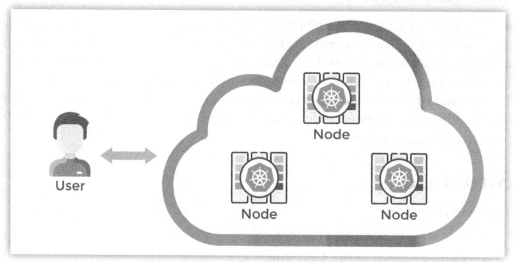

Figure 15.1: Kubernetes Cluster on Cloud

My dear Alice… think about a wonderland (*there, I even gave all the readers a nickname for a cheesy reference!*). A wonderland where all you need is a working desktop browser; you have to do a few clicks here and there and boom! Your containerized application is LIVE! That is serverless Kubernetes:

Figure 15.2: *Serverless Kubernetes*

Serverless Kubernetes is a relatively new member of services falling under the Serverless Computing category. After the success of hosted / managed distributed computing infrastructure (like managed database, managed Hadoop, or managed Kubernetes), cloud providers started to offer a new class of services that handled both backend infrastructure as well as its management. This left users with less burden, more cost-efficient billing, and only frontend to take care of. Such offerings are collectively called **Serverless Computing**. Amazon Web Services (AWS) Lambda, BigQuery, Google Cloud Run, and so on are examples of Serverless Computing.

Behind the scenes, or in the backend; the Serverless Kubernetes service provider also has lots of Kubernetes clusters deployed, but you do not have to worry about it. This has a few implications as follows:

- You do not know the full details of the cluster you are operating on. There are exceptions, but we will get into them later.

- The smallest unit of acquisition is NOT a bunch of virtual machines anymore. You are merely given a separate namespace and it is highly, likely, that other users are also operating the cluster your containers are on, but you will never clash because of namespace isolation and RBAC access policies.

- This makes deploying your applications even faster, economical, and easier!

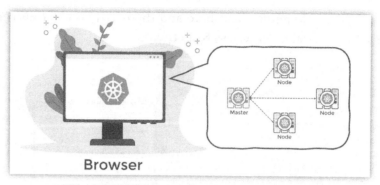

Figure 15.3: Backend of Serverless Kubernetes

Google's Cloud Run is a Great example of Serverless Kubernetes Offerings. Of course, much like everything we have encountered in this book so far, Cloud Run also has a fair share of competitive alternatives like AWS EKS on Fargate or Azure Serverless, but Cloud Run is a couple of steps ahead of them at the time of writing this book. Let's see how to work with it in practice.

Getting started with Cloud Run

Cloud Run is a part of Google Cloud Platform offerings; so much like Google Compute Engine VMs, or GKE's Hosted Kubernetes, the way to navigate is through the hamburger icon. Before we start using Cloud Run, we need to make sure that we have enabled its API in our GCP project. Go to API and Services. Once navigated, you will find stats about a list of APIs relevant to the products used under your GCP project.

Once navigated, you should find a bunch of APIs divided by categories of usage. If you want to avoid scrolling for eternity, use one of the best inventions of computer science… the search function!

Type Cloud Run and the first result you see should be our target API shown as follows:

Figure 15.4: Cloud Run API

Once you land on the Cloud Run API page, you can notice a lot of details like the latest update time, one-liner description, overview, and even links to documentation. Focusing on the overview of Cloud Run, it is a managed compute platform as it runs on a Kubernetes cluster in the backend. It enables you to run stateless containers invocable via HTTP APIs. To be honest, HTTP APIs are fine because everything that we have done in this book so far has used HTTP requests in one way or another. The crucial detail here is the specific mention of stateless applications (*#NoStatefulSetsOnCloudRun*).

This is where the glitters and gold analogy used in the introduction of the chapter becomes relevant. Cloud Run **can** host Kubernetes services without having to create or manage a cluster, but it does not give all of the privileges of a traditional or even a hosted Kubernetes cluster.

You can even sense the pattern here, the easier an implementation becomes, the less control and customizations you get. Does this mean you cannot run any stateful applications on Cloud Run? Not necessarily, you can still trigger one stateless service from another, but you have to tailor the app architecture to meet Cloud Run caveats as well as Business logic demands.

For example, deployments are stateless, so we should be able to play with them. Click on the **ENABLE** API button shown as follows:

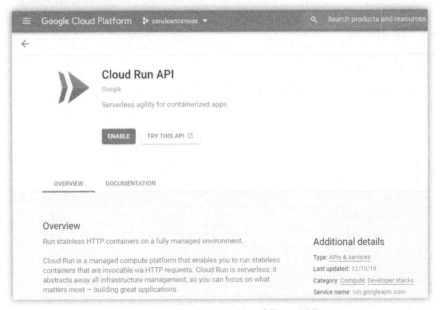

Figure 15.5: Enable Cloud Run API

Once the API is enabled, navigate to the Cloud Run page using the same hamburger icon and you should see an empty list of services. This means our Cloud Run is ready to host containers!

Hosting your first Serverless Container

In the beginning of the chapter, I had mentioned that hosting a serverless container is a matter of a few clicks... well, let's start clicking! Click on the **CREATE SERVICE** button as shown below and you will be guided to the service settings page:

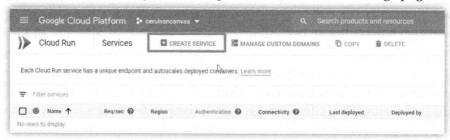

Figure 15.6: Create a Cloud Run Service

As we navigate to the service settings page, you can notice that Google is being elaborated with the descriptions as shown below. They are elaborating on what service is. This is helpful and frustrating at the same time because we have already seen docker swarm and Kubernetes objects called services leading to different interpretations:

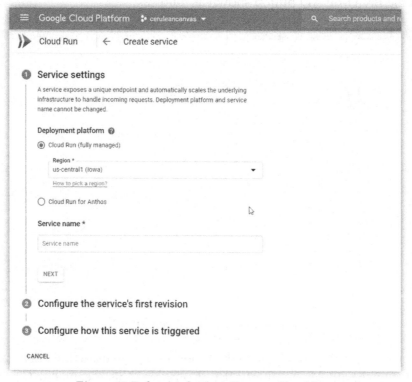

Figure 15.7: Service Settings Page on Cloud Run

Regardless, for Cloud Run, service is like a combination of Kubernetes deployments and Kubernetes services. It is an endpoint as well as an orchestration unit of stateless workloads. Also, it is important to note that the services created by Cloud Run **scale automatically**. This removes another burden from our fragile little DevOps shoulders.

Moving on, we have a deployment platform that is set to Cloud run by default. We have already seen what Cloud Run is. The other option called **Cloud Run for Anthos** is for the users who want to host their containers on their own clusters, but still want serverless features for the end developers. Anthos allows you to setup a Cloud Run on your GKE cluster on Google's servers or on your own servers. We will stick to Cloud Run and we will pick a region. Next, provide a name to the service *e.g., hello-cloud-run)*. Finally, hit **Next** button to get the following screen:

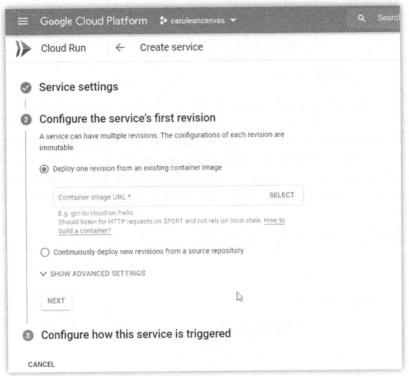

Figure 15.8: *Configure the first revision of the Cloud Run service*

These are the configuration options. A service can have multiple revisions, but the configs of each revision are unchangeable. In other words, whenever you make changes to any of the service configurations like the container image or port exposure, it will be served as a new version of your service; unlike previously where we could just Kubectl apply any change and deployments would get modified.

First, this new approach provides great version control and revision accessibility. On top of that, since every change is a new version of the service, rolling out blue-green or canary deployments becomes even more intuitive since all you have to do is manage traffic between two running versions of a service.

Then, we get to choose between using a container image from the Google container Registry of our project or from a source repo like Github shown as follows:

Figure 15.9: Sample container image on Google Container Registry

Second option is useful when we want to setup a continuous deployment pipeline. We will stick to a single version. Click on select and choose a demo container image called hello. This is one of Google's built-in image provided to every GCP project for enthusiasts to try out Cloud Run. Click **Next** to move to the third setting shown as follows:

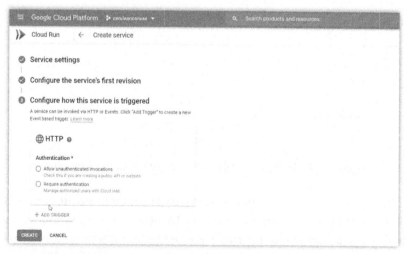

Figure 15.10: Configure HTTP triggers for Cloud Run Service

Finally, we get to choose just like Compute Engine VMs or GKE Cluster if we want to allow external connections without authentication. Set it to yes. Click on the create button to see the status of the service being created. Once the service is created, you should see a page looking like the following screenshot:

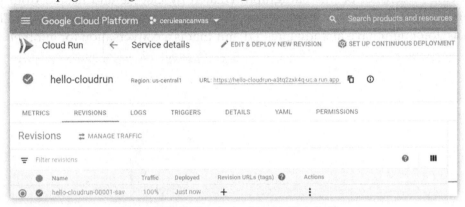

Figure 15.11: *Cloud run Service Details Page*

It is amazing how many complex processes like deploying the revision, setting up access policies, routing traffic, everything is done under just a few clicks. We also get a bunch of information about the container like the image URL, exposed port number, which is **8080**, the command is inherited from the docker image's entry point instruction and below are some resource allocation stats:

hello-cloudrun-00001-sav	
Deployed by csametriya@gmail.com using Cloud Console	
CONTAINER VARIABLES CONNECTIONS YAML	
General	
Image URL	gcr.io/cloudrun/hello@sha256:83709febe214d7f174c...
Build	(no build information available)
Source	(no source information available)
Port	8080
Command and args	(container entrypoint)
Service account	863842034203-compute@developer.gserviceaccount.com
Capacity	
CPU allocated	1
Memory allocated	256Mi
Concurrency	80
Request timeout	300 seconds
Autoscaling	
Min instances	3
Max instances	1,000

Figure 15.12: *Resource details of a Cloud Run Service*

Most importantly, right beside the name of our service, we can see the region that we had selected and the link where the service is being exposed.

You can simply click on this to enjoy A beautiful, little landing page (resembling the following screenshot of this paragraph) created by Google and hosted from your account without you having to provision anything. You can do **a lot more** with Cloud Run as you might have already guessed, but that is a conversation for another day:

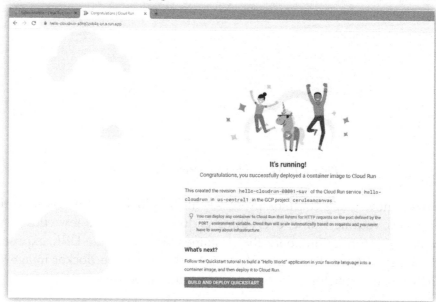

Figure 15.13: Landing page of the hello-cloud run service

Finally, you can go back to the services page and see your service listed with the settings you had applied and explore it further. Of course, you can select the service and delete it using the button on the top when you don't need it (*In fact, delete it. You don't need it. Cloud Run is cheap, not free*).

This is an example of how serverless containers are scheduled. You may wonder, is that the only way? Of course not. The market is growing with tools offering competitive pricing and novel solutions. One such example is **KEDA** that stands for **Kubernetes Event Driven Autoscaling**. Instead of managing the infrastructure around resource utilization, KEDA scales up or down your K8s objects depending on user-defined event triggers. Such solutions may not be used ubiquitously, but sometimes they can suite niche use cases more accurately. The best way to make the optimized choice for your use case is to stay relevant and up to date with the updates.

Conclusion

This was a short introduction to Serverless Kubernetes with an example of Cloud Run. Just like everything else, even Serverless Kubernetes can demand an entire book for itself with all of the complexities and challenges but with all of the knowledge and understanding built from previous chapters, nothing should stop you from making calculated experiments!

Multiple choice questions

1. Which of the following is Google's offering for serverless Kubernetes?

    A. Google Compute Engine

    B. Google Kubernetes Engine

    C. Google Cloud Run

    D. AWS Fargate

    Answer: C

2. Which of the following Kubernetes objects cannot be deployed with Google Cloud Run?

    A. Deployment

    B. Services

    C. Stateful set

    D. Replica set

    Answer: B

3. Which of the following Google Cloud Platform APIs is not required to be enabled to run serverless containers?

    A. Cloud Run

    B. Compute Engine

    C. Kubernetes Engine

    D. Big Query

    Answer: D

4. How many revisions can a running Cloud Run Service support?

    A. 0

    B. 1

    C. 2

D. Many

Answer: D

5. Which of the following sources can be used to obtain container images in Google Cloud Run?

A. Docker Hub

B. Google Container Registry

C. Github

D. All of the above

Answer: D

CHAPTER 16
The Checkpoint

The journey...

We started our conversation around containers with topics as basic as Web applications, DevOps, Linux Containers, etc. Once the foundation was setup, we discussed various aspects of Containers, Container Runtime Environments, the process of Containerization, Container Orchestrators, Wrapper objects, Cloud Services, and even application-specific solutions. All of them collectively create a container ecosystem.

This book is intended to be an entry point, a friendly guide, and a handy reference for the Containers. The grouping of topics and chapter arrangement were carried out in a way that you as readers could feel the connection between the tools and the progression of your own comprehension of containers as well as containerized applications. We went from writing a simple Ubuntu container to set up a working CI/CD pipeline on Cloud using Kubernetes and other DevOps tools.

Using the knowledge and skills gained from this book, you can envision solutions centered around containers. After all, solving real-world challenges is the end-goal of any form of technical document. Here is an example *Figure 16.1*:

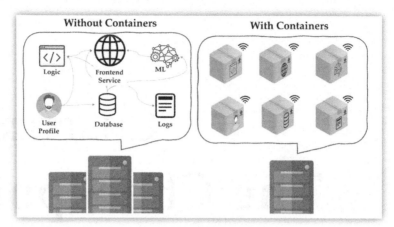

Figure 16.1: Conceptual representation of a Container-based solution

Cleartrip, a leading online tourism planning company migrated to containers during the pandemic. Through the migration, they not only decreased the cost of infrastructure and operations but also managed to optimize various components of their code base. They realized that a lot of their blocks were unnecessarily tightly integrated. By moving to containers, they were able to decouple independent services making them more fault tolerant and covering them under tighter access control.

We particularly chose **Cleartrip** as a reference because the solution they opted for is the same as the solution you have learned in the book, Google Kubernetes Engine. This single reference should immediately ring multiple bells in your head with thoughts like they must have used high availability, they must have used Identity and Access Management for access control, they must have used CI/CD for rolling out discounts and updates on the fly and so on. More importantly, there is someone in their team running Kubectl CLI as or more frequently than you do! Their services are containerized using Docker, which resonates with your compose file and Dockerfile writing skills! Your excitement is legitimate, and you should rightfully pursue it further by practicing different use cases and interpreting various problem statements before finally landing on your dream job or dream role.

While this was a fulfilling experience for us (and hopefully for you too), we understand that all of us have a curious appetite to know where and how to progress further. While this little chapter is literally the conclusion of the book, it is figuratively **a checkpoint** for the authors and the readers *(and the publication too!)*.

So, what next?

The tools and technologies of the Container Ecosystem will continue to grow further, trying to make the user experience smoother, while addressing difficulties and challenges faced by people working on DevOps at the moment. Docker and Kubernetes will continue to release their updated versions. Many of the beta and alpha features will make their way to General Availability while some of them will be deprecated for good.

Since these technologies are not laws of physics, but market-driven products, you might see unexpected mergers, discontinuation of support for some tools or features, strong and competitive alternatives, or even ground-breaking replacements! Does that mean the validity of your skills is in danger? Not at all. You should embrace the progress with an open mind and catching up with the updates will be way easier than you think. The most important takeaway from this (or any) book is the thought process and understanding that you have built throughout the chapters. Even when you encounter newer challenges, the learnings from your sought-out expertise will stack up; it will help you get your priorities in correct order to make technically, logically (and hopefully financially) efficient decisions and solutions for your project and/or your company. The show must and will go on.

As for your immediate progression, the best thing you can do is continue practicing what you have already learned and set sight for what to learn next *(the learning should never stop)*. The second-best thing would be to come out of the cocoon of solo learning. If you have read the book completely and if you have been practicing alongside it, your knowledge and skills on Docker and Kubernetes are more than enough to make productive conversations with like-minded and skilled professionals. You can participate in forums, groups, and social media activities to help absolute beginners get started with containers while getting expert advice on different use cases and problems from veterans.

That is not all, you should also leverage your containerization skills to step up your job profile (and pay scale) since Docker, Kubernetes, and Hosted Cloud solutions are some of the most in-demand and well-paid skills in the current IT landscape *(this fact is not going to change at least in near future of writing this book, since a large section of IT industry is yet to migrate to containers and bring down their resource consumption)*.

Official Certifications are a great investment to establish the credibility of your skills and knowledge. Docker provides an all-rounder certification (Docker Certified Associate) with a unique examination pattern, while the Cloud Native Computing Foundation provides three different certifications for Kubernetes. They are targeted at Administrators (Certified Kubernetes Admin), Developers (Certified Kubernetes Application Developer), and Security specialists (Certified Kubernetes Security Specialist) respectively. That is not all, Kubernetes and containers are also part of some of the certifications offered by Public Cloud Platforms such as GCP, AWS, or Microsoft Azure. If you are unsure about which certification to prepare for and apply for, you can ask your colleagues, higher management, or potential employer about which one will make the most positive impact on your career graph and will match the most with your job role or with the future directions of your job role.

Finally, you can always reach out to us via social media or BPB Publications for any questions, discussions, or constructive feedback. Once the pandemic stops affecting the lives, livelihood, and lifestyles of people, we would also love to have you for a cup of hot chocolate *(because one of the authors doesn't drink coffee... or tea)*!

Thank you so much for reading this book. We wish you all the best for your journey further.

Index

Made in the USA
Coppell, TX
16 August 2024

36087741R00293